THE FIRST TEN

BY ALFRED STEINBERG

THE FIRST TEN

The Founding Presidents and
Their Administrations

ALFRED STEINBERG

Garden City, New York
DOUBLEDAY & COMPANY, INC.

To Florence, for whom I wrote this book

ACKNOWLEDGMENTS

I should like to thank especially the Library of Congress, the Enoch Pratt Library in Baltimore, the New York Public Library and the Silver Spring, Maryland, Library, for the books and materials made available to me.

I must also thank Elsa Anderson of Doubleday for her interest in this work.

ALFRED STEINBERG
October 4, 1966

☆ ☆ ☆

CONTENTS

CONTENTS

☆ ☆ ☆

FOREWORD

Harry S. Truman once recalled that as a young man he came running out of the Kansas City Bank, where he worked as a clerk, to join the immense street crowd gawking and shrieking at the sight of Theodore Roosevelt, then the President of the United States.

Every President has been the object of such attention, for the institution of the Presidency is one of continuing, tremendous awe by the American people. From the time that George Washington repeated the oath, and bowed down and kissed the sacred volume until the current day, national veneration for the Office has never diminished.

Nevertheless, Americans tend to make a clear distinction between the Presidency and the President. The Presidency is a solid granite affair that combines the ceremonial activities of the Chief of State with the operational activities of the Chief of Government. The operating Presidency runs the Executive Branch, commands the armed forces, promotes legislative programs through Congress, directs foreign policy and relations with other nations, leads a political party and informs the public on the state of the Union. On the other hand, the President is a mere man—but one who usually possesses the belief he is best able among his fellow Americans to occupy the nation's highest office.

Since the days of the founding Presidents, custom makes it sacrilegious to attack the Presidency, while it is always open season on the man who happens to be President. Will Rogers once remarked that following the stock market crash in 1929, a man bit into a wormy apple and bellowed, "Damn that Hoover!" One important difference between the Presidency and the President shows itself distinctly when a new President takes office. There is an unseemly impatience on the part of the public that the man losing the mantle of the Presidency leave the scene of his decisions, challenges or triumphs with all speed and sink into oblivion. As for the new President, fair play toward him means giving him a short honeymoon before subjecting him to sledge hammer attacks.

No doubt a large part of the mystique of the Presidency is due to the fact that rational men know how powerful this office is. Lincoln's Secretary of State, William H. Seward, observed: "We elect a king for four years, and give him absolute power within certain limits, which after all he can interpret for himself." The existence of such an office in a land that professes individual equality is such an enormous incongruity that it must be given an unquestioned status in the minds of men.

Americans want to believe that theirs is a government of laws and not of men. No matter who happens to administer the law, so goes the legend, it will be meted out in precisely the same manner. Yet study shows that even though every President comes to the Presidency with the same authority, each will use his powers in his own unique way. It is my purpose to detail the proposition that the Office of the Presidency in practice has been as weak or as strong as each occupant has made it.

The men included are the founding Presidents, from George Washington through John Tyler, men who took a raw institution and put brick and mortar on its basic structure. Without a Washington, there would have been neither the awe toward the Presidency nor the vast powers of that office. Only six years before his inauguration, a small body of eighty belligerent soldiers of the Pennsylvania Line forced the Articles of Confederation Congress to flee in the night from Philadelphia, the capital, to safety at Princeton.

Without a John Tyler at precisely his point in American history, the precedent that a Vice-President succeeds a dead Chief Executive with full title and powers would probably never have resulted. By the time Tyler left Washington in 1845 to return home to the deprecating job as road overseer, to which his frowning neighbors had elected him, his Vice-President-to-full-President principle was never again challenged. Considering that one out of five Presidents has died in office, this stubborn, ambitious Virginian did much to bring about a smooth continuity of government.

The Presidency has always been an area of great interest to the historians. Many volumes are biographical. Others examine the functions of the Presidency, and the differences in practice which history reveals. *The First Ten* attempts a new approach. I have concentrated on the administration of each President: what he did from the time he took office until he left; how he was affected by the issues of his day, his own past, his personality and philosophy; and how he dealt with the contending politicians who strode across his path. In a broad sense, it is a panoramic view of the development of the United States from its colonial old age to its vigorous spread westward and its shift from aristocratic leadership of powder-wig Virginia planters and diary-writing New England intellectuals to the push and shove of muddy-booted frontiersmen.

☆ 1 ☆

GEORGE WASHINGTON

Man With a Country

In the spring of 1789, fifty-seven-year-old George Washington started out from Virginia on a journey that would climax his life. He realized well he was embarking on a task as fateful as his eight years commanding the Continental Army in the fight of the thirteen colonies for freedom from Mother England. What he now faced as the first President of the United States was the enormous task of creating a functioning government and establishing a national policy.

Two years earlier he had served as presiding officer of the Constitutional Convention of 1787 and helped bring about the ratification of the 5000-word document which the delegates had written in Philadelphia's State House. But how to explain the section dealing with the office he was now to occupy? It lacked essentially the clarity and preciseness that would have eliminated all the groping and testing he knew would occupy much of his time. He could only feel apprehensive that his own conduct in office would establish precedents binding those who followed. Yet on the other side of the ledger, the lack of clarity would permit each occupant to follow his own personality and philosophy in dealing with the problems of his day. The Office of the President would therefore be as large or as insignificant as each holder made it.

Opinions differed regarding the scope of the Presidency. Virginia's Thomas Jefferson believed that the national Executive must make himself subservient to Congress. On the other hand, the man soon to become Washington's Vice-President assessed the Constitution's brief Article II as creating an immensely powerful President. John Adams of Massachusetts wrote in 1789: "I know of no first magistrate in any republican government, except England

and Neuchâtel, who possesses a constitutional dignity, authority and power comparable to his. The power of sending and receiving ambassadors, of raising and commanding armies and navies, of nominating and appointing and commissioning all officers, of managing the treasuries, the internal and external affairs of the nation, nay, the whole executive power, co-extensive with the legislative power as vested in him, and he has the right, and his is the duty, to take care that the laws are faithfully executed. These rights and duties, these prerogatives and dignities, are so transcendental that they must naturally and necessarily excite in the nation all the jealousy, envy, fear, apprehensions and opposition that are so constantly observed in England against the crown."

Master-builder of the Constitution and a man who helped create the dimensions of the Presidency was "my particular friend Mr. Madison," as Washington addressed the brilliant political scholar from the rolling Piedmont of Virginia. It was James Madison, a member of the Continental Congress, who parlayed the abortive Annapolis Convention of September 1786, which was supposed to consider an interstate trade agreement, into a call for the Philadelphia Convention of May 1787, to consider all the ills of the Confederacy. Washington had been aware of the strategy to bring about the latter convention: Madison had paid a visit to him at Mount Vernon and against the background of a heavy rainstorm they had discussed the advisability of a general conference. Calling a convention without the approval of the Confederation Congress was unconstitutional under the Articles of Confederation, yet "something must be done or the fabric must fall," said Washington. "All the courage and suffering of the war might be lost in the confusion of a peace without policy or system."

In June 1776, the Continental Congress had appointed a committee to prepare a constitution and in August that committee submitted the Articles of Confederation written by John Dickinson of Delaware, whose Farmer's Letters of 1767–1768 contributed heavily to the original movement toward independence from England. For five years after submission the Articles of Confederation lay unpassed. Not until March 1781 was the final vote in: Maryland approved the Articles, only after being assured that seven states holding western lands would turn them over to Congress. The Confederacy, as stated in the constitution, was a "league of friendship," a loose association of the states, each retaining its independence and equality.

"A rope of sand" was the apt way that Washington described the sorry political organization. Under the thirteen-article constitution, Congress could not lay or collect taxes to meet its obligations. It could merely make annual money assessments on the states and pray that most would live up to their moral commitment to keep the Confederacy solvent. Nor could Congress regulate commerce among the states, a serious deficiency considering the trade wars some practiced on their neighbors. Congress had authority to settle squabbles between states, but it lacked coercive powers to enforce its decisions. The same applied to treaties: Congress could effect a treaty with a foreign nation but the states were free to ignore its provisions. As a member of the Continental Congress, Madison had made several attempts with Washington's blessings to correct these deficiencies by amending the Articles of Confederation. But in not a single instance did an amendment win the required approval of all thirteen states. "It is at an end," Washington wrote Thomas Jefferson, American Minister to Louis XVI's Government. "Unless a remedy is soon applied, anarchy and confusion will inevitably ensue."

The record of the Confederacy did not reveal a complete failure, however. Despite the existence of only a shadowy central government the Confederacy had fought a war and won a peace treaty that exceeded fondest hopes, abolished slavery on the northwest frontier and laid out a program for democratic settlement and future statehood by the Northwest Ordinance of 1787. There had even been a spurting prosperity under the Confederacy until the gold and silver coins France and England brought to the United States during the war again crossed the Atlantic in 1783 and 1784 to pay for enormous imports from those countries.

Then had come the "Panic of 1785" and serious new troubles. Paper-money political parties made their appearance in every state and demanded the printing of large amounts of paper money unbacked by gold or silver. Seven states fell under their power and printing presses worked overtime as the paper depreciated rapidly. By the end of 1786 the depression reached rock bottom and prosperity slowly returned. In Massachusetts, creditors gained political control and turned the tables on the large debtor group. A moratorium on debt-collecting was now rescinded and the courts filled with cases against debtor farmers. In the western part of the state, Daniel Shays, a former Revolutionary officer, led mobs of farmers in breaking up court sessions and in laying siege to the

U. S. Arsenal at Springfield. The state militia easily dispersed the
so-called Shays' Rebellion, but Washington heard that groups in
other states were planning similar disorders. "There are combusti-
bles in every state which a spark might set fire to," he said in
alarm.

The paper-money craze with its threat to property owners, the
threatened rebellions, the jealous states and undernourished Congress, continued British violations of the peace treaty and Spanish
occupation of American territory along the southern border—all
these and more contributed to Washington's concern that there
was little time left to save the stumbling nation. And yet even
when the Virginia assembly named him to the state's seven-man
delegation to the Philadelphia convention, his first instinct was not
to "intermeddle in public affairs." Then, too, he was not well.
"A rheumatic complaint in my shoulder . . . At times I am hardly
able to raise my hand to my head," he explained to urging friends.
But Madison and others insisted he must attend because his influence was so great that if he stayed home the convention was
doomed to failure.

The May 14 opening date for the convention found only the
Virginia and Pennsylvania delegations present in the second-floor
meeting room at the State House. Delegates straggled into town
and not until May 25, when twenty-nine delegates from seven
states took seats, was a working quorum present.

One of their first acts was to elect Washington presiding officer by a unanimous vote. Now began the debate whether to propose amending the Articles of Confederation or create a new form
of national government. "Temporizing applications will dishonor
the councils that propose them," Madison vowed and Washington
thoroughly agreed with his young friend, nineteen years his junior.

This was a young man's convention, though the dean of the
delegates, eighty-one-year-old Benjamin Franklin, then governor of
Pennsylvania, helped raise the average age to slightly higher than
forty. A total of seventy-four delegates had been appointed, but
only fifty-five eventually made an appearance and average daily
attendance was about thirty. Of the fifty-five, half were lawyers
and the rest were planters and merchants. Almost all were political
leaders of their states, three-fourths served as members of the
Continental Congress and thirty held military posts at one time
or another in Washington's army. Jefferson later hailed the convention as "an assembly of demigods," a heroic description for

mortal men torn between personal interest, duty and patriotism. They considered it wiser to meet in closed, secret sessions than to permit newspapers and the country to know what they were doing.

Taking the initiative, the Virginia delegation, through Governor Edmund Randolph, presented Madison's plan to the convention on May 29. After a pious resolve that the Articles of Confederation be corrected and enlarged, this Virginia Plan offered a long series of resolutions that would effectively destroy the Confederacy. In its place there would be a supreme national government and subordinate states, with the central authority holding power to "negative all laws passed by the several states . . . and to call forth the force of the Union against any member failing to fulfill its duties under the articles thereof."

Two weeks of discussion of the Virginia Plan alarmed the small states who believed they were to be overwhelmed by their larger neighbors. They reached this conclusion from the fact that the plan proposed a two-house national legislature with representation based on population. So on June 15 came the New Jersey, or small state, Plan, expounded by William Paterson, which called merely for a revision of the Articles of Confederation. Among its resolves were those to grant power to Congress to levy taxes and regulate commerce. However, each state would retain its equal vote in Congress.

While the two sides threatened and ridiculed each other in the blistering summer heat, Washington sat on his raised dais and faced the delegates with mounting animosity. "I almost despair of seeing a favorable issue to the proceedings," he remarked at the close of June, "and do therefore repent having had any agency in the business." He revealed his bias in a further comment—"The men who oppose a strong and energetic government are, in my opinion, narrowminded politicians, or are under the influence of local views."

On July 2 came the vote on whether representation in the Senate should be by population or by state equality. One delegate overslept and another was hurrying from Philadelphia to fight a duel. Thus the large states' majority vanished and the vote was a tie. This now made possible the Great Compromise of the convention. The issue, once shifted to the Committee of the States (consisting of a delegate from each state), emerged as a compromise proposal by Benjamin Franklin. Finally on July 16, the convention adopted the compromise by the narrow margin of five states to four. There would be representation in the House by population and an equal vote for each state in the Senate. As a concession to the large states, all money bills would have to originate in the House, where it was assumed the large states would be in control.

Once the Great Compromise was reached, the small states dropped all pretense that they favored only a rejuvenation of the Articles of Confederation. Washington later agreed with Madison that they now "exceeded all others in zeal for granting powers to the general government." On July 26 things were moving along so well that a five-man Committee of Detail was ordered to prepare a draft constitution on the basis of the general principles of government so far accepted by the convention.

The committee filled in most of this outline of principles with sections lifted bodily from the Articles of Confederation and from various state constitutions. For instance, the Congressional powers enumerated in the Articles were placed with little change into the proposed draft Constitution. On August 6, the committee submitted its draft and the next month passed by as the convention argued out the document word by word. By only a single-vote majority did the convention vote down a grant of power to Congress to declare state laws null and void. Toward the end of August subjects that had been postponed were given to the Committee of Eleven, or, as some called it, the Committee on Unfinished Parts. These now came back as a report on September 4 and on September 8, with its work almost completed, the convention appointed a five-man Committee on Style. What remained after the document came to the floor on the twelfth were some last-minute changes and the signing on the seventeenth of the Constitution of the United States.

One of the subjects that had baffled the convention almost to the end was the structure, selection and authority of the national Executive. There was hardly any argument about the Virginia Plan proposal for a separate Executive, even though it was totally unlike the situation in the Confederation Congress where the President was a member of Congress. However, beyond agreement that the Chief Executive should not be part of the legislature, delegates were perplexed regarding all other attributes of the office.

The Virginia Plan first proposed a single Chief Executive, while the New Jersey Plan adherents demanded a plural head. Then

Governor Randolph called a one-man Executive head an alarming step toward monarchy. Madison quickly suggested that a group of national judges form a council of legislative revision with the single Executive. Other ideas poured forth and a tangle developed until the idea of a single Executive won general favor over that of a plural head.

How was the President to be selected? The Virginia Plan proposed that Congress elect him. Pennsylvania delegate James Wilson wanted him chosen directly by the people. Then he and Madison devised a plan whereby the people would choose electors and the electors would choose the President. Several times the convention voted to make the President the choice of Congress, but at other times a majority opposed this method. On one occasion the convention agreed to a system of electors selected by the legislatures of the states, and on two other occasions they disapproved of this scheme. Three further attempts to settle the question of selection brought votes to reconsider everything that had so far been approved. As one delegate now put it: "We seem to be entirely at a loss." Finally at the end of August, the convention dumped the entire problem into the lap of the Committee on Unfinished Parts with a suggested article "providing for election of President by Congress for seven years and forbidding re-election."

While the problem of the President's selection bogged down, the convention was also perplexed about what duties to assign him. Some delegates wanted the office modeled after that of the governor of Virginia, a figurehead executive. Roger Sherman of Connecticut demanded that the President be restricted to carrying out the will of Congress. Gouverneur Morris of Pennsylvania went to an opposite extreme and insisted that "the Executive should appoint the Senate." James Wilson excitedly called for giving him an absolute veto on all legislation. Madison's suggestion that the President have the power to veto, with Congress able to override his veto by a two-thirds vote, finally won convention approval. Madison also changed a single word in one sentence that added significantly to the President's power. The sentence in question read that Congress had power to "make" war. Madison changed "make" to "declare."

With the growing belief that the President would be chosen by the legislature, delegates began to add to the list of his duties. However, there was a more compelling reason for this phenomenon. As Pierce Butler of South Carolina put it in a letter to a relative:

"Entre nous, I do not believe they would have been so great, had not many of the members cast their eyes toward General Washington as President; and shaped their ideas of the Powers to be given a President, by their opinion of his Virtues." Had the eleven members of the Committee on Unfinished Parts acted without this assumption that Washington would serve as first President, there is little doubt that the historic course would have taken a vastly different turn.

By the time the committee took up its eleven proposals, there appeared unofficially to be a majority for the proposition that the President should be elected by ballot by the legislature for a seven-year term and be ineligible for re-election. Also of apparent popularity was another proposal: "The Senate of the United States shall have power to make treaties, and to appoint Ambassadors, and Judges of the Supreme Court."

The report of the committee four days later and its acceptance by the convention were events of immense magnitude in the making of the Office of the Presidency. First, the President was to be chosen by electors selected in each state by a method determined by the state legislature. His term of office would be for four years and he would be eligible for re-election. In case no candidate won a majority of the electoral votes, the Senate would select a President "from the five highest on the list." The convention later shifted this selection scheme to the House.

The committee report also provided for the Office of the Vice-President "in case of the Removal of the President from Office, or of his Death, Resignation, or Inability to discharge the Powers and Duties of the said Office." Electors were to vote for two persons who did not reside in the same state, with the person receiving the majority of the votes becoming President and the runner-up, Vice-President.

There was yet another important change made by the Committee on Unfinished Parts. Their report of September 4 shifted the treaty-making power from the Senate to the President, "by and with the advice and consent of the Senate." In addition, appointment of "ambassadors, and other public Ministers, Judges of the Supreme Court, and all other Officers of the United States" not otherwise provided for was transferred from the Senate to the President.

When the Presidential Office in this form cleared the convention, an outsider asked Benjamin Franklin: "Well, Doctor, what have we got, a republic or a monarchy?" "A republic," Franklin snapped, "if you can keep it."

The old doctor, voice-weary, gouty and physically feeble, well understood Washington's role. His presence had given the convention great dignity and authority; his character spelled safety and optimism for the country's development under the new Constitution. While the delegates signed the document on September 17, 1787, Franklin pointed to the painting of the sun on the back of Washington's chair. His comment was: "I have often and often in the course of the session, and the vicissitudes of my hopes and fears as to its issue, looked at that sun behind the President without being able to tell whether it was rising or setting. But now at length I have the happiness to know it is a rising and not a setting sun."

"I wish the Constitution offered had been made more perfect," said Washington. "But I sincerely believe it is the best that could be obtained at this time."

There was still an uncertain road to travel before the Constitution became effective. Madison had insisted that the Constitution be submitted to special conventions elected by the people in each state instead of to state legislatures. Ratification by nine state conventions would put the Constitution into effect. The surprising opposition that emerged in various states was offset to some extent by the written propaganda of Alexander Hamilton, John Jay and Madison. As "Publius," they penned eighty-five essays, collectively known as *The Federalist*, in a stirring defense of the Constitution.

However, the single most important factor in the ratification struggle was that Washington favored the new government proposed by the document. In a country divided so far by state boundaries, he represented national unity. As a result, said Colonel William Grayson, at the Virginia ratifying convention, "Were it not for one great character in America, so many men would not be for this government." And as soon as New Hampshire became the ninth state to ratify the Constitution and the big states of Viriginia and New York agreed to join the Union, there was little question throughout the country that Washington would be called upon to serve as the first President under the Constitution. He had no desire for this office, and he said that the pressure on him produced "a kind of gloom upon my mind." But the clamor rose that "Farmer Washington—May he like a second Cincinnatus be called from the plow to rule a great people." After a long period of thought on the subject, Washington finally agreed to become a candidate.

With the ratification of the Constitution, the Confederation Congress set the first Wednesday in January, 1789, for the choosing of Presidential electors. Then on the first Wednesday in February the electors were to assemble to make their choice, the top candidate becoming President and the next highest the Vice-President. It would be on the first Wednesday in March that the Federal Government would begin business in its capital, New York City.

Washington made no campaign for office, though the helpful political efforts of Alexander Hamilton insured his unanimous selection. That first election proved wildly chaotic because of bungling delays and uncertainties regarding the proper method for choosing electors. In five states, the legislatures chose the electors; three states held popular elections; one combined popular election and appointment by the legislature. New Hampshire held a popular election but when no elector won a majority vote, the state senate chose its own Presidential electors. New York failed to elect or choose electors and did not cast any vote in that first election. Two states, North Carolina and Rhode Island, had not ratified the Constitution and did not consider themselves part of the new government.

Despite all these goings-on, sixty-nine electors of a possible ninety-one finally assembled in New York City on February 4, 1789, to cast ballots for President and Vice-President. Every elector cast one ballot for Washington, and John Adams, the next highest, collected thirty-four of the second ballots. Ten others divided the remaining thirty-five votes.

The United States Congress was to convene on March 4 to count the electoral ballots and notify the winners. But not until April 6 did a majority quorum of twelve Senators appear in the Senate chamber in Federal Hall at the corner of Wall and Broad streets. "Suffer me, Sir, to indulge the hope, that so auspicious a mark of public confidence will meet with your approbation," wrote Senator John Langdon of New Hampshire, the Senate's first President Pro Tempore, in notifying Washington that day of his unanimous election.

The gravity of the moment produced sudden qualms in Washington's breast. "My movement to the chair of government," he wrote a friend, "will be accomplished by feelings not unlike that of a culprit, who is going to his place of execution." Short of ready cash, he was forced to take a loan before his departure. Fortunately, Richard Conway of Alexandria was willing to lend him six hundred pounds at six per cent interest "to discharge what I owe and to leave the state."

Washington also visited his mother, Mary Ball Washington, at Fredericksburg, before beginning the 260-mile trip to New York on April 16. The eighty-one-year-old woman was dying of cancer, and the farewell had the mystique of sadness, despite a general lack of warmth between the two. "The last act of personal duty," he bluntly labeled the visit. As a fatherless boy of eleven, he had been shunted off by his mother to his two half-brothers, Lawrence and Augustine, to grow up in their care. Over the years, Washington's letters to his mother had been few; almost all began with "Honour'd Madam" and ended with "Your Most Affect. and Dutiful Son." Although he was the oldest of her six children he was not her favorite, despite her reliance on him in financial matters. She had hurt him deeply during the Revolutionary War when she charged him publicly with being "unjust and undutifull" in not providing for her needs. When Washington learned in 1781 that the Virginia Assembly had proposed a pension for her, he wrote to the Assembly Speaker: "Before I left Virginia, I answered all her calls for money, and since that period have directed my Steward to do the same. Whence her distress can arise, therefore, I do not know." During the thirty years of his marriage to Martha Custis, his mother had never visited Mount Vernon, which he had inherited from his half-brother Lawrence. Once when he feared that she planned to spend her last years living with him, he discouraged her by calling Mount Vernon not a home but "a well-resorted tavern." He said she would "be always dressing to appear in company; to come in dishabille; or to be as a prisoner in your bed-chamber. The first you'ld not like, the second I would not like and the third would not be pleasing to either of us."

After his visit with his hot-tempered, fault-finding mother, Washington was soon on his way north. All along the route great crowds turned out to greet him with resounding cheers. It was not a tribute to the new government he would head but a personal show of regard for the most popular American of the day. It seemed that at Baltimore the entire population greeted him and hundreds marched behind his carriage as he left the city. At Trenton, the scene of his spectacular victory over the Hessians on Christmas

of 1776, "Virgins fair and matrons grave" spread flowers in his
path and serenaded him. The specially-built barge carrying him
across the Hudson from New Jersey to New York had thirteen
rowing pilots dressed in white, and choirs aboard Hudson sloops
sang odes in his honor while ship and shore batteries pounded out
deafening thirteen-gun salutes.

April 30 dawned, the day the first President would be sworn
into office and deliver his inaugural address in the Senate chamber.
"Gentlemen, I wish for the direction of the Senate," Vice-President John Adams called out in agitation to the Senators as the
great hour neared. The Constitution had failed to provide guidelines for the occasion. "The President will, I suppose, address the
Congress. How shall I behave? How shall we receive it? Shall it
be standing or sitting?" One Senator insisted that Washington
should be received by the sergeant-at-arms bearing a mace on
his shoulder. But the Senate had neither sergeant-at-arms nor
mace, and time evaporated in uncertainty as Washington arrived
at Federal Hall at twelve-thirty following religious services and a
parade of troops in his honor.

For the occasion Washington came attired in a homespun suit
of brown broadcloth to emphasize native production and commerce.
The metal suit buttons carried a spread eagle motif, and he was
otherwise dressed in white silk stockings, square silver buckles on
his black shoes; a dress sword hung at his side and his hair was
powdered and tied in a queue. He was tall, with superb posture;
his shoes were size thirteen; and his hands were unusually large—
"the largest I have ever seen on a human being," his young
war aide, the Marquis de Lafayette, once commented. His face
still showed the effects of smallpox he had contracted in the
Barbados at eighteen.

Not a single foreign government except France had bothered
to send a diplomatic representative to the inauguration. Nor was
Martha Washington present; she had chosen to remain at Mount
Vernon until May. After a desperate search for a Bible because
one had been forgotten in the excitement, Chancellor Robert R.
Livingston of New York State administered the oath of office to
Washington on the balcony of Federal Hall in view of a tremendous crowd. After repeating the oath, the first President added
a spontaneous "So help me God," which all succeeding Presidents
were also to say. Then General Washington returned to the Senate
chamber where he delivered his inaugural address, a precedent not

demanded by the Constitution, but one that his successors would follow without exception.

In his speech, Washington expressed his appreciation for the confidence the country had in him, made a modest reference to his "inferior endowments," asked Congress to consider amendments to the Constitution (many who had opposed ratification had done so because the document did not contain a Bill of Rights), said that he planned to exercise his authority under Article II to recommend legislation, spoke out for a Congress that would operate with "no local prejudices, or attachments; no separate views, nor party animosities," and requested that he be paid no salary, only expense money.

He spoke in a low voice, and one Senator noted: "This great man was agitated and embarrassed more than he ever was by the leveled cannon or pointed musket. He trembled, and several times could scarcely make out to read." One time he pointed a finger to emphasize a remark and his extended arm remained frozen in place well into the next paragraph. It was the solemnity of the occasion rather than the gathering that upset him, for he knew half the twenty-two Senators facing him as well as many members of the House.

Following his talk, Washington retired from the light blue, high-ceilinged room, and escorted by committees from the House and Senate plus a troop of cavalry, he went to his home at No. 1 Cherry Street, near the base of what is now the Brooklyn Bridge. Here it was that he began his eight years as President, with his office in his residence.

Under the circumstances of the many problems facing the new nation in a world of ill-wishers, Washington knew that his Presidential years would be demanding. But such a condition would not be overwhelming because almost all of his life had been a hectic undertaking. He had begun the swift race with only a rudimentary education and without the favor of his father's will in which the family's three farms had been left to his mother and two half-brothers, Lawrence and Augustine. At sixteen, George was already at work as a surveyor's helper to chart the five million acres of the Northern Neck of Virginia owned by Thomas Lord Fairfax. The next year he moved up to become Culpeper County surveyor and a budding landowner.

Then in 1753, when he was only twenty-one, he began his military career when Royal Governor Robert Dinwiddie appointed

him a major and sent him on a 500-mile trip to order the French
Army to quit the Ohio Valley. "They pretend to have an un-
doubted design to the river from a discovery made by one LaSalle
sixty years ago," he reported on the failure of his mission. The
next year he won the opening skirmish of the French and Indian
War that would determine whether the French or British would
be chased from North America. This was a clash in the wilderness
in which he unconcernedly left the wounded French to the Indians who, he said, "believ'd them of their scalps." But there was
no time to gloat, for soon afterward he was forced to surrender
his hastily erected Fort Necessity following a nine-hour battle in
a downpour. The French allowed him to go home after he signed
a document that referred to him as an "assassin."

It was in July 1755 that he played a hero's role in the ambush
and slaughter of General James Braddock's two thousand Redcoats
in the Monongahela forest in that ill-fated expedition to capture
Fort Duquesne. Weak and shaky from dysentery, he nevertheless
displayed faultless courage in rough fighting that saw four bul-
lets rip his clothes and two horses die beneath him. For this Governor Dinwiddie appointed him a colonel with command of all
Virginia troops despite his youth. However, he quit the military
at the end of 1758 following his participation in the capture of
Fort Duquesne, because he had come to despise many of the
snobbish British officers as much as he did the French enemy.

After writing to Sally Fairfax, the wife of his closest friend,
that "the world has no business to know the object of my love,
declared in this manner to you," he married twenty-seven-year-old
Martha Dandridge Custis on January 6, 1759. Then, two years
later, he joined the planter class on his own when Lawrence Washington's widow and child died, leaving him as owner of Mount
Vernon. There were a dozen years now filled with farming, buying
more land, entertaining hundreds of guests each year, serving in the
House of Burgesses and meeting with interested citizens on local
political matters. Business dealings taught him to be shrewd and dis-
trustful even of friends. When he considered buying property from
Tom Marshall, his boyhood friend, fellow surveyor and father of
John Marshall, he wrote that Tom would "practice every deception
in his power to work me up to his price." There were only two
individuals who invariably bested him; they were Martha's spoiled
children, Jacky and Patsy.

When the British imposed the Stamp Act on the colonies in

1765 to force their American wards to meet the costs of garrisoning the frontier and protecting the seacoast, Washington did not join in the crescendo of howling that greeted this "taxation without representation." Not until successive retaliatory acts by the British culminated in the Quebec Act and Intolerable Acts of 1774 was Washington moved to protest. The Quebec Act placed the Ohio country in Quebec Province, while the Intolerable Acts in retribution for the Boston Tea Party closed the port of Boston and ended civil government in the Bay Colony. At this point, Washington agreed that the cousins Sam and John Adams and Virginia's firebrand, Patrick Henry, were right in their demand that the colonies must unite in their opposition to such arbitrary action.

He began as a member of the Virginia delegation to the First Continental Congress in Philadelphia that September. Then in June of 1775, he swept to leadership when the Second Continental Congress named him Commander-in-Chief of the Continental Army. "The peaceful plains of America are either to be drenched with blood or inhabited by slaves. Can a virtuous man hesitate in his choice?" he asked.

In December 1793, when Washington resigned his commission, he said that future historians would be puzzled "that such a force as Great Britain has employed for eight years in this country could be baffled in their plan of subjugating it by numbers infinitely less, composed of men often half starved, always in rags, without pay, and experiencing every species of distress which human nature is capable of undergoing."

Washington had once given the answer to this question in explaining the war strategy he planned to employ. As he put it: "We should on all occasions avoid a general action, nor put anything to the risk unless compelled by a necessity into which we ought never to be drawn." It was this identical strategy that he intended to use again in creating a new and functioning government.

It was apparent to those about Washington at the outset that he was constantly under a strain because, as he himself put it, he operated on "untrodden ground." He believed it best to proceed slowly with the "hopeful experiment" before arriving at decisions. "Many things which appear of little importance in themselves and at the beginning," he noted, "may have great and durable consequences from their having been established at the commencement of a new general government. It will be much easier to commence the Administration upon a well-adjusted system built on tenable grounds, than to correct errors or other inconveniences after they shall have been confirmed by habit."

This concern with establishing precedents revealed itself in the amount of attention he paid to determining the proper conduct of a President. He realized that a President was a chief of state like the King of England. But he was also a chief of government like the British Prime Minister. So far as the American Chief Executive was concerned, it was impossible to divorce the ceremonial activities of the former from the work activities of the latter. A President, therefore, had to wear two hats, doffing one and then the other as the situation demanded.

Washington knew that the ceremonial duties could interfere with the work of the President unless he took precautions to hold them in place. At the same time he wanted to "avoid as much as may be the charge of superciliousness, and seclusion from information, by too much reserve and too great a withdrawal of himself from company on the one hand, and the inconveniences as well as a diminution of respectability, from too free an intercourse and too much familiarity on the other." On this latter score, he was well aware that most of the sixteen Presidents of the Continental Congress had impaired their effectiveness and dignity by their promiscuous hospitality until they were generally considered in the same fashion as a major-domo of an inn.

Eleven days after he took office he wrote a letter with nine pertinent questions "by the President, respecting the system of conduct to be adopted by him" and sent it to John Jay, John Adams and Alexander Hamilton. Should he adopt "a line of conduct, equally distant from an association with all kinds of company on the one hand and from a total seclusion from Society on the other? And in that case, how is it to be done?" Would "one day in every week . . . be sufficient for receiving visits of Compliment?" Would it "tend to prompt impertinent applications and involve disagreeable consequences to have it known that the President will, every Morning at eight Oclock, be at leisure to give Audience to persons who may have business with him?" Could he invite "six, eight or ten official characters (including in rotation the members of both Houses of Congress) . . . to dine with him on the days fixed for receiving Company, without exciting clamours in the rest of the Community?" Would it "be satisfactory to the Public for the President to make about four great entertainmts. in a year on such occasions as . . . the Anniversary of the Declaration of Independence . . . the Alliance with France . . . the Peace with Great Britain . . . the Organization of the general Government?" Another question brought up the problem of whether the President possessed a private as well as a public character. For instance, question seven asked "whether there would be any impropriety in the President's making informal visits . . . calling upon his Acquaintances . . . for the purposes of sociability or civility?"

On the basis of the Adams reply and his own thoughts on the subject, Washington made it known that he would return no visits; that his dinner entertaining would be restricted to "official characters and strangers of distinction"; and that he would hold public receptions on specified days. Most members of Congress agreed with this course of conduct. But one Senator who found it monarchial said that for Washington "to suffer himself to be run down, on the one hand, by a crowd of visitants as to engross his time, would never do, as it would render the doing of business impracticable; but, on the other hand, for him to be seen only in public on stated times, like an Eastern Lama, would be equally offensive."

One of the precedents Washington established was that a President must encloak himself in paragon virtues, no matter what he was like as a private man. It was his belief that the public would be affronted to learn that the President was a human being after all. He must attend church regularly, even though as Washington confessed in agony in his diary, he was subjected to some "very lame discourses." He must live well and with great formality. Those who were invited to Washington's home found the residence attended by fourteen white servants and seven slaves. Yet this was the same man who bellowed at an officer who knelt to help him pull off a tight boot during the war: "I can take off my own damn boot, thank you!" A diner who sat down at the Washington table found the typical meal to consist of soup, fish, roast, gammon, fowl, apple pie, pudding, ice cream, watermelon, apples, peaches and nuts. Had that diner watched Washington he would have noticed that the President always restricted himself to a single dish. Moreover, he could not banquet because of ill-fitting false teeth. John Adams wrote in his diary: "My friend Washington attributed his misfortune to cracking walnuts in his youth." To increase public awe toward his office, Washington traveled through the city in a canary-colored, fancy coach pulled by six cream-colored horses and serviced by liveried lackeys and outriders. He walked daily for exercise, but only with his secretary, Tobias Lear, and never with politicians, administration officials or private citizens.

One of Washington's firm beliefs was that the President should always show a serious, unsmiling face in public, and at his wife's Friday levees he was "invariably grave." The public image of the aloof chief of state was further enhanced by his habit of bowing to guests, never shaking hands. It was only in private, said Thomas Jefferson, where he could be "unreserved with safety," that Washington "took a free share in conversation," and sometimes his mask of serenity would fall and he could be "most tremendous in his wrath" when the occasion demanded it. He would not wear the glasses he needed to correct his poor vision if outsiders were to be present, for he considered glasses a sign of weakness to the public. Back home at Mount Vernon, he could dress as a farmer in managing the plantation's affairs. However, at the weekly levee, Tobias Lear, his secretary, noted on one occasion, he was attired "in black velvet, his hair in full dress, powdered and gathered behind in a large silk bag, yellow gloves on his hands, holding a cocked hat with cockade in it, and the edges adorned with a black feather about an inch deep."

Martha Washington, or "Lady Washington" as she was called, found her husband's social rules a binding strait-jacket. "I lead a very dull life here," she wrote. "I never go to any public place. I am more like a state prisoner than anything else, there is certain bounds set for me which I must not depart from—and as I cannot doe [sic] as I like I am obstinate and stay at home." Unlike her husband, she returned social calls, though she waited until three days passed before doing so. On visiting day, her carriage pulled up at the house of call, the footman rapped loudly and announced her; then she and Tobias Lear went inside for a swift visit.

Martha, reputedly the richest widow in the Colonies at the time of her marriage to Washington, had inherited her wealth from her first husband, Daniel Parke Custis. He had inherited his fortune in turn from his father after the mysterious death of a Negro lad who had entered into the will because of the fondness of the elder Custis for him. Martha was a short, plump woman with snow-white hair and beautiful teeth. Abigail Adams called her "dignified and feminine." Washington's chief concern with Martha was that she could not be left alone but required a companion at all times.

Despite Washington's desire to set a precedent of aloof dignity, he was displeased by the fight made by certain members of Congress to provide him with royal titles. Fully a week before his inauguration, House and Senate committees had begun such discussion. The House had quickly and unanimously voted against additional titles, but the Senate would not let the subject die. The false rumor spread that Washington was demanding the title "His Mightiness, the President of the United States and Protector of their Liberties."

Chief culprit in the demand for titles was Vice-President Adams. It was undignified to call Washington simply "the President of the United States," he argued. "The President must be himself something that includes all dignities of the diplomatic corps and something greater still. What will the common people of foreign countries, what will the sailors and soldiers say, 'George Washington, President of the United States'? They will despise him to all eternity." A proposal that Washington be addressed as "His Excellency" failed to win a majority Senate vote; and a Senate committee report that a proper address was, "His Highness, the President of the United States of America, and Protector of their Liberties" was postponed indefinitely from consideration by the chamber.

However, Adams would not permit the subject to lapse, and after Washington's inaugural address he told the Senate clerk to refer to it in the minutes as the President's "most gracious speech." This had prompted Senator William Maclay of Pennsylvania to leap to his feet and cry out: "We have lately had a hard struggle for our liberty against kingly authority. The words prefixed to the President's speech are the same that are usually placed before the speech of his Britannic Majesty . . . I consider them as improper. I move that they be struck out." And they were. By mid-May, with reports of public anger and ridicule reaching them, Senators agreed to shelve the fight over titles and go on to other business.

During all this nonsense, Washington wrote to David Stuart, who had married the widow of Martha's son Jacky, about his uneasiness lest his countrymen believed he favored titles. Word had also reached him that Patrick Henry, who had opposed the Constitution, had smugly pointed to the "squints toward monarchy" the new government was making. Washington told Stuart that the subject had arisen before he reached New York, and despite his opposition once he was apprised of the Congressional moves, others had continued to urge titles. "I foresaw and predicted the reception it has met with, and the use that would be made of it by the adversaries of the government," he wrote. "Happily this matter is now done with, I hope never to be revived."

Years afterward, John Adams admitted that Washington did not need any fancy titles to add to the ceremonial pomp with which he surrounded himself. "He was the best Actor of the Presidency we have ever had," he wrote, operating "in a strain of Shakespearean and Garrickal excellence in Dramatic Exhibitions."

Washington's code of self-conduct was actually an important factor in winning public approval for the office he held. But more important to the survival of the country itself was the task of organizing a functioning government that would act with dispatch and energy, unify the nation, improve the economy and establish itself abroad as an independent nation.

Just how enormous was the task he faced is readily evident from a study of conditions at the outset of his stewardship. From the Confederation he had taken over a debt of about $54,000,000, almost no revenue and a non-existent credit. Of this debt, $12,000,000 were owed to foreign governments. Rhode Island and North Carolina stubbornly refused to join the Union and several of the states sent men to Congress who had openly opposed the ratification of the Constitution. On the western frontiers, Washington had plentiful complaints that the British were holding on to military posts in defiance of the 1783 peace treaty, while Spain throttled the western economy over the Alleghenies by barring Americans from using the Mississippi.

In the ratification fight, Washington had insisted that the new Constitution laid the foundation for "an efficient and responsible Executive." But now that he held the office, how was flesh to be put on the skeleton? How could he make the most of the vague power assigned to him in the short section of the Constitution that dealt with the Presidency?

Only in an offhand way did the Constitution refer to government agencies to help the President execute the laws passed by Congress. Article II, section 2, paragraph 1, provided that the President "may require the Opinion, in writing, of the principal Officer in each of the executive Departments." Paragraph 2 permitted Congress to "vest the Appointment of such inferior Officers, as they think proper, in the President alone, in the Courts of Law, or in the Heads of Departments."

The old Confederation Congress had operated a tiny foreign office under John Jay of New York, a bankrupt Treasury Board and a War Department overseeing 840 officers and men. With nothing else to rely on at the beginning, Washington continued these agencies as his shadow Executive Branch during his first few months as President. Then late in July 1789, three months after his inauguration, Congress established the first department, the Department of Foreign Affairs. Not long afterward when Congress assigned to this agency the task of preserving the laws passed by each session of Congress, it changed the name to the Department of State. In August came the passage of the War Department Act, establishing this agency to control both an army and a navy. Then in September one act authorized the Treasury Department and another, the Judiciary Act of 1789, prescribed a six-member Supreme Court, thirteen district courts, three circuit court districts on which Supreme Court justices and district court judges would work together, and laid out the legal work involved. The Judiciary Act also provided for an Attorney General.

For his departmental Secretaries, Washington nominated Thomas Jefferson as Secretary of State after John Jay rejected the position for the later opportunity to become the first Chief Justice of the Supreme Court. Henry Knox, Washington's old Revolutionary War Chief of Artillery, became Secretary of War and Alexander Hamilton, Washington's wartime secretary and now thirty-two years old, became Secretary of the Treasury. Edmund Randolph, successful Richmond attorney, governor, sponsor of the Virginia Plan at the convention and for a time opponent of ratification, accepted the nomination as Attorney General.

As an excellent wartime administrator, Washington fully understood that direction within the Executive Branch must come from the top. Jefferson called him a phenomenal administrator: "He was always in accurate possession of all facts and proceedings in every part of the Union, formed a central point for the different branches, preserved an unity of object and action among them, and met himself the due responsibility for whatever was done."

The truth was that he was so concerned that the government should get off to a good start that he needlessly took part in the details of activities he should have avoided. His Secretaries were always under the impression they were under close surveillance.

Frequently he dropped into their offices to discuss current business, while they in turn were forever being asked to come to his house on official matters. Even when it came to minor appointments, such as custom collectors and lighthouse keepers, he decided who would get the jobs. Then there were the streams of Presidential notes and chits that flowed steadily to the departments. Secretary of War Knox, whose three hundred pounds almost upset the barge crossing the Delaware that fateful Christmas Eve of 1776, was not only an inept administrator but also operated in a field Washington knew well. The result was a constant bombardment of notes demanding explanations, computations and copies of mail received by the hapless Secretary. "Who is Mr. Rosencrantz and under what authority has he attended the councils of the Indians at Buffalo Creek?" was a typical query from Washington.

The other Secretaries also felt his pressure. On one occasion he wrote to Jefferson: "Have you formed an opinion on the subject I submitted to you on Tuesday?" In 1791, when Hamilton devised a plan for an Internal Revenue Service, a messenger brought him another plan written by Washington, with orders to install it.

As soon as Washington had reached New York, he found himself deluged by three thousand applications for Federal jobs. A week before his inauguration, he wrote, "Scarcely a day passes in which applications do not arrive. . . . As it is, I have found the number of answers, which I have been necessitated to give in my own hand, an almost unsupportable burden to me." Several months later while wrestling with complex matters he announced: "Nomination to office is the most irksome part of the executive trust." Sometimes he consulted with Vice-President Adams, whose experience led him to write his sons: "Make it a rule never to become dependent on public employment for subsistence."

One of Washington's firmest convictions was that any show of nepotism on his part would only serve to disillusion the public. To his favorite nephew, Bushrod Washington, a one-eyed, snuff-dripping lawyer of modest abilities to whom he would one day leave Mount Vernon, Washington wrote a letter rejecting his plea to be made U. S. Attorney for Virginia. "My political conduct in nominations, even if I was uninfluenced by principle," he informed Bushrod, the son of his brother John Augustine, "must be exceedingly circumspect and proof against just criticism, for the eyes of Argus are upon me."

However, by the time he left office he believed that on occasion exceptions should be made to the rule against nepotism. For instance, on his last day as President, he wrote John Adams, his successor, of his "strong hope that you will not withhold merited promotion [from John Quincy Adams] because he is your son."

A second rule Washington enforced was to permit no applicant to promote himself in person. Applicants had swarmed in the vicinity of his Cherry Street home and office and made a nuisance of themselves. "I only wish that candidates for office would save themselves the trouble and consequent expense of personal attendance," Washington insisted. "All that I require are the names and such testimonials with respect to abilities, integrity and fitness, as may be in the power of the several applicants to produce. Beyond this, nothing is necessary or will be of any avail in my decisions." On the other hand, some individuals, like young John Marshall of Richmond, who had suffered through Valley Forge and played a vital role in the Virginia ratifying convention, applied for no positions yet were beseeched by Washington without avail to join his Administration.

Like "nepotism," "seniority" was another word Washington despised. The best man, rather than the one with the longest service, deserved the job. Once when he brought in an outsider to be Chief Justice of the Supreme Court instead of elevating one of the sitting justices, Thomas Jefferson applauded. Jefferson's observation was that Washington had "intended to establish a precedent against the descent of that office by seniority and to keep five mouths [from] always gaping for one sugar plumb."

Still another Washington rule was to judge candidates without regard to their political beliefs. On one occasion when a close personal friend and a political enemy were under consideration for the same position, he selected his enemy. His explanation was: "My friend I receive with cordial welcome to my house and welcome to my heart, but, with all his good qualities, he is not a man of business. His opponent is, with all his politics so hostile to me, a man of business; my private feelings have nothing to do in this case. I am not George Washington, but President of the United States."

He was soon to learn, however, that lofty as his standards were, he would not be permitted to be a free agent when it came to selecting his own underlings. For the Senate planned to squeeze what power it could from its constitutional authority to give its "advice and consent" to Executive appointments.

His rude awakening came when he sent the Senate a list of about one hundred names for appointments as collectors, naval officers and surveyors on August 3, 1789. He expected the list to be confirmed as routine. But two days later the Senate informed him that upon the personal objection of the two Senators from Georgia, the upper chamber had rejected his nomination of Benjamin Fishbourn to serve as naval officer for the Port of Savannah. Washington's reaction was one of wrath at this beginning of the institution of "Senatorial courtesy," whereby the Senate would reject a nomination solely on the ground that the nominee was personally obnoxious to a Senator from his home state.

He might have chosen to make an issue over Senatorial courtesy by fighting for a reconsideration of Fishbourn's nomination. Instead, he submitted a new nomination in a special message on August 7 and sharply criticized the Senate's action. After pointing out that Colonel Fishbourn had served under his watchful eye during the Revolution and was exceptionally qualified for his proposed government post, Washington bitingly added: "Permit me to submit to your consideration whether on occasions when the propriety of nominations appear questionable to you, it would not be expedient to communicate that circumstance to me, and thereby avail yourselves of the information which led me to make them." Yet from that time on he carefully queried Senators from the states involved prior to submitting nominations, thus accepting Senatorial courtesy. Chiefly as a result of this, the Senate withheld its consent from only five Washington nominees in eight years.

The Senate's appetite to control his appointments extended far beyond this political consideration. One minor point was whether the Senate could downgrade the level of a nominee. This issue had come up on Washington's very first nomination when on June 15, 1789, he informed the Senate that Thomas Jefferson wanted to return to the United States from the Court of France. "To take charge of American affairs at the Court in his absence," Washington's message went on, "I nominate William Short, Esq., and request your advice on the propriety of appointing him." Vice-President Adams had then raised the question regarding the rank Short should hold. Although the Senate did not on that occasion settle this question, Washington was determined to fight it as "an abuse of the power confided to the Senate."

A more important struggle between Washington and the Senate arose on the issue of what authority the Senate held on removing Executive officials. Washington assumed that his employees would hold their positions so long as their work pleased him, and when it no longer did he could discharge them. The Constitution failed to consider this problem beyond Article II, section 4, which stated that "the President, Vice-President and all civil Officers of the United States shall be removed from Office on Impeachment for, and Conviction of, Treason, Bribery, or other high Crimes and Misdemeanors." However, during the course of the ratification fight, Alexander Hamilton in *The Federalist* had expounded the position that for appointed officers there was another way to oust them. Just as with nominations, wrote Hamilton, the President would request the approval of the Senate to remove an official. "The consent of that body [the Senate] would be necessary to displace as well as to appoint."

The issue over the Senate's power of removal appeared when Congress considered the bill to establish the Department of Foreign Affairs in July 1789. One of its provisions stated that the Secretary was to be appointed by and with the advice and consent of the Senate and "to be removable by the President."

A harsh three-day debate on this single phrase took place in the House. Some members took the position that since the only method mentioned in the Constitution was the impeachment route, Secretaries could be removed only in this way. Alexander White of Virginia argued that since the Senate shared the appointive power, it must also share the removal power. The view of Representative James Madison, who had shared Hamilton's pen name of "Publius," was to prevail, and it was a view totally opposite from the ratification period *Federalist*. Madison's reasoning now was that the Chief Executive could not perform his duties unless his subordinates were responsible to him and therefore removable by him alone. The consent of the Senate, moreover, was not necessary to remove as well as to appoint, said Madison, because it must be assumed that the general Executive authority contained the implied power to dismiss an official.

Madison also pointed out that the bill's phrase making the Secretary "removable by the President" suggested that the Senate had this power but was in this single instance conferring it on the President. Chiefly because of the veneration in which Washington was then held, the House by a vote of 29 to 22 passed the bill with the phrase in question changed to read that "whenever said principal officer shall be removed by the President" the chief clerk should perform his functions. In this way it appeared that the power of removal was inherent in the Presidency.

In the Senate the debate was just as fiery. The final vote proved to be a 9 to 9 tie, which was broken in favor of the President by the deciding vote of Vice-President Adams. In later years Adams was to hail this vote as one of the most important acts in his life.

If the problem of controlling appointments and removals was a knotty one, even more vexing was the treaty-making process. As chairman of the Constitutional Convention, Washington was aware that at one time the delegates considered creating a council of advisers for the President and at another time giving the Senate full power to make treaties. But the final decision was to eliminate the council and hand over only part of the treaty-making functions to the Senate. One such function, outlined in Article II, section 2, paragraph 2, said that the President "shall have Power, by and with the Advice and Consent of the Senate, to make Treaties, provided two-thirds of the Senators present concur." What did this mean? Was the President to seek the Senate's advice in the actual writing of treaties? Was he to consult the Senate in person?

The Senate had appointed a committee to meet with Washington to determine the proper method of communication regarding nominations and treaties. Washington told the committee he would submit nominations by written messages because: "It could be no pleasing thing, I conceive, for the President, on the one hand, to be present and hear the propriety of his nominations questioned, nor for the Senators, on the other hand, to be under the smallest restraint from his presence from the fullest and freest inquiry into the character of the person nominated."

However, Washington took a different view on treaties, and told the committee that "oral communications seem indispensably necessary." He gave as his reason: "Respecting treaties . . . in these a variety of matters are contained all of which not only require consideration, but some of them may undergo much discussion; to do which by written communications would be tedious without being satisfactory." On this basis, the Senate passed a resolution that when the President visited the upper chamber, he should occupy the Vice-President's chair on the dais, while Adams should sit with the Senators facing him. The Senate resolution also said that when the President came, in all cases questions put to Senate members were to be voted on viva voce and not by written ballot.

This resolution had hardly passed when Washington's secretary delivered the following message:

Gentlemen of the Senate: The President of the United States will meet the Senate, in the Senate chamber, at half-past eleven o'clock tomorrow, to advise with them on the terms of the treaty to be negotiated with the Southern Indians.

Gº. Washington

New York, Aug. 21, 1789.

At the appointed time Washington arrived and stated that he came for their advice and consent to seven propositions regarding the pending treaty which would end the border dispute between the state of Georgia and the Creek Indians. Adams quickly read the seven proposals to be included by three negotiating commissioners. At the end, he came to "seven heads," to which the Senate was to give its advice and consent.

"But carriages were driving past and such a noise," said Senator William Maclay of Pennsylvania, "I could tell it was something about Indians, but was not master of one sentence of it." After a complaint about the outside noise by Senator Robert Morris, Adams reread the "first head," then put the question, "Do you advise and consent?"

No one stirred and finally Maclay jumped up, later writing in his *Journal* that if he had not, no one else would have dared to protest and "we should have had these advices and consents ravished in a degree from us." To Washington he declared, "Mr. President, the business is new to the Senate. It is of importance. It is our duty to inform ourselves as well as possible." He called for a reading of the treaties and documents mentioned in the paper Adams had read, and as he did so, he said, "I cast my eye at the President of the United States. I saw he wore an aspect of stern displeasure."

A tedious reading of papers began. Decision on the "first head" was postponed when someone said new information might be obtained from a man who had recently returned from the Cherokee country. The second head was rejected and the third was post-

poned after a heated debate. Finally a motion was made that
all the papers be referred to a Senate committee for a two-day
study and then reported back to the floor. Senator Pierce Butler
of South Carolina called this improper and quoted Washington that
the Senators were "acting as a council." No council ever committed
anything to a committee. But the motion carried.

"The President of the United States started up in a violent fret,"
said Maclay. "'This defeats every purpose of my coming here'
were the first words that he said. He then went on that he had
brought his Secretary of War with him to give every needed information; that the Secretary knew all about the business, and yet
he was delayed and could not go on with the matter. He cooled
down, by degrees . . . but declared that he did not understand the
matter of commitment. . . . He rose a second time, and said that
he had no objection to postponement until Monday at ten o'clock.
. . . A pause for some time ensued. We waited for him to withdraw. He did so with a discontented air . . . with sullen dignity."

One report was that as Washington stamped out he declared
"that he would be damned if he ever went there again." But he
returned the following Monday. Maclay reported that Washington "was placid and serene, and manifested a spirit of accommodation; declared his consent that his questions should be amended."
After a long debate, the work was finally completed and Washington left with his advice and consent.

This single experience had a vital effect on both Washington
and the Senate. No more would he meet with the upper house
to discuss a treaty. Instead he turned generally to the practice of
submitting treaties to the Senate only after completing negotiations
with the other governments involved. And these he sent by special
message. So far as the Senate was concerned, the intention of the
Founding Fathers to make it the President's privy council was not
to be fulfilled. It was simply a legislative body.

Although Washington would no longer come to the Senate to
seek its advice and consent, he continued to come each year to
Congress to read his Annual Message on the State of the Union.
Here a clumsy precedent began that ran on for twelve years. After
listening to the Message, each House prepared an address in reply
and sent a committee to call on the President and read it to
him. He was then expected to make a reply to their reply.

A great deal of legislative time was wasted preparing these addresses. The more democratic Congressmen called them "sycophantic" and "the most servile echo," while Washington considered them a bore that he could not avoid. Senator Maclay reported that at one committee reading of its address in reply, "the President took his reply out of his coat pocket. He had his spectacles in his jacket pocket, having his hat in his left hand and his paper in his right. He had too many objects in his hands. He shifted his hat between his forearm and the left side of his breast. But taking his spectacles from the case embarrassed him. He got rid of this small distress by laying the spectacle case in the chimney piece. . . . Having adjusted his spectacles, which was not very easy considering the engagement of his hands, he read the reply with tolerable exactness and without emotion." But his false teeth made his voice "hollow."

Besides extending feelers to determine how far his executive authority extended, Washington had to face problems at the start involving the financing of the new government. The first revenue bill he recommended to Congress was the Tariff Act of July 1789, a bill written by Representative James Madison, which placed duties on imports and protected domestic manufactures from foreign competition. In addition, his Administration's first budget won Congressional approval in September 1789, without any examination of its details. The total was $639,000, and of this, $216,000 covered civil expenses, $137,000 military expenses, $190,000 for payment on the public debt that he inherited and $96,000 for pensions.

Washington gave no consideration to promoting members of each house to act as his floor leaders to further his legislative recommendations. For it was his philosophy that just as the Chief Executive must guard to prevent the legislature from encroaching upon his authority, he must refrain from openly encroaching on the prerogatives of Congress. Nevertheless, James Madison, his close friend and the accepted leader of the House, made himself available to assist the President where he could. "What do you think I had best do?" Washington would bluntly write him on an important matter that needed deciding. Another time he wrote Madison: "I am very troublesome but you must excuse me. Ascribe it to friendship and confidence, and you will do justice to my motives."

It was Madison who handled the first revenue bill, and wrote

Messages to Congress for the President. When Washington asked Congress to add a bill of rights to the Constitution, as amendments to the document, Madison undertook this task. He collected the more than one hundred proposals made by various state conventions and sent in from other sources, and after culling out the duplicates and trivia, he introduced the rest in the House in June 1789. Twelve passed and went to the state legislatures for action. In the end when ten amendments were added to the Constitution, Washington was then able to say he had kept his promise to the country. The two that failed dealt with Congressional pay and the number of House members, hardly Bill of Rights material.

When the first session of the First Congress adjourned in September 1789, Washington thought it was time to use his prestige to stir popular interest in the new government and strengthen national pride. He did this by making a grand tour of New England that fall where his presence evoked an enormous and joyful response from the people. The only tense moment came in Massachusetts where gouty Governor John Hancock insisted that the President pay his respects to him by making the first call. Washington recognized that this was Hancock's way of telling the people of his state that the national government was inferior to the state government. He, therefore, coldly requested Hancock to come to him. The governor finally complied, thus giving the President a symbolic victory of great importance in the eyes of his four million countrymen.

This desire to add to the prestige of the Presidency and the new government was a constant endeavor. For instance, when Washington returned from his tour, he proclaimed the last Thursday in November a national Day of Thanksgiving. With the country acting in unison to celebrate this day, national unity was further strengthened.

Having carefully set the stage during the first year, Washington's Administration quickened the pace in 1790. At the opening of the second session of the First Congress on January 8, he told members in joint meeting that they should derive encouragement from the reflection that the measures of the last session had been as satisfactory to their constituents as the novelty and difficulty of the work allowed one to hope. He asked Congress to examine defense measures because: "To be prepared for War is one of the most effectual means of preserving peace." He also requested Congress's patronage for the promotion of science and literature and

said it was its duty to promote education because "the enlight-
ened confidence of the people . . . by teaching themselves to know
and value their own rights . . . to distinguish between oppression
and the necessary exercise of lawful authority" was the "valuable
end of government."

That second year steps were taken to establish a national
census, and pass legislation involving naturalization, patents, copy-
rights, territorial government and relations with Indian tribes. Congress also determined the site of the future permanent capital
and approved a plan to pay off national and state debts. That year
North Carolina and Rhode Island had representation in Congress
for the first time. Washington had assented to the legislative
scheme of Senator Oliver Ellsworth to force them to join the Union
—by levying taxes on their exports to other states, as though
they were foreign nations.

It became noticeable that year that Secretary of the Treasury
Alexander Hamilton was providing the impetus for this outpouring of legislative activity. He even gave it a name—"Executive
impulse." Washington had stated flatly: "Motives of delicacy have
uniformly restrained the P—— from introducing any topick which
relates to legislative matters to members of either house of Congress lest it should be supposed that he wished to influence the
question before it." Even with Representative Madison, he carefully restricted his association to asking his aid on Executive matters, not on ways to promote legislation through Congress.

Unlike the President, Hamilton felt no such compunctions for
maintaining a wall between the Executive and Legislative
branches on the legislative procedure. To a large extent he was
helped by the wording of the act establishing the Treasury
Department. Differing from the acts setting up the other departments, the Treasury Act made it the duty of the Secretary to
"digest and prepare plans for the improvement and management of the revenue and for the support of the public credit." He
was also to "make reports and give information to either branch of
the legislature, in person or in writing as may be required."

In a meeting with Washington, Hamilton explained that the act
made his department subject to a large extent to Congress. The
organic acts establishing the other departments, he pointed out,
directed their Secretaries to perform those duties the President
entrusted to them. If Congress wanted information from the State
Department, it would ask the President to direct the Secretary

to give it to him for submission to Congress. However, in the case of the Treasury Department, Congress would call directly on the Secretary. Washington offered no objection to this interpretation, which made the Treasury Department both an executive and a legislative agency. However, Secretary of State Thomas Jefferson sarcastically remarked that Hamilton's interpretation would let him "place himself subject to the house when the Executive should propose what he should not like, & subject to the Executive when the house should propose anything disagreeable."

By taking this double position for his department, Hamilton moved quickly to bring the Legislative Branch under his control, by providing it with his legislative leadership. Within a week after he became Secretary, the House discharged its tax committee as superfluous and turned over to him the function of preparing tax legislation, by requesting him to submit a report on the subject. It was a simple process to move on from making reports to submitting actual legislation, and from here to working for their passage.

So while Washington personally refrained from controlling Congress, his lieutenant worked at it constantly, and thus increased the Executive power with his "Executive impulse." Hamilton not only took to preparing legislation, but, as some legislators accused him, he also worked behind the scenes selecting committee members, attending committee meetings and holding evening sessions with Congressional assistants to plan strategy. "Nothing is done without him," one Senator charged, referring to Hamilton's interference in the Senate's activities through his "Senatorial gladiators." Hamilton's contempt for legislators led Senator Maclay to comment that "a schoolboy should be whipped for such pitiful evasions" practiced by "his Holiness [Hamilton]."

Hamilton's legislative leadership grew bolder early in 1790 when Washington fell desperately ill. During his many years of warfare, Washington had seldom slept more than four hours a night. This had permanently lowered his resistance to disease and made him look far older than his actual years. For a short time in 1789 an attack of pneumonia put him to bed, but now in the spring of 1790 a recurrence made doctors despair of his life. "I have already within less than a year had two severe attacks, the last worst than the first," Washington wrote matter-of-factly. "A third probably will put me to sleep with my fathers."

While Washington lay ill, Hamilton pushed ahead with pet

financial proposals. One would fund the national debt of $54 million through the sale of Treasury bonds paying 6 per cent interest. Another would have the Federal Government assume the war debts of the states and pay off the $21.5 million involved at full par value. The two proposals soon acquired the names of "Funding" and "Assumption."

Both schemes ran into immediate opposition, though the attacks on Assumption were more violent. Leading opponents were Congressmen from Virginia which, as they pointed out, had already paid off most of her wartime debts and now would be called upon through taxes to the Federal Government to pay off the debts of lax neighboring states. In addition, as other Congressmen argued, the wartime certificates the thirteen states had issued could now be purchased at ten to fifteen cents on their original dollar value. To pay them off at face value, as Hamilton was proposing, would give speculators an enormous windfall.

These facts were of little interest to Alexander Hamilton. By assuming the wartime debts of the states, he argued in return, the Federal Government would be showing foreign governments that it was stronger than the states. It would also reveal an intention of stability and reliability on the part of the Federal Government that would make foreign loans available. Moreover, he added, the bill would bind the well-to-do in the population to the new government. This group held most of the languishing state certificates. His plan was to exchange national bonds paying 6 per cent interest for these state certificates. The bondholders would therefore have a prime interest in seeing to it that the Federal Government prospered. "A public debt," said Hamilton, "is a public blessing."

While Hamilton's Assumption Bill languished in Congress, so did another bill favored by Southerners to place the permanent capital in their midst. It was known that Washington preferred Georgetown near the Potomac River, though he did nothing to promote it. Energetic Hamilton was quick to perceive that a trade might be made with the southern faction whereby he would get Assumption and they would gain a capital.

Hamilton made it appear to be an accidental meeting when he stopped Jefferson, newly arrived from France, on the street one morning. They walked along Broadway while Hamilton told him that the Union was doomed without the Assumption Bill. "He walked me backwards and forwards before the President's door for half an hour," said Jefferson. The talk led to dinner the following evening, and here the two Secretaries arranged the first instance of log-rolling, or an agreement to help one another gain votes for unrelated bills. Jefferson agreed to get two Virginia legislators, Alexander White and Richard Bland Lee, to change their votes and approve Assumption, while Hamilton promised to persuade other legislators to vote for a Potomac River capital site, following a ten-year interim shift by the National Government from New York to Philadelphia, or from 1790 to 1800.

When both measures passed Congress, the first harsh words against Washington were heard. Senator Maclay charged that "the President has become in the hands of Hamilton the dish-clout of every dirty speculation, as his name goes to wipe away blame and silence all murmuring." Jefferson later tried to absolve himself from blame for the log-rolling deal by lamely charging he had not wanted to provide "pablum for stock-jobbers," but was so new to national politics that he was "most ignorantly and innocently made to hold the candle to Hamilton's wicked scheme." Yet seven years earlier when James Madison included Assumption in a tax bill under the Articles of Confederation Government Jefferson then called it "one palatable ingredient at least in the pill we were to swallow."

Having recovered from his almost fatal bout with pneumonia, and with these two issues settled, Washington visited Rhode Island in August to welcome her into the Union. After a rest at Mount Vernon, Washington hired a large public-service coach to drive him in November 1790 to Philadelphia, the second national capital. It rained the entire trip, the roads were slippery trenches and his driver was drunk from the beginning to the end of the frightening ride. Unlike his arrival in New York for his inauguration, his entrance into Philadelphia was unheralded and he quietly moved into the home of Senator Robert Morris, who besides being the financier of the Revolution, built the first hothouse and icehouse in America. A few years later, Morris would be languishing in a debtors' prison.

By mid-passage in his first term, Washington could consider with pleasure the virility and success of the "hopeful experiment." Most fortunately, during those critical first two years the country had been blessed with booming prosperity, which naturally redounded to the credit of the new government. Little wonder that Washington's fifty-ninth birthday on February 22, 1791, was treated as a national holiday. And later that year his two-month grand tour of the South brought him ear-splitting cheers and as many as sixty toasts in such places as Charleston, Savannah and Augusta. But the trip was a physical ordeal. During one coach ferry river crossing, he said he had "lain all night in my Great Coat and Boots, in a berth not long enough for me by the head, and much cramped." He also found the southern inns and taverns, which were run mostly by widows, "extremely indifferent." Nevertheless, he was pleased with the personal attention accorded him and with the prosperity he found everywhere. "They begin to feel the good effects of equal laws and equal protection," he noted. "Tranquillity reigns among the people with the disposition towards the general government which is likely to preserve it." But there were future problems to consider, he told the South. Among these were "the direful effect of slavery" and the growing "daemon of party spirit and local reproach."

To preserve his health, Washington began to spend more time outdoors, either walking or riding. He did not smoke; he drank moderately; and with few exceptions he was in bed by nine P.M. A serious drain on his time and energy was the time he had to spend on official and personal correspondence. Almost the entire Sunday was given over to writing instructions to his farm manager at Mount Vernon. There were also the letters that he wrote for Martha which she then copied in her own hand because her inability to spell even simple words was an embarrassment to him. In addition, he wrote letters of advice to young people. To Martha's eighteen-year-old granddaughter, Eleanor Parke Custis, who contemplated marriage, he wrote: "Love is too dainty a food to live upon alone." To his dentist, he complained of the false teeth that "bulge my lips out in such a manner as to make them appear considerably swelled."

Besides his Sunday work on Mount Vernon, Washington began to spend many Presidential days and weeks developing the nation's capital that was to spring into existence on the banks of the Potomac River in 1800. Not only did he select the three Federal district commissioners who were to handle the preparation but he also kept close watch on them and shared their duties. When it came to buying the land, he rode down from Philadelphia on several occasions for personal talks with the owners, for he was an experienced and shrewd bargainer and was determined to buy cheap. He was to find that his chief obstacle to success was David Burnes, a heavy-drinking, argumentative farmer who lazed away his time on the river or in his small cabin. Burnes was not the least impressed that the man who dickered with him was the President of the United States. Washington's tactics ranged from a show of disinterestedness to displays of sharp talk and a loud voice. Finally Burnes gave up the vital plot on which Washington had determined for the President's residence. Washington also played a key role in selecting the Capitol site. One of his proudest moments came two years later, in September 1793, when he donned his masonic apron and laid the cornerstone of the Capitol Building that would house the Congress in 1800.

The year 1791 also saw a beginning in the development of a major Presidential institution. Washington's unhappy experience with the Senate in a direct confrontation regarding the Southern Indians treaty in 1789 had led him to reject using the Senate as his advisory council. But this had created a void, for he required a body of this sort to aid him in determining policy. He did not immediately think of his Secretaries as a possibility, but considered them as separate entities to assist the Chief Magistrate in discharging the duties of his trust. For instance, when he decided to veto the Congressional bill to apportion Representatives among the states according to the 1790 census, he asked Representative Madison to draft his veto message, rather than any of his Secretaries. In his view, the rules prescribed in the Constitution had not been followed in the bill.

However, early in 1790, Washington had begun the practice of calling upon his Secretaries for written opinions on various matters. But it was not until April, the following year, when he prepared to leave on his southern tour that he asked the Secretaries and the Vice-President to meet as a group during his absence. Later Jefferson sent him a report of their discussion.

Washington's first conference with all of his department heads came in March 1792, as a result of a government crisis. Trouble with the Miami and Wabash Indian tribes in Ohio and Kentucky had forced Washington to send Major General Arthur St. Clair to establish a military post and give the Indians a "thorough drubbing." Only a few miles from his goal in November 1791, St. Clair's forces suddenly were pounced upon by the Miamis led by Little Turtle and suffered nearly one thousand casualties. The decimation of the American force had led the House to establish its first investigating committee. Washington called his Secretaries into conference to consider how the Executive Branch should deal with the investigators who were demanding that the Secretary of War supply papers relating to that costly fiasco.

It was Madison who first used the term "Cabinet" in 1793 to label the conferences of the President with his department heads. But long before he invented the word, the Cabinet was already a primary institution, providing the President with a council of advisers on national policy.

In time, the Cabinet came to be an organization bound together by loyalty to the President's aims and goals. However, at the outset this was not true, for Washington had in Secretary of the Treasury Hamilton and Secretary of State Jefferson two brilliant men whose views were not reconcilable. Born in the West Indies on the island of Nevis, his lineage uncertain, the insatiably ambitious Hamilton married into the highly respectable Schuyler clan in New York and became the strong champion of the rich and well born. As he viewed things, this group should be given "a distinct, permanent share in the government" to "check the imprudence of democracy." To his way of thinking a government run for the benefit of the moneyed groups meant a strong central government using the Constitution as a guideline and not as a limiting force. To promote his views for a national financial program, he wrote three excellent reports: *Public Credit* (January 1790); on *A National Bank* (December 1790); and on *Manufactures* (December 1791). Jefferson's views ran the opposite—for an agrarian economy, expanding democracy, states' rights and a weak central government and President.

At the beginning, the antagonism between Hamilton and Jefferson was not readily apparent to Washington or to others. It first appeared in the fall of 1790 when Washington asked for written opinions on American policy should England go to war with Spain and attempt to conquer the Spanish Floridas and Louisiana. Jefferson wanted war with Britain if this should happen because it would ruinously affect the future of the American frontier. Hamilton's view was that the British Government was the best in the world and should be dealt a slight protest if this came about.

Their next squabble came over whether or not Congress had authority to charter a Bank of the United States. In December 1790, Hamilton wrote a report for the House proposing a privately-owned bank with the government owning $2,000,000 of its $10,-

000,000 capital stock and laying down conditions for its management. Its purpose, said Hamilton, was to provide sound money.
The paper money issued by the states during the Confederation era was disappearing and under Article I, section 10 of the
Constitution the states were forbidden to issue more. However,
there was such a shortage of gold and silver coins that several
states were considering chartering local banks of issue without
requiring that the paper money they issued be backed by gold or
silver reserves. This would not only result in a wild inflation but
would also ruin the public credit and banking system. Hamilton
argued that a strong central bank with branches throughout the
country would maintain a sound national currency by pledging to
redeem on demand in gold or silver the notes it issued. Not only
would this help business and trade, he pointed out, but the bank
would also serve to help the Government by acting as its agent to
obtain loans through the sale of Treasury securities, collect taxes
and store and transfer government money from one section of the
country to others as needed.

When the bill passed Congress, Washington asked Jefferson and
his other Cabinet officers for their opinions. Jefferson quickly
charged that Congress lacked the right to establish the bank; "The
Constitution allows only means which are 'necessary,'" he wrote
Washington, "not those which are merely convenient for effecting
the enumerated powers . . . a bank is not necessary, and conse-
quently not authorized."

In rebuttal, Hamilton argued that the Federal Government was
not bound by the enumerated powers, but could do anything so
long as the Constitution did not expressly forbid it: "The powers
. . . ought to be construed liberally in advancement of the public
good." Besides, he continued, there were more powers than the
enumerated powers that Jefferson saw. There were also "implied
powers," or the *means* for executing an enumerated power, and
"resultant powers," or the necessary and proper *consequences* of
enumerated or implied powers. If Congress had the power to
collect taxes, it was *implied* that Congress could establish an internal revenue service; if the Constitution sanctioned the acquisi-
tion of territory, this would necessarily *result* in power to control
persons living there.

Washington was greatly embarrassed by the emotion stirred up
by Jefferson and Hamilton on the bank issue. But the Hamilton
view was more to his liking, for it would provide the means for

adapting the Constitution to the changing requirements of a growing nation without resorting to the time-consuming and uncertain amendment process. Moreover, as a practical man he could see that the bank would help the nation's financial stability. So in February 1791, when he signed the act creating the Bank of the United States, he was in reality telling Jefferson he did not agree with his theory of strict construction of the Constitution and its resulting weak central government.

By the late fall of 1791, Hamilton and Jefferson were like two mastiffs with bared fangs. "Mr. H. and Mr. J.," noted an observer, were eager to battle over most subjects, especially whether "Tom Paine or Edmund Burke are the greatest fools." With their respective followings in Congress also taking sides, Washington began to grow alarmed at the rising system of political parties.

While he pondered what to do, both Cabinet members organized political newspapers to attack each other. Hamilton's organ was the *Gazette of the United States,* edited by John Fenno, for whom Hamilton acquired public printing contracts, including the printing for the Senate. Jefferson chose to meet Fenno's harsh attacks by inducing Philip Freneau, "the poet of the Revolution," to come to Philadelphia, where the Government had moved in December 1790, and establish the *National Gazette.*

Hamilton's forces took to calling themselves Federalists, while Jefferson's protagonists were known as Democratic-Republicans, later to be shortened to Republicans. By the spring of 1792, Fenno was already portraying Democratic-Republicans as radical fiends, and Freneau was performing a comparable hatchet job on the Federalists. Washington hinted broadly to Jefferson that he did not believe it proper for him to employ Freneau as translator in the State Department. However, Jefferson did not take the hint, but retained him, pointing out to others that Freneau was doing a necessary job by publicizing an Administration that was "fast galloping into monarchy."

As the attacks gathered steam, Hamilton aided Fenno by writing anonymous articles against Jefferson in the *Gazette of the United States.* One of Hamilton's charges was that Jefferson was hiding behind pseudonyms in shooting newspaper broadsides at the Washington Administration and at him in particular. To this, Jefferson issued a flat denial: "Some people here are insinuating that I am Brutus, that I am Agricola, that I am Philodemus, &c., &c. I am none of them."

In May 1792, Jefferson believed he had enough ammunition to warrant Washington's dismissal of Hamilton, and he sent the President a long list of charges against the Treasury Secretary. He accused Hamilton of seeking to establish a monarchy, creating a "corrupt squadron" in Congress to serve his legislative purposes, forcing a national debt on the country, establishing odious taxes and excessive interest rates on government obligations.

Washington made no attempt to answer Jefferson, but laboriously drew up the charges under twenty-one titles. These he sent to Hamilton and asked him to submit his comments, in order "to obtain light and pursue truth." The criticisms, he said, had come from "sensible and moderate men." However, Hamilton was aware of the source and made a complete denial, point by point, in an essay running to 14,000 words.

Because he valued both men, Washington attempted a reconciliation between them. In August, he wrote Jefferson and a month later to Hamilton "how much it is to be regretted then, that whilst we are encompassed on all sides with avowed enemies and insidious friends, that internal dissensions should be harrowing and tearing our vitals . . . Without more charity for the opinions and acts of one another in Governmental matters, I believe it will be difficult, if not impracticable, to manage the Reins of Government or to keep the parts of it together."

However, his appeal was in vain and constituted an additional reason for contemplating retirement when his term ended in March 1793. To Madison he wrote: "I find myself deficient in many of the essential qualifications, owing to my inexperience in the forms of public business, my unfitness to judge legal questions and the questions arising out of the Constitution; that others more conversant in such matters would be better able to administer them."

For these and other reasons, Washington asked Madison to decide on the proper time and mode of announcing his intentions: "Turn your thoughts to a Valadictory [sic] address from me to the public; expressing in plain and modest terms, that having been honored with the Presidential Chair, and to the best of my abilities contributed to the Organization and Administration of the government, that having arrived at a period of life when the private Walks of it, in the shade of retirement, becomes necessary, and will be most pleasing to me; and the spirit of the government may render a rotation in the Elective Officers of it more congenial with their ideas of liberty and safety, that I take my leave of them as a public man." Although Madison complied with the request, he nevertheless remonstrated with Washington to accept a second term. So did Jefferson and Hamilton, who made this one of the few matters on which they did not disagree in 1792. Jefferson's plea that "North and South will hang together if they have you to hang on" made Washington pause in his thoughts on retiring to Mount Vernon.

Washington had planned to make his farewell address in November. But that month when he read his Annual Message to Congress, he made no mention of retiring. Because of this, it became widely accepted that he would serve a second term, and when the electoral vote was counted in the Senate on February 13, 1793, once again he won unanimous election.

In his first term, Washington had cautiously but emphatically laid a solid foundation for his office and provided the necessary leadership for guiding the birth of the new government and insuring its continuation. His second term was to be significantly different. These next four years were to test the permanence of his reputation and his ability to keep his small nation from becoming entangled "in the crooked policies of Europe."

Almost all Americans had been thrilled when the French Revolution broke out in July 1789. French aid during the American Revolution, which had made possible the decisive victory over the British at Yorktown, Virginia, in October 1781, had resulted in a strong bond of friendship between a grateful United States and a France happy at the opportunity to humiliate Britain. Washington deeply felt this kinship and debt, and when his former French aide, the young Marquis de Lafayette, sent him the key to the stormed Bastile, he responded by hailing the key as "a token of victory gained by liberty over despotism."

Ironical, French aid against England had played a key role in bankrupting the French monarchy and bringing on the thunderous uprising of the French people. However, when the French Revolution led to savage excesses, Washington's initial enthusiasm rapidly evaporated and he condemned the Revolutionists as being given more to "haste than good speed in their innovations." This opinion was further solidified in January 1793 when Louis XVI was beheaded, and again the following month when France declared war on Britain.

In the wake of these events floated vital constitutional problems in foreign relations. With the monarchy overthrown, France was sending a new minister to the United States. Washington realized that receiving him would mean recognizing the new French Government. But could the President do so without the Senate's approval? Also, what authority did he possess to prevent his country from being dragged into war?

Over in Paris, the French Government assumed that Americans would soon join forces on the firing lines facing Britain. Not only did they assume so because of their own wartime aid to Americans fifteen years earlier, but also because of the 1778 Treaty of Alliance. In the midst of their war for independence, grateful Americans had agreed by this treaty to defend French possessions in the West Indies forever. If the British were now to attack in that area did this plunge the United States automatically into the war?

On April 18, 1793, Washington addressed thirteen questions to his Cabinet on the problems relating to the French treaty and the new French Government. Question thirteen asked whether it was necessary or advisable to call together the two houses of Congress with a view to the posture of European affairs.

From the replies, Washington drew certain conclusions. It was imperative that the United States take immediate action to prevent being drawn into a war in which she had no particular interest. Second, the President had authority to do this without waiting for Congressional approval. As for the Treaty of Alliance, several loopholes existed to nullify its permanent nature. First, Washington reasoned, the French alliance had been a defensive agreement. Now that France was the aggressor against Britain the United States was no longer under obligation. Furthermore, the treaty had been made with the French monarchy, which no longer existed. In addition, the treaty of peace with Britain in 1783 outmoded the defensive alliance with France.

Cabinet members offered no verbal resistance to the issuance of a Presidential proclamation, and on April 22, Washington declared that the United States would follow "a conduct friendly and impartial towards the belligerent powers." Nowhere in his statement that was drawn up by Attorney General Randolph was the word "neutrality" used. Nevertheless, it came to be universally known as "Washington's Proclamation of Neutrality."

Although Jefferson had consented to the proclamation, shortly after it was released his second thought was that it was an unconstitutional action. For if the President had the right to proclaim American neutrality, he was thereby asserting that the United States would not go to war. Jefferson felt this encroached on the legislature's rights and concluded that if Washington had not issued his "milk and water" proclamation, he could have won concessions from the warring nations and thus obtained "the broadest privileges of neutral nations."

When Jefferson stirred against the proclamation, his Democratic-Republicans in Congress and throughout the country began shouting. As "Pacificus," Hamilton was quick to come to Washington's defense with newspaper articles backing neutrality. Jefferson, close to Madison since 1779, now asked Madison to forget his warm friendship with Washington and reply to Hamilton. "For God's sake, my dear Sir, take up your pen, select the most striking heresies and cut him to pieces in the face of the public." By now Jefferson was convinced that "a secret Anglomanny" had mothered neutrality and that the Administration's proclamation favored Britain. His fellow Cabinet member Hamilton, he said, was "panic-struck if we refuse our breath to every kick which Gr. Brit. may choose to give it."

Up and down the country, Democratic clubs began springing up to champion France. Members hailed each other as "Citizen" and "Citizeness" in slavish imitation of the French Revolutionists, sang revolutionary songs, wore red liberty caps and raised liberty poles. Jefferson hailed the clubs as a popular movement toward greater democracy, while Hamilton's Federalists spat at them as "filthy Jacobins," seditionists, "frog-eating, man-eating, blood-drinking cannibals." As their noise and activities increased, Washington in disgust called them self-created societies intent on fomenting resistance to neutrality and laws applying to the nation. "I want an *American* character," he later told Patrick Henry, "that the powers of Europe may be convinced we act for *ourselves* and not for *others*."

The pro-French partisans were given great stimulation by the arrival of the new French minister, Edmond Genêt, at Charleston, South Carolina, in the same month Washington issued his proclamation. Impressed by his wild reception, young Genêt felt like a conquering hero. In a slow, twenty-eight-day trip to Philadelphia that was replete with banquets, ovations and speeches, he sponsored Democratic clubs, outfitted several American privateers to prey on British shipping and organized American expeditions to seize Spanish Florida and Louisiana. One of his commissions named George Rogers Clark, a Revolutionary War hero, as "Commander-in-Chief of the French Revolutionary Legion on the Mississippi." To the Government back in Paris he wrote: "I provision the Antilles, I excite the Canadians to free themselves from the yoke of England, I arm the Kentuckians."

Washington received him coldly, uncertain at first how to handle his rude, undiplomatic behavior. Genêt reacted to this frigidity by demanding that Congress be called into special session so that the legislators could judge between Washington's neutrality stand and his own insistence on full American aid against England. By June, even Jefferson, who had found the "old spirit of '76 rekindling" by his triumphant tour north, called Genêt hot-headed, and remarked that "never was so calamitous an appointment made." Two months later after Genêt continued to swagger about and referred to Washington as "this old man," Jefferson considered him "absolutely incorrigible" and voted with all other Cabinet members to demand his recall, as Washington suggested. Genêt was stunned when he heard the news. He denounced Jefferson for having encouraged him, declared that Jefferson had told him Washington was "controlled by the English," and pleaded for permission to remain in the United States as a private citizen, on the ground that the changed French Government would send him to the guillotine. Washington graciously permitted him to stay, and he later married the daughter of Governor George Clinton of New York. After the Genêt affair, when Martha Washington found a greasy spot on her sofa one day, she said that this indicated the presence of "a filthy Democrat."

The close of the Genêt incident did not put a damper on the Democratic clubs. Attacks on Washington by the Democratic-Republican press grew so vicious in the summer of 1793 that at one Cabinet meeting, Jefferson said, "The President was much inflamed; got into one of those passions when he cannot command himself; ran on much on the personal abuse which had been bestowed upon him; defied any man on earth to produce one single act of his since he had been in the government, which was not done on the purist motive . . . that by God he had rather be in his grave than in his present situation."

Years later, Vice-President Adams with failing memory recalled that summer: "Ten thousand people in the streets of Philadelphia, day after day, threatened to drag Washington out of his house and effect a revolution in the government, or compel it to declare war in favor of the French Revolution and against England." Adams claimed that only the yellow fever epidemic that killed about 4000 of Philadelphia's 40,000 inhabitants prevented a revolution.

Despite these continuing attacks by the Jeffersonians, Washington did not entirely lose his sense of humor. Once when he stayed overnight in Baltimore, three small boys knocked on his inn door and he invited them to enter his room. Two wore the Jeffersonian tricolor cockades of the French Revolution on their caps, while the third lad's cap had none. Washington found out his name was David Hoffman, and he said to him, "I see you have no cockade. Will you allow me to make one for you?" He sent a servant to buy some ribbon, and cut out a Jeffersonian rosette which he pinned to young Hoffman's cap.

But that summer Washington and Jefferson reached a parting of the ways. On July 31, Jefferson wrote a letter of resignation and on August 5, Washington drove to his home and argued on the lawn with him to stay on. But Jefferson charged that to do so would "oblige me always to move exactly in the circle which I know to bear me peculiar hatred." At this, Washington agreed that Jefferson should resign, though he asked him to stay on until 1794. After that, whether by chance or agreement, neither was in Philadelphia while the other was there, and at the end of the year Jefferson was to quit the Administration.

That summer, too, Washington was convinced he could not get loyal advice from his entire Cabinet and he attempted to make use of the Supreme Court as an advisory council. He sent the justices a list of twenty-nine involved questions relating to the treaties between the United States and France. The justices, however, refused to offer their opinions, replying that they could do so only if the issues reached the Court in the form of lawsuits.

Washington's first serious domestic problem came in 1794, with the Whiskey Rebellion in western Pennsylvania. Four years earlier when he signed the measure calling for the Federal assumption of the wartime state debts, it was apparent that the cost would have to be met by an increase in revenue. This money could have been obtained by increasing import duties. However, Washington had listened to Hamilton who advocated instead an excise tax on distilled spirits. Hamilton's argument had been that it would be wise for the Federal Government to create a precedent in the area of internal taxation. His fear was that if this were not done under the popular Washington Administration, it might be interpreted under future administrations to mean that the right did not exist.

Unfortunately, whisky producers were not the best guinea pigs for this precedent. Poor roads made it difficult for farmers along the Pennsylvania, Virginia and North Carolina frontier to send bulky grains across the Allegheny Mountains to eastern markets. For this reason they converted corn and rye to whisky, which was easier to transport. Every farm family over the mountains was a whisky producer and resentment against the excise tax of 1791 turned to physical resistance. Finally in 1794, the farmers in the Pittsburgh area drove out Federal tax collectors and an open rebellion followed. Listening to Hamilton, who eagerly called for military action, Washington viewed the insurrection as the "first formidable fruit" of the Democratic clubs and said that if it were not put down "we may bid adieu to all government in this country, except mob and club government."

Under the Constitution, Congress had authority to call out the state militias "to execute the Laws of the Union, suppress Insurrections and repel Invasions." In 1792, Congress had enacted a law authorizing the President to call out the militia of a state or states in case of invasion or the expectancy of one. Where the problem was an insurrection, he was required to secure permission from the state legislature or the governor. As for the Federal use of a state militia "to execute the Laws of the Union," the 1792 Act empowered the President to do so only after a Federal judge informed him that regular judicial processes could not halt a disobedience.

On August 7, 1794, after getting the opinion of Associate Justice James Wilson of the Supreme Court that ordinary court orders were not effective in western Pennsylvania, Washington issued a proclamation ordering the Pennsylvania farmers to end their rebellion by September 1. He also requested the governors of four states to supply him with 15,000 men in case they did not. There was some doubt whether the states would acknowledge his authority over their internal forces, and in fact Pennsylvania recruits were few because of local loyalty to the Whiskey Rebels. But his prestige brought the proper response from the other states. Washington went personally to investigate the situation and Hamilton accompanied the large militia contingent as a second boss behind the Commander-in-Chief. The insurgents disbanded before the military forces arrived but several leaders were arrested and two were convicted of treason. Washington later pardoned them, for he believed it was sufficient that he had produced a proper respect for the Federal Government with his show of force. The importance of the incident was that it helped establish the principle that where there was an extended disorder in a state or states, or even the threat of a widespread disturbance, the President's authority could be dictatorial in nature.

Hamilton's role in the Whiskey Rebellion kept the supposedly retired Jefferson awake nights at Monticello where he worked under the light of spermaceti candles writing letters to his followers attacking what he considered the pro-British monarchial philosophy of his former colleague. This attack broadened that year and during the rest of Washington's term, until it included Washington as well as Hamilton.

The chief charge of the Jeffersonians was that the Administration was being cruel to ally France and subservient to foe England. The former Mother Country still clung to fur posts on the frontier in violation of the peace treaty and was thought by Westerners to be encouraging Indian scalpers to prey on pioneer settlements. She was also seizing American vessels bound to or from the French West Indies, claiming a large part of Maine and impressing American seamen off American ships into the Royal Navy.

Even before he quit the Administration, Jefferson had advocated war against England if she tried to conquer the Floridas and Louisiana. Four months after he was gone, his Senate followers managed a tie vote on a bill to bar importation of British goods. This would have been a harsh blow against the British because 90 per cent of American imports came from that source. Only Adams' tie-breaking vote prevented this.

Washington's position was that without a navy or a standing army the United States was in no position to take bold action against Britain for her arrogant deeds. On March 27, 1794, he had induced Congress to authorize the construction of four forty-four-gun ships and two thirty-six-gun vessels, but construction lay far in the future, and the clamor by the Jeffersonians for direct action never abated.

If not war, there was only one honorable course left, Washington concluded, and this was to settle outstanding differences by negotiation. While the Whiskey Rebellion was working its way to its climax, Washington gave much thought to making a second peace treaty with Britain. Four Federalist Senators, who were stalwarts of Hamilton, proposed in the spring of 1794 that Washington send his young Treasury Secretary to London on such a mission. However, despite his fondness for Hamilton, Washington rejected the proposal on the ground that Hamilton was too unpopular politically throughout the country to gain approval for any treaty.

Chief Justice John Jay, whom he finally selected for the British mission, was almost as great a liability as Hamilton. A sour, long-beaked man of forty-nine, Jay was of French Huguenot descent and was known for his strong anti-French views. Jay's aristocratic tendencies were also well publicized and served as the chief issue against him when he ran for governor of New York in 1792. He ascribed his loss to the crooked vote manipulators in the hire of George Clinton, the boss of New York, though the fact that he had not resigned from the Court to make the local race was probably another reason for his defeat.

In a rousing Senate debate over Jay's confirmation, a strong minority of members called it a violation of the doctrine of separation of powers to send a judge to do work that involved only the President and the Senate. Jay also came under attack as a foe of the frontier. During the Confederation years, he had made a report to the Congress justifying Britain's unyielding control over the western fur posts despite the peace treaty. Also, in 1786 he had negotiated a treaty with Spain in which the United States agreed to relinquish navigation rights on the Mississippi for twenty-five years in exchange for some commercial rights. The treaty won approval from seven of the thirteen states in the Confederation Congress, but it failed to become effective because nine affirmative votes were necessary.

At the same time that Washington sent the Anglophile Jay to London as envoy in April 1794, his strategy was to send a Francophile to Paris to balance the other side of the foreign seesaw. Gouverneur Morris was then the American minister to France. The peglegged Morris, a bosom friend of Hamilton and the stylist who wrote the final draft of the Constitution and a master's degree thesis at Kings College (Columbia) on "Love," had openly intrigued with Louis XVI and his court to overthrow the Revolutionists and taunted French leaders with his aristocratic mode of living.

To replace Morris as American envoy to the gruesome French Government of the Committee of Public Safety, which Robespierre the beheader was then directing, Washington dispatched Senator James Monroe to Paris. The thirty-six-year-old Monroe was the protégé of Thomas Jefferson and a young man who saw only good in the French Revolution, though he opposed another war with England.

The balance of Jay in London and Monroe in Paris was far from perfect. Jay reached England with instructions to seek a treaty of friendship and commerce, while Monroe was told that his job was essentially "to strengthen our friendship with that country [France]." Among Washington's instructions to Monroe, as transmitted by Secretary of State Edmund Randolph, was a directive to tell the French Government that "the motives of that mission [the Jay mission] to be to obtain immediate compensation for plundered property and restitution of posts."

Once in touch with the British Government, Jay proceeded to draft a treaty that would eliminate the major causes of friction between his government and the British. His work went on steadily despite the open animosity of Thomas Pinckney, the American minister to England, who resented the fact that he was being ignored. On September 20, Jay submitted to Lord William Grenville, the British negotiator, a treaty that would end impressment of American sailors into the British Navy and recognize the rights of neutral nations by belligerents.

At first, Grenville considered accepting this treaty because he had been secretly opening Pinckney's diplomatic mail and was concerned that the United States planned to join Sweden and Denmark in an armed neutrality convention. This would mean the combination of the three fleets against the molesting ships of the belligerents. However, Lord Grenville dropped his concern when he heard from George Hammond, the twenty-seven-year-old British minister to the American Government at Philadelphia. Hammond reported that Hamilton had told him in confidence that Washington and his Cabinet had rejected armed neutrality. With nothing to fear from the United States, Grenville now discarded the Jay Treaty draft of September and proceeded to fashion another one based on his superior bargaining position. The result was the Treaty of Amity, Commerce and Navigation, which Jay signed on November 19, 1794.

Nowhere did the treaty mention an end to impressment and Indian depredations, respect for neutral rights in trading with France, or payment for slaves the British had stolen when they quit New York after the Revolutionary War. Actual provisions contained British agreement to abandon their western posts by mid-1796, and to establish joint commissions to determine the boundary of Maine and settle claims arising from the seizure of merchant ships. Regarding mutual commerce, the United States agreed to open the Mississippi to British trade while England opened her West Indies ports to American ships under seventy tons. Even so, these small vessels were not to be permitted to carry sugar, coffee, cocoa, cotton or molasses to any country other than the United States.

When Washington received the Jay Treaty in March 1795, he was greatly displeased with its contents. Even Hamilton called it "execrable," though he said he would accept it if the Twelfth Article were amended to permit cotton to be carried to Europe. Washington held the treaty for three months before he decided that, obnoxious as it was, Jay could not have done much better under the circumstances. Finally, in June, he reluctantly submitted it to the Senate, and insisted that copies be kept from the press and the treaty debated in secret.

For eighteen days the Senate chewed over the treaty, with the Jeffersonians denouncing it as a humiliating sellout to the British. Finally, after rejecting the article limiting West Indies trade, the Senate consented to the rest of the treaty by a small margin. The oath of secrecy had kept news of the treaty from the public, but immediately after the Senate's action, Senator Stevens Mason of Virginia, who was an ardent Jeffersonian, leaked it to the press.

A violent storm of outrage swept the country. "D— John Jay! D— every one who won't d— John Jay!" read a popular placard of that day. Long before August 18, when Washington finally signed the treaty after a further seven-week study, he was complaining to Hamilton: "The cry against the treaty is like that against a mad-dog; and every one, in a manner, seemed engaged on running it down." Hamilton had quit the Cabinet in February 1795 for private law practice in New York City, but angry mobs charged him with being the true author of the Jay Treaty and stoned him on New York streets. Jay escaped such physical damage, for mobs gave vent to their hatred of him by burning him in effigy.

Once the fire of party animosities reached this fever pitch there was no way to put it out and return to the good old days before the Jefferson and Hamilton antagonism had kindled. Washington

added to the excitement between the Federalists and the Democratic-Republicans at the very moment he prepared to sign the Jay
Treaty by dismissing Edmund Randolph, an opponent of the treaty,
from his Cabinet. Randolph had succeeded Jefferson as Secretary
of State in February 1794, after serving as Attorney General. A
dispatch from French minister Joseph Fauchet to his government
now come to light implied that Randolph had asked Fauchet for
a bribe in return for softening American policy toward France.
Washington immediately demanded an explanation from his Secretary of State. When Randolph, insulted to the point of rage, withdrew, Washington was reported to have bellowed, "A damn'der
scoundrel God Almighty never permitted to disgrace humanity!"
It was after Randolph's forced departure from the government to
write his 103-page pamphlet, "A Vindication," that Washington
belatedly came to the conclusion that all Cabinet members must
show unity behind the President's policies.

Jeffersonian broadsides against the Administration were directed
chiefly to the western frontier where Jay's name was a household
swear word. This opposition centered primarily in Kentucky, where
there was added resentment that Washington had done nothing to
force Spain to reopen the Mississippi. Inflammatory public meetings called for direct local action against Spain. "Let this communication then be received," Washington wrote to Kentucky's hot-
headed political leaders, "as a warning against the danger to which
these unauthorized schemes of war may expose the United States,
and particularly the State of Kentucky."

He had already sent Thomas Pinckney, American minister to
England, to negotiate a treaty with Spain. Fearing that the Jay
Treaty meant a close alliance between Britain and the United
States, Spain decided to settle her differences with the new nation.
The Godoy-Pinckney Treaty that resulted in October 1795 did
much to raise the drastically low opinion of the Washington Administration along the frontier. It also raised doubts about the wisdom
of employing Jay on the British treaty instead of Pinckney. For
Spain agreed to grant the United States the right of navigation on
the Mississippi and the right of duty-free deposit at New Orleans
for American goods destined for overseas markets. Spain also
agreed to recognize the 31st Parallel as the northern border of her
Florida provinces and promised to take action against Indians raiding across the border.

The furor against the Jay Treaty extended into 1796 when the House declined by a vote of 50 to 38 to adjourn at noon on February 22, as it had in previous years on the President's birthday. But worse chagrin came to Washington when he asked the House to appropriate the money necessary to carry out the treaty. Jefferson's stalwarts, through Representative Edward Livingston of New York, demanded that the President submit copies of his instructions to Jay; their contention was that they required the facts to judge whether the treaty deserved an appropriation.

After consulting his Cabinet, Washington refused to comply with the Livingston resolutions. The papers, he said, were not related to any functions of the House unless it wanted to consider his impeachment. He also said that only he and the Senate were involved in treaty-making, according to the Constitution, and that the House had a legal and moral obligation to appropriate money needed to carry out the terms of a treaty binding the United States. "I have resolved to resist the principle," Washington wrote to Hamilton, as the House wrangled over the matter. The debate was long and bitter, and only the oratorical brilliance of Fisher Ames, a Federalist Representative from Massachusetts, changed the tide and produced a 51 to 48 vote in favor of the appropriation. Even so, by a vote of 57 to 35 the House stubbornly affirmed its "Constitutional right . . . to deliberate on the expediency or inexpediency of carrying such Treaty into effect."

Still another arrow off the Jay Treaty bow involved John Rutledge of South Carolina. Chief Justice Jay had resigned during the furor to run again for governor of New York, after learning that the Jeffersonians planned impeachment procedures. Washington had named Rutledge, an Associate Justice of the Court from 1789 to 1791, to succeed him. But Rutledge combined his service as Chief Justice in the August 1795 Court term with emotional speechmaking in his home state against the Jay Treaty. As a recess appointee, Rutledge's nomination did not reach the Senate until the December 1795 Congressional session. By then, the Hamilton Federalists charged him with being insane and unfit, and he failed of confirmation.

Another victim of the Jay Treaty was James Monroe. After he publicly denounced the treaty, Washington considered him a disgrace to the diplomatic service and recalled him in August 1796. His replacement was C. C. Pinckney, brother of Thomas.

Washington's second term had been a difficult period. He had fought against the rise of political parties and in the end had himself become a Hamilton partisan. The whisky-making farmers and Kentucky frontiersmen had proved trying in their efforts to upset the national authority. He had kept the United States from being forced to honor the French Treaty of Alliance of 1778 and going to war with Britain. From the Spanish he had gained a treaty that seemed to insure prosperity and the good life along the southern frontier. As for the Jay Treaty, no matter how poor its contents, it represented a beginning stab at peaceful relations with Britain.

Yet with this treaty as an excuse, the Jefferson Republican press lost all restraint in attacking him personally. He found himself referred to as "a front for tories, speculators and indeed all the British party" and as "the step-father of his country." A piece of Thomas Jefferson's writings—a copy of a letter to Philip Mazzei in Italy—that came to his attention wounded him deeply, for it snidely mentioned "men who were Samsons in the field and Solomons in the council, but who have had their heads shorn by the harlot England." After forty-five years in public service, said Washington, he was weary of being "buffeted in the public prints by a set of infamous scribblers." In a letter to Jefferson, he poured out his hurt because "every act of my Administration" was subjected to "such exaggeration and indecent terms as could scarcely be applied to a Nero; a notorious defaulter; or even of a common pickpocket."

Attempts by some Republicans to picture him as living on a scale of a King George III were errant nonsense. Thomas Twining, a young officer in the British colonial service, delivered a painting to Washington at his Philadelphia home in 1795 and had this to say: "He lived in a small, red brick house on the left side of High Street. . . . There was nothing in the exterior of the house that denoted the rank of its possessor. Next door was a hairdresser. . . . I was conducted up a neat but rather narrow staircase, carpeted in the middle, and was shown into a middling-sized, well-furnished drawing room on the left of the passage. Nearly opposite the door was a fireplace with a wood fire in it. The floor was carpeted. On the left of the fireplace was a sofa which sloped across the room. There were no pictures on the walls, no ornaments on the chimney piece. Two windows on the right of the entrance looked into the street."

Mrs. Washington came in. "Mrs. Washington was a middle-sized lady, rather stout, her manner extremely kind and unaffected. . . . I saw the tall, upright, venerable figure of this great man advancing toward me to take me by the hand. . . . So completely did he look the part of the great and good man he really was that I felt rather respect than awe in his presence. . . . I mentioned the particular respect with which Lord Cornwallis always spoke of him." Washington did not raise an eyebrow over this reference to his conquered foe. Instead, "he received this communication in the most courteous manner, inquiring about his lordship, and expressed for him much esteem. . . . His hair was powdered and tied behind. Although his deportment was that of a general, the expression of his features had rather the calm dignity of a legislator than the severity of a soldier."

During 1796, Washington established his last important Presidential precedent, one that would stand one hundred and forty-four years. This was his refusal to accept a third term. He took this position not because of principle but because he wanted to return to Mount Vernon. It was time, he said, to rest his mind, which had been "constantly on the stretch since the year 1753, with but short intervals and little relaxation."

It was on September 19, 1796, that he made public his Farewell Address in the pages of Claypool's *American Daily Advertiser*. This was a four-person collaboration based on Washington's 1792 letter of outline to Madison, the Madison draft and now a new Hamilton draft based on the earlier work, revisions by John Jay and final corrections and additions by Washington. Referring to himself as an "old and affectionate friend" of "my countrymen," Washington called for unity in government, decried "the banefull effects of the Spirit of Party" and "the insidious wiles of foreign influence." He pointed out that "the Unity of Government which constitutes you one people is also now dear to you," and he cautioned that "much pains will be taken, many artifices employed, to weaken in your minds the conviction of this truth." Under all circumstances, he said, "steer clear of permanent Alliances, with any portion of the foreign world . . . take a Neutral position."

When Americans now realized that Washington's long services to his country were nearing an end, mellow huzzas for the first First Citizen took on a non-partisan ring. On his birthday in 1797, twelve hundred persons honored him and Martha at a dinner and an evening of dancing at Rickett's Amphitheatre. Martha sobbed at the fine tributes paid him, and Supreme Court Justice James

Iredell noted that Washington's "emotions were too powerful to be concealed. He could sometimes scarcely speak."

On Saturday, March 4, 1797, the first President walked alone to Congress Hall in Philadelphia to attend the inauguration of his successor, John Adams, in the chamber of the House. His success at establishing a thriving new government was undeniable. Yet he was anxious to turn over the torch to others. "He seemed to me to enjoy a triumph over me," said Adams. "Methought I heard him say 'Ay! I am fairly out and you fairly in.'"

☆ 2 ☆

JOHN ADAMS

Matter Over Mind

At a more settled period in history, John Adams might have fared better as Chief Executive. He was brilliant, courageous and experienced. His background was indeed awesome: a leading colonial lawyer in the legal center of Boston, energetic chairman of more than twenty-five committees in the Continental Congress, a diplomat with a decade of experience in France, Holland and Britain, author of profound philosophic writings, and a two-term Vice-President of the United States.

An early demander of independence, it was Adams who nevertheless successfully defended British Captain Preston and eight Redcoats who fired into a rowdy Boston mob on March 5, 1770, and killed five Americans in what became known as the Boston Massacre. It was also Adams who astutely won the approval of the Continental Congress in June 1775 to send Colonel George Washington of Virginia to lead the little ragtag local army encamped at Cambridge, six miles from Boston where the British were in control. By this clever move, a full year before the Declaration of Independence, Adams enlarged the war from a New England struggle against the Intolerable Acts to a Continental effort. It was again Adams whose eloquence in July 1776 ensured the passage of the Resolution and Declaration of Independence, when those who favored this course would not take a chance with the high, squeaky voice of Thomas Jefferson against the strong opposition. A thrilled Jefferson later recalled that "the deep conceptions and nervous style gave Adams a power of thought and expression which moved members from their seats."

Yet Adams was the same man who almost succeeded in reducing the Office of the President to a shabby, innocuous post.

His failure to recognize Cabinet treachery, his inability to influence fellow political party members in Congress and his false assumption that he could run a government by remote control made a mockery of his belief that the office he held was the most powerful executive position to be found in any republican government.

During most of his single term, he made so little of his position that he became a joke of sorts to friend and foe. Then when the roof was off his structure and the walls were shaking, he rose from his stupor and boldly asserted the authority of his office. In his final hour, he ruled as well as reigned, only to find ironically that his belated strong action meant the end of his long political career and the doom of his political party.

Part of his inability to take a firm grasp on the Presidency stemmed from personality factors, part from outside forces. The combination of the two was ruinous. In personality and outlook, Adams was almost a double for England's Dr. Samuel Johnson. On the one hand, he was a man of complex abstract reasoning power, a thorough scholar and a remarkable conversationalist; and on the other, he was rude, undignified and given to wild outbursts of temper. Like Johnson, Adams was a realist who believed that idealism was interesting for mental stimulation but entirely unrelated to actual human nature. Man was not perfectible, said Adams, but merely a generation-after-generation repetition of a few decent traits and a host of faults. Once he dampened Jefferson's optimism by noting that: "The loss of Paradise, by eating a forbidden apple, has been many thousand years a lesson to mankind, but not much regarded." From experience and readings in history, he believed that men "will not fail to show that natural depravity of heart whenever they have a fair opportunity." Idealism was nonsense, he said, because "the first want of every man is his dinner and his second want is his girl."

Unlike the slovenly Johnson, Adams lacked sycophantic disciples waiting breathlessly to applaud every word emanating from his lips and then race through the town to repeat his latest remarks. The sad truth was that he was quite friendless and suffered the pangs of a deep persecution complex. In this case, his independent, outspoken nature and sharp tongue drove would-be adherents away. Even the marginalia found in the books of his extensive library attested to the type of language he sometimes employed. In one book, he scribbled alongside the name of Rous-

seau, "Coxcomb"; alongside that of Voltaire, "Liar," and alongside d'Alembert who helped edit the excellent *Encyclopédie*,
"Thou Louse, Flea, Tick, Ant, Wasp, or whatever Vermin thou
art!"

Most men who later became President were able to create a
fresh image of themselves while serving as Chief Executive. In
the case of Adams, however, his image was hardened long before.
Deliberate misinterpretations and correct interpretations of his
writings and stories about his temper and language were in common vogue. Those whom he had intentionally and unintentionally
insulted would have filled a banquet hall.

His intemperance knew no chivalry. Mercy Otis Warren, an old
family friend, was the sister of James Otis who coined the expression "Taxation without representation is tyranny" and the sister-
in-law of Dr. Joseph Warren who hung two signal lamps in the Old
North Church tower for Paul Revere. When Mercy Warren au-
thored the three volumes on the "Rise, Progress and Termination
of the American Revolution," Adams wrote her that she was
guilty of a "malignity of heart" and was "determined to be enrolled
in the glorious list of libelers of John Adams . . . Most of these
have already come to a bad end, and the rest will follow." On another occasion, he described a woman as "breathing like a porpoise
and prating like a magpie."

Nor was Adams a respecter of age. In September 1776, he and
Benjamin Franklin had traveled together to Staten Island for the
Continental Congress to discuss peace with Admiral Lord Richard Howe. At an inn along the way, the two had to share a room
and argued into the night whether to open the bedroom window
or keep it closed. Later in Paris, Adams found his fellow diplomat
Franklin a base character for practicing the opposite of the high
morality he preached in his *Poor Richard's Almanac*. Franklin, in
turn, characterized Adams as "always an honest man, often a wise
man, but sometimes, and in some things, absolutely out of his
senses."

In the opening months of the new government in 1789, Adams,
as the first Vice-President, had added to the picture of ridicule
his insistence on royal-sounding titles. Perhaps this stemmed from
the fact that he was a farmer-shoemaker's son who had discovered
at Harvard that students were ranked according to the social
status of their families. Nevertheless, the spectacle of the short,
pudgy, bald Vice-President demanding titles did his reputation

no good. Behind his back fellow politicians awarded him several titles of their own, winking and calling him "His Superfluous Excellency," "His Rotundity," "The Duke of Braintree" and "Bonny Johnny Adams." Throughout the long, coastal nation of four million souls the story spread that after the 1792 election Adams had revealed his monarchial tendencies to several Senators by an outburst against the electorate. The story went that he shouted: "Damn 'em, damn 'em, damn 'em! You see that elective government will not do." The truth was that Adams believed, as he wrote his cousin Sam Adams, "Good government is and must be Republican." But he also believed (to the fury of the Jeffersonians) that "there never was a democracy that did not commit suicide . . . It soon wastes, exhausts and murders itself."

When Adams had first read a copy of the Constitution while in Europe, he wrote Jefferson: "We agree perfectly that the many should have a full, fair and perfect representation. You are apprehensive of monarchy, I of aristocracy. I would therefore have given more power to the President and less to the Senate." Jefferson's view was that without specifying the number of terms a President might serve and by limiting the authority of the House of Representatives, the President was a "bad edition of a Polish king." But on the whole, Adams offered, the new Constitution was "admirably calculated to cement all Americans in affection and interest as one great nation," though "I cannot pretend to promise immortality to liberty or to virtue."

As for the Vice-Presidency, the office he held and studied for eight years, Adams was inclined throughout to belittle it unmercifully as a kind of duty not adapted to his character—too inactive and mechanical. "My country," he wrote his brilliant wife Abigail, "has in its wisdom contrived for me the most insignificant office that was the invention of man . . . or his imagination conceived; and as I can do neither good nor evil, I must be borne away by others and meet the common fate." Its chief saving grace, he believed, was that it provided an understudy should something unfortunate overtake the President. "I am possessed of two separate powers, the one in *esse* and the other in *posse*," he said. "I am Vice-President. In this I am nothing, but I may be everything."

Nevertheless, Adams breathed so much life into the Vice-Presidency while he held it that future Vice-Presidents would not have recognized it as the same office they occupied. In fact, in 1960,

Franklin Roosevelt's Vice-President, John Nance Garner, replied to Senator Lyndon Johnson's query whether Johnson should accept the Vice-Presidential nomination offered him by Senator John F. Kennedy: "I'll tell you, Lyndon, the Vice-Presidency isn't worth a pitcher of warm spit."

In the first session of Congress, Vice-President Adams joined freely in the discussions in the Senate chamber. This brought him much criticism, and even his wife told him sharply that he talked too much. When the French National Assembly sent Congress eulogies on the death of Franklin, Adams read sarcastically the appendaged list of Franklin's honorary Ph.D.'s and told the Senate it was strange that the French, who claimed to have abolished titles, would have given so many to Franklin. A friend wrote him that Senators were angered by his contempt for the opinions and reasonings of his adversaries and his "force of argument and strength of language, approaching to sarcasm." "He who mingles in debate," came another bit of advice, "places himself on the same ground with his inferiors in rank and renders it more difficult for him to support the dignity of the chair and preserve order in the debate." In time, Adams subsided into silence, demanding exacting decorum from Senators by glowering and rapping sharply on his small brown table with his silver pencil case if he caught one whispering during debate.

In the early Senate, because of the almost equal division on many crucial issues, his tie-breaking vote on twenty-nine occasions established important policy. During the spring of 1794, the British fleet at war with France seized 250 American ships in the Caribbean. This brought on a wide clamor for retaliation, and a bill barring all commerce with Britain quickly passed the House. In the Senate, the vote was even and Adams broke the tie by killing the bill. It was his belief, and that of Washington, that passage would have resulted in a second war with the British. The defeat of the bill bought time for Jay's peace mission to London. Another tie-breaking vote, which gave the President undivided power to remove government officials, was, as we have seen, one that Adams long afterward included among the most vital actions of his lengthy career.

John Adams was the first President elected by a political party, yet he was not a politician. The times called for a President who would expand his constitutional authority by wielding leadership of a political organization. Then, by using the power and patronage of his office, he could prod party members toward voting for his programs. But control of others through any type of organization was foreign to a man of such independence and individuality as was Adams. Reasoning and patriotism were the only tools he cared to employ.

To his way of thinking political parties made sheep of men; from the outset he had watched with misgivings as the American parties took shape. At first there had been Federalists, men like Madison, Hamilton and Jay, who supported the ratification of the Constitution, and Anti-Federalists, like Patrick Henry and Monroe, who opposed ratification by the states. The bitter fights between these two groups had spread into every state and occasioned polemics and political trickery that spoiled lifetime friendships.

Once the new government began, these original parties vanished. However, when Alexander Hamilton's financial program became known early in Washington's first term, political alignments appeared again. Simply put, there were the Federalists led by Hamilton who argued for a strong national government and a loose interpretation of the Constitution, acting for the benefit of the well born. In opposition were the Democratic-Republicans (later known as the Republicans), led by Thomas Jefferson. The Republicans espoused the cause of states' rights and the strict interpretation of the Constitution, denounced city dwellers and laborers and championed farmers and frontiersmen.

Inclined to the Federalists, Adams nevertheless regarded warily both the wealthy man's government by Hamilton and the agricultural society put on a pedestal by Jefferson. Government, he believed, had to strive for equilibrium between the desire of the elite to exploit the mass of the population for personal gain and the irrational demands of the common people for vengeance on the rich. Later, especially after war broke out between Britain and France in 1793, the parties took on further distinctions. The Federalists came to be regarded as pro-British and the Republicans as Francophiles. Adams saw no virtue in the Republicans' slavish attachment to bloodthirsty French Revolutionists. Yet he could not subscribe to his own party's theme that Britain was on the side of good and France on the side of evil.

So Adams was neither a political leader nor a follower, though he earnestly sought the support of Federalists to put him into office. But once there, his refusal to promote Federalist ideals or blindly follow party objectives helped keep his Administration in an uproar. Strangely, it was his independence from party dictate that would in the end provide him with his only successes.

If political control did not center on Adams, who led the Federalists? Adams well knew it was forceful and dynamic Alexander Hamilton, now out of government service but still boss of the party. From his own recent experience in the 1796 campaign, Adams realized the potency of the Federalist chief. However, he could not believe that Federalist Congressmen meeting in Philadelphia would legislate according to orders from a man engaged in private law practice in New York.

Nor could he believe that his own Administration would make no major or minor move without Hamilton's approval. Thus the story of Adams as President is the tale of a man who did not awaken until his time was nearly gone to the fact that Hamilton was actually directing the Executive Branch and making national policy!

On March 3, 1797, George Washington performed his final acts as President. He remitted a smuggler's fine and pardoned ten men convicted of high treason in the Whiskey Rebellion. On the next day Adams delivered his inaugural address, and two days later when he met with his Cabinet for the first time he considered his powers under the Constitution "much greater than that of an avoyer, a consul, a podesta, a doge, a stadtholder; nay, than a king of Poland; nay, than a king of Sparta." What he failed to realize was that the power was meaningless until he used it. And three of the men facing him—Secretary of State Timothy Pickering, Secretary of War James McHenry and Secretary of the Treasury Oliver Wolcott—were determined that Hamilton should exercise that power and not Adams.

Back in 1795, President Washington had called it "a sort of political suicide to bring a man into any office of consequence whose political tenets are adverse to the measures which the general government are pursuing." Adams might well have heeded this advice and extended it to establish the principle that Cabinet members must be personally loyal to their Chief Executive. The three in question not only considered Adams a pseudo-Federalist, they also despised him. In their view, it was essential that they serve in the Adams Cabinet, if only to keep an eye on him. There was never any question of either implicit obedience or resignation. As Pickering once argued, "I should think it their duty to prevent, as far as practicable, the mischievous measures of a wrong-headed President." Pickering's chief tactic for thwarting Adams was interminable delay in carrying out orders; McHenry's, copying Hamilton's written arguments in his own hand and presenting them to Adams; while the perennially false-smiling Wolcott relied on flattery.

Like the concept of political parties, the Cabinet was an extra-constitutional growth stumbling along to institutional status. Adams was of course the first President to face the question: should each new Chief Executive select his own department heads or retain those of his predecessor? His logical mind should have led him to make a clean sweep when he took office, and select like-minded men who would be loyal to him. Instead, he continued the old Cabinet and blundered badly.

Certainly Adams knew that Washington was not satisfied with the caliber of his final Cabinet. After Secretary of State Jefferson left at the end of 1793 and Hamilton in February 1795, he could not get first-rate men to enter the Cabinet. Timothy Pickering was a hooknosed, bony Puritan with a dour personality, who had served in the non-policy position of Postmaster General. When Washington's old military comrade, General Henry Knox, resigned as Secretary of War at the close of 1794 in order to raise money to meet the gambling mania of his wife, Washington gave his post temporarily to Pickering. Then in 1795, after five men rejected Washington's plea to become his Secretary of State, he assigned it to Pickering, a rabid Federalist but hardly qualified, according to Washington's high standards, to manage foreign policy.

Nor was James McHenry, whom Adams inherited as Secretary of War, qualified to run his department. An Irish immigrant, former surgeon and wartime secretary to Washington, McHenry had spent seven years pestering Washington for a government job. It was only after three excellent choices refused the nomination that Washington finally weakened at the beginning of 1796. To Hamilton, who had given McHenry a negative recommendation, Washington abjectly wrote, "Your opinion accords with mine. I early discovered that his talents were unequal to great exertions, or deep resources."

The last member in this triumvirate was Oliver Wolcott, who had begun as auditor of the Treasury Department in 1789 at the age of twenty-nine. After rising to comptroller, he became Secretary following Hamilton's departure in 1795, despite a lack of imagination and ability to comprehend fiscal theory.

Since Pickering and Wolcott had once worked for Hamilton and McHenry idolized him, it was small wonder that they were anxious to serve him during the Adams Administration. They were also agreed that because they had been appointed by Washington, they owed Adams nothing. Moreover, they could point to the numerous times that Washington himself had asked Hamilton for advice, even though he was no longer in government service. In fact, the three had kept up a flood of correspondence between Philadelphia and Hamilton's New York office to get his advice and guidance on fiscal matters, foreign policy, contract letting and patronage.

Even though it had become a normal routine of the Executive Branch to ask Hamilton for advice, the inauguration of Adams gave the three Secretaries momentary pause. They knew that Adams would never knowingly tolerate the intrusion of Hamilton. Yet they required his continued aid and leadership. What were they to do? Their decision was to continue their relationship with Hamilton as in the past—but in secret. If they flattered Adams and if Hamilton did not appear in person in the capital, with luck Adams might never learn that Hamilton was actually President while he was merely a figurehead.

Another good reason for their need for secrecy was that Adams had a basic dislike not only for Hamilton but for friends of Hamilton. This antipathy extended as far back as the first national election in 1788. At that time, thirty-one-year-old Hamilton sent word to electors in the states that Washington was to be elected unanimously but second votes were to be widely scattered so that Adams would win the Vice-Presidency by only the slimmest margin. The beginning of the Adams-Hamilton feud dated from the hour Adams learned why he got only 34 electoral votes compared with 69 for Washington. "Is not my election to this office in the scurvy manner in which it was done, a curse rather than a blessing?" he asked.

In 1792, Hamilton had ordered all Federalist electors to support Adams for a second term as Vice-President solely because the Jeffersonians were scheming to saddle Washington with a Republican Vice-President, Governor George Clinton of New York. This was hardly reason to make Adams drop his distaste for Hamilton.

Washington again won unanimously with 132 electoral votes, while Adams got only 77 and Clinton 50.

Then in 1796 came the point of no return in their relationship. That year Hamilton yearned after the Presidency but realized he could not win it because of personal scandal and continued opposition to the financial policies he had installed while serving as Washington's Secretary of the Treasury. Nevertheless, he could still determine who would be the Federalist candidates for President and Vice-President.

By the time Washington's Farewell Address was printed in September 1796, and the first President was now out of contention for a third term, Hamilton was already searching for his candidate for the short campaign period that remained. Patrick Henry, the fire-eater of the Revolution and chief opponent of the ratification of the Constitution, was the first man to whom he turned. Then when Henry rejected his offer, he decided on Thomas Pinckney of South Carolina, who had won a highly popular treaty from Spain, opening the Mississippi and New Orleans to American commerce in 1795.

Hamilton realized that Adams could not be dropped from a place on the ticket because New England votes were necessary to the Federalists for victory. However, since the Constitution did not order electors to designate separately which of their two votes was their choice for President, it was the person with the most votes rather than the Presidential candidate with the most votes who would become President. Let Adams consider himself the Presidential candidate, but why not see to it that Pinckney received more votes than he?

The first step in this nefarious scheme came when the Federalists in Congress held their nominating caucus and voted to support Adams and Thomas Pinckney on a ticket with the slogan "Peace and Prosperity." The Republican ticket consisted of Jefferson and Aaron Burr of New York. Its slogan was "Rights of Man." Now came Hamilton's second step. To Federalists in the North, he passed word along to vote equally for Adams and Pinckney. But to southern Federalists, he sent orders to vote solidly for Pinckney and to throw away many of their second votes on men other than Adams. "Ambitious as Julius Caesar, a subtle intriguer," Abigail Adams denounced Hamilton. "His thirst for fame is insatiable . . . I have read his heart in his wicked eyes many a time. The very devil is in them."

But like the best-laid plans, Hamilton's devilish scheme back-fired. Adams got wind of it from New Englanders who wanted a northern President more than they treasured Federalist unity. The upshot was a temporary revolt against Hamilton that resulted in Adams' winning all 39 electoral votes in that section, while Pinckney's New England vote was deliberately cut to only 22. The effect was even more noticeable in the national totals. Adams was elected President with 71 electoral votes, but Pinckney with only 59 lagged nine votes behind Jefferson. So the country faced four years with a Federalist President and a Republican Vice-President; and Hamilton had to ponder the fact that if his unwanted Federalist President died in office, he would be succeeded by the leader of the opposition party.

If this were Hamilton's concern, it did not disturb Adams at the outset. He was already determined to have no further association with Hamilton, but toward Jefferson he felt no sharp animosity. Both men could recall a friendship that went back to the early days of the Continental Congress when they served as members of the five-man committee in 1776 to write the Declaration of Independence. For a time when Adams served as America's first minister to Britain, Abigail Adams had cared for Jefferson's motherless younger daughter Polly. The two men enjoyed poking holes in each other's philosophy, with Adams considering Jefferson naïve for believing that Americans were democratic in nature. If the Dauphin of France should want to marry one of Jefferson's "beautiful and most amiable daughters" Adams told the lanky Virginian one time, "all America from Georgia to New Hampshire would find their vanity and pride so agreeably flattered by it that all their sage maxims would give way." During the period when Jefferson and Hamilton were feuding in Washington's Cabinet, Adams lowered his opinion of Jefferson. Early in 1794 when Jefferson retired to Monticello with the announced purpose of carrying on his private interests, Adams said jeeringly, "Instead of being the ardent pursuer of science some think him, he is indolent and his soul is poisoned with ambition."

Other events separated the two men further, yet the 1796 election seemed to bring them together again. Fortunately, neither Adams nor Jefferson had made public statements during the campaign, with the result that the election ended without mutual bitterness. In fact, Jefferson wrote Adams of his "solid esteem," and he permitted James Madison to publish a letter Jefferson had

written earlier in which he asked that the House choose Adams
as President if their electoral votes were equal. In a letter of December 1796, Jefferson apologized that circumstances had put them
in opposite corners. He also warned Adams he might yet be
cheated out of his election "by a trick worthy of the subtilty of
your arch-friend of New York [Hamilton] who has been able to
make of your real friends tools to defeat their and your best
wishes." Then before Jefferson left his Virginia home he sent a
message to his first lieutenant, James Madison, that he was willing
to serve under Adams because "he is perhaps the only sure barrier
against Hamilton's getting in." Once arriving in Philadelphia, Jefferson pointedly moved into Francis Tavern, where Adams resided
before the inauguration. "Adams is cordial and talks of administering the government with me," he noted.

Yet from this high point of cordiality, Adams was soon to hold as
deep a hatred for Jefferson as he did for Hamilton. What would
ruin their friendship was their position on the most vital issue of
the day—whether or not there was to be war with France. This
single issue was also to pervade the struggle between Adams and
his Cabinet, between Adams and Hamilton; it would tarnish Washington's reputation; and in the end it would determine the fate of
the Federalist party.

"The President is fortunate to get off just as the bubble is bursting, leaving others to hold the bag," Jefferson remarked when
Washington left office. The "bag" was a foreign situation that had
gone from bad to worse. Since 1793 when France declared war
against Britain, she had been snarling in anger waiting for the
United States to come to her aid under their 1778 treaty of mutual
defense. Washington's Neutrality Proclamation in April 1793 had
been the first blow. Then the successive blows of the Genêt recall,
the Jay Treaty and the unfortunate Monroe diplomacy in France
had reduced French-American relations to cold animosity.

Unfortunately, Monroe had acted as though he represented the
Republican party rather than the Government of the United
States. Not only had he slurred the British while serving as minister but he also took it upon himself to insist that the United States
stood alongside France against Britain.

Washington had possessed no recourse other than to recall Monroe and send a replacement who would explain more faithfully
the views of his government. This decision in itself had brought on

a strong reaction against the American Government in Paris. Paul Barras, head of the French Directory, told the departing Monroe, who did not protest, that Americans should rise against their leaders and fight alongside France. When Charles Cotesworth Pinckney arrived in December 1796 to take Monroe's place, the French refused to receive him and he retreated to Holland in confusion. Then in violent anger the French undertook vicious sea action against neutral American shipping involved in British trade. Ships and cargoes were seized and some American crewmen were tortured.

While Adams awaited his inauguration in March 1797, C. C. Pinckney still languished in Holland. Two months earlier Hamilton had advised Washington to send an extraordinary three-man mission to France. It was Hamilton's belief that such action would "prove" that the Federalists were not a pro-British party, even though they were. As a show of non-partisanship, Hamilton also suggested that Washington name Madison to the French mission. There was still another gain from sending a mission, Hamilton believed, for no doubt it would fail and the Federalists could then openly champion hostilities with France. Washington, however, was tired of his official duties, and decided to pass the entire French problem on to his successor. This left Hamilton with the job of managing Adams through his Cabinet to carry out his proposal.

First came the hint that Federalist Senator Theodore Sedgwick of Massachusetts was to carry to Adams—"Were I Mr. Adams, then I believe I should begin my Presidency by naming an extraordinary commission to the French Republic." After this Hamilton wrote to his allies, the Cabinet trio, that they must see to it that a mission was sent, with Jefferson as a member. To Wolcott, who questioned the advisability of sending any Republican, Hamilton replied with a sharp rebuke for his "passions that prevent the pliancy to circumstances which is sometimes indispensable." Wolcott immediately jumped back in line with: "You know that I am accustomed to respect your opinions. If you are known to favor the sending of a commission, so the thing must and will be done." Pickering's first reaction was that the proper step was an outright declaration of war against France. To him, Hamilton caustically pointed out that the mission was "indispensable to silence the [Republican] Jacobin criticism and promote union among ourselves."

While these letters were making their rounds, Adams also was giving some thought to France. When he asked his Secretaries for their opinions on what to do, they were not long in passing on to him the proposal for a mission. A moment of peril arose for the sly Cabinet members when Elbridge Gerry, a Massachusetts politician, with whom Adams had served in the Continental Congress, wrote that Hamilton and the Cabinet were plotting something. But Adams scoffingly replied that Hamilton was completely innocent of any intrigue and "Pickering and all his colleagues are as much attached to me as I desire."

There is, of course, no way of determining whether Adams would have decided on a mission without Hamilton's pressure. Nevertheless, he concluded one was necessary and asked Jefferson to become a member. When Jefferson turned him down on the ground that "the Constitution strictly limits my duties to the Legislative Branch," Adams was furious. He could not believe that his old friend would spurn him, and when he thought about it later he concluded that Jefferson's manner had been offensively cold. From this time forward he considered Jefferson another on his formidable list of enemies. Yet after a while he agreed with Jefferson's decision because "the nation must hold itself very cheap that can choose a man one day to hold its second office, and the next send him to Europe to dance attendance at levees and drawing rooms." For a time he thought of substituting James Madison for Jefferson on the mission, but when he mentioned this at a Cabinet meeting Wolcott objected with "Mr. President, we are willing to resign."

In May 1797, Adams decided that a mission had to be sent without delay and he called a special session of the Fifth Congress. For two months he had basked in a political honeymoon: no attacks had emanated from the Republican press; Hamilton was not on the scene; and his Cabinet Secretaries seemed to be operating smoothly. A man starved for compliments found joy in reading the Republican press's pleasure in having a President whose carriage was hauled by two horses and not six like his predecessor and who employed no lackeys with white wands to part the crowd.

But Republican friendliness curdled when he presented his Message to Congress on May 15. There were cheers for his proposal to send special envoys to France, but there were protests when he called for strong defense measures in case negotiations failed. Merchant ships must be armed, the Navy expanded and the militia strengthened, he warned, to "convince France and the whole world that we are not a degraded people, humiliated under a colonial spirit of fear and sense of inferiority."

The Republican press trampled on him by labeling his speech a "war-whoop." But what hurt him more was "The President by Three Votes," the sneering reference to his electoral margin over Jefferson. Nor did he feel better when an acquaintance told him that Jefferson had expressed a poor opinion of his Message. Adams flared out with a wild attack: "It is evidence of a mind soured, yet seeking for popularity, and eaten to a honeycomb with ambition, yet weak, confused, uninformed and ignorant."

The change in feeling was made apparent from another quarter that same day. Senator Uriah Tracy of Connecticut, a Hamilton lieutenant, laid a letter from Hamilton before Adams. As Adams read it his anger mounted, for it turned out to be a document detailing "a whole system of instructions for the conduct of the President, the Senate and the House of Representatives." Adams, who tossed it back at Tracy, later recalled, "I really thought the man was in a delirium." Nevertheless, it still did not occur to him that Hamilton intended to dominate his Administration.

C. C. Pinckney, John Marshall and Elbridge Gerry were finally approved for the French mission before Congress adjourned in July. There was a fight over Gerry, whose name has entered the language as "gerrymander," because of his political division of a county. The objection to Gerry by the Federalists was that he was a radical Republican. As members began streaming out of Philadelphia for home, Adams foolishly began a practice that was to slash whatever remaining Presidential powers he held. He would go home to Quincy when Congress was not in session and return to Philadelphia when the next session convened.

During his four years such absences were to total 385 days, long stretches of months when he was not on hand to keep personal watch on his treacherous Cabinet. Mail took nine days from Philadelphia to Quincy and back again. But, said Adams, "the post goes very rapidly, and I answer by the return of it, so that nothing suffers . . . The people elected me to administer the government, and I do administer it here at Quincy as really as I could do at Philadelphia. The Secretaries transmit me daily by the post all the business of consequence, and nothing is done without my advice and direction." From his vantage point as Vice-President, Jefferson drew quite a different conclusion: "His long and habitual absences from the seat of government . . . removed him from any share in the transaction of affairs, and parcelled out the government, in fact, among four independent heads."

These absences only increased the arrogance and contempt of Pickering, Wolcott and McHenry. McHenry expressed his opinion of his superior in this fashion: "Whether he is spiteful, playful, witty, kind, cold, drunk, sober, angry, easy, stiff, jealous, cautious, confident, close, open, it is always in the wrong place or to the wrong person." While Adams was away, his Secretaries sent him Hamilton's suggested nominations for government positions, along with copies of reports dictated by Hamilton and Hamilton-inspired opinions on a host of subjects. But much of the departmental business they concluded without informing the President. This game of "hide-and-seek" palled occasionally and at one point, Secretary Pickering complained to Hamilton: "I wish you were in a situation not only 'to see all the cards,' but to play them. With all my soul, I would give you my *hand,* and engage in any other game, in which I might best co-operate on the same side, to *win the stakes.*"

In the fall of 1797, the three envoys were on French soil, but the lack of swift communications shrouded their reception in silence. When the new session of Congress convened in November, Adams' warlike Message was one Pickering had written and Adams and Abigail had edited. Abigail had become his chief adviser, though she was also unaware of the activities of the Cabinet trio. After the Message was delivered, Adams asked his Cabinet for advice on what course to follow should the mission fail. Charles Lee, his Attorney General and also a holdover from the Washington Administration, had little to offer. In fact, Lee, who had been severely criticized by Washington for inattentiveness to his duties, was even less interested now in public affairs. Whatever advice Pickering, Wolcott and McHenry gave Adams would generally meet with Lee's approval.

In the winter, the Cabinet trio met privately and decided that McHenry should write to Hamilton for the advice Adams requested. "I am sure I cannot do justice to the subject as you can," McHenry wrote, almost apologetically. Hamilton sent him recommendations and McHenry transcribed them in his own hand before delivering them to Adams. There should be war taxes, said Hamilton, and twenty new sloops of war, plus the floating of a Treasury security issue, the addition of 36,000 more soldiers and the abrogation of the French Treaty of Alliance of 1778. Tension mounted in

Philadelphia throughout January and February 1798, as no word came from the Americans in Paris. In March Adams received a report written by his envoys the previous October. Not only had their mission failed but they had been treated with indignity. Acting through three agents named Hottenguer, Bellamy and Hauteval, said envoy John Marshall, French Foreign Minister Talleyrand had demanded a bribe of $250,000, a $13,000,000 loan to France and an apology from Adams for his Message to Congress the preceding May, in which he condemned France for her harsh treatment of Pinckney. All these conditions would have to be met before the French would consider any settlement of differences, said the confidential statement.

The report infuriated Adams, and on March 19 he requested the passage of war preparation legislation that Hamilton had laid out for McHenry. Abigail was so certain of war that she ordered fifty pounds of coffee and one hundred and fifty pounds of sugar before inflation set in.

It was impossible, the Republicans cried, that the French would have refused to receive the American envoys properly. Adams' Message was "insane," Jefferson declared; he merely thirsted for war like all other Federalists. If Adams would only send Congress the mission's papers, the Republicans said, the country would know that he had no justification for his call for war legislation.

At first, Adams was opposed to sending Executive papers to Congress, just as Washington had refused Congress the Jay Treaty papers in 1795. But by this time, with the Republican clamor growing, the Cabinet trio had informed Hamilton of the nature of the mission's report. Quickly he saw the opportunity to paralyze the Republican party and turn the entire country into a Federalist stronghold. Adams must transmit the papers to Congress, he wrote to Pickering. "Nothing certainly can be more proper. Confidence will otherwise be wanting."

On April 3, Adams finally sent Congress the papers after his Cabinet convinced him that this was necessary to prove the need for war preparation. Adams also unwittingly accepted another Hamilton recommendation when he proclaimed May 9 a day of fasting and prayer.

He had changed the names of the three French blackmailers to X, Y and Z, and by this the mission's experience became known. The XYZ Papers stunned the Republicans. An immediate sensation, they set the country aflame with demands for war. "Millions

for defense, but not a cent for tribute" became the rallying cry
for hostilities. Down came the French flags that had flown over
Republican coffee houses; the tricolor cockade of France on American hats gave way to the black cockade of the Federalists; and
Republicans went into hiding as young men paraded through
Philadelphia streets in patriotic fervor. "Yankee Doodle" drowned
out "Ça Ira," the marching song of the French Revolutionists.
Crowds gathered at the home of the President, and Adams, who
had always regretted his lack of military experience, greeted them
dressed in a military uniform and a dangling sword. In one of the
few aggressive Republican reactions to the Federalist body blow,
Bache's Republican *Aurora* printed a description of the President
as the "old, querulous, bald, blind, crippled, toothless Adams!"

While the Republicans lay shocked by the duplicity and lack
of idealism in their French heroes, the Federalists in Congress
swiftly followed Hamilton's directions to capitalize on the war
hysteria. Within a few months, twenty war measures became law.
Even more would have been done, said Abigail, if Albert Gallatin,
the Republican House leader, hadn't "constantly thrown down
balls" to the Federalists. In April 1798, one bill established the
Navy Department and Adams made his first Cabinet appointment,
selecting Benjamin Stoddert as Secretary. Other bills abrogated
existing American treaties with France, brought an arming of merchant vessels, installed high taxes on houses, land and windows.
Still another gave Adams authority to establish a provisional army
of volunteers for three years. There were already rumors that the
French were preparing an invasion, and frightened Federalists
demanded that Adams lose no time in creating an army to meet it.
"The Army was none of my Work," Adams later derided the
hysteria. "I only advised a few Companies of Artillery to garrison
our most exposed forts. Hamilton's Project of an Army of fifty
thousand Men, ten thousand of them to be horse, appeared to me
proper only for Bedlam."

Nor did Adams propose the anti-civil rights legislation that Congress passed. To silence the Republican leadership, Congressional
Federalists threatened to impeach Jefferson. But, hungry to destroy
the Republican party, the Federalists did more than threaten.
First came the Alien Act aimed at Irish immigrants who were
almost all Republicans. Adams was given authority to deport any
alien he deemed dangerous to the peace and safety of the country.
The Enemy Alien Act, aimed at French aliens, authorized him to

arrest and imprison enemy aliens during wartime. Last, but worse than these two laws in its effect on constitutional freedoms, was the Sedition Act. Here fines up to $5000 and prison sentences up to five years were to be imposed upon persons who wrote, printed, uttered, or published . . . "false, scandalous and malicious writings" about Congress and the President. It is difficult to believe that with his background as a protector of civil rights Adams put his signature on the Sedition Act. Yet Adams lightly tossed aside his lifetime beliefs because hysteria had momentarily taken control over his reasoning. On the other hand, Hamilton's first reaction to the laws was to utter the sane words: "Why establish a tyranny? Energy is a very different thing from violence."

While the prospect of filling jails with Republicans on charges of sedition made Federalist hearts beat faster, the last important member of the Adams cast of characters was playing a big part on the Presidential stage. In office, George Washington had been a severe critic of political parties, but in retirement, he had become a rabid Federalist. In his eyes, Republicans were anti-American. Not only did he favor prosecuting them under the Sedition Act, but he was also insistent that they be kept out of the Provisional Army. His late-developing interest in political maneuvering had even brought him to urge certain Federalists to run for office and to pressure Adams to appoint his protégés. One of these was Bushrod Washington, his nephew and heir, whom he induced Adams to appoint as Associate Justice of the Supreme Court in 1798, even though Bushrod was an inconsequential lawyer.

When Adams became President, he had hoped to be rid of Washington for good. He even went so far to sour their relationship as to decline to attend a Washington birthday ball. He said a President could not attend a function honoring a private citizen. Washington's latter-day interest in politics did not disturb Adams to any extent because the former Chief Executive did not attempt to interfere with Adams' Presidential prerogatives. However, when Congress authorized the Provisional Army in May 1798, Adams realized with distaste that he would have to deal directly with his predecessor. There appeared no alternative other than to appoint Washington commander-in-chief.

Adams was aware that Washington had accepted him as his running mate in 1788 primarily because Hamilton was too young and had not held prestige posts during the Revolutionary War.

He found this hardly gratifying to his easily affronted nature for the entire country knew that it was he who had proposed Washington as head of the Continental Army back in 1775. Yet though he patted his own back for putting Washington on his road to glory, he insisted that Washington's ability was a mirage, that he "owed his talents to his height, his grace, his gift of silence, a large imposing fortune and the fact that he was a Virginian and Virginia geese are all swans." Few would remember, Adams wailed, that his own civilian role in the Revolution was second to none. "The history of our Revolution," he noted bitterly, "will be one continued lie from one end to the other. The essence of the whole will be that Dr. Franklin's electrical rod smote the earth and out sprang General Washington. That Franklin electrified him with his rod—and thenceforward these two conducted all the policies, negotiations, legislatures, and war."

Long after he was out of office, Adams glanced back on that hot summer of 1798 and commented ruefully, "I should have said no to an appointment of Washington and Hamilton." Actually, he had no choice in the matter. In the spring, Hamilton was already planning an enormous army engaged in grandiose undertakings, with Washington serving as figurehead commander-in-chief and himself in real command. In May, he wrote Washington in a tone that suggested he was directing the government: "In the event of an open rupture with France," he said, "the public voice will again call you to command the armies of your country."

Washington was so pleased with Hamilton's grant that he failed to point out in his reply that someone named John Adams would have to make that decision. Instead, he acted as though he were accepting a firm commitment and inquired whether he could count on Hamilton's assistance in managing military affairs. Early in June Hamilton wrote him again, spoke about the immense personal sacrifice he would be making if he joined Washington, but expressed his willingness if he were named at least the inspector general. This time he mentioned Adams and cleverly planted the idea that Washington was to be given independent control of the Army if he would insist on it. For instance, on the selection of the officers of the Army, he said he assumed that Washington's "choice would *regulate* the Executive."

During the time these two were secretly making their plans, Adams was also thinking about the Army. One day he asked Secretary Pickering to suggest a man to lead the Army and the instant

reply was "Colonel Hamilton." This was not to Adams' liking. On
another occasion when Pickering gave the same reply, Adams remarked angrily, "It is not his turn by a great deal."

After these rebuffs, Pickering attempted to convince Adams that
Hamilton merited second place behind Washington. When he again
met with failure, he appealed to Washington to bring pressure on
Adams. A letter to Mount Vernon on June 6, 1798 read: "From
the conversation that I and others have had with the President,
there appears to us to be a disinclination to appoint Colo. Hamilton
in what we think is his proper station, and that alone in which
we suppose he will serve: the Second to You; and Chief in your
absence."

Adams could no longer delay appointing a chief for the Army
and on June 22 he wrote Washington: "We must have your name.
There will be more efficacy in it than in many an army." Once
Washington accepted, Adams expected he could then take his
time determining who would be appointed to the posts immediately under him. But his Cabinet and Hamilton had done
their work well, for Washington's letter of acceptance also called
on Adams to relinquish his constitutional authority. He would lead
the Army, he said, only on the condition that no staff officer would
be appointed who did not meet with his "entire confidence." Adams
recognized this usurpation of Presidential authority. Nevertheless,
he sent Washington's nomination as commander-in-chief with the
rank of lieutenant general to the Senate in July and Washington
was quickly confirmed.

The formal selection was the signal for Hamilton and his Cabinet aides to make their last push. The chief immediate problem
facing the conspirators was that Washington had so far refused to
commit himself on whom he wanted for second place. An opportunity to tackle this situation came when Adams sent Secretary
of War McHenry to Mount Vernon to deliver Washington's commission. Adams told him to bring back some suggestions from the
general regarding possible appointments of staff officers, but Mc-
Henry went prepared to work solely in behalf of Hamilton. He
also carried with him a letter from Pickering demanding that
Hamilton be named his second man. When he returned, he was
in a happy mood, for he had a note in the general's own hand
to deliver to Adams. Washington's list of major generals he desired
were Hamilton, C. C. Pinckney and former Secretary of War
Henry Knox, in that order.

However, Adams took no action before leaving for Quincy on July 25, 1798, other than to send the names on Washington's list to the Senate for confirmation. His beloved wife Abigail had contracted malaria, and not even the expected French invasion would have kept him from her side. In horror, his Cabinet trio realized that their task was made triply more complicated because he was not available. Seniority among the three suggested major generals would be determined on the basis of which commission Adams signed first. What if he took the time to consider that Washington had no business interfering with the nominating process?

Adams was doing just this as he sat with Abigail. In mid-August he wrote McHenry that he intended to make Knox Washington's deputy, with Pinckney following and Hamilton third. Knox had come to Quincy to register a strong protest against being put behind the less experienced Hamilton, and he had also informed Washington that he would not serve under Hamilton. Adams had heard that Washington himself was beginning to waver in favor of the battle-scarred Knox.

The Adams letter to McHenry caught Hamilton at a bad moment, for he was already mapping the conquest of New Orleans, the Southwest and Mexico. Washington now found himself deluged with strange self-praising letters from Hamilton, while Knox received a Hamilton-dictated note from McHenry fixing him at a lower military status. Then on September 17, the Cabinet trio composed a letter to Adams, which Wolcott signed. Washington was insisting on Hamilton as his deputy, Wolcott wrote. "Public opinion" demanded this also. Besides, Knox had "no popular character." After posting this letter, Wolcott smugly wrote Hamilton that "measures have been taken to bring all right" and he advised him to say or do nothing "until you hear from me."

The letter from trusted Wolcott so jarred Adams that he backed away from his newfound intention to maintain his Presidential rights. On September 30, he sent the three commissions to McHenry and explained that he had made no decision on their seniority, making them "all dated on the Same Day."

This was better than nothing but still not the answer Hamilton demanded. The time had come to work on Washington's ego and lead him to force the hand of Adams. Accordingly, word was sent to Washington that the President had no intention of honoring his agreement to abide by Washington's choice of officers. The desired result came quickly. As President, Washington had fought off all attempts to cut Presidential authority. But now as an employee of a President, he saw things differently. Washington harshly demanded that Adams tell him "at once and precisely . . . whether your determination to reverse the order of the three Major Generals is final, and whether you mean to appoint another Adjutant General without my concurrence." He added that if Hamilton were not given second place he would not serve, and the loss would be "irrepairable."

This letter completely deflated Adams, and in his reply on October 9, he notified Washington he could do as he pleased. His weak explanation was that he had dated the three commissions simultaneously with the hope that he and Washington might work out a friendly solution. "But if these hopes should be disappointed and controversies should arise they will be submitted to you as Commander-in-Chief, and if, after all, any one should be so obstinate as to appeal to me from the judgment of the Commander-in-Chief, I was determined to confirm that judgment."

Hamilton had triumphed, but the experience had opened Adams' eyes to some strange carryings-on in his own official family. The sting of this degrading defeat could lead to a future explosion.

When the third session of the Fifth Congress convened on December 3, 1798, Adams was aware of a significant change in the national political climate. The much heralded French invasion had not come off and only the most hardbitten Federalists still believed it would. The high war taxes were already being felt and resentment was growing. Military recruitment had brought only the youthful scum into the Army, and the soldiers were behaving so badly in the towns that Adams likened them to "a ferocious wild beast let loose upon the nation to devour it."

There were other matters that Adams noted. The British had stepped up their nefarious practice of impressing American sailors, hauling them off American ships with total disregard of naturalization laws. Then there was the Sedition Act, which was proving to be the most unpopular law in the nation's short history. Even its minor enforcement was ending the earlier widespread animosity toward the French-loving Republicans. Each prison sentence for criticizing either Congress or the President served only to increase the popularity of the Jeffersonians.

Adams was also aware that the Federalist leadership hoped to turn the current undeclared war against France into a formally declared war through Congressional action. But Adams was already pondering whether even an undeclared war was necessary. In October, Elbridge Gerry of the ill-fated French mission had come to Quincy to report that Talleyrand wished to renew negotiations. Shortly afterward, Adams had also heard from William Vans Murray, his minister to The Hague, that the French feared continued hostility would push Adams into closer alliance with Britain.

When Adams arrived in Philadelphia for the December 1798 Congressional session, his Cabinet had already prepared his Message for the legislature. It was a document actually written by Hamilton, who had come to Philadelphia to guide the Cabinet ghostwriters in the writing of a strong anti-peace speech. Adams was reading through the Message at a Cabinet meeting when he stopped at one paragraph. This contained the statement that France would in effect, have to come begging on her knees for any renewal of negotiations, and that a new attempt at negotiation by the United States would be an act of humiliation. This would never do, Adams said. The fuming Secretaries were forced to watch Adams rephrase the paragraph so that it offered his willingness to send an envoy if the French gave assurance of a proper reception. Later in the Philadelphia Capitol, when he read this to Congress, eyes turned in concern toward Washington, Hamilton and Pinckney who sat listening in full military regalia.

The offending paragraph in the original Message added greatly to Adams' growing doubts about the loyalty of certain of his Cabinet Secretaries. But it was Secretary Pickering for whom he reserved the most distaste. In October, Pickering made public a devastating report he had written on Elbridge Gerry's role in the XYZ Affair. Adams had thought it only fair that Pickering print Gerry's rebuttal, but with astounding arrogance his Secretary of State refused. Pickering went on to threaten to publish a further attack, which would reveal not only Gerry's "pusillanimity, weakness, and meanness alone, but his duplicity and treachery." In another action, Pickering had gone on his own to Congress for a law because a Quaker meddler, Dr. George Logan, had told Adams that the French wanted peace. Logan had traveled to France to discuss the undeclared war with Merlin, President of the Directory. Pickering's Logan Act made it a high misdemeanor for a private citizen to discuss foreign affairs with officials of a foreign government in an attempt to influence their conduct on matters in dispute with the United States.

However, what irked Adams most was Pickering's villainy toward Colonel William S. Smith, who was the President's son-in-law. In sending a list of officer nominations to the Senate late in 1798, Adams included Smith's name as commander of a regiment of provisionals. Upon learning this, Pickering immediately hurried to the Senate chamber, where he urged Federalist Senators to vote against Smith's confirmation. Pickering later explained his strange behavior as necessary because, he said, Smith was incapable, a crooked businessman and a nominee solely because of nepotism. This last was odd coming from Pickering because he had installed his eldest son and nephew in the diplomatic service, another son and nephew in the Navy, a cousin as a postmaster and his brother as insurance agent for the Navy.

Adams might have forgiven Pickering his lobbying except for one factor: Every person on the list of nominations was confirmed but Smith. His total was a dismal three votes. One Senator reported that when Adams heard the news "his resentment appeared implacable." Pickering admitted that he expected to be fired, but despite his feelings Adams did not request his resignation. Instead, Adams submitted Smith's name for a lower rank, which won approval. Pickering's mean opinion of Adams' son-in-law was later confirmed by Albert Gallatin of the Republicans who wrote to Jefferson: "Colonel Smith is a bad officer; he does not attend to the duties of his office; he has presented fallacious statements of his emoluments, with intention of keeping a portion which by law ought to be paid in the Treasury."

On January 21, 1799, while the undeclared sea war between the United States and France grew even more vicious, Adams received a message from the French Government requesting a reconciliation. A short time later came a letter from William Vans Murray, American minister to The Hague, saying he had read a note from Talleyrand assuring him that an American envoy would be "received as the representative of a great, free, powerful and independent nation." These notes left Adams with two clear choices. He could be loyal to the Federalist party and ask Congress for an open declaration of war. Or he could take his own counsel and try to end the current hostilities.

Adams decided to seek peace with honor, but he carefully refrained from discussing it with his Cabinet. "I knew that if I called the heads of departments together and asked their advice," he explained later, "three of them would very laconically protest against the measure. The consequence would be, that the whole would be instantly communicated to A, B, C, D, E, F, etc., in the Senate, and G, H, I, etc., in the House; the public and the presses would have it at once, and a clamor raised and a prejudice propagated against the measure, that would probably excite the Senate to put their negative on the whole plan."

On February 18, while the Senate debated further war preparations, a messenger knocked on the door of the chamber. He had a note from Adams, requesting the confirmation of Minister to Holland William Vans Murray as Minister Plenipotentiary to France.

Pandemonium immediately broke out. The Republicans were wild with joy; the Federalists, outraged. Some Federalists muttered that "they wished the old woman [Abigail] had been there; then it wouldn't have taken place." One Federalist threatened to assassinate Adams. Hamilton's reply to a Senator who broke the news to him was: "The step announced in your letter just received, in all its circumstances, would astonish, if anything from that quarter could astonish." But he *was* astonished—and hurt. For if there would be no war, how was he to fulfill his grandiose dream of leading an army of conquest through Louisiana and Mexico and returning home a greater hero than Washington?

When he recovered from his initial shock, Hamilton devised a scheme to prevent an end to the French troubles. Five Federalist Senators were appointed to a committee to consider Murray's nomination, and Hamilton requested them to visit Adams one evening to tell him the nomination would be rejected. Adams recognized the five as members of the committee and had a good idea why they had come. He greeted them with a reminder that the doctrine of separation of powers made their visit illegal. "Gentlemen, I am glad to see you as friends and Senators," he was reported to have said, "but as a committee interfering with my executive duties, I cannot consent to receive you. I protest against all such interference." With annoyance, he told them, "If you are determined to interfere in diplomatic matters, reject Mr. Murray." Hamilton had asked them to suggest that if he sent a mission of three envoys instead of Murray alone, they would approve it. They brought this up, and, as Hamilton had hoped, Adams rejected this compromise angrily and ended the meeting.

Later that evening, filled with confidence that Adams' peace-seeking venture had been successfully stifled, the caucus of Federalist Congressmen agreed to reject Murray. But peace with France was more important to Adams than upholding Presidential prerogatives. In a surprise move on February 25, he accepted the committee's offer that he had previously spurned and added the names of Patrick Henry and Chief Justice Oliver Ellsworth to Murray's as envoys to France.

Two days later the Senate confirmed the commission. Pickering charged that "the President's character can never be retrieved." Hamilton's view of the President's clever stratagem was expressed in a letter to Washington: "All my calculations lead me to regret the measure. I hope that it may not in its consequences involve the United States in a war on the side of France with her enemies." But Hamilton and his Cabinet assistants were not yet finished. They had one last hope—time; and their plan now became one to stop the mission from sailing.

Early in March 1799, shortly after the Senate approved the mission, with Governor Davie of North Carolina replacing old Patrick Henry who rejected the appointment because of ill health, Congress adjourned and Adams deserted the capital for Quincy as usual. Before leaving, he had ordered Pickering to write to Murray for an official assurance from the French Government that the envoys would be properly received. Talleyrand's assurance came in July, much too early to suit the dour Secretary of State. In August, he sent it to Quincy, calling the President's attention to one paragraph in which Talleyrand had objected to the delay in proceedings. Pickering suggested that Adams demand a full explanation for the tone of that paragraph. But Adams realized this would serve no purpose other than to delay things several months more, and he adamantly ordered Pickering to ignore it, send the commission to the envoys and warn them to get ready for imminent departure.

A yellow fever epidemic hit Philadelphia that summer and the government moved temporarily to Trenton, New Jersey. Here, while Pickering dawdled over the writing of instructions for the envoys, his fellow conspirators induced various Federalists to visit Adams in an effort to have him call off the mission. Secretary of the Navy Stoddert finally wrote the President, telling him it was necessary that he come to Trenton and take personal command.

Adams delayed until mid-October after he received a second Stoddert note warning him that "artful and designing men" were plotting in his absence "from the seat of government to make your next election less honorable than it would otherwise be." When he finally reached Trenton, he was surprised to find Hamilton and British minister Robert Liston there. Hamilton brazenly demanded in a personal meeting that Adams delay the mission. The evening of October 15, Adams called a Cabinet meeting. The Hamiltonian Secretaries were primed with arguments for ordering an end to the mission, but Adams refused to discuss anything beyond the instructions for the envoys. Then he bade the Secretaries good night and ended the meeting. They were at an early breakfast the next morning when a note came from Adams. A frigate was to be made ready for the envoys, who were to depart within two weeks. The entire subject was closed to further discussion.

When the envoys sailed on November 5, their departure represented Adams' first victory over Hamilton since he had taken office almost three years earlier. It also gave notice that the rift between the two men was now complete. Washington's death on the fourteenth of the following month pointed up this situation; Adams refused to elevate Hamilton to commander-in-chief of the Provisional Army.

But toward the treacherous Cabinet officers, Adams did not appear to be inclined to take any action. Then on May 5, the Secretary of War received the following note: "The President requests Mr. McHenry's company for one minute." McHenry had not noticed any change in the President's attitude toward him since the mission fight and he blithely went to Adams' house on Market Street. Calmly, Adams discussed a nomination with him. However, when this matter was finished, Adams suddenly broke into wild rage, and in a screaming voice that could be heard far down the street told McHenry that Washington had saddled him with three untrustworthy Secretaries. He bellowed out charges that McHenry had refused a commission in the Provisional Army to the sole elector in North Carolina who had voted for him in 1796; that McHenry had "biased" Washington to give Hamilton preference over Knox; that in a report to Congress he had eulogized Washington and praised Hamilton; and that he had pressured Adams to suspend the French mission. Hamilton was "a bastard and as much a foreigner as Gallatin!" Adams bellowed. In a final roar,

Adams demanded his resignation. Early the next morning McHenry complied. He told others that Adams was "mad, indecorous, and at times outrageous." He described the President's mind as "like the last glimmerings of a lamp, feeble, wavering and unsteady."

Adams knew too well his inability to control his temper to chance a face-to-face meeting with Pickering. Five days after his outburst against McHenry, he informed his Secretary of State by letter "that he may have the opportunity of resigning, if he chooses." But Pickering stubbornly refused to quit and sent back a letter calling attention to his personal financial problems. Adams then notified him that he was discharged from further service. In a sneering portrayal of Pickering's two-faced role, Adams later described him as having "a bald head and straight hair." When Hamilton heard the news, he quickly sent his regrets to Pickering and ordered him before leaving the department to "take copies and extracts of all such documents as will enable you to explain both Jefferson and Adams."

Secretary of the Treasury Wolcott, as deceitful as the others, waited for word that he was also fired. But none came. He was to repay Adams for keeping him on during 1800 by supplying Hamilton with secret data for attacking the President. Then a decade later he would suddenly become a Republican and serve ten years as governor of Connecticut.

The year 1800 was a Presidential election year, and Hamilton was determined to bar Adams from a second term. He made a tour of New England solely to induce Federalist leaders there to refrain from supporting the President. However, leader after leader refused. In the meantime, the Federalist Congressional nominating caucus met and recommended that Adams and C. C. Pinckney be supported equally. Hamilton lost little time approaching Pinckney with his bearded scheme to have more electors vote for him than for Adams, but Pinckney would have none of it. Nevertheless, from his department office, Treasury Secretary Wolcott busily wrote letters to other Federalists, proposing that "Adams ought not to be supported."

Early that year, Hamilton the Federalist had pitted himself against Aaron Burr the Republican in a contest to see who could elect the majority of members in the New York state legislature. The significance of this struggle was that the legislature would choose the state's Presidential electors. Burr's surprising victory meant that Adams had lost the state's twelve electoral votes and insured a place for Burr on the Republican ticket because of the potency of the votes he controlled. It was right after Adams had learned of the New York loss that he fired McHenry and Pickering.

Without New York, Adams realized he needed widespread support in the South. A study of the situation there convinced him he would collect many electoral votes, and if some unforeseen tragedy did not occur his chance for re-election was promising. But whatever chance he had disappeared that summer when in choking anger Hamilton ruined both the President and the party. The sequence was as follows: After he was fired, Pickering blasted Adams. Adams retorted that a "British faction" existed in American politics with Hamilton serving as its boss. On August 1, Hamilton demanded an explanation. When Adams ignored him he grew furious, and with the aid of private material supplied him by Wolcott, he wrote a vicious pamphlet titled: "Letter containing the Public Conduct and Character of John Adams." Influential Federalists who heard of it pleaded with Hamilton not to release it, but he would not listen and ordered the tract distributed privately to select Federalists. One favorable comment came from Wolcott who wrote him that "the style, temper and spirit of the composition are well suited to the object and will do you honor."

The dirty linen he washed in public about Adams supposedly offered "irrefragable proofs of his unfitness for the station of Chief Magistrate." Adams revealed "vanity, extreme egotism" and as far back as the Revolution there had been strong doubts about "the solidity of his understanding." Hamilton denied the existence of any conspiracy against the sending of the French mission, yet said that Adams' "capricious and undignified negotiations with France" were to be condemned. He went on to denounce the dismissal of the Cabinet Secretaries, declaring that Adams had fired McHenry without cause and in "paroxysms of rage," while Pickering's only crime was that he had been "justly tenacious of his own dignity." Then, after moaning because Adams had failed to name him commander-in-chief, he concluded his name-calling with the announcement that he planned to support Adams!

The Republicans were no doubt making some headway against Adams even before the pamphlet appeared. They were throwing the entire burden on him for the existence of the Sedition Act and charging that he was responsible for the high taxes to create a war machine that he himself had shown was unnecessary.

But the election remained in doubt until one morning when

Aaron Burr rose early and intercepted a boy on the New York streets who was delivering copies of Hamilton's diatribe. Burr seized a copy from him and gave it immediate wide circulation by supplying it to Republican editors.

Adams no longer had a political future. "The bastard brat of a Scotch pedlar," he referred to Hamilton. "He is no more fit for a prompter than Phaeton to drive the chariot of the sun." But nothing could alter the election results, which showed Jefferson and Burr tied, each getting 73 electoral votes, and Adams trailing with 65. Under the circumstances, it was remarkable that Adams had done so well. A decisive blow had come in South Carolina where the eight electoral votes had gone to the Republicans.

It was a sad Adams who moved to primitive Washington in November 1800 to become the first President to live in the permanent capital. Not long afterward, Vice-President Jefferson came to the Executive Mansion to request his aid against the Federalist plot to make Burr President. The House of Representatives, which would decided between Jefferson and Burr, had a Federalist majority. "You have turned me out, you have turned me out!" Adams berated him. Then, instead of offering aid, he demanded that Jefferson pledge himself to carry out certain political measures Adams favored if he defeated Burr and became President. Jefferson refused.

The Hamiltonian Federalists were still not finished with their hated President. The new Secretary of State was John Marshall, and Hamilton's crew remembered that as a member of the House, Marshall had been Adams' sole Federalist defender. They also remembered Marshall as the Federalist who had opposed the Alien and Sedition Acts and favored the French negotiations. Marshall was now handling the French negotiations for Adams and it was the Hamiltonians' hope that if he sent a new French treaty to the Senate, they could muster sufficient votes to defeat it.

In November 1799, Napoleon Bonaparte had overthrown the Directory and become First Consul. With the conquest of Europe and England on his mind, the undeclared war was a nuisance to him, especially since the fourteen American naval vessels and two hundred armed merchant ships were doing so well against French ships. He was anxious to negotiate an end to hostilities, yet he was a strong bargainer and when Marshall and Adams read the terms of the treaty they received in November 1800, there was nothing in it that favored the United States. But the treaty did not call for a bribe, loan or apology, and it was an honorable document in this sense. For calling off the war, Napoleon was to gain a "most favored nation" trading status for France. In return, he agreed to end the 1778 Treaty of Alliance and to accept the principle that "free ships make free goods."

New England die-hard Federalists fought savagely for two months to prevent this peace convention from passing the Senate. But despite their bombast, they were unable to do so. After the Senate consented to the treaty, Adams remarked: "I desire no other inscription over my gravestone than: 'Here lies John Adams, who took upon himself the responsibility of the peace with France, in the year 1800.'" The prevention of a full war with France, a negative achievement, was to be his chief success as President.

But there was another success. In January 1801, he nominated Marshall as Chief Justice of the Supreme Court. Republicans angrily charged that the office should be kept vacant for Jefferson to fill, while many Federalists condemned the selection of Marshall. For almost a month the Senate debated and stalled before confirming Marshall. Years later Adams said, "My gift of John Marshall to the people of the United States was the proudest act of my life."

The last few months in office were sad ones for John and Abigail Adams. Not only did they believe he had been cheated out of a second term but they were also griefstricken by the death of their thirty-year-old son Charles, a victim of acute alcoholism. "Oh, that I had died for him," Adams weepingly told his youngest son, Thomas. Early in 1801, Congress passed the Judiciary Act, which added several judges, marshals and attorneys to the Federal court system. Adams sat at his desk until midnight on March 3, his palsied hand signing commissions that would burden the incoming Republican Administration with Federalist office holders. This gesture was unworthy of the man. So was his lack of dignity in creeping out of Washington at four A.M. the next day so that he would not have to witness his successor's inauguration. "You have no idea of the meanness, indecency, almost insanity of his conduct," Albert Gallatin wrote his wife about Adams' early morning departure.

The man who understood that the constitutional powers of a President were vast knew fully well at the close of his four-year term that he had not even scratched the surface of his office's potential. Yet from the vantage point of passing centuries, we must conclude that he did well to prevent a war that might have brought irreparable harm to his country's future.

☆ 3 ☆

THOMAS JEFFERSON

The Practical Idealist

Probably no man came to the Presidency with a political philosophy and program so clearly defined as did Thomas Jefferson. Yet in the course of eight tempestuous years dealing with vexing domestic and foreign problems, no man departed further from his ideals in practice than he.

The master of Monticello, noted thinker and humanitarian, author of the stirring Declaration of Independence, governor of Virginia, successor to Benjamin Franklin as minister to France, Washington's Secretary of State, John Adams' Vice-President and emotion-arousing political leader, had spent decades considering the composition and regulation of his ideal society.

In his view the function of government was to nurture a simple agricultural economy, which, he believed, would fulfill man's yearning for independence and individualism. The Arcadia of his blueprints allotted no space for industry, a laboring class, bankers, a merchant marine, a standing or sailing military force or cities. He saw Europe as a place where class was set against class with the advent of industrialization, until human degradation and oppression resulted. The laboring class, unable to provide for its own needs, became "the mobs of great cities," adding "just so much to the support of pure government as sores do to the strength of the human body." His conclusion was that "when we get piled upon one another in large cities, as in Europe, we shall become as corrupt as in Europe, and go to eating one another as they do there."

The simple life demanded a simple government; one that would "restrain men from injuring one another" but "leave them otherwise free to regulate their own pursuits of industry and improvement." Even the few restraining political powers that were permissible would have to be decentralized because "centralization has destroyed the liberty and rights of men in every government which has ever existed under the sun." The chief province of the central government would be the foreign relations that involved all the states.

Jefferson's ideas extended also to the anemic national government he proposed for his Arcadia. Presidential leadership must be prevented because it was monarchial in nature. Congress—especially the House, which was more representative of the average citizen than the Senate—must originate policy and maintain close scrutiny over the way the President executed its will.

In the flush of the political victory in 1800, Jefferson wrote in excitement, "We shall now put her [the ship of state] on her republican tack, and she will show by the beauty of her motion the skill of the builders." The Federalists—or "Monocrats," the term he coined for the opposition—had passed "infernal" laws, cloaked the President with monarchial trappings, decoyed "the laborer from his plow," misread the Constitution's restrictions on the national government. "We shall see the reign of witches pass over," he declared, "and the people recovering their true right, restoring the government to its true principles."

It was Alexander Hamilton, the dynamic leader of the Federalists, who first predicted that Jefferson would not be paralyzed by his philosophy. Scoffing at Jefferson's vow to reduce the Presidency to shadow without substance, Hamilton said: "It is not true that he is an enemy to the power of the Executive, or that he is for confounding all the powers in the House of Representatives. While we were in the Administration together, he was for a large construction of the Executive authority and not backward to act upon it in cases which coincided with his views."

This observation was an important factor in the contested election of 1800. The Constitution had revealed a flaw that year because electors were not permitted to designate separately their choice for President and Vice-President. The resulting tie vote of 73 electoral ballots each for Jefferson and Aaron Burr had thrown the contest into the House for final decision, a House controlled by lame-duck Federalists.

To most Federalists the fact that the Republican electors had meant Jefferson to be President and Burr the Vice-President was of no consequence in the face of this superb opportunity to de-molish Jefferson. However, Hamilton would not hear of this. "If there is a man in the world I ought to hate, it is Jefferson," he wrote. "But the public good must be paramount to every consider-ation." Jefferson might mouth radical doctrines, Hamilton warned his fellow Federalists, but Burr was a potential traitor, conspira-tor, "the Catiline of America, extortionist and bankrupt beyond redemption except by the plunder of his country."

Federalists remained unconvinced and ballot followed ballot be-tween Jefferson and Burr that February of 1801. The first ballot gave Jefferson eight states and Burr six, with nine needed for election. Succeeding ballots brought no change. Then rumor spread on the Federalist side of the aisle that Representative James Bayard from Delaware had won indirect assurance that Jefferson would continue Federalist policies in exchange for Presi-dential votes. Bayard later said that word had come that Jefferson would not tamper with the Hamiltonian internal tax program and the funding of the national debt; nor would he cut naval strength or oust any Federalists from government jobs except a handful at the very top. Then there was Timothy Pickering's belief that on the basis of the abuse poured on Jefferson in the 1800 campaign, he would "make no great strides from the old Administration and would look more to the Federalists than to the Jacobins for his support." So it came to pass that on the thirty-sixth ballot, Jef-ferson the scholar, philosopher, musician, inventor, amateur scien-tist, architect, author, planter, lawyer and politician won over Burr and became President.

The Federalist belief that "the serious mischiefs that had been foretold" would not come true was apparent even on Inauguration Day, the day of days for each new President, when their generous optimism was jolted chiefly by the refusal of John Adams to wit-ness his successor's oath-taking. One of the wariest of Federalists was Chief Justice John Marshall, the loose-jointed cousin of the new President and his longtime opponent. Before administering the oath of office to Jefferson, Marshall had begun a letter in which he wrote: "The Democrats are divided into speculative theorists and absolute terrorists. With the latter I am disposed to class Mr. Jefferson." However, after listening to Jefferson's ad-dress, Marshall continued his letter with: "I have administered the oath to the President. His inaugural speech well judged and con-ciliatory . . . is in direct terms giving the lie to the violent party declamation which has elected him." The remark that did most to bring Marshall and the last of the die-hards to this position was Jefferson's statement, "We are all Republicans; we are all Federalists," uttered in a tone that augured conciliation between former political enemies.

The special session of the Seventh Congress ended on March 5, 1801, after only a two-day meeting. Other than being on hand for the inauguration, its work consisted chiefly in approving the three Cabinet nominations Jefferson submitted covering the departments of State and War and the Attorney General.

As his Secretary of State, Jefferson chose James Madison, the "Father of the Constitution" and his close friend. Madison was a profound thinker but inexperienced in foreign affairs except for his work in the Continental Congress on Spanish-American relations. However, this was of little concern to Jefferson because he planned on managing his own foreign policy. Some contemporaries considered the relationship between the lanky President and the small, frail-appearing Secretary of State to be that of father and son. But Madison was closer to being an equal, differing with Jefferson where he thought necessary and attempting to bring him to his own point of view.

General Henry Dearborn, whose military career found him at Bunker Hill in 1775 and at the British surrender at Yorktown in October 1781, became Secretary of War; and Levi Lincoln, ardent Massachusetts Republican, the Attorney General. The brilliant financial expert, thirty-five-year-old Albert Gallatin became Secretary of the Treasury; Robert Smith of Baltimore, Secretary of the Navy, after three others rejected the post; and Gideon Granger, an excellent publicist but mentally unstable person, Postmaster General.

After the special session adjourned on March 5, 1801, Congress was not scheduled to meet again until the following December. When Jefferson, too, deserted the capital for Monticello, leading Federalists looked forward with happy anticipation to nine months of Republican inaction, with Federalists near the helm in all departments. But Jefferson was back in Washington after a short vacation and in the midst of the first major test of his professed ideals.

He knew that one obvious way to curtail the activities of the national government and make the states dominant was to slash

the roll of government employees. However, even before his inauguration, loyal Republicans clamored for patronage rewards.
The job-hungry swarmed about him with demands both subtle
and broad. Some expressed initial shock to learn that the total
number of government jobs was so small, while Jefferson bluntly
commented that they would be fewer shortly.

Bitter reaction soon set in. Writing to James Monroe, his former
law clerk and disciple, Jefferson spelled out his dilemma. He had
not said "We are all Republicans; we are all Federalists" at his
inauguration because he wanted to lie in the same bed with his
political enemies. Instead he had hoped to win over thousands
of persons who were lukewarm Federalists, having joined that
party only after the XYZ sickness in 1798, upon the exposure of
Talleyrand's bribe demands. If he should now fire Federalist employees "on the ground of political principles alone," he wrote
Monroe, "it would revolt our new converts and give a body to
leaders who now stand alone." Therefore, removals would necessarily be "as few as possible, done gradually, and bottomed on
some malversation or inherent disqualification," even though "out
of about six hundred offices named by the President, there were
six Republicans only when I came to office, and these were chiefly
half-breeds."

But the outraged cries from Republicans did not abate and soon
Jefferson complained about the patronage pressures: "The torrent
has been pressing me heavily, and will require all my force to
bear up against." By mid-1801, he found the Federalists charging
him with wholesale firings of government employees and the Republicans with foot-dragging. Slowly he changed his view that
Federalist office-holders held some job rights. When he fired the
Federalist collector of customs at New Haven and merchants there
demanded a reinstatement, he sent them a letter on July 12, 1801
that he made public to clarify his new patronage stand. "If a due
participation of office is a matter of right, how are vacancies to be
obtained?" he wrote. "Those by death are few; by resignation,
none. Can any other mode than that of removal be proposed?
This is a painful duty, but it is made my duty, and I must meet
it as such."

After that he called his job "the office of the executioner, that
of lopping off" Federalists from the payroll and finding places for
Republicans. His activity in this area was so great, he wrote a
Republican editor two years later, that of 316 offices that fell under

his appointive power, only 130 were still held by Federalists. Although Andrew Jackson has come to be considered the father of the spoils system, Jefferson actually removed and replaced a greater percentage of government employees than he. Even so, Jefferson complained of his role as patronage boss, "You would find yourself in most cases with one loaf and ten wanting bread. Nine must be disappointed, perhaps become secret, if not open enemies." But there was one area in patronage he would not open, and this was nepotism. To a relative who asked for a government job, he wrote a rejection, saying: "The public will never be made to believe that an appointment of a relative is made on the ground of merit alone."

When Congress convened for business on December 7, 1801, Jefferson's first Annual Message omitted any mention of the patronage fiasco and other problems "capable of being chicaned and furnishing something to the opposition to make a handle of." He informed Congress by messenger that he was herewith ending the custom of Washington and Adams to read the Annual Message to Congress in person. For years Republicans had charged that the personal appearance of the President before Congress smacked of a "speech from the throne." Not only was he eliminating the oral Message, said Jefferson, but he was also requesting Congress to end the custom of preparing a reply to his address and sending a committee to read the reply to him. This, he calculated, would save them ten working days a year, as well as the needless ceremony of replies to replies. There is little question that everyone benefited from the change, though no doubt the most compelling reason for it was Jefferson's thin, high reed of a speaking voice.

In his first Message, Jefferson unfolded a tale to prove that Republicans could handle a vexing problem and still hold fast to their principles. The case in point was the trouble with Tripoli while Congress was not in session. Both Presidents Washington and Adams had paid annual bribe tributes to the Barbary pirates of North Africa. A treaty signed by Washington on March 7, 1796 paid the Dey of Algiers $800,000 to ransom American ships he was holding and gave him an annual tribute of $24,000. But when the Pasha of Tripoli now demanded similar payment, Jefferson refused and the Pasha declared war. Jefferson then related to Congress how he had sent Commodore Dale into the Mediterranean and how Dale had captured one of the Pasha's ships, inflicting "a heavy slaughter of her men." But Congress need have no fear, said Jefferson, that the President usurped the legislature's power to declare war. Once the fight ended, the Administration was well aware it was "unauthorized by the Constitution, without the sanction of Congress to go beyond the line of defense." So "the vessel, being disabled from committing further hostilities, was liberated with its crew."

This struck the Federalists as inane, but what they heard next pained them more deeply. The supposed agreement by Jefferson to continue Hamilton programs in exchange for Federalist House votes to make him President was no longer operative—if it ever was. The national government must be weakened, said Jefferson, because the "states themselves have principal care of our persons, our property and our reputations." Congress must slash the Federal budget and dispense with all internal taxes. Congress must also dominate the Executive Branch "by appropriating specific sums to every specific purpose" and keep close watch on how every dime was spent.

In working toward this program, Jefferson now had another major test of his adherence to his philosophy. He had asked Congress to make itself supreme over him. But the more he studied the Republicans in Congress the greater was his realization that they had little unity and even less natural leadership.

Northern Republicans were uncomfortable in the company of their southern brethren, who were for the most part plantation aristocrats. Both groups voiced the same Jeffersonian principles but had little in common socially or intellectually. Then there was the problem of a political party that stressed individualism as its mark of distinction. The House, where Republicans outnumbered Federalists two to one, would have turned into a battleground if some members had attempted to assume leadership over others. Speaker Nathaniel Macon of North Carolina, holding the Number One spot in the House under the Republicans, found his authority negligible. Had he attempted to act the role of boss, said one observer, "the majority would split into violent coteries." Much worse for Macon's tender pride, he found himself the butt of cloakroom jokes that characterized him as being frequently incoherent and ungrammatical. In the Senate, where the Republicans outnumbered the Federalists by only three votes, the vaunted rugged individualism of the members provided an even greater hazard to

Jefferson's program. Moreover, the Senate's presiding officer was Vice-President Burr, hardly a Republican enthusiast since his defeat in the House for the Presidency.

There was still another major point on the minus side of the ledger. Ever since the Republicans had come into existence during Washington's Administration, the party's total experience had been as the party of the "outs" reacting negatively to the plans of the "ins." The Republicans had therefore developed as masters at sneering and jeering at promoters and programs and setting up roadblocks to legislation. It was too much to expect that such men would change abruptly into positive, responsible politicians.

Jefferson best expressed his quandary with the lament: "Our leading friends are not yet sufficiently aware of the necessity of accommodation and mutual sacrifice of opinion for conducting a numerous assembly." What to do? If he let the Republicans in Congress do as they pleased, the Federalists, "drilled," he said, "to act in a phalanx on every question," would control Congress. Yet if he interfered with the legislature he would make a mockery of his dogmatic declaration that Congress must be supreme over the President. His solution was the one that seemed simplest to him to save the Republican legislative program from complete disaster. Publicly, he continued to preach and pay homage to Congressional domination of the President. But behind the scenes he made himself master of the legislative process in all its stages.

It was a ruthless sort of mastery. The necessity for having his own agents on the spot produced the Jefferson innovation of the floor leader, who sponsored the President's legislative program, lining up votes for him by promising patronage and threatening punishments. If a member failed to meet the floor leader's demands, he might find his friends losing government jobs or contracts, or his next campaign would be without the popular President's blessing.

The Federalists had installed a milder form of the floor leader during their years in control. In the House, the Speaker selected several members who served as his assistants to move legislation along without promises or threats. The Jefferson floor leaders, however, served at the President's pleasure and were subject to dismissal when they displeased him. If he could not find the man he wanted among the current lot of Congressmen, he would induce an outsider to run for Congress and take on the post of floor leader. For instance, on one occasion he wrote to Wilson Cary Nicholas, a Virginia Republican: "Never did the calls of patriotism more loudly assail you than at this moment. After excepting the federalists, who will be 27., and the little band of schismatics, who will be 3. or 4. (all tongue), the residue of the H of R is as well disposed a body of men as I ever saw collected. But there is no one whose talents & standing, taken together, have weight enough to give him the lead. The consequence is, that there is no one who will undertake to do the public business, and it remains undone. Were you here, the whole would rally round you in an instant," Jefferson knowingly assured him. "Let me beseech you then to offer yourself. You never will have it so much in your power again to render such eminent service." Nicholas ran for the House, won and, as promised, became the floor leader.

This was not Jefferson's only tool for controlling Congress. Republican Congressmen were called together in party caucuses to discuss legislative programs. Before the caucuses adjourned, leaders took a vote that bound members to allegiance when the issues later emerged in the House and Senate chambers. Leaving nothing to chance, Jefferson determined when a caucus would be held, what topics would be considered and occasionally appeared in person to preside over these secret conclaves.

Still another Jefferson technique was to select the chairmen of Congressional committees instead of leaving the choice to members of the two houses. Again, the chairmen served only as long as they continued to please him. In fact, so did the Speaker, as Macon found out when Jefferson tired of Macon's association with a rebellious element of the party.

A further strategic weapon to bend the motley Republican membership to his will was Jefferson's use of Treasury Secretary Albert Gallatin as his legislative watchdog and hatchetman. The dark, thin-faced, Swiss-born Gallatin was a man of enormous ability, energy, drive and loyalty. Although he retained his European manners and foreign accent throughout his life, he was thoroughly American in interests and outlook. His family had expected him to carry on the tradition of serving as head of the Republic at Geneva, as five Gallatins before him had done since the Republic was established in the sixteenth century. Instead, after graduating from college at seventeen, he emigrated to the New World where he put in a short stint in the Revolutionary Army, taught at Harvard for a year, then went south to the land of the planter aristocrats. John Marshall was so impressed with him that he invited him to join his Richmond law firm, but Gallatin took the advice of Patrick Henry to "go West." He finally settled on an estate in Pennsylvania, went into business, served in the state legislature and was named by that body to the United States Senate in February 1793.

His financial brilliance soon antagonized the Federalists. When an effort to indict him as a ringleader of the Whiskey Rebellion against the excise tax on distilled liquor failed, the Federalist-controlled Senate used another method to rid themselves of his company. In February 1794, the Senate ousted him on the ground that he had failed to meet the minimum nine-year citizenship requirement of the Constitution. This ouster fight was in itself an important milestone in the Senate's history. Previously, the Senate had met in secret session, but at Gallatin's trial the doors were voted open to the public and they remained so afterward except on executive business (nominations and treaties). Following Gallatin's ouster, the Federalists had only a short time to gloat, for he won election to the House, where he served as a powerful Republican leader until Jefferson's election.

Gallatin saw Jefferson almost daily to exchange advice on party matters. "You will always find a plate and a sincere welcome," Jefferson said, encouraging him to barge in at mealtime or any other time. Gallatin's spacious residence became a legislative headquarters where floor leaders and committee chairmen gathered frequently to go over plans and programs. One man pointed out that "much of the confidential communications between Mr. Jefferson and his party in the legislature passed through this channel."

However, this was only one of the many uses Jefferson made of his Treasury Secretary. Gallatin also attended committee meetings at the Capitol as though he were a member, prepared questions for committees to use in interrogating witnesses (including himself), drafted committee reports and helped floor leaders hold wavering members in line on key votes. Gallatin was without diplomatic niceties where Jefferson's legislative program was involved and operated at the Capitol like a bee-stung bull. Yet Senator John Quincy Adams who admired him said he possessed an "extraordinary combination of stubbornness and flexibility." Like Hamilton in Washington's era, he also wrote bills to be introduced directly in Congress. Once, for example, he wrote to Senate floor leader John Breckinridge of Kentucky: "I send in the shape of a bill, the substance of what the President seems to think necessary."

The Federalists were not so naïve as to be unaware that Jefferson was talking one way and acting the opposite. "With affected modesty and deference," said Senator Pickering, "he secretly dictated every measure which is seriously proposed."

If only they could find him at the Capitol on a legislative day, they might have been able to expose him. But he came to the legislative chambers only on Sundays, and this for church services since Washington lacked even a single church. This unfailing Sunday arrival at the Capitol and the sight of the reddish gray head and freckled face bowed in prayer galled the Federalists, for their campaign cry was that he was an atheist.

Jefferson was so conscious of the Federalist hunt for evidence of his interference with the legislature that he insisted on secrecy when writing letters to Republicans on Congressional business. On one occasion, in sending a bill to Senator Breckinridge, he cautioned: "With more boldness than wisdom I therefore determined to prepare a canvas, giving it a few dabs of outline and tend it to you to fill up. I must do it in confidence that you will never let any person know that I have put pen to paper on the subject and that if you think the enclosed can be of any aid to you, you will take the trouble to copy it and return me the original. I am this particular because you know with what bloody teeth and fangs the Federalists will attack any sentiment or principle known to come from me and what bloody blackguardisms and personalities they make it the occasion of vomiting forth."

Thus Jefferson failed abjectly in his goal to reduce the Office of the President to subserviency to Congress. He now held powers never dreamed of by John Adams.

What puzzled Federalists about Jefferson's control over the Legislative and Executive branches was that he was thorough and efficient. In previous administrative posts he had done poorly, especially as governor of Virginia during the war. Late in 1780, Washington had sent him word that General Cornwallis and the traitor Benedict Arnold were planning invasions of Virginia. Washington's warning that Jefferson should prepare the militia went unheeded, and after Jefferson and the Assembly fled to Charlottesville, Arnold put Richmond, Virginia's capital, to the torch. Cornwallis followed this up by dispatching General Banastre Tarleton's cavalry raiders to capture the governor as a war prize. While Tarleton's men sped up one side of the mountain to Monticello, Jefferson, alerted only minutes before, was fortunately galloping down the other side. Afterward, the state legislature made an effort to try Jefferson for his shortcomings. Even though he won exoneration, Jefferson wrote at the time that the legislative charge "had inflicted a wound on my spirit which only will be erased by the all-healing grave."

Jefferson the governor was hardly the same as Jefferson the President, for the Chief Executive was a man certain of his abilities. He had benefited from Adams' Cabinet troubles insofar as no doubts were ever expressed by Cabinet members that he was in command. Recalling the Washington Cabinet, Jefferson once commented: "In those discussions, Hamilton and myself were daily pitted in the Cabinet like two cocks. We were then but four in number, and according to the majority, which of course was three to one, the President decided." Jefferson had carefully constructed his Cabinet so that there would be no repetition of this scene of squabbling Secretaries. In addition, he directed his infrequent Cabinet meetings like an orchestra conductor, taking charge at the outset and calling the tune throughout. As a result, even though he gave himself but a single vote in Cabinet balloting on an issue, he knew in advance he held the majority.

His chief fault as an administrator was his insatiable curiosity, which sometimes led him into the pettiest departmental business. For instance, he asked that all letters to the departments that required answers be sent to him as well as proposed replies. He considered himself the equal of any engineer and on one occasion spent time he could not afford advising Postmaster General Granger on the kinds of post-road river crossings to construct in the western frontier. "I would propose that all streams under 40. f. width not fordable at their common winter tide shall be bridged," he wrote. "And over all streams not bridged, a tree should be laid across, if their breadth does not exceed the extent of a single tree."

This attention to small matters was to bring on recurrences of violent migraine headaches from which he had suffered intermittently since youth. And with them came his complaint: "It is not because I do less than I might do, but that I have more to do than I can do."

If Jefferson ever had misgivings about his failure to make the Presidency an anemic branch compared with Congress, he could nevertheless point to one area where his theories and practices matched. This was his success in chopping away the monarchial trappings appendaged to the Presidency by his Federalist predecessors. In their place, he tried to reshape the Presidency into a living embodiment of democracy, so that by example the principles of liberty and freedom and human dignity regardless of status would spread throughout the country. He began by walking to his own inauguration and returning afoot afterward to take his usual place at the table at Conrad's boardinghouse near the Capitol. Some imaginative Republicans who thought he could have been even more unassuming than this spread the story that he rode horseback to the Capitol, tossed his reins over a picket fence and strode inside covered with the road's dust to accept his nation's highest office.

A month after his inauguration, when he had his fifty-eighth birthday, he announced that Presidents were no longer to be venerated by the monarchial custom of national birthday celebrations. Furthermore, he had no intention of making Presidential tours to the various parts of the country, where the chief results previously had been the bowing, scraping and staring of thousands of citizens.

His lack of interest in clothes also helped picture him as the complete democrat. A diplomat coming to call one day noted his "slippers down at the heels" and likened his appearance to "a tall, large-boned farmer." Senator William Plumer described the President as being "dressed or rather undressed in an old brown coat, red waistcoat, old corduroy small clothes much soiled." Earlier another Senator of his own party made this observation: "His clothes seem too small for him; he sits in a lounging manner, on one hip commonly, and with one of his shoulders elevated much above the other; his face has a sunny aspect, his whole figure has a loose, shackling air. He has a rambling, vacant look. I looked for gravity, but a laxity of manner seemed shed about him. He spoke almost without ceasing." Residents of the Federal City, as Washington was then called, had the opportunity to see their President do his own marketing, if they were early risers. Those who were not might be fortunate to meet him on a dirt road during the day, for he enjoyed an afternoon horseback ride and frequently stopped to converse with passers-by.

His political setting, too, added to the picture of the simple man. One observer noted that the Palace, as the President's residence was then known, "stood in a naked field overlooking the Potomac with two awkward department buildings near it . . . Across a swamp, a mile and a half away, the shapeless unfinished Capitol was seen, two wings without a body." The East Room was unplastered and rain leaked through the slate roof of the two-story, boxlike Palace. Visitors found the interior of the Executive Mansion filled with President Washington's worn furniture plus the cheapest additional furniture Jefferson could buy. Outdoors, the grounds were devoid of shrubs and trees. For a time the primitive atmosphere was heightened by the antics of two grizzly bears living on the Palace grounds. These were souvenirs given Jefferson by his secretary, Meriwether Lewis, who brought them back from his historic Lewis and Clark Expedition. "Jefferson's Zoo" included some sheep to nibble the White House crab grass, and when he erected a rough sheep fence a Senator called it "not fit for the yard of a barn." Yet despite the many discomforts of living in the Palace, Jefferson found it wise to label it as too elegant for him—"a great stone house, big enough for two emperors, one pope and the grand lama in the bargain."

Washington and Adams had held weekly levees, or formal receptions. These must end, said Jefferson, because they were imitations of royal gatherings. Instead, there would be only two receptions annually, one on New Year's Day and the other on the Fourth of July. And at these receptions, there would be no stiff bows as at the Federalist levees. The President would mingle with guests and shake hands, and unlike the highly restricted guest list of his predecessors, the doors were open to all Washingtonians to wander through the Palace, eat Jefferson's food and converse with him. At one of these gatherings, wrote a diplomat in disgust, "All who chose attended, and even toward the close blacks and dirty boys who drank his wine and lolled upon his couches before us all."

Of disquieting concern to the diplomatic colony was his complete disdain for protocol, which he wrote off as rules for monarchial behavior. Perhaps if his wife had been alive, he might not have taken this extreme position. However, he was already a widower of nineteen years when he became President. He had married Martha Wayles Skelton in 1772, when she was the twenty-three-year-old widow of Bathurst Skelton. A mutual interest in music—she played the spinet and he the fiddle—had brought them together initially. But Martha bore him so many children at such short intervals that she died as the result of the birth of their sixth child in 1782. Jefferson's two surviving children, plain Martha, better known as "Patsy," and beautiful Mary, or "Marie" or "Polly," served as their father's hostesses when they were in the Federal City. During their frequent absences, Dolley Madison and her sister, Anna Payne, took on this duty at Jefferson's request. But none of these ladies had the slightest influence on the social conduct at the Palace.

It was Jefferson's contempt for protocol that precipitated a social and diplomatic squabble with notes sailing back and forth across the Atlantic. President Adams had invariably conducted the British minister's wife to the table at Presidential dinner parties. However, when British minister Anthony Merry and his wife came to the Palace, Jefferson gave his arm to Dolley Madison. Merry found he had to escort his wife into the dining room and when he started to sit down a Congressman pushed him out of the chair. Then to heap one shock upon another, Merry discovered that the French minister, whose country was at war with England, was also at Jefferson's table. When Merry complained of this to Secretary of State Madison, the reply was, "A liberal oblivion of all hostile relations ought to take place" at the President's table.

From that time on, imperious Mrs. Merry declared war on this strange pell-mell etiquette and refused to attend further Presidential affairs. Meanwhile Merry added to the social war by informing his ministry in London that Jefferson was making a studied effort "to degrade the character of a foreign minister" and set him "on a level with the lowest American citizen." The diplomatic headquarters of both England and the United States were busy for some time after the incident answering charges and countercharges. But Jefferson blithely continued the pell-mell practice and labeled Mrs. Merry "a virago who has already disturbed our harmony extremely."

Instead of stiff diplomatic gatherings, Jefferson preferred bringing poets, artists, writers and scientists to his dining room for good food and long talk. This infuriated some Federalists, for the Republicans could thus claim that culture was on their side. On the occasions when Jefferson vaccinated some Indians at the Palace and operated a corn-shelling machine, Federalists complained that he was also trying to equate science with his political party.

Nevertheless, Federalists sought invitations to his groaning board because he served the best meals in town. Patrick Henry, once his political sponsor and then his enemy, remarked, "Thomas Jefferson came home from France so Frenchified that he abjured his native victuals." Federalists who gorged themselves at his expense later spread the tale that Jefferson's annual wine bill came to $10,000.

The person made angriest by Jefferson's announced efforts to wipe the Presidential slate clean of monarchial glitter was his predecessor, John Adams. Said Adams: "In the differences between speeches and messages, I was a monarchist because I thought a speech more manly, more respectful to Congress and the nation. Jefferson preferred messages. I held levees once a week, that all my time might not be wasted by idle visits. Jefferson's whole eight years was a levee. I dined a large company once or twice a week. Jefferson dined a dozen every day. Jefferson was for liberty and straight hair. I thought curled hair was as Republican as straight."

In Jefferson's view, making the President the living embodiment of democratic principles was essential because most Americans, he believed, considered government their foe and not their friend. For this reason, it was important that they see their President as someone not apart from them but as a person concerned with their welfare. Only then could he hope that the "Revolution of 1800" would be "as real a revolution in the principles of our government as that of 1776 was of its form." Only by ending "bigotry in politics and religion" and enlarging "the suffrage of the people" would the Revolution of 1800 become a reality.

The harsh truth was that the Spirit of '76 had thus far not invaded men's social and political relations except on the frontier. Even in Virginia where, after a fight lasting almost a decade, Jefferson and Madison finally succeeded in disestablishing the Anglican Church to bring about a complete church-state separation, they had failed to win a public school system. Their effort to limit capital punishment to treason and murder was also unsuccessful. As a result, when Jefferson took office, Virginia still decreed the death penalty for destroying a will or swearing falsely on oath. In Maryland, a person convicted of seditious libel suffered the fate of having a large "S" branded on a cheek; a counterfeiter, an "F"; a vagrant, a shoulder "R." Delaware branded a "B" on the forehead of blasphemers; New Hampshire did the same to those who stole on the Sabbath; while Pennsylvania ordered paupers to wear special armbands.

Voting and office-holding were highly restricted affairs, with only 5 per cent of the white population eligible to cast ballots. In New Hampshire, for instance, only Protestants could vote, and in Maryland Jews could not go to the polls. Besides religious restrictions, most states permitted only property owners to vote. Candidates for office also came from a select group. Unless a man could furnish proof he was worth from 500 to 5000 British pounds, he could not run for governor in most northern states. To run for the upper house in a northern state, a candidate had to show a worth from 200 to 1000 pounds, while in the South he had to prove title to a minimum of 300 to 500 acres.

Ending bigotry in law and religion and extending the suffrage were basic goals in Jefferson's philosophy. Five months before taking office he wrote: "I have sworn upon the altar of God eternal hostility against every form of tyranny over the mind of men." Yet as President, he believed he would be violating the authority of the states if he now interfered in their domestic affairs. Furthermore, his chief political supporters in the South were aristocratic planters who feared the spread of democracy. Some were his floor leaders and committee chairmen, and to antagonize them meant political disaster. So, the President held their support by avoiding undue stress upon democratic principles, and hoped that local Republicans would take the lead on these basic issues.

Just as serious a clash between Jefferson the philosopher and Jefferson the politician came over the Federal court system. Jefferson firmly believed in the separation of powers, but what he saw in the courts infuriated him.

In the dying gasps of the Adams Administration, the Federalists had enacted the Judiciary Act of 1801, providing for sixteen new circuit court judges plus several attorneys and marshals. Then with unseemly haste, President Adams had filled these new court posts and a large number of other court vacancies until the very midnight when his authority finally expired. The result was that when Jefferson took office, the judge in every Federal court chamber was a Federalist.

"The Revolution is incapable so long as that strong fortress [the Federal courts] is in the possession of the enemy," Representative William B. Giles of Virginia, a future House floor leader, warned him in June 1801. Jefferson did not need this warning, for he already realized that the laws passed by a Republican Congress were to be interpreted solely by Federalist judges, many of whom were his militant opponents. In addition, as followers of the Hamilton philosophy of a strong central government they would no doubt continue to encroach on the work of state courts and take over local jurisdiction.

He was convinced that the staffing of the courts with Federalists and the establishment of the new circuit court system was a well-considered Federalist plot. "They have retired into the judiciary as a stronghold," he fumed. "There the remains of federalism are to be preserved and fed from treasury, and from that battery all the works of republicanism are to be beaten down and erased. By a fradulent use of the Constitution, which has made judges irremovable, they have multiplied useless judges merely to strengthen their phalanx."

Jefferson's first approach to the Federalist court monopoly was to demand that the late appointees resign. In one pronouncement he declared that all appointments made between December 12, 1800, (when the Republican victory in the Presidential contest became known) and March 4, 1801, (when he took the oath of office) were null and void. These appointments were the responsibility of the new Administration, he insisted. That such a procedure would have usurped the constitutional authority of the outgoing President, who remained in charge until the hour his term expired, did not appear to be a valid argument to Jefferson. Needless to say, not a single Federalist judge resigned.

It was plain to all politicians at the time that the single judge Jefferson had most in mind when he wanted late appointees disqualified was Chief Justice John Marshall. Once it had become known that Chief Justice Oliver Ellsworth had resigned after taking on the French peace mission for Adams, Jefferson assumed the vacancy would stand until he selected Ellsworth's successor. It had come as a shock to him when he learned that Adams had appointed Marshall on January 20, 1801, for Jefferson had already decided on his own new Chief Justice.

The man Jefferson chose was Spencer Roane, son-in-law of Patrick Henry, rabid Republican and judge on the Virginia Superior Court of Appeals. Roane was a strict constructionist and an extreme proponent of states' rights, contending that only a state legislature and not the U. S. Supreme Court could declare an act of Congress unconstitutional. The Supreme Court, he asserted, was only a "subordinate agent" in the Federal establishment and not a "master."

Marshall had no intention of quitting the Supreme Court and making his post available to Roane simply because Jefferson called his appointment null and void. In fact, Marshall now decided on his own bold step to humiliate Jefferson. Adams had appointed forty-two Federalists as Justices of the Peace for the District of Columbia, but even with last-minute haste some of their commissions had not yet been delivered at the time Jefferson became President. When Jefferson ordered Secretary of State Madison to throw the undelivered commissions in the waste basket, William Marbury, whose commission was in this group, petitioned the Supreme Court. In December 1801, Marshall taunted the Administration by directing Madison to appear at the following year's court session and show cause why Marshall should not issue a writ of mandamus to force him to deliver Marbury's commission.

Jefferson had been considering several proposals to weaken the Federalist grip on the courts. One plan would have been an amendment to the Constitution, giving him authority to remove judges with the consent of Congress. Another, which came to light years later, would have permitted him to appoint judges for a four- to six-year term renewable by the President with the consent of the Senate. But neither approach lent itself readily to the quick action he desired.

At the time Marshall made his move in Marbury vs. Madison, Jefferson had already decided on his own course of action. In his first Annual Message on December 7, 1801, Jefferson denounced the "Midnight Judges" appointed by Adams as "excrescences on the Judiciary." He told Congress the moment had come that the Federal court system "should present itself to the contemplation of Congress—especially that portion of it recently erected."

On January 8, 1802, at Jefferson's request Senator Breckinridge, his Senate floor leader, introduced a bill to repeal the Judiciary Act of 1801. If the new judges, attorneys and marshals appointed under that act would not resign, why not repeal the enabling act and abolish their courts?

It was the fight over repeal that proved conclusively to Jefferson that his Vice-President was not a Republican. When a Federalist Senator had made a motion to return the repeal bill to committee, a 15 to 15 vote resulted. Burr now had the opportunity to cast a vote and he shocked some Republicans when he broke the tie by siding with the Federalists. A short time later he attended a Federalist celebration and proposed a toast—"A union of all honest men."

Jefferson's demand for Senate Republican unity brought a favorable vote to return the repeal bill from committee. Then on February 3, the bill skinned through the Senate by a vote of 16 to 15 and a month later it met with favorable House action. Jefferson now had his first major victory over the Federalist judiciary. One of the purposes of the Judiciary Act of 1801 was to create regular circuit court judges. The original Judiciary Act of 1789 had forced the six Supreme Court justices to ride horseback and sit with outlying district court judges to hear circuit court cases. With the repeal of the 1801 Act, Supreme Court justices would once more have to ride the circuits, a hardship to men no longer young. Marshall called his fellow justices to a special meeting where he proposed they refuse to return to circuit duty and "risk the consequences." However, the others were unwilling to contest Jefferson and rejected his plea.

During the fight over erasing the Judiciary Act of 1801, Republicans heard that Marshall planned to declare its repeal unconstitutional. Senator Breckinridge, in close touch with Jefferson, warned Marshall that "the Legislature has the exclusive right to interpret the Constitution, and the judges are bound to execute the laws they make." Besides this warning, Breckinridge wrote into the repeal bill a provision that eliminated the Supreme Court's next regular session in mid-1802 and set one for the following February. By keeping the Supreme Court inactive for a year, Jefferson hoped meanwhile to destroy all trace of the new circuit court structure to prevent Marshall from taking any meaningful action.

As a result of Congress's action regarding the repeal act, the show cause case of the commissionless Marbury vs. Madison did not reach its climax before the Supreme Court until the winter of 1803. At this time, Marbury's commission had only a few more months to run before it expired, and Marshall could have taken the easy way out by laying the case over to the next court term. However, he would not do this, an action that pleased the Republicans. For if he ordered Madison to deliver the commission, Madison intended to ignore him. Thus the Supreme Court would have stood revealed as a toothless old crone. On the other hand, if he denied Marbury's request, Marshall would then stand exposed as a coward. For it was he who had carelessly failed to deliver Marbury's commission while serving as Secretary of State to John Adams.

Under these circumstances, Marshall did not appear to have any avenue of self-respect left. Yet he managed to hand down an opinion that completely outmaneuvered Jefferson. First, he delivered a long lecture on the duties of the President. As to the case at hand, he then affirmed Marbury's right to his commission. But before Republican onlookers could gloat over the prospect of ignoring him, Marshall added that "the authority given to the Supreme Court by the [1789 Judiciary] act to issue writs of mandamus to public officers appears not to be warranted by the Constitution." In other words, he argued that Congress had granted the Supreme Court an illegal power. Therefore, although he said he sided personally with Marbury, the Chief Justice claimed that the Supreme Court lacked original jurisdiction over the matter because the section of the Judiciary Act of 1789 granting it was unconstitutional.

By this decision which established judicial review, Marshall enlarged the authority of the Supreme Court to its widest possible extreme. It brought great rage to Jefferson who realized that through little Marbury, Marshall had made his court the judge over the acts of Congress and the President. "The opinion which gives to the judges the right to declare what laws are unconstitutional," he thundered, "would make the judiciary a despotic branch."

The repeal of the Judiciary Act of 1801 had been met by the assertion that the Supreme Court was specially endowed with authority to interpret the Constitution. But this did not end the war between Jefferson and Marshall.

From the outset of the development of political parties, the Federalist bench had acted in a highly partisan fashion. Jefferson knew of many instances when Federalist judges campaigned for their party at election time. Several judges barred Republicans from jury duty, harassed Republican witnesses and used the bench as a political pulpit. Former Chief Justice Ellsworth had used the prestige of his position to call Jefferson "the apostle of anarchy, bloodshed and atheism." Judges held "their Offices during good Behavior," according to the Constitution. But were the Federalist judges showing good behavior? They were not, Jefferson decided, and it was time to use the impeachment power to remove them.

First on Jefferson's list was Judge John Pickering of the New Hampshire Federal district court. During the very month that Marshall handed down his landmark opinion in Marbury vs. Madison, Jefferson sent a special message to the House with documents revealing Pickering as a habitual drunkard in court as well as a profane judge. The House quickly impeached him and the Senate set trial for March 2, 1804. Pickering did not appear, but his attorney produced evidence that he was insane. This immediately split the Republicans, with northern members arguing that impeachment was a criminal process and that insanity was not a crime. Senator James Jackson of Georgia offered the point that if Pickering could avoid removal because of his insanity, then all other Federalist judges would immediately declare themselves insane in order to retain their places on the bench. "It will take two years to try this impeachment," Jefferson snapped when he learned of the dispute. Finally on March 12, the Republicans worked out a compromise that enabled the different factions to vote to remove Pickering. Instead of finding Pickering guilty of high crimes and misdemeanors, the Senate removed him on the vague ground of being "guilty as charged," without defining that expression.

Having cleared that first low hurdle, Jefferson now decided that the time was ripe to go after bigger game. On the same day that the insane judge was ousted, Jefferson requested the House to impeach Justice Samuel Chase of the Supreme Court. Not only would Chase be removed, boasted Senator William Giles, who had moved to the upper chamber to become another floor leader there for Jefferson, but so would "all other judges of the Supreme Court." Senator John Quincy Adams also saw something much deeper than a case against Chase. In a letter to his father, the former President, he wrote, "The assault upon Judge Chase was unquestionably intended to pave the way for another prosecution, which would have swept the Supreme Judicial Bench clean at a stroke." The final objective was undoubtedly the Chief Justice.

There were many good charges against Chase. One was his lack of propriety in the case of John Fries, a Pennsylvania Dutchman who led a raid on a prison in 1798. Fries had hoped to free some inmates who were in jail because they had refused to pay the Federal property tax whose revenues would help meet part of the

expenses of the undeclared French war. Chase had informed the
jury before the trial that he considered Fries guilty of treason,
and the panel of jurymen did his bidding. President Adams had
pardoned Fries shortly before he was to be hung. In the Sedition
Act trial of journalist James Callender, a sharp-tongued Republican extremist who had called Adams a tyrant and warmonger,
Chase had remarked while en route to the courtroom, "It is a
pity they had not hung the rascal." Among the long list of his un-
judicious acts at the Callender trial was his order to the Richmond
marshal "not to put any of those creatures called Democrats on
the jury."

Jefferson wanted these charges ignored so that Congress could
concentrate on a more recent action by the obese, redfaced Chase.
This was his harangue to a Baltimore grand jury on May 2, 1803,
when he bellowed from the bench: "The late alteration of the
Federal judiciary by the abolition of the office of the sixteen circuit judges and the recent change in our state constitution by the
establishing of universal suffrage, and the further alteration that
is contemplated in our state judiciary will in my judgment take
away all security for property and personal liberty. . . . Our republican Constitution will sink into a mobocracy—the worst of
all possible governments. . . . The modern doctrines of our late
reformers that all men in a state of society are entitled to enjoy
equal liberty and equal rights have brought this mighty mischief
upon us."

Unfortunately for Jefferson, House Republicans considered
Chase a monster and added seven other charges to the one on
which Jefferson wanted him impeached. It was the confusion of
these numerous charges plus the legal superiority of Chase's lawyers to the House battery of managers that turned his trial before the Senate into a chaotic farce. In his final summation, John
Randolph, one of the House managers, mislaid his notes and burst
into hysterical sobs before the Senate court. Nevertheless, John
Marshall, who had testified against his fellow Federalist judge, was
so certain Chase would be found guilty and that his turn was
next that he proposed a compromise in a letter to another Federalist. His suggestion was to permit a Congressional majority to
override a Supreme Court decision! Fortunately for Marshall, his
letter was not made public at the time. Twenty-three votes were
necessary to convict Chase, but the Republicans were so divided

on which charge to find him guilty that on not a single charge were they able to muster the necessary total.

With the Chase trial a debacle, Jefferson gave up his fight with the judiciary. Years later he assessed his resort to impeachments as "a mere scarecrow." Yet his efforts did yield one bonus. After the Chase trial most Federal judges took on the non-political decorum by which they are known today.

Not until 1804 was Jefferson able to appoint his first Republican to the Supreme Court. This was William Johnson of South Carolina who rated his fellow judges in this fashion: "Cushing was incompetent; Chase could not be got to think or write; Paterson was a slow man; and the other two judges [Marshall and Bushrod Washington] are commonly estimated as one judge." Jefferson filled two other vacancies on the Supreme Court before his Administration ended, but he still had only a minority of the seven justices.

During these years of warfare with the Federalist court, Jefferson, of course, had other important matters to settle. The most vital of these was Louisiana. Here again Jefferson the philosopher and Jefferson the practical politician were at serious odds.

In 1762, to repay a debt to Spain for her aid in the French and Indian War against England, France ceded to her New Orleans and the vast Louisiana Territory stretching westward from the Mississippi. The following year, when England concluded the successful Seven Years' War against both nations, Spain ceded Florida to her and France gave up a strip of territory east of New Orleans to the Perdido River. England then divided these new acquisitions at the Apalachicola River into East and West Florida. Then twenty years later, the 1783 Treaty of Paris ending the American Revolutionary War forced England to cede both Florida provinces to Spain.

For decades after her loss of an American empire, France coveted the return of Louisiana. Opportunity came when Napoleon ousted the Directory in November 1799 and took charge as First Consul of France. Less than twenty-four hours after the Treaty of Morfontaine in October 1800, ending the undeclared war between France and the United States, Napoleon forced the Treaty of San Ildefonso on his vassal Spain. In exchange for a small kingdom (Etruria), which was to be carved out of part of Italy,

Spain agreed to cede Louisiana back to France and give her six warships.

From personal experience and his regard for the ideals of the French Revolution, Jefferson had heretofore been pro-French. But when rumors first reached him shortly after he became President that France had reclaimed her American empire, he grew alarmed. As a decadent power, Spain had presented no real problem to the United States once the Pinckney Treaty of 1795 opened New Orleans to American commerce. However, France in possession of Louisiana could be expected to be aggressive and troublesome, for Napoleon was in essence a vulgar and despotic conqueror.

With obvious concern, Jefferson wrote to Robert Livingston, his minister to France, with whom he had served on the Continental Congress committee charged with writing the Declaration of Independence. The cession of Louisiana, he wrote, "completely reverses all the political relations of the United States . . . There is on the globe one single spot, the possessor of which is our natural and habitual enemy . . . New Orleans, through which the produce of three eighths of our territory must pass to market. France placing herself in that door assumes to us the attitude of defiance. Spain might have retained it quietly for years. . . . The day that France takes possession of New Orleans . . . seals the union of two nations. From that moment on we must marry ourselves to the British fleet and nation."

The year 1802 was a time of suspenseful watching for Jefferson. In March, Napoleon had ended his war with England with the Treaty of Amiens, seemingly giving him the freedom to move into his recently acquired empire. However, he could not do so. The fleet to carry French occupation forces to New Orleans was bottled up in Dutch harbors because of a prolonged winter freeze. Moreover, Napoleon's effort to put down the revolt on the French Caribbean island of St. Domingo was draining him of his best troops. There Toussaint L'Ouverture, a Haitian Negro general, had led a half million freed Negroes to war against the French, and the fighting had so far cost Napoleon thousands of soldiers.

Jefferson was at the point of observing that Napoleon might never take Louisiana, when disquieting word reached him about supposedly innocuous Spain, still in physical possession there. Morales, the Spanish Intendant at New Orleans, had suddenly withdrawn the American right of deposit at the port, in violation of the 1795 Treaty. Flatboats that brought produce down the

Mississippi were not ocean-worthy, and now that goods could no longer land at New Orleans for transfer to larger sailing vessels, the prosperity of the West appeared doomed.

With the West thoroughly aroused and demanding war, Jefferson took quick action. He requested the Spanish minister to Washington to seek an immediate return to the 1795 Treaty by Madrid. He also sent word to Livingston to negotiate with the French for the purchase of New Orleans and the two Floridas. Then in January 1803, he sent the Senate the nomination of James Monroe, the recent governor of Virginia and a man who had the confidence of Western leaders, to work with Livingston as his special envoy.

But just as the Republicans had thought nothing of acting in an irresponsible manner during the Adams Administration, Federalists now proceeded to do the same to the Republicans. Previously antagonistic toward the frontier people, they now emerged as their forensic champions. Why did Jefferson insist upon wasting his time on negotiations when war was the only solution? How dare he claim to be a friend of the West when he would not take the only proper steps to end the Spanish threat? Sending Monroe to attempt a peaceful solution through bribery was both cowardly and immoral. The Federalists, Jefferson commented wearily, had "caught as a plank in a shipwreck" the issue at New Orleans.

Loud Federalist argument almost defeated Monroe's confirmation, but he squeaked through the Senate by an uncomfortable three-vote margin. Then while the Federalist press denounced Jefferson as a coward, trimmer and shyster, Federalist Senator James Ross of Pennsylvania offered a resolution on February 15, 1803 to order the President to assemble an army of 50,000 and spend $5,000,000 to take New Orleans. In fury, Jefferson denounced this as a scheme "to derange our finances, or if this cannot be done, to attach the western country to them, as their best friends, and thus get again into power."

Only after an angry debate was the Ross resolution defeated. Then to end talk that he was seeking a soft solution, Jefferson promoted through the Senate a substitute measure, giving him authority to request governors to hold their state militias in readiness and to make a public call for Regular Army volunteers. He also pushed through Congress a $2,000,000 appropriation for use by Livingston and Monroe to buy New Orleans and the two

Floridas from the French, though costly Republican absences
from the Senate gave him only a 14 to 12 margin.

The hour was late to get Monroe off on his mission, but
Jefferson suffered sudden qualms about adhering to his Republican principles. Having sworn to achieve government economy, he believed it hypocritical to provide his emissary with a
swift Navy frigate. "Mr. Madison's friendship and mine for you
being so well known," he informed Monroe, "the public will
have an eagle eye to watch if we grant you any indulgence
out of the general rule." So Monroe had to book passage on an
ordinary commercial vessel, though Jefferson assured him he would
have free postage privileges while abroad. Jefferson also told him
he was to offer up to $10,000,000 for the areas in question, but if
France would not sell them to settle for a renewal of the right
of deposit at New Orleans. Failing both, he and Livingston were
to cross the Channel to London and effect a treaty of alliance with
England.

Events moved quickly before Monroe arrived at Paris. The uneasy truce between France and England of March 1802 was
drawing to a close with war again in the offing for spring 1803.
Napoleon knew this would end his dream of an American empire,
for the powerful British Navy could easily occupy New Orleans.
On April 11, while Livingston discussed with Foreign Minister
Talleyrand the sale of the Isle of Orleans, Talleyrand suddenly
inquired, "What would you give for the whole of Louisiana?"

The stunned Livingston began negotiations on the enlarged
area with Barbé-Marbois, the French Finance Minister. His excitement at being offered a loaf of bread when he had asked for
a slice was unbounded. By the time Monroe arrived and likewise
gasped when he heard the news, Livingston and Marbois had already begun preparation of a treaty. Napoleon had instructed
Marbois to get 100,000,000 francs. But when the two Americans appeared staggered, he dropped the demand to 60,000,000 francs, or
about $15,000,000. Finally he had to warn them that if they hag-
gled further there would be no sale. Livingston's comment when
he signed the treaty dated April 30, 1803, was: "This is the noblest
work of our whole lives." Napoleon said with a smile: "I have
given England a rival who, sooner or later, will humble her pride."
But the disposal of Louisiana also brought trouble within the Bonaparte family. Napoleon's brothers, Joseph and Lucien, quarreled

bitterly with him not to sell the vast territory and engaged in a free-for-all one morning in his bathroom over this subject.

Jefferson first received word from Spain that spring that the arrogant Spanish Intendant at New Orleans, Don Juan Ventura Morales, had been ordered to re-establish the right of deposit there. Then in June came the astounding news from Paris about the Louisiana Territory. Jefferson's first reaction was one of jubilance, for by this fortuitous stroke the size of the country was "more than doubled," he said, "and the new part is not inferior to the old." But doubts soon set in on two scores.

First of all, the treaty was vague, making no mention of the geographic boundaries. When Livingston had queried Talleyrand on this point, the reply was a shrug and "I can give you no direction. You must take the territory as France received it from Spain." Napoleon's comment was: "If an obscurity did not already exist, it would perhaps be good policy to put one there." Livingston had specifically inquired about the Floridas. No, they were not included, said Napoleon, but he promised vaguely to use his influence to persuade his ally to sell them to the United States. Livingston's suggestion to Jefferson was that he claim part of West Florida to the Perdido River in order to control both sides of the Mississippi.

As a strict constructionist, Jefferson also had doubts about the constitutionality of the purchase. "The Constitution has made no provision for our holding foreign territory, still less for our incorporating foreign nations into our Union," he wrote Senator Breckinridge on August 12, 1803. "The Executive, in seizing the fugitive occurrence which so much advances the good of their country, has done an act beyond the Constitution." What Jefferson proposed was that the treaty be approved first, followed by an amendment to the Constitution to legalize it. "The legislature must ratify and pay for it, and throw themselves on their country for doing for them unauthorized what we know they would have done for themselves had they been in a position to do it. It is the case of a guardian, investing the money of his ward in purchasing an important adjacent territory; and saying to him when he came of age, 'I did this for your good; I pretend to no right to bind you; you may disavow me, and I must get out of the scrape as I can; I thought it my duty to risk myself for you.'"

Twice Jefferson discussed a constitutional amendment to cover the Louisiana Purchase in meetings with his Cabinet. He argued that he would have to set an example against broad construction by appealing for new power to the people. He would not accept the notion that the treaty-making power could be stretched to encompass the purchase of territory. As a good Republican, he did not believe in implied powers, for to assume powers by construction would mean that the Federal Government could develop into a monstrous entity and make blank paper of the Constitution. But what if Congress approved the treaty and then the state legislatures rejected the constitutional amendment? asked his advisers.

Reluctantly, he decided to forego his principles and not press for an amendment. To Breckinridge, he again wrote on the eighteenth, "I wrote you on the 12th inst. on the subject of Louisiana and the constitutional provision which might be necessary. . . . Nothing must be said on the subject . . . we should do *sub silentio* what shall be found necessary."

The treaty contained the stipulation making it void if not ratified within six months after the signing on April 30, or by the end of October 1803. Washington was enveloped in a yellow fever epidemic when Jefferson called Congress back for a special session on October 15. Two days earlier, Senate Republicans had met in caucus and agreed on unity to ratify the treaty before it expired. When the Senate approved the treaty 24 to 7 on October 19, this was legally all that was required to put it into effect. However, one of Jefferson's well-publicized pronouncements was that the House possessed the right to pass on treaties, too, even though the Constitution made no mention of this.

Earlier, House Federalists had demanded war measures to seize New Orleans. But now they argued that the treaty acquiring New Orleans peacefully should not be approved. One objection was that the enormous addition of territory meant that the northern states would be eclipsed in power by the South and West. The treaty pledged the United States to incorporate the inhabitants of Louisiana into the Union. This was unconstitutional, cried the Federalists, because the power to admit new states was restricted to the original territory of the United States. It was all right to buy or conquer new lands and subjects, but "they must remain in the condition of colonies and be governed accordingly." Furthermore, if the government could add states by treaty then it could cede states by the same method. The final House vote came on

October 25, with a straight party alignment approving the treaty by 90 to 25.

With the treaty ratified, Jefferson moved on to other important matters regarding the new territory that stretched from the Mississippi to the Rockies and from Canada to the Gulf of Mexico. First, he sent Congress a bill authorizing him to take possession of Louisiana and direct its affairs. When Federalists howled that this conferred unconstitutional powers upon the President, Republicans replied that "the limitations of power found in the Constitution are applicable to states and not to territories." This bill passed both houses by an overwhelming vote, and next came another measure from the Palace to authorize an appropriation to pay France for the new territory. Jefferson proposed a fifteen-year bond issue of $11,250,000 with 6 per cent interest to pay off the French Government. Another $3,750,000 would be spent to pay claims of American citizens against France for French spoliation during the undeclared war.

But now came unexpected trouble. Spain was arguing that Louisiana still belonged to her because Napoleon had failed to win recognition from other European powers for the kingdom of Etruria, which he had carved out of Italy for Spain's Duke of Parma. This had been a basic condition of the retrocession in their Treaty of San Ildefonso. Spain had another ground for claiming ownership, and this was Napoleon's promise never to alienate Louisiana. When it did not look likely that Spain would withdraw from the Territory without a fight, Jefferson called on Ohio, Tennessee and Kentucky to prepare their militias for action.

This was sufficient to reduce Spanish bluster and on November 30, 1803, the Spanish flag came down from the staff at New Orleans and the French flag went up. Then on December 20 the French governor general formally turned over the purchased area in a ceremony watched by "white, black, yellow, red, Frenchman, Spaniard, African, mulatto, Indian and most visible of all by his height and boisterous triumph on the occasion, the tall lanky Westerner in coonskin cap and leather hunting shirt." It took two years before the old Spanish officials, still plotting openly to regain Louisiana, were ousted from the Territory.

Once in physical possession, Jefferson asked Congress to approve a bill he had drawn up with Madison to establish a government there. Senator Breckinridge had proposed that slavery be barred from the Territory, but Jefferson overruled him. The Jefferson bill divided Louisiana into two parts at the 33rd Parallel. The District of Louisiana, or the northern part, which would include the entire area except for a small piece approximating the state of Louisiana's present boundaries, was to be placed temporarily under the government of Indiana Territory. Jefferson first considered barring the area to settlement, but Senator Breckinridge talked him out of this.

It was in the small southern section, or the proposed Territory of Orleans, that Jefferson drafted controls entirely at odds with his beliefs regarding civil rights. He also disregarded the treaty, which guaranteed the residents of the territory "all the rights, advantages and immunities" of American citizens. His plan called for a governor and a council of thirteen, all of whom would be appointed by him from property-holders residing there. These appointees would not require Senate confirmation and would serve at Jefferson's pleasure. Jury trial would be severely limited and local residents were to suffer taxation without representation. Senator John Quincy Adams charged that Jefferson had set Louisiana's subjects "lower in the political scale than the meanest tribe of Indians." Another Senator later called Jefferson's handiwork "startling . . . putting the President in the place of the King of Spain; putting all the territorial officers in place of the King's officers, and placing the appointment of all these officers in the President alone without reference to the Senate . . . a mere emanation of Spanish despotism." Jefferson justified his action on the ground that the inhabitants were almost all foreigners, not Americans, and not ready for such blessings.

The Louisiana Purchase added further to Jefferson's already immense national popularity. That the Orleans Territory inhabitants were not awarded all American rights and privileges did not disturb his following; as one Federalist leader noted disgustedly, whatever Jefferson did he still held the "infatuation of the people." Another sighed hopefully, "When the people have been long enough drunk they will get sober, but while the frolic lasts, to reason with them is hopeless."

In 1804, another Presidential contest was at hand, with the Federalists fully aware that they had no chance to win. Nevertheless, the Federalist Congressional caucus met and nominated C. C. Pinckney of South Carolina and Rufus King of New York. Jefferson's candidacy for a second term was not seriously in doubt, though he announced publicly: "I sincerely regret that the un-bounded calumnies of the Federal party have obliged me to throw myself on the verdict of my country for trial, my great desire having been to retire at the end of my present term." Privately, he wrote that he needed the salary from a second term to clear up his heavy debts.

On February 25, 1804, when the Jefferson-controlled Republican Congressional nominating caucus met, it unanimously selected him to head the ticket. Vice-President Burr had sent an emissary to ask Jefferson whether he still considered Burr a member of the party. Jefferson's reply was a "yes" too weak to do Burr any political good, for the President had already decided to drop him and replace him with elderly Governor George Clinton of New York. Clinton's dislike of Jefferson was matched by the Presi-dent's low regard for the cunning New York boss. Friends had pro-posed forty-three-year-old Senator Breckinridge for Vice-President, and though Jefferson regarded him highly, he believed a Virginia-New York ticket provided more equitable Republican representa-tion than a Virginia-Kentucky ticket. Even with the President's authority over the caucus, Clinton won the nomination only by a vote of 67 to 41.

Jefferson made no campaign speeches or tours, but confined himself to other conclusive means to insure victory. In fact, sad-dened by the loss of his lovely daughter Mary, who died in childbirth in April 1804, he remained at Monticello throughout that summer. Nevertheless, from this remote place, he promoted a striking development in the political campaign process. In every state he named a leader, or national committeeman, to manage the party's campaign. Every state leader had town and district managers under him, who recorded the politics of every voter in their area and made strenuous efforts to win support from those who still called themselves Federalists.

In addition, Jefferson promoted the creation of Republican news-papers to offset a press overwhelmingly Federalist. Led by Gideon Granger, the Postmaster General, Republicans also turned out pamphlets written in simple English and gave them wide cir-culation. Jefferson had barred the use of the country's 1200 post-masters to take subscriptions and help deliver copies of Chief Justice Marshall's biography of George Washington, which Jef-ferson called "that five-volumed libel." But Granger suffered no con-science-guilt when it came to spreading Republican pamphlets. His own pamphlet noted that Jefferson had eliminated all internal taxation, reduced the national debt by $8,000,000 and still managed to have a $5,000,000 Treasury excess. Federalists countered with references to Jefferson as an alcoholic, a tool of France, an anti-Christ, "Mad Tom, Jacobin, apostle of the race track and cock-pit." Federalists also attacked Jefferson's appearance, pointing out that his classmates had considered him to be "the homeliest scholar at William and Mary College." They spread stories that he possessed bright red hair and a bulbous nose. Long afterward, when this description failed to die, James Madison defended his friend as having not "red but between yellow and red hair" and a nose "rather under, certainly not above, common size."

Until shortly before the election, Jefferson was concerned that 1804 would be a repetition of the 1800 contest when his tie with Burr forced the Presidential decision on the House. In 1802, he had proposed an amendment to the Constitution requiring electors to designate separately whom they were voting for as President and whom as Vice-President. Not until December 1803 did it get the necessary two-thirds approval of Congress. Then before this Twelfth Amendment to the Constitution could go into effect, it had to be ratified by three-fourths of the state legislatures, or by thirteen of the seventeen. Only a persistent effort by Jefferson finally produced the thirteenth approval on September 25, 1804. This came as a severe disappointment to supporters of Governor Clinton, Jefferson's running mate, who had hoped to use the old rules for mischievous purpose to give their man the Presidency.

The 1804 results showed a Republican landslide with 162 of the 176 electoral vote total. The Congressional picture looked even as promising. The Ninth Congress would have 119 Republicans and 25 Federalists in the House and a Senate with 27 Republicans and only 7 Federalists. Five of the 34 Senators were named Smith, giving rise to the title of the "Smith Senate" for the Ninth Congress.

All indications were that Jefferson's second term would prove as successful as his first. But this was not to be the case. Across the Atlantic, the war between Napoleon's France and England was already threatening the neutralist rights of the United States to a free carrying trade. Jefferson saw the two warring powers as "one man bestriding the continent of Europe like a colossus, and another roaming unbridled on the ocean." There were also disruptive clouds at home where rumors were flying that Aaron Burr was treasonously conspiring to separate the West from the Union and make himself master of the Southwest and Mexico. In addition, despite the overwhelming Republican victory, faint rumbles of dissatisfaction and unrest were beginning to be heard in Congress against Jefferson's tight control over the Legislative Branch.

This control had indeed been thorough during his first term. An observer noted that on one nomination, "The Senate had agreed to the appointment when not a single Senator believed he was qualified for the office. And Genl. Bradley said that the President's dinners had silenced them—& that Senators were becoming more servile." During that first term, he had only to suggest a need for money and an appropriation followed. When he wanted to send his secretary, Meriwether Lewis, and Captain William Clark to explore the Louisiana Territory and beyond, he did not bother to send a written request to Congress. Instead he discussed the proposed expedition with Congressmen who came to the Palace. Triumphantly, he then wrote Clark, "I have proposed in conversation, and it seems generally assented to, that Congress appropriate 10–12,000 dollars."

It was apparent to observers that Jefferson's control over Congress in his first term had been made easier by his fortunate selection of floor leaders. Senator John Breckinridge of Kentucky, who had worked closely with Jefferson in the drafting of the Kentucky Resolutions in 1798, arguing that a state could declare an act of Congress null and void, had served as the personification of Jefferson's will in the Senate. But now his strong influence was gone from the upper chamber because he had agreed to become Attorney General.

Jefferson's House floor leader, John Randolph of Virginia, had also performed brilliantly for the President during the first term. But he was growing erratic and spoiling for a fight with the Administration. When seated, Randolph looked like a small boy, but when he rose he showed extremely long legs and arms. An observer noted that the standing Randolph had "the appearance of a sort of pyramid." From a distance his face seemed that of a youth, but up close it was a mass of deep wrinkles. Mumps had erased his manhood, leaving him with a shrill, effeminate voice. Yet he had a brilliant mind, an amazing command of language and a hot-tempered call to dueling. "He chatters away like a magpie," Abigail Adams characterized him. Jefferson had installed him as chairman of the powerful House Ways and Means Committee, and when Randolph was not at home riding about his plantation named "Bizarre," or busily handling money legislation for the President, he was pouring political spleen over House members who failed to please him. He was fond of saying he would "shoot an impertinent fellow down as [he] would a mad dog." Randolph attributed his fighting qualities to the fact that he was the direct descendant of the Indian princess Pocahontas. But Dr. Benjamin Rush took another view of Randolph when he wrote to ex-President John Adams: "I have long considered him as a mischievous boy with a squirt in his hands, throwing its dirty contents into the eyes of everybody that looked at him. A kicking or a horsewhipping would be the best reply that could be made to his parliamentary insolence."

A minor squabble between Jefferson and Randolph developed in 1804 when Randolph opposed Jefferson's bills to permit textbooks to enter the country duty free as class legislation and to authorize Georgetown to build a dam on the Potomac as a violation of strict construction of the Constitution. Yet although Jefferson angrily charged Randolph with engaging in "metaphysical subtleties," he did not remove him from his post as floor leader.

The first major fallout between Randolph and the Administration came in February 1805 on the Yazoo scandal. The Yazoo was the vast area owned by Georgia, which later became the states of Alabama and Mississippi. Back in 1795, the Georgia legislature had approved its sale to four land-speculating companies for $500,000. Almost immediately it became known that every member of the legislature except one had taken bribes for this cheap sale of the Yazoo's 35,000,000 acres. Public whippings, shootings and lynchings followed, and a new legislature was installed that declared the sale invalid. However, before this news was spread, the original purchasing companies hurriedly sent agents throughout the country, especially into New England, where they unloaded Yazoo parcels on local citizens.

Because so many unsuspecting purchasers now faced ruin, shortly before President Adams left office Congress authorized the President to appoint a commission to work out some sort of solution to this mess. When Jefferson came in, he appointed three of his Cabinet members, Madison, Gallatin and Levi Lincoln, men of complete integrity, as his Yazoo Commission.

The trio worked closely with Georgia officials and reached the following agreement: Georgia was to accept $1,250,000 from the United States for the Yazoo lands stretching to the Mississippi. In turn, the Federal Government promised to grant statehood to these territories, extinguish Indian titles there and declare legal those Yazoo land purchases where settlers already resided. To satisfy other claims that might arise, the United States also agreed to set aside five million acres of the original thirty-five million. The three Cabinet members admitted that while the title of the claimants could not be supported, they had made their purchases in good faith and deserved lenient treatment.

Jefferson considered the Yazoo settlement fair. However, when he asked Randolph to appropriate the money to be paid to Georgia, Randolph grew wild with rage. In a self-righteous pose to the House, Randolph denounced it as a corrupt job, an infamous piece of legislation forced on Congress by a hired lobby. All honesty and purity in government had vanished forever, he cried. And the culprit and true "Yazoo Man" was James Madison!

Jefferson was stunned when he learned of this vicious attack on innocent Madison by his House floor leader. This was only the opening gun to be trained by Randolph on the Secretary of State, for his cruel tongue vilified him endlessly far into the future. For the immediate period, Randolph's attack doomed the Yazoo settlement, and it was not until five years later in the case of Fletcher vs. Peck that Chief Justice Marshall decided for the purchasers, as the Yazoo Commission had recommended.

Randolph's second major attack was not long delayed. Spain had continued sullen over the loss of Louisiana, and her forces in the Floridas harassed American commerce heading for the Gulf of Mexico. In addition, her soldiers made frequent raids across the American border both from Florida and across the Sabine River from Spanish Texas into Louisiana. Jefferson realized that Spain was essentially weak, for in 1804 when he established the Mobile Revenue District in Spanish West Florida, Spanish officials were unable to interfere.

Knowing that Spain was subservient to France, Jefferson sent word to General John Armstrong, American minister to Paris, that he favored a peaceful settlement with "France as the mediator, and the price of Florida as the means." Talleyrand took the hint and through an agent informed Armstrong that if Emperor Napoleon brought about a settlement, he would expect commercial privileges in the American Floridas, a settlement of French claims relating to the Undeclared War of 1798 and a peace-maker's fee of about $4,000,000 for arranging the deal. Madison was appalled by the demand for a bribe, but Jefferson did not find it offensive. He and his Cabinet finally agreed to a $5,000,000 top offer, and his comment was that "moral duties make no part of the political system of those governments of Europe which are habitually belligerent."

By the time Congress met in December 1805, Southerners and frontiersmen were hoarse in their cries for military action against Spain to seize her American holdings and end her depredations. Jefferson now did an odd thing. On December 3, he sent Congress an Annual Message which hinted broadly that he would go to war if necessary to acquire the Floridas. Then came a second Message, on December 6, that was not to be made public: Monroe had been sent to Spain to negotiate a treaty of sale. Jefferson's second Message explained the history of the negotiations and the possibility of a peaceful solution, by cash purchase. Unlike the bellicose tone of the public Message, the secret Message assured Congress that "formal war is not necessary."

Randolph had gone to the Palace to consult on various matters, and while he was there Jefferson told him he would require an initial $2,000,000 appropriation to buy Florida from Spain through the offices of France. This infuriated Randolph, and in a vicious attack on the House floor he charged Jefferson with talking from both corners of his mouth at the same time. The duplicity of the Messages, Randolph screamed, was intended to make the President appear as a stalwart military leader to the public, and the House to appear as a cringing coward using money instead of the nation's manhood to achieve justice. And was not all of the money merely a bribe to France? The culprit, he added, must be that "Yazoo Man" and "imbecile" Madison.

Congress eventually appropriated the $2,000,000 but the harsh and rowdy demonstrations ruined the Spanish negotiations. Jefferson was now completely aroused by Randolph's coarse exhibition and he removed him both from his committee chairmanship and as House floor leader. In a further move he induced another Virginian to run against Randolph for his House seat, but Randolph was too well entrenched. Afterward, the two had only unkind comments to make about each other: Randolph's usual nickname for Jefferson became "St. Thomas of Cantingbury"; while Jefferson referred to any long-winded filibusterer as someone pulling "a John Randolph."

Another violent, disrupting factor during his second term was Aaron Burr. Burr knew a full three years before the end of his term on March 4, 1805, that Jefferson would not make him his running mate again. Early in 1804, therefore, without resigning the Vice-Presidency, he ran for governor of New York. Jefferson, however, threw his support behind Morgan Lewis, the regular nominee of the party, and Burr was swamped.

Burr was still smarting from his loss when he read some published letters purporting to be strong comments against him made by his Federalist enemy, Alexander Hamilton. Burr demanded a denial and when he received an equivocal reply, he challenged Hamilton to a duel. At Weehawken, New Jersey, close to the spot where his favorite son Philip had earlier been killed in a duel, Hamilton fell fatally wounded on July 11, 1804, at the age of forty-seven. Ironically, the great financial expert died penniless.

Burr fled south afterward under indictment for murder in New York and New Jersey. He stopped in Washington, safe from extradition, and as Vice-President he officiated at the Senate's impeachment trial of Justice Samuel Chase early in 1805. At the time Jefferson had only contempt for Burr, but to elicit his co-operation at the trial, he appointed Burr's stepson as Secretary of Louisiana, a brother-in-law as judge of the New Orleans Superior Court and Burr's friend, General James Wilkinson, governor of Upper Louisiana.

The expiration of Burr's term found him politically disgraced, bankrupt and a fugitive from justice. In a visit with British minister Anthony Merry, he requested $500,000 and some British frigates to separate Louisiana and the West from the Union. This proposal was treasonous, of course, though it did not come to light for almost a century after he made it. His partner in this venture was to be General Wilkinson. Neither Burr nor Jefferson knew that the stout, rednosed Wilkinson was actually on the Spanish payroll as a spy and secret agent #13.

While Merry dispatched a report to London, Burr toured the West in the spring of 1805, receiving a hero's welcome wherever he stopped. Upon his return to Washington, he learned that the British Government was little interested in his scheme. This occasioned a visit to Jefferson and a request for a diplomatic post. But the President reacted stonily.

Burr was now more desperate than ever. Another confederate, former Senator Jonathan Dayton, was sent to Spanish minister Yrujo for money. Dayton poured out a wild tale—Burr would capture Jefferson, Vice-President Clinton and House Speaker Nathaniel Macon, seize the Treasury, rob the banks and take the arsenal at Washington. But if he were unable to maintain control over the Federal City after that, he would burn the ships in the Navy Yard and sail to New Orleans, where he would proclaim independence for Louisiana and the West. Yrujo transmitted the strange conversation to his government at Madrid. But like England, Spain would not lend financial support.

After failing to attract several prominent military men with grudges against Jefferson, Burr set off in August 1806 to stir up action on his own. He wrote Wilkinson that he was coming with an army and money. Burr stopped en route on an island in the Ohio River, where he stayed with its owner, Harman Blennerhassett, a wealthy Irish expatriate, and so charmed his host as to win his co-operation. If the revolt failed, Blennerhassett was to become his partner in purchasing the million-acre Bastrop land grant on the Washita River in northern Louisiana. By the time Burr left, Blennerhassett was already preparing to collect a group of young men to settle on the Bastrop grant. All would come down the river by barges and meet Burr later at a designated point on the Mississippi.

In the meantime, Spanish troops were continuing to cross the Sabine into Louisiana and Jefferson ordered General Wilkinson into hot pursuit. But this would have meant an end to his pay as a Spanish agent. So the general met secretly with his Spanish employers and effected an oral agreement whereby both armies would not enter territory in dispute between their governments. Then he sent word to Jefferson, asserting his success in driving the Spanish beyond the Sabine.

Wilkinson now panicked on his deal with Burr and wrote Jefferson on October 21, 1806: "A Numerous and powerful Association, extending from New York to the Mississippi had been formed to levy & rendezvous eight or Ten Thousand Men in New Orleans & from thence to carry an Expedition against Vera Cruz." In a follow-up letter, Wilkinson announced his patriotic willingness to throw his "Little Band into New Orleans to be ready to defend that Capital against Usurpation and violence."

Jefferson already knew that Burr was on his way westward, and had dispatched John Graham of the State Department to trail "and to arrest Burr, if he makes himself liable." In Kentucky, Joseph Daviess, Chief Justice Marshall's brother-in-law and U. S. Attorney for that state, met Burr's arrival there with a court charge that he planned a Mexican expedition and a western revolt against the Union. Twice a grand jury considered action, but the eloquence of Henry Clay, Burr's twenty-nine-year-old attorney, won him his freedom.

Jefferson also issued a Presidential proclamation. Without mentioning Burr by name, he declared that a conspiracy against Spain had been discovered and all military and civilian officials in the affected area were to detain and seize the culprits. On December 13, a mob raided Blennerhassett's island, plundered his house and molested his wife. Blennerhassett escaped on the river with about thirty young men in a half dozen boats for the rendezvous with Burr at the mouth of the Cumberland.

Wilkinson was now writing Jefferson: "With my handful of veterans, however gallant, it is improbable I shall be able to withstand such a disparity of numbers." With the cry that Burr was approaching with "at least two thousand strong," Wilkinson ordered martial law for New Orleans, filled the jails with persons he disliked and sent Army officers in civilian garb to hunt Burr down and kill him.

Burr first learned of Wilkinson's treachery when he read a newspaper carrying a translation of a coded letter he had sent the general. Then aware that Wilkinson wanted him dead, he surrendered in Mississippi to the acting governor of the Territory, who expressed surprise that Burr's entire army "has eventuated in nine boats and one hundred men, and the major part of these are boys." Burr later escaped, was recaptured and finally sent on horseback a thousand miles to Richmond, Virginia, to stand trial for treason.

Jefferson's high regard for the rights of all individuals failed him in the case of Burr. In a Message to Congress in December 1806, he said he was "bringing to justice" all the conspirators. Then he sent a Special Message before the trial began in which he assured Congress that Burr's "guilt is placed beyond question." For authority, he pointed to General Wilkinson, calling him a man "with the honor of a soldier and the fidelity of a good citizen." Burr's treason, he added, was to be "the severance of the Union of these States beyond the Allegheny mountains; the other, an attack on Mexico." He called "the settlement of a pretended purchase of a tract of country on the Washita, merely a pretext."

Burr's seven-month trial was in essence another contest between Jefferson and his cousin, John Marshall, for the Chief Justice heard the case on his circuit court duty, made necessary by the repeal of the Judiciary Act of 1801. First came grand jury action to determine whether Burr should be tried for treason. By happenstance or otherwise, Jefferson's former House floor leader, John Randolph, sat as foreman as the grand jury began hearing evidence on May 22, 1807. Angry crowds outside wanted Burr lynched. But screaming in his favor was Andrew Jackson, Burr's friend, who was described then as "a tall, lank uncouth-looking personage, with long locks of hair hanging over his face and a queue down his back tied in an eelskin." Jackson had been subpoenaed as a prosecution witness even though it was not Burr he disliked but Wilkinson, whom he called "a double traitor" and a "felon." As for Burr, Jackson charged that Jefferson was spending "millions to persecute an American; not a cent to resist England."

On June 9, Burr demanded that Jefferson deliver to the court a letter Wilkinson had written, plus all Presidential orders relating to Burr. Marshall ruled this preposterous request was reasonable and issued a subpoena to Jefferson to produce these papers. In his cold reply, Jefferson retorted that this could not be done because "it would amount to laying open the whole executive books." The defense would not hear of this and demanded that Marshall haul Jefferson into court. The Chief Justice ruled that the Constitution entitled "any person charged with a crime to compel the attendance of his witnesses." The only excuse available to the President was that "his duties demand his whole time for national objects," said Marshall. But in his opinion, the Presidency was but a part-time job. Therefore, Jefferson would have to appear in court with the papers Burr requested.

In choking rage, Jefferson wrote to George Hay, James Monroe's young son-in-law who was the Government's prosecutor, that "if he alludes to our annual retirement from the seat of government during the sickly season," then Marshall should be told that the President carried on his various Executive duties while at Monticello. In a statement he asked Hay to read to Marshall in court, Jefferson strongly asserted Presidential independence from court orders. "I am persuaded the court is sensible that paramount duties to the nation at large control the obligations of compliance with the summons in this case, as it would should we receive a similar one to attend the trials of Blennerhassett and others in the Territory of Mississippi. . . . What if the several courts could bandy him from pillar to post, keeping him trudging from north to south and east and west, and withdraw him entirely from his constitutional duties?" The Presidency, Jefferson concluded, "should not be withdrawn from its station by any co-ordinate authority." He would send some of the papers Burr requested, but he would decide which ones to send. In no case would he bring them in person.

Wilkinson, after a long delay, arrived in Richmond where he was expected to be the prosecution's star witness. "I saluted the Bench," he wrote Jefferson, "and in spite of myself my Eyes darted a flash of indignation at the little Traitor." After four days of the general's testimony, John Randolph declared, "Wilkinson is the only man I ever saw who was from the bark to the very core a villain." He pressed for Wilkinson's indictment for treason and failed only by the close margin of 9 to 7. "Merciful God, what a spectacle I did behold," Wilkinson wrote Jefferson again. "Integrity & Truth perverted & trampled under foot by turpitude & Guilt, Patriotism appaled & Usurpation triumphant."

On June 24, after hearing forty-eight witnesses, the grand jury indicted Burr and Blennerhassett for treason. When Burr's case came before the trial jury on August 3, the Chief Justice's brother-in-law was serving as foreman. The Chief Justice had also set tongues wagging by attending a party where Burr was a guest. His excuse was that he didn't know Burr would be there. Marshall made it plain that the trial hinged on the meaning of the word treason. According to the Constitution, he read: "Treason against the United States shall consist only in levying war against them, or adhering to their enemies, giving them aid and comfort."

The Government was hinging its entire case against Burr on an earlier opinion by Marshall in a related case involving two Burr associates. At that time, the question had arisen as to the meaning of the words "levying war." Marshall had said then this meant "an actual assemblage of men for the purpose of executing a treasonable design." Going further, he explained that "all those who perform any part, however minute, or however remote from the scene of action, and who are actually leagued in the general conspiracy, are to be considered as traitors." On the basis of this earlier opinion, the Government decided to claim that the necessary overt act of treason was the assemblage of men on Blennerhassett's island. This would also implicate Burr, even though he was remote from the scene of action.

But the case exploded on August 31, when Marshall came to court armed with a fifty-page opinion that erased his earlier definitions and produced new standards for defining treason. What the Government desired, said Marshall, having Jefferson in mind, was the use of the concept of "constructed treason." This was the British concept which made it simple for the Government to get rid of its enemies merely by charging them with plotting an insurrection or being friendly to those accused of plotting. Henceforth it would no longer be sufficient, he asserted, to define levying of war to be any assemblage for a treasonable purpose. It would also be necessary to prove that the assemblage was "in a condition to make war" and was not merely "a secret, furtive assemblage." To be more precise, "Plotting treason is not treason itself." On this basis, Marshall charged the jury to reach its verdict; and, of course, it was "Aaron Burr is not proved to be guilty."

Jefferson had little time to brood over the Burr trial fiasco at the Richmond court. There were more compelling matters on his mind now. For a time after the British and French had resumed their war on May 15, 1803, American trade had benefited immensely from the needs of the belligerents, and the fruits of prosperity were apparent in the rich port towns and cities on the East Coast. British goods had to go to market regardless of the war in order to maintain that nation's economy. The United States bought a great deal for her own consumption but in addition bought millions of dollars' worth to be carried on American vessels to Napoleon's Europe. At the time the British did not resent supplying Napoleon, though her shipping interests regarded with concern the swift growth of the American merchant marine.

After Lord Nelson's smashing victory off Cape Trafalgar on October 21, 1805, the annihilation of the French and Spanish navies gave England supremacy of the sea. Her policy now became one of reducing the American carrying trade to British vassalage and impressing naturalized American sailors of English origin into the British Navy. Jefferson well described what the British were doing in his outraged Message to Congress in December: Not only had the British Navy blockaded European ports, but "our coasts have been infested and our harbors watched by private armed vessels. They have captured in the very entrance of our harbors, as well as on the high seas, not only the vessels of our friends coming to trade with us, but our own also. . . . They have plundered and sunk them on the way; maltreated the crews and abandoned them in boats on the open sea or on desert shores without food or covering."

It was Jefferson's desire that Congress give him authority to punish the British by curtailing their trade. However, John Randolph was still chairman of the House Ways and Means Committee when the Message was referred there, and as an extreme Anglophile he refused to call a committee meeting for eight weeks. Finally, when questioned in the House chamber, he scathingly denounced Jefferson for illegally trying to impose his will on a supposedly independent Congress and for misleading the legislature as to his real purposes: "I speak of backstairs influence," he shouted, "of men who bring messages to this House, which, although they do not appear on the journals, govern its decisions." As for Jefferson, "You gave him money to buy Florida and he bought Louisiana. You furnish means; the application of those means rests with him. Let not the master and the mate go below when the ship is in distress and throw the responsibility on the cook and the cabin-boy."

Despite Randolph's cries that Jefferson's proposal for commercial conflict would only mushroom "this fungus of war," Congress in March 1806 gave Jefferson a Non-Importation Act, permitting him to exclude imports from Britain that were available from non-British sources. Jefferson had asked that it not be made effective for nine months, for he hoped that James Monroe, American minister to London, and William Pinkney, Maryland Federalist lawyer sent by Jefferson as special envoy to work with Monroe could use the impending law to effect a treaty that would end impressment, violations of neutralist shipping rights and make the British agree to pay an indemnity for attacks on American commerce in 1805.

Congress was in its final day of the session on March 3, 1807, when the Monroe Treaty arrived at the Palace. A Senate committee called on Jefferson and asked if he wanted to submit it for ratification. "Certainly not!" he bellowed. He had been furious when he read the treaty earlier. No mention had been made of impressment or any of the other basic matters. Furthermore, the British insisted they would repudiate even the Monroe failure if Jefferson remained at peace with France.

That June, in the midst of the Burr trial, British efforts to humiliate the United States reached a climax. The American frigate *Chesapeake,* leaving Hampton Roads, was fired upon twenty-two times by the British cruiser *Leopard*. Three sailors were killed and eighteen wounded as a result of the American naval commander's refusal to submit to search. A later boarding party then carried off three American sailors who had previously been impressed into the Royal Navy.

The country was in an uproar when word spread about this outrage, and a declaration of war would have been eagerly accepted. But Jefferson knew how ill-prepared the nation was. Six years of Republican policies in opposing a standing army and in severely curtailing government spending had rendered her almost helpless. "America is a bugbear," scoffed British Lord Sidmouth. "There is no terror in her threats!"

Jefferson's first reprisal was a proclamation in mid-October 1807, ordering British warships from American ports. Monroe was ordered to get the British to apologize for the *Chesapeake* abuse and to return the impressed sailors. Instead of this, Britain published fresh Orders in Council in November, installing a blockade on every European country excluding the British flag and making all ships bound for those countries subject to seizure unless they first stopped at a British port and purchased licenses. Napoleon met the orders in December with the Milan Decree, declaring any ship bound to or from Britain or a British colony subject to capture or sinking.

Because war was out of the question and because American shipping was now in great danger with the belligerents unwilling to accept the rights of neutrals to freedom of the seas, Jefferson decided on a new foreign policy. He called it "commercial coercion," a course that he hoped would prove as effective as a successful war.

This untrodden path would be a self-imposed blockade, an embargo on American trade with the belligerents. He reasoned that both Britain and France were dependent on the United States for materials, and the abolition of trade with them would bring them to their knees. But Treasury Secretary Gallatin told him, "As to the hope that it may induce England to treat us better, I think it entirely groundless. I prefer war to a permanent embargo." Secretary of the Navy Smith called it a "mischeif[sic]-making busybody," while Vice-President Clinton predicted it would result in "damning the principle of Republicanism." When British Foreign Secretary Canning heard of Jefferson's embargo plan, he was delighted because Britain would now absorb the carrying trade of her upstart competitor.

On the morning of December 18, 1807, Jefferson's call for "an inhibition of the departure of our vessels from the ports of the United States" went to Congress. So complete was his control over the Senate that within a few hours after the bill reached the chamber it won approval. Action in the House was almost as swift.

Despite his ease in winning the Embargo Act from Congress, Jefferson soon found little support for it. So many coastal vessels slipped off for foreign ports that within a month Jefferson got Congress to pass a second Embargo Act putting coastal vessels under heavy bond. A violator was subject to a $20,000 fine, loss of his ship and was barred from future sailing. In March 1808 came his third Embargo Act forced by a previous loophole that did not take American enterprise into account. A swelling of trade across the Canadian border prompted the act which made it unlawful to export any merchandise by land as well as by sea.

Evasions of the Embargo Acts were an everyday occurrence, especially in New England, where jeering Federalists turned the word around and called it the "O Grab Me Act." Led by Senator Pickering, Federalists in the Northeast considered calling a convention to declare the act unconstitutional, similar to the Jefferson-Madison Kentucky and Virginia Resolutions of 1798 against the Alien and Sedition Acts. As Secretary of State to John Adams, Pickering had pushed the Logan Act through Congress, making it a crime for an American citizen to confer with foreign officials with a view to influencing their negotiations with the United States. Now Pickering chose to violate his own law by plotting secretly with British minister George Rose against the Jefferson Administration.

When Washington had used troops to put down the Whiskey Rebellion in 1794, Jefferson had cried "shame." Yet to enforce his embargo, he proposed measures just as harsh. His first Enforcement Act of April 25, 1808 gave Treasury agents authority to seize goods in ports adjacent to foreign territory if they *thought* the goods might be exported to evade the embargo, to seize any coastal ship merely on the ground that they considered it suspicious. No ship could get clearance unless a revenue officer inspected its loading, and even on the high seas a ship could be stopped by revenue cutters at will. A howl came even from previously loyal Republicans when agents were everywhere prying into local business and seizing goods. By late 1808 embargo evading was so prevalent that Jefferson in anger proposed that towns involved in wholesale violations be quarantined.

The greater the resistance the more determined he grew to coerce compliance. "I did not expect a crop of so sudden & rank growth of fraud & open opposition by force could have grown up in the U.S.," he wrote Gallatin, who asked that his collectors be given the power of "taking the rudders" from ships to prevent their departure. Jefferson actually considered destroying ships to prevent evasion, but he did not include this in the second Enforcement Act that he pushed through Congress early in January 1809. Nevertheless, this Act gave the President such dictatorial power as would have evoked the fiercest opposition from the Jefferson of eight years earlier before he took office. He could blacklist any coastal vessel he desired and thus bar it from leaving port. His collectors could refuse to permit the loading of a ship if it aroused their suspicions, and they could seize cargoes even on wagons or sleighs if they suspected an eventual foreign destination. In addition to using Army and Navy forces to enforce the embargo, Jefferson or an authorized subordinate was given the extraordinary power to call out state militias.

Although Congress obligingly passed this last act for Jefferson, a wide-scale revolt against his embargo was already in progress. The South and West were almost destitute as a result of being deprived of normal European markets for their cotton, rice, tobacco and wheat. Port towns were crowded with unemployed sailors and many ships rotted in harbors. Many sailors, rather than starve, signed to sail under the British flag. The only apparent bright spot was in New England where infant industries sprang up to produce goods previously imported.

Leadership of the revolt came from New England Republicans concerned that they would be swept from office if the embargo continued. Among the ringleaders were two young Massachusetts Congressmen, Joseph Story, who was under thirty, and Ezekial Bacon, thirty-two. Some time afterward, Jefferson said that Story, whom he called a "pseudo-Republican," convinced Bacon that the country would be enveloped in civil war unless the Embargo Act were repealed; Bacon then worked on House members to vote repeal. Story later recalled: "The whole influence of the Administration was directly brought to bear to seduce us from what we considered a great duty to our country, and especially to New En-

gland. We were scolded, privately consulted, and argued with.
. . . I knew, at the time, that Mr. Jefferson had no ulterior measure
in view, and was determined on protracting the embargo for
an indefinite period, even for years. I was well satisfied that such a
course . . . would bring on a direct rebellion. Yet Mr. Jefferson,
with his usual visionary obstinacy, was determined to maintain it.
Mr. Bacon and myself resisted, and measures were concerted by
us, with the aid of Pennsylvania, to compel him to abandon his
mad scheme."

Severe headaches attacked Jefferson as he watched his complete
domination over Congress vanish in a matter of weeks. He became
inattentive to his Presidential duties, and it was said that Madison
and Gallatin took them over in that final period in order to prevent
a governmental collapse. On March 1, 1809, he found himself
with no alternative to signing a bill repealing the embargo and
substituting for it an Act of Non-Intercourse with France and
England alone. American ships could now return to trade except
with the two belligerents. Congress then showed a final contempt
for him when the Senate rejected the nomination of William Short,
his protégé, to a diplomatic post in Russia. With relief, Jefferson
wrote to Monroe, whose failure to write a decent treaty with
England had led directly to his current troubles. Soon, wrote Jefferson, he would be free "from a drudgery to which I am no
longer equal" and restored "to a scene of tranquillity amidst my
family and friends more congenial to my age and natural inclinations."

On March 4, 1809, discouraged by his own years as President,
he turned over his office to James Madison and departed for
Monticello one week afterward. Later he declared that the final
eruption against his authority had led directly to the War of 1812;
he was convinced that continuance of the embargo for two months
longer would have prevented war.

Nevertheless, history would assess him kindly as President,
chiefly because he pushed his country's boundary across the muddy
Mississippi to the Rockies. That he presented such contrast between his expressed philosophy and his Presidential activities
would in time be forgotten by all except his small group of
enemies. What would be remembered were tales of a democratic
President, stories that brought closer kinship between Americans
and their national government. Stripped of its quaint desire for a
simple agricultural economy, his philosophic goal of a broadened
democracy would inspire other men to action.

☆ 4 ☆

JAMES MADISON

Man With a Past

If circumstances had not operated to reduce the Office of the President to a secondary role during James Madison's Administration, his out-of-character behavior would have produced the same results.

At the trying hour in 1809 when he became President, the need for Executive leadership was great. But Madison chose to remain passive. Jefferson before him had also announced his adherence to the Republican doctrine of legislative supremacy. In Jefferson's case, of course, this was only lip service, for he busied himself behind the scenes. Madison was different. As a late convert to Republican belief in legislative leadership, not only did he speak out for it, he was much more zealous in practice than original believers. Only when Congress was away from the capital did he come to life and permit the Office of the President to show leadership. When Congress returned, he dwindled to a shadow and became its servant. The combination of his philosophy and the character of the times marked his terms of office as periods of chaos.

Yet the pity is that Madison was one of the few Presidents of intellectual bent and a man who revealed a profound creative ability in every office he held until he reached the heights. He was a man of fighting heart and bold, relentless drive—until he became temporary master of the Executive Mansion.

As a thinker, the earlier Madison could claim to be an originator of the field of economic history, viewing mankind's development in terms of contending economic forces. A specious use of his work helped Karl Marx formulate his class struggle doctrine. Before Thomas Malthus conceived his famous law, Madison expounded the similar theory that food production could not keep pace with the increase in population. Madison was also a leading authority on government administration and international law. One literary effort in this area was on the rise and fall of confederation governments, a study that encompassed the confederations of Lydia, Amphictyons and Achaea, as well as the Helvetian, Belgian and German confederations. Madison's well-reasoned conclusion, that each failed because it lacked a central authority with powers to enforce its decisions over equal and independent subparts, led to his fiery determination to replace the American Articles of Confederation Government with a strong central government in 1787.

Seldom are thinkers men of action. In Madison's case, however, he managed to combine the two areas with brilliance before he rose to the Presidency. Even his political writings were not directed generally to an academic audience but were instead keyed to influence those who might be persuaded to join him in controlling the course of events. Some critics have decried Madison's writing style as a pallid imitation of Joseph Addison's in *The Spectator*. Madison himself acknowledged a debt to Addison, to concern himself with clarity rather than maxims or emotional phraseology in order to put "proper words in their proper places."

Yet if his language lacked searing fire, it still pleased his contemporaries. The Continental Congress turned to him whenever a eulogy had to be written or when states had to be exhorted to cooperate with the Confederation Government; Hamilton pleaded with him to join him and John Jay as the anonymous "Publius" trio in composing the classic, eighty-five explanatory essays known as *The Federalist*, to propagandize the Constitution during the critical ratification fight; Jefferson was forever urging him to seize his quill pen and scratch out a bitter attack on a mutual enemy—whether it be Hamilton for his financial policy or the entire national government for the Alien and Sedition Acts of 1798. And Washington made frequent use of him as chief Presidential ghostwriter. It was Madison who wrote Washington's First Inaugural Address and his unused Farewell Address in 1792. Not only did he write the First Inaugural Address but the House of Representatives also called on him to write its reply to the Address. Then to complete the writing circle, Washington had him write the Presidential reply to the House's reply.

Madison's slight frame belied the enormous stamina within. During the twilight period between the demise of the Virginia colony

and the establishment of the state of Virginia, he played a vital
role directing Orange County's affairs and helping to write the
state's first constitution at the May 1776 Williamsburg convention.
Then as a member of the Virginia House of Delegates, he brought
freedom of religion to the state by pushing through the legislature the Jefferson bill to disestablish the Virginia Anglican Church
as the state's church and tax beneficiary. Later, as a delegate to
the Continental Congress, he singlehandedly prevented approval
of the Jay Treaty with Spain, which would have closed the Mississippi River to Americans for twenty-five years in exchange for a
commercial deal. He also served as Congressional liaison with General Nathanael Greene's southern army fighting General Cornwallis' Redcoats; saved the venerable Benjamin Franklin from being recalled in disgrace from his Paris post; worked out actuarial
tables for postwar pay that satisfied Continental Army officers and
prevented a general mutiny; and fought valiantly but unsuccessfully to give the Confederation Government powers to tax, control
commerce and enforce its decisions.

Certainly Madison's greatest contribution was his service as
"Father of the Constitution" when he was thirty-seven years old.
It was his planning and dogged determination which finally
brought the Philadelphia Convention into session from May into
September 1787. And it was he who more than any other single
individual determined the new form of government and the scope
of Presidential power. Afterward, he masterminded the grueling
ratification fight in Virginia against his enemy, Patrick Henry,
who contemptuously but erroneously called him a "bookworm."
Had he died at this point and been laid to rest in the red earth of
the small, hillside family cemetery at Montpelier, he would have
merited indelibly a rank held by few other American statesmen.

From this lofty perch, his career could go in only two directions. He could continue at that level, or he could tarnish
his reputation and standing. During Washington's first Administration, he was a whirlwind of brilliance as the leader of the House
of Representatives. He introduced the first tax bill; proposed
the establishment of the State, Treasury and War departments;
prevented the Senate from having a voice in removing Executive
officials; and took charge of the drafting and promotion of the
Bill of Rights. But all the while, he was undergoing an internal
philosophical struggle and a completely new Madison emerged.

The early-day Madison had fought for "a due supremacy of the national authority" and "subordinately useful local authorities." He had even gone so far as to propose to the Constitutional Convention that Congress be authorized to pass final judgment on the legislative acts of the states in all cases. The latter-day Madison was a states' rights champion. In the Virginia Resolutions that he wrote in opposition to the Alien and Sedition Acts of 1798, he advanced the doctrine that the states could declare an act of Congress unconstitutional "in the case of a deliberate, palpable and dangerous exercise of powers not granted by the said compact."

Madison No. 1 had promoted the concept of a strong President at the Constitutional Convention and considered with delight the prospect of a continued increase in Executive power. But Madison No. 2 came to the conclusion that the experiences of the Washington and Adams administrations showed that Federalist Presidents threatened to transfer the Republic of the United States into an absolute or, at best, a mixed monarchy. Legislative mastery was the best hope for the Republic, he now believed.

But the legislature must also be cut down to size. In 1780, as a delegate to the Continental Congress, he was the originator of the concept of implied powers, or those powers necessary to carry out specifically enumerated constitutional powers. Then in No. 44 of *The Federalist,* he wrote: "No axiom is more clearly established in law, or in reason, than that wherever the end is required, the means are authorized; wherever a general power to do a thing is given, every power necessary for doing it is included." This was the doctrine, in almost these identical words, that Chief Justice John Marshall expounded in McCulloch *vs.* Maryland in 1819 to make implied powers part of the authority of the Federal Government. In writing the Tenth Amendment, Madison had successfully fought for implied powers in 1789 by preventing a legislative attempt to insert the word "expressly" before "delegated" in the clause "powers not delegated to the United States by the Constitution, nor prohibited by it to the States, are reserved to the States respectively, or to the people." Yet only two years later he opposed Hamilton's bill to establish a Bank of the United States because this activity was not "expressly" enumerated in the Constitution as a national power.

Historians have generally credited Thomas Jefferson with exerting a powerful influence on Madison but the simple truth is that Madison had already begun to shift his philosophic sack from one shoulder to the other before Jefferson arrived in New York in 1790 to become Washington's Secretary of State. The change in Madison stemmed from his own interpretation of events. His championing of a strong central government resulted originally from his belief that the Confederation Government would disintegrate without this alteration. But once the new government began operating, he viewed it as working in behalf of the merchant and creditor classes and against the interests of farmers and debtors. Hence he shifted sides.

This shift was not without its penalties. Most of all, he became a man with a past that he believed necessary to hide. Although he had taken almost complete daily records of the proceedings at the Constitutional Convention, he dared not publish this invaluable legal and historic work during his lifetime for fear his enemies would quote him against himself until he became a national laughingstock. Whenever a letter reached him to verify or disclaim a statement in behalf of Federalist principles that had been attributed to him, Madison would either reply evasively or ignore the request. As for the attitude of many leading Republicans toward him, even Madison's close relationship with Jefferson did not erase the finger of suspicion pointed in his direction as the man who held two diametrically opposed philosophies.

By 1808, when Jefferson began his final year as President, the national political scene had begun to turn grim. Discontent with the Embargo Act was rapidly reaching national hysteria. And as Jefferson's political authority disintegrated, Republican factions began the fight to name his successor.

The bitterness of the internal party struggle was premised on the assumption that only a Republican could win election as President, that the Federalists had dwindled in support to a New England political party. In August, when the Federalists repeated their 1804 ticket of C. C. Pinckney of XYZ Affair fame and former Senator Rufus King of New York, this was ample evidence to the Republicans that the Federalists were acknowledging an expected electoral thrashing.

It was well known to both parties that Jefferson wanted Secretary of State Madison to succeed him. However, Republican malcontents spoiled for a fight to humiliate both men. Vice-President George Clinton yearned after his nation's top honor plus the destruction of Virginian domination of the party. On the southern front, John Randolph, ousted as House floor leader by Jefferson, had organized his own tight political faction of Republicans, whom he called the Tertium Quids, or a middle course third party. Randolph's hatred of Madison was well advertised by rambling, emotional speeches. Madison was not a true Republican, he cried: Madison was a Federalist, kin to Hamilton in philosophy. When Madison refrained from answering him, Randolph's fury grew. By 1806, the sound of Madison's name sickened him; for that year when Randolph requested appointment as minister to England, Madison's negative report to Jefferson ended consideration. The Quids would put up their own candidate, Randolph determined, and destroy both Madison and Jefferson with one blow.

James Monroe, protégé of Jefferson, was envoy to England when the Quids decided on him as their candidate. "The friends of Mr. Madison have left nothing undone to impair the very high and just confidence of the nation in yourself," Randolph wrote him temptingly. When Monroe had first heard of the attempt to make him President, despite his insatiable political ambitions, he had replied that he would "sooner be a constable" than run for President against his friend Madison.

But letters from Randolph and other Quids continued coming and with his ego bathed in political honey, he began to waver. When William Pinkney was sent to London to help him negotiate a British treaty in the spring of 1806, Monroe received the Quid explanation that it was done "to take you from the task of settling our differences with England." Monroe's pride suffered another blow when Jefferson offered him "the choice of the two governments of Orleans and Louisiana" in order that he might be "just that much withdrawn from the focus of the ensuing contest [1808] until its events should be known." Then when Monroe rejected the offer, Jefferson responded: "I see with infinite grief a contest arising between yourself and another, who have been very dear to each other, and equally so to me. . . . One piquing thing draws on another . . . with increasing acrimony, until . . . it becomes difficult for yourselves to keep clear of the toils in which your friends will endeavor to interlace you. . . . I have ever viewed Mr. Madison and yourself as two principal pillars of my happiness. Were either to be withdrawn, I should consider it among the greatest calamities which could assail my future peace of mind."

Monroe fell completely into the Quid trap despite Jefferson's plea. When he and William Pinkney wrote an abominable treaty that Jefferson refused to transmit to the Senate, in shame and shock Monroe saw Madison behind this episode as a jealous rival. Finally, when he returned home from Europe in December and Jefferson did not ask him to call at the Palace, he determined to erase his humiliation by running against Madison.

Although Jefferson informed Monroe he would remain neutral in the Presidential contest, he had no intention of letting Madison be defeated. Despite the unpopularity of his embargo policy, he still dominated the machinery of the Legislative Branch. But how much longer would he be able to boss the internal operations of Congress, and especially the caucus to select his successor? To nail down the nomination for Madison without delay, he therefore passed word along to Congressional lieutenants to call the nominating caucus for January 23, 1808.

The Quids were outraged at this unseemly rush, but once he recovered, Randolph selected the strategy of calling for an even earlier Virginia Assembly caucus vote; he believed Madison's Assembly friends would stay away because the call was a Quid maneuver. This would obviously result in a landslide for Monroe and become a vital factor to sway the following Congressional nominating caucus. However, Madison's Washington managers, Senator William B. Giles and Representative Wilson C. Nicholas, who also functioned as Jefferson's floor leaders in Congress, got wind of this scheme and called for a Virginia Assembly caucus on the same night as the Quid call. The Giles-Nicholas caucus took place at Bell's Tavern in Richmond the night of January 21, and here Madison was unanimously favored 123 to zero. At the same time, the caucus at the state capitol showed a vote of 57 for Monroe and 10 for Madison. Then the following night both groups of legislators met together and Madison won over Monroe by 136 to 57.

Jefferson had selected Senator Stephen R. Bradley of Vermont to preside over the Congressional nominating caucus, as he had in 1804. Bradley realized trouble was brewing when his note for the January 23 caucus, which he had pinned on the curtain near the Speaker's chair, acquired a companion note denouncing the caucus and demanding that members stay away. The Republicans claimed 139 of the 179 members of Congress, but on that vital Saturday evening only 89 members came. Madison won the nomination with 83 votes to 3 for Vice-President Clinton and 3 for Monroe. Clinton was then named his running mate with 79 votes.

Madison was chagrined by the small number attending the caucus, for he realized he would now be subjected to attack as an unpopular candidate forced on the party. How right he was soon became apparent when Randolph and sixteen other Quids, who called themselves "The Protesters," published an address to the American people, denying the authority of Republican Congressmen to hold a nominating meeting and denouncing Madison as lacking talent and energy and as being a secret Federalist.

Nor was this all. Clinton had accepted the Vice-Presidential nomination. However, he prompted his supporters to decry the caucus that had named him as a "corrupt" gathering. On this basis, he declared himself a Republican Presidential candidate against Madison, though he carefully refrained from eliminating himself as Madison's running mate on the caucus ticket.

Like orchestras that had been waiting impatiently for the raised baton, the backers of each candidate broke into their campaign tunes that spring and summer. Because custom at that time frowned on political speechmaking by candidates, the chief means of communication had to come from whispering campaigns and newspaper attacks or praise. Since Madison's voice was faint, custom was to his advantage. Clinton also gained, for if he had gone on a speaking tour audiences would have noted, as Senator William Plumer of New Hampshire did, that he was old, feeble, and had "no mind, no intellect, no memory."

As the front-runner, Madison had no need for a whispering campaign against his opponents. This was not true of the others. There was much ear-whispering that Madison stood hardly higher than a midget, though he was slightly above five feet, four inches in height—he was "Little Jemmy." Then there was the tale promoted by John Randolph and others that his wife Dolley and her sister, Anna Cutts, the wife of a Massachusetts Congressman, were "loose" women involved in countless affairs with men in the capital. A third effort was promoted by Edmond Genêt, Clinton's son-in-law and the same former French minister to the United States who had caused President Washington so much anguish in 1793 before he was ordered recalled. Genêt now tried to equate Madison and Jefferson with Robespierre the Beheader by charging that both had accepted French citizenship from him. The truth was that Washington, Madison and Hamilton had been offered French citizenship a year before Robespierre came to power.

The campaign in the newspapers was hardly at a higher level. When the influential New York *Public Advertiser* prepared to run a series of pro-Madison articles, Clinton pushed city and state printing contracts on the publisher, who promptly dropped the series. Several Clinton papers hammered away at Madison, calling him a Federalist who saw to it that in the State Department "under his immediate control, were fostered a most vigorous set of aristocrats, monarchists and tories." Other sympathetic newspapers chose the theme of a Madison who would be a puppet of Napoleon; still others of a Madison who would continue the "present visionary, corrupt management of our national affairs." A theme of all the pro-Clinton papers was that Madison was physically unfit for the Presidency. "Unfortunately for his country," one lamented, "he is sickly, valetudinarian, and subject to spasmodic affections which operate unfavorably on his nervous system." As for the Federalists, Timothy Pickering set the party line by calling Madison "as visionary in politics as Mr. Jefferson, who, from the top of Monticello, will direct all the movements of the little man at the Palace." One peculiar Federalist attack on Madison was the charge that he was "a disciple of Confucius," thus making him an adversary of both commerce and agriculture and an exponent of grazing.

Not until Senator John Milledge of Georgia, the Senate's President Pro Tem, opened the ballot box and counted the electoral votes for the assembled House and Senate on February 8, 1809, did the name-calling end. Madison was the winner with 122 votes to 47 for C. C. Pinckney, 6 for Clinton and none for Monroe. By this time, Monroe had turned over to Jefferson his entire correspondence with Randolph to prove there was "nothing in them to sanction what has been by some ungenerously insinuated." The reaction at the time of both Jefferson and Madison was that Monroe go into exile as governor of Louisiana. His rejection of the offer, he said later, was like "the answer given by the king of Prussia to Count Saxe when he offered him the Island of Barbadoes . . . that he must find another Sancho for his Barataria." In the contest for Vice-President, Clinton won re-election with a 113 to 47 votes over Rufus King.

Republican party harmony seemed to have been restored by March 4, 1809, when Madison was inaugurated President. An eyewitness noted that he was extremely pale and trembled excessively when he first began to speak, but soon gained confidence. That evening's festivities included the first inaugural ball, at which, remarked the wife of a Republican editor, Dolley looked like a queen. Her headdress was a turban of velvet and white satin matching her gown from Paris with two superb plumes, the bird of paradise feathers.

Even though Madison's victory was of almost landslide proportions, he had little reason to hope he would be able to provide effective Presidential leadership.

Part of his troubles were inherited. The attacks on Jefferson's Embargo policy had led to a revolt of New England Republicans by the beginning of 1809. Jefferson, who had loomed larger than life to his following, was now just a man whose orders could be ignored with impunity. More than that, he had reacted to the revolt by abandoning his stewardship of the Executive Branch. Because Madison, as Secretary of State, had been forced to take over many of his responsibilities, he had been compelled to deal personally with an angry Congress for three months before he took office as President; and because he had fought to sustain Jefferson's hated embargo, he found himself tarred with the same brush as Jefferson. Members who now smiled derisively at Jefferson's naïve statement on proposing the embargo—"Our commerce is so valuable to them [England and France] that they will be glad to purchase it when the only price we ask is to do us justice"—turned their scorn on the man who would succeed him. The most he could salvage for Jefferson was the repeal of the embargo on all foreign trade and its replacement with the Non-Intercourse Act of March 1, 1809, which banned all commerce with England and France but permitted American vessels to leave port to conduct trade elsewhere. Yet from the enterprise of American shippers it was obvious that they would evade the restrictions imposed by the new law and send their ships to France and England. John Randolph derided the Non-Intercourse Act as "a leaky vessel."

Besides an increasingly chaotic relationship between the Executive and Legislative branches, Madison also inherited the soured fruits of his predecessor's military program. With a policy that opposed standing military forces as a threat to democracy, Jefferson had enthusiastically cut the Army to impotence, forcing officers on low pay with little chance for advancement in rank and scattering them and their men among isolated frontier posts. His basic Army legislation in 1802 authorized only a single artillery and two infantry regiments totaling about three thousand men. Then in

1808, with a mounting tension on the international scene and the embargo in operation, Congress authorized eight more regiments. However, Jefferson's policy continued, for operational money was not appropriated. And in the Navy, where his anti-preparedness policy was also in operation, his restrictive course halted the construction of all double-deck frigates. Instead, the six Navy yards turned out only cheap little sailing gunboats, capable of carrying a few men and a small cannon. So there existed no deterrent to the violently anti-American stand of British Foreign Secretary George Canning or the double-dealing of Napoleon.

But not all of Madison's troubles had been passed down. The harsh truth was that even before he took office Madison gave up a large part of his Executive prerogatives in order to placate certain Senators. Months before his inauguration he had decided on the brilliant Gallatin as his Secretary of State, advancing him to primacy in the Cabinet after eight years as Jefferson's Secretary of the Treasury. However, this news came as a shock to Senator William Giles of Virginia, one of his campaign managers and a Jefferson floor leader in both the House and Senate. Intemperate "Farmer" Giles coveted the State post and took it as a personal insult that Madison did not proffer him the Cabinet seat.

He quickly dispatched angry letters to Madison and advanced a long string of arguments why the President-elect must not make Gallatin his Secretary of State. Here was a "foreigner," he argued, who could not be trusted to uphold the American view; furthermore, Madison could not count on Gallatin's loyalty because Jefferson liked him. Charging it was well known in party circles that Jefferson had appointed Gallatin even though he knew he lacked ability, Giles went on to threaten Madison. "Nothing could be more unfortunate for you during your whole Administration," he wrote, "than the transfer of the opinion in relationship to Mr. Jefferson to yourself, that favoritisms should be ingredients in the inducements to office. The nomination of Mr. Gallatin will have a greater tendency towards producing this impression than any other act you could decree."

Had the ill-tempered, bitter-tongued Virginia Senator stood alone, Madison might have ignored him. But he soon learned that Giles had teamed with Senator Samuel Smith of Maryland, a seething Gallatin hater whose incompetent brother Robert had managed Jefferson's Navy Department. Imperious Sam Smith was a wealthy Baltimore shipping merchant who was restless when not engaged in intrigues. He saw every adverse financial undertaking as a personal vendetta on the part of Gallatin to ruin him.

Because Smith's Senate colleagues had frequently elected him President Pro Tem, Madison considered it necessary to appease him now to squeeze Gallatin past the necessary Senate confirmation. He therefore broached to Smith his plan to shift Gallatin to the State Department and brother Robert Smith to the Treasury Department. The Smiths wanted time to think this over, although Robert Smith visited the Treasury for a long dry-run on the Secretary's duties. However, before the Smith brothers advised Madison as to their decision, Gallatin hurried to Madison with word that Robert Smith was so thickheaded he had not been able to comprehend even simple financial and taxation matters. This news worried Madison, who was beginning to see that the Smith brothers would cause him a mountain of trouble unless he gave them a major payoff. In addition, even if he complied, he could not be assured of their support. He had fallen into a muddy hole that he had dug himself.

Another misstep at this time was his request to Wilson C. Nicholas, his other campaign manager and Jefferson's House floor leader, to conduct a Senate survey on Gallatin's chances for confirmation to the State Department. Nicholas was the brother-in-law of the Smiths and his pessimistic report noted that Gallatin would be rejected. Nicholas also said he had spent several days arguing with Giles to vote for Gallatin but had not made any headway.

Madison likened himself to the general who could attack a superior force and die courageously or withdraw to fight another day. If he submitted Gallatin's name to the Senate, he believed, he faced not only probably defeat but also continued warfare with Giles and Smith. The result would be that his Administration would lose all momentum at the outset and never recover.

Gallatin, therefore, had to be sacrificed, though not eliminated, for this latter act would be interpreted by his enemies as a show of complete Presidential impotence. This left only one road open to Madison. He would retain Gallatin as Secretary of the Treasury, where he would not require Senatorial confirmation since he was merely continuing in the post he had held under Jefferson.

But like many men who take an action against their true desire, Madison compounded his troubles. With the State Department post still open, Giles pursued it with renewed hope. However, Madison settled the problem by nominating Robert Smith, despite his awareness of the man's incompetence. So at one stroke, Madison humiliated Gallatin, debased the State Department, angered mean-tempered, influential Giles and made Senator Sam Smith contemptuous of him for his act of appeasement.

The Smith appointment set the tone generally for other Cabinet assignments. As his Secretary of the Navy, Madison named former South Carolina governor Paul Hamilton who knew nothing of the sea and was absorbed in a losing bout with alcoholism. Dr. William Eustis, a physician of excellent reputation, became Secretary of War and an observer noted that the burly doctor from Massachusetts "consumes his time in reading advertisements of petty retailing merchants to find where he may purchase one hundred shoes or two hundred hats . . . instead of forming general and comprehensive arrangements for the organization of his troops." Gideon Granger, a Jefferson carryover as Postmaster General, was already tarnished by publicity of his involvement in the Yazoo land scandal and an unhealthy connection with Aaron Burr. He was also close to the Smith-Giles Senate ring. Caesar Rodney, the Attorney General and also a carryover, was a man of first-rate ability. Only after repeated Presidential pleas would he leave his thriving law practice at Wilmington, Delaware. Even then, he stayed in Washington only a few days at a time before rushing home. Besides this odd combination of ability and disinterest, Rodney was renowned as a patriot, having galloped his horse eighty miles to Philadelphia in 1776 to cast a prime vote for Independence. His chief serious drawback was his appearance. John Adams once noted that "his face is no bigger than a large apple."

With his motley force of departmental Secretaries, Madison began managing the national government from the confines of his narrow house on F Street between Thirteenth and Fourteenth streets. Two blocks away, Jefferson had made no effort to pack his belongings, and it was not until March 11 that he climbed into his carriage and started off toward Monticello.

The first session of the Eleventh Congress was not scheduled to convene until May 22, and Madison, who had made a botch of his office so far, was determined to return to his previous, high operating level. In his waning months as Secretary of State, he had begun to meet privately with affable David Erskine, the British minister, a thirty-year-old inexperienced diplomat who replaced Anthony Merry, in an effort to straighten out the tense situation between both nations. Then when he became President, he stepped up the pace of his meetings with Erskine.

Madison wanted an end of impressment of American sailors and the rescinding of the hated British Order in Council of November 11, 1807, which required neutral ships to enter a British port and purchase a license in order to trade with the European Continent under Napoleon. Erskine in turn said he had some basic British positions to consider. These instructions, he told Madison, were: (1) The United States was to withdraw her trade embargo against England but was to continue it against France; (2) The United States was to renounce all commercial relations with the colonies of England's enemies with whom she had not dealt before the Napoleonic War; and (3) The United States was to agree that Britain was at liberty to seize all American vessels trading with France or the countries abiding by Napoleon's decrees.

When Madison called points two and three an insult to American sovereignty, Erskine quickly agreed to abandon them in the interest of reaching a peaceful accord between both nations. Jefferson's embargo and the national turmoil it had created seemed so unnecessary as Madison and Erskine now drew up a treaty in an atmosphere of good fellowship. Madison was only a month in office when he produced resounding joy across the nation by issuing a proclamation noting the end of trouble with England over neutral rights. England had agreed to withdraw her Orders in Council by June 10, he announced, and in return Americans could once more engage in trade with her. There was peace with honor for both sides.

The relief he brought to the nation found even previously unfriendly editors cheering him as a remarkable President. Late in May when Congress convened this high regard was translated into congratulatory speeches and eulogies that occupied almost all of the legislature's time before adjournment on June 28.

The arrangement with Erskine had laid the groundwork also for a jubilant Presidential social season. This was important to the national and international set in Washington, for the capital was still a primitive village. A visiting Frenchman said it reminded him of "those Russian towns traced in the deserts of Tartary, in whose enclosures we behold nothing but naked fields and a few glimpses of houses."

On May 31, Dolley Madison held her first Wednesday evening levee, complete with military music and refreshments and visitors seeking to stare at the President or greet him obsequiously. Dinners and balls also became a regular feature of the Madison Executive Mansion as the Jeffersonian plainness in entertaining gave way to an elaborate social existence. Styles had begun to change, with men now attired in cloth coats and pantaloons. Madison would not change, however, and clung to his colonial dress with its knee breeches, long silk hose, silver shoe buckles and powdered hair. He always dressed totally in black and was as immaculate as Jefferson was careless. To add to his height, he liked extra-high hats and he combed his hair over his forehead to hide bald spots. Women's styles, which had fallen under French influence, were revealing. When Elizabeth Patterson, the lovely niece of Senator Sam Smith and Secretary of State Robert Smith, attended a ball with her husband, Jerome Bonaparte, young brother of Napoleon, it was reported that because of her low-cut gown "no one dared look at her but by stealth." Rivaling her was the American wife of British Minister Erskine.

Despite her Quaker upbringing, Dolley Madison was born for laughter and parties. She was seventeen years younger than her husband, about three inches taller and perhaps thirty pounds heavier. Washington Irving, who visited the Palace, described them in this fashion: "Mrs. Madison is a fine, portly, buxom dame, who has a smile and a pleasant word for everybody. But as to Jemmy Madison—ah! poor Jemmy!—he is but a withered little Apple-John." Dolley applied cheek circles of thick, red rouge, doused herself in perfume, wore odd hats and revealing gowns and used snuff. Once when she took a pinch of Henry Clay's Maccoboy Snuff, she was holding a bandanna kerchief in one hand and a dainty lace square in the other. "Mr. Clay, this is for rough work, and this is my polisher," she explained.

Madison and Dolley complemented each other well and had a mutual affection that was evidenced in Dolley's warm references to her husband in letters. When Burr first brought them together in 1794, she wrote to a friend: "Aaron Burr says that the great little Madison has asked to be brought to see me this evening." They lived out their lives in what would have been complete harmony, were it not for one major irritant. This was the surviving son of her first marriage, Payne Todd, a wastrel who in time forced Madison to pay $40,000 of his gambling debts and caused his mother to lose the ancestral estate at Montpelier and become an object of charity. Another persistent irritant was the continuing slander of Dolley as an unfaithful wife. Aaron Burr, in self-imposed European exile, told Jeremy Bentham, the English philosopher, that he had slept with the wife of a President, a tale that spread across the Atlantic to the United States.

Strangers who met Madison at his wife's levees said he had "rather a sour, reserved and forbidding countenance." Actually, among friends he revealed a sparkling wit and was at his best telling stories on himself. Perennial favorites were those related to his hectic two years at Princeton getting the four-year B.A. degree under Dr. John Witherspoon who made all students wear the academic cap and gown; the campus oratorical fights between the Whigs and the Cliosophic Society, with Madison and his fellow Whigs, especially Philip Freneau and Hugh Henry Brackenridge, penning more obscene poetry as the battle lengthened; most of all the humorous tales of his long political career. One frequently told story was about the aftermath of his successful fight for ratification of the Federal Constitution in 1788 at the Virginia convention. Patrick Henry, his chief opponent at the convention, and "The Voice," as he called him, had punished him by getting the Virginia Assembly to reject him as the state's first Senator. Then when Madison ran for a House seat, Patrick Henry "henrymandered" the Congressional district against him and put up young James Monroe, an opposer of the Constitution's ratification, as his opponent.

The two candidates had traveled together throughout the district and engaged in debating their views of the Constitution. At one place, said Madison, "service was performed and then they had music with two fiddles. When it was all over we addressed these people and kept them standing in the snow listening to the discussion of constitutional subjects. They stood it out very patiently—seemed to consider it a sort of fight in which they were required to be spectators." That night Madison's nose suffered severe frostbite that left a permanent "campaign scar." And when voting day came, he was certain the vote would be so close that he rode far out of his way to pick up an old man and bring him to the polling place. After he helped the tottering old fellow out of his carriage, the elderly gentleman finally reached the polling table and announced, "I'm voting for Monroe." The final outcome showed Madison winning by three hundred votes.

Madison's impish wit especially delighted Jefferson, who called on him endlessly to provide wall-shaking laughs. A typical Madison twist occurred when he was Secretary of State and Mellimelli, ambassador from the Bey of Tunis, demanded that the United States Government provide him with concubines. He made such a pest of himself that the State Department finally supplied him with "Georgia, a Greek." Madison had to find an unobtrusive way of charging the expense to the department's budget in order not to arouse newspapers or Congress. His decision was to call it an "appropriation to foreign intercourse."

There were also sadder stories with ironic twists that told a great deal about the temper and biases of the American people. For instance, on September 11, 1790, while returning to Virginia from the New York national capital, Madison and Jefferson stopped for breakfast with Mrs. Margaret Adams, an old colored woman of Bladensburg, Maryland, who used her home as an inn. Mrs. Adams told them that President Washington and his wife Martha had stayed overnight with her, preferring her place to the dirty lodge in the village. Then on September 10, an outraged white mob collected before her residence and threatened to burn it to the ground because she had taken in white guests. This threat collapsed when it was pointed out that the great Washington had slept in her place. However, the mob insisted on doing symbolic damage, Madison noted. Rushing into her back yard, the wild crew took revenge by destroying her outhouse.

American joy with the Madison-Erskine settlement was shortlived. New England sailing vessels were just back from their first trip to the English market when the bubble burst. Angry words emanated from London where Foreign Secretary Canning, the outspoken, anti-American member of the Duke of Portland's Ministry, ordered Erskine recalled and the Orders in Council reaffirmed. Canning charged that Erskine had been instructed to win agreement on points two and three before proceeding with a treaty, and by ignoring binding instructions he had produced an invalid agreement. On hearing the bad news, the humiliated Madison on August 9, 1809, was forced to issue a second proclamation, resuming the Non-Intercourse Act against England.

To pour salt into the wound, Canning now dispatched Francis James "Copenhagen" Jackson to succeed Erskine. Jackson had won his nickname in 1807 while serving as special envoy to Denmark. He had ordered the Danish Government to surrender its fleet for British use during the war with Napoleon, and when the Government refused, he decreed the bombing and destruction of

Copenhagen and the death of hundreds of women and children.

Jackson arrived in Washington filled with belligerence and contempt. If the United States wanted to improve relations with Britain, he told Secretary Smith, it would have to apologize for hoodwinking Erskine and in addition offer concessions. Madison let the rude minister cool his heels for a month before receiving him. Then in their conversation, he warned Jackson that he had no further compromises to make but would be amenable to British proposals for relieving the tension between both nations. A furious Jackson reported to London that Madison was a "rather mean-looking little man." As for Dolley Madison, he erroneously reported later that she "must have been a comely person when she served out the liquor at the bar of her father's tavern."

It was in his dealings with "Copenhagen" Jackson that Secretary of State Robert Smith revealed both his inadequacy and his disloyalty to Madison. He proved so apologetic that Madison was finally forced to order him to deal with the envoy only by letter, with Madison ghostwriting all correspondence for his signature. At first, the rough Jackson was puzzled because the complexities and arguments in Smith's letters did not match his oral stupidity. But he soon found himself overwhelmed in attempting to refute the American points against the British violations of neutral rights on the high seas. Finally, in violent anger he exploded, called Madison a liar and accused him of bad faith in dealing with Erskine. This closed the door on his short stay in Washington, for Madison wrote him via Smith: "It only remains to inform you that no further communications will be received from you."

Only a few short months before, when Congress had met in its brief session, members had acclaimed Madison for his diplomatic brilliance. Now, in November 1809, when the Eleventh Congress's second session met, the atmosphere changed. A few members demanded war with England, but most seemed lost and looked for Presidential guidance on a third route between physical combat and appeasement.

Yet in his Message to Congress, Madison revealed that they could not rely on him for Executive leadership. After summarizing the problems facing the nation, he announced he was leaving the solution of those problems to "the wisdom of the national legislature." As a result, all through December, Congress floundered, wasting day after day debating a resolution offered by Senator

Giles denouncing "Copenhagen" Jackson. Finally in January 1810, when Congress wearily agreed with Giles that Jackson's conduct had been "indecorous, insolent, affronting, insidious, false, outrageous and premeditated," Madison sent over a vague semblance of a defense program. He thought it might be worthwhile if Congress permitted as many as 20,000 Americans to volunteer for the Army. As for the Navy, he proposed that Congress consider "how far further provision may be expedient for putting into actual service, if necessary, any part of the Naval armament not now employed."

This language especially outraged Senator William Crawford, the tall Georgian who wanted to use his growing Senate prestige in Madison's behalf and for his own future. Crawford had fully expected Madison to show the same strength he possessed as Secretary of State and gird the country unequivocally for climactic action if necessary. "This Message, in point of obscurity," thundered Crawford, "comes nearer my idea of a Delphic Oracle than any state paper which has come under my inspection. It is for war, it is for peace. It is so cautiously expressed that every man can put what construction on it he pleases."

But if Madison vaguely called for a stronger defense posture, his position was being undermined with his own approval by Secretary of the Treasury Gallatin. In his financial report to Congress, which Madison agreed should be sent, Gallatin informed the legislature that the Government was racing toward a dangerous financial crisis. He blamed the sharp drop in import duty revenues on the ravaging effects of the Embargo and Non-Intercourse acts. But rather than ask Congress to install excise taxes on domestic products and services and thus raise the necessary revenue, Gallatin went far afield and proposed a 50 per cent cut in military spending, or an annual slash in appropriations of $3,000,000.

Congressional confusion followed the receipt of the shadowy pro-defense Madison proposal and the anti-defense and budget-cutting Gallatin program. The result was that nothing was done either to strengthen the military establishment or to improve the Treasury's weakened condition. In the Senate, Sam Smith and William Giles pushed through legislation to fit out the frigates retired by Jefferson to various Navy yards. Their action was quickly perceived by Gallatin as a step toward national bankruptcy and designed to force him from the Cabinet. For their bill did not provide permission for the frigates to proceed to sea once readied for duty but contained them in the Navy yards to rot once again. His view that they were not motivated by defense considerations was borne out when they pigeonholed in a Senate committee a bill to increase the Army.

In his desperate search for revenue, Gallatin prevailed upon his friend, former Speaker Nathaniel Macon, to introduce a bill for him. This became known as Macon No. 1, which proposed to continue to bar British and French ships from American ports but to permit their goods to enter the United States if carried on American ships. Since import duties from these two countries—and especially from England—provided the bulk of American revenue, Gallatin considered this a major legislative action. But after the House passed Macon No. 1, Smith cut out the heart of the bill by an amendment. When the House in turn rejected the bill with the Smith Amendment and returned the original to the Senate, Smith successfully killed it.

After this, the Eleventh Congress proceeded like a carriage without brakes on a winding downgrade. While Giles and Smith were scheming against Gallatin, young Senator Henry Clay from Kentucky sneered at Madison and said that America needed "a new race of heroes" to carry on the "deeds of glory and renown" of the "illustrious founders of our freedom." Meanwhile, in the House, John Randolph was denouncing Giles and Smith and calling for sharp cuts in the already almost non-existent military forces. When he won two to one approval for his resolution to reduce the Army and Navy, he then undertook at the House's request the job of making his resolution specific. His resulting substantive bills ordered all of Jefferson's gunboats sold, all but three Navy yards dismantled, and the Navy cut to three frigates, the Army to three regiments and the Marines to two companies. Fortunately for Madison who was concerned but would not interfere, the Randolph military cyclone failed to pass the House.

In April 1810, Congress prepared to adjourn its chaotic and unproductive session. At this point, Representative John Taylor of South Carolina induced Macon to introduce Macon No. 2, even though Macon personally opposed the bill and would later vote against it. Macon No. 2 cast aside entirely the "peaceable coercion" doctrine of Jefferson by reopening trade with the entire world. On the surface, this appeared to be a reaffirmation on the part of a neutral nation that it had rights it expected belligerent nations to respect. However, Macon No. 2 was not actually so forthright, for one clause was specifically designed to play off the two belligerents against each other. This was the qualification that if either Britain or France repealed its Orders or Decrees against neutral shipping, the President was then authorized to install non-intercourse with the other. The tired Congress found Macon No. 2 to its liking, although Senators Smith and Giles managed to eliminate a Gallatin provision for a 50 per cent increase in duties on British and French goods.

Madison, who had abstained entirely from the legislative pits, came to life once Congress left town. This was to be his pattern throughout his two terms.

During that summer of 1810, John Armstrong, American minister to France, sent him word on Napoleon's reaction to Macon No. 2. "The Decrees of Berlin and Milan are revoked," the Duc de Cadore, Napoleon's Minister of Foreign Affairs, wrote Armstrong, "and after November 1 they shall cease to have effect. It being understood that in consequence of this declaration the English are to revoke their Orders in Council; or that the United States, conformably to the Act you have just communicated [Macon No. 2], cause their rights to be respected by the English."

Madison did not consider Napoleon's solemn oath to revoke his trade Decrees against neutral commerce to be trustworthy in the slightest degree. In fact, he soon was made aware that the wily French Emperor sent no orders to his subordinates to quit molesting and seizing American ships and property. Nevertheless, Madison decided to pretend publicly that the French Decrees had ended because this gave him leverage to force Britain to rescind her Orders in Council or face the loss of a third of her total exports. He had reason to believe that Britain would revoke her Orders because of the growing critical condition of her economy. The English laboring class was being impoverished by the price of wheat which was already at famine levels, a rapid increase in population which depressed wage rates, and the industrial revolution following the discoveries of Watt and Arkwright which ended the handicraft system and introduced machines. All over England machine-wrecking riots were beginning to break out as the poor-rate jumped 50 per cent.

Accordingly, on November 2, 1810, Madison proclaimed: "It has been officially made known to this government that the said edicts of France have been so revoked as that they ceased, on the first day of the present month, to violate the neutral commerce of the United States." Then, as provided for in Macon No. 2, he also announced that Non-Intercourse would be reinstated against Britain on February 2, 1811, unless she revoked her Orders in Council in the interim.

While Congress was away, Madison also attended to a daring Florida venture. In 1808, Napoleon forced King Ferdinand VII to resign the Spanish throne and installed his brother, Joseph Bonaparte, in his place. Madison was President only a month when Jefferson wrote him: "I suppose the conquest of Spain will soon force a delicate question on you as to the Floridas and Cuba, which will offer themselves to you. Napoleon will certainly give his consent without difficulty to our receiving the Floridas, and with some difficulty possibly Cuba."

What was happening was that from the Rio de la Plata to the Rio Grande, Spanish colonies in Latin America had risen in revolt against the new regime and established revolutionary juntas. Madison decided to help this revolutionary spirit along in West Florida Spanish Province, a narrow run of coastal land from the Mississippi River eastward to the Perdido, which kept Americans from the Gulf of Mexico. Here along the numerous bays that filled with onrushing water from the large rivers to the north lived 100,000 persons, most of whom were Americans who chafed under foreign rule.

Governor Claiborne of New Orleans and Governor Holmes of Mississippi received secret orders from Madison to prepare an insurrection in West Florida. By the summer of 1810 their work was so well done that the "Movement for Self Government" broke into the open. However, to allay the suspicions of the Spanish Commandant De Lassus, the resident American leaders assured him they loved Ferdinand VII and wanted only to correct local abuses. The Baton Rouge convention of the Madison-inspired insurrection farcically announced on July 25 that it was "legally constituted to act in all cases of national concern with the consent of the governor to promote the happiness of our beloved king."

Orders were passed out to watch De Lassus' every move in order to find justification for the next step. Americans carefully read all his mail, and finally in mid-September they found his "act of perfidy" in an intercepted letter to the Spanish governor. This was his request for troops, and it became the excuse for the convention to seize the fort at Baton Rouge and declare West Florida's independence. Then when the convention sent him a petition, drawn up long beforehand, asking that their area be made part of the United States, Madison on October 27 issued a proclamation incorporating West Florida into the Orleans Territory.

There was still East Florida to consider. This Spanish province stretched from the Pensacola section on the Gulf of Mexico, around the peninsula and up the Atlantic to the St. Marys River along the border of Georgia. In a secret message to the third session of the Eleventh Congress on January 3, 1811, Madison asked for authorization to seize possession of East Florida if the local Spanish authorities asked him to do so or if a foreign power (England) tried to occupy it. This secret message was a vital turning point in Presidential direction of foreign policy for it formed the basis of the future Monroe Doctrine. In it Madison recommended a declaration "that the United States could not see without serious disquietude any part of a neighboring territory [like East Florida], in which they have in different respects so deep and so just a concern, pass from the hands of Spain into those of any other foreign power."

Congress quickly consented, and Madison dispatched General George Mathews, a former governor of Georgia, and Colonel John McKee to inspire a revolution in East Florida on the order of West Florida. This bizarre episode was to be executed in a land populated by smugglers, pirates and cutthroats.

In the fall of 1810, the people of the United States had taken revenge on Congress in the elections for members of the House of Representatives. Great dissatisfaction with the Eleventh Congress existed for not settling the crisis involving the neutral rights of the United States with the continuing struggle between His Majesty's Government and Napoleon. As a result, almost half the members of the House failed to win re-election; yet the irony of the situation was that the newly elected members would not meet until a year later when the Twelfth Congress convened on November 4, 1811.

In the meantime, the same wrecking crew of the House and Senate would be in command to thwart adequate defense and combat Gallatin. John Randolph chose to show his contempt for fellow legislators by coming to the House, bringing "two pointers with him, which set up a barking when members rose to speak.

No one dared turned the dogs out," said one disgusted observer. One day when Representative Willis Alston of North Carolina was shoved and mauled by the dogs, he struck at them and suffered a sword-cane beating from their master. Speaker Joseph Varnum decided afterward not to take action against Randolph who was quick to challenge others to duels.

While Randolph was creating turmoil in the House, Giles and Smith continued at their old stand in the Senate. The most crucial piece of legislation to be considered that session in the Upper Chamber was the renewal of the charter of the Bank of the United States. The twenty-year charter of the Bank was to expire on March 4, 1811, and Madison considered it essential that the Bank continue. This private financial institution, part of whose stock was owned by the Government, served as the Government's fiscal agent by safekeeping public money, collecting taxes, lending money to the Government and issuing paper money backed by adequate gold and silver reserves. To end the Bank meant that the Treasury would be at the mercy of small bankers for loans, the currency would depreciate and a horde of new and untrained employees would have to be hired to collect revenues and distribute Government monies in the various sections of the country.

Madison had been the original promoter of the doctrine of implied powers, giving Congress authority to pass all laws which were necessary and proper to carry the enumerated powers into effect. Yet in 1791, when Hamilton promoted the Bank's charter, Madison called it unconstitutional, arguing that there were no implied powers. Because the Bank was not listed among the enumerated powers, he insisted, it could not legally exist. Over the years, he watched the Bank in operation and by 1811 he realized that its continuation was vital. Nevertheless, he believed his earlier position made it impossible for him to declare himself publicly for the Bank.

So he left the task to Gallatin, the Bank's ardent supporter. But Gallatin no longer held sway over the Senate as he had during Jefferson's day, and he turned the job over to his friend, Senator William Crawford. With Madison and Gallatin on the sidelines, Giles and Smith immediately jumped into the fray to inflict another stinging defeat on the Administration. With delighted sarcasm, Smith told his colleagues that Madison's arguments against the Bank in 1791 "add another wreath to his fame." Giles, who was weak on economics and constitutional matters, gave a long, rambling speech that led one of his own supporters to annouce that he "discussed both sides of the question with great ability . . . that it was constitutional and unconstitutional, highly proper and improper." When the vote came after weeks of debate, the result was a 17 to 17 tie. This gave Vice-President George Clinton the opportunity to decide the fate of the Bank: filled with hatred for Madison and Gallatin, he voted for its end.

On March 3, 1811, the Eleventh Congress died and carriages carrying Congressmen oozed out of town through the sticky yellow mud. Once again Madison came alive. Discouraged by the defeat of the Bank bill, Gallatin sent him the following note: "I clearly perceive that my continuing a member of the present Administration is no longer of any public utility, invigorates the opposition against yourself, and must necessarily be attended with an increased loss of reputation by myself. Under these impressions . . . I beg leave to tender you my resignation."

Madison had no intention of letting Gallatin go and he refused to accept his resignation. While he brooded about his weak political situation, Secretary of State Robert Smith came to see him on departmental business. Unaware of the Gallatin letter and Madison's mood, Smith began their talk by casually mentioning a newspaper story of that day which told about John Adams' dismissal of his Secretary of State, Timothy Pickering, in 1801.

A gleam suddenly appeared in Madison's eyes. He stared at Smith and remarked (according to his own later account): "That in coming over, Smith had anticipated my intention of sending for him . . . for a frank talk on a delicate and disagreeable topic." Madison then told him he was fired and recited charge after charge that the Secretary attempted to refute in a loud and angry voice. Madison told him he was incompetent, lazy and that "whatever talents he might possess, he did not, as he must have found by experience, possess those adapted to his station." Furthermore, he said, Smith was disloyal to the Administration, spoke to outsiders against the President and Cabinet members, conveyed confidential Cabinet matters and diplomatic correspondence to those who had no business knowing about them, and worked against the President's foreign policy.

Smith charged that he had been subject to hostility and plots by members of the Administration "to which he himself would never deign to stoop." Madison heard him out and at the close offered him a face-saving avenue of departure with the suggestion that he could go to St. Petersburg as American minister. "London more so," Smith countered.

Madison: "No! For London is a place calling for talent in negotiations."

Smith: "I would accept the coming seat on the Supreme Court likely to be produced ere long by the death in Baltimore of Justice Chase."

Madison: "The Senate might be hard to please." Smith said he stood well there, to which Madison added, "You don't know how greatly you have lost ground there." For the sake of mutual friends, Madison continued, he was willing to ease Smith out gently.

"May I say that the Russian appointment is offered to me?"

"I have no objection."

When Smith did nothing, Madison sent for him a few days later. Smith willingly handed over his Cabinet commission but rejected the diplomatic post. He gave as his reason the advice of friends not to supply Madison with a cover for his removal. Another major argument now took place and Smith left with cold formality.

Madison knew that the full fury of the Smith family would now be turned loose against him. Shortly before he fired Robert Smith, Senator Sam Smith had let him know that he expected to be appointed minister to France. This would have been an opportunity to get rid of the Senator, but Madison was no longer in a mood to appease him. When he appointed the poet Joel Barlow instead, said an eyewitness, "Our General Smith raved like a madman about it." The Baltimore newspaper organ of the Smiths noted shortly after Madison's slap at both brothers: "The opinion is gaining ground rapidly that it is in the power of Robert Smith to disclose further high crimes and misdemeanors committed by Mr. Madison, throwing far into the shade the crimes of Charles II of England." But the revenge for the Smith brothers would have to wait two years, until 1813. Meanwhile, Barlow accompanied Napoleon on his invasion of Russia in 1812 and died of exposure and illness on the retreat from Moscow.

Madison also took strong action in another field while Congress was away. Non-intercourse had gone into effect again against Britain in February 1811, despite Madison's hope that the British would react favorably to the escape clause in Macon No. 2. But

Prime Minister Spencer Perceval, whose hatred of the United States exceeded his desire to improve the British economy, would not offer even a false revocation of the Orders in Council as Napoleon had with his Decrees. Instead, Perceval sent Augustus Foster to Washington to succeed "Copenhagen" Jackson and to threaten further British reprisals unless Madison dropped non-intercourse. As emphasis for this policy, British frigates blocked New York harbor, boarded all incoming and outgoing vessels and impressed American sailors at an increasing rate.

Madison realized he lacked a proper Navy to clear the British from New York harbor or any other zone. Nevertheless, he gave Commodore John Rodgers, in command of the *President,* permission to patrol the coast as he saw fit. On May 16, 1811, Rodgers sighted what he thought was a large British frigate fifty miles off Cape Henry. He gave chase, shelled the vessel and claimed a major victory, even though his adversary, *Little Belt,* turned out to be far smaller than the *President.* News of Rodgers' victory swept the nation and momentarily raised the spirit of long downtrodden Americans. Chests swelled when word came that British newspapers had called the United States a bully.

The firing of Robert Smith had left a vacancy in the State Department. Jefferson had been busy trying to effect a reconciliation between Madison and Monroe, and now Madison offered the top Cabinet post to his former nettlesome rival. Not content with accepting a position he had failed to earn through friendship and previous aid, Monroe laid down conditions. In his opinion, Madison's foreign policy was entirely pro-French and anti-British. He would take the position, he said, if Madison permitted him "to make an accommodation with England, the great maritime power, even on modest terms, rather than hazard war." Madison, who was striving toward this same goal, assured him he would be delighted, and Monroe accepted.

The appointment of Monroe was to add to the Congressional animosity toward Madison. On learning of it, John Randolph, Monroe's Presidential sponsor, took time out from his public pose as a man "devoted to sick and retarded nephews" to scribble in his diary: "Monroe, Traitor . . . Judas." Later he cursed Monroe and Madison with the bitter comment of "Glamis and Cawdor." Senator Giles in a letter to Robert Smith denounced Madison for having made "the wickedest of all his contrivances" and called him the "dupe of the most wretched intrigues."

The promotion of Monroe for the Cabinet post was only one of Jefferson's many attempts to play an important role in his successor's Administration. However, Madison did not permit Jefferson to make his decisions for him. When a vacancy occurred on the Supreme Court in 1811, Madison nominated Joseph Story over Jefferson's angry protestations that Story had forced an end to his embargo scheme in 1809. Later when Story became Chief Justice John Marshall's close ally, Jefferson believed himself vindicated in his view that Story was a Federalist in disguise. The gossip in Washington was that Marshall, whose academic training was nil, would say, "That, Story, is the law. Now you find the precedents."

An explosion occurred in Washington with the arrival, finally, of the Twelfth Congress in November 1811. Seventy new members took their seats in the House along with eighty-five returning members and helped elect thirty-four-year-old, former U. S. Senator Henry Clay, who was also a House newcomer, as Speaker. The air smelled of war, for Clay and his Congressional followers were promising this, even though few of the new members had campaigned on this issue. They were the young War Hawks, eager to battle Britain and confident of success at that enterprise.

Clay had made a study of Jefferson's selection of floor leaders and committee chairmen and his direction of the party caucus. With such machinery Jefferson had been able to master Congress from his office in the Executive Mansion. Clay now determined to fill the gap left by Madison's lack of leadership, adopt Jefferson's tools as his own and thus gain control over the President.

The first step toward this end was to gain symbolic control over all House members. This meant stifling John Randolph, something that no one previously had been able to accomplish. Their encounter came early when the long, cadaverous Virginian strode onto the House floor with a barking dog. Clay glanced once at the smirking Randolph and immediately ordered the doorkeeper to remove the beast. The House watched to see Randolph's reaction. But he was silent as his pet was dragged away. Never again did he bring any of his dogs to the House. Much later he said about Clay: "He is a man of splendid abilities, but utterly corrupt. Like rotten mackerel by moonlight, he shines and stinks."

Clay soon called his first secret caucus and his rash group of War Hawks agreed to abandon any effort to conciliate England. So far as they were concerned they made foreign policy, not the President. Madison seemed to be on their side when he sent the House a Message on November 5, 1811, listing the various British and French violations of neutral rights, and commenting: "Congress will feel the duty of putting the United States into an armor and an attitude demanded by the crisis and corresponding with the national spirit and expectations." Clay noted with approval that while Madison had criticized both belligerents, he had emphasized British crimes. This is what the leader of the West wanted to believe, for the frontier, where the loudest calls for war emanated, wanted military action both from a concern that the British were instigating Indian depredations and from a desire to take over British land.

With what appeared to be Presidential concurrence in his own foreign policy, Clay now set out to implement his stand. As the boss of the House, he decided on all committee assignments, putting his most energetic and devoted War Hawk followers into key slots. For his chairman of the House Foreign Affairs Committee, he selected thirty-eight-year-old Peter B. Porter of New York. Porter, a Yale man, represented the Niagara frontier and had earlier supported the Burr conspiracy. Other nationalist supporters named to Porter's committee were thirty-four-year-old Felix Grundy, former Tennessee judge, and twenty-nine-year-old John C. Calhoun of South Carolina, whose long black hair fell back in a defiant pompadour and whose piercing eyes that changed color according to his emotions were already set in sunken sockets. Young David R. Williams, also from South Carolina and an arrogant showoff, headed the Committee on Military Affairs with twenty-nine-year-old Richard M. Johnson of Kentucky, a fancier of mulatto slave mistresses, and a future Vice-President, named to assist him. Clay chose a third South Carolinian, Langdon Cheves, an obese man with remarkable oratorical abilities, to run the Naval Affairs Committee. Cheves also found a seat on the Ways and Means Committee, from which Clay callously excluded all Federalists.

While Madison made no overt move to hold on to Presidential control over foreign policy, Porter's committee began hearings. As Secretary of State, James Monroe had pledged himself to seek an accommodation with the British. This should have brought a protest from him that Porter was interfering with the function of the State Department. But Monroe's initial talk with British minister Foster had made him forget his vow. Instead of suggesting a compromise to ease the situation between both nations, Foster demanded that non-intercourse be reinstated with France and asserted that unless Madison announced the falsity of Napoleon's claims to have revoked his Milan and Berlin Decrees, the British would begin further measures of retaliation for the Non-Importation Act. Monroe was so discouraged by his talk with Foster that he went to the other extreme. He was soon a conspicuous diner at the "War Mess," as the boardinghouse where leading War Hawks lived was called. At one of their final sessions, said Foster, he and Monroe "endeavored to frighten one another for a whole hour by descanting on the consequences of war."

On November 29, 1811, the Porter Committee made its report, and, as expected, England was thoroughly condemned and France slapped. But the report went further than a probe of the foreign situation. Porter also called for strong war measures, including the addition of ten regiments for the Army, authority to Madison to call for fifty thousand volunteers, expansion of the Navy to war power and the arming of merchant ships. There were loud rumors that Monroe had written the Porter Report.

No word came from the Palace to caution Clay against extremist talk in the floor discussion to follow on the Porter Report that might harm continuing diplomatic activities of the Executive Branch. Instead, bombastic talk became the order of the day and it soon was apparent that the War Hawks were not so much concerned with British high sea misactivities as they were with territorial aggrandizement for the United States. As Felix Grundy stated the War Hawk case: "This war, if carried on successfully, will have its advantages. We shall drive the British from our continent. . . . I am willing to receive the Canadians as adopted brethren. . . . It will preserve the equilibrium of the government. When Louisiana shall be fully peopled, the northern states will lose their power and be at the discretion of others; they can be depressed at pleasure, and then the Union might be endangered. I, therefore, feel anxious not only to add the Floridas to the south, but the Canadians to the north of this Empire."

This cry for Canada and Florida—especially for Canada, which western farmers coveted—grew into such a mammoth roar that the original problem with Britain seemed forgotten. John Randolph, who opposed war, shouted: "Agrarian cupidity, not maritime right, urges the war. Ever since the report of the Committee on Foreign

Affairs, we have heard but one word—like the whippoorwill, but one eternal monotonous tone—Canada, Canada, Canada!" Should war come, he predicted, it would not be "a war for our homes and fire-sides, but a war of rapine, of privateering, a scuffle and scramble for plunder."

Many of those who had misgivings about war now swung over into the ranks of the War Hawks with the news from Tippecanoe in the west central Indiana Territory. Jefferson had inaugurated a selfish land program in that area when he wrote to Governor William Henry Harrison in 1803: "To promote this disposition [on the part of the Indians] to exchange lands which they have to spare and we want, . . . we shall push our trading houses, and be glad to see the good and influential individuals among them in debt; because we observe that when these debts get beyond what the individuals can pay, they become willing to lop them off by a cession of land."

Harrison had followed this policy into Madison's time. But this was too slow for his greedy desires, and on September 30, 1809, he signed the Treaty of Fort Wayne with five tribes he called "the most depraved wretches upon earth." The treaty, by which Indian title to 3,000,000 acres in the Wabash Valley was extinguished, was illegal because the signing tribes did not own the land.

In November 1810, Madison, who had been a political associate in Virginia of Benjamin Harrison, William Henry Harrison's father, ordered the governor not to occupy the treaty lands. The great Indian chief Tecumseh and his brother, The Prophet, were disputing the treaty and further negotiations were in order. In the summer of 1811, Tecumseh left for the South to promote the union of all tribes from Canada to Florida. He planned afterward to go to Washington for a conference, unaware that since childhood Madison held a strong bias against all Indians. Harrison lost little time after Tecumseh's departure to crush his tribe in his absence. With 1000 men he struck across the Shawnee hunting grounds and paused near The Prophet's town. Indian envoys came to talk peace, but Harrison would not listen. Through fear of an imminent attack by Harrison, the Indians took the offensive and attacked him at Tippecanoe Creek on November 7, and in the battle that followed Indian casualties were so high that Tecumseh's confederation was permanently broken. Harrison's casualties, which numbered 188 Americans, became a rallying point of the War Hawks to show that the British were promoting Indian trouble.

While Madison maintained a steady silence during the Congressional tempest, Clay set to work to bring about "the new United States," as he called it. To implement the Porter Committee Report recommendations, he and David Williams pushed through the House bill after bill to strengthen the Army—adding six thousand men to old regiments, creating new regiments with ten thousand men and authorizing Madison to acquire fifty thousand temporary volunteers. Chairman Langdon Cheves of the Naval Affairs Committee now offered a bill to appropriate $7,500,000 for twelve frigates each carrying seventy-four guns and for twenty other armed ships. However, Clay could not overcome the great Republican fear of a large Navy and the bill went down to defeat 56 to 52. This meant that if war should come the United States would have to do battle with only sixteen old frigates and armed brigs plus the 165 laughable Jefferson gunboats. These would hardly constitute a match for Britain's mighty armada of about a thousand ships. For that matter, when Gallatin nagged Congress for a new tax program to meet the expected $50,000,000 war costs, Congress brushed him off by giving him authority to borrow $11,000,000, even though the government's credit was poor. As a result, the War Hawks revealed a strange turn of mind: they wanted war but they did not want to prepare for it or pay the costs.

In the midst of all this threshing about, the country was getting ready for another Presidential contest. Ordinarily, the Republican party chose its candidates in the first months of an election year, but the winter of 1812 passed without action. When he took over Jefferson's political machinery, Clay also fell heir to commanding the selection in caucus of the Republican candidate. The Speaker was now the party's kingmaker, and he was in no hurry to call the caucus.

Many historians have assumed that because Madison wanted a second term and because he recognized Clay's power, he agreed to do his bidding in order to remain in residence at the Palace. The basis of this story goes back to Representative James Fisk, a Vermont Republican House member of the Twelfth Congress. Fisk said at the time that a Congressional committee called on the President, and told him that Clay had decided upon war and that if he did not recommend a declaration of war he would not get the Republican nomination. Representative Josiah Quincy later repeated this story in the House and was not challenged. What makes this story unlikely is that Madison was not the sort to prostitute himself for the sake of personal ambition. Yet doubt remained because neither Madison nor Clay denied the Fisk-Quincy statements.

As though to emphasize that Madison was opposed to the position of the War Hawks until election fever got the better of him, one Republican Congressman declared at the time that "he could not be kicked into a fight." The truth disproves this. Madison had hoped that the British would come to their senses before it was too late. But by late 1811, he doubted that they would. Shortly after the Porter Committee Report appeared, Dolley wrote to one of her sisters, "I believe there will be war. Mr. Madison sees no end to the perplexities without it." Yet unlike Clay who was born in 1777, Madison had lived through the Revolutionary War, understood its horror and wanted to keep the door open, even if only slightly ajar, for British concessions.

Monroe, who was now among the worst of the fire-eaters, began to exert anxious pressure on Madison to slam the door on Britain. A French adventurer who called himself the Count de Crillon, but was actually an agent of Napoleon's secret police named Soubiron, offered to sell to Monroe for $50,000 the secret papers of one John Henry, an alleged spy for the Governor General of Canada. Crillon claimed that Henry had been a go-between with disgruntled New England Federalists. Madison, who had read for pleasure the Comte de Buffon's forty-four volumes on European animal species, took Monroe's word that the papers were authentic without even a glance at them and agreed to pay the $50,000. Then on March 9, 1812, he sent the Henry papers to Congress with the comment that they proved Federalists had planned "forming the eastern part" of the United States "into a political connection with Great Britain."

A Congressional examination of the Henry papers found no evidence of this plot. When a Senate resolution requested Madison to supply names of the plotters, he was forced to admit that someone had erased all the names in the papers. But the War Hawks wanted war with England and not a fight with Madison. So instead of condemning him for wasting money on a fraud, they called Henry's "evidence" the crowning British insult to date.

Madison was drifting rapidly into the war-call area when an event occurred that drove the War Hawks frantic. A French squadron had accosted two American ships in the Atlantic and destroyed both. Monroe harshly told the French minister, "You know what warlike measures have been taken for three months past. . . . It is at such a moment that your frigates come and burn our ships, destroy our work and put the Administration in the falsest and most terrible position in which a government can find itself."

On March 15, Clay grew bold and sent a note to Madison requesting him to "recommend an embargo to last say thirty days, by a confidential message. That a termination of the embargo be followed by war." Madison pointed out that England had a new Foreign Secretary, Lord Castlereagh, and that the U.S.S. *Hornet* was expected to arrive soon with a statement of Castlereagh's policy. The *Hornet* had been sent to Europe in December with copies of the Porter Report of the House Foreign Affairs Committee. Clay still urged the embargo and added, "The *Hornet* will have returned with good or bad news and of course the question of war may then be fairly decided."

On April 1, Madison sent Congress a secret Message, asking the two houses to consider a sixty-day embargo on foreign trade. The purpose was to give American ships at sea time to return home safely before the possible war. When Congress passed a ninety-day embargo, British minister Foster requested Madison to tell him if this were a war measure. "Oh, no, embargo is not war," Madison replied. "But the United States would be amply justified in going to war with Great Britain, for Great Britain is actually waging war upon us." For proof, he cited the recent British capture of eighteen American ships.

On May 13, according to Joseph Gale, an editor of the semi-official Republican newspaper, the *National Intelligencer,* the War Hawks met with Madison. Gale reported that Clay asked him his position on a war with England and Madison replied that he hesitated to ask openly for a war declaration only because he did not believe the House would sustain him. Clay quickly asserted there was a "readiness of a majority of Congress to vote the war if recommended."

On the evening of May 18, Clay finally held the Congressional nominating caucus. Of the 135 Republicans in Congress, about 60 per cent came to the Senate chamber for the voting. The unanimity of those present was revealed by the caucus tally—"For James Madison, 82, no other person being voted for." Vice-President George Clinton had died on April 21, and the caucus chose former Senator John Langdon of New Hampshire as Madison's running mate. But Langdon declined because of his age and a later caucus chose Elbridge Gerry, of "gerrymandering" and "XYZ" notoriety. When Gerry died in 1814, Madison gained the distinction of being the only President to have two Vice-Presidents die in office.

The day after Madison won renomination the *Hornet* arrived with bad news from England. Instead of dropping the Orders in Council, Lord Castlereagh's dispatch of April 10 declared that since Napoleon had not actually withdrawn his Decrees the British intended to maintain her Orders.

To Madison, all rays of hope were now completely beclouded. On June 1 he sent Congress his War Message, justifying action for five reasons. First, there was the impressment of 6000 Americans into the British Navy—"Thousands of American citizens have been torn from their country . . . dragged on board ships of war of a foreign nation . . . to be exiled to the most distant and deadly climes, to risk their lives in the battles of their oppressors." He also condemned British ships that "hover over and harass our entering and departing commerce"; British paper or "pretended blockades" under which "our commerce has been plundered in every sea"; British efforts to destroy American vessels in order to gain her own monopoly; and British schemers for "the warfare just renewed by the savages on one of our extensive frontiers." Whether this recitation merited a declaration of war, he said, "is a solemn question which the Constitution wisely confides to the Legislative Branch."

Two days later Calhoun, who had been elevated by Clay to chairman of the Foreign Affairs Committee, introduced a war resolution. "What! Go to war when you have not the courage to lay taxes!" shouted John Randolph. "To go to war without money, without men, without a Navy!" "So far from being unprepared, sir," said Calhoun, "I believe that in four weeks from the time that a declaration of war is heard on our frontiers, the whole of Upper and a part of Lower Canada will be in our hands."

Speaker Clay sent word down the line for quick action, and on June 4 the House voted for war, 79 to 49. The Senate was much more evenly divided, and the vote did not come until two weeks later when the totals on June 17 showed 19 for war and 13 opposed. On signing the resolution the following day Madison made the war official. Unknown to him at the time, Prime Minister Perceval had been assassinated by a maniac on May 11, 1812. Lord Liverpool, who replaced Perceval, favored a more moderate American policy in order to separate the United States from

France. Accordingly, on June 16, he had Castlereagh tell Commons that the Orders in Council were to be suspended on the next day. So the chief cause of the war was removed before Madison signed the declaration. Later he remarked ruefully that had he known of the suspension there would have been no war. But communications could not keep pace with events.

With the coming of the War of 1812, an American President was confronted for the first time with the meaning of the undefined provision of the Constitution making him Commander-in-Chief of the Army and Navy. Madison began by taking his power literally, and, on June 19, the day after the war started, a friend noted that he visited "in person—a thing never known before—all the offices of the departments of War and Navy, stimulating everything in a manner worthy of a little commander-in-chief, with his little round hat and huge cockade."

Madison also attempted to dominate fighting strategy at first by personal selection of top military leaders. The Navy did not present a complex personnel problem for him because there were so few ships. But those naval commanders he did name proved in general to be both brave and mean. Commodore David Porter later characterized the war's typical naval officer as "the little tyrant who struts his few fathoms of scoured plank." In naming his Army generals, Madison blundered woefully. He had his choice of taking older men with some Revolutionary War experience or daring, young men without battlefield grounding. He took the old crew and thus deprived the country of a healthy and enthusiastic command. Only a single man among his eight generals was actually a professional soldier, and he was the same James Wilkinson who was a secret Spanish agent and former Burr conspirator. A few years before the war, Wilkinson had been ordered to Natchez, where he was to fix his camp on high ground. He chose the river delta swamp instead and his army of northern recruits died almost as a unit from disease. Madison had then ordered a court of inquiry, which tried him at Frederick, Maryland, on eight charges, including the Burr charge, his Spanish pension and neglect of duty. After reading the court's records for a month, Madison found the evidence inconclusive and returned Wilkinson's sword to him.

Almost as soon as he signed his name to the war declaration, Madison realized that the war was not popular except in the West and in some parts of the South. The War Hawks were scream-

ing, "Free trade and sailors' rights," but young men did not flock
to the colors and the Army expansion legislated by Congress remained a paper deal. Nor did Gallatin's public appeal for an
$11,000,000 loan to the Government result in more than a feeble
response. Further on the debit side, shortly after formal war began
thirty Federalist Congressmen flooded the country with an anti-
war pamphlet called "An Address of the Minority to Their Constituents." Then there were stings from Randolph's "Quids." But
also formidable were the activities of DeWitt Clinton, who had
inherited his late uncle's New York political machine and was
challenging Madison for the Presidency just as George Clinton
had four years earlier. With the guidance of a young, shrewd campaign manager named Martin Van Buren, DeWitt Clinton was
running on a peace platform designed to entice Federalist votes.

It was the Federalists who threw a major roadblock into Madison's
concept of Commander-in-Chief. With a Regular Army of only
6700 men scattered throughout the country, and a long coastline
to safeguard, Madison issued a call to New England governors to
put quotas of their militias under national command outside their
states. However, the governors of Connecticut and Massachusetts
refused to comply. When told that the Constitution warranted the
President to call up the state militias to repel invasions, Governor
Caleb Strong of Massachusetts said that it was his own responsibility to judge when this exigency existed. The mere threat of an invasion, he argued, was not an actual invasion. He also insisted
that the President lacked authority to place militiamen under officers of the Regular Army.

Because no semblance of national unity existed, Madison started
the war with secret diplomatic efforts to end it. With an ill-
disguised bluff, he ordered Jonathan Russell, the American chargé
d'affaires who oddly continued living in London as though no war
existed, to warn the Liverpool Ministry that if it did not agree
to an early armistice, he would find it "difficult to relinquish
territory which had been conquered." For a year it had been
known that Napoleon planned to lead his Grand Army to
Moscow because Alexander I refused to suspend all trade with
England. Madison had no way of knowing that Napoleon's army
had finally crossed the Niemen into Poland only five days after
the Anglo-American War started. But he had been counting on its
occurrence and hoped to use that threat to bring on an armistice.

Years later he said: "Had the French Emperor not been broken down, as he was, to a degree in variance with all probability, and which no human sagacity could anticipate, can it be doubted that Great Britain would have been constrained by her own situation and the demands of her allies, to listen to our reasonable terms of conciliation?"

Madison realized that an American military victory, small or large, might hasten the British to agree to an armistice and honorable terms. All signs pointed to a land, rather than a sea, engagement and an effort directed toward Canada, as the most auspicious place for this victory. Here Madison now turned for his trump card.

To the north, the thousand-mile water border along the Great Lakes and up the St. Lawrence into the Atlantic found a defense force of only 7000 British regulars. Nevertheless, British frigates controlled the waters and thus restricted a possible invasion chiefly to Detroit at the western end of Lake Erie, Niagara Falls at the eastern end, and the Plattsburg line toward vital Montreal on the St. Lawrence. Lower Canada, or Quebec Province in the east, had 5000 British regulars; while Upper Canada, or Ontario Province to the west, had only 2000 regulars and 600 Canadian militiamen standing guard all the way from Detroit to Montreal.

Madison decided that Brigadier General William Hull, the palsied governor of the Michigan Territory, would strike south from Detroit, take Canadian Fort Malden eighteen miles below and then crash eastward to seize Upper Canada. At the same time Hull attacked along the Detroit River, the senior American commander, Major General Henry Dearborn, a Revolutionary War hero, Congressman and Jefferson's Secretary of War, was to strike at Niagara and divert British strength from Hull.

At the end of August 1812, in a mood of optimism Madison began the 110-mile carriage ride from Washington to Montpelier near the Blue Ridge Mountains. Suddenly a military messenger halted his carriage and delivered devastating news. Hull had gone toward Fort Malden and then had returned to Detroit. Here British General Isaac Brock, in command of only 700 regulars, had demanded that Hull and his 2500 men surrender. Hull had done exactly this. "No one anticipated the surrender until he saw the white flag displayed," said an American colonel later, after Hull surrendered on August 16 without firing a shot. Hull was found sitting on the ground within his tent and shaking almost uncontrollably. Brock's report to his superior said: "Your excellency will be astonished."

Hull's surrender had important repercussions. The British, who had shown eagerness to end the war, now believed they could achieve an easy total victory. As for Madison, he took a position that found expression through Monroe: "When our honor shall be avenged, when our generals shall occupy the best part of your Canada, then I shall be disposed to listen, and to treat of peace."

Hull's failure plus other setbacks played a role in the bitter Presidential contest that fall. General Stephen Van Rensselaer took his army across the Niagara where it was decimated in full view of other American militiamen who refused to cross the border; Indians massacred the Americans they found at the Fort Dearborn garrison; and General Dearborn, suffering painful rheumatism, led his forces to the Canadian border and then back to Plattsburg, New York, when they would not venture into Canada.

In the meantime, DeWitt Clinton had been approached by Republicans to withdraw from the race against Madison and become the party's choice in 1816. Clinton refused, then courted the Federalists, who held the first national convention in American history that September in New York City. Here the seventy delegates from eleven states nominated Clinton and mild Jared Ingersoll of Pennsylvania as their ticket, and proceeded to flay Madison as both a warmonger and an inept Commander-in-Chief. "It's time to have a change," became Clinton's campaign cry.

The campaign grew further confused because of sensational American victories at sea. Shortly after the Detroit disaster, Captain Isaac Hull, nephew of General Hull, evoked national cheers when his frigate, the *Constitution*, captured the British *Guerrière* off Bermuda. The *Constitution*'s success won her the nickname of "Old Ironsides." Then the American *Wasp* took the twenty-two-gun *Frolic* and Captain Stephen Decatur captured the newest and largest British man-o'-war, the *Macedonian*, off the Canary Islands. The Federalists let out a roar that they were responsible for these victories because they had voted for Navy appropriations while the Republicans opposed them.

Charges and countercharges filled the air until December 3, 1812, when the total electoral vote became known. In nine of the eighteen states, the legislatures, not the people, chose the electors. Clinton won every coastal state from New Hampshire to five of Maryland's eleven electoral districts and the entire Middle Atlantic zone except for Pennsylvania. But that state, plus Vermont, the solid six southern states and Kentucky and Tennessee on the frontier provided Madison with a victory of 128 electoral votes to 89 for Clinton.

Once assured of re-election, Madison revamped his Administration. Dr. Eustis was permitted to quit the War Department in December without the public condemnation he warranted for ineptness. Secretary of the Navy Hamilton also left after Madison told him that Congress would not appropriate money for the department so long as he remained. The French minister to Washington noted that for two years Hamilton was drunk by noon each day and "Mr. Madison and his friends tried by every means to cure him; it was hopeless."

As Hamilton's successor, Madison selected William Jones of Philadelphia. Jones had served as a third lieutenant under Captain Truxton on Pennsylvania's privately armed ship St. James during the Revolution and was wounded twice and taken prisoner twice. Jones, who had been a Congressman and also a shipper in the China trade, was a serious, energetic man and he proved invaluable in reorganizing the Navy, building fleets of line ships and planning naval strategy.

Finding an adequate successor to Eustis proved more difficult. After General Hull's surrender, the keenly ambitious Secretary of State Monroe envisioned himself as the "George Washington of the War of 1812." First, he convinced Madison that he should be appointed head of a combined Kentucky-Ohio army to retake Detroit. The governor of Kentucky spoiled his plan by naming William Henry Harrison as major general over Kentucky soldiers. But Monroe rebounded when Eustis left and agreed to add to his duties as Secretary of State a temporary appointment as Secretary of War on the belief that Madison had agreed to appoint him lieutenant general in charge of all field armies.

After a few weeks Monroe refused permanent appointment to the War Department because he learned that Madison did not intend to make him field general. In addition, Monroe's friends convinced him that the Secretary would be blamed for all war troubles and this would seriously jeopardize his chances in 1816 to succeed Madison. Madison then turned to ailing General Dearborn, who declined, and then to his Senate stalwart, William Crawford, who also turned him down.

Madison's final choice infuriated Monroe, for he selected John Armstrong of New York, whom Monroe considered his leading opponent for the Republican Presidential nomination in 1816. Armstrong was a bombastic man who picked up enemies wherever he went because he was forever plotting how to ruin one person's career or make another person subservient to him. After a diplomatic career in Europe, he was named a brigadier general in June 1812, even though Madison knew he had been a chief instigator of the officers' revolt against the Continental Congress in 1783. In June of that year when drunken, rowdy soldiers had forced Madison and other Congressmen to flee Philadelphia for Princeton in the middle of the night, Armstrong, who had egged the soldiers on, wrote that Congress had left Philadelphia "where their wisdom has long been questioned, their virtue suspected and their dignity a jest."

After barely winning confirmation to the War Department post, Armstrong soon had the Cabinet in an uproar. Gallatin referred to him as a "devil" because his closest Congressional friends were Gallatin's enemies. Jealous Monroe warned Madison that Armstrong planned to make himself field commander and then emulate Napoleon in taking over the government. Although Monroe went so far as to write Madison his recommendation for the summary removal of his rival, Madison refused to consider the recommendation seriously, for he saw the remarkable changes Armstrong was making in the Army. The old Revolutionary War generals found themselves retired and young men, such as Andrew Jackson, Jacob Brown and Winfield Scott, gained commands. A general staff began to function as the planner for the entire Army, instead of continuing the custom of permitting each general officer to be his own boss. One analyst commented that the "energy thus infused by Armstrong into the Regular Army lasted for half a century." Armstrong's achievements in his first year were outstanding, considering that Congress established a competing system of military supplies outside his control, cheating contractors produced defective weapons and ammunition, and soldiers' pay was less than that of common laborers.

When Congress returned to the Capitol in November 1812, Madison again reverted to passivity in his relations with the legislature. This was disastrous for Gallatin who told Congress he needed $20,000,000 immediately to pay mounting war costs. Gallatin suggested a novel excess profits tax applicable to those engaged in foreign trade. However, his enemies said this would interfere with the free enterprise system. Instead, they gave him authority to float another government loan, even though he told Congress his earlier effort had failed.

By 1813, many who had screamed loudest for war were now blaming the President for the miserable Army showing and were denouncing the fight as "Mr. Madison's War." It was customary for the Vice-President to absent himself from the Senate one day, so that the upper chamber could elect a Senate Pro Tempore. However, in the spring of 1813, newly-elected Vice-President Elbridge Gerry would not absent himself. He gave as his reason the fact that the Senate Pro Tem was next in line for the Presidency should Madison and he die. Since the Senate leadership was anti-Madison, the lack of a Senate Pro Tem made Speaker Henry Clay next in line, and Clay was friendly to the Administration.

Following Madison's second inauguration in March 1813, Czar Alexander I, elated by his unexpected success against Napoleon, sent him word that he was anxious to mediate the trouble with Britain. After Napoleon's 400,000-man army reached Moscow in October 1812, the Russians had set fire to the city. With the coming of freezing winter, the French Army had no alternative other than to begin its retreat in November, and only a few thousand lived to recross the Niemen in December. Alexander now wanted to play a larger role on the world scene; hence his desire to preside at a settlement between the United States and Britain.

Madison understood that Napoleon's fiasco would give the British the opportunity to send more troops to Canada. He was also aware by now that the British blockade was growing tighter despite the victories of individual American ships; the New England towns were not only playing host to British crews but were also outfitting their vessels; and that there was growing New England talk of secession. For all these reasons, Madison sent word to the czar that he was willing to let him end the war. Madison proposed to send two special envoys to work with American minister John Quincy Adams at St. Petersburg, and on learning of this, Gallatin asked to be named to the mission. Madison hesitated, for he was loath to lose Gallatin's services. However, he

agreed that Gallatin should become a temporary envoy and retain his Treasury post, to which he was to return after his foreign
assignment.

Gallatin had already departed with Federalist Senator James
Bayard of Delaware when Senator Sam Smith decided the time
had come to get his revenge for the firing of his brother
Robert. With the special help of Senator Giles, who was chairman
of the select committees handling foreign affairs and military
matters, Smith insisted it was illegal for Gallatin to serve as
Secretary and envoy at the same time. Instead of pointing out
that Washington had established a precedent in 1794 by sending
Chief Justice John Jay to London to write a treaty, Madison
replied that Secretary of the Navy Jones was handling Gallatin's
duties in his absence. Smith now said that this, too, was illegal,
and by a vote of 20 to 14 the Senate agreed that Gallatin's two
jobs could not be "united in the same person."

Then came the second blow to Gallatin. The Smith-Giles
"Malcontent Junto" began a buttonholing campaign of other Senators to humiliate Gallatin further. Even Senator Joseph Anderson
of Tennessee, who had agreed to head the Senate force to win
Gallatin's confirmation as envoy, now announced he would vote
against him. Secretary of War Armstrong was also reported in the
Capitol to line up Senate votes against confirmation. Finally on
July 19, 1813, by a vote of 18 to 17, the Senate rejected Gallatin
while confirming Adams and Bayard.

Madison had not come to Gallatin's aid in 1809 to make him
Secretary of State, nor did he now. However, he had a legitimate
excuse in this latter instance. For he fell deathly ill in June 1813,
and doctors despaired of his recovery. After a five-week vigil at his
bedside, Dolley Madison wrote to Mrs. Gallatin late in July: "I
watch over him as I would an infant, so precarious is his con-
valescence." Then when his high fever began to subside, she
wrote, "But now that I see he will get well, I feel as if I should die
myself from fatigue."

Chagrined as he was by Gallatin's defeat, Madison was nevertheless happy that Gallatin would soon return to Washington
to resume his duties as Treasury Secretary. The Republican financial genius, however, was so embarrassed by the Senate vote
that he would not return. This news pleased Smith and Giles, who
then pushed through a Senate resolution declaring the Treasury
post vacated. Their joy was complete when Madison docilely ac-

cepted their verdict and replaced Gallatin at the Treasury with incredibly incompetent Senator George Washington Campbell of Tennessee. With Gallatin now ousted from the Cabinet by their wily strategy, Smith and Giles relented slightly and the Senate confirmed Gallatin as a peace commissioner.

Madison's physical recovery was not hastened by reports on the British Navy or news from his field armies. While he was still in bed, a British squadron cruised into Chesapeake Bay and proceeded to raid shore villages at will. "All the city and Georgetown (except the Cabinet) have expected a visit from the enemy," wrote Dolley Madison. Congress considered a bill giving arms to "all able-bodied men." But the bill failed when the House Committee on Military Affairs called this expenditure wasteful and unnecessary. Fortunately, the British ships did not move on the capital. Madison's view was that the British abstained because such action would have aroused the nation and endangered the enormous contraband trade being conducted up and down the Atlantic seaboard.

There was military action elsewhere during 1813. Further defeats came on the Detroit front, but on September 10, Captain Oliver Hazard Perry, who had been urged to action personally by the President, thrashed a British squadron in the western part of Lake Erie and gained control of the lake for the United States. Loyal Americans echoed his report: "We have met the enemy and they are ours!" Perry's victory cut the British communication and supply lines at Detroit, and when the enemy retreated eastward, William Henry Harrison gave chase and defeated them decisively twenty miles away at the Battle of the Thames River on October 5. The Thames fight also ruined the northwest Indians, for Tecumseh, their leader, died here fighting for the British.

On orders from Secretary of War Armstrong, General Dearborn came to marching life on the New York-Canada border. In April he took his troops around Lake Ontario to capture York (Toronto), the capital of Upper Canada. His men acted like savages, burning the parliament building and terrorizing the seven hundred residents. Afterward, the British seeking revenge issued a manifesto to its fleet "to destroy and lay waste such towns and districts upon the coast as may be found assertable." This meant, of course, the Middle Atlantic region, for New England was too valuable a British ally.

In December 1813, the Thirteenth Congress reconvened and
Madison sent it a Message praising the nation for its wartime
unity. But only days later, he sent Congress a second Message,
this time in secret, to recommend an embargo on foreign trade to
punish New England for supplying British ships stationed off the
coast. Madison also knew that American grain was going to Spain
to feed the Duke of Wellington's army and some cotton was reaching Liverpool. The War Hawks pushed the embargo through Congress, bringing on loud cries from New England Federalists for
secession. But the embargo had to be revoked the following spring
at the request of the South and the frontier, for the skyrocketing
prices of New England goods drained gold and silver specie from
those areas. To add insult to injury, Boston Federalist bankers,
who refused to subscribe to Treasury loans, sent much of the
specie to Canada to pay for their purchases of British Treasury
notes.

Madison began 1814 with the belief that his envoys were negotiating a peace treaty with British diplomats at St. Petersburg
under the auspices of Czar Alexander. This picture was spoiled
by the arrival of the "Flag of Truce" British schooner *Bramble*
with double-barreled news. First, Napoleon, who had reassem-
bled a strong army, suffered a vital defeat at Leipzig on October 18, 1813, which saw his army collapse in rout back across the
Rhine. Napoleon's final defeat was now in view, thus freeing British ships for American coastal duty and battle-hardened soldiers
for offensive action. Second, the *Bramble* brought a message from
Lord Castlereagh, in which he rejected the Czar's mediation offer.
However, Castlereagh said he was not averse to direct negotiations
and Madison quickly accepted this offer, sending Speaker Henry
Clay and American minister to Sweden Jonathan Russell to join
Adams, Bayard and Gallatin at a site to be agreed upon by the
participants.

British battle plans for 1814 were based on Prime Minister Liverpool's policy to insist that territory captured during the war be
made a permanent possession under the peace treaty. One British
army was to attack through Niagara; another along Lake Champlain, which would cut off New England from the rest of the
country; while a southern force would come by water to take New
Orleans. There was also a fourth line. This was to capture Wash-

ington to seek revenge for the ravaging of York and to seize Madison in order to exhibit him abroad like a caged animal.

Early that summer when the British increased their forces in the Chesapeake, Madison grew concerned that they planned an assault on Washington. Armstrong called this ridiculous and said if the British were to attack the objective would be Baltimore. This failed to mollify Madison who ordered the establishment of the Potomac Military District and appointed Brigadier General William Winder as commander. These actions so incensed Armstrong that he refused to take any responsibility for the capital's defense.

Madison was, of course, correct in his decision, but the appointment of Winder was among his worst. Winder was a Baltimore lawyer turned soldier who had recently returned from a Canadian prison camp to which he had been sent following his capture in June 1813. He was neither acquainted with the rudiments of strategy nor temperamentally fitted to direct a campaign. As one person judged him, "When he retreated, he retreated in the wrong direction; when he fought he thought only of retreat; and whether scouting, retreating, or fighting, he never betrayed an idea."

The six thousand residents of Washington were leading a carefree life of parties and balls, dancing the newly introduced waltz step and becoming acquainted with Beethoven's music, when concern spread throughout the city that an attack was imminent. Madison assumed that Winder was at his headquarters planning the defense, training troops and acquiring supplies. Instead, Winder had left town for a six-week scouting expedition.

Armstrong was still denying that the British would attack Washington when Monroe noted: "Calling on the President on the morning of the 18th of August, he informed me that the enemy had entered the Patuxent in considerable force, and were landing at Benedict [Maryland]. I remarked that this city [Washington] was their object. He concurred in the opinion." With Madison's permission, Monroe now became a rival scout to Winder, and on the nineteenth he sent back word he had counted twenty-three square rigged vessels at Benedict. That day British Major General Robert Ross disembarked with four thousand men and began a march on Washington. Monroe, who was hiding in the bushes, lost sight of the advancing British force for a while as it headed for Marlboro. As for Winder, he would not agree with junior officers that Ross planned an approach through the village of

Bladensburg outside the capital and he sent back word to his
army to scatter along all the roads leading into Washington. On
the night of August 22, Ross camped a few miles outside of the
village and early the next morning Madison realized Winder had
acted idiotically when he received a request from him for "assistance of counsel from yourself and the government."

The Battle of Bladensburg came on August 24 and was the low
point of the war for the Americans. Monroe was with Madison
that morning when word came of Ross's advance on the village.
Madison agreed with Monroe's request that he be permitted to
join General Tobias Stansbury's Maryland militia to help save the
day. An hour later Monroe reached the high ground held by
Stansbury, and without telling the general he ordered the Fifth
Regiment of Baltimore volunteers to quit the orchards that concealed them and advance into the open. Stansbury later called
this officious action detrimental, while Armstrong flayed Monroe
as an "amateur, blundering tactician."

Nor was this the extent of the day's folly. Shortly before the
battle began the first Washington units arrived with Madison and
his Cabinet. Only the stern shout of a volunteer scout kept Madison and his Secretaries from riding across the bridge southwest
of town and into the British preparatory camp. Then came the
British assault and Attorney General Richard Rush who watched
along with the President said that "their rockets flew over us as
we sat on our horses." Madison stayed until Winder gave the order
to retreat, said Madison, and "it became manifest that the battle
was lost." Winder's order came, strangely, before the two thousand
American soldiers who were present had fired a single shot.

While Madison was riding into Washington ahead of the stam-
peding army, Dolley Madison wrote her sister that she was "calmly
listening to the roar of cannon, and watching the rockets in the
air, when [she] perceived our troops rushing into the city, with
the haste and dismay of a routed force." She had expected her
husband to return for three P.M. dinner with good news, but instead, she said, "Our kind friend, Mr. Carroll, has come to hasten
my departure, and is in a very bad humor with me because I
insist on waiting until the large picture of George Washington is
secured, and it requires to be unscrewed from the wall." In the
end, it was necessary to break the picture frame in order to extricate the Gilbert Stuart portrait of Washington. Then she added
to her letter: "And now, dear sister, I must leave this house, or

the retreating army will make me a prisoner in it, by filling up the road I am directed to take."

Madison returned to the Palace at four P.M. only to find Dolley gone and dinner in the kitchen. A British soldier later reported finding the dining room table set for forty and in the kitchen "spits, loaded with joints of various sorts, turned before the fire." By the time the weary victors reached Washington that evening to set the capital to the torch, Madison was safely in Virginia at the home of Rev. John Maffitt near Chain Bridge, while Dolley was at the Love home at Rokeby, Virginia. The next day Madison went in search of her, and when a hurricane hit, he took refuge in an old house. He finally found Dolley at Wiley's Tavern near the Great Falls of the Potomac, about fifteen miles from Washington. But he left her at midnight to cross the river by ferry to Brookville, Maryland, because of the rumor that a British party was hunting him.

Madison returned to Washington on the twenty-seventh to find the papers were denouncing him as a "serpent," and a "coward" who hid in "midnight hovels." One lie that was never to be stamped out was the story that an angry wife of a militiaman had chased Dolley from Mrs. Love's house. Madison knew that local citizens were making him the recipient of their anger and contempt, and he was described as "miserably shattered and woebegone." One verse that children took up in their play ran: "Fly, Monroe, fly! Run, Armstrong, run! were the last words of Madison."

The Madisons could not return to the Palace because it was a charred box. That the capital was not in worse condition was the result of two factors. First, the hurricane had put out the raging blazes set by the British. Second, on the twenty-fifth, Washingtonians falsely reported to the British that a large American force was rapidly approaching the capital. This prompted Admiral Cockburn and General Ross to call off further damage and order troops back to their transports. Madison first moved back into the small F Street house he had once occupied, then he moved to Octagon House, two blocks from the Palace, and he finally finished out his term in the House of the Seven Buildings at Pennsylvania Avenue and Nineteenth Street. Until the Capitol was restored, Congress moved into Blodget's Hotel, now called the Post and Patent Office Building, which had escaped burning. Then the following year, fearing the Congress might vote to leave Washington, local citizens raised funds to build the "Brick Capitol," at the site of the later Supreme Court Building, and here Congress remained from 1815 until 1819.

Armstrong returned on the same day as Madison and the President lost no time calling him to a meeting. Madison later reported that he told Armstrong: "Violent prejudices were known to exist against the Administration . . . particularly against me and himself as head of the War Department; that threats of personal violence had, as it was said, been thrown out against us both, but more especially against him; that the temper of the troops was such as made it expedient, if possible, that he should have nothing to do with them; that I had within a few hours received a message from the commanding General of the Militia informing me that every officer would tear off his epaulettes if Genl Armstrong was to have anything to do with them." Armstrong offered to resign or visit his family in New York until the agitation blew over. Madison told him to go off to New York, but the next morning Armstrong submitted his resignation. Madison also told General Winder to tender his resignation. Winder fought this request with more vigor than he did the British at Bladensburg, but when Madison would not change his mind he complied.

To pick up the broken pieces of government and glue them in place, Madison made more Cabinet changes. Now that his chief rival was destroyed, Monroe agreed to serve as Secretary of War and commander of the Potomac District while retaining his State Department post. Secretary of the Treasury Campbell was on his way out, with Alexander Dallas, the leading member of the Philadelphia bar, waiting for Senate confirmation. The third Attorney General was also in office, while Gideon Granger, who had served as Postmaster General since 1801, found himself summarily dismissed for insubordination, with the Madison conclusion that "his bodily infirmity with its effects on his mental stability" were additional reasons for firing him.

Granger had been given a free hand in naming the thousands of postal employees, and he stopped consulting Madison on any appointments. Granger suffered from a seething hatred of Madison, stemming from the President's refusal to appoint him to the Supreme Court in 1810. In 1814, a problem arose when Michael Leib, Senator from Pennsylvania and a Smith-Giles supporter, found he could not expect the state legislature to name him to another Senate term. Granger was a friend of Leib and sent his nomination to the Senate to become postmaster of Philadelphia despite the Leib-Madison antagonism. Madison then ordered him to withdraw Leib's name and submit that of Richard Bache, a Madison supporter, but Granger ignored him and won confirmation. It was at this point that Madison notified Granger he was submitting the nomination of Return J. Meigs, former chief justice of the Ohio Supreme Court and governor, as the next Postmaster General. The infuriated Granger then attempted to blackmail Madison into withdrawing the Meigs nomination. He would find it necessary, he informed Madison, to show his true Republican loyalty by telling the public how he had defended Dolley and her sister against unchastity charges in 1804 by offering to duel a vilifier and how he had prevented the Jefferson-Mrs. Walker affair of 1768 from gaining notoriety by killing a sedition case in which it would have been mentioned. But Madison refused to be frightened and Granger left his Administration in disgrace, after failing by a single vote to win a Senate investigation of his firing.

Less than a month after Washington was burned, Madison called Congress into special session on September 19, 1814. The gloom that had settled on the capital was already disappearing because of good news from the fighting fronts. After Bladensburg and Washington, British Vice-Admiral Alexander Cochrane led his fleet into the Patapsco River close to Fort McHenry, which barred the path to nearby Baltimore. Cochrane proposed to bomb the fort into submission while General Ross advanced on the city by land, in a combined effort to subdue the forces under Major General Sam Smith, now on temporary leave from the Senate and his anti-Madison activities. On September 12, the British land attack collapsed when Ross was killed in a skirmish, and the sea bombardment of Fort McHenry with 1500 shells from early morning on September 13 to seven A.M. the following day did not result in the lowering of the fort's flag. Baltimore was saved and the British fleet sailed to Jamaica.

From elsewhere, the news Madison received cheered him. In July, Winfield Scott overran the British at the Battle of Chippewa and ten days later Jacob Brown won a classic, tactical victory at Lundy's Lane near Niagara Falls. With Brown's 2600 men attacking the 3000-man British force, Lundy's Lane became the scene of the biggest battle of the war. After burning Washington, the British also put into motion the plan to cut the country in two in the north. A force of 9000 veterans of Wellington's Peninsular Army marched south to attack Plattsburg, the strategic point on the northwestern side of Lake Champlain, under cover of a strong flotilla on the lake. But American Commodore Thomas Macdonough, who had spent a year in the area under orders from Madison to construct his own fleet from nearby forests, was ready for Captain Downie's armada. The two fleets locked in Plattsburg Bay on September 11 and Macdonough emerged with the decisive victory of the war. The British land forces, who had been bragging that they were "driving the Doodles in all directions," reacted to Plattsburg Bay by racing back to Canada in wild disorder.

The peace negotiations had been under way since August at Ghent, Belgium, a British garrison town controlling the water routes of Flanders, and the three British negotiators had been arrogantly insisting on outrageous terms. They demanded recognition of an independent buffer-Indian country comprising Ohio, Indiana, Illinois, Michigan and Wisconsin; American withdrawal from the Great Lakes; cession of much of Maine; recognition of British navigation rights on the Mississippi; and American relinquishment of fishing rights off Canada.

The American commissioners immediately got into a hassle among themselves regarding the parts of the British demands they might accept. Gallatin, who had assumed nominal leadership of the five-member American delegation found his chief task was to keep a semblance of peace between Henry Clay and John Quincy Adams. "Harry of the West" adamantly opposed British use of the Mississippi, but was not averse to giving up American fishing rights off Canada. As a New Englander, Adams, of course, took the opposite position.

General pessimism among the American envoys disappeared in November when they learned of Macdonough's victory. A different effect overtook the British. Lord Liverpool had asked Wellington to take charge of the war and thrash the United States. But on November 9, with information on hand regarding Plattsburg Bay, Wellington wrote him: "I feel no obligation to going to America. . . . That which appears to me to be wanting in America is not a general, or a general officer and troops, but a naval superiority on the Lakes. . . . In regard to your present negotiations, I confess that I think you have no right, from the state of the war, to demand any concessions of territory from America." Wellington's advice, the warlike cries of Friedrich Wilhelm of Prussia and

Alexander of Russia against England at the Congress of Vienna where European territorial adjustments were being considered, and the growing opposition of Britishers to rising, harsh taxes to support the endless American war convinced Liverpool that a simple peace treaty was in order.

Madison had been anxiously waiting to hear from his envoys, because, despite the improved military situation, ugly problems had arisen. On November 9, 1814, his Administration was forced to admit bankruptcy. Even the promise not to publish the names of Treasury note purchasers had failed to increase sales. Specie was out of circulation and paper money was so depreciated that few merchants would accept it as payment. Treasury Secretary Dallas' report to the House Ways and Means Committee read: "When I perceive that more than 40 millions of dollars must be raised for the service of the year 1815, by an appeal to the public credit through the medium of Treasury notes and loans, I am not without sensations of extreme solicitude." Soldiers were long without pay, some lacked shoes and coats, and mutinies were beginning to take place.

Another Madison problem was New England. In October, the Massachusetts General Court called for a convention to consider grievances against the Madison Administration. A visitor at Octagon House reported that the President's mind was full of the New England sedition. Nevertheless, Madison did not propose to take any action against the disloyal New Englanders, which was opposite the advice Jefferson gave him for dealing with northern Federalists—"You may there have to apply the rougher drastics of Governor Wright, hemp and confiscation." His reference was to the hanging of Eastern Shore Tories in 1776 by Maryland Minutemen.

In December 1814, five states sent twenty-six delegates to Hartford, Connecticut, where they praised the British, advocated acceptance of the original British terms and talked secession. However, members of this Hartford Convention refused to put themselves on record with these stands. Instead their approved resolutions called for a constitutional amendment to require a two-thirds vote of Congress to declare war or admit a state into the Union; a ban on more than a single term for a President; a prohibition against two successive Presidents from the same state; and the exclusion of naturalized Americans from government jobs.

While the Hartford Convention was at work, still another problem disturbed Madison. Intelligence reported that fifteen thousand battle-tried Redcoats had arrived in Jamaica from Ireland in September, for an early effort by Sir Edward Pakenham, Wellington's brother-in-law, to take New Orleans. Lord Liverpool's strategy was to send Pakenham into the Delaware River and the Chesapeake after New Orleans if Madison refused to sign a peace treaty. Then if raids there did not change his mind, Liverpool said, "We must immediately propose to make a separate peace with them [the New England states], and we have good reason to believe that they would."

Madison's concern was how to get Major General Andrew Jackson of the Tennessee militia and hero of the Battle of Horseshoe Bend against the Creek Indians, to quit Florida and head for New Orleans defense. Monroe had sent him urgent orders, but Jackson calmly replied that he had to capture Pensacola first. It was Jackson's luck that Pakenham was behind schedule. In addition, after the British took the American flotilla at the entrance to the city, a fog set in and what should have been an easy victory became a retirement to reconsider strategy. On January 8, 1815, a week later, Pakenham returned with a frontal attack but Jackson had ample time to prepare and his frontier sharpshooters slaughtered more than two thousand of the enemy, including Pakenham.

The Hartford Convention had sent "ambassadors" to warn Madison to accept its resolutions or face New England disunion. They had not reached Washington when they learned of Jackson's great victory at New Orleans. Then in the capital they heard worse news. On December 24, 1814, the American and British commissioners had agreed to the Peace Treaty of Ghent. Such national derision now descended on the Hartford ambassadors and New England disloyalists that the Federalist party vanished from the American scene as a national political organization.

The peace treaty did not appear to have warranted the expenditure of blood and other sacrifices. Madison had not accepted the initial, severe terms proposed by the British that would have dismembered and constricted his nation. Nor would Liverpool and Castlereagh discuss the questions of impressment or neutral rights, which Madison considered basic matters. The final document recognized this total impasse by ignoring all demands and becoming chiefly an agreement to restore territory captured during the war.

Yet the War of 1812 had enormous consequences for the American state of mind. Americans no longer felt weak or helpless in an aggrandizing world. Furthermore, ties with European nations became unemotional as Americans turned inward to get on with the exciting business of expanding across the continent. As Gallatin so knowingly explained the result of the fighting: "The war has renewed and reinstated the national feelings and character which the Revolution had given, and which were daily lessened. The people . . . are more American; they feel and act more as a nation."

Once the treaty was signed, Madison found himself in the unfamiliar position of being treated with admiration by the press. Nor did his popularity dwindle during his two remaining years as President. The earlier bankruptcy of the Treasury gave way to government and national prosperity as wartime industries converted and expanded to meet pent-up demand. Madison was concerned with the wartime national debt which reached $99,000,000, but excise taxes passed by Congress plus import duties filled Treasury vaults. The changed financial status best indicated itself by the heavy investment in Treasury notes by foreign governments.

During his last period in office, Madison revealed the influence of his past by reverting to various Federalist policies he once favored. He was willing on occasion now to use his office in a more aggressive fashion to promote those principles he believed essential at a younger age. To the dismay of Jefferson, he came out in favor of granting a charter to reinstate the defunct Bank of the United States. He also favored the Protective Tariff Act of 1816 and the establishment of a permanent Army General Staff, as well as a strong, standing peacetime Army and Navy. Other Madison proposals that went against the grain of old-line Republican statesrighters called for the expansion of the Federal court system by establishing a separate circuit court layer to relieve Supreme Court justices from riding the circuit; the creation of a Department of the Interior; and a Federal aid-to-education program.

It was only in his final Presidential action that he reverted to Republicanism. When the Second Bank of the United States was chartered in 1816 by Congress, the Bank gave the Government $1,500,000 as a bonus. Representative John C. Calhoun quickly introduced a bill to utilize this sum to build roads and canals in each state. The desire of Americans to move westward and to ship goods cheaply from state to state made transportation improvements essential. But on his final day in office Madison declared that internal improvements were not among the enumerated powers of the Constitution, and he vetoed the bill.

As he prepared to leave office in March 1817, even the remnant Federalist press praised him. John Adams, whose own Federalist Administration was almost as chaotic as Madison's, had only words of sympathy and commendation for his former political opponent. Said Adams: "[Despite] a thousand faults and blunders, his administration has acquired more glory and established more Union than all three predecessors, Washington, Adams and Jefferson."

☆ 5 ☆

JAMES MONROE

Era of Good and Bad Feelings

John Quincy Adams, who observed President James Monroe closely from 1817 to 1825 as his Secretary of State, noted that Monroe's Presidential philosophy was to seek out equilibrium and inertia. Tranquillity, said Adams, was "the pole-star of his policy . . . There is slowness, want of decision and a spirit of procrastination in the President, which perhaps arises more from his situation than his personal character." In a complexity such as politics, a highly personal affair where emotions pour out over trivia and where fights are commonplace, a seeker of tranquillity cannot expect to maintain leadership. Monroe was no exception. As Supreme Court Justice Joseph Story observed in 1818: "The Executive has no longer a commanding influence. The House of Representatives has absorbed all the popular feeling and all the effective power of the country."

Nevertheless, when this passive President left office, he could point to an Administration record that an aggressive President would have been proud to claim. He sealed one agreement with England in 1817 that brought permanent disarmament between Canada and the United States at their Great Lakes boundary. Neither side would again maintain warships on the five lakes. The next year another agreement brought acceptance of the 49th Parallel for the boundary between the Lake of the Woods and the Rockies, and joint occupancy of the disputed Oregon Territory for ten years with options for renewal rather than war. For Latin America, his Administration recognized revolutionary native governments in 1822, and the following year his historic Monroe Doctrine put the Americas under the protection of the United States against European despots. Monroe's Administration also added to his country's territory in 1821 by purchasing the Floridas from Spain and by winning Spanish agreement to limit her territorial claims to the area south of the 42nd Parallel, from Louisiana to the Pacific Ocean.

Nor were the significant changes only in the field of foreign affairs. Domestically, Monroe's Administration witnessed the opening struggle of the slavery drama, with the Missouri Compromise of 1820 separating North and South by a high emotional fence, yet holding both sections together in an uneasy truce that would savagely explode in fratricide forty years later. Before leaving office, the Monroe Administration also dug a shallow grave for the stentorian Republican demand for states' rights and adherence to enumerated powers in order to bar the Federal Government from engaging in road building and canal construction. In a literal sense, the vast Federal power, reclamation, highway and river projects that cover the United States stem from a $30,000 general surveys bill that Monroe signed in 1824 in a peace-making effort with zealous expansionists.

Oddly enough, this passive President was by nature the most aggressive of politicians. All his previous life he had clawed, fought and schemed against competitors. Everywhere he saw plots to humiliate or destroy him. He was so suspicious of his contemporaries and so sensitive a soul that he could turn any unrelated action into a personal attack. Once while he was American minister to England and the Queen hurried through a crowd, he said she had intentionally failed to greet him. From early youth on he determined to spend his life in public service, and as such was his country's first important professional politician. Unlike earlier Chief Executives, who considered their political careers more a burden than a reward, Monroe found the political atmosphere the only worthwhile air to breathe. Higher and higher he rose, battling all the way, making serious blunders that would have ruined others but always rebounding to new heights. Yet when he reached the final pinnacle, he subsided in pious self-satisfaction that would keep him essentially apart from the fierce political struggles whirling about him.

The blunt truth is that Monroe's political career was not keyed to his ability, nor to promoting political principles. It rested instead on exerting influence and attaching himself to men of stature. So when he moved into the White House and found he no longer needed to continue his tactics to rise further, he was without a sound basis for using his vast Presidential powers. One of his apologists frankly admitted, "He was not the equal of Washington in prudence, of Marshall in wisdom, of Hamilton in constructive power, of Jefferson in genius for politics, of Madison in persistent ability to think out an idea and to persuade others of its importance." But Monroe did not suffer as a result of his shortcomings, for he had influence and good fortune.

At the outset it was his uncle, popular Judge Joseph Jones, neighbor and friend of Washington, Jefferson, Madison and other important Virginians, who carefully heeded his ward's request to promote him into avenues of sure advancement. Born on April 28, 1758, Monroe was a student at William and Mary College when his carpenter-farmer father, Spence Monroe, died in 1774. He was seventeen when the boys poured out of the school and joined the fight for independence from England. As a second lieutenant in the 3rd Virginia Regiment, he fought bravely in Washington's retreating army at Harlem Heights and White Plains, then took part in the ragged race from advancing Redcoats across the Hudson, through New Jersey and across the Delaware. The high point of his military service occurred at the successful attack on the Hessians at Trenton after the Christmas Eve crossing of the icy river. Here he received a ball in the shoulder that he carried with him throughout life.

He was a captain now and saw that rapid advancement would come through commanding troops. So his Uncle Joseph suggested to Washington: "I wish Cap'n Monroe could have made up his company on his own account." But Washington did not have extra soldiers available to accommodate the young warrior. Instead, Monroe attached himself as a major to the Earl of Stirling, a British general fighting on the American side. Again he fought bravely at the Battle of Brandywine on September 11, 1777, Germantown on October 4 and at Monmouth, the last major northern battle, on June 28, 1778. But according to Aaron Burr, Monroe's service to Lord Stirling, who was a Washington favorite, was chiefly spent filling his alcoholic lordship's cup with ale and listening to his long-winded stories.

When Monroe left the army in 1779, he returned to Virginia armed with letters of praise from Lord Stirling, Alexander Hamilton and Washington himself. The helpful letter he asked Washington to write contained the following: ". . . the esteem I have for him, and a regard for his merit, conspire to make me earnestly wish to see him provided for in some handsome way." His presentation of the Washington letter convinced the Virginia Assembly to appoint the twenty-one-year-old Monroe as a lieutenant colonel of the militia. But he had no troops to lead and precious time was fleeing. So a short time later he asked his uncle to help him decide whether to study law under the country's great jurist, George Wythe at William and Mary, or under Governor Thomas Jefferson, who had practiced law only a short time. Judge Jones was aware of what his nephew had in mind, and his reply made clear that Jefferson provided the better bridge to a political career—"and while you continue to deserve his esteem he will not withdraw his countenance." Backstage maneuvers then took place, and a harassed wartime governor found himself with the additional burden of serving as Monroe's law teacher.

Monroe's appearance was at that time relatively similar to what it would be forty years later. He was tall and lean with an athlete's stance and walk. His pale blue eyes peered out of a face expressionless in repose yet like a strong beam when he smiled. A contemporary noted that "there is often in his manner an artificial and even an awkward simplicity."

In 1782, when Monroe wanted to begin his political career, Judge Jones induced his friends in King George County to send him to the Virginia Assembly. Always careful to maintain contacts, he quickly informed Washington, Jefferson and Lord Stirling when he won office and told them that without their help "I could not have expected, among so many competitors, at my age, to have attained, in this degree, the confidence of my countrymen." Jefferson sourly commented: "Public service and private misery are linked together."

Monroe's superb connections catapulted him only a few months later into the eight-man Executive Council, the cumbersome legislative cabinet which shared the conduct of the state administration with the governor. The momentum of this meteoric rise was not dispelled, for in 1783, when his uncle left the Confederation Congress, Monroe moved onto the national scene as a member of the Virginia delegation. Here, despite an exceedingly poor speaking voice, he became the champion of western interests. He also met James Madison that year and added his name to those with whom Madison regularly corresponded.

In 1786, when he married, he needed to earn money, which

prompted him to win admittance to the Virginia bar. He hoped to move to Richmond, the thriving new capital, but Judge Jones advised Fredericksburg because Monroe's boyhood schoolmate, John Marshall, had Richmond's legal business fairly well cornered. Jones provided his nephew with money for a carriage and had a house and office waiting for him at Fredericksburg, so he might begin his career free from debt and competition.

The year 1787 witnessed the Constitutional Convention at Philadelphia. Monroe believed he merited a place on the Virginia delegation with Washington and Madison. When he was not chosen he wailed to Jefferson, then in France, that "the Governor, I have reason to believe, is unfriendly to me & hath shewn a disposition to thwart me," while "Madison, upon whose friendship I have calculated, whose views I have favor'd, and with whom I have held the most confidential correspondence, [is] in strict league" with Governor Edmund Randolph.

However, Monroe later had an opportunity to undo Madison's work in Philadelphia when he served as Patrick Henry's assistant to fight the Constitution at the Virginia ratifying convention in June 1788. Henry was then the strongest political figure in the state. He pushed Monroe forward to speak for the veterans of the Revolution, but Monroe was demolished by the oratorically brilliant John Marshall, whom Madison sent into the speaker's box to represent the veterans for the Constitution. In his argument, Monroe feebly expressed concern that a President might seek re-election and that the President and the Senate might easily conspire to establish an aristocratic, dictatorial government of their own design. Despite Patrick Henry's loss and the Constitution's ratification, Monroe had picked the winning side, for Henry dominated the Assembly and selected as Virginia's first Senators two men who had opposed ratification. Henry failed in his effort to bring Monroe in as a winner against Madison for a seat in the House of Representatives, but he elevated Monroe as successor to Senator William Grayson who died early in 1790.

By now Monroe had definitely decided that Patrick Henry's enemy, Secretary of State Thomas Jefferson, was *the* man with *the* future. Not only did he move to Charlottesville to become a neighbor of "the great sachem of his tribe," but he also became Jefferson's echo in the Senate. This meant throwing away his friendship with Washington and Hamilton and becoming a junior member of the Republican board of strategy under Jefferson and Madison. Heretofore an acknowledged admirer of Washington, he now called him a fairly witless dupe of Hamilton and his Federalist faction. "I thought that Washington was opposed to their schemes," he would later explain in an attempt to justify his stand, "and not being able to take him with them, that they were forced to work, in regard to him, under-handed, using his name and standing with the nation, as far as circumstances permitted, to serve their purposes."

Yet despite Monroe's attacks, Washington sent him to France as minister in 1794. In Paris, Monroe saved both Thomas Paine and Madame Lafayette, who were languishing in prison for opposing Robespierre. However, as a diplomat he proved an abject failure. He permitted the Committee of Public Safety to use his name and presence to show American support for their terrorist activities. When he delivered a fervent, pro-revolutionary address to the French National Convention in August 1794, Secretary of State Edmund Randolph scathingly warned him that "the dictates of sincerity do not demand that we render notorious all our feelings in favor of that nation." But Monroe did not take the advice. He spoke out against the Jay Treaty of November 1794 with England, permitted Tom Paine to write virulent attacks on President Washington while Paine was his house guest and refused to drink a toast to Washington at an affair.

All these factors brought his recall in mid-1796, and when he returned to the United States the next spring he found himself the center of a huge political controversy. While the Republicans wined and dined him, the Federalists condemned him as a villainous failure. In addition, he narrowly avoided a duel with Alexander Hamilton. Five years earlier, Monroe had served on a three-man Congressional delegation to investigate the charge that Hamilton was speculating in government funds. In self-vindication, Hamilton had at the time poured out a sordid tale: how a young woman had come to his house to plead for money to return to her family in New York, how he brought the money to her at her boardinghouse room. "After that I had frequent meetings with her at my own house, Mrs. Hamilton and her children being absent," Hamilton confessed. The affair later led to the blackmail of Hamilton by the young woman's husband, James Reynolds. It was Reynolds, caught in Treasury speculation with one of Hamilton's clerks, who had tried to implicate the Secretary of the Treasury.

The Congressional delegation had agreed to lay the matter to rest and Monroe left the papers pertaining to the Reynolds matter with Jefferson at Monticello. Now five years later, without Monroe's knowledge and with the Republican-Federalist battle at full tide, Jefferson slipped the Reynolds papers to a Republican editor who published them. Hamilton confronted Monroe the day after he arrived from France, called him a liar and a scoundrel, accused him of treachery and won agreement for a duel. Witnesses talked them out of it, though later Hamilton wrote him a violent, accusatory letter, which was in effect a couched challenge to a duel. However, Monroe knew that the law prosecuted the formal aggressor in a duel and he refused to make the actual challenge. Instead, he ironically induced Aaron Burr to speak to Hamilton to end his demand for a duel.

While this was proceeding, Monroe bickered with Secretary of State Timothy Pickering to supply him with the reasons for his recall. Pickering refused to be direct. Nevertheless, he delivered Monroe and his defending Republicans a hammer blow when he replied that *any* diplomat might be ordered home because he was unskilled, lacking in judgment, diligence or sincerity or was hostile to his own government. Stung to the core, Monroe now sat down and wrote a hundred-page refutation, "A View Of The Conduct Of The Executive." This effort evoked a comment from President Adams that Monroe was "a disgraced minister, recalled in displeasure for misconduct." Washington was so aroused by Monroe's pamphlet that he scribbled blistering comments on the margins throughout his own copy.

Monroe directly contributed to Washington's death. In 1799, Republicans in the Virginia Assembly proposed Monroe for governor, and a harsh battle of words broke out with Federalist members. On December 6, the Assembly finally elected Monroe governor by a vote of 101 to 66, which prompted the Richmond *Federalist* to declare "a day of mourning." The news was late reaching Mount Vernon where Washington had expressed horror that Monroe might become governor. That day, December 12, Washington had ridden about his farms on an inspection despite a steady snowfall. Upon his return home, he learned of Monroe's victory and instead of changing clothes, he sat in his wet garments for hours, angrily denouncing the new governor. Then a sudden chill sent him to bed and two days later he was dead.

Despite Monroe's earlier failure as a diplomat, President Jefferson sent him to France in 1803 as special envoy. Here he increased his political stature by participating with American minister Robert R. Livingston in the Louisiana Purchase. Each realized that credit for the purchase might open the gate to the Presidency, and each belittled the other's role, even though it was Napoleon alone who proposed the cession. Monroe hoped to gain on Livingston by getting a treaty with Spain for the sale of the Floridas. However, this proved unsuccessful. He had a further opportunity for diplomatic brilliance when Jefferson requested him and William Pinkney to negotiate a treaty with England to end impressment and to honor neutral rights during the Napoleonic War. But the two envoys ignored instructions and produced a treaty that Jefferson denounced. Again Monroe returned from abroad in disgrace.

He fell prey to the false kindness of John Randolph for a while and lost Jefferson's friendship when he became Randolph's candidate for President against Madison in 1808. A period of rehabilitation followed, however, and he returned to the Virginia Assembly in 1810 and to the governor's chair for a second term. But it was the national scene he yearned for. It took some effort by Jefferson to overcome Madison's animosity. This was accomplished and in 1811, Monroe joined Madison's Cabinet as Secretary of State and heir apparent.

In Washington, he gave unquestioned loyalty to Madison during the trying years of the War of 1812, though he helped botch the defense of the capital. Also, on occasion he nakedly revealed his personal ambitions. When General John Armstrong, former minister to France and Spain as well as U. S. Senator, became Secretary of War, Monroe recognized him as his chief rival to succeed Madison. Now began a campaign to ruin Armstrong's reputation. On December 27, 1813, for instance, he wrote Madison the following letter: "It is painful to me to make this communication to you, nor should I do it if I did not most conscientiously believe that this man, if continued in office, will ruin not you and the administration only, but the whole Republican party and cause. He has already gone too far, and it is my opinion, if he is not promptly removed, he will soon accomplish it."

In 1816, with General Armstrong in disgrace because of his inept stewardship over military strategy, there seemed little likelihood Monroe would face Republican opposition for the Presidency. Yet a threat appeared that year in the person of William Crawford, former Senator from Georgia, minister to France and Madison's latest Secretary of War. The blond, affable giant would easily have captured the Republican nomination had an early Congressional nominating caucus taken place. Over the years, Crawford had nurtured a personal political machine among his Congressional colleagues and his gregarious nature made him well liked. Colleagues roared when he told how he had fallen seriously ill in Paris during Napoleon's Hundred Days and how French doctors could not help him. He cured himself, he said, by ordering his servant "to fetch me a peck of turnip salad, a fat hog's jowl and a black old pot big enough to hold them both. Then get me some cornmeal bread well baked." Another favorite story related to the occasion when Napoleon approached him at a public gathering and sneeringly asked, "Is your Mr. Madison tall?" "Not at all," replied Crawford. "He is on the contrary quite small—no taller than that." He stretched out an arm so that the palm of his hand rested two inches above Napoleon's head. Napoleon beat a stumbling retreat.

Aware of Crawford's strength in Congress, Jefferson planned to delay the calling of the nominating caucus in order to win more support for Monroe. Fortunately, this strategy met with favor from Speaker Henry Clay and Sam Smith, now a member of the House and caucus chairman, for both disliked Crawford. However, when Crawford's support failed to dwindle, Senator Abner Lacock of Pennsylvania, presumably on Jefferson's orders, arranged a private meeting with the Georgian. After appealing to Crawford not to stand in the path of "the last of the Revolutionary worthies," he hinted that if Crawford stood aside he would win Virginian support for 1820. On this oral promise, Crawford agreed to withdraw as a candidate and his promise won hasty publicity in influential Republican papers. Nevertheless, his followers were loud in their demands at the caucus on March 16. The outcome finally turned on the New York delegation where four-fifths favored Crawford. However, young boss Martin Van Buren, who was not in Congress at the time, used political pressures and the final caucus vote read 65 for Monroe and 54 for Crawford.

The unpatriotic Hartford Convention had reduced the Federalist party to tiny proportions, and because of a lack of party competition for the Presidency, voter interest centered on the Congressional elections in 1816. Congress had passed the Compensation Act of 1816, an act to raise Congressional pay from $6.00 a day to $1500 a year. On the basis of the length of sessions, this amounted to only a slight increase. But the electorate considered it a money grab and the chief political issue that year was whether an incumbent seeking re-election had voted for the act. New York returned only five members of its twenty-seven-man delegation in the Fourteenth Congress to the Fifteenth; Georgia returned only two out of seven; and in general a vast army of new legislators won seats.

Forgotten for the most part was the Presidential campaign. This proved a quiet matter with Monroe capturing all states except three, which went to Rufus King, the persevering Federalist. King now publicly proclaimed that the Federalists were no longer a national party and urged his supporters to give their future assistance to "the least wicked section of the Republicans."

Not long after his victory, it was Monroe's selection of a Cabinet that revealed his intention to seek tranquillity. He was determined, he wrote to Major General Andrew Jackson, to put at ease sectional rivalry by choosing a man from each of the four sections—the East, Middle, South and West—to head the four major departments. However, to his great dismay, even so simple a plan failed.

John Quincy Adams of the East became his Secretary of State; his rival, William Crawford, of the South his Secretary of the Treasury. For his western Secretary, Monroe offered the War Department to Henry Clay, but Clay believed he merited the State Department as his future stepping stone to the Presidency, and he angrily refused to become War Secretary. After this, Monroe offered it to General Isaac Shelby, who turned it down, as did General Jackson. Finally Monroe picked young Congressman John C. Calhoun from South Carolina. There were now two Southerners in the Cabinet and soon a third appeared when William Wirt of Virginia became Attorney General.

The theme of Monroe's inaugural address was tranquillity, yet Speaker Clay did his best to bring chaos on that occasion. As was customary, Monroe expected to come to the Capitol and take his oath before a joint House-Senate gathering in the chamber of the House of Representatives. However, Clay flatly refused to permit the use of the House. His offhand excuse was that the floor of the House chamber would buckle under the weight of the expected throng. As a result, the inauguration committee was forced to hold the ceremony on a raised portico in front of the Capitol. Thus because of Clay's anger a new Presidential tradition had its beginning.

A month later Monroe decided to carry his theme to the people. This he hoped to accomplish by making a tour of New England and healing the wounds brought on by Federalist disloyalty in that region. In order to give the trip a non-political label so that he would not have to pay for it out of his own pocket, he announced he would make an examination of the forts and harbors in the North. Since Congress had appropriated a great deal of money for defense and since it was his responsibility to administer the programs, it was his duty he said, to check on their adequacy.

The three-and-a-half-month trip proved an enormous personal triumph. He was wined and dined, kowtowed to and applauded all along the Atlantic Coast to Portland, across New Hampshire, Vermont and New York, westward to frontier Detroit and back to Washington via Pittsburgh. It was in the Federalist Boston *Centinel* of July 12, 1817, on the occasion of his visit to Boston that the news story carried this caption: "Era of Good Feelings." This phrase was immediately picked up by the country and made descriptive of Monroe's period in office. It seemed at the time a proper synonym to describe the end of the two-party system and the end of bondage to England and France in their international activities.

If the rest of the country expressed pleasure in his tour, his Cabinet did not, for it meant inactivity during his absence. In Crawford's opinion: "The President's tour through the East has produced something like a political jubilee. . . . If the bondmen and bondwomen were not set free, and individual debts released, a general absolution of political sins seems to have been mutually agreed upon." Nevertheless, the trip had certain value. A glimpse of their President had a profound effect on citizens to whom the national government seemed remote: it helped cement their nationalism and made them feel he was one of them and not an abstraction. Most who saw him believed they had found a link with the Revolution of '76 because of his quaint attire. In an age when men wore trousers, this "last of the Revolutionary farmers" dressed in knee breeches and silk hose. He wore silver buckles on his shoes and carried a sword at his side and the cockade of the Revolution on his cocked hat.

During Monroe's absence the long effort to repair the Executive

Mansion was completed, and he was able to move in upon his return to Washington. Several thick coats of white paint covered the smoke and fire damage to the gray sandstone structure by the British on August 24, 1814, and the President's residence assumed the name White House. It was from the White House that the Administration's activities now began unfolding late in 1817.

Unfortunately for a man who wanted to be a passive President, the country was beset with many problems that required resolute leadership. The first major problem facing Monroe was what to do about the South American revolutions against tyrannical Spain by Simón Bolívar in the north and José de San Martín in the south. Monroe's newfound Presidential caution overrode his strong sympathy for the native revolutionists, and his policy became one of delaying their recognition until all doubts were removed regarding the permanency of the newly established governments.

This policy of neutrality was the first to shake the complacency of the Era of Good Feelings, for it gave Speaker Clay his initial opportunity to denounce Monroe. In order to push the problem into the future, Monroe proposed to Congress that an appropriation be made to send three commissioners of inquiry on a sloop-of-war to cruise along the coast of South America and determine the degree of independence enjoyed by the revolutionists. Clay found this, in effect, callous and inhuman and in a fiery address to the House demanded immediate recognition and an exchange of diplomats. Secretary of State Adams noted in his diary on December 6, 1817 that Clay had "mounted his South American great horse" in an attempt "to overthrow the Executive by swaying the H of Reps." Adams also wrote that Monroe was so stunned by this intraparty attack that he could not talk of anything else. The argument was settled temporarily when Clay's colleagues would not give him control over foreign policy and voted $30,000 for the commissioners of inquiry.

However, Monroe was not to enjoy peace for long because a new matter intervened to rock the Administration. In 1814, Major General Jackson had forced the Creek Indians of Georgia to give up 23,000,000 acres at the Treaty of Fort Jackson. Many Creeks crossed into Spanish Florida afterward and joined the Seminole tribe in the Everglades in a running border war with Americans. For a time the attacks were only a nuisance, but in 1817 they grew serious.

About 800 Negro runaway slaves had taken over an old British fort on the Apalachicola River in Florida. Brevet Major General Edmund Gaines had erected Fort Scott on the river across from the slaves in Georgia in order to keep an eye on them. In 1816, the Negroes attacked a convoy on its way to Fort Scott and in retaliation, American troops fired into their fort. One burning cannon ball landed in the Negro fort's magazine, and the explosion killed 350 men, women and children. The Seminoles then took whatever weapons remained in the fort and early the next year stepped up activities against American frontiersmen.

In November, General Gaines set the Seminole village of Fowltown in Georgia to the torch, and the Indians struck back by ambushing an American hospital ship, killing forty-one soldiers and women. Monroe could no longer delay a policy decision. The Cabinet agreed that Gaines must take strong action against the offenders and, if necessary, cross into Spanish East Florida to attack the Seminoles "unless they should shelter under a Spanish post."

From past performance, Gaines was a man who obeyed orders and probably would not have gone out of his way to flout Spanish authority in Florida had he been forced to give hot pursuit of the Seminoles. However, there was at that time a malignant situation on Amelia Island, a no-man's-land in the Atlantic off the border of Georgia and Florida. Gaines was told to seize the pirate-held island, while the original orders to him regarding the Seminoles were transferred to General Jackson in late December. Monroe's troubles were multiplying.

The Virginia Republican dynasty had taken a jaundiced view of Jackson since his implication in the Burr scandal during Jefferson's second term. Since that time Monroe had consciously worked to improve his own relationship with the headstrong Tennessean. In turn, Jackson supported him against Madison in 1808 and made Monroe his chief government contact during the War of 1812. No warmth developed between the two men, though a false friendship that was too hearty in public and too suspicious in private did exist.

Republicans raised to abhor militarism found it difficult to praise the victor at New Orleans, even though he had saved their hides. They spoke of his arrogance to higher authority, his cruelty to his foot soldiers and his absorption with money-making schemes. So far as Monroe was concerned, the trait he disliked most in Jackson was the general's unwillingness to treat him with the respect due a

President. As soon as his victory was assured, Monroe was pep-
pered with letters from Jackson, advising him how to comport himself as President and whom to select for his Cabinet. One letter
advised Monroe that "the Chief Magistrate of a great and powerful
nation should not engage in party feelings." Others to Monroe and
Secretary of War Calhoun insisted that all orders to the Southern
Division must clear with him and must not be sent directly to
other generals there. When Monroe wrote him in August 1817,
"Every order from the dept. of war, to whomever directed, must be
obeyed," Jackson replied, "I will continue to support the government in all respects when the orders of the War Dept. do not,
in my opinion, go to infringe all law and strike at the very root of
subordination and the discipline of the Army." When Monroe protested this and also refused to swallow all of Jackson's outpouring
of advice, the general took this as a sign of the President's ill-will.

Although Monroe sent Jackson orders on December 26, 1817, to
go after the Seminoles into Florida if necessary but not to attack
them if they moved into Spanish forts, his letter crossed with one
written him by Jackson on January 6, 1818. The aggressive general
wrote from Tennessee that raids against the Indians into East
Florida were not sufficient. All of Spanish East Florida should be
seized, he said. "This can be done without implicating the government. Let it be signified to me through any channel (say Mr. J.
Rhea) that the possession of the Floridas would be desirable to the
United States, and in sixty days it will be accomplished." Mr. Rhea
was a Congressman from Tennessee and a close friend of Jackson.

The "Rhea Letter" reached Washington at a time when Monroe
was ill. Twelve years later Monroe recollected its fate to Calhoun:
"I well remember that when I received the letter from Gen'l Jackson . . . I was sick in bed, and could not read it. You were either
present, or came in immediately afterwards, and I handed it to you
for perusal. After reading it you replaced it with a remark that it
required my attention, or would require an answer, but without
notice of its contents. Mr. Crawford came in soon afterwards, and
I handed it also to him, for perusal. He read it and returned it,
in like manner, without making any comment on its contents, further than that it related to the Seminole war, or something to that
effect. . . . Having made all the arrangements respecting that war,
and being sometime confined by indisposition, the letter was laid
aside, and forgotten by me, and I never read it until after the conclusion of the war."

Filled with military ambition and excessive energy and daring, and assuming that whatever he did would be acceptable to the Administration, Jackson reached Fort Scott near the border on March 9 with two thousand men. Then he crossed into Florida, occupying the bombed runaway Negro fort and capturing the Spanish fort of St. Marks. At St. Marks, he found Francis and Peter, the Seminole prophets, and he hung them. He also took prisoner an old, white-haired Scotsman named Alexander Arbuthnot, the kindly father adviser to local Indians and a trader with a remarkable resemblance to Aaron Burr. Jackson next hurried eastward to the Suwannee River, through waist-high swamps, to capture Boleck's village and its chief, Boleck, or Bowlegs as he was called. But through his own son, Arbuthnot had warned Boleck and the village was almost deserted. By coincidence, a young British officer, Lieutenant Robert C. Ambrister, a veteran of Waterloo and a Napoleon guard on St. Helena, walked into the village while Jackson was there and was taken prisoner. Jackson gave quick approval to the hanging of old Arbuthnot, and although a military court sentenced Ambrister to fifty lashes and a year in jail, Jackson ordered him shot. Nor was this the end of Jackson's adventuring. He now turned westward on a 200-mile march to capture Spanish Pensacola. When the Spanish governor ran away to Fort Barancas on the Gulf of Mexico, Jackson forced him to surrender along with his archives.

Monroe was enjoying a quiet spring when the first news reached him on June 18, 1818. His inclination was to ignore the report as false rumor, but on July 6 Jackson's official dispatches arrived confirming the worst. Secretary of State Adams was exasperated with Monroe because he had gone to his home in Loudoun County, Virginia, "and though the moment is very critical and a storm is rapidly thickening, he had not read many of the papers I left with him, and he puts off everything for a future time." Adams also wailed that Spanish minister Don Luis de Onís had just "received new instructions from Spain, which would have enabled him to conclude a treaty with me [to sell East Florida] with satisfaction to both parties if it had not been for this unfortunate incident."

The capital was tense on July 15 as Monroe returned and met with his Cabinet for five hours to consider British and Spanish protests over the execution of two British subjects on Spanish soil and the seizure of Spanish posts. Adams later wrote in his diary: "The President and all the members of the Cabinet except myself are of the opinion that Jackson acted not only without, but against, instructions: that he has committed war upon Spain . . . in which, if not disavowed by the Administration, they [the Cabinet] will be abandoned by the country." Secretary of War Calhoun proposed that Jackson be court-martialed and bitterly commented that Jackson also was motivated by his interest in Florida land speculation and by a desire to bring on war with Spain in order that he might lead an army into Mexico. Crawford said that unless Monroe disavowed Jackson "for having commenced a war in violation of the Constitution; that the people would not support the Administration in such a war; that our shipping, navigation and commerce would be destroyed by privateers from all parts of the world, under the Spanish flag, and that the Administration would sink under it."

Had Adams gone along with the others the issue would have been settled immediately by a disavowal of the general and full apologies to England and Spain. But Adams saw disavowal as cringing cowardice and he alone insisted that Jackson must be supported. For five days the Cabinet wrangled with Adams, who lamented that the arguments brought "a weakness and palsy" to his right hand. Adams steadfastly insisted that Jackson's action "was defensive, that it was neither war against Spain nor violation of the Constitution," that he "took Pensacola only because the governor threatened to drive him out of the province by force if he did not withdraw . . . and that his only alternative was to prevent the execution of the threat." Finally on July 20, Attorney General Wirt swung over to his side, and then Monroe adopted his view. Agreement was reached that Wirt, a part-time novelist, would write an article to be planted in the Republican organ, the *National Intelligencer*, defending a soft policy on Jackson; while Adams was detailed to tell the Spanish minister that the Jackson-captured forts would be returned.

It became Adams' task to brazen out the matter with England and Spain by diplomatic correspondence. Richard Rush, American minister to England, reported that the execution of the two Britishers had aroused national fury in England and Jackson was commonly called a "ruffian" and "murderer." He also reported that Foreign Secretary Castlereagh told him that war would have come "if the ministry had but held up a finger." But Prime Minister Liverpool would not countenance another war and dropped the subject without even demanding an apology. So far as Spain was concerned, Adams took the offensive and in a bullying note declared that Spain's inability to control the Indians had forced the United States to take "defensive" measures. The Spanish forts would be returned—this time.

Fear now overtook Calhoun and Monroe that Jackson would be incensed to learn of the Cabinet dispute over him and the decision to return the forts to Spain. Calhoun found it political to tell a lie, one that would be exposed a decade later and ruin his ambition to become President. He told Captain James Gadsden, Jackson's close friend, that he abhorred the attitude of his colleagues who had been anxious to sacrifice "their best friend" in order to save their own political hides.

Monroe revealed the greatest difficulty in telling Jackson what had been decided. "When I am talking to him about the proposed negotiation in England, the instructions for Everett, or even South America," Adams said, "he stops in the middle of the discourse and says something about Jackson and Pensacola." Monroe finally rationalized his action to Jackson on a constitutional argument. "If the Executive refused to evacuate the posts, especially Pensacola, it would amount to a declaration of war. I would be accused of usurping the authority of Congress, and giving a deep and fatal wound to the Constitution." He also told Jackson that his military dispatches would have to be rewritten so that their public release would show he had acted only in defense, in his Florida undertaking. Monroe diplomatically added that Jackson probably had not written his dispatches in this fashion originally because of "haste and under the pressure of fatigue and infirmity, and in a spirit of conscious rectitude."

This was the first letter in a series that followed between the two men until December. At no time would Jackson admit he might have done something wrong. Nor did he justify his conquest by claiming Presidential approval. This was to come as an afterthought. Much later, in the face of harsh denials by Monroe, Jackson claimed that Monroe had given him permission through John Rhea to seize Spanish East Florida. He also claimed that he had saved the letter until April 12, 1818, when Rhea told him Monroe wanted the letter burned. When first questioned, Rhea said he had not had dealings with Monroe, nor had he written the letter in question to Jackson.

The Florida Affair argument now shifted to Congress. Henry Clay recognized that Jackson's popularity had been enhanced by his East Florida venture. Unless Jackson were immediately struck down, Clay reasoned, his own Presidential chances would decline. Clay made his move following Monroe's second Annual Message to Congress in December 1818, in which the President justified Jackson's conduct. For twenty-seven days, to the exclusion of all other business, Clay saw to it that the House debated four resolutions condemning the general for the Florida invasion and for executing Arbuthnot and Ambrister. Jackson got wind of the attack and hurried to Washington where he stalked the halls of the Capitol and intimidated many legislators. On February 8, 1819, the House was caught between its loyalty to Clay and its esteem for the general. The vote that day vindicated Jackson. Over in the Senate, Treasury Secretary Crawford duplicated Clay's effort and for the same reason—to strike down a looming Presidential threat. Crawford succeeded in getting the Senate to condemn Jackson two weeks after the House praised him. However, the two efforts were politically unwise, for the attacks served only to win Jackson national sympathy, as he now found on his triumphant tour of the North.

The entire controversy over Jackson and Spanish Florida appeared academic on February 22, 1819, when Secretary Adams concluded a treaty with Spanish minister Onís for the transfer of that area to the United States. This was a protracted negotiation that had begun in December 1817 when Adams learned that Spain's Foreign Minister, Don José Pizarro, announced his willingness to cede Florida if the United States would agree to abandon all territorial claims west of the Mississippi. Of course, Adams and Monroe considered this absurd, for since 1803 the American Government had claimed the Rio Grande, including Texas, as the boundary of the Louisiana Territory. Now began the battle between Adams and Don Onís, who scoffed at the American claim to the Rio Grande and Texas. Spain, he said, owned the West and the Pacific Coast up to 56° north, or well into Canada. When Adams grudgingly agreed to move the American boundary halfway through Texas to the Lower Colorado River, Pizarro told Onís to settle for the Colorado River line. But Onís maintained a gruff and curt manner and Adams agreed to retreat to the Trinity River in East Texas. However, he insisted on a further stipulation: the Spanish-American border was to end at the 41st Parallel in what is now Wyoming and then run directly west to the Pacific.

Monroe had paid little attention to the negotiations because the details of following river lines and chunks of latitudes and longitudes bored him. But when he heard of the possibility to extend the United States in a contiguous sweep to the Pacific, he grew excited. At the turn of the century it had seemed impossible that any future President might rule a nation that stretched acre after acre from the Atlantic to the Pacific. Now less than twenty years later, the possibility was not only present, it actually beckoned.

All that was needed was for Adams to yield a little more ground to Spain. With the two-ocean vision now his overriding desire, Monroe thus ordered his Secretary of State to offer an immediate settlement with Spain at lines far narrower than weak Spain would have been willing to accept. Adams was to give up all of Texas by moving his western boundary eastward from the Trinity to the Sabine River. He was even to relinquish a latitude or so north of the 41st Parallel if this would hasten the treaty.

On February 22, 1819, Onís and Adams signed what became known as the Transcontinental Treaty. One part dealt with Florida: Spain was to turn over Florida to the United States. In exchange, the American Government agreed to pay $5,000,000 to American citizens for commercial damages they claimed to have suffered from Spanish privateers. The other chief feature of the treaty gave Texas to Spain and acknowledged her claim to western territory only as far north as the 42nd Parallel. Adams wrote after the signing: "It was near one in the morning when I closed the day with ejaculations of fervent gratitude . . . the acknowledgement of a definite line of boundary to the South Seas forms a great epoch in our history."

Despite the angry charge by Speaker Clay that the United States had needlessly and dishonorably given up Texas, the Senate ratified the treaty unanimously two days later. However, two years were to elapse before it became effective. For Adams learned that King Ferdinand VII had slyly granted most of Florida to two Spaniards. Under the treaty, existing grants were to be honored, but Adams would not accept this treachery. It took until October 1820 before the Spanish tyrant agreed to cancel his grants, and on February 19, 1821, the Senate reconsidered and again approved the treaty. Monroe's dream had now come true.

Yet as things turned out, it was the very growth and spread of the United States that plunged the nation into its most emotional problem, one that ripped to shreds the tranquillity which was

Monroe's abiding desire. This was the question of slavery, which by a gentleman's agreement had scrupulously remained outside the pale of public discussion.

It came to the limelight now not because of moral implications but because its spread or contraction would seriously affect sectional political strength on the national scene. The original thirteen states had presented a lineup of seven northern states with a growing tendency to oppose slavery within their boundaries and six slave states, all in the South. In the face of an expanding nation, Congressional politicians had carefully devised a scheme for maintaining sectional balance. New states would be admitted in pairs, one free and one slave state. How honorably this plan was followed is apparent from the division at the beginning of 1818. Of the twenty states in the Union, ten were free and ten were slave.

In 1818, Illinois would win admission as a state, and then the South would balance the scale with Alabama. But now came the problem. Except for the sparsely populated Michigan Territory, statehood existed over the entire area east of the Mississippi River. In the future, the new states would all be western; and was the North to help in the spread of slavery merely to appease southern politicians? This was a question some Northerners were asking themselves.

The test case came early in 1819, on the question of creating states west of the Mississippi. Without fanfare, a House committee reported an enabling bill to the House floor that would permit the people of Missouri to organize a government and then apply for admission as a state. It was obvious that Missouri would join the ranks of the slave states, for her population was chiefly of southern origin and her farm labor basically Negro slaves.

Southern politicians looked forward complacently to the acceptance of Missouri as a slave state and the proliferation of slavery in the West. But a bombshell hit them when Representative James Tallmadge, Jr., of New York proposed an amendment to the Missouri Enabling Bill. Under Tallmadge's amendment, there would be a prohibition against any further introduction of slavery into Missouri and all slave children born there would be freed when they reached the age of twenty-five.

Southern reaction was immediate. Representative Thomas Cobb of Georgia cried: "You have kindled a fire which all the waters of the ocean cannot put out, which seas of blood can only extinguish." Speaker Clay recognized the seriousness of the situation. As the leader of the West, he might have taken the view that the West was unique and not bound either to the North or South; instead, he followed the bent of his Virginia origins and supported the southern position on Missouri.

Despite Clay's prestige, the House adopted the Tallmadge Amendment 87 to 76. But the Senate's rejection returned it to the House. The House then repassed it and the Senate again voted to send the unamended version of the bill back to the House. With both chambers stubborn, the Missouri Enabling Bill was put over until the Sixteenth Congress met in December 1819.

During the summer following the Congressional stalemate, Monroe was aware of the fierce sectional animosities that the Tallmadge Amendment had aroused. In the North, mass meetings and newspaper editorials condemned any extension of slavery through the admission of more slave states. In the South, where leading citizens had considered slavery an evil to be eliminated at some future time, the tone changed under northern attack to a defense of slavery as being economically necessary, morally condoned by the Bible and the Constitution and socially a humane effort to care for ignorant former African tribesmen.

As a true Virginian in heritage and training, Monroe, of course, held the southern position regarding Missouri's unencumbered entrance into the Union. He based his position on legalities, writing privately that "all states composing our Union, new as well as old, must have equal rights . . . that they cannot be incorporated into the Union on different principles or conditions. As slavery is recognized by the Constitution, it is evidently unjust to restrain the owner from carrying his slave into a territory and retaining his right to him there." Nevertheless, Monroe was careful to keep his opinion quiet and to stay out of the whirling controversy.

In general, the overriding fear in the South was that its 1,500,000 Negroes would revolt and treat the white population to a blood bath. Because Monroe had himself engaged in stamping out a slave revolt, Southerners considered him a hero, despite his unwillingness to use his Presidential office to force a southern solution for the Missouri question. The story was well known. Back in 1800, while he served as governor of Virginia, he was confronted with a slave insurrection. Not far from Richmond, a Negro slave who called himself General Gabriel and his confederate,

Jack Bowler, a huge slave on a nearby plantation, organized a thousand-man slave army to attack the whites in Richmond.

However, when the day for the contemplated slaughter approached, a slave named Pharaoh, traitorous to General Gabriel and Bowler, crept into Richmond and warned Monroe. The capital immediately went into siege and the militia dashed out to do battle. Unfortunately for the slaves, a torrential downpour swelled the rivers and the insurgents were hindered in reaching their rendezvous point and fell easy prey to the militia. The government had time to act with effect now, and the rebellion collapsed as General Gabriel, Bowler and other ringleaders were executed.

When the Congress convened in December, Monroe refrained from mentioning the most important current issue in dispatching his Annual Message to the legislators. He informed them instead about the Transcontinental Treaty and announced he was maintaining his position of watchful waiting and neutrality on the question of recognizing Spain's former colonies in South America.

The new Congress quickly assented to statehood for Alabama as the twenty-second state, thus balancing sectional strength again. This pointed up the fact that Missouri would unbalance things once more. Fortunately, a solution seemed available for returning to the old gentleman's agreement. The northern area of Massachusetts was a Republican hotbed whose fighting tactics were a continuing irritant to the Federalists around Boston who controlled the state. Why not let that Northern, or Maine, Territory go its own way so that Federalists might live in peace?

The Maine Territory found this admirable and in December 1819 asked Congress to admit it into the Union. Maine coupled with Missouri would help restore the hand-in-hand entrance of free and slave states and put the lid back on the slavery question, Clay argued. But Representative John W. Taylor of New York, who had succeeded Tallmadge as House leader of the antislavery states, had no intention of permitting this. To the Missouri Enabling Bill, he proposed an even more drastic amendment than Tallmadge had: Missouri could not attain statehood until she adopted a Constitution that barred slavery. Clay reacted with a fiery threat not to permit Maine to become a state so long as restrictions were put on Missouri. However, Taylor led a larger army on this issue and the House passed the Maine Enabling Bill without Missouri on January 3, 1820. Missouri would have to be handled separately now and not made part of any southern scheme to promote slavery by calling for sectional political equality.

Crowds choked the Capitol as the issue now moved on to the Senate. Senator William Pinkney of Maryland, Monroe's fellow envoy to Britain and one of the country's leading attorneys, pleased the throngs by dressing in ruffled sleeves and blouse, soft long trousers and tinted gloves. In a heady flight of flowery rhetoric, he found slavery for Missouri a positive virtue. Pinkney's chief opponent was Federalist Senator Rufus King of New York who was treated to hissing and threats when he denounced slavery as immoral and against natural law. In anger at King's attack, Senator James Barbour of Virginia, a friend of Monroe, made the rounds of southern Senators to propose a convention to dissolve the Union.

There seemed no way out of the impasse as speaker after speaker heaped acrimony on the other side. Yet a solution was suggested before the debate ended. It came in the form of an amendment by Senator Jesse B. Thomas of Illinois: Missouri would be admitted as a slave state, but all future states carved from the Louisiana Territory north of 36°30' north latitude would exclude slavery. Tired of continuing the wrangle further, the Senate agreed to the Thomas Amendment by a vote of 34 to 10 on February 17. Once again "the Misery Debate," as the newspapers called the goings-on, returned to the House.

With the Missouri question on everyone's lips, it had to intrude into Monroe's Cabinet sessions, even though he wished to keep it out. Adams reported that he told the President that in his opinion "the present question is a mere preamble—a title page to a great tragic volume." But Monroe, he continued, "thinks this question will be winked away by a compromise. . . . Much am I mistaken if it is not destined to survive his political and individual life and mine." In letters to Jefferson, Monroe did not mask his southern sympathies, as he did when speaking with Adams. He desired a Missouri unrestricted in her choice of slavery. "The object of those, who brought it [the Thomas Amendment] for'd," he wrote on February 7, 1820, "was undoubtedly to acquire power."

While he kept his views from Congress, the House debated the Taylor and Thomas proposals with little respite. Taylor was not willing to accept the Thomas Amendment to the Missouri Enabling Bill with its promise that only Missouri in the Louisiana Territory north of 36°30′ would become a slave state. On the other hand, do-or-die Southerners led by erratic John Randolph demanded that no geographic line bar slavery anywhere. Finally the debaters collapsed in exhaustion and the anti-Thomas Amendment line wavered. Taylor could not pull them together, and the "Doughfaces," the name by which Randolph contemptuously labeled Northerners with southern sympathies, helped provide the large margin by which the House approved the Missouri Enabling Bill with the Thomas Amendment.

Even then, Randolph would not quit. The following day he was on his feet with a motion to reconsider the bill. Clay put him off by declaring his motion out of order until the House Journal was read. Then while this was being done, Clay hastily signed the bill and smuggled it out to the Senate. When Randolph again made his motion, only to learn that the bill was no longer before the House, he cried out, "A dirty bargain!"

On March 3, 1820, the bill came before the man who had publicly ignored its existence. Monroe had no choice now other than to enter into the controversy, and he found the pressures enormous. Two weeks earlier, George Hay, his son-in-law, who had served as prosecuting attorney in the Burr trial, sent him word from Richmond that the Virginia caucus was preparing to select its slate of Presidential electors for the forthcoming election. If Monroe signed the bill, the caucus would probably order the electors to support another candidate. "I have never said how you would act, but simply that you would do your duty," said Hay. "The members have gone up to the caucus under the conviction that you will put your veto on this infamous cabal and intrigue; this I would certainly and promptly do. You may be injured in the northern and eastern states, but you will be amply repaid by the gratitude and affection of the South."

With a troubled mind Monroe wrote a draft of a Veto Message on the Missouri Compromise Bill, but whether this was prompted by his son-in-law's letter is uncertain. In this undelivered Message, he wrote: "That the proposed restriction to territories which are to be admitted into the Union, if not in direct violation of the Constitution, is repugnant to its principles."

It was Monroe's policy to submit all major issues to his Cabinet for debate and to ask for written replies to vexing questions. He now asked his Cabinet for opinions on the following questions: (1) Did Congress have the constitutional right to prohibit slavery in the *territories?* (2) Did the prohibition of slavery north of the 36°30' line apply only to territories or did it also apply to the *states* made from those territories?

A major argument broke out among Cabinet members, but in the end Crawford, Calhoun and Wirt—all from the South—assented to Adams' view on the first question that Congress could bar slavery in a territory. The question whether Congress had the right to do this in a state did not meet with similar assent. Finally Calhoun proposed that the second question be changed to whether the bill as it affected Missouri was constitutional. By this clever change of language, those who were previously in disagreement could now give unanimous assent. On this show of support for the bill, Monroe signed it on March 6.

He could say with honesty that signing the bill prevented civil war, even though he personally opposed the legislation, finding it obnoxious and unconstitutional. And because the immediate problem disappeared into thin air when he affixed his almost undecipherable signature on the bill, he could not agree with Jefferson's long-range view that the compromise was "a fire-bell in the night . . . We have the wolf by the ears, and we can neither safely hold him, nor safely let him go."

The spleen-spilling battle over slavery beyond the Mississippi came at a time when another grievous problem was leaking acid onto Monroe's Era of Good Feelings. In his inaugural address, Monroe had described the American people as "happy" and the nation as "prosperous." This was aptly put for the country was enjoying an unprecedented economic boom. Pent-up wartime hunger for consumer goods gave impetus to a demand for labor and raw materials. In the East, infant industries, spawned by the wartime barring of European products and invigorated by the protective Tariff of 1816, were adding immeasurably to the factory population and the manufacturing class. In the farm belt, cotton producers watched excitedly as cotton shot up to more than thirty cents a pound. As a direct result, cotton land values sought new ceilings and a great speculative urge overtook the American people. By the thousands, people began buying high-priced land on usurious credit terms, with no money down and an expectation that the principal would be endlessly renewed by the lender.

Americans were an optimistic breed and they thought the future held only immense wealth for the industrious and the risk-taker.

But things changed suddenly. Great Britain had emerged from the Napoleonic War with a need to sell her products abroad or fail. The United States had been a prime selling area before the war and this market had to be recaptured at all cost. To circumvent the Tariff of 1816 and home-grown American manufacturing, the British soon developed their strategy. This was simply to dump their goods on the American market at the outset, because in the words of a member of Parliament, it would "stifle in the cradle those rising manufactures in the United States which the war has forced into existence contrary to the usual course of nature." Later, prices would be raised.

British goods now began pouring into the United States, but by clever planning they avoided normal trade channels in sales and distribution. Instead they were sold directly at ports of entry at auctions. Their prices were far below cost, and as the pressure of this grossly unfair competition broadened, American manufacturers in the North and East were forced to close their doors with a resulting widespread unemployment among their workers.

The British also tightened the neck knot by closing their West Indies ports to American ships, thus eliminating the $6,000,000 a year in produce sales for American farmers. Furthermore, British manufacturers closed off the American cotton export trade by importing cheap and shoddy cotton from the East Indies. Thirty-two-cent cotton on the Liverpool market suddenly collapsed to fourteen cents a pound for American exporters, and with this catastrophe land rigidly mortgaged at one hundred dollars an acre could not be sold even for twenty dollars.

The Panic of 1819, as it was called, was the first major depression in the United States. With ruin and inactivity extending from border to border, the people searched for a scapegoat other than themselves to blame. In later depressions, whoever was President would be blamed; but no one pointed a finger at Monroe as the culprit bringing on the hunger, poverty and financial disaster. Among those ruined by the Panic was seventy-six-year-old Thomas Jefferson. He had endorsed the $20,000 note of Wilson Cary Nicholas, his friend and his former leader in the House of Representatives, as well as a recent governor of Virginia. When Nicholas did not make repayment, Jefferson was legally responsible and was left destitute as a result. Not even a later cash gift of $16,000 from well-wishers saved his last few years from financial worries.

Whatever unity the euphoria of prosperity had brought to their country vanished and with it went the Era of Good Feelings. Businessmen and politicians found their scapegoat in the Second Bank of the United States, even though their chief accusation was that the Bank had been too lenient in its loans policy.

The First Bank, the dreamchild of Hamilton, had functioned as a powerful tool for national stability before its charter expired in 1811. Among its activities, it operated as the Treasury's banker. People paid their Federal taxes at any of the Bank's branches in the bank notes of private bank origin. The U. S. Bank then presented these money certificates to the banks of origin for payment in gold and silver. To a large extent, this kept private banks honest. The U. S. Bank also paid off Federal obligations throughout the country.

When the Bank's charter expired and Congress refused to grant it a new lease, wildcat local banks took over the financial system. Uncontrolled as they were, they were soon working printing presses night and day, producing bank notes entirely unbacked by gold or silver reserves. It was simple for a man to get a loan to buy overpriced land. The bank gave the seller a pile of dubious paper certificates and tied the buyer to a high-interest mortgage. Those who could not be bothered to go through this process frequently counterfeited bank notes. Jefferson characterized the frightening situation as "a dropsical fullness of circulating medium."

In 1816, Republicans who had made their opposition to the First Bank a major plank in their program now rechartered the Second Bank of the United States. Its capital was $35,000,000 at the outset with $7,000,000 subscribed by the U. S. Government and five of its twenty-five directors named by the President. With wildcat paper money looked upon as a disease carrier by those engaged in trade, it was the hope of the Bank's exponents that it would speedily correct this situation. Foremost on its agenda were to be the tasks of (1) forcing state banks to tidy up their paper money mess and resume specie payment; and (2) issuing paper money of its own that would be redeemable in specie anywhere in the country on demand at any of its branch banks.

Unfortunately, William Jones, the first president of the Second Bank, who had proved a first-rate Secretary of the Navy under Madison, was a totally inept banker. He did not want to jar local financing abruptly, so he agreed to continue to accept unconvertible state bank notes as payment for public land. Jones also put the Bank itself into the wild land speculation business in the South and West with direct loans to speculators. He further compounded his ineptness by not establishing an examiners' unit to scrutinize the Bank's branches, where mismanagement and thievery flourished.

It was in July 1818 that Jones learned that the Bank's demand liability stood at $22,000,000, while its specie holdings were only $2,000,000. This in itself did not constitute a serious problem because paper money kept circulating and was seldom turned in for specie. However, the Monroe Administration would soon demand $2,000,000 in specie from the Bank's holdings of its deposits to make payment due on the Louisiana Purchase stock. And this spelled possible disaster.

The auctioning of British goods at ports of entry and the sharp cut in American exports had by now brought the country's economy close to disaster. Jones hastened the course, ordering his branch banks to accept no notes as payment for debts or taxes except the Bank's own notes. He also ordered the branches to present immediately all state bank notes they held for payment and to prohibit further renewal of personal loans.

Treasury Secretary Crawford, who had no authority over Jones, noted: "The banking bubbles are breaking . . . and distress universal in every part of the country." It was like a castle built with cards. Pressed by the Bank, the state banks could not meet specie demand on their unconvertible paper money. Land speculators could not meet payments on their loans, nor could they save their property by loan extensions. The crash came overnight.

In wrath, the now penniless debtors envisioned the Second Bank as the cause of their troubles. While many were without food or shelter, "the monster," as they called the Bank, waxed rich as the vast owner of defaulted land, cotton farms, retail businesses and local bank buildings. In state after state came demands that legislatures drive its branches from their borders.

It was in the case of McCulloch vs. Maryland that Monroe put his Administration into the Bank fight. In May 1818, the Maryland legislature passed a law requiring the Bank's Baltimore branch to pay an annual tax of $15,000. James W. McCulloch, the branch cashier, refused to pay the tax, and after the highest Maryland court ruled for the state, he brought the case on a writ of error to the U. S. Supreme Court. William Wirt, Monroe's Attorney

General, defended the Bank with the legal help of Daniel Webster and William Pinkney.

Maryland's attorneys argued three points: (1) Congress could not incorporate a bank because such authority did not exist under the enumerated powers in the Constitution; (2) Congress could not authorize a corporation to do business inside a state without the permission of that state; and (3) A state had the sovereign power to tax any corporation operating within its borders, despite Congressional incorporation.

Chief Justice John Marshall, ardent advocate of a strong central government, handed down his opinion in this historic case on March 6, 1819. Congress had authority to establish the Bank, he ruled, citing the language of Madison against the Jeffersonians who opposed expansion of Federal power beyond the enumerated powers. "Let the end be legitimate," he followed Madison's argument for implied powers, "let it be within the scope of the Constitution, and all means which are appropriate, which are plainly adapted to that end, which are not prohibited, but consist with the letter and spirit of the Constitution, are constitutional." Having ruled that the Bank was legitimately created by Congress, Marshall then struck down the state's power to tax it. The power to tax, he said, was equal to the power to destroy. In this case, the power to destroy would defeat the Federal Government's "power to create." It was, therefore, unconstitutional.

Those who had denounced the Bank as the cause of their financial ills now turned their anger on the Supreme Court. Forgotten was the fact that Monroe had placed his Administration on the side of the Bank. In an effort to quiet public animosity after this landmark decision, Speaker Clay brought on a House investigation of the Bank with the intention of instituting reforms. The spotlight now revealed that the Baltimore branch had engaged in a monumental, fraudulent operation. Sam Smith, former Senate tormentor of Albert Gallatin and President Madison, military defender of Baltimore, chairman of the Republican Presidential nominating caucus and now Representative from Maryland, was found to be involved in the shenanigans. His partner in the thriving firm of Smith & Buchanan, James Buchanan, was also serving as president of the Baltimore branch bank. With the collusion of McCulloch, the cashier whose name became part of judicial history, the firm looted the branch of its assets and used its authority to engage in dishonest stock transactions. However, the

House committee and the Attorney General did not believe criminal action could be taken. This led one of the Bank's directors to write Monroe: "This seems a dangerous inequality in the punishments inflicted by our legislation. If any person employed in the General Post Office embezzles or secretes the smallest amount of property confided to him he may be publicly whipped and imprisoned for ten years—whilst any officer of a Bank in which the revenue of the U.S. is deposited may defraud the institution of millions & escape the criminal law of the United States."

However, Monroe did not request Congress to change this inequality in the criminal code. His solution was in terms of personalities. William Jones and the entire Bank board resigned in disgrace, and Monroe induced Langdon Cheves of South Carolina, one of the original young War Hawks of 1811, to become president of the Bank in the spring of 1819. Common sense called for easing the harsh rulings of his predecessor in order to expand credit to some extent. However, in the face of continuing economic agony, Cheves ordered a further contraction of credit. More businesses now went under, the economy slid into a deeper hole and hatred of the Bank gained new adherents as the Bank took possession of additional millions of dollars' worth of property and businesses. As one man judged Cheves: "The Bank was saved, and the people were ruined."

Monroe, who had made no study of economics, took the view that the depression simply had to be endured until it went away. He also believed that adversity improved people and that they might learn important lessons from the depression to help them in the future. "I cannot regard the pressures to which I have adverted otherwise than in the light of mild and instructive admonitions," he said in his Annual Message of November 14, 1820, when the depression still continued in full force.

In the spring of 1819, with everything seeming to be falling apart in the political and economic arena, Monroe sought escape with a tour of the South. His travels took him to Augusta, then through Cherokee country to Nashville and then on to Louisville and Lexington. At Savannah, he had the pleasure of watching the steamship *Savannah* prepare for her first transatlantic voyage. At Athens, Georgia, where many were concerned about the growing sectional animosity over slavery, he pointedly toasted the Colonization Society. As governor of Virginia, he had tried unsuccessfully to acquire land outside of Virginia in which freed Negroes might settle by themselves. Then later while he was President and the Colonization Society acquired African territory, he gave his blessing to the effort to send freed Negroes there. In his honor, that territory, called Liberia, named its capital Monrovia.

In all the excitement over the Missouri Compromise fight during the early months of 1820, Congressional politicians forgot that another Presidential election was due that year. Finally in April, several Congressmen asked Representative Sam Smith to call a nominating caucus. Smith did so and to signify that the Federalist party no longer existed, he asked all members of Congress to attend.

A surprisingly small group of only forty members showed up that Saturday evening. Their handiwork before adjournment consisted in adopting a resolution declaring it unnecessary to make any nomination. With only the Republican party in existence, the caucus thus signified by its silence that the Republican standard bearer, Monroe, was the sole candidate in the field. Treasury Secretary Crawford, who had believed he had been given a veiled promise in 1816 that 1820 was to be his year, now had to hold off four years more.

Because voters in states where electors were popularly elected had no choice among alternate candidates, the election of 1820 proved the most apathetic in history. Only in Pennsylvania was an electoral ticket proposed against the Monroe slate, but the charge that Monroe was the candidate of the slavery party failed to yield more than yawns. In Philadelphia, where 4700 had voted for governor shortly before, only 2000 turned out to choose between Monroe and DeWitt Clinton, the anti-slavery slate candidate. In Connecticut only one out of each seventy eligible voters came to the polling stations. Worst of all was Richmond, Virginia, where only seventeen persons bothered to vote!

On December 5, 1820, when the Electoral College met, Monroe would have received all 232 electoral votes were it not for William Plumer, former U. S. Senator and governor of New Hampshire, who deprived Monroe of a unanimous election by voting for John Quincy Adams. Plumer's reasons, as stated at different times, were that he did not want Monroe to share this unique honor with hallowed Washington, that he distrusted Monroe and that he wanted to give Adams publicity to help him in the 1824 Presidential election.

Monroe viewed the one-party election of 1820 as a sign of the nation's growing maturity. He was so pleased with winning a second term that his enthusiasm overpoured onto the pages of his last Annual Message of his first term. He astounded legislators constantly beleaguered by constituents to do something about the continuing economic depression when he expressed "the greatest satisfaction at our wonderful prosperity."

As for his lack of Presidential competition, he wrote: "Surely our government may get on and prosper without the existence of parties. I have always considered their existence as the curse of the country, of which we have sufficient proof, more especially in the late war. How keep them alive and in action? The same causes which exist in other countries do not here." Jefferson found the view of his protégé naïve. "You are told, indeed," he wrote to Gallatin, then minister to France, "that there are no longer parties among us; that they are all now amalgamated; the lion and the lamb lie down together in peace. Do not believe a word of it."

Monroe had hoped that the Missouri Compromise of March 1820 would put to rest the sectional struggle over slavery. But a second Missouri debate came the next winter. Following passage of the Enabling Act, the Missouri constitutional convention met to write a state constitution. The product contained one provision barring free Negroes from entering Missouri and another prohibiting the state legislature from freeing slaves without the permission of their owners. This constitution was then sent to Washington when Congress convened in November for its approval in order that Missouri be granted statehood.

The arrogance of Missouri politicians made northern Congressmen see red and the second Missouri debate turned out to be much more acrimonious than the first. Northern legislators ripped into the two offending provisions of the Missouri constitution as being flagrantly in violation of Article IV of the Federal Constitution which declared that "the citizens of each State shall be entitled to all privileges and immunities of citizens in the several states." They denounced the Missouri constitutional convention as arrogant and venal. Through Dr. William Eustis, Madison's inept Secretary of War, now a Massachusetts Congressman, Secretary of State Adams led the fight to expunge from the Missouri constitution the clause barring free Negroes from the state. But this effort met with defeat as did a counter move to win acceptance of the constitution as presented to Congress.

For two months the debate raged with both sides unwilling to compromise. The Southerners' offensive pointed out that northern states had no business criticizing Missouri because of their own discriminatory practices: Indiana barred Negroes from appearing as court witnesses against whites; Kentucky barred all but free whites from voting; and the District of Columbia permitted only free whites to run for mayor, even though, said one speaker, "a swarm of mulattoes have been reared in the city, many of whom, no doubt, had as illustrious fathers as any in the nation."

The debate was still on when Congress met in the House chamber on February 14, 1821, to count the electoral vote. Henry Clay had resigned the Speakership the previous October (but he retained his House seat) when he found it necessary to return home to Kentucky to earn money to repay gambling debts. In his place, the House had elected John W. Taylor of New York, the leader of the anti-slavers. However, Clay now cut short his Kentucky stay to be on hand for the eventual settlement of the Missouri problem.

To prevent disputes among the warring debaters during the electoral vote count, the leadership decided that Vice-President Daniel D. Tompkins would announce the results in two forms: (1) with the vote of Missouri included; and (2) with the vote of Missouri omitted. He was then to say, "But in either case James Monroe is elected President of the United States."

However, when Missouri was reached during the count, John Randolph leaped to his feet to scream that Missouri was a state and that Congress lacked authority to decide on the vote of a state. Clay made a reply, but bedlam had taken over. When it was suggested that perhaps the Senate should withdraw, Tompkins declared the motion carried and led the Senators from the House chamber. House members continued their fight until dusk came and candles were lighted. By then members were exhausted and Clay asked Speaker Taylor to recall the Senate. But again when the Vice-President came to Missouri, Randolph and John Floyd, also from Virginia, were stamping and yelling that the Missouri vote should be counted without questioning. However, Taylor refused to recognize either, and above their din, the count was completed and announced in its dual form.

Afterward, Clay succeeded in getting a joint committee appointed on Missouri's status. The committee recommended a solution the House had already rejected, that Missouri be granted statehood if her legislature agreed to respect "the rights and privileges of all citizens of the United States." This was meaningless so long as her constitution said the opposite, but Congress passed this Second Missouri Compromise in order to adjourn. The reaction of the Missouri legislature came in its resolution that Congress had no authority to bind it to certain action. Nevertheless, anxious for peace, Monroe proclaimed Missouri a state.

Monroe's second inauguration was hardly a gay occasion, for the depression still lingered and the Missouri bitterness had yet to subside. March 4, 1821 came on a Sunday and he waited until the fifth for his ceremony. Wind and sleet turned historic Pennsylvania Avenue into a deserted mud patch as Monroe rode unescorted by carriage to the Capitol. He arrived as the proud Revolutionary, wearing a "suit of black broadcloth of somewhat antiquated fashion," with knee and shoe buckles and his hair powdered and tied behind in a queue. He found a large crowd inside the building on his day of days, and British minister Stratford Canning noted: "We had a tremendous crowd of sturdy and ragged citizens to squeeze through on our way into the House of Representatives. We stood about ten paces from the door and were utterly unable to get through until the arrival of the President, who to our great concern and satisfaction was squeezed as handsomely and detained as long as ourselves. . . . In addition to the squeezing and shoving which the poor Prezzy experienced at the door, his speech, which was indeed rather long, was occasionally interrupted by queer sounds from the gallery." The disorder and agitation in the gallery, which Adams also mentioned, may have arisen when Monroe spoke of the "extraordinary prosperity" of the country.

Monroe's philosophy of non-interference with the Legislative Branch's activities did not change during his second term. For example, in November 1821 Speaker John Taylor ran for re-election against a field of four other Representatives. Taylor called on Secretary of State Adams, and with the hope of gaining Monroe's support he pledged his allegiance to the Administration. Adams immediately informed Monroe of his opportunity. However, Monroe quickly scotched him with the declaration that "he believed the proper course would be to take no part in it at all."

Monroe's hands-off policy did not deter Treasury Secretary Crawford from promoting his own choice, James Barbour of Virginia. When Barbour defeated Taylor, Adams was in a fury, scribbling in his diary that the new Speaker was "a shallow-pated wildcat, fit for nothing but to tear the Union to rags and tatters." Adams recognized that, through default, Monroe had turned over control of the House to a Crawford lieutenant who was anti-Administration. More than that, through Barbour, Crawford could now attack Adams and reduce his Presidential hopes for 1824. This was not long in coming true, for Barbour lost little time appointing Jonathan Russell of Massachusetts, an enemy of Adams since their peace treaty days at Ghent, as chairman of the House Committee on Foreign Affairs.

The Era of Good Feelings was never apparent in Washington, whether at the Capitol or at the White House. The troubles at the White House stemmed from the attitudes of Monroe's wife, the former Elizabeth Kortright of New York, who was known as a "stately snob." The warmth and good cheer Dolley Madison brought to the Executive Mansion disappeared when Mrs. Monroe, the daughter of a British Army officer, took charge. Formality was reinstated, Dolley's open house entertaining thrown out and set visiting hours for a carefully selected guest list established. For a week or more before an important social function, Mrs. Monroe kept slaves fully occupied producing the thousands of candles needed. Levee guests were warmed by great fires of hickory wood in the large open fireplaces and were served wine by colored waiters dressed in dark livery, gilt buttons, etc. Dolley Madison had called on official Washington with great enthusiasm, but Mrs. Monroe deemed outside calls beneath the dignity of the First Lady. Eliza Monroe Hay, Monroe's older daughter, proved even more snobbish than her mother when Mrs. Monroe because of illness had to delegate social duties to her. Eliza, whose claim to fame was her schoolhood friendship with Hortense de Beauharnais, Napoleon's stepdaughter who became Queen of Holland, was widely regarded as an "obstinate little firebrand" who spoiled parties by ignoring some guests and scolding others. When she tried to find a basis for her high-handed manners, she began intruding on Secretary of State Adams' time with endless questions regarding "etiquette visiting." This spilled over into Cabinet meetings where President Monroe actually held discussions on protocol. At one Cabinet meeting he instructed Adams to make a thorough study of the subject, and although Adams found this offensive he prepared a volume on the matter for Monroe.

Eventually social Washington decided it had had enough of the Monroe women and instituted a boycott of White House affairs. What remained to the First Family now were its dull and gloomy official dinners. Yet there were occasions when the unexpected managed to enliven the parties. One time, for instance, Sir Charles Vaughan, British minister, sat opposite Count de Sérurier, who kept biting his thumb when Sir Charles spoke. "Do you bite your thumb at me, sir?" he finally asked the Frenchman.

"I do," the Count shouted, and the two immediately left the table.

Monroe, who had been watching them, found this peculiar and went out after them. He found the two with their swords crossed in an adjoining room. Quickly pulling out his own sword, he uncrossed theirs with an angry upward swing and ordered them to leave.

For a time Monroe employed his brother Joseph as his White House secretary. A ne'er-do-well who was a constant problem because of his associates and his desire to make use of his brother's position, Joseph had been married three times and continually nagged James to pay his bills and "to be so kind as to put him in the way to make money." Monroe then employed his wife's nephew, Samuel Gouverneur, a young man known as a sport, who had a dream he would one day make his fortune at the race track. Monroe's younger daughter, Maria, was only twelve when he was inaugurated. When she was sixteen, she fell in love with Gouverneur, and despite the fact that he was primarily interested in gambling, horse racing and drinking and had run through his large inheritance, her father consented to their marriage. She was married on her seventeenth birthday, in the Blue Room at the White House, with Eliza barring the diplomatic corps from attending the wedding reception despite pleas from Maria. This marriage brought on new trouble at the White House, for her older sister Eliza detested Sam Gouverneur and instigated a continuing family row.

Monroe had put off making decisions in his first term on a host of questions of vital concern to Americans. Now he could no longer remain entirely impassive, for explosions were bound to occur. Nevertheless, he found ways to continue his stifling tactics as long as he could.

One urgent problem that he had inherited and kept inactive

went back to the year 1816, known as the "year without a summer." In usually hot areas, it was necessary to light coal and wood fires in July. Many New Englanders deserted the frigid Puritan soil for what they hoped would be a warmer West. Others found the weather an excuse for seeking new adventure and a fresh start.

When Monroe became President the clamor for roads and canals was already enormous. Madison's last official act had been to veto a bill putting the Federal Government into the internal improvements field. Monroe found it expedient to continue the old Republican philosophy: in his inaugural address, he admitted the importance of roads and canals, but insisted that such works could not be done without an amendment to the Constitution. Construction would be costly, and this would interfere with Monroe's intention to pay off the national debt and to eliminate internal taxation. This immediately stirred Henry Clay to vicious attack, for he was well aware that Monroe had not objected to the chartering of the Second Bank, a parallel activity not included among the enumerated powers. Clay refused to promote an amendment through Congress, for he said that none was needed. To Monroe's chagrin, both Secretary of War Calhoun and Treasury Secretary Crawford agreed with Clay and submitted reports to Congress on vital military and civil projects that should be undertaken. However, before Clay could test his own view in Congress, the Panic of 1819 occurred and the Calhoun-Crawford reports gathered dust during the long retrenchment period that followed.

In 1822, when the country finally emerged from the depression, the issue once more became pressing. States and localities had drawn up plans to alleviate the lack of communication between settlements, but costs were far beyond the meager limitations of local revenues. A test case now arose to see whether Monroe would change his mind. In 1802, Jefferson had signed a bill providing for the construction of the Cumberland Road from Maryland to Ohio at the time Ohio became a state; funds were to come from a percentage of the receipts from the sale of public land in Ohio. At the time no one appears to have questioned how Jefferson managed to approve this construction while declaring all Federal internal improvements to be unconstitutional. Madison later attempted a justification in a letter to President Monroe: "The Executive consent was doubtingly or hastily given. Having once become a law, and being a measure of singular utility, additional appropriations took place, of course under the same Administration, and, with the accumulated impulse thence derived, were continued under the succeeding one, with less of critical investigation perhaps than was due to the case."

The Cumberland Road had been extended as far as Wheeling when the Panic of 1819 halted work. With economic recovery, Clay advocated extending the road through the Northwest to the Pacific. Meanwhile repair work was needed and in April Congress appropriated $9000 and authorized Monroe to construct toll gates and fix toll charges to pay for future repairs. Imagine the Congressional consternation when a Veto Message arrived a few days later from the White House.

When Congress failed to muster the necessary two-thirds vote to override his veto, there appeared to be no solution to this urgent problem other than to go through the cumbersome, time-consuming process of passing a constitutional amendment. Monroe had sent General Jackson a copy of his long Veto Message and the general had fortified the President with his comment: "My opinion has always been that the Federal Government did not possess the constitutional right." Had the Jackson letter been made public, his immense popularity in the West would have ebbed.

Congressional leaders still resisted promoting a constitutional amendment. Sharp eyes had noted in Monroe's Veto Message the stress the President had put on the unconstitutionality of the authorization for toll gate construction. So they wrote a simple bill calling only for necessary repairs on the Cumberland Road and sent it to the White House after passage. By now, Monroe was well aware that the first western anger was being directed at him. For decades he had been considered the champion of the West, and this new turn hurt him deeply. He quickly signed the new bill and justified it with the comment that the obnoxious sections had been removed.

Henry Clay had dropped out of Congress during the Seventeenth Congress. But he returned for the Eighteenth in March 1823, and easily won election as Speaker again. This time he was determined to settle the roads and canals question, and in 1824 he promoted the General Surveys Bill. This legislation authorized the President to use the Army Engineers to make surveys costing up to $30,000 for "a system of roads and canals as he might deem of national importance from a postal, commercial or military point of view."

In the long debate, Clay ridiculed Monroe's professed belief in strict construction of the Constitution. How illogical and foolish was the President, he charged, to oppose internal improvements yet approve lighthouse construction and harbor improvements— "Everything on the margin of the ocean, but nothing for domestic trade; nothing for the great interior of the country." Fearful that Clay's arguments might impress Monroe, John Randolph spewed out a long tirade against a loose construction of the Constitution. If Congress could authorize road construction, he argued, then Congress could also free slaves.

Clay's argument pushed the bill through Congress and Monroe could no longer hide the problem under the rug. His veto would uphold his position, but it also would make him hated in the West. He chose popularity. When he signed the bill, he pointed out that it called only for surveys and not for actual construction. But with his signature, he opened the gate to future Federal appropriations for public works projects.

Another problem that could not be delayed indefinitely was what to do about the South American revolutions. Despite recurring attacks on him by Clay, Monroe managed to get through his first term without recognizing the revolutionists. Monroe was personally as avid a liberationist as Clay, but he found several reasons for doing nothing. His primary concern was that recognition might involve the United States in war with European nations who spoke of intervening in South America against the revolutionists. A secondary consideration was his agreement with Secretary Adams that the revolutionists "had not the first elements of good or free government. Arbitrary power, military and ecclesiastical, was stamped upon their education, upon their habits, and upon all their institutions." This view was also borne out by his three-man commission sent cruising into Latin American waters to study the rebels.

Until the Transcontinental Treaty with Spain for Florida and a quit-claim above the 42nd Parallel was finally signed in 1821, Monroe had a further excuse for delaying recognition. Action sooner might have jeopardized the treaty. Nevertheless, 1821 passed and Monroe still did not act. It was early in 1822 that Adams gave him word that decisive rebel victories had been achieved in South America. Simón Bolívar had liberated Venezuela and Colombia the previous year, while José de San Martín had led rebel forces from liberated Argentina across the Andes to free Chile and from there had traveled by sea to oust the Spanish from Peru.

On March 8, 1822, Monroe finally sent a Special Message to Congress, in which he reviewed the history of the revolutions in Mexico, Argentina, Peru, Chile and Colombia and declared that Spain no longer controlled those countries. Members of Congress expected to read that he had recognized their revolutionary governments, but a passive President to the end, he said that if Congress would appropriate money for diplomatic representatives he would *then* recognize their independence. Congress thus exercised Presidential authority when it acted on his request and appropriated $100,000.

There was only one foreign piece of land which might have enticed Monroe to take aggressive action. This was the island of Cuba, a prime target for annexation by all Republican Presidents. "I have always concurr'd with you in sentiment," Monroe wrote Jefferson, "that too much importance could not be attached to the Island, and that we ought, if possible, to incorporate it into our Union, availing ourselves of the most favorable moment for it, hoping also that one would arrive, when it might be done, without a rupture with Spain or any other power. I consider Cape Florida & Cuba, as forming the mouth of the Mississippi; & other rivers, emptying into the Gulph of Mexico."

The favorable moment never seemed to come. An opportunity presented itself when a revolution took place in Spain and in the turmoil, Spain's "Pearl of the Antilles" would have been an easy island to capture. But Monroe did not act. Then in 1823 when despotic France invaded Spain to restore Ferdinand to the throne, Monroe grew tortured with concern because of reports that Spain would give Cuba to Britain in return for aid against France. His policy now became one advocated by Adams: to support Spanish retention of Cuba but to consider annexing the island if any other country tried to take it over.

There were other problems besides Cuba and Latin American revolutions to disturb Monroe's peace during his second term. Britain had agreed in 1817 to demilitarize the Great Lakes border and Lake Champlain. A convention of 1818 also provided for joint occupation of the disputed Oregon Territory. This upturn in good relations was jolted in 1820 when Congress authorized American settlements on the Columbia River. The British, who had considered the Pacific Northwest as primarily an area for trade and not for settlement, registered an angry objection to American immigration between the 42nd and 54th Parallels. However, Secretary Adams made use of his sharp tongue to warn British minister Stratford Canning during a two-day word-lashing, "Keep what is yours, but leave the rest of the continent to us!"

Continuing problems with Britain included her monopoly of West Indies trade and her desire to gain Cuba. At the prodding of Adams, Monroe recommended that Congress retaliate and in May 1820 he signed a bill which barred British ships from bringing goods into the United States from any British colony barring American ships. Monroe was fearful that this would lead to further British trade retaliation; however, it had the opposite effect, for in June 1822, Prime Minister Liverpool pushed legislation through Parliament granting American ships free trade in the West Indies.

Monroe and Adams had also been watching the spread of the Russians into American-claimed territory in the West. In 1811, the Russians had established a trading port at Bodega Bay, not far from San Francisco. The Monroe-Adams policy was to consider the Russians at San Francisco as having a commercial but not a territorial interest there. However, this was not the Czar's intent, for in 1822 he claimed the entire Pacific coast from the Bering Strait to the 51st Parallel deep into the Oregon Territory as his alone, and he barred all ships from approaching within a hundred miles of this coast.

Monroe considered the Czar's proclamation with anger, and following several meetings with his Secretary of State, he insisted that a strong line be taken. In July 1822, Adams formally contested the right of Russia to any territorial establishment and assumed "distinctly the principle that the American continents are no longer subjects for any new European colonial establishments." The Administration then followed up by ordering American minister Middleton at St. Petersburg to demand a settlement before a serious collision took place. Czar Alexander took offense at the outset, but Adams would not weaken his pursuit. Finally almost two years later, on April 17, 1824, Alexander agreed by treaty not to settle on the Pacific coast below 54°40′ and to drop his absurd hundred-mile maritime claim. In exchange, Monroe pledged not to settle above 54°40′ north latitude.

Alexander's ukase in 1822 was the first real factor leading to Monroe's most important contribution to American foreign policy. Another factor was the proposal by the Holy Alliance to intervene in South America and recapture the former Spanish colonies.

Following the Napoleonic War, the victors made three arrangements. First, the Vienna Congress led by Britain's Castlereagh, Austria's Metternich, France's Talleyrand and several of Czar Alexander's aides attempted to restore Europe's balance of power by territorial and governmental adjustments. Second, the Quadruple Alliance (Austria, Britain, Prussia and Russia) set future periodic meetings of the foreign ministers to discuss what was needed to maintain peace in Europe. The third arrangement was the Holy Alliance of Austria, Prussia and Russia with ostensible pretensions of living a Christlike national existence but dedicated to quelling revolutionary revolts in Europe and subsequently in Latin America. In April 1823, the Holy Alliance showed itself to be more than "a loud-sounding nothing," as Count Metternich had laughed it off. Through the military offices of French Bourbon Louis XVIII, cruel Ferdinand of Spain was that month restored to his throne. Flushed with success, Chateaubriand, the French author and representative to the Holy Alliance meeting at Verona, proposed that the House of Bourbons establish kingdoms in the former Spanish colonies in South America.

British Foreign Secretary Castlereagh had based British foreign policy on a European balance of power that took little interest in outside areas. In mid-1822, he became deranged, a condition that manifested itself when he shouted at King George IV: "Have you heard the news, the terrible news? I am a fugitive from justice." Then on August 12, he gazed out a window and slit his throat from ear to ear.

George Canning, who succeeded Castlereagh, operated the Foreign Office under entirely different guidelines. He found the idea of a concert of Europe offensive and he revealed great concern with the Holy Alliance's plans for South America. Although Canning had displayed a strong anti-American attitude in previous ministries, he now saw a distinct advantage to Britain in a close association with the United States. Therefore, on August 20, 1823, he sent the following confidential note to Richard Rush, the American minister to the Court of St. James: "Is not the moment come when our governments might understand each other as to the Spanish American colonies? And if we can arrive at such an understanding, would it not be expedient for ourselves, and beneficial for all the world, that the principles of it should be clearly settled and plainly avowed?"

Canning then proceeded to state a five-point summary of his position—that the British believed the recovery of the colonies by Spain to be hopeless; recognition of them as independent nations was a matter of time; England would not impede amicable negotiations between them and Spain. For his last two points, Canning wrote: "We aim not at the possession of any portion of them ourselves. We could not see any portion of them transferred to any other power with indifference."

To Canning's urging that Rush join him in signing a two-nation convention on these points, the American minister replied that if Britain would immediately recognize the former Spanish colonies as independent nations, he would agree to "make a declaration in the name of my government that it will not remain inactive under an attack upon those states by the Holy Alliance." However, Canning would not accept Rush's proposal that he announce recognition of the new governments without delay. Nevertheless, with some suspicion and yet with great excitement, Rush sent Canning's note and copies of their correspondence to Washington. Canning then turned his persuasive charm on the French ambassador, the Prince Polignac, in an effort to head off Holy Alliance action in South America. Polignac proved agreeable and after several talks, the two men evolved the Polignac Memorandum of October 9–12, 1823. In this secret pact, France agreed to accept the Canning points sent to Rush, plus other provisions not to assist Spain against her former colonies nor to seek exclusive commercial relations with Latin American nations.

Unaware of the Polignac Memorandum, Monroe was in despair that France intended to take military action in South America. When Rush's papers reached him on October 9, 1823, Adams was not at hand to help explore their significance. Monroe read through them and then hurriedly wrote Jefferson and Madison for advice. He pointed out that he favored a joint declaration with England, even though this would violate previously established American policy to avoid European entanglements.

Both Jefferson and Madison replied that they also favored a joint declaration. Jefferson went so far as to call the proposal "the most momentous since that of Independence . . . By acceding to her [England's] proposition, we detach her from the bands [Europe],

bring her mighty weight into the scale of free government, and
emancipate a continent at one stroke. . . . Great Britain is the
nation which can do us the most harm of anyone on all the earth;
and with her on our side we need not fear the whole world."
To obtain this, he was even willing to sacrifice his great desire to
make Cuba part of the United States.

Monroe called his Cabinet to discuss Canning's proposal on November 7, and for a month a free debate produced heated sessions.
Monroe and Calhoun were fearful of Holy Alliance action, while
Adams scoffed at the possibility of such intervention. Adams also
found himself alone in arguing against a joint declaration with Britain. In his opinion, the United States should announce her own
policy that would take in Russian adventures on the West Coast
as well as Holy Alliance threats to Latin America. The United
States should not, he argued, "Come in as a cock-boat in the wake
of the British man-of-war."

Toward the end of November, Monroe and the others accepted
the principle of going it alone. In discussing the mechanics best
suited for transmitting the policy, it developed Adams advocated
diplomatic correspondence, but Monroe believed this would be a
low-pitch approach. The proper vehicle, he said, would be his
Annual Message to Congress in December.

With these matters settled, Monroe next read his proposed Message draft to his Cabinet. Adams preened as he heard the almost
verbatim memo on the declaration he had sent Monroe a week
before. But his joy disappeared in face of a vicious attack on
France for invading Spain and overthrowing a constitutional government. Nor was he pleased to listen to an attack on Turkey and
praise for Greek revolutionists in their war for independence
against the sultan, in addition to Monroe's recommendation that
Congress should appropriate money to send an American minister
to Greece.

Monroe, who had been such a cautious President, was suddenly
imbued with the desire to use the strength of his office to help
the cause of freedom everywhere. But Adams, who had been so
critical of his passive nature earlier, would not hear of it: the
latter part of the President's Message was too strong as well as useless, for mere words of praise would not actually help the revolutionists in Spain and Greece. Yet American encouragement coming
from the nation's highest official would serve only to bring a rupture in diplomatic relations with Russia, France and Spain. "The

ground that I wish to take," said Adams, "is that of earnest remon-
strance against the interference of the European powers by force
with South America, but to disclaim all interference on our part
with Europe." When Monroe's momentary resurgence of his revolutionary spark faded and he agreed to eliminate the paragraphs,
Adams expressed pleasure that the Message was now "in the spirit
that I had so urgently pressed."

The Monroe Doctrine, as the foreign policy portion of Monroe's
seventh Annual Message was called, reached Congress on December 2, 1823. It called not for legislative approval, but asserted itself
as fundamental law on the sole basis of Presidential prerogatives
over foreign relations. That it could have come from a notorious
avoider of policy decisions must have mystified some of his contemporaries. Yet to Monroe must go the credit for a doctrine that
dictated American foreign policy until World War I.

Old Republicans found it essentially a restatement in more compelling language of ideas Jefferson and Madison had earlier
espoused. But the application seemed so much more vital now, for
it established the United States as a world power warning other
nations of serious consequences should they defy American policy.

In brief, the Monroe Doctrine was contained in paragraphs of
the Message separated by other subjects. One part clearly announced "that the American continents . . . are henceforth not to
be considered as subjects for future colonization by any European
powers," and "we should consider any attempt on their part to
extend their system to any portion of this hemisphere as dangerous to our peace and safety." In another section, Monroe pledged
that in return the United States would not "interfere in the internal
concerns" of any European power, but would always "consider the
Government *de facto* as the legitimate government for us."

At the time Monroe promulgated his Doctrine, it failed to receive widespread attention at home. The reason was obvious. At
the outset of his re-election victory, Monroe had expressed joy that
contending political parties had vanished from the American scene.
Yet the truth was that after the demise of the Federalists, the Republican party had splintered into several parts behind various
candidates who hoped to succeed Monroe. In fact, Monroe's entire
second term was a raucous battleground drowning out the sounds
from his Administration.

The 1824 campaign formally began when the South Carolina
legislature nominated Representative William Lowndes for Presi-

dent in 1821. Yellow-haired Lowndes was a superb orator of outstanding intellect and integrity and was viewed since his Congressional years of leadership among the young War Hawks as a man
destined for greatness. But Lowndes was already ill and had not
long to live. When he died in October 1822, while en route to
England, his friends were at least thankful he had died at sea
and thus was spared having John Randolph at his funeral. In
recent years, Randolph had developed a "strange obituary zeal."
When a member of Congress died, or even when there was only a
rumor that one may have perished, Randolph was on his feet and
uttering long orations. If he appeared at a funeral, he was liable
to come on a prancing horse that leaped back and forth across the
grave and into the crowd of mourners as he did at the funeral of
Commodore Stephen Decatur, killed in a duel with Captain James
Barron.

A second prominent candidate was General Andrew Jackson.
When "Old Hickory" was first asked in 1821 if he was running, he
replied with feigned modesty: "Do they think I am such a damn
fool as to think myself fit for the Presidency? No, sir, I know what
I am good for. I can command a body of men in a rough way, but
I am not fit to be President."

Jackson faced a serious problem in March 1821 when Congress in
an effort to curtail government spending during the depression designated Jacob Brown as top Army officer at a rank of major general
and cut the ranks of brigadier generals to two. Since Jackson lacked
the seniority of Winfield Scott or Edmund Gaines, he could not
retain his single star. When Monroe learned of this, he tried to
rectify the situation by appointing Jackson as governor of East and
West Florida. Jackson, however, betrayed this act of kindness when
he learned that Monroe had appointed lesser Florida officials without consulting him and had omitted any of his coterie. The result
was that the President was soon sorry he had kept Jackson in the
limelight. Once he reached Florida, Jackson imprisoned the outgoing Spanish governor on the charge of failing to turn over certain
public papers. Then when a Federal judge issued a writ of habeas
corpus, Jackson refused to release the Spaniard but appealed instead to Monroe to support his position.

The entire matter received a Cabinet airing in October. As was
his custom, Adams strongly defended Jackson, while Monroe, Calhoun and Wirt argued that Jackson had no authority to act as judge
over the Spaniard. When news of the Cabinet squabbles became

public, the Republican press was full of inflammatory hatred toward Monroe because of Jackson's popularity. Several letters threatening Monroe's life reached the White House. Jackson finally solved the problem by resigning and returning home. Here he took to bombarding Monroe with unpleasant letters, calling him a warm-weather friend. Then in 1823, he came to Washington as a Senator from Tennessee to take personal charge of his campaign.

Another strong candidate was Speaker Henry Clay, who competed with Jackson as the spokesman for the West. While Jackson had no political program and ran solely on the basis of widespread popularity for a tried and proven military leader, Clay had a program that he expected to boost him into the White House. Clay was a man of sporting blood, a whisky drinker, gambler and a man of honor, as was expected of their politicians by Kentuckians. So far as the rest of the country was concerned, he knew he would have to offer more than these, and he did.

One important aspect of his candidacy was to show himself as the real leader of the nation by making himself master of the Monroe Administration. Secretary Adams, who watched the effect Clay had on Monroe's serenity, called him "essentially a gamester" with a keen intellect and "a very undigestible system of ethics." He decried Clay's constant violent systematic opposition to the Administration, as well as Monroe's unwillingness to descend from his plane of aloofness and give battle. Certainly Monroe had ample cause for fighting Clay, for the Speaker eroded Executive power almost without letup. Clay would taunt the Administration, daring it to stand up for its rights. Attorney General Wirt cited the instance when Clay entered a personal money claim for past diplomatic services rendered. "If you reject the claim," said Wirt, "Mr. Clay and his friends may impute it to hostility to him. If you admit the claim, it may be imputed to a dread of his further opposition and a wish to bribe him to silence." The claim was paid.

As the House's leader, he instigated several unfriendly investigations of the Post Office. He also established standing committees to scrutinize spending and efficiency in the State, Treasury, Navy, Post Office and Public Buildings agencies. These standing committees wrote new legislation affecting these agencies and controlled their appropriations. So in effect, Clay controlled their day-to-day operations rather than their chiefs.

It was a postal appointment that showed how unstable Republican unity actually was. In 1822, when the Albany postmaster was fired for corrupt accounting, twenty-two of the twenty-seven members of the New York Congressional delegation asked Postmaster General Return Meigs to appoint their House colleague, General Stephen Van Rensselaer, who was penniless, in his place. Monroe was willing to do so, even though the general had been an ardent Federalist. However, Secretary of the Navy Smith Thompson, who was from New York, voiced strong objections. So did the two New York Senators, Martin Van Buren and Rufus King. Worst of all was the vitriolic exasperation of Vice-President Tompkins, once New York's governor. It was reported that Tompkins "broke out into the most violent language against the President himself, and in the presence of a person who he must have known would report all he said to him." A bitter Cabinet meeting followed, with Monroe asking for advice on the proposed appointment and his Secretaries fighting among themselves. Monroe's final decision was to pretend that he had never heard of the vacancy. Left on his own, Meigs appointed Van Rensselaer and shouldered all responsibility for it.

Besides his effort to stamp himself as a strong leader, Clay presented a political program that he labeled "The American System." There were three chief planks in his program: (1) the establishment of a high protective tariff; (2) a large Federal program for road and canal construction financed from the sale of public land; and (3) increased authority for the Second Bank of the United States.

Unfortunately for Clay, only his second plank proved popular, and this chiefly in the West. Any general esteem that may have existed for the Second Bank, of course, vanished with the Panic of 1819. So far as a protective tariff might have contributed to his political status, Clay learned in 1824 that it was a handicap. Support from the West, which produced for the domestic market, and from eastern manufacturers, who feared foreign competition, was offset by strong opposition from the exporting southern planters and the New England shippers who carried their cotton and tobacco abroad. The division over the Tariff of 1824 was apparent from the close margin by which it won approval in Congress: 105 to 102 in the House and 25 to 22 in the Senate.

This disturbed Clay who knew the importance of holding an enthusiastic backing if he were to win the Presidency. He was also disturbed by the severe attacks that now descended upon him from supporters of the various other candidates. "It seems to me as if every liar and calumniator in the country was at work day and night to destroy my character," he cried out. "It distracts my attention from public business and consumes precious time."

To Monroe, the most unpleasant aspect of the 1824 contest was that three of the leading candidates were members of his Cabinet. Their brawls in his presence and the tales brought to him about their efforts to destroy each other politically were painful reminders to him that he had failed in his object of attaining Presidential tranquillity. The pity was that the three men, John Quincy Adams, John C. Calhoun and William Crawford, were among the most able men of their day, or any day, for that matter.

Secretary of State Adams was in many ways like his father, who was forever engaged in a self-analysis of his faults, like a good Puritan. "Pride and self-conceit and presumption lie so deep in my natural character," he admitted to his diary. He had a superb training for his position, having begun at fourteen his work in the diplomatic service; and as Secretary of State he was without peer. He was wise, patriotic, far-visioned and daring in his work, but in politics he was naïve. Adams made the assumption he was Monroe's heir-apparent because the last three Presidents had also served as Secretary of State. But the truth was that an imporant consideration by Monroe in naming him was his intention to end that tradition. Writing to Jefferson before he chose his Cabinet, Monroe said: "I have thought that it would produce a bad effect to place anyone from this quarter of the Union in the dept. of State, or from the South or West. You know how much has been said to impress a belief, on the country, North & East of this, that the citizens from Virga., holding the Presidency, have made appointments to that dept., to secure the succession from it, to the Presidency, of the person who happens to be from that State."

John C. Calhoun had purposely left Congress to become Secretary of War. He hoped that his record as an administrator would convince voters he had executive ability as well as legislative prowess. Calhoun was thirty-five when he joined the Cabinet, and he had made his reputation in the House as a War Hawk leader and strong nationalist. He possessed mystic eyes and a commanding appearance, but he was not yet the "cast-iron man, who looks as if he had never been born." In Congress, he had favored a loose construction of the Constitution, which would sanction the Second

Bank and internal improvements. In Monroe's Administration, he was slowly emerging as the philosopher of slavery, states' rights and free trade.

Treasury Secretary William Crawford was biding his time until he could collect on the 1816 debt the Republicans owed him when he took himself out of the race with Monroe. The President gave Crawford a free hand in running the Treasury; first, because he had little interest in financial matters, and second, because Crawford insisted on continuing the Hamilton tradition of submitting his financial programs directly to Congress without discussing them with the President. Crawford also involved himself in legislation that did not specifically relate to his department. Most important was his Tenure of Office Act of 1820, which he drew up and which his Senate lieutenant, Mahlon Dickerson of New Jersey, introduced for him. Under this act, the job terms of intermediate-grade government employees expired after four years. Adams said that the real purpose of the act was to promote Crawford's candidacy for 1824 because almost all government employees were at the mercy of Crawford and of the Senate, which he controlled. He also said that "Mr. Monroe unwarily signed the bill without adverting to its real character." It was the view of Madison that the act was "an encroachment on the constitutional attributes of the Executive." For, he said, "if a law can displace an officer at every period of four years, it can do so at the end of every year, or at every session of the Senate, and the tenure will then be at the pleasure of the Senate as much as of the President, and not of the President alone." Monroe chose to ignore the act, but it remained on the record for future use.

With three Cabinet members in such open contention, Monroe led a miserable existence. What was principle and what was politics became impossible to separate. Crawford submitted a program to Congress to curtail government activities during the depression, and Calhoun discovered that his own department was to be skeletonized. Monroe's carefully drawn up plan for coastal defenses was also a victim of retrenchment. Then in 1822, when Monroe in his own economy move attempted to reduce the number of Army officers, the Senate forced him to keep many officers he planned to discard. Crawford's supporters charged that Calhoun was using Army patronage for his own electioneering purposes, while Calhoun's followers charged Crawford with mismanagement of the Treasury.

Even Adams, one of the fighters, commented, "All public business in Congress now connects itself with intrigues, and there is great danger that the whole Government will degenerate into a struggle of cabals." Monroe, already aware that things were fast getting out of hand, nevertheless chose to maintain a hands-off policy. A blunder, this, for it removed any need of the candidates to gain his good will. In writing to Madison, Monroe complained woefully: "I have never known such a state of things as has existed here during the last Session, nor have I personally ever experienced so much embarrassment and mortification. While there is an open contest with a foreign enemy, or with an internal party, in which you are supported by just principles, the course is plain . . . but now we are blessed with peace, and the success of the late war has overwhelmed the Federal party, so that there is no division of that kind to rally any persons together in support of the Administration. The approaching election, 'tho distant, is a circumstance that excites greatest interest in both houses, and whose effect, already sensibly felt, is still much to be dreaded. There being three avowed candidates in the administration is a circumstance which increases the embarrassment. The friends of each endeavor to annoy the others."

That Monroe was even more annoyed than the candidates came clear in August of 1823, when Adams noted with concern: "[he] was suddenly seized . . . with cramps or convulsions of such extreme violence that he was at one time believed dying and he lay upwards to two hours in a state of insensibility."

Crawford was the front-runner by 1822 because of his Congressional phalanx, Jefferson's blessing and the support of the official party organ. This made the other candidates seethe and they filled letters and diaries with their denunciation of him. Made in the heat of jealousy and expected disappointment, their comments were unjustified. Yet they served to supply undiscerning historians and biographers of anti-Crawfordites with a ready-made villain. A Clay biographer, for instance, disdainfully characterized Crawford as having merely "the reputation of a reputation."

Since there were no issues in the campaign, the politicking consisted solely of name-calling. The influential *Niles' Register* referred to Crawford's following as "a quirking, spouting majority"; Adams described him as "a worm preying upon the vitals of the Administration within its own body"; while Jackson denounced him as an Indian-lover for proposing legal intermarriages between whites and redskins and for allowing Cherokee claims to Creek lands Jackson had wrested from the Creeks in 1814. Calhoun and Crawford had both attended the academy run by Calhoun's brother-in-law, Dr. Moses Waddel, where Waddel preached against "the rich, the rice and the slaves." The boy Calhoun was silent through shyness and a speech impediment. But in 1824, the man Calhoun spoke easily in denouncing Crawford as the father of the Federal spoils system. However, while the field ganged up on Crawford as "corrupt," the bitterness also enveloped them. Jackson found himself called a murderer, Clay a gambler and Adams a liar.

In August 1823, when many believed Crawford was unbeatable, the unbelievable happened. While on a short vacation in Virginia, the Georgian giant developed a fever and itching. A doctor diagnosed his trouble as erysipelas and gave him a dose of lobelia. But the dosage was said to have been improper, and Crawford suffered a stroke that left him temporarily blind and paralyzed. All other candidates were comforted when the news reached them, because for the first time they had a chance. While he lay in bed, there was talk that Monroe should relieve him from the Treasury Department. Crawford's daughter had prepared a stamp with her father's facsimile signature, and angry charges emerged that a mere girl was actually functioning as Secretary of the Treasury. But Monroe chose to ignore the wagging tongues.

Because of the Georgian's political machine in Congress, all candidates except Crawford naturally opposed the Congressional nominating caucus to select the official party candidate for the Presidency. To make "King Caucus" appear obsolete and illegal, they scrambled for nominations by state legislatures and legislative resolutions condemning the caucus method. Clay gained nominations by this method in Kentucky, Illinois, Ohio, Missouri and Louisiana; Calhoun in South Carolina; Adams in the New England states; and Jackson in Tennessee and at mass conventions in various counties throughout the country. Calhoun realized he had so little support that he dropped his candidacy and attached himself to all other tickets as the Vice-Presidential candidate.

The chaos in the number of nominees and their lack of campaign issues prompted Crawford's followers to call for a caucus to unify the Republicans around a single candidate. The caucus came at seven P.M. on February 14, 1824, in the House of Representatives, with Representative Benjamin Ruggles of Ohio in the chair, and for the first time the public was invited to watch. But though the galleries were crowded, floor attendance was dismal for only 66 of the 261 members came. With the assemblage constituting a Crawford party, he won the nomination with 64 votes and Albert Gallatin became his running mate with 57. Other candidates immediately labeled the caucus as a fraud.

When charges spread during the campaign that Crawford was near death and insane, his campaign advisers, who included Senator Martin Van Buren and Representatives Nathaniel Macon and John Randolph, suggested he be put on public exhibition despite his continuing paralysis. Servants carried the huge, limp figure to his carriage, propped him up with pillows and drove him through the streets of Washington so people could witness that he was not on his deathbed or a babbling idiot.

As the campaign reached its fever pitch President Monroe was forgotten until a scurrilous attack on Crawford put Monroe in the news again. Senator Ninian Edwards of Illinois, an ally of Calhoun, had been appointed minister to Mexico. Before he left, he gave his son-in-law, Representative Daniel P. Cook, (for whom Cook County was named) a statement charging Crawford with depositing public money from Illinois land sales in insolvent banks during the Panic of 1819. Cook carried out the intrigue by giving Clay the statement and also by repeating it in public.

By now, Monroe realized his own reputation was at stake. The campaign air had been clouded with so many charges of skulduggery in his Administration that it was time to take action. Although Adams tried to persuade him to wait until after the election was settled, Monroe refused to let the charge against Crawford stand. Crawford's friends in the House agreed and the sergeant-at-arms was sent on a 1500-mile journey through unsettled country to find Edwards and bring him back to Washington. Here a select committee composed of Daniel Webster, John Randolph and Edward Livingston questioned Edwards and charged him with spreading a falsehood. Monroe then removed his diplomatic status.

In December 1824, the electoral vote became known. Gallatin had withdrawn from the Vice-Presidential race in October after persistent charges that he was a "foreigner." Twenty-four states had taken part, and of these, six gave their legislatures the job of selecting electors. In Delaware, for instance, thirty legislators determined the state's Presidential vote. The national totals gave Jackson 99 electoral votes, Adams 84, Crawford 41 and Clay 37.

Because no man had a majority, the House had to make the final determination from among the top three men.

Crawford was bitter when it became obvious that Adams would be the choice of the House. His was a bitterness verging on violence as one event showed. Secretary of the Navy Sam Southard reported that he came to see Monroe on business one day and found him shaking. In explanation, the President said that Crawford had visited him earlier with recommendations for jobs in the customs service. Monroe had objected to each candidate. "Mr. Crawford at last rose in much irritation," John Quincy Adams quoted Southard's story in his diary, "gathered the papers together, and said petulantly, 'Well, if you will not appoint the persons well qualified for the places, tell me whom you will appoint, that I may get rid of their importunities.'" Monroe replied heatedly that he considered Crawford's language extremely improper and unsuitable to the relation between them; Crawford, turning to him, raised his cane, as in the attitude to strike, and said, "You damned infernal old scoundrel!"

Monroe seized the tongs at the fireplace for self-defense, applied a retaliatory epithet to Crawford, and told him he would immediately turn him out of the house. Beginning to recover himself, Crawford said he did not intend, and had not intended, to insult him, and left the house. They never met afterward.

In his last months in the White House, Monroe suffered heavy broadsides from a Congress that had heretofore refrained from attacking him. One charge that never died was that he had personally pocketed $20,000 of the $50,000 Congress had appropriated to refurnish the White House. Sam Lane, the unscrupulous Commissioner of Public Buildings and in charge of the refurnishing, had unfortunately died leaving only scribbles of accounting records. When a Congressional committee called Monroe a thief and demanded that he appear for questioning, Monroe replied that the chairman was a scoundrel and that it was the only answer he would give him. When the committee protested a $6000 payment to Monroe for his furniture, he bought it back to escape further attacks.

Before he left office, Monroe said good-by to his Secretaries, with whom he had held a total of 180 Cabinet meetings during his eight years. He also sent Congress a few remarks, as he put it, on his experience in office. Those who expected sagacious comments and analysis were to be disappointed. For his remarks

centered on his concern that the President was not given assistants
to help him handle the onerous, petty duties of his office. In his
own case, he pointed out, personal attention to inferior duties
stole precious time away from his supervision and control of the
several departments, preparing Messages to Congress, replying to
requests for information and meeting with members of Congress.

When the "last cockade" turned over his office to President Adams,
he was almost sixty-seven and in declining health. His lavish mode
of living, which he thought important for the maintenance of Presidential dignity, coupled with declining land values on his Virginia
property and Congressional failure to pay his diplomatic expenses
incurred in previous administrations were fast pushing him to
the brink of bankruptcy.

Monroe knew he had failed in his quest for tranquillity in
office. Yet the question remained: Would history be as passive in
judging him as he was in managing it? Even with the limited use
he made of his Presidential power, he had brought significant
advances in foreign policy, opened the floodgate to manifest des-
tiny with the establishment of an ocean-to-ocean nation and finally
made possible Federal internal improvements. What pleased him
most was the message sent him by Chief Justice Marshall, his childhood schoolmate—"that I feel sincere pleasure in the persuasion
that your administration may be viewed with real approval by our
wisest statesmen."

☆ 6 ☆

JOHN QUINCY ADAMS

Like Father Like Son

John Quincy Adams was a short, stout, bald, brilliant and puritanical twig off a short, stout, bald, brilliant and puritanical tree. Little wonder, then, that he took the same view of the Office of President as had his father.

He saw the Presidency as an office of immense scope and power, presiding over a Federal Government that could enter into an infinite variety of activities. In fact, he became the first President to propose to the nation a positive program for expanding economic and cultural affairs. As he told the country in his first Annual Message to Congress, if the central government did not use all the power available to it "for the benefit of the people themselves," this "would be treachery to the most sacred of trusts." Then to a Congress that might be persuaded not to act for the public good because of a fear of local voter retribution, he added that the government must not "proclaim to the world that we are palsied by the will of our constituents."

Unfortunately, like his father before him, John Quincy Adams' view of the Presidency and the Federal Government had to remain an academic goal. Both men were lacking in leadership qualities, troubled by treachery inside their political house and beset by an opponent who had popular support to spare. In John Adams' case, of course, it was Thomas Jefferson; for John Quincy Adams it was Andrew Jackson. Thus an excellent background, honest intentions, patriotic standards and a positive program all went down the drain and into the muddy river.

Until 1824, Adams had never found himself in the fiery general's dungeon. In fact, during his eight years as Monroe's Secretary of State, he had defended Jackson's military ruthlessness and illegal operations against the shouting demands of other Cabinet members that he be punished. In each instance, Adams had stood alone, talking relentlessly until the others gave in.

As the 1824 campaign had progressed, both Adams and Jackson considered the other his chief rival and an animosity crept into their relationship. For a time, Adams, who had little political sense, believed he could toss Jackson a small bone and get him out of the contest. This foolish move was to ask his supporters to vote for Jackson for Vice-President, an appeal that could only move the Jacksonians to extreme fury. As the frank New Englander put it, the Vice-Presidency was "a station in which the general could hang no one, and in which he would need to quarrel with no one. . . . It would afford an easy and dignified retirement to his old age."

The Adams-Jackson crash came with the indecisive 1824 election and Adams' selection of Henry Clay as Secretary of State. In this Presidential contest, in which no candidate held a majority of the 261 electoral votes, Clay had needed only a few more than his total of 37 to emerge third behind Jackson with 99 and Adams with 84. But he had been cheated out of this position by twenty-six-year-old Thurlow Weed, who violated the agreed-upon distribution of New York's electoral votes. Clay was not a man to let public dignity stand in the way of his ambitions, and had he stood among the magic three from whom the House chose the nation's next President, there is every reason to believe he would not have been shy about using his power as Speaker to gain the coveted honor. However, this was not to be, for William Crawford of Georgia was the third man with his 41 electoral votes. Therefore, as Clay assessed the situation: "I found myself transformed from a candidate before the people to an elector for the people." It did not take long for the friends of these three contenders to begin courting him. Both Adams and Jackson were personally active on the political scene, one as Secretary of State and the other as Senator from Tennessee, and thus readily available to oversee efforts in their own behalf.

Actually, Clay had made up his mind which man he would support before December 15, 1824. This date is significant because the chief lobbying did not commence until afterward. Furthermore, Clay made known his choice to Senator Thomas Hart Benton of Missouri, Mrs. Clay's cousin and a Jackson lieutenant. He could not support Jackson because he did not believe a military man should hold the Presidency. Crawford's views were too radical and besides, he was ailing. Therefore, by a process of elimination, he favored Adams.

While Clay lapsed into pleasant silence, the lobbyists rushed into action. Young Representative James Buchanan of Pennsylvania, a rich bachelor whose tall, heavy body rested on tiny feet, sought out Jackson. One of Buchanan's blue eyes had a distracting, blinking tic that never subsided. Perhaps this is why Jackson's story differed from his, though the general had a reputation for drawing different conclusions and summaries from conversations and letters than the other participants. Jackson claimed Buchanan promised him Clay's support if he would publicly declare he would not name Adams as his Secretary of State. There was also the strong implication that the post should go to Clay. Jackson said his reply was to the effect that he planned to hide his Cabinet choices even "from the very hairs of my head." Buchanan's retort later was that Jackson owned a vivid imagination, that it "never once entered my head that he believed me to be the agent of Mr. Clay or one of his friends, or that I intended to propose to him terms of any kind from them."

Robert Letcher, Representative from Kentucky and a close friend of Henry Clay, called on Adams on December 17. Adams believed the visit was important when Letcher asked him point-blank what he thought of Clay. Adams might easily have recalled that he thought of Clay as a "gamester," how the two had fought at the peace treaty-making at Ghent, and how Clay later had taken strong measures to control the Monroe Administration's policies regarding public works and Latin America. When Clay put John Randolph on the Foreign Affairs Committee in December 1819, Adams had considered this as a personal attack upon himself as Secretary of State "to prevent anything's being done congenial to the view of the Administration." As late as March 1824, he had written in his diary that Clay was "absurd upon the tariff" and "it is extremely difficult to preserve the temper of friendly society with him." But his reply now to Letcher was that he "harbored no hostility" toward Clay.

Letcher returned for two more talks, hinting at the first that it would be possible for Adams to win the contest in the House on the first ballot. The second visit on January 1, 1825, brought Adams' agreement that perhaps he should meet directly with Clay. That very night Washington was the scene of a banquet for Lafayette, and Adams and Clay sat side by side. Here they agreed to meet on January 9. The suspicion of the Jacksonians that a Presidential egg was about to be hatched was substantiated later by Francis Blair, an editor working for Clay who became afterward Jackson's propagandist and adviser. When Clay wrote Blair he would support Adams as "a choice among evils," Blair called Adams "the safest choice, therefore the best."

At their private meeting, Clay demanded to know how Adams stood on various issues. Then after a long period of questions and answers, Clay told him he would have his support. Clay had no need to say he expected high office in return; nor did Adams have to press a reward on him. There was something implicit, however, in their talk that the fortunes of both were now bound together.

The Jacksonians grew alarmed at reports of their meeting, and the faction's more astute schemers came up with a plan to separate the two by public scandal. On January 28, the Philadelphia *Columbia Observer* ran a letter claiming that "the friends of Clay have hinted that they, like the Swiss, would fight for those who would pay best." The damning part of the letter was the statement that Adams had offered Clay the post of Secretary of State for his aid.

Certainly the Jacksonians should not have expected Clay to step forward and deny he would take any post with Adams. This might have implied that he did not favor Adams. Yet had Clay not been rash, he would have found it best to ignore the letter. Instead, he foolishly gave it mileage throughout the country when he had his card printed in the *National Intelligencer*, demanding that the author reveal his identity. The Jacksonians countered by having Representative George Kremer of Pennsylvania step forward and claim authorship of the letter. Kremer, who was well known because he wore a leopardskin coat, was also known as a semi-literate. Obviously he could not have composed the letter, and Clay realized he had been made to look the fool. After labeling Kremer "a base and infamous calumniator, a dastard and a liar," Clay dropped the argument.

The formal counting of the electoral vote was set for February 9, after which the House would then select the President. Since each state, regardless of size, would have only one vote, the winner required the support of thirteen state delegations. While Clay

went to work on undecided state delegations, Adams, who believed
he could count only on the six New England states, for the first
and only time in his life tried to play the part of the political
promiser. Representative Daniel Webster was given the impression
he would be appointed minister to England if he lined up the
Federalist remnants behind Adams; Senator Martin Van Buren,
who was Crawford's campaign manager, believed he had an
understanding that one of his friends would be appointed to the
consular service; while Missouri's lone Representative came away
with the belief that his brother, a Federal judge, would not be
prosecuted for killing a fellow judge who dissented with one of
his legal opinions.

The 1828 Presidential campaign began on February 9, 1825,
when the House bowed to Clay's politicking and voted Adams
in on the first ballot with the necessary thirteen states, to seven
for Jackson and four for Crawford. Two days later came the issue
for 1828 when Adams named Clay as his Secretary of State.
As angry Andrew Jackson read the events: "So you see, the Judas
of the West has closed the contract and will receive the thirty
pieces of silver. His end will be the same."

From the outset, Adams sensed that his Administration would
prove to be a cipher, for the antagonism of Jackson was not
something easily overcome. The air was filled with the cry, "Bargain and Corruption!" Thus were the names of Adams and Clay
linked in a derisive shout that became their synonym. Even before
his Inauguration Day, Adams felt the fear of a man whose stalkers
were closing in and screaming for revenge. When the Congressional committee came to present him with formal notification of
his victory, he began to perspire badly. His reply to the committee was that he would have declined the office if this would
bring about another election; but since the Constitution made no
provision for this, he added weakly, he was forced to become
President.

Even if Adams did not have to put up with the heavy albatross
of "Bargain and Corruption!" he would still have made little of
his office. Like his father, he failed to understand that a President had to deal with people as a politician in addition to handling
issues as a statesman. A political following was held together by
rewards and patronage, not by pious policy statements. Only by

passing out jobs and contracts could he effect a united group of backers to support his policies.

Because of this lack of acumen, when juicy political plums fell vacant, John Quincy Adams gave no thought to the antecedents of aspirants; as things turned out, he revealed a penchant for rewarding his enemies. In New York, for instance, young Thurlow Weed and former Congressman James Tallmadge had been instrumental in helping him win that state. Yet he ignored them to offer his disdainful enemy, DeWitt Clinton, a post as minister to Britain and one of Clinton's henchmen a Federal judgeship in upstate New York. The Tenure of Office Act, with its four-year term for government employees, gave Adams a great opportunity to get rid of any civil servants he cared to at the outset of his Administration and staff the departments with Adams Republicans. But he refused to fire anyone, even though he knew the Customs Service was almost totally a Jackson rooting assembly. In similar fashion, he failed to appoint men of his own choosing to his Cabinet, with the exception of Clay. He continued William Wirt, Samuel Southard and John McLean from the Monroe Cabinet as Attorney General, Secretary of the Navy and Postmaster General respectively. Southard and McLean were Calhoun lieutenants, though it was becoming known that McLean had shifted his loyalty to Jackson. When asked about McLean, Adams said that all that mattered was his ability on the job and that a President had no claim to a Cabinet member's "active, partisan exertions." Adams also named former Senator James Barbour of Virginia as Secretary of War and Richard Rush, former minister to Britain, as Secretary of the Treasury. Barbour, formerly chairman of the Senate Foreign Relations Committee, had been a vociferous William Crawford booster in the Upper Chamber. Adams had actually asked Crawford to stay on at the Treasury, and when he refused Adams then plugged the gap with Rush who had returned to the country.

Regardless of his belief that "perhaps two-thirds of the whole people were adverse to the actual result," Adams bravely determined to restore Presidential government, a practice that had gone out of style after Jefferson. Congressional primacy was wrong, he believed, for the President was the "Chief Magistrate of ten millions of people." Instead of acting as though he were on one side of a high fence and Congress on the other side, Adams scoffed at the doctrine of separation of powers. The President must interfere where necessary, he believed, with Congressional activities in order to retain leadership of the government, for Congressmen took a small view of events and were primarily interested in grubby matters. "About one-half the members of Congress are seekers for office at the nomination of the President," he said. "Of the remainder, at least one-half have some appointment or favor to ask for their relatives." John Taylor, who was elected Speaker of the House, credited the personal intercession of Adams for his success.

Adams also believed that the President should offer the country a blueprint of its immediate future, for, as he said in his inaugural address, the government must be vitally concerned with the "moral, political and intellectual improvement of man." This was to be his revolutionary contribution to the art of the Presidency, though the audacious scheme met with considerable Cabinet opposition, particularly from Clay and Barbour who preferred vague generalities to specifics in discussing the future. At one four-hour Cabinet session, with each of the two Secretaries raising loud objections, Adams stated: "I am like the man with two wives—one plucking out his black hairs, and the other the white, till none were left."

In the Message that he finally dispatched to Congress in December 1825, he chose to ignore his timid advisers. The nation soon learned that he proposed establishing a national university, a Department of the Interior, Federal sponsorship of scientific explorations, reform of patent laws, Federal construction of astronomy observatories—"lighthouses of the skies"—and the survey and construction of roads and canals and river improvements.

There was nothing in this program that should have offended anyone. Yet the Jacksonians lost little time announcing their opposition to every feature. The picture of "lighthouses of the skies" made them laugh hysterically, while the proposal to plunge the government into large-scale internal improvements activities brought out their warning that Adams intended to halt settlement of the West and make slave laborers of pioneers.

In self-defense after continuing Jacksonian attacks, Adams said that the great effort of his Administration was to put all surplus revenue into internal improvements. This would have resulted, he added, in "high wages and constant employment to hundreds of thousands of laborers, in which every dollar expended would have repaid itself fourfold in the enhanced value of the public lands. With this system in ten years the surface of the whole Union would have been checkered over with railroads and canals."

Jackson had quit the Senate in 1825 on the advice of friends who pointed out that if he remained in Washington he would find himself involved in specific legislation proposed by Adams. By remaining at The Hermitage, he would not have to take such stands and would thus avoid criticism. For instance, only the year before, after writing President Monroe that he opposed Federal public works, Senator Jackson had voted for internal improvements. Now with the necessity of opposing everything Adams favored, he would find himself embarrassed if he were still in the Senate.

The Jacksonians did not find it difficult to reset the minds of the great body of citizens who had been asking for internal improvements. Their argument was this: President Adams, half of the "Bargain and Corruption" team, planned to finance road and canal construction from the sale of public land. This would boost the price of the land and put it out of reach of most settlers. Also, if there were a large internal improvements program, the expanded worker force would have to come from the would-be settlers group. By becoming laborers, they would reduce the number of settlers, the Jacksonians preached speciously.

How successful the Jacksonians were in their arguments can be seen from the record of the Adams Administration. In four years, Adams was able to win from Congress only authorization to survey a Florida Canal route, Federal stock subscription in the Louisiana & Portland Canal and the Virginia Dismal Swamp Canal, Federal land grants for state-built canals in Illinois and Indiana and a stump and snag removal program in the Ohio River.

The Jacksonian policy of opposition per se regardless of the issue became the monotonous feature of the Adams years. For instance, several Latin American countries planned a Panama Congress for June 1826, and invited the United States to send delegates. Adams accepted, for he believed it would be useful to bring Western Hemisphere nations together, even though he said he would make no alliances or take part in negotiations of a belligerent character.

Adams, sublime in his policy decision, was totally unprepared for what followed when he submitted the names of his two proposed delegates to the Senate for confirmation. Senator Van Buren

of New York was looking for the proper moment to insure the
Jacksonians he was ready to join them. He now found his moment. On February 15, 1826, Van Buren introduced two resolutions condemning this "usurpation of power" by the President in not asking for the Senate's advice first on whether to
attend the Panama Congress. Van Buren also demanded that Adams
inform the Senate if the related documents submitted to the
Senate could be made public. To this Adams sent a scathing reply that executive business of the Senate (treaties and nominations) was a closed-door business.

The nominations were sent to the Jackson-controlled Senate
Foreign Relations Committee, which printed a savage attack on
the Panama mission. And so matters dragged along until March
30 when new horror was added. At the time Barbour joined the
Cabinet, his Senate seat had gone to John Randolph, the Republican scourge of the Republicans for a quarter century and the
Adams family's unrelenting enemy. Randolph was now taking dope
and falling deeper into insanity, but he still managed to attend
the Senate and make use of his genius for invective.

"This Panama mission is a Kentucky cuckoo's egg laid in a
Spanish-American nest," Randolph derided the harmless proposal.
"This miserable Constitution of ours, crucified between two
gentlemen suffering for conscience' sake under the burden of the
two first offices of the government," he shrieked, warming to
personal attack on Adams and Clay. The name "Adams" came
out of his throat like a poisoned fume. Randolph hated the
Adams family because of the humiliating experience his sick
brother Theodoric had suffered in 1789, when Theodoric had
approached the carriage of Vice-President John Adams like any
ordinary well-wisher, only to have the coachmen shove him
aside. John Randolph blamed Adams personally, though the Vice-
President had not been involved. Henceforth, the Adamses were
"The American House of Stuart," and when the son became President, Randolph charged, "The cub is a greater bear than the old
one."

With each paragraph, Randolph grew louder and wilder. Senators expected Vice-President Calhoun to call him to order, but
Calhoun who had worked on such cordial terms with Adams
in the Monroe Cabinet, let him rave on without caution. Calhoun
had also joined the Jackson camp and looked forward to succeeding Jackson one day as President. Randolph went on to say

that Colombia and Mexico had not invited the United States to attend the mission but that Clay had arranged the conference from the outset. Then came his damning comment on the Administration, declaring that Adams and Clay were a "coalition of Blifil and Black George . . . the combination of the Puritan with the black-leg."

Clay's reaction was one of fury. Newspapers gave the speech wide play and pointed out that the references were to Henry Fielding's *Tom Jones*—Blifil, the hypocrite, and Black George, the scoundrel gamekeeper. The reference to the "black-leg" was a bald charge that Clay was a dishonest gambler and a swindler. No man from Kentucky could accept an insult of this nature, and on April 8, the two met in a duel on the Virginia side of the Potomac. Both Clay and Randolph missed on their first shots. On the second shot, Randolph withheld his fire while Clay's bullet tore his jacket. Randolph then fired into the air. "You owe me a coat, Mr. Clay," he said as they rode together back to Washington the best of newfound friends. "I'm glad the debt is no greater," said Clay, a foolish romantic who did not realize that Randolph actually owed him the debt of having destroyed the Adams Administration.

For Randolph had supplied a picture—Blifil and Black George—that the Jacksonians would not let the country forget in their smear campaign against Adams and Clay. Nor did the duel halt Randolph's condemnation of the Administration. In fact, he grew so raw in further attacks that Senators fled the chamber when he gained the floor. Adams writhed under what he called Randolph's "drunken speeches," and wrote in his dairy, "Randolph is the image and superscription of a great man stamped upon base metal. His mind is a jumble of sense, wit and absurdity." The Virginia legislature was to replace Randolph with John Tyler for the next session of Congress in order to get him out of the Senate. But Randolph's constituents would send him back to the House in 1827 to continue his attacks.

More weeks sped by in cascading Jacksonian slanders before the senate finally confirmed the two delegates for the Panama meeting. However, the House did not pass the $40,000 appropriation until April 22. It was late now and the Panama Congress fizzled with only four countries in attendance. One of the American delegates died en route and the other did not leave the United States before the Panama sessions were over.

Adams was stunned by the pettiness of his political opposition
and chagrined that Clay had fought a duel over a charge that
had also involved himself. All of this he blamed on Vice-President
Calhoun for permitting Randolph to rant. Adams had helped
organize the Washington *National Journal* in 1823 to function
as his political mouthpiece, and on May 1, 1826, an article he
signed "Patrick Henry" appeared in the *Journal*, attacking Calhoun
for not using his power to silence Randolph. Unfortunately, the
writing style was readily recognized. Then on May 20, the *National
Intelligencer* carried a harsh reply signed by "Onslow," who was
obviously Calhoun. Adams disguised once more as Patrick Henry,
hit at him again; "Onslow" replied, and the nation watched its top
officials brawl almost the rest of the year before Adams finally
quit. Even the Senate, under Jacksonian control, had found Calhoun too obvious. "Patrick Henry" had pointed out that Calhoun
had put only "a single Senator who was not hostile to the Administration" on the Foreign Relations, Finance, Indian Affairs
and Judiciary committees. First the Senate stripped the Vice-
President of his power to appoint committee members and restored the rule of selection by Senate ballot. Then over Calhoun's
protestations that he had lacked the power to call Randolph to
order, the Senate amended its rules to make this a specific power
of the Vice-President.

Yet Calhoun continued his laxity when it came to controlling the
tongue of mad John Randolph. The Virginia Senator would come
striding into the Senate chamber in his blue riding suit, buckskin
breeches and top boots and followed by his Negro servant. Once
he gained the floor, his colleagues were in dread of what he
might say. On the occasion of the death of Senator Gaillard in
1826, Randolph interposed this thought: "I have been ill here
and have feared death; feared it because I would not die in
Washington, be eulogized by men I despise and buried in the
Congressional burying ground. The idea of lying by the side of
—— ——; Ah! that adds a new horror to death."

Adams had other miseries in the first session of the Nineteenth
Congress. With a change in the British Government, the United
States was barred from trading with the West Indies. Van Buren
led the attack, blaming Adams for a situation that reduced the
income of farmers who depended on that trade. Senator Thomas
Hart Benton of Missouri, who had once fought a gun battle with

Jackson but was now his ally, ran a select committee in 1826 to "inquire into the expediency of reducing the Patronage of the Executive Government of the United States." Benton's purpose was not to reduce patronage but to picture Adams as a man with deep control over all parts of the country through his Presidential powers to appoint public officials. Benton proposed that the President lose his authority to relieve military officers at will and that he submit an explanation to the Senate if he planned to remove a civilian official. Benton did not get anywhere with his proposals except in the newspaper publicity he sought. Adams reacted to Benton by dubbing him "the doughty knight of the stuffed cravat."

If Adams' efforts to create a strong Presidency were not already largely nullified by the Jacksonians, his encounter with Governor George Troup of Georgia would in itself have been disastrous. During the last months of the Monroe Administration the Government had approved the Treaty of Indian Springs. Under the treaty, the Creeks and their chief, William McIntosh, agreed to relinquish 4,700,000 acres in western Georgia and move beyond the Mississippi. McIntosh, the son of a full-blooded Indian mother and a British father, had served as a brigadier general in the American Army during the War of 1812 and later with Jackson in the 1818 Seminole fighting. For a price, he was willing to sell out his people. When Adams became President, he determined that the treaty was fraudulent and he composed a new agreement, returning a million of the acres to the Creeks. He sent this new treaty to the Senate in January 1826 and proclaimed it as the law of the land in April. In the meantime, the Upper Creeks, who had opposed the original treaty, took revenge on McIntosh and killed him.

Trouble over the second treaty now arose with Governor Troup, a William Crawford lieutenant and first cousin of Chief McIntosh, who was determined that it not go into effect. The million acres in question were excellent cotton fields and Georgians had rushed in to occupy them. But regardless of occupation the land still belonged to the Creeks and Adams called upon Troup to honor the legal treaty posthaste. An angry exchange of letters took place when Troup refused and announced that any Federal officials who attempted to interfere with the Treaty of Indian Springs would be arrested. Moreover, if the Federal Government sent in the Army, he warned, he would repel it with the state militia.

At the time, this did not seem to disconcert Adams who quickly related the details of the controversy to Congress and called for its backing in the use of the Army to enforce the second treaty. However, when Congress gave its reluctant approval to uphold the national honor, Adams did not act. The thought of fomenting bloodshed troubled him to such an extent that he would not send the Army into Georgia, even though this made a mockery of his philosophy of Federal supremacy. In the end, the second treaty and the Creeks were abandoned. Worst of all, Adams had permitted the national government to suffer a blow to its prestige, giving other southern states and politicians the idea that they, too, might humiliate the Federal establishment with impunity.

The second session of the Nineteenth Congress, which ran from December 4, 1826 to March 3, 1827, was a Jacksonian nightmare for Adams. The Senate either ignored or voted down every recommendation he dispatched to Capitol Hill. These ranged from proposals for internal improvements to one raising benefits for the few surviving Revolutionary War veterans. Vice-President Calhoun found another opportunity to slap Adams when the President recommended a bill to raise the tariff. A tie vote on the measure resulted in the Senate when Senator Van Buren decided to make himself scarce, on the ground that either a pro or con vote would hurt him politically. So he abstained from casting his vote, with the excuse that he had "promised to accompany a friend on a visit to the Congressional Cemetery." This gave the Vice-President the opportunity to vote, and Calhoun broke the tie by killing the bill. Adams labeled Calhoun "the sabled genius of the South who opposed northern property."

The year 1826 was a bad one for Adams in several other respects. Worst of all was the death of his father on the Fourth of July. The old man, almost ninety-one, died after uttering, "Thomas Jefferson survives," unaware that Jefferson also died that day. "I feel it is time for me to begin to set my house in order," the younger Adams said, "and to prepare for the church-yard myself." He had been so close to his parents that now that both were gone he felt alone and old.

That year also, the Jacksonians established the Washington *United States Telegraph* as a party paper with Duff Green, an expert at billingsgate, as editor. To give Green extra funds, the Senate awarded the paper its printing business. The *Telegraph* was soon attacking Adams with the ridiculous charge that he was planning to revive the Alien and Sedition Acts of his father's Administration. He was also painted as the most wasteful and high-living President.

Of course, neither charge was true. "I rise about five; read two chapters of Scott's Bible & Commentary and the corresponding Commentary of Hewlett," he wrote in his diary. "Then the morning newspapers, and public papers from the several departments . . . breakfast an hour from nine to ten; then have a session of visitors, upon business, in search of place, solicitor for donations, or from mere curiosity, from eleven till between four and five o'clock. The heads of departments of course occupy much of this time. Between four and six I take a walk of three or four miles. Dine from about half past five to seven, and from dark until about eleven I generally pass the evening in my chamber, signing land-grants or blank patents. . . . About eleven I retire." Except for some expensive chairs and a few tables, the White House that he and his wife, Louisa, and their three sons, George Washington, John and Charles Francis, occupied was an ill-furnished place now that James Monroe had moved all his exquisite furniture out.

Besides his work and general routine, Adams involved himself in other activities. During warm weather, he noted in his diary, he took "two morning hours for bathing and swimming in the Potomac." On June 13, 1825, he almost drowned and on other occasions he wrote of his exhaustion in swimming against the swift current. On one occasion, Mrs. Anne Royall, a reporter known to Washington politicians as the "widow with the serpent's tongue" for her penetrating analysis of political events, discovered Adams swimming in the nude in the Potomac. Mrs. Royall, who prided herself in watching Congress "as a cat watches a rat hole," quickly sat on the President's clothes and refused to leave until he gave her an interview on state banks while treading water. Adams denounced her as a "virago-errant in enchanted armor." Adams' interests included designing statues for the Capitol and the completion of the building, his concern with his son Charles' progress in Latin and his own exertions in the White House garden. He wrote about his wife's "winding silk from several hundred silk-worms that she is rearing," and of his own botanical interests: "This has been a harassing day; but I perceived a tamarind heaving up the earth in the center of tumbler No. 2; and I planted in tumbler No. 1 three whole Hautboy strawberries." He would not dine out, for, he said, "It is established by custom that the President of the United States goes not about into any private companies." But he sometimes attended lectures and once reported: "I heard Dr. Caldwell's lecture upon the organ of amativeness, which I thought more indelicate than philosophical."

Although in his last Message to Congress Monroe had complained that a President required additional help, Congress did not provide Adams with more than a personal secretary. His twenty-two-year-old son John was his sole assistant, laboring in an amateurish way to be of aid to his father. As a result of having so little help, Adams could make no arrangements to screen visitors or to provide himself with the privacy he needed. He was particularly beset with women who sought pardons for brothers and husbands, and he complained that they "operated with the usual female weapon, a shower of tears . . . It seldom fails to disconcert my philosophy." Other callers wanted appointments. Judge Thurston, whom he described in his diary as "partially insane," came one day to scold him because his son had not been appointed a lieutenant in the Marine Corps. Adams' worst experience with unwanted visitors came with Dr. George P. Todson who had been court-martialed by the Army and sought reinstatement as an assistant surgeon. Adams learned "that Todson had come to the most and inflexible determination to murder me." Nevertheless, he let Todson into his office. When told nothing would be done in his behalf, especially under the threat of murder, Todson did not act surprised. He did say, however, he had given up the idea. A few days later he returned to ask Adams for money to pay his inn bill and this time insisted that any notion the President entertained that he had wanted to kill him was "absurd." After several further calls, Adams finally placed him on a ship returning Negroes to Africa. Then when he returned and pestered further, Adams pawned him off accompanying a group of displaced Indians.

The worst political blow Adams suffered in 1826 was in the general election when the Jacksonians gained control over the House as well as the Senate. For the first time in history, a President faced a Congress belonging overwhelmingly to the opposition. Nevertheless, Adams would not give up easily and sought to help Speaker Taylor in his fight to retain his place on the dais. However, straight entreaty proved no match for the smear tactics of Jacksonians, who charged Taylor with sexual irregularities. As Taylor summarized the story being spread, the opposition said he had "brought my girl from Baltimore, established her in quarters and lodged with her every night." Taylor claimed he did not speak to women to whom he had not been introduced except for the occasion when he met two ladies on the stage at Baltimore and conversed with them until he and his friends climbed off the coach at Washington. From all of Taylor's too numerous denials, Adams believed that Taylor's argument of complete innocence was as unlikely as the Jacksonian charge. But for politics' sake, he backed Taylor only to see him lose out as Speaker to Representative Andrew Stevenson of Virginia by a vote of 104 to 94. "This settles the complexion of the House," he said glumly afterward.

During the Twentieth Congress, no measure came to be considered on its own merit. Everything was weighed by the Jacksonians on the scale of the 1828 Presidential contest. Even the paintings in the Capitol were involved. James Hamilton of South Carolina introduced a resolution in the House to fill one of the large panels in the rotunda with a colorful oil painting of Jackson at the Battle of New Orleans. The House debated this resolution an entire month before deciding by a vote of 103 to 97 that it would be a trifle undignified.

Next Representative John Sloane of Ohio, a stalwart of the President, introduced a resolution to hold an inquiry into the court-martial and execution of six Tennessee militiamen by Jackson during the War of 1812. Sloane's resolution went to the House Committee on Military Affairs, which was entirely in the control of the Jacksonians. Friends of the President pleaded with him to let them copy the public record dealing with the courts-martial and executions. But Adams refused because "it would be construed as a measure of hostility against General Jackson." As a result, the House committee turned its inquiry into a hearing of redundant praise for Jackson. Its report, which completely exonerated him, was ordered printed as a public document by the House by a vote of 103 to 97.

A third resolution was destined to crown the campaign of smears against Adams. James Hamilton headed the select House committee to investigate the expenditures of the Administration. It soon became apparent that Hamilton intended to "prove" that Adams was wasting a ruinous amount of money. Adams called the majority report "One hundred and fifty pages of invective upon every department of the government except the Post Office for extravagance and waste of money." The key invective was reserved for the White House. Hamilton had discovered a $61 billiard table and a $23.50 chess set in the Executive Mansion. Although Adams bought these with his own money, the committee majority conveniently accused him of spending *public* money for the "purchase of gaming tables and gambling furniture." If he did this, the committee report went on, "why not, also, faro banks, playing cards, race horses and every other article necessary to complete a system of gambling at the President's Palace?" The House ordered the printing of six thousand copies of this nonsense for distribution by Congressmen to constituents.

The major legislative issue during Adams' last year was the tariff question. Jackson Republican politicians in Pennsylvania believed that a wool tariff increase was essential to promote their cause in their state. But the dilemma of the Jacksonians was that this would redound to the credit of Adams. Van Buren found what he thought was a foolproof scheme: raise the wool tariff to show that the Jacksonians wanted to help Pennsylvania and other affected states; but load the bill with so many high raw-material tariff schedules harmful to New England business interests that New England Congressmen, who were almost solidly behind Adams, would be forced to vote against the bill and thus kill it. Wily Van Buren also considered it essential that Jackson not be involved personally in the legislation in order not to alienate any voters. "I am entirely confident that all that is necessary to make the election perfectly safe is that we be discreet," he wrote Jackson. While Jackson had served as Senator, he had favored a protective tariff policy. Now copies were made and distributed of a safe Jackson statement that he favored a "judicious examination and revision" of the tariff.

John Randolph, now in the House, correctly judged the bill when he introduced a motion to call it "A Bill to Manufacture a President of the United States." In line with the Van Buren scheme, besides raising the duty on raw wool to protect the sheep states, the bill contained sharp import duty increases for molasses, iron and hemp. These brought the expected loud outcry from New England's rum producers, machinery makers and ship-builders. But something unexpected also occurred. Van Buren's strategy backfired when sufficient New England Congressmen voted for the bill and it passed. "The Tariff of Abominations," Southerners screamed when Adams signed the bill into law on May 19, 1828.

By this time, the Congressional nominating caucus lay discredited and dead. In its place, state legislatures, state conventions and public gatherings nominated Jackson, while Adams arranged to be nominated at the "Administration" convention of Pennsylvania at Harrisburg in January 1828.

Pessimism pervaded the Administration regarding the election. In April, Clay complained of a "paralytic numbness and torpidity" in his left leg. Rush and Barbour expressed keen desire to leave the country and become the minister to Britain. Adams sourly recognized their "anxiety to save themselves from the wreck," and said that Clay's ailment was really "one and the same thing" with Rush's "preference of the harbor to the tempest." But Rush reluctantly agreed to run for Vice-President, Clay said he would stay and Barbour happily departed for London. Clay's political troubles were magnified by personal troubles. His son, Thomas, a boisterous young fellow, would land in a Philadelphia jail before 1828 was out. Another son, Theodore, was rapidly going insane.

Adams' personal troubles were also a heavy extra load during this period. He and his invalid wife Louisa were unhappy with their daughter-in-law Mary, who was wed to John, II, secretary to his father. All three Adams boys had fallen in love with Mary and now there was dissension among them. John had earlier caused his father pain when he and the entire Harvard senior class had been expelled for rioting in 1823. But the worst family problem of all was first-born, George Washington Adams, his father's favorite, who had become an alcoholic and was threatening suicide after mismanaging the family's money. George's threat became fact in April 1829, a month after his father left office, when he leaped over the side of the *Benjamin Franklin* on its trip from Providence to New York.

The collapse of the government seemed imminent in this year of pessimism. General Winfield Scott was fighting with pamphlets and words against other prominent generals, such as General Gaines, Macomb and Porter, in an attempt to become the chief general. In his meetings with Scott, Adams found the six and a half foot tall general insubordinate and rude. Yet he would not fire him. Adams also concluded from the politicking of the Customs Service that four-fifths of the employees were talking in behalf of

Jackson. As for Postmaster General McLean: "He has been three years using the extensive patronage of his office in condemning" the Administration. Yet despite the pleas from Clay and others, he would not fire McLean or anyone else for merely preferring another candidate for the Presidency.

There was probably more political mudslinging during the 1828 campaign than in any other in history. Nor was Adams able to avoid its loud overtones even when he left Washington on trips. On August 5, he went to bed in Barnum's Tavern in Baltimore, but he could not sleep because a Jackson meeting got under way and one speaker shouted for three hours. "I heard his voice, like the beating of a mill-clapper," Adams wrote in his diary. "A stranger would think that the people of the United States have no other occupation than electioneering." To differentiate between the two opponents, the Adams forces were known as the National Republicans, while the Jacksonians clung to the Republican tag. No issues were raised between the factions; Adams' opposition being content to yell, "Hooray for Jackson!"

The year dragged along until December 3 when Adams learned he had lost. Of twenty-four states, all but two now enjoyed popular election of Presidential electors. The popular vote stood at 1,155,340, with Jackson holding a total of 647,276, or 55 per cent. His electoral total, however, was 178 to 83 for Adams. The defeated President's mood showed in his diary entry on New Year's Day: "The year begins in gloom. My wife had a sleepless and painful night. The dawn was overcast, and, as I began to write, my shaded lamp went out, self-extinguished."

According to an observer, members of the outgoing Administration took the defeat hard as Inauguration Day approached. Clay was thin and wan, with his eyes "sunk into his head"; Rush was "alarmingly ill"; Southard unable to leave his bed; General Peter B. Porter, the new Secretary of War, was "almost blind from an inflammation of the eyes"; while Attorney General Wirt was in agony from vertigo. Only Vice-President Calhoun was happy because he had been re-elected to serve with Jackson.

Like his father, Adams could not bear to watch his successor take his oath of office. At nine P.M. on March 3, he silently left the White House and joined his family for dinner at Meridian Hill. His four-year fiasco and torture were at an end.

☆ 7 ☆

ANDREW JACKSON

Hickory Stick President

Andrew Jackson of Tennessee, gangling, grizzled warrior, came tottering to the Presidency in March 1829, leaning on his hickory cane. He was sick and weary and dressed in the black suit that well befitted his enormous grief at the recent passing of his beloved wife Rachel. He brought with him no specific political program or goals except for the heavy chains of the Jeffersonian dogma of states' rights and strict construction of the Constitution. Yet during the eight years that followed, he kept the nation in a constant state of turbulence, vigorously brandishing his hickory cane at a host of real and imaginary enemies. And he left office one of the few Presidents who, in vital respects, stretched the powers of the Presidency and the authority of the central government over the states to their utmost.

To his noisy followers—the poor of the cities, the downtrodden southern farmers, the mud-booted western frontiersmen, scheming spoilsmen, itchy-fingered speculators, paper money enthusiasts and Indian haters—he was Everyman's David doing battle with the twin Goliaths of landed wealth and established privilege. To them, he was the great equalizer whose heart bled to give them all a chance to grow rich and politically powerful regardless of their lack of education, experience or beginning money stake.

But to his enemies, he was "King Andrew," dictatorial, fanatically ruthless, narrow, prejudiced, unprincipled and vindictive. Henry Clay described him as "ignorant, passionate, hypocritical, corrupt and easily swayed by the base men who surround him." John C. Calhoun considered him a traitor to the land of his birth and to his political origins because he would not accept the right of a state to nullify a Federal law. On the occasion when Harvard

awarded Jackson an honorary degree, John Quincy Adams, twice
his Presidential opponent, complained bitterly that he was unde-
serving, on the ground that he was "a barbarian who could not
write a sentence of grammar and hardly could spell his name."

Who was Jackson in reality? Was he a revolutionist who fought
relentlessly to bring about "Jacksonian Democracy"—a national government committed to the interests of the common man? Or was
he a spoiler who replaced stability with chaos and advanced the
worst elements and ideas current in his day? The truthful answer
to both questions must be the same: "No, but . . ."

Like a widening accordion, national support for Jackson's candidacy began with a loud shout of national thanks for his victory
over the British at New Orleans in January 1815. Ten years later
it grew into a deafening roar at his repeated charge of "bargain
and corruption" hurled at President Adams and Secretary of State
Clay when they deprived "The Hero" of the Presidency. By 1828,
the roar was greater than Niagara for the general, The Hero and
now the President.

As he prepared for his inauguration, Andrew Jackson could look
back on a highly dramatic life. The Hero's background contained
all the ingredients of an emotional blood-bath by his legion of
followers, a plot of a story far beyond the imagination of admirers
such as Washington Irving, James Fenimore Cooper and Nathaniel
Hawthorne. It began with the frontier, proceeded into Revolutionary War miseries, orphanhood, then forged on to a legal career,
self-made wealth, adventure and, of course, military feats. There
were flaws, many of them, some serious. But by the time the flaws
were uncovered, the myth had taken over and acquired such a
thick coat of armor plate that it could not be pierced without
indicting the exposer.

He was born on the border between North and South Carolina
on March 15, 1767, the third son of Irish immigrants. His father,
another Andrew Jackson, died a few days before the baby's birth
from the strain of lifting a heavy log. In later life the general
recalled that his mother was determined to make him a preacher
and started him at school at five after teaching him to read. But
the redheaded, skinny boy possessed an explosive temper and a
caustic tongue, like his mother, and preaching was out. Nevertheless, his mother instilled in him an urge toward social compassion,
and he remembered his entire life the winter nights she told
him about the suffering of his grandfather at the siege of Carrick-
fergus and the oppression by the nobility of Ireland over the

laboring poor. But compassion was combined with a combative nature that early revealed itself. As a classmate recalled: "Jackson never would give up, although he was always beaten."

The British general Lord Cornwallis came South in 1780 and after General Benjamin Lincoln surrendered his five thousand men at Charleston without a fight, Cornwallis began his campaign to despoil the lower colonies. Although Andy Jackson was only thirteen, an American officer made him a mounted orderly or messenger, for which he was well fitted, being a good rider familiar with all the roads. His view of the enemy was that he enjoyed "popping them," but at fourteen he was captured and imprisoned. When a Redcoat officer ordered him to clean his boots, the boy refused and the officer slashed at his head with a sword. Fortunately, he raised his hand to save his face. But the hand was slashed to the bone and his head cut. These scars remained throughout his life and served as a continuing reminder of a bursting dislike of the British. During his Presidency when the will of an Englishman, James Smithson, left $500,000 to establish a scientific institute in the United States, Jackson saw to it that Congress rejected the offer. It was not until 1846 that Congress established the Smithsonian Institution.

Not long after his prison incident, he found himself an orphan, for his mother died as did his two older Irish-born brothers. For six months after his release from jail, he existed by serving as an apprentice to a saddle maker. Then he attended schools spasmodically but horse races, gambling tables and cock fights religiously. He squandered an inheritance from a deceased Irish Jackson, taught school awhile and at eighteen began reading law in a lawyer's office. Here associates remembered him as "the most roaring, rollicking, game-cocking, horse-racing, card-playing, mischievous fellow, that ever lived in Salisbury . . . the head of the rowdies, more in the stable than in the office." Yet despite his inattentiveness to the law and his concentration on gaining the reputation as the biggest spender, gambler, female chaser and fanciest dresser, he won admission to the bar in September 1787, a week after the Constitutional Convention completed its four months of labor at Philadelphia. He now appeared in courtrooms, relying excessively on Francis Bacon as his legal authority. When an older lawyer scoffed at his use of Bacon, Jackson had his first duel, though neither man was injured.

In 1787, Jackson crossed the wilds to dirty, lawless Nashville, fighting Indians and panthers along his route. Nashville was to serve henceforth as his permanent arena. Here in what was then the western district of North Carolina, he began as solicitor of the superior court, with jurisdiction over the five thousand residents living in the fifty-mile-long Cumberland Valley. At twenty-one, he stood six feet one inch tall, weighed less than 140 pounds, possessed red wiry hair flattened with grease, bold steel-blue eyes and a long, pockmarked face. It took only a short time before he garnered a reputation as the champion of creditors with his zealous efforts to collect from a community of debtors.

Andrew Jackson was also involved in a love that would trouble his next forty years. The cause of all this anguish was Rachel Donelson Robards, the youngest and prettiest daughter of his landlady. Rachel Donelson had been married in 1785 when only seventeen to Lewis Robards, scion of a prominent Kentucky family. The marriage soon proved a failure because of Robards' jealousy. She was irresistible to men; they gravitated to her without any encouragement on her part, and her husband thought the worst. Once finding her talking to a young man on their porch, he ordered her never to show her face in his house again.

Jackson met Rachel upon her return home on this occasion. Not long afterward, Robards showed up for a reconciliation, only to quarrel with her over Jackson. On learning of this, Jackson argued with Robards "respecting the injustice he had done his wife." Robards proposed they settle things with a fistfight; Jackson with a duel. Neither occurred and Robards returned to Kentucky with Rachel following him.

The arguments were worse this time and in July 1790, at the request of her family, Jackson helped her escape from Robards' house. Robards came to Nashville, doggedly determined to effect another reconciliation that summer. After Jackson told him he was considering cutting off Robards' ears, Robards swore out a warrant and left. Word came next to the widow Donelson that Robards planned to kidnap Rachel. Because of this threat, Jackson took her to Natchez to stay with friends.

In December 1790, Robards petitioned the Virginia General Assembly for a divorce, for Kentucky was still part of that state. The Assembly rejected his request, though it granted him the right to sue in court for one. Robards then maliciously wrote to Tennessee with the false news that he and Rachel were divorced. On the basis of this lie, Jackson then rushed to Natchez and married Rachel in August 1791.

But two years later the bad news came. Jackson's friend and partner, John Overton, later claimed he had gone on business to Harrodsburg, Kentucky, and while there skimmed through the court records. He said he chanced upon the record of a court case of September 27, 1793, in which Lewis Robards had been granted a divorce on the ground that Rachel Robards "doth still live in adultery with another man."

Shame overtook Rachel and anger claimed Jackson. Although they went through a second marriage ceremony on January 7, 1794, throughout the rest of his life Jackson spent an inordinate amount of time, thought and energy protecting his wife from slander and libel. He had his pistols and his hickory cane, and the duels and clubbings he engaged in were too numerous to count. "I can assure you that whenever my enemies think it worthwhile to investigate the character of Mrs. J.," he informed one man, "I fear not as I know how to defend her." There was Tennessee's great governor, John Sevier. When Jackson invited him to a duel, he noted that Sevier had smeared "the sacred name of a lady in your polluted lips." In another duel over Rachel's name with a blasphemer named Dickinson in 1806, Jackson shifted the lines of his jacket so that the central button was on one side instead of over his heart. He permitted Dickinson a free shot at the button, then although wounded by a bullet that would remain forever in his body, he calmly killed Rachel's detractor. Dueling was so much on his mind that he turned to it as a solution for other problems as well. The fear of opponents to engage him led in turn to an unbridled use of his caustic tongue and pen. Once when General Winfield Scott ran away from a challenge, he swallowed a Jackson description as "a hectoring bully" and one of a group of "intermeddling pimps and spies of the War Department."

Meantime, Jackson's law practice at Nashville prospered. He dreamed of becoming the wealthiest man in the West and soon involved himself in large-scale land speculation ventures, the operation of a general store and slave trading. His outspoken manner and strong personality attracted admirers and in 1796 he won election as a delegate to the state's constitutional convention. Then that same year, as the champion of the well-to-do, he defeated the Sevier candidate of the less fortunates and became Tennessee's first member of the U. S. House of Representatives.

He served a year in the House, with his chief interest apparently the demand that President Washington be impeached for approving the Jay Treaty with the hated English. At home, he had considered himself a gentleman. But in Philadelphia, where the capital was then located, a Tennessee gentleman lacked the gloss of the East. Self-consciously he described the House as being filled with "aristocratic Neebobs"; and in turn, Albert Gallatin, the Jeffersonian leader there, described Jackson's manners as "those of a rough backwoodsman."

In 1797, he moved to the United States Senate. This time he wore a black coat with a velvet collar. However, he revealed his frontier manners by challenging William Cocke, his predecessor, to a duel when Cocke was slow about relinquishing his seat. Jackson was a Jeffersonian in the Senate, although he could not work up enthusiasm for Jefferson personally. In turn, Vice-President Jefferson recalled that Jackson attracted unfavorable comment because whenever he rose to speak he would choke with rage.

Less than a year after he took his Senate seat, Jackson resigned to become a judge on the Tennessee Supreme Court. A worldwide depression that began in 1796 now belatedly affected Jackson, and he watched helplessly as his accumulations dissolved to save him from debtors' prison. Yet although he found himself struggling to remain solvent, his economic views remained unchanged and his six years on the bench saw a continuation of his championing of rich merchants and land barons. In 1804, he thought he had a way to exit from his financial morass. This was to take a desperate trip to Washington to apply to President Jefferson for the post of governor of Louisiana in the newly acquired territory. However, Jefferson appointed twenty-nine-year-old William C. C. Claiborne of Tennessee instead.

Upon his return home emptyhanded, Jackson and Rachel were forced to move from their fine home at Hunter's Hill to a 640-acre tract eight miles from Nashville. This was the place he named the Hermitage, and from here he began his slow rise again to financial success as a partner in a mercantile firm, as a cotton planter and race track owner. One of his horses earned him $40,000. Far more important than wealth, so far as his future was concerned, Governor Archibald Roane broke a tie vote between Jackson and John Sevier and named Jackson major general in charge of the Tennessee militia.

It was on the basis of his elected military status that he became involved in the periphery of the Aaron Burr conspiracy in 1805. Suave Colonel Burr paid a call to Nashville and spoke vaguely but enthusiastically about going to war with Spain to liberate the

Southwest and Mexico, with the approval of the Jefferson Administration. Jackson thought this commendable. Later when Burr was arrested and charged with treason, Jackson appeared at his trial in Richmond, Virginia, to denounce Burr's treacherous, double-dealing partner, General Charles Wilkinson. One day Jackson harangued a crowd on the courthouse stairs for an hour in his shrill voice with his denunciation of Jefferson as "cowardly."

Little wonder then that when the War of 1812 began, Jefferson's friend and successor, James Madison, refused to give Jackson any field orders despite his many pleas. Worse for Jackson, his Tennessee militia troops were ordered to New Orleans and to Florida without him. But the fiery Jackson would not remain ignored, and finally Governor William Blount scribbled in his name as major general of U. S. Volunteers on one of the blank commission forms sent him by the War Department. Thus by trickery did he make his ignominious entrance into a war in which he would emerge as The Hero to the nation and as "Old Hickory" to most of his troops.

Jackson had hardly marched his army to Natchez when Secretary of War John Armstrong sent him an order to disband his troops on the spot. But Jackson refused, for he viewed this as a maneuver on the part of Burr's old fellow conspirator, General Wilkinson, the beloved general of the Administration, who was now in charge of the southern army. Jackson gathered that if his men disbanded so far from home, Wilkinson would add them to his own forces with a promise of bread and meat. So instead of following orders, he marched his men home as a unit and kept them intact.

His major break came when a Creek uprising occurred in the Alabama section of the Mississippi Territory. Keeping the Federal Government in the dark, Governor Blount dispatched Jackson to the troubled area with 2500 men in September 1813. Almost dead after being ambushed by Thomas Hart Benton and his brother Jesse in a Nashville tavern, Jackson rode off into glory with a useless left arm in a sling.

Ill as he was, he craved action. He had his first battle with the Indian friends of the British at Tallushatchee, where "we shot them like dogs," reported Davy Crockett. Seven major victories over the Creeks came in seven months, including the decisive Battle of Horseshoe Bend on the Tallapoosa River on March 27, 1814. With almost all other American generals involved in disastrous action with the British, Jackson's success naturally received sensational praise in the nation's press. Grudgingly, on May 28, 1814 Madison elevated him to the rank of major general in the Regular Army and placed him in command of the Seventh Military District, covering Tennessee, Louisiana and the Mississippi Territory. But to make the honor hollow, the War Secretary followed this with an order to disband most of his army because the war was over on the southern front.

However, Jackson had no intention of falling idle. After forcing a cruel treaty on the Creeks, which he had no authority to impose and which resulted in their relinquishing 23,000,000 acres, he disobeyed orders and invaded Spanish Florida where the British were ensconced. He soon chased them from Mobile and Pensacola. Then on orders from the new Secretary of War, James Monroe, who was now his champion, he went to the defense of New Orleans, a city quaking from reports of an impending large-scale British invasion from the sea. It was here that he brought off the ultimate American victory of the war on January 8, 1815. This was the victory that wiped out memories of earlier catastrophes up North and the burning of Washington, and won Jackson grateful status as "The Hero." Not even disquieting tales of his occasional cruelty to enforce discipline among his men could tarnish his image.

As The Hero, he used his new status to advise President Monroe freely on how to run his Administration and whom to appoint to his Cabinet. Now in command of the Southern District, Jackson ordered his military subordinates to ignore all orders from the War Department that did not meet with his specific approval. Monroe, who feared him, rebuked him gently for placing himself above the Constitution's insistence upon civilian control of the military. He would not rebuke him, however, on reported land speculation deals and horse racing activities while holding his post.

Jackson's red hair had already turned spiky gray by late 1817, when he received orders to attend to the Seminoles who were raiding across the border of Georgia from Spanish Florida. Here his highhanded seizure of Spanish posts and the execution of Indian prophets and two Britishers led to international squabbles with the British and Spanish governments and precipitated Cabinet crises. When Speaker Henry Clay led the Congressional fight against Jackson's behavior in the Seminole fighting, Jackson hurried to Washington to confront his attackers. Members saw him roaming through the Capitol with his hickory cane held in readiness to club opponents. But the House exonerated him and he departed on a triumphant tour of the North.

There was growing talk now that The Hero should be President. But what were his views on civilian matters? When the Panic of 1819 devastated the country, he took the reactionary position in Tennessee against legislative proposals to postpone debt payments and to set up state loan offices for hard-pressed debtors. As a creditor, he considered these laws that passed to be unconstitutional. How was he as a civilian administrator? In the 1821 Federal retrenchment program, his military rank was a casualty, and he accepted President Monroe's offer to become the first governor of Florida, after treaty ratification. Three years earlier Monroe had queried Jefferson about sending Jackson on a diplomatic mission to Russia. "Good God," Jefferson replied, "he would breed you a quarrel before he had been there a month!"

Prophetic words. Secretary of State John Quincy Adams admired the military man of action and he considered Monroe's appointment of Jackson admirable. But he soon found he trembled at the prospect of opening each day's mail and reports from the new governor's realm. By October 5, 1821, when The Hero resigned, he had thrown the outgoing Spanish governor in prison and threatened and lectured an American Federal judge.

When The Hero returned this time to the Hermitage, he found an eager army prepared to promote him for the Presidency. Twenty papers reached the Hermitage regularly and almost to a man their editors wanted him to run. Physically, this should have proved an impossibility, because he suffered from tuberculosis, dropsy and from the severe pain of the bullet imbedded in his left arm near the shoulder. The bullet near his heart did not pain him. Moreover, his habit of chewing tobacco and his constant pipe-smoking gave him fierce headaches. But he possessed a will that was far stronger than his collective ailments. Later on, John Quincy Adams assessed Jackson as a man who was "always dying," like John Randolph who threatened to do so for forty years. Adams wrote of Jackson in his diary that "four-fifths of his sickness is trickery, and the other fifth merely fatigue."

By 1820, a strategy board began forming around Jackson. Among its members were six-foot-six Sam Houston, his protégé; John Henry Eaton, who had gone to the U. S. Senate in 1818 at twenty-eight, despite the Constitution's minimum age requirement of thirty; John Overton, his law and business partner; and William B.

Lewis, his neighbor and friend. These and others decided early in 1821 that they must get to work immediately on a nation-wide campaign if The Hero was to be a strong candidate for 1824. To wait until election year meant defeat because Treasury Secretary William Crawford, with his powerful lobby in Congress and a favorite of Jefferson, would certainly be the choice of the Congressional nominating caucus. So it was wise to start the campaign early and make the prime issue that of discrediting the caucus method of nominating the Republican candidate. Accordingly, in July 1822, Jackson's board of strategy won unanimous nomination for him from the Tennessee Assembly.

Not long afterward, President Monroe nominated Jackson as minister to Mexico. After Senate confirmation, Jackson suspiciously concluded that it was merely a scheme to get him out of the country and out of the 1824 contest. "I cannot accept," he wrote Monroe. "The app. of a minister from the United States might help Tyrant Iturbide [the self-proclaimed Mexican emperor who had overthrown the Republic] in rivitting Despotism upon his country."

Jackson's strategy was one of feigned modesty, to make it appear that he was being "drafted" for the Presidency half against his will. But in 1823, he had to cast this role aside and jump into politics. For Tennessee Senator John Williams was spreading stories in Washington that Jackson was not a serious candidate and was weak even in his own state. To counter these stories, Jackson induced the Tennessee legislature in 1823 to replace Williams as Senator and send The Hero to Washington in his place.

Jackson's return to the Washington scene was not wasted, for he was especially careful to be reserved and courtly, to overcome his ferocious reputation, and he charmed even his opponents in the nation's capital. But so far as his candidacy was concerned, he could not win over to his side his western rival, Speaker Henry Clay, who held the balance of power when no candidate obtained a majority of electoral votes. On issues, Jackson had supported Clay's American System proposals for Federal internal improvements and a protective tariff. When Clay threw his support to Adams, giving him the Presidency, Jackson resigned from the Senate in October 1825, after voting to reject Clay as Secretary of State. Then he returned home, wailing about the "corrupt bargain" between Adams and Clay. Little did Clay realize that his decision to support Adams would rob him of future opportunities to become President.

Jackson's struggle for the Presidency finally ended in success in 1828. While his junto collected the 1824 political managers of Crawford, Clay and Calhoun, his lieutenants in Congress had carried on a four-year war of ridicule against Adams and Clay. All the while, Jackson remained close to home, having decided "to say nothing and plant cotton." Once when a speaking engagement was pushed on him, he escaped by saying, "Having lost many of my teeth it is with difficulty I can articulate." But his vocal silence did not stop him from writing many letters that should not have been mailed. For instance, he heard that Secretary of the Navy Samuel Southard had claimed at a dinner that the chief glory for the New Orleans victory actually belonged to Monroe, then Secretary of War. Jackson, quickly reaching his low boiling point, wrote Southard that the War Department had been so unhelpful to him at New Orleans that either Monroe or the ordnance chief should have been executed for criminal neglect. He also admonished Southard to watch his tongue at his "wine drinkings hereafter."

The 1828 contest proved many things. The political axiom has it that if one side fights dirty, it can expect the other side to retaliate in kind. The Jacksonians found this to be true after libeling and slandering Adams with seeming impunity. "King John the Second," the Jacksonian Republicans repeated endlessly, was a waster of public funds, a crook and a gambler who broke the Sabbath riding "like mad" on Sundays in a jockey's suit, hated the poor and despised democracy.

Then the gun muzzles turned and the National Republicans began printing stories about the harsh court-martial sentences meted out by Jackson. The Hero's mother was called a "common prostitute" and his father a "mulatto man." But the worst was soon forthcoming. Clay's supporter, Charles Hammond, editor of the Cincinnati *Gazette,* attempted to help Adams by spreading the story of Jackson, Rachel and Lewis Robards across the nation. "Ought a convicted adulteress and her paramour husband to be placed in the highest offices of this free and Christian land?" Hammond asked. False and lurid accounts of the marriage mess now became the meat of the National Republican press.

Duff Green, editor of the Jacksonian *United States Telegraph,* retaliated with a tale that Adams and his wife had engaged in pre-

marital relations. And Isaac Hill, the crippled little editor of the
New Hampshire *Patriot*, came out with the libel that Adams, while
envoy to Russia, had procured a beautiful American girl to satisfy
the lust of Czar Alexander I. Jackson was sickened by these coun-
terattacks, and he admonished Green: "I never war against females
and it is only the base and cowardly that do."

After Jackson's smashing defeat of Adams, stout little "Aunt
Rachel" wrote, "The enemys of the Genls have dipt their arrows
in wormwood and gall and sped them at me." Even though she
had gone to Washington four years earlier when Jackson had been
Senator and enjoyed herself, she grew depressed now at the
prospect of becoming First Lady. "I had rather be a doorkeeper
in the house of God than to live in that palace at Washington,"
she wrote. On December 17, 1828, she suffered a heart attack,
was bled three times in a single day, but recovered sufficiently to
smoke her clay pipe. However, she died five days later. At her
grave, her stricken husband said, "I know 'tis unmanly, but these
tears are due her virtue. . . . Those vile wretches who have slandered her must look to God for mercy!"

The roar of expectancy prevailed in Washington even before the
bereaved Hero arrived. "No one knows what he will do when he
comes," wrote Senator Daniel Webster. "My opinion is, that when
he comes, he will bring a breeze with him. Which way it will
blow I cannot tell." Great crowds flooded the taverns and inns
awaiting "the Revolution of 1828." One man described the scene
as "like the inundation of northern barbarians into Rome." Webster
added: "They really seem to think the country is rescued from
some dreadful danger . . . that democracy had won over aristocracy."

On Inauguration Day, Jackson emulated Jefferson's simplicity.
Leaving Gadsby's Tavern on Pennsylvania Avenue, he walked
bareheaded along the sidewalk up the hill to the Capitol where
he delivered an inaudible address to the enormous, cheering
crowd. It was a dull talk, of a conservative nature, and hardly
one to please followers who demanded an ineffable revolution. He
promised to handle the duties of the President without exceeding
their constitutional limitations, to practice strict economy and
eliminate the national debt. So far as the controversial topics of
the times were concerned, he carefully straddled the questions
of the protective tariff and internal improvements and he made

no mention of the emerging slavery issue. Almost apologetically he said: "The task of reform . . . inscribes itself on the list of executive duties." This above all would have brought resounding cheers, for "reform" to his followers meant changes in government personnel and recipients of government contracts.

Then on horseback Jackson rode back to the White House, deserted the previous day by John Quincy Adams. He led a great walking and riding crowd, who followed him into the Executive Mansion for the reception. In a moment, frontiersmen stood with muddy boots on satin-covered chairs, and the throng became "a mob—scrambling, fighting, romping." An observer wrote that he saw "a stout black wench eating a jelly with a gold spoon." The rooms grew crowded and suffocatingly hot. The more unruly drinkers smashed china and glasses and tore clothing; women fainted, and Jackson's friends discovered him crushed in a corner and sinking into exhaustion. A cordon helped him escape the Mansion by a rear exit for Gadsby's. Then the crowd was tricked outdoors by the setting of tubs of liquor on the lawn. In the view of a Jacksonian, this was "the people's day and the people's President." But Supreme Court Justice Joseph Story, once a Jeffersonian and now the disciple of Chief Justice Marshall, characterized the event and the new Administration as "the reign of King 'Mob.'"

It was apparent to Jackson that the crowds that had descended on Washington had not come merely to cheer him. The city remained swollen and bulging after Inauguration Day with job seekers and would-be contractors. They heralded the vast decline in public and business morals that was fast settling over the country. Too long, they charged, had the appointees of the previous aristocratic-minded Presidents controlled the day-by-day activities of the Federal establishment. "Turn the rascals out," they shouted until they were hoarse. William L. Marcy, a New York Jacksonian politician, coined the battle cry for this army—"To the victors belong the spoils!" Duff Green's *Telegraph* offered its own repetitive war whoop: "Cleanse the Augean stable" of Adams men.

All this posed a problem to Jackson, who had not taken office with any fixed program on party patronage. In fact, years before he had gone on record favoring the merit system in government. In one letter to President Monroe he had urged him to keep the Federal service free of the taint of special Administration patronage. When William Crawford's Tenure of Office Act became law in 1820, permitting each Administration to replace employees after a four-year tenure, Jackson found the law detestable.

But now the shouts and demands of his followers were too loud and strenuous to ignore. They jostled their way into the White House and Government buildings, beset officials and insisted on their reward for having supported The Hero. "It appeared that instead of love of principle it was love of office that had induced them to support the good cause," Jackson said with disillusionment. "Self-exertion was about to be abandoned and dependence for a livelihood placed upon the government."

But if he found it disgusting that so many of his followers had only pretended to work in his behalf for nothing, he also saw much merit in developing a government service that would be loyal to him. Rotation in office would get rid of the superannuated hirelings of his "neebob" predecessors, satisfy the most deserving of his helpers and form a sound base for future political action.

Accordingly, he sent the departments an "Outline of Principles." They were called on to retrench and improve their economy. Then so far as their employees were concerned, they were to investigate the "moral habits" and fire those found wanting. Nor was this the only cause for dismissal. The Outline said it was the duty of every department head "to dismiss all officers who were appointed against the manifest will of the people or whose official station, by a subserviency to selfish electioning processes, was made to operate against the freedom of elections." These standards, of course, provided total leeway to officials to establish a Jacksonian bureaucracy. And by what standards were new employees to be rated? Not on the basis of experience and specialization, he said flatly. Nothing the Federal Government did could not be made "so plain and simple that men of intelligence may readily qualify themselves for [its] performance."

With the unveiling of the Jackson spoils system, a reign of terror enveloped jobholders. It was not long before the Adams-Clay National Republican press reported suicides and tales of starving, fired employees and denounced the "clean sweep" of the Government service. Yet the spoils system, though severe, never affected more than 20 per cent of employees during Jackson's Administration.

When rotation in office went into effect, Jackson summoned Postmaster General John McLean. McLean controlled the most patronage and the President expected him to co-operate, for he had been a Jacksonian while serving in Adams' Administration. However, McLean stunned him when he boldly announced he would not fire capable personnel no matter what their politics. "Mr. McLean," Jackson cut in, "will you accept a seat on the bench of the Supreme Court?" McLean caught the look of violence in Jackson's eyes and he nodded. Martin Van Buren, Jackson's new Secretary of State and a man who understood the importance of patronage, calculated that there were 5200 postmasters, each with four helpers, plus hundreds of single-man post offices. These were a potentially large voting bloc and were best kept in safe hands, such as his own.

Frequently, Jackson permitted sentiment to interfere with rotation. Any Revolutionary War soldier or 1812 veteran could appeal to him to save his job and expect a warm reception. "By the Eternal! I will not remove the old man!" he saved one Revolutionary War government employee. "Do you know that he carries a pound of British lead in his body?"

There could be no Jackson Revolution so long as the Administration was engrossed with patronage, and Jackson soon had his fill of the hordes of favor-seekers. They would have to leave town in order to let the Government settle down to its tasks, he finally uttered in rage. This shocked those who had yet failed to find their reward, and many grumbled that they would start a new political party to get their due. But Jackson's wrath and the desire for quiet by his exhausted, besieged Cabinet officers, especially his Secretary of State, promoted the exodus from town. Jackson was well aware of the anger that the disappointed carried home with them, and he wrote a friend: "If I had a tit for every one of those pigs to suck at they would still be my friends."

Once in office, Jackson revealed in other ways besides the adoption of the spoils system his flexibility regarding former principles. For instance, in 1825 when House Speaker Clay was up for confirmation as Adams' Secretary of State, Jackson had urged a constitutional amendment "rendering any member of Congress ineligible to office under the general government during the terms for which he was elected, and for two years thereafter." Yet when he chose his own Secretaries, he pulled five of his six top officers from Congress. True, Senator Martin Van Buren of New York had quit Congress to serve two months as governor before becoming Secretary of State. But Representative Samuel Ingham of Pennsylvania (now Secretary of the Treasury) and Senators

John Branch of North Carolina (Secretary of the Navy), John Berrien of Georgia (Attorney General) and John Henry Eaton of Tennessee (Secretary of War) came directly from the Hill.

If this preponderance of former members of Congress was calculated to result in camaraderie with the Legislative Branch, it yielded a poor return on the investment. The Jacksonians held a 26 to 22 margin in the Senate, but most had been too well trained in opposing the Executive. When Jackson sent the Upper Chamber seventy-six nominations for key posts, great arguments arose over confirming many of them. A significant number had not been acted upon when the Senate blithely adjourned on March 17, 1829, for a nine-months' vacation.

For a President who was supposed to be leading a revolution, Congressional adjournment with so many nominations unconfirmed seemed a slap in the face. Yet it also gave him the opportunity to act without annoyance from legislators. Unfortunately, he misused these precious months by involving himself in a cause that had nothing to do with government management.

The "cause" was Margaret (Peggy) O'Neale Timberlake Eaton, the wife of Secretary of War Eaton. Back in 1818, after John Henry Eaton, a wealthy Tennessee lawyer and planter, completed a biography of the general, Jackson helped reward him by supporting him for a seat in the United States Senate. Young Eaton, then two years younger than the permissible Senate age of thirty, became Jackson's most vociferous booster for the Presidency. It was Eaton who had offered the Senate resolution that permitted Missouri to become a state in 1821 despite Missouri's constitution, which was in contempt of Congress.

In Washington, Eaton boarded on different occasions at the O'Neale Tavern. Here he met O'Neale's small but voluptuous daughter Peggy, a young girl with an apple-cheek complexion and "the prettiest teeth in Washington." Almost from childhood, Peggy was a femme fatale. One suitor killed himself, two others dueled each other and an old general almost went insane in his desire for her. Then in 1816 when she was sixteen, she married a Navy purser named John Timberlake after a five-hour acquaintanceship. Timberlake was then on furlough from the Navy because he had stolen from his accounts.

Senator Eaton was a widower when he moved into the O'Neale Tavern for the first time in 1818. Not long afterward he was madly

in love with Peggy. Using his Senate influence, Eaton straightened out Timberlake's troubles with the Navy and soon had him
out to sea again. But now he and Peggy disported themselves so
openly that their relationship became common gossip. Peggy was
so much regarded as a woman who would "dispense her favors
wherever she took a fancy" that Mrs. Monroe bluntly ordered her
to stay away from Presidential receptions.

When Jackson came to the Senate in December 1823, he stayed
with Eaton at the O'Neale Tavern, and he met Peggy. Timberlake
also turned up in more trouble with the Navy over his bookkeep-
ing. This time Eaton posted a $10,000 bond in his behalf and saw
to it that he was given a berth on the frigate *Constitution*, which
was destined to be gone four long years. Afterward he and Peggy
went on as before. Jackson, who never saw what all of Washington claimed, wrote home to Rachel that "in the evening Mrs.
Timberlake the maryed daughter whose husband belongs to our
Navy plays the piano delightfully, and every Sunday evening en-
tertains her pious mother with sacred music."

In April 1828, while in the Mediterranean, Timberlake committed suicide. The Navy said he died from "pulmonary disease,"
but Washington tongues said he slit his throat because he knew
of Peggy's affair with Eaton. After Jackson won his election as
President, Eaton came to him for advice. "Major," Jackson told
him, "if you love Margaret Timberlake go and marry her at once
and shut their mouths." Eaton heeded this advice and on January 1, 1829, he and Peggy were married by the Chaplain of
the Senate. However, the gossip did not die but became in fact
louder and coarser. Jacksonians and anti-Jacksonians alike considered the newlyweds with contempt. Representative Churchill
Cambreleng of New York, a close associate of Martin Van Buren,
wrote him, "There is a vulgar saying of some vulgar man, I believe Swift, on such unions—about using a certain household . . .
and then putting it on one's head."

When Jackson considered candidates for his Cabinet, he offered
the War Department to his old friend, Senator Hugh Lawson
White of Tennessee, and sent a note to White to pass the letter
offer on to Eaton if he would not accept. Although Eaton and
Peggy panted over Cabinet status, when White rejected the post
and sent him the letter, Eaton coyly told Jackson he could not
accept it. To Jackson, who knew that Washington society considered the Eatons as social lepers, this refusal could not stand

and Eaton "very reluctantly," said Jackson, joined the Cabinet. This defense of the Eatons by elevating them socially became part of Jackson's dialogue in interviewing other Cabinet prospects. Berrien, the would-be Attorney General, denied he agreed with the general opinion of the Eatons, while Branch, who wanted the Navy Department told Jackson that he "disavowed any knowledge of anything disreputable to Mrs. Eaton, or any belief of the rumors."

Trouble started at the inaugural ball when Floride Calhoun, the wife of the Vice-President, refused to acknowledge Peggy's existence. Then after the Cabinet was made official, Branch would not let his wife call on the Eatons, nor would the widower Berrien let his daughters visit there. Trouble also came at the White House, where Rachel's niece, Emily Donelson, who was Jackson's hostess, would not associate with Peggy. Emily's husband, Andrew Jackson Donelson, son of Rachel's brother Samuel and reared by Rachel at the Hermitage after his father died, served as Jackson's private secretary. Donelson agreed with his wife, and Jackson suffered a double hurt.

Instead of going about his work, Jackson became obsessed with the belief that Peggy Eaton was a woman wronged—like his Rachel. And by the Eternal! he would not let Peggy suffer the same fate.

At first he blamed the Eaton troubles on "Clay and his minions." To this, Clay issued his humorous broadside on Peggy—"Age cannot wither nor time stale her infinite virginity." Jackson then turned in fury on his own official family for ignoring the Eatons in the spring social season. With a show of wrath, he exploded at his Cabinet: "I did not come here to make a Cabinet for the ladies of this place, but for the nation." Most vulnerable was Emily Donelson, and he ordered his niece to be pleasant to Peggy. But Emily refused. On a Presidential excursion boat to Norfolk, Peggy offered Emily some of her cologne. When Emily refused, Peggy shrieked that if she did not change, the President would banish her to Tennessee. Later the Eatons sent Emily a threatening letter, to which the young White House hostess foolishly replied with a hot rejoinder.

All spring and summer, Jackson labored to win acceptance for Peggy. As one good Jacksonian remarked in disgust at this enormous waste of Presidential time and effort, "God knows we did not make him President to work the miracle of making Mrs. E.

an honorable woman." Martin Van Buren, the dapper Secretary of State, was one of a few who perceived that "the Eaton Malaria," as he called Jackson's affliction, might become an important political weapon. There was much to be gained for his own political future by being friendly with the Eatons, since this meant so much to the President. Van Buren's advantage in playing this fakery was that he was a widower and thus did not have the handicap of a wife in society. So he proceeded to join Eaton and his wife in their empty dining room and to see to it that Jackson learned of his conduct. Immediately, as he knew it would, his stock rose sharply while that of Vice-President Calhoun, his rival as Jackson's successor, fell. One day Jackson determinedly left the White House and went to the Calhoun home where he ordered Floride Calhoun to include Peggy in her social sphere. But Floride would not agree. Acquaintances of the Calhouns in Washington were amused by Floride's airs because her temper tantrums were much discussed. Once she dented a water pitcher on her husband's head and on another fiery occasion she threw her best china service at him.

On one occasion, Van Buren, who was a magnificent actor, told Peggy: "General Jackson is the greatest man that ever lived—the only man among them all without a fault. But don't tell him what I said, I would not have him know it for the world." When she rushed to Jackson and told him, she said Jackson stared at her "with tears in his eyes" and commented, "Ah, that man loves me."

The height of Jackson's strange obsession in the Eaton Malaria came in September 1829. Perhaps the weirdest Cabinet meeting in history took place at that time when Jackson ordered his Secretaries to a meeting to discuss Peggy's virtue. Eaton had been forewarned and remained away. In his seat sat Major William B. Lewis, Jackson's longtime associate and a relative of Eaton's first wife. Jackson had also ordered Vice-President Calhoun to be present and had requested the Reverend John Campbell, pastor of the Washington Presbyterian Church, which Jackson attended, and the Reverend Ezra Stiles Ely of Philadelphia, an old friend, to join the Cabinet for the meeting.

The meeting opened with Jackson presenting a wide array of testimonials he had asked Lewis to collect to prove the high virtue of Mrs. Eaton. Earlier Reverend Ely had written Jackson that Peggy's reputation had been bad since girlhood, that she and

Eaton had traveled together before they were married and that when Peggy failed to say hello to a man at Gadsby's the gentleman remarked she had "apparently forgotten the time when she slept with me." After offering Lewis' testimonials, Jackson demanded that Ely offer positive proof or shut up. "She is chaste as a virgin!" Jackson silenced him. The Reverend Campbell had earlier told Jackson that a Dr. Craven said he had taken care of Peggy when she had a miscarriage in 1821 at a time when her husband had been long at sea. Campbell was now called upon to repeat his story and he had hardly begun his explanation when Jackson ordered him to "give evidence, not discuss it!" Campbell stamped out of the room, shouting that he could prove his case in court. Jackson then ended the sordid discussion by ordering everyone to leave, and his expression was that of a man who had won an important case.

The next day Eaton confronted Reverend Campbell in his rectory where they had hot words and a fistfight. Peggy stepped between and was accidentally hit and felled by her husband with a head gash.

The Eaton Malaria had a long course to run. Jackson stopped attending Campbell's church and he eventually banished Emily and Jack Donelson to Tennessee, where they stayed a year before resuming their duties as hostess and secretary. He postponed his dinner for the Cabinet because Cabinet members were expected to give dinners later for their colleagues and more embarrassment might befall Peggy. Eventually he held his dinner, but his worst fears were realized when his officers held theirs. "Calhoun leads the moral party," John Quincy Adams commented drily, "Van Buren that of the frail sisterhood." Peggy was not invited to Cabinet member parties other than those staged by Van Buren. Even here, when she had a loud argument on the dance floor with the wife of a general, she was dubbed "Bellona, the Goddess of War," a name by which Washingtonians called her afterward. His venom rising anew, Jackson hailed Secretaries Ingham, Berrien and Branch to appear before him. When they came he read a prepared statement in which he said: "You and your families have . . . taken measures to induce others to avoid Mrs. Eaton and thereby to exclude her from society and degrade him." Each declared his innocence, to which Jackson snapped, "An indignity to Major Eaton is an indignity to me."

Little did he know that Peggy was trading on his image of her

as another wronged-Rachel. With the power of the President behind her, Peggy found it simple to slip her father and brother-in-
law onto the government payroll. She also used her influence to
help Major Lewis, her strong ally, win the post of second auditor
of the Treasury. There were also unsavory schemes, such as her
offer of a carriage as a bribe to a Treasury official to approve
a padded mail-carrying contract.

So the months of the first year of the Jackson Administration
flew by, portending on the basis of what took place the most
chaotic and nonsensical administration in the nation's history. Chief
immediate casualties were the government service and the Cabinet.

There seemed to be either no co-ordination of government activities or a calculated contempt for the way of business of previous
Administrations. For instance, in 1829, with Congress away,
Jackson made recess appointments to a commission to go to
Turkey to discuss diplomatic relations. When Congress returned,
he failed to send the names of the commissioners to the Senate
for confirmation. But two years later he had his House supporters
insert an item in an appropriations bill to compensate the commission for its completed mission.

The Cabinet's importance had been established in the Washington Administration, but now because of the Eaton affair it had
become a crippled institution. Nevertheless, its functions remained
necessary and Jackson turned elsewhere for advice and help. These
personal advisers later came to be known collectively as the
"Kitchen Cabinet," a derisive term covering their general lack of
high formal positions. Although a jealous Cabinet officer denounced
the Kitchen Cabinet as "unknown to the Constitution and to the
country," his description would have aptly covered the Cabinet
itself at the outset of the Washington Administration.

The Kitchen Cabinet was not a set group, but had a changing
membership, depending on Jackson's inclinations and the key issues
of the moment. Over the years, its most prominent members included editors Amos Kendall and Francis Preston Blair, Isaac Hill,
Major William B. Lewis, Martin Van Buren, Maryland attorney
Roger Taney, Jack Donelson and Edward Livingston.

Next to Van Buren, the man with the most influence in the
Kitchen Cabinet was Amos Kendall, who, like the others, specialized in press, patronage and policy matters. In addition, Kendall
was frequently used by Jackson as a ghostwriter. He had come

originally from Massachusetts, moving to Kentucky after schooling at Groton and Dartmouth. Here Mrs. Henry Clay befriended him and he became the tutor of her two oldest sons who were wild-tempered boys. Lucretia Clay did much to change Kendall's sour, negative personality and to teach him public manners. She also nursed him through an almost fatal illness, "with the kindess of a mother," he said. Later he passed the Kentucky bar and then became editor of the Frankfort, Kentucky, *Argus,* attached to Clay's cause. Kendall had opposed the Kentucky relief laws for debtors following the Panic of 1819, but he dropped this conservative Clay-Jackson position when pressed by two of the paper's backers to do so. The two were Colonel Richard M. Johnson, one of the original 1812 War Hawks in Congress, and William Barry, who was chief justice of the self-created "New Kentucky Court" when the established court declared the relief laws unconstitutional.

When Clay became Secretary of State under President Adams in 1825, he found a government job for Kendall, but the editor turned it down because he would not work for only $1000 a year. Not long after this, rich Kentucky Jacksonians threatened to establish a rival paper unless the *Argus* supported their man for 1828. Kendall then switched allegiance, issuing broadside after broadside against his former benefactor and President Adams. These attacks so infuriated Clay that he removed the paper's Federal printing contracts. When Kendall came to Washington, Jackson interviewed him and then found him a place as fourth auditor of the Treasury. Here he uncovered a $7000 default in accounts by his predecessor, Tobias Watkins, a personal friend of former President Adams. When Watkins fled and then was captured, tried and convicted, Kendall's stock shot sky-high and he became a member of Jackson's inner circle.

Anti-Jacksonites feared Kendall's influence and called him the sinister mystery man of the Administration. Harriet Martineau, a visiting English writer of that period, reported: "A member of Congress told me he had watched through five sessions for a sight of Kendall and had never obtained one until now. . . . In a moment he was gone." Kendall's unwillingness to discuss his activities, plus his strange appearance, added to the mystery. His back was bent, his hair prematurely white and his body was wracked continually by coughing. He often circled his head with a handkerchief. "Poor wretch," a Congressman once described him, "he looked like Death on the pale horse." Kendall's primary function was to write state papers for Jackson, but his enemies made him out to be de facto President. Congressman Henry A. Wise of Virginia insisted that Kendall was "the President's thinking machine, and his writing machine—ay, and his lying machine . . . He was chief overseer, chief reporter, amanuensis, scribe, accountant general, man of all work—nothing was well done without the aid of his diabolical genius." Harriet Martineau added: "He is supposed to be the moving spring of the Administration, the thinker, the planner, the doer; but it is all in the dark. Documents are issued the excellence of which prevents them from being attributed to the persons that take the responsibility. . . . Work is done with goblin speed which makes men look about them with superstitious wonder; and the invisible Amos Kendall has the credit of it all."

Also a key member of the Kitchen Cabinet was Francis Preston Blair, who had earlier succeeded Kendall as editor of the pro-Clay *Argus*. Kendall had spoken highly of Blair and was instrumental in bringing him to Washington to edit a newly established Jackson paper, the Washington *Globe*. However, Kendall had failed to mention Blair's odd appearance, and when he first arrived, Major William Lewis took a look at him and blurted, "Mr. Blair, we want stout hearts and sound heads here." Blair was about six feet tall, weighed one hundred pounds and came with a black patch over a head wound. However, an earlier dour expression was no longer present, because Jacksonians had promised to pay off his debts of $40,000. In contrast to Blair was his partner on the *Globe*, John C. Rives, an obese giant of six and a half feet. Rives referred to himself and Blair as "the ugliest looking pair in the country." The importance of "Blar," as Jackson called him, was his wonderfully vitriolic pen that gave the President's enemies sharp indigestion and his friends rallying euphoria. Blair fashioned the motto for the *Globe* from the states' rights and Federal-enumerated powers view of the Jeffersonians—"The world is governed too much." "I expect you all to patronize the *Globe*," Jackson warned government employees when the paper began operations. In addition to giving the editor free rein on the paper, Jackson consulted with him on vital matters of state.

In December 1829, with the Eaton Malaria still raging, Jackson sent the returning Congress his first Annual Message. For months politicians had waited expectantly to learn how he intended to reverse what the campaigning Jacksonians had called Big Government run by the Aristocrats for the benefit of the Rich. They were to find now that he had no revolutionary plan.

After noting that the twenty-four states contained "12,000,000 happy citizens," he asked Congress to amend the Constitution to provide for the direct election of Presidents. He also declared himself in favor of limiting "the service of the Chief Magistrate to a single term of either four or six years." On foreign policy, he advocated a strong line against France for refusing to pay for the damages to American commerce by Napoleon and against England for closing her West Indies ports to American commerce. He said he would "ask for nothing that is not clearly right and to submit to nothing that is wrong." Regarding the growing problem with eastern Indians, he opposed a policy of leniency and would push them beyond the Mississippi. On the national debt, he was against the Hamiltonian principle that one should be maintained and the bonds sold to the rich in order to keep them attached to the welfare of the Federal Government. The national debt would be paid off and surplus Federal revenues distributed among the states. To a West earnestly in need of roads and canals, he said he would permit only "constitutional" projects, a term that made Westerners gulp with concern. He also had an opinion on the Second Bank of the United States, whose twenty-year charter would expire in 1836. He suggested that Congress "and the people" consider a new arrangement because the private institution had failed to establish a uniform and sound currency." One further item: the protective tariff. The South had labeled Van Buren's bill of 1828 the "Tariff of Abominations," and there were rumors that South Carolina planned to "nullify" it. Jackson had been a protective tariff Senator in 1824, but now he advocated peaceful compromise.

Jackson's first order of business was to have the Senate confirm the many nominations he had made to posts under him. However, even a pro-Jackson Upper Chamber was in no mood to become his rubber stamp. When he submitted 319 nominations, he was chagrined by rough treatment, especially harsh toward his Kitchen Cabinet. Because no appropriation existed for a White House staff, he had been forced to arrange other government jobs for his important advisers. Even though Jack Donelson lived and worked in the White House as his secretary, Jackson had to provide him a salary as an official at the Land Office. To his embarrassment, the duties of even that minor post required Donelson to sign his name to land patents, and one summer there were forty thousand for him to sign.

Donelson's nomination evoked no real opposition, but those involving other advisers and aides did. Jackson had named Isaac Hill, former editor of the New Hampshire *Patriot* and the spreader of the falsehood that Adams had been a procurer for the Czar, as second comptroller of the Treasury. The Senate now boldly rejected Hill. Jackson's fury was equaled by that of Hill, who got his revenge when the New Hampshire legislature sent him back to Washington as a Senator.

Amos Kendall teetered on the brink of rejection. The final vote to confirm him was a tie and only Vice-President Calhoun's ballot saved him as fourth auditor of the Treasury. Henry Lee, third son of Henry "Light-Horse Harry" and brother of Robert E., suffered the worse defeat of all. Known as "Black-Horse Harry," he was mentally and socially unsteady. He had come to live at the Hermitage years earlier when Jackson took him in out of pity after Lee had seduced his own sister-in-law and fled to avoid legal troubles. Before being elected President, Jackson utilized Black-Horse Harry as a letter writer and minor adviser. His reward now was an appointment as consul general to Algiers. But the Senate chose to reject him—unanimously. In anguish, Lee wrote Senator John Tyler, his college classmate, that his only "crime" was exactly the one committed by Thomas Jefferson on his sister-in-law.

Another man was rejected by a vote of 43 to 1; others by less embarrassing totals. Senator Daniel Webster's opinion was that "were it not for the outdoor popularity of the President, we would have negatived more than half his nominations." One nominee winning confirmation was John Randolph, the old troublemaker, as minister to Russia. Van Buren had suggested this to Jackson in order, as he put it, "to get Randolph's tongue out of the country." Van Buren had added: "It would expose him to an unfavorable climate . . . and little harm would be done if it should turn out we had made a mistake." As things did turn out, when Randolph reached St. Petersburg he immediately detested the place and fled after ten days to England, where he remained a year as a visitor. Later Congress ordered the Treasury to pay him $21,407 for "services in Russia."

Jackson was not a man to restrict himself to private cursing when the Senate rejected his men. On many occasions he resubmitted the names of rejected nominees. He entertained no fear of or high regard for the Senate, considering it subservient to the President but possessed of annoying weapons. His later advice for President John Tyler was "to do as I did. Whenever the Senate rejected a good man, on the ground of his politics, I gave them a hot potatoe, and he will soon bring them to terms, and if not, if they leave the office not filled, the vengeance of the people will fall upon them." This advice notwithstanding, Jackson suffered one of the highest casualty rates on nominations of all Presidents.

The first major policy battle of the Jackson Administration came in January 1830 and found the President on the sidelines until the crucial point. One of Jackson's innovations was to post aides at the Capitol to relay to him each day's Congressional activities. On a cold day Major Lewis, the nominal second auditor of the Treasury and Presidential observer of Congress, reported that an important debate on public land policy and states' rights was under way.

The essential background, which came clear later, was that after Congress passed the Tariff of Abominations in 1828, Vice-President John C. Calhoun went home to his Pendleton, South Carolina, plantation and secretly wrote a treatise, known as "The South Carolina Exposition and Protest." Then on December 19, 1828, the state legislature ordered part of it printed as a public document without revealing authorship, for Calhoun, who had been Adams' Vice-President, was to hold the same office under the President-elect, an admirer of his open show of opposition to Adams.

The "South Carolina Exposition" promoted the view that the Union was only a compact of state governments; that the authority of the Federal Government was severely limited in scope and methods; and that when Congress acted beyond its authority a single state could nullify that act. Applying this philosophy to the tariff, Calhoun argued that the Constitution's grant of the tax power was limited strictly to the task of raising revenue. Since protective tariffs were devoted instead to providing northern industries with freedom from foreign competition, the Tariff of 1828 was, therefore, "unconstitutional, unequal and oppressive," in his view. Under it, he said, Southerners became "the serfs of the system, out of whose labor is raised not only the money paid into the Treasury, but the funds out of which are drawn the rich rewards of the manufacturer and his associates. Their encouragement is our discouragement." What the 1828 Tariff actually did, he explained further, was to place a 45 per cent tax on southern agricultural exports, for this was how much more Southerners had to pay for domestic manufactured goods under a 45 per cent import umbrella for the protected industries.

The situation presented a classic problem of democratic governments, he reasoned—a situation where the majority was oppressing a minority. For the North, which enjoyed the benefits of the protective tariff, held two-thirds of the population, while the South, which was burdened by the tariff, held only a third of the nation's population. However, there was one way in which the minority could protect itself, he argued, and that method could be found in the work of Jefferson and Madison in the Kentucky and Virginia Resolutions of 1798 against the Alien and Sedition Acts. Because majority rule would continue to oppress the beleaguered South, he said, the minority states had the right of *interposition* against the despotism of the many. This power, said Calhoun, was legal, for even though the Constitution failed to enumerate such powers it was in accord with the principles on which the Constitution was framed. By interposition, a state, then, could convene a state convention to declare a Federal act null and void. And if this were not done now, Calhoun contended long before Karl Marx began his revolutionary writings, after the planters were bankrupted by the tariff there would be a class war between "capitalists and operatives . . . wages must sink more rapidly than the necessaries of life."

Although the South Carolina legislature had ordered most of the "Exposition" printed, it did not put Calhoun's handiwork to a vote. For there was good reason to believe that Jackson, who raised cotton and owned one hundred slaves, would promote southern interests. Moreover, Calhoun believed he would dominate the Jackson Administration, for he was not only heir apparent but had also put three of his henchmen into the Cabinet as Secretaries of the Navy and Treasury and Attorney General.

However, Calhoun's initial smugness soon gave way to rising concern. His wife's leadership in snubbing Peggy Eaton was a blunder, for it made Jackson consider him with narrowed eyes. Then Duff Green's continuing campaign in the *Telegraph* hailing him as the President-to-be in 1832 had irritated Jackson and the Kitchen Cabinet to the point of establishing another paper, the *Globe*, under Francis Blair. There was still another breach between Jackson and Calhoun, for neither the inaugural address nor the first Message to Congress on December 8, 1829, had called for the removal of the protective tariff.

In order to promote this last event, southern politicians had entered into an alliance with western Congressmen. The Westerners wanted cheap public land; the Southerners, an end to the Tariff of Abominations. Just as Southerners had counted on Jackson's aid for their cause, so had the Westerners counted on him to promote large-scale internal improvements. But he had stunned the West by his ominous stand against Federal aid for road construction that was not "constitutional." In addition, by proposing to extinguish the national debt and distribute excess revenues among the states, he would not have funds available to build roads.

The South-West alliance had its first test on December 29, 1829, when Senator Samuel A. Foote of Connecticut offered an anti-western resolution to inquire into the expediency of limiting the sale of public lands. At the White House, Jackson had a running report of the surprising aftermath. Foote's resolution brought Senator Thomas Hart Benton, champion of the West, to his feet. This large, hooknosed man with a voice dripping with rasping sarcasm and a penchant for obtaining government jobs and contracts for relatives, was at his most furious. He lashed the East with the old whip that it opposed settlement of the West in order to maintain a cheap labor force. As a corollary to Foote's resolution, Benton shouted, he would just as soon inquire into the expediency of setting fire to cities or flooding fertile farm land.

What began as a simple argument now turned into the greatest debate in American history. Senator Robert Y. Hayne of South Carolina, handsome lieutenant of Calhoun and personal friend of Jackson, followed with a firm approval of Benton's arguments. But he did not stop with a defense of a cheap land policy. Instead he went on to attack Clay's American System planks of a protective tariff, public works programs and a stronger Bank of the United States. Hayne attacked most harshly the protective tariff proposal of Clay's platform and spoke in horror of a strong national government with large revenues. Then he turned on the East and said, "The South will always be sympathetic with the West, unlike the East whose attitude toward western public lands is selfish and unprincipled."

While Hayne spoke, Senator Daniel Webster entered the chamber following his appearance at a law case before the Supreme Court, which was located directly below the Senate chamber in the

Capitol. An impressive figure with his massive chest, bulging fore-head and a skin so dark he was called "Black Dan," Webster considered leaving the chamber, but he soon joined the battle. "I rise to defend the East," he said at the outset of the famous Web-ster-Hayne debates. "I deny that the East has at any time shown an illiberal policy toward the West. . . . I deny the sum total and I deny the detail." To Hayne's statement that "no evil was more to be deprecated than the consolidation of this government," Web-ster offered a deriding "Consolidation! that perpetual cry, both of terror and delusion." Consolidation served only to strengthen the Union, he said, and he hoped Hayne and other Southerners had not intended to "speak of the Union in terms of indifference, or even disparagement." So far as public land was concerned, he did not favor taking it off the market but would sell it at a low price.

Hayne returned another day to vent his anger on Webster but his tone and subject matter were changed: he glorified slavery and condemned the miserable condition of northern factory work-ers. The Senator from Massachusetts was a fine one to attack the patriotism of the South, he said. What about the treasonous ac-tivities of New England Federalists during the War of 1812 and tales of the demands for separation from the Union at the 1814 Hartford Convention?

Had he stopped after this attack on the patriotism of New En-gland, Webster would have been on the defensive. However, Hayne strayed from this subject to expound Calhoun's theory of interposi-tion. Any state, he repeated, had the right to declare a Federal act null and void when the Federal Government violated the Con-stitution.

It seemed that all of Washington tried to crowd into the Capitol to hear Webster's reply to Hayne's latest attack. He filled two after-noons with remarkable oratory from twelve pages of notes at a pace of one hundred words a minute. He spoke without anger and his rich voice was set at a conversational tone. The Hartford Conven-tion was far in the past, he said. Furthermore, how could Hayne deride its philosophy when what he now proposed was at least as obnoxious? Nullification was a false and dangerous doctrine. "The Constitution is not the creature of the state government. The very chief end, the main design for which the whole Constitution was framed and adopted, was to establish a government that should not . . . depend on state opinion and state discretion."

As for Hayne's attack on New England and especially on Massachusetts, said Webster, "I shall enter no encomium of Massachusetts. For she needs none. There she is. Behold her and judge for yourselves. . . . There is Boston, and Concord, and Lexington and Bunker Hill; and there they will remain forever. The bones of her sons, falling in the great struggle for Independence, now lie mingled with the soil of every state from New England to Georgia." As for South Carolina, he went on, "I claim them for my countrymen, too, one and all. The Rutledges, the Pinckneys, the Sumters, the Marions—Americans all."

Hayne had argued that tax money collected in one state could not be used to improve another. Webster ripped this apart: "We look upon a road over the Alleghenies, a canal round the falls of the Ohio . . . as being an object . . . for the common benefit. We look upon the states not as being separated but as being united." Hayne was also wrong to praise slavery, he added, for Negro bondage was "one of the greatest evils, both moral and political." So was Hayne in error, he repeated, in stating that the Constitution stemmed from a compact among the states who retained a right to nullify Federal action. "The Constitution is the people's Constitution, the people's government. It is made for the people, by the people and answerable to the people," he said in language Abraham Lincoln would later borrow. "The people of the United States have declared this Constitution shall be the supreme law of the land. . . . The main debate hinges on whose prerogative it is to decide the constitutionality of our laws. The people have at no time, directly or indirectly, authorized any state legislature to construe or interpret their high instrument of government. The people have preserved this, their chosen Constitution, for forty years and have seen their happiness, prosperity and renown grow. Overthrown, evaded, nullified, it will not be, if we, and those who shall succeed us here, shall vigilantly discharge our public trust."

He closed with an eloquent peroration that became world-famous. "When my eyes shall be turned to behold, for the last time, the sun in heaven, may I not see him shining on the broken and dishonored fragments of a once glorious Union; on states dissevered, discordant, belligerent; on a land rent with civil feuds, or drenched, it may be, in fraternal blood. Let their last feeble and lingering glance, rather, behold the gorgeous ensign of the republic . . . not a stripe erased or polluted, not a single star obscured, bearing for its motto no such miserable interrogatory as . . . 'Liberty first, and Union afterwards': but everywhere . . . that other sentiment, dear to every true American heart—'Liberty and Union, now and forever, one and inseparable!'"

The Webster-Hayne debate had stirred the entire nation. How would The Hero react? On April 13, 1830, the answer came. This was the day of the Jackson party's subscription dinner at Brown's Indian Queen Hotel to celebrate Jefferson's birthday. Both Jackson and Calhoun attended, and it became obvious to those who were present that the nullifiers dominated the roster of speakers. Then there were twenty-four prearranged toasts glorifying states' rights, the Virginia Resolutions of 1798, Georgia's defiance of President John Quincy Adams in seizing Indian lands, and veiled praise of South Carolina's stand against the tariff.

The volunteer toasts followed, with Jackson offering the first. He spoke his with stabbing punctuation, his eyes staring directly into Calhoun's. "Our Federal Union. It must be preserved!" Ike Hill was watching Calhoun and he said that the Vice-President's hand trembled so much at Jackson's words "that a little of the amber fluid trickled down the side" of his glass. "An order to arrest Calhoun where he sat could not have come with more blinding, staggering force," Hill added.

Calhoun recovered sufficiently to offer the second toast. Jackson had taken a stand alongside Webster's view against nullification. Calhoun had no intention of giving up his own philosophy despite the presence of the President. In his biting, hurried tone, he said emphatically: "The Union—next to our liberty the most dear."

Jackson's position, which put him squarely in opposition to Calhoun's nullification doctrine, constituted another peg in Calhoun's political coffin. The final showdown was not far off.

From the outset, Secretary of State Van Buren knew he would have to destroy Calhoun in the eyes of Jackson if he were to become The Hero's successor. "The Red Fox of Kinderhook," "the Little Magician" and "the American Talleyrand," as Van Buren was variously nicknamed, early diagnosed Jackson's intense but inane defense of Peggy Eaton. With Calhoun on the opposite side, Van Buren wisely courted the Secretary of War and his bride. Van Buren had also seen that while Jackson had instituted a spoils system, he early tired of the hungry job seekers. It was Van Buren who took the lead in pushing this rapacious crew from Washington, and for this he earned Jackson's appreciation. He still had far to go after this because the original Jackson coterie remembered him as William Crawford's campaign manager in 1824. But he knew he was on his way so long as he did not appear in a hurry. This was not too difficult for him because for years now he had practiced the art of pleasant self-control and clever caution. John Randolph, who had observed him over a long stretch of time, characterized him by saying that he "rowed to his object with muffled oars."

Two things had always bothered Van Buren—his short stature and his lack of formal education. He sorely regretted not having gone to Yale like Calhoun or to Harvard like Adams because, as he put it, a college degree would have helped "to sustain me in my conflicts with able and better educated men." Nevertheless, Van Buren was considered by his associates a first-class lawyer and a man of dignified manner and courtly bearing. He was a dandy of sorts, standing out in any crowd, for his daytime attire included "snuff-colored coats, white trousers, lace-tipped cravats, yellow gloves and morocco shoes." When he first joined the Jackson Cabinet, he rode about in a fancy carriage. But he soon perceived that the President enjoyed a daily horseback ride, so he changed to a saddle, even though he did not enjoy it, and he became The Hero's companion. Jackson was especially taken with his wit. A popular newspaper humorist at the time was "Major Jack Downing," the pen name of Seba Smith of the Portland *Courier*, who punctured pomposity and wrote as though he were in the inner circle. Downing pretended he accompanied Jackson on trips and the words he put into the President's mouth were widely quoted as gospel. For instance, when Jackson was awarded an honorary degree by Harvard, said Major Jack, "I says in his ear, 'You must give 'em a little Latin, Doctor!' . . . 'E pluribus unum,' says he, 'my friends, sine qua non.'" After many horseback rides in Van Buren's company, Jackson commented, "Depend upon it, Jack Downing is only Van Buren in masquerade."

There was more to their relationship than clever quips. As they rode along, Jackson also discussed his business with Van Buren and asked for advice. Van Buren was aware that Jackson liked the "sincere" compliment, and he carefully devised those that could pass muster. What pleased Jackson most of all was to be regarded as a missionary in politics. Years later, in his autobiography, Van Buren wrote that Jackson believed that "to labor for the good of the masses was a special mission assigned to him by his Creator and no man was ever better disposed to work in his vocation in season and out of season."

Because he was short, Van Buren stood on chairs at banquets and dinners to see the speaker. He stood on a chair at Brown's Indian Queen Hotel to see the President engage in his toasting duel with Calhoun. Exactly a month later he propelled Jackson into writing a letter to Calhoun that ruined the Vice-President's political future. The chain of events had begun a few years earlier when Van Buren learned that Calhoun had played a dirty game during the Seminole fighting in 1818. Van Buren was wildly excited when he found out that as War Secretary in Monroe's Cabinet, Calhoun had urged Jackson's court-martial for executing two Britishers he had captured in Spanish Florida and for seizing the Spanish governor. Later when asked about his stand on the matter, Calhoun had insisted he had supported Jackson.

Since William Crawford had also served in Monroe's Cabinet as Secretary of the Treasury, Van Buren could easily ascertain Calhoun's true role. An agent was quietly dispatched to Georgia, where Crawford was now a local judge. The man who traveled south was Colonel James A. Hamilton, the third son of Alexander Hamilton. The colonel was an aide of Van Buren and a peripheral Kitchen Cabinet member whose chief interest was to destroy the Second Bank of the United States, an institution considered most essential in concept by his father. Intimates blandly passed along the story that young Colonel Hamilton had been friendly with Aaron Burr, his father's murderer.

Hamilton went to Georgia, but instead of asking Crawford for a letter stating the facts of the Monroe Cabinet, he spoke only with Crawford's friend, Governor John Forsyth. The governor willingly wrote a letter purporting to be what Crawford had said about Calhoun's role in the court-martial Cabinet meeting. Major Lewis, who saw the Forsyth letter, considered it too weak to show to Jackson. And so the affair seemed to have collapsed.

However, in November 1829, after Jackson entertained former President Monroe at dinner and all the guests had left, Lewis mentioned the Forsyth letter to Jackson. Jackson had to see it. At this time, Forsyth had come to the Senate, and although a Jackson man he would not permit Hamilton to turn over his letter to the President. Again the subject was dropped.

But the Calhoun nullification dinner in April 1830 once more revealed the importance to Van Buren of a final stabbing of his opponent. The timing was now perfect for a letter directly to Jackson from Crawford. Senator Forsyth agreed to write to Crawford, and the reply that came charged Calhoun with having advocated a court-martial.

On May 13, Jackson wrote Calhoun regarding Crawford's letter and asked "whether it is possible that the information given is correct." Calhoun pleaded for time. Then two weeks later he sent Jackson a fifty-two-page letter in a shaky script, denouncing Crawford for betraying the deliberations of the Cabinet, and called it the first instance in the country when their secrets had been made public. He put up a strong case for his actions in 1818, but did not explain why he had given Jackson to understand the opposite when asked earlier. "Understanding you now, no further communication with you on this subject is necessary," Jackson replied. This permanently severed the cord between the two men, and Van Buren rose to undisputed heir apparent.

Martin Van Buren saw a need for consolidating his new status. One minor victory came when Jackson ordered government printing contracts removed from Duff Green's *Telegraph*. Green was not only continuing his rooting for Calhoun but his daughter was married to Calhoun's son. However, Green's paper was a small matter compared with the more vexing problem of how to rid the Cabinet of the three Calhoun supporters. In addition, the continuing Eaton issue would eventually debilitate Jackson's political strength and hence harm Van Buren's candidacy as his successor. How to knock all of them out with one quick blow?

Van Buren's solution was ingenious. On a horseback ride with Jackson one day, he suddenly blurted that there was only one thing that would give the President peace, and that was Van Buren's resignation from the Cabinet. The general was stunned. Van Buren went on to explain that he was taking this course solely from a sense of loyalty. He also said that the Cabinet should be dissolved, so that Jackson could reorganize his government and begin anew.

Still surprised but certain that Van Buren was making his offer for the good of the nation, Jackson accepted his resignation reluctantly. With this example, Eaton angrily submitted his own resignation. The three Calhounites—Ingham, Berrien and Branch—had to be thrown out almost bodily, leaving only Postmaster General William Barry of the original top crew. If ever a man deserved to be fired it was Barry, for by incompetency he was ruining the mail service built up by McLean and was permitting its plunder.

Peggy Eaton was furious with her husband, Van Buren and other Jacksonians when she found herself deprived of stellar billing at the White House. She baited her weak husband into taking action against the three Cabinet Calhounites whose families had refused to recognize her socially. Eaton challenged Branch to a duel through the columns of the *Globe;* Branch answered in the *Telegraph* that he would not demean himself. Then Eaton hunted through Washington for two days, carrying a loaded pistol that he planned to discharge on former Secretary of the Treasury Ingham. When Ingham sneaked out of town, Eaton next challenged Berrien and again failed to win acceptance.

Jackson's respect for Eaton rose in his defense of his wife, while he had only condemnation for his former Secretaries. He shouted about Branch's "treachery" and "the disgraceful flight of Ingham," in a review of events with the happy Van Buren, who had agreed to become the next minister to Great Britain. As for Berrien, Jackson cursed, "What a wretch! This southern hotspur will not fight. My Creed is true— There never was a base man a brave one." But eventually, Eaton's bravado grew boring to Jackson, especially when he took heavily to the bottle, and Jackson was pleased to see him and Peggy quit Washington in September 1831. As bait, he promised vaguely to help the man who had almost ruined him return to Washington again as U. S. Senator from Tennessee. Van Buren had achieved remarkable success.

To replace his depleted Cabinet, Jackson appointed Senator Edward Livingston as Secretary of State; Lewis Cass, former civil governor of the Michigan Territory and a general in the War of 1812, as Secretary of War; Louis McLane, Senator from New York and more recently minister to England, as Secretary of the Treasury; Levi Woodbury, Senator from New Hampshire, as Secretary of the Navy; and Roger B. Taney, (pronounced Tawney) a lawyer from Maryland, as Attorney General. Of this group, Livingston and Taney were expected to do chores of a Kitchen Cabinet nature. Livingston, former mayor of New York, had moved to New Orleans after serious graft was uncovered in his administration, though he was in no way involved. In 1815, he had served on The Hero's staff in the defense against the British attack. Livingston was also notorious for having sued Jefferson for $100,000 in 1810, bringing the case to collect damages for property seized from him by the Jefferson Administration. At the time, Jefferson feared that he would lose and be ruined, but his cousin and enemy, Chief Justice John Marshall,

ruled against Livingston. The new Secretary of State possessed a
facile pen and would be of great help to Jackson when a vital paper
had to be written. John Randolph's caustic view of Edward Livingston was that he was the "most degraded of beings, whom no man
ought to touch, unless with a pair of tongs."

Taney had started in politics as a Federalist. With time and
events prodding him, he had now veered to the opposite pole,
but he would veer back again by 1857, when as Chief Justice
of the Supreme Court he would rule in the Dred Scott case
that the Missouri Compromise with its territorial limitation on
slavery was unconstitutional. When he became Jackson's Attorney
General in 1831, he was a shockingly homely and unkempt fifty-
four-year-old man. His mouth was too large and contained yellow,
spaced teeth. He squinted, shuffled and spoke with a speech impediment. His black suit was never clean and did not fit him,
making him look like a seedy countryman. But he had a sharp
mind, dogged determination and an outspoken nature. The Hero,
who generally made decisions on the basis of emotions rather
than from the facts involved, considered Taney to be attuned
to his way of operating, and quickly accepted him into his inner
circle of advisers.

The chief concern of the Kitchen Cabinet was to consolidate
political power and thus insure continued control of the national
government by the Jacksonians far into the future. For two years
the Eatons had been an albatross but now they were gone. The
spoils system had its plus and minus qualities, but sufficient rewards were distributed to yield strong support across the country
at the next election. On a class basis, farmers and exporters were
being helped by Van Buren's success in reopening the British
West Indies to trade after it had been shut off by the British
during the Adams Administration. In the first year of the renewed
trade, the value of American shipments was a sizable $2,250,000.

Another group to receive attention from the Kitchen Cabinet
was city workers. The beginning of the Industrial Revolution had
produced the first labor organizations and these had begun to
make demands regarding wages and working conditions. Hard
times in 1828–1829 gave impetus to unionists to devise specific
political demands and to promote them through their own party.
Workingmen's papers at the time Jackson was first growing accustomed to living in the White House called for the abolition of

imprisonment for debt, equal universal education instead of education for those who met a means test, an end to monopolies, abolition of state militias, a cheaper law system, equal property taxation (Virginia taxed slaves at a far lower rate than horses) and popular election of all public officials.

It was important for the Jackson party to befriend this group, for as Mathew Carey, a sympathetic Philadelphia writer and publisher, estimated, they numbered more than eight million. The significance of this number (even if inflated 100 per cent) was that the bars against universal white male suffrage were rapidly being dropped. Jackson had not personally known labor leaders or factory workers, nor did he understand their motives and interests. Indian fighters, soldiers, planters, slave traders and land speculators he knew well, and could speak their private language. In past crises, he always landed alongside those upholding the views of the well-to-do and the creditor group. But now he began to talk about "the people," and in an early Message declared, "It should be the care of a republic not to exert a grinding power over misfortune and poverty." He did not mean by this that he he would carry out the Workingmen's political program, even though his own party found it valuable to steal planks from the "Workies" platform in order to kill off the threat of a separate Labor party. For Jackson was not a Federal legislation President, but a Jeffersonian in philosophy, favoring government economy and a strict construction of the Constitution. What he meant was that he would not countenance legislation that benefited solely the rich. His only aid to the poor would be negative, to "remove" or "eliminate" burdens by law, not to promote social welfare bills. A case in point was his successful action in 1832 to get Congress to eliminate imprisonment for debt.

Geographically, the Kitchen Cabinet strategists divided the country into three sections—the East, West and South. Eastern support was predicated on the continuing protective tariff and on Jackson's stand against Calhoun's advocacy of nullification. Although these key Jacksonians held strong antipathy toward the growing business community, they were nevertheless not remiss in pointing to the business prosperity in the East.

As a Westerner, Jackson enjoyed the blanket loyalty of the frontiersmen. But a problem he often considered was that the Westerner possessed a big heart and his affections might also include Henry Clay. "Harry of the West" had returned to Kentucky in dejection following the demise of the Adams Cabinet and Administration. But at Ashland his spirits revived and he once more entertained the vision that he was one of the chosen few to become President. Because Adams had not bothered to hold candidacy control of the National Republicans, Clay began asserting himself as Adams' heir. Once more the air was filled with talk about Clay's American System with its focus on a strong central government busily building roads and canals at Federal expense, developing local industry through a high protective tariff and adding to the authority of the Second Bank of the United States.

Most of all the Westerner wanted roads and cheap money. He desired wealth, great holdings in land; and he needed roads to move products to market and inflation to pay off his speculations in lower value money. In his raw setting he was not a man of culture and was often crude, rude and boisterous. Even his circuit-riding preachers were frequently illiterate men, and the admonitions he received to practice the Sermon on the Mount were meaningless in an "eye for an eye and a tooth for a tooth" society.

Jackson did not like the idea of a watered currency, even though so many of his western following were hounded debtors. His view on internal improvements had been expounded in his first Message, in which he promised only "constitutional" projects, a term that seemed to mean he might do little. When Clay began his work to strengthen the National Republicans, Jackson decided to attack him on the issue of internal improvements. However, he did not want to harm the West, nor his own standing in that section. In addition, he wanted to put fear in the hearts of Congressmen who were entering the new game of logrolling, promising support for each other's road and canal projects regardless of merit.

Early in 1830, he asked Van Buren to keep an eye on the internal improvements bills before Congress and spot one he could safely attack. Later Van Buren announced he had found one that could be worked on both sides of the road. This was a bill to construct a turnpike between Maysville, Kentucky, on the Ohio River and Lexington. Not only was the proposed project vulnerable on the ground that it was entirely local and without a national purpose, but it also provided that the national government buy $150,-000 of the stock of the private corporation that would build and own the road. If these reasons were not sufficient, said Van Buren, there was still another to consider. This was that Clay personally had promoted the Maysville Road primarily because the sixty-four-mile road from the Ohio River at Maysville to his plantation was a quagmire that often required four days of difficult travel to reach.

Jackson vetoed the Maysville Road, despite the frenzied cry of Jacksonian Congressmen from Kentucky. His Veto Message asserted he was taking this course because of his concern for the welfare of the common people. It was inexpedient, he said, to spend money for an unconstitutional, purely local project at a time when he was trying to eliminate the national debt.

Clay screamed at the veto and worked up National Republican mass meetings, which voted to censure Jackson. But Van Buren had calculated for Jackson that the Maysville Road affected the smallest number of voters of all the road bills and would hurt him least politically, and Jackson was unconcerned. Moreover, the veto was highly popular in Pennsylvania and New York, which were building their own roads and canals, and in the South, more than a half century away from becoming the leading pork barrel demander in the nation. Once he had his desired political mileage from the Maysville Road veto, Jackson went quietly back to approving other road bills, some just as local.

As a conglomerate party, the Jacksonians also needed the South. Here the problem was that the Calhoun doctrine of disunity might gain the South Carolinian adherents in other states below the Mason-Dixon Line. A lowering of the tariff would appease many. So would a strong anti-Indian policy, for land-hungry Southerners coveted the 33,000,000 acres held by sixty thousand Creeks, Choctaws, Chickasaws and Cherokees.

The Cherokees of Georgia were as modern as their white enemies. They lived in houses, operated farms and taverns, built roads and maintained a fair legal system. During the previous Administration, Georgia had violated Federal treaties with the Indians without retribution from the Federal Government. Georgians had crossed Cherokee lines to seize lands and a movement began in other southern states to do the same with their Indian tribes.

Concern arose in Georgia, Mississippi and Alabama that Jackson would not tolerate their violation of Federal treaties, even though The Hero was an old Indian fighter who enjoyed putting Indian villages to the torch. But Jackson calmed their fears in a Message to Congress, in which he put himself on the side of the marauding states by suggesting that the tribes undergo a "voluntary" removal west of the Mississippi. On hearing this, the Cherokees hired William Wirt, the astute former Attorney General under John Quincy

Adams, to institute a suit in Federal court. Jackson was soon apprised that Wirt planned to argue that a state had no right to annul a Federal contract. Since Chief Justice Marshall had a fetish about the sanctity of contracts that went back to the Dartmouth College Case in 1818, Jackson realized that Wirt would win his suit.

Jackson decided he must act personally before Marshall rendered an opinion. Therefore, in the summer of 1830, he traveled to the Indians for a personal powwow with chieftains of several tribes. He sent agents ahead of him to soften the Indians with firewater and pieces of silver. "Sharp Knife," as he was ominously called by the Indians, smoked the peace pipe and then warned them, "Your Great Father . . . asks . . . you . . . to submit . . . and make a surrender of your ancient laws. . . . Reject the opportunity which is now offered to obtain comfortable homes, and it may not come again."

The Chickasaws and Choctaws eventually agreed to cross the Mississippi in 1832. However, the Choctaws cleverly insisted that their proposition be submitted to the Senate for advice and consent before a formal treaty was arranged. Jackson had no alternative other than to ask for the "previous advice of the Senate," but that body chose to ignore the vague recommendations of its committee.

By this time, Indian cases had reached the Supreme Court. In one case, an Indian named Corn Tassel killed another Indian on Cherokee territory. The Georgia court sentenced him to be hanged, and Corn Tassel applied to the Supreme Court for a writ of error on the ground that Georgia lacked jurisdiction. Chief Justice Marshall issued the writ, but Georgia ignored him and hanged Corn Tassel. In another case, Marshall ruled that the state of Georgia could not force white missionaries in Cherokee country to take loyalty oaths to the state. He ordered two missionaries who had been arrested to be released. When Georgia refused, the Court had to depend on Jackson to enforce its decision. But Jackson openly supported Georgia. A Congressman later attributed the following statement to Jackson: "John Marshall has made his opinion. Now let him enforce it."

Calhoun supporters pointed out with obvious contempt that Jackson favored states' rights for Georgia but not for South Carolina. But Jackson saw no threat to the Union in Georgia's defiance of the Supreme Court because his own authority had not been questioned. Besides, only Indians were involved. To settle the entire issue of the Redman in the South, he asked Congress to set aside territory west of the Mississippi where he could send them. Only by a straight party vote did the proposal pass and a forced migration get under way.

The Indian move was fiendishly cruel. Politicians stole much of the money appropriated to finance it; southern whites seized their property before sale was completed; their new lands were unfertile and unhospitable. The Creeks were marched in heavy chains from their ancient lands in Alabama; Choctaws from Mississippi in the cold winter of December 1831, without warm clothing or moccasins. Henry Clay, who came to the Senate that very month, led the protest against the Administration's Indian policy, but Jackson prevailed.

From the start of his Administration, Jackson considered the Marshall Supreme Court with the same hatred that Jefferson did almost three decades earlier. The old judge seemed indestructible. With his views favoring a strong central government and the Bank of the United States, Marshall was like a brick wall against which the Jacksonians could only dent their heads in cases involving these issues. That was why Jackson enjoyed himself so much in the Court's fight with Georgia.

Again, as Jefferson had earlier attempted, Jackson tried to cut the Court down to size. First, his party members in the House promoted legislation to remove the Court's power to declare an act of Congress unconstitutional. But on sober thought, the House rejected this overwhelmingly by a vote of 137 to 51. As in the Jefferson Administration, the attack on the Court then centered on an effort to impeach judges and thus frighten Marshall into submission. Judge James Peck, Federal district court judge in Missouri, was most vulnerable and the impeachment routine began with him. Peck had sentenced a lawyer named Luke Lawless for contempt of court after Lawless wrote an article criticizing one of his decisions. The judge was hauled before the Senate for trial, pitting his attorney, William Wirt, against the inferior manager for the House, Representative James Buchanan. When Peck won acquittal in January 1831, proposed action against other judges was dropped. Marshall could not last forever, the Jacksonians now hopefully prayed.

When the Twenty-second Congress met on December 5, 1831,

Jackson could point to little positive action in two and a half years. Congress had generally ignored the vague proposals he offered in his Annual Messages. In return he did little pressing of the legislators. In fact, in his second Message he warned of a liberal use of his veto power. Yet it seemed to editors, at least from what they printed, that the National Government was enveloped by a titanic struggle between heroic and despicable forces. There was an aura of high excitement that did not diminish and an outpouring of emotions as though the fate of the universe hung in the balance. But what had transpired to that time was just an appetizer for what was to follow.

Part of the continuing political fever was due to the Presidential election scheduled for the following year. Already the Jacksonians were crying that The Hero's Revolution must be carried through to completion. To this many National Republicans were replying, in effect, with—"What Revolution?"

Throughout much of his first term Jackson's health had been poor and he did not believe he would survive. In December 1829, when his leg swelled from dropsy to an alarming extent, he wrote a political will and sent it to his old friend, John Overton, to be used in case he died. "Permit me to say here of Mr. Van Buren that . . . he, my dear friend, is well qualified . . . to fill the highest office in the gift of the people. . . . I wish I could say as much for Mr. Calhoun. . . . However, of him I desire not now to speak."

Jackson recovered, though, and in the autumn of the following year, while enjoying a ride through Georgetown with Van Buren, he confided that he planned to run for a second term with the New Yorker as his running mate. At the end of one or two years, Jackson assured him, he would then resign, thus elevating Van Buren into the White House. Van Buren later wrote that he gasped at this astonishing offer, but on second thought he rejected it because his enemies would denounce it as "a selfish intrigue designed to smuggle me into the Presidency and to gratify his [Jackson's] own resentment against" Calhoun. In addition, a forthright rejection of the offer would reassure the old Hero that he was sincerely without personal ambitions.

Jackson's health took another turn for the better in January 1832, shortly before a yellow fever epidemic ravaged Washington. Since 1813 when he had been bushwhacked in a Nashville tavern by Tom Benton (now his Senate leader) and his brother Jesse, Jackson had suffered excruciating pain as a result of the bullet that remained in his left arm. The arm was almost useless, but doctors earlier had refused to remove Jesse's bullet because it might overshock Jackson's heart near which lay the bullet taken in his 1806 duel over Rachel's reputation. However, a surgeon now said that the arm bullet could be safely removed, and Jackson, bare to the shoulder, pressed his hickory stick cane for comfort while the doctor operated. Afterward, Senator Benton refused to accept the bullet because Jackson had "acquired clear title to it in common law by twenty years' peaceable possession."

With the use of his arm restored, Jackson turned gay and reminiscent. At a White House party, said a Treasury official, "the old hero gave a very minute account of the manner in which his arm was broken all to pieces in his conflict with Benton and of its dreadful situation when he took command of the army to go into the Creek country— It remain'd in a sling for Six Months. In a violent effort to draw his sword to cut [the demoralized and retreating Colonel] Stump's head off in the battle of Enichopco [Enotachopco], he tore the broken bones of the arm to pieces again."

In order not to stir up the political puddle more than was necessary before an election year, Jackson sent a mild Message to the first session of the Twenty-second Congress. This disturbed Senator Clay, for he needed issues and victories over Jackson in the legislative arena if he was to defeat him at the polls. Left to his own devices by Jackson's shrewd move, Clay cast about for subjects that would lead him to triumph over the "ignorant . . . corrupt" President.

His first attempt boomeranged. Vice-President Calhoun, seething over the ascendancy of the Van Buren star, anxiously desired revenge. Clay was willing to co-operate with him because the Jacksonians were praising Van Buren for having won the concession from England to reopen her West Indies possessions to American trade. They were also blaming Clay personally for the closing of that trade in the first place, charging him with ineptness as Adams' Secretary of State.

Van Buren had already gone to London as minister to the Government of King William IV, one of the fifteen children of mad George III. So sure was he of the Senate, he had left without waiting for Senate confirmation. There, with the aid of Washington Irving, his loyal secretary of legation, he was busily conducting his country's business with Lord Palmerston when Calhoun and Clay decided on their scheme to humiliate him. On a freezing January night in 1832, the two contrived a tie Senate vote on confirming him. This gave the Vice-President the opportunity to vote and he cast his deciding vote to reject Van Buren. Calhoun was so overcome with delight at his deed that he was overheard in his hysterical self-praise: "It will kill him, sir, kill him dead. He will never kick, sir, never kick." Senator Benton held a more realistic view: "You have broken a minister, and elected a Vice-President."

The hope of Calhoun and Clay to see Van Buren return home in disgrace was not fulfilled. Instead, Van Buren was treated like a returning hero and undisputed running mate of the President by eastern party members. When word was first carried to the White House of the Calhoun-Clay action, Jackson bellowed: "By the Eternal! I'll smash them!" John Randolph saw it in the same light as Benton. In a letter to Jackson he exulted: "Calhoun, by this time, must be in Hell. He is self-mutilated like the Fanatic that emasculated himself."

With the election contest approaching, Clay believed he might challenge Jackson on the tariff and western land issues. To entice the western vote, he proposed legislation to maintain fairly high land prices, but to award 10 per cent of the gross to the states where the lands were and to divide the rest of the money among all the states according to their votes in Congress. However, House Jacksonians prevented his bill from reaching a vote.

Clay also moved to win southern support by discussions with southern leaders on the tariff question. He now claimed that protection was really a minor concern of his in setting the tariff levels, that they should be set chiefly to raise necessary revenue. What protection they did bring would surely create in time a high-paying market for southern raw materials. Then to conciliate the South further, he announced his opposition to using tariff revenues to build roads and canals.

While Clay was making these assurances, John Quincy Adams reappeared on the Washington scene and proceeded to act on them to the horror of Clay. After leaving the Presidency, Adams found himself reduced to the brink of bankruptcy as had Jefferson, Madison and Monroe before him. Swallowing his pride in order to eat, he had won election to the House and a salary of $8.00 a day while Congress was in session. "Old Man Eloquent," fellow members and editors called him, for he had his father's oratorical ability. A Washington reporter described the former President in the House as "alone, unspoken to, unconsulted, never consulting with others, he sits apart . . . looks enfeebled, but yet he is never tired, worn out, but ever ready for combat; melancholy, but let a witty thing fall from any member, and that old man's face is wreathed in smiles."

When Adams appeared in the House, Speaker Andrew Stevenson named him chairman of the Committee on Manufactures, and he proceeded to write a new tariff bill. To the disgust of Clay, who had not been serious in his talk with Southerners about slashing import duties, Adams' bill reduced tariffs to the 1824 level, with a host of cuts in the steep 1828 protective tariff schedule. In the Senate, as the threat of reduced tariffs grew, Clay was forced to come into the open in defense of a high protective tariff. This brought a collapse in his alliance with Calhoun and a sharp attack on Clay by Calhoun's mouthpiece, Senator Hayne. To this, Clay turned on the smirking Vice-President and reminded him that "in 1816, we worked together in Congress side by side" in producing a protective tariff law.

When the Adams tariff bill passed Congress and won Jackson's signature, Clay was again bereft of a major issue on which to campaign. He could condemn Jackson for the Maysville Road veto and for vetoing other bills on grounds of expediency instead of constitutionality. The truth is that he did, proposing, for example, that the Constitution be changed to permit Congress to override a veto by majority vote, instead of by the two-thirds requirement. But the veto usage was not an issue to excite voters.

By a process of elimination among slim pickings, Clay finally found what he believed would be the issue to break the rule of the Jacksonians. He would base his campaign on Jackson's opposition to the Second Bank of the United States. The Bank was then operating under a twenty-year charter from Congress that was not due to expire until 1836. Why rock the boat until that time? Top Bank officials expressed concern when Clay told them about his plan. The Bank was a private institution with complex Federal connections. The Government subscribed to 20 per cent of its $35,000,000 capital and appointed five of its twenty-five directors, with the Bank serving as a depository for Government funds, center for individuals paying taxes, payer of Government bills and regulator of the nation's currency supply. As a financial institution in the commercial marketplace, the Bank could print notes to the extent of its initial capital investment of $35,000,000 but it was obliged to make payments in specie on request.

Head of the Bank was handsome, aristocratic Nicholas Biddle, a Jeffersonian Republican by background, who sat in the glistening, Greek marble temple on Chestnut Street in Philadelphia and directed its multifarious operations. Biddle had been a child prodigy, graduating from the University of Pennsylvania at thirteen, from Princeton at fifteen as valedictorian and at eighteen, while serving as secretary to the American minister in France, handled the financial details of the Louisiana Purchase. Shortly afterward, he became an editor, an acknowledged expert on ancient Greek culture and the author of the standard history of the Lewis and Clark Expedition. Biddle's return to finance was heralded by the burning of Washington by the British in August 1814, when he helped obtain loans that saved the Madison Administration from a threatened total collapse. At the time, James Monroe took notice of the young economist, and when Congress chartered the Second Bank he named Biddle as one of the five Government members of the Bank's board. Finally in 1823, Nick Biddle at thirty-seven became the Bank's president, after the first head had almost brought the Bank to ruin, and the second had damaged the economy in order to save the bank.

Those who understood central banking agreed that Biddle was a brilliant manager. He afforded the Federal Government a ready market for its bond issues, and through the Bank's branches, the nation's farmers, businessmen and foreign trade operators were assured of simple and fast service on commercial transactions. Also by requiring state banks to redeem their own notes in hard gold and silver specie on demand by the Second Bank, state banks did not dare to enter into extensive production of unbacked currency. True, the Biddle Bank amounted only to about a 20 per cent factor in the nation's total banking business, but as the Government's agent and banker this prestige gave it pre-eminence and influence so that it dominated the field. In 1831, Biddle could accurately boast that through the Bank's efforts the American currency was the soundest in the entire world.

During the 1828 campaign, the Bank had not been a political issue, and there was no reason why it should have been one before 1836 when it would come up again for its recharter. Jackson's earlier stand on money was well known to his chief supporters—his favoritism toward creditors and his opposition to cheap money through unbacked and heavily discounted printing press bank notes to help debtors wriggle out of legitimate payment of bills.

As for the Bank, he had not gone on record pro or con on its recharter until after the election. Ike Hill, who had tried so hard to paint poor John Quincy Adams as a sex immoralist, told Jackson that the Portsmouth, New Hampshire, Branch Bank had discriminated in the election against Jackson supporters. Those who had supported Adams, he claimed, found loans easy to obtain. Other reports of discrimination reached him, by what was probably a careful plan to indoctrinate him until in rage he denounced the "Monster" as a "hydra of corruption—dangerous to our liberties by its corrupting influence everywhere."

When Jackson made up his mind on an issue, he could not be deterred by reason and argument. His emotional apparatus was so intense, in fact, that he easily forgot that he had once held differing views on various matters. As governor of Florida in 1821, he had asked the Bank to establish a branch there and he had owned stock in the Nashville Branch Bank. But with his opposition to the Bank now firm, he told "Young Hickory," as his Tennessee protégé Congressman James K. Polk was called, "Everyone that knows me does know that I have been always opposed to the United States Bank, nay, all banks."

Not until his first Message to Congress in December 1829 did Jackson publicly reveal his opposition to the Bank. He said it had failed in the great end of establishing a uniform and sound currency and suggested a study to find how best to replace it. Biddle's reaction was to placate Jackson by finding out what minor Bank changes would remove his opposition, then to establish a corps of Jacksonians to hold the President in check. He had paid a call on The Hero before the Message to present a sound proposal to pay off the national debt of $48,522,000 by January 8, 1833, the anniversary day of Jackson's victory at New Orleans. Jackson's charm on that occasion had misled Biddle into believing all would turn out well for the Bank in the end.

Biddle now knew he would have to play a tight political game to keep the President in line. Josiah Nichol, rich merchant who handled Jackson's financial affairs back home, was president of the Nashville Branch Bank and he accepted Biddle's orders to pour into Jackson's ear the wonders of the Bank. Gleefully he reported that Jackson "speaks of You in the most exalted terms and says No Gentleman would manage the Bank better." Major William Lewis was also enlisted in the Bank's cause; Postmaster General Barry got his long-overdue note extended; Asbury Dickens, chief clerk of the Treasury, was permitted to settle his loan for 50 per cent of what he owed; Amos Kendall received a $5000 loan; and influential newspaper editors throughout the country got such large loans that if the Bank called for early repayment they knew they would be ruined. Biddle also gained further aid in the Administration with partisanship for his cause coming from three Cabinet members named after the first Cabinet breakup. These pro-Bank men were Secretaries McLane, Livingston and Cass. In addition, a host of top Jacksonians in every section of the country were put on the board of Branch Banks.

Congress took no action on Jackson's suggestion to study the Bank, though lines were beginning to form throughout the nation either for or against the Bank. The forces on each side were a strange mixture. For instance, among the opponents were the inflationists, western speculators and eastern state bankers who wanted the Bank ended so that there would be no check on state bank notes issued; those from all sections who wanted to establish banks but felt restrained from doing so because of the Bank's competition; and those who believed that with the Bank out of business paper money would end and only hard currency would circulate. This last view was held by Senator Tom Benton, who talked so much on the subject that his colleagues named him "Old Bullion."

By late 1831, Biddle had wisely decided not to rock the boat on the recharter issue, but to wait out the Bank's charter life before coming to Congress for a new grant. However, it was at this point that Clay reached the conclusion that the Bank should be his campaign issue, and he proposed an immediate rechartering fight. Although Biddle had misgivings, he reluctantly agreed to make a check of Congressional sentiment for Clay, who was one of the Bank's attorneys. The Bank's Washington lobbyist, Thomas Cadwalader, took a canvas and found that the bill would pass, but would be vetoed by Jackson. To the possibility of such a course, Clay later bragged, "Should Jackson veto it, I shall veto him!" Clay argued that with three Cabinet members and probably a fourth Secretary favoring the Bank, Jackson would be talked out of a veto. Overwhelmed by Clay's enthusiasm, Biddle gave the signal to institute Congressional action without delay. Thus he put into motion a train of events that ruined the Bank, himself and the country's stable financial system and made a still more popular idol of Jackson.

On June 11, 1832, the Senate by a vote of 28 to 20 voted to grant a new fifteen-year charter to the Bank. The new charter sharply curtailed the Bank's power in order to meet many objections voiced against the Second Bank by leading Jacksonians. Three weeks later when the House approved this bill by a vote of 107 to 85, Biddle was observed on the House floor accepting congratulations from members. Both Biddle and Clay took the position that Jackson faced a dilemma. A veto would put Pennsylvania behind Clay, for the Bank was popular in that state. If he signed the bill, he would lose southern support, for Congressmen from that section had almost unanimously voted against the Bank.

Jackson awaited the bill with pleasure, for he had long determined to veto it. As he told Van Buren, "The Bank is trying to kill me, but I will kill it." With the help of Amos Kendall, Attorney General Taney and Secretary of the Navy Levi Woodbury, he drew up a Message of explanation, and on July 10, the publication of the "Monster's" veto was like an explosion across the land.

Jackson's veto stands out as the most revolutionary Message sent to Congress by any Chief Executive. It began ordinarily enough with a charge that the changes made in the Bank's charter were inconsequential. It also called the Bank a dangerous "concentration of power in the hands of a few men irresponsible to the people." Then came the argument that the Bank was unconstitutional, buttressed by the strange position that: "It is as much the duty of the House of Representatives, of the Senate, and of the President to decide upon the constitutionality of any bill or resolution which may be presented to them for passage or approval as it is of the supreme judges. . . . The opinion of the judges has no more authority over Congress than the opinion of Congress has over the judges, and on that point the President is independent of both. The authority of the Supreme Court must not, therefore, be permitted to control the Congress or the Executive when acting in their legislative capacities, but to have only such influence as the force of their reasoning may deserve."

If this were not sufficient to make the veto unusual, there was still to come a blatant philosophizing effort to make Jackson the great champion of the "common people." In Jackson's view the law operated to make the rich richer and the potent more powerful. Therefore, "the humble members of society—the farmers, mechanics and laborers—who have neither the time nor the means of securing like favors for themselves, have a right to complain of the injustice of their government." And their complaints would be received in good hands, he vowed, pledging to stand like a barrier against "the advancement of the few at the expense of the many."

Little wonder that Daniel Webster, who recognized the artful propaganda, denounced the Veto Message as "endeavoring to stir up the poor against the rich." Biddle called it "a manifesto of anarchy." When Congress failed to override the veto, Biddle realized to some extent the folly of the charter fight. Yet he did not believe his cause was lost, for there were yet four years of Bank life remaining. With Clay elected President, the situation would again be altered. As he had earlier written: "If he [Jackson] pursues us till we turn & stand at bay, why then—he may perhaps awaken a spirit which has hitherto been checked and reined in—and which it is wisest not to force into offensive defense."

The Bank veto cannoned off the intensive fight for the Presidency, among candidates all chosen for the first time by national conventions. There had been one previous national convention, that of the Federalist party meeting in New York to nominate DeWitt Clinton for President in 1812. But no followup occurred until now. Henceforth, instead of spending their time influencing Congressional leaders in nominating caucuses or state legislatures for nominating resolutions, Presidential candidates would have to control delegates from the various states who would sit in nominating judgment on their future. Their task would be much more complex and demanding.

First of the modern conventions came in September 1830, when the Anti-Masonic party held its conclave in Philadelphia. This party of demagogues was started in 1826 when William Morgan, a stonesetter, announced plans to publish a book exposing the "secrets" of Freemasonry. Morgan, the town drunkard of Batavia, New York, lay in a western New York jail for an unpaid debt of $2.69, and when he was released, he was kidnapped in front of the jail. He was believed to have been drowned in Lake Ontario by the fraternal order men, who were told he planned to make public the secrets of the Blue Lodge, or the first three degrees of Masonry.

Morgan's kidnapping touched off the rise of the Anti-Masonic political movement. This was a phenomenon explainable only in terms of the willingness of people to believe that the snobbish, secretive Masons held special privileges in government and business. The slowness of politicians and judges in taking action on Morgan's disappearance served to fortify this view. Thurlow Weed, the ultraconservative boss of New York, stepped in early to spur on this movement, with the help of William Henry Seward and Millard Fillmore of New York and Thaddeus Stevens of Pennsylvania. When a body came to the surface on Lake Ontario and was buried as the remains of Morgan, only to be revealed as the remains of another person, Weed was reported to have said, "He is a good enough Morgan until after the election." Weed's Albany *Evening Journal*, established in 1831, served as the official organ of the Anti-Masonic party.

The first Anti-Masonic convention called a second convention at Baltimore in September 1831. Here 113 delegates, equal to the number of Congressmen from the New England and middle states, Ohio and Indiana, met to select candidates for President and Vice-President. In the balloting, William Wirt, the former Attorney General, amassed 108 of 111 votes for President and Amos Ellmaker, former Congressman and attorney general of Pennsylvania became his running mate. Wirt, puzzled by his selection, addressed the convention. He told the gathering he had been a Mason, that he had never seen any danger in the order and that the Masonry the delegates were railing against with such venom "was not and could not be Masonry as understood by Washington." But despite his speech, the convention voted to retain him as its candidate.

In December 1831, the National Republicans also held a convention at Baltimore, and 167 delegates came from seventeen states. Clay won unanimously with John Sergeant, a rich Philadelphia lawyer, as his running mate. The following May a convention of young National Republicans (popularly called "Clay's Infant School") met in the capital and approved a series of ten resolutions, which became the first party platform. Essentially, this platform was a call for Clay's American System.

Not to be outdone by the opposition's pomp and excitement, the Jacksonians also held their convention at Baltimore, meeting on May 21, 1832. There was, of course, no opposition to Jackson, though much was in evidence against Van Buren for Vice-President in southern delegations, and also in those from Pennsylvania,

Kentucky and Indiana. In order to save Van Buren, who was on his way home from England, Jackson's lieutenants pushed through the two-thirds rule, requiring nominees to win the votes of two-thirds of the delegates rather than a simple majority. Since no candidate who opposed Van Buren could expect to get that large a vote, the convention bowed to Jackson and nominated the Red Fox of Kinderhook. The convention issued no platform, relying on a resolution extolling "the purity, patriotism and talents of Andrew Jackson."

The campaign proved bitter and vitriolic. Clay tried without success to swing the Anti-Masons behind his candidacy, even though he was a Mason. Jackson was so proud of being a Mason that he would not permit his followers to attempt a similar union. Moreover, it soon became evident that the third party served only to split the National Republican vote and lessen Clay's chances of victory. But to split the Jackson vote, the National Republicans, though the conservative party, had helped organize local Workingmen's parties in some states.

Leaders of the Anti-Masonic party, professing to seek greater democracy and the end of mutual favoritism by members of the fraternity, revealed themselves as crackpots, shrill demagogues and highly undemocratic political technicians. As for Clay's campaign, it blustered into a personal clash with "King Andrew I." There were fulsome details of the Eaton Malaria and the spoils system. Van Buren was pictured as an aristocrat pretending to be a champion of the masses and Jackson's vetoes as "a common means of making executive discretion paramount." But Clay's big issue was Jackson's specific veto of the Bank's recharter. Naïve Mr. Biddle had so misread the popular opposition to his Bank that he printed and distributed thirty thousand copies of the Veto Message as a Clay campaign document! This was a horrible blunder, although the results would have been the same.

Calhoun's force, though nominally part of the Jackson party of Democratic Republicans, aided Clay. Duff Green's *Telegraph*, ever faithful to Calhoun, hoped to reduce the dignity of the Jacksonians by labeling their party derisively as "Democrats." But the Jacksonians liked the flavor of the name and adopted it as their own. Afterward, they called themselves the Democratic party. Blair, whose *Globe* led the attack on the National Republicans, centered his attention on "Czar Nicholas," his Bank as the "hydra of corruption," and portrayed Jackson as the champion of the common man against the Bank aristocrats. Ike Hill's New Hampshire *Patriot* was again up to old tricks, offering as one of "Twenty-one Reasons Why Henry Clay Should Not Be Elected President"— "Because . . . he spends his days at the gambling tables and his nights in a brothel."

Jackson was right in showing no concern about the outcome. "Isaac, it'll be a walk," he told Ike Hill. Nevertheless, great splashes of emotion poured out among partisans of the candidates until the results were known. In New York, for instance, William Cullen Bryant, editor of the New York *Post,* the Jackson organ that had started life as Alexander Hamilton's newspaper, was so carried away that he caned a Clay man on Broadway.

The results were even more impressive than some of the Jackson aides had hoped they might be. "Hurrah for Old Hickory" proved much more attractive than the Clay promise of "A Full Dinner Pail." The general had 219 of the 286 electoral votes. Clay had only 49, Wirt 7 and John Floyd of Virginia the 11 protest votes of Calhoun's South Carolina. National Republicans looked forward to a grim future unless the party could make an appeal to the vastly enlarged voting rights among poorer citizens. One paper argued that "if all who were unable to read or write had been excluded from the polls, Andrew Jackson could not have been elected." Said Wirt with only Vermont's electoral votes, "My opinion is that he may be President for life if he chooses."

Jackson's joy was unbounded, for in addition to his election victory he learned he had become a grandfather. Although Rachel was childless, in 1810 they had adopted one of the twin male infants born to the wife of Rachel's brother Severn. Little Andy Jackson was raised along with several other Jackson wards, including an Indian boy whom Jackson found in a village he had destroyed. Andy Jackson, Jr., was married now and his wife, Sarah, gave birth to a baby named Rachel, after the mistress of the Hermitage.

But Jackson's joy was short-lived. In signing the Adams tariff bill of 1832, he had believed that the lowering of duty ceilings to the 1824 level would appease South Carolina. However, in November, a state convention controlled by the "Nullies," the general name of the Nullifiers, denounced the Tariff Acts of 1828 and 1832 as null and void and declared they would not be enforced in South Carolina after February 1, 1833. Should the Federal Government attempt to coerce South Carolina, said the convention, the state would secede from the Union "and will forthwith proceed to organize a separate Government."

Jackson's reaction was one of blazing fury. South Carolina Democrats were divided into the Nullies and Unionists, and he wrote to Joel Poinsett, former minister to Mexico, a Unionist leader and the man for whom the flower poinsettia was named, condemning a further legislative resolution to call out the state militia to fight Federal "aggression." Jackson wrote he would have the leaders arrested and arraigned for treason: "The wickedness, madness and folly of the leaders and the delusion of their followers in the attempt to destroy themselves and our Union has not its parallel in the history of the world."

Nevertheless, Jackson did not take this drastic step. On December 4, 1832, his Message to Congress was awaited with great expectations by Unionists. But these men were disappointed by the President's conciliatory tone. He gave as his excuse for not annihilating the Nullies the fact that with the national debt almost wiped out, the importance of the tariffs as a source of revenue had dropped. He proposed therefore that all existing duty levels should be severely curtailed or dropped, except for products the country needed in time of war. John Quincy Adams called Jackson's Message "a complete surrender to the nullifiers," while John Randolph had the effrontery to write The Hero: "You are now in a situation to recede with dignity."

But Jackson had no intention of receding beyond this bland Message. His next move was to put Secretary of State Livingston to work dressing up his thoughts on "A Proclamation to the People of South Carolina," revealing his unyielding determination against nullification and secession. "Fellow citizens of my native state, let me admonish you," he said. "Secession does not break a league, but destroys the unity of a nation. . . . To say that any state may at pleasure secede from the Union is to say that the United States is not a nation. . . . Admit this doctrine [of nullification] and every law for raising revenue may be annulled. . . . The laws of the United States must be executed. I have no discretionary power on the subject; my duty is emphatically pronounced in the Constitution. Those who told you that you might peaceably prevent their execution deceive you; they could not have deceived themselves. They know that a forcible opposition could alone prevent the execution of the laws, and they know that such opposition must be repelled. Their object is disunion. But be not deceived by names. Disunion by armed force is treason. Are you ready to incur its guilt?"

To make certain his Proclamation would not be interpreted as a paper affair, Jackson sent seven revenue cutters and a sloop-of-war to Charleston. General Winfield Scott was also sent there to build up harbor defenses in case the armed Nullies attacked from shore. To help lead the Nullies, Jackson's friend, Senator Hayne, had resigned his seat to become governor of South Carolina, and he ignored the Proclamation and the show of national military strength to organize "Mounted Minute Men," an elite squadron of 2500 men. Then on December 28, Calhoun resigned the Vice-Presidency and on January 4, 1833, took Hayne's vacated Senate seat, to direct his state's fight against Jackson. The story circulated that a furious Jackson had shouted that "if one more step was taken he would try Calhoun for treason and, if convicted, hang him as high as Haman."

Van Buren advised Jackson that the raising of troops by Governor Hayne was no reason for extreme action against him. "You will say I am on my old track—caution—caution—caution," wrote the Vice-President-elect, "but my Dr Sir I have always thought that considering our respective temperaments there was no way perhaps in which I could better render you service." However, the South Carolina nullification day of February 1 was not far off, and Jackson was in no mood to give in to the Nullies, as Vice-President-elect Martin Van Buren so cautiously suggested.

Therefore, on January 16, he sent Congress a Special Message, requesting authority to use military force to collect the customs in South Carolina. Powers to do so were embodied in the Force Bill, which reached the Senate floor from committee on January 21. Henry Clay and Daniel Webster, leaders of the National Republicans, closed ranks with Jackson to support the Force Bill, or the "Bloody Bill," as Calhoun labeled it.

It seemed impossible after these developments, but the showdown was avoided. While the Force Bill was moving through Congress, the House was also considering the Verplanck bill, which had Jackson's backing. Representative Gulian Verplanck of New York, following orders from Van Buren, was proposing a 50 per cent cut in tariffs by 1834, or a reduction to a general level of a 20 per cent duty in two years. When the bill cleared the House Ways and Means Committee, Clay suddenly feared that a continuing protective tariff would disappear entirely. So on February 12, 1833, he introduced his own tariff reform, a bill to save the general principle of protection while cutting duties to the Verplanck ceiling of 20 per cent by 1842. Both free traders and protectionists attacked his measure, yet his parliamentary abilities enabled him to promote it successfully as a substitute for the Verplanck bill in both the House and Senate. Curiously, Calhoun rejected the Verplanck bill, which would have accomplished in two years what Clay's bill would in ten. He turned instead to support Clay's bill, torn as he was between saving face or gaining the best economic deal for his state. In Clay's private view, South Carolina and the rest of the South would gain little from his tariff bill, for he purposely designed it to bring slight reductions in duties during the first seven years. He believed that before the drastic cuts proposed during the last three years went into effect, the country's mood would change and he would no doubt be able to shoot tariff levels back to a high-level position.

Both the Force Bill and Clay's Compromise Tariff of 1833 worked their way through Congress to passage on March 1, 1833. Calhoun had attempted to delay action on the Force Bill by offering three Senate resolutions for debate. He demanded that the Senate approve the state compact theory of the Constitution, the doctrine of limited Federal powers and the principle of state sovereignty. But Webster rose and demolished his arguments, just as he had demolished Hayne in 1830. On the Senate vote of February 20 on the Force Bill, Calhoun ordered his southern lieutenants to leave the floor. All did except Virginia's rabid states'-righter John Tyler, who cast the only vote in opposition to the Jacksonian measure, making the vote 32 to 1 in favor of Force.

Jackson signed both the Force Act and the Tariff Act on March 2. Little did he care that Clay took bows as "the Great Pacificator" and was again the bosom ally of Calhoun. More important at the moment was that a major crisis had ended. Since the tariff compromise removed the cause of the trouble with South Carolina, the Force Act was actually unnecessary. With relief, South Carolinians now bragged that they had forced Congress to do their will. Then to have its cake and eat it, the South Carolina legislature first rescinded its nullification ordinance and followed this with an act calling the Force Law unconstitutional and "null and void." Arrogance had its day, yet for the time being the threat of disunion was averted. But the South Carolina example was one the South would remember and copy until 1861. "I thought I w^d have to hang some of them & w^d have done it," said Jackson. Then about the future he prophesied, "These men would do any act to destroy this Union and form a southern confederacy bounded, north, by the Potomac River."

The crisis with South Carolina over nullification did not perceptibly alter Jackson's White House routine. After four years of experience, it was fairly well set. He enjoyed the power and attention, though he publicly complained that being President was "dignified slavery." The Presidency did not change his personal philosophy toward his fellow men. He continued to hold blind loyalty to friends, hatred for those who opposed him, general distrust of all men as potential favor-seekers and steamy sentimentality toward women and children.

The memory of Rachel continued to absorb him. Around his neck, attached to a cord under his shirt, he wore a miniature of Rachel painted by Anna Peale in 1815. Rachel's protégé, Ralph E. W. Earle, a wandering artist whom she had given a home at the Hermitage, was a part of Jackson's White House family and he spent his time painting portraits of The Hero. "Blair's the King's printer and I'm the King's painter," Earle liked to say. He did a large portrait of Rachel that was a Jackson favorite and Jackson hung it on his bedroom wall. Every night, George, his mulatto personal servant, would help him into his floor-dragging white nightgown, and after studying the wall painting, Jackson would prop the miniature on the table adjoining his bed. As he pressed back on the pillows, he would read a chapter from Rachel's old Bible before asking George, who slept on a thin straw mattress next to his bed, to snuff out the candle. In the morning, Jackson would begin his day by looking at the miniature before slipping it back on the cord.

Jackson's White House was alive with hordes of visiting young relatives and their broods. One room was set aside as a nursery, and frequently he made a middle-of-the-night trip here to check on his "pets." To make life easier for visitors and White House occupants, workers installed running water in the Mansion and provided hot and cold shower stalls. But nothing worked for long to rid the place of bedbugs. Every morning "farmer" Frank Blair of Silver Spring, now the closest associate of Jackson, delivered a pail of milk for the President and his young guests before hurrying on to the office of the *Globe*. Jackson's letters were filled with reports of teething and toddling, and to many young friends he wrote letters of advice. But to two girls who did not write after being treated to a White House stay, his letter chastised them as "lasy toads."

During the day, the White House was a scene of noise and excitement with the large Donelson clan of in-laws, young visitors and flirting military officers all about the place while Jackson tried to handle his business in the upstairs study. An enormous amount of wine and hard liquor was consumed during Jackson's stay. Jackson personally had lost his taste for liquor and he avoided the heavily laden dining room table delights. He preferred sipping wine at meals and making the old army meal of rice his chief and often his sole dish. He was seldom without his corncob—"the sweetest and best pipe"—and in little time the puffing smoke filled the room. He also chewed tobacco and spat, characteristic of the mountain people of his day. Protocol forced him to host formal gatherings, where he was rarely at ease. Four P.M. was the hour for more informal dinners and a stay of about three hours around the table was usual. The hated diplomatic dinners came at seven-thirty. One consisted of soup first, then beef bouilli, wild turkey boned and dressed with brains, fish, chicken, slices of tongue, canvasback ducks and celery, partridges with sweetbreads and last, pheasants and old Virginia ham. Drinks included sherry, port, champagne and claret and the desserts were jelly and small tarts in the turkish style, blanche mode and kisses with dried fruits in them, ice cream, grapes and oranges.

Because of his temper, harsh tongue and the authority of his office, few men dared talk back to him. "He had never studied the niceties of language," Taney commented, "and disliked what he was apt to regard as mere verbal criticisms." He could blister people outrageously, yet later claim he did so in jest or just for effect. After one wild display of rage at a visiting group, he said laughingly, "They thought I was mad." Aides tried to shrug off his angry words. Typical was the comment that he was "mild by nature and putting himself into a rage only when it would serve a purpose." Said another: "He would sometimes extemporize a fit of passion in order to overwhelm an adversary, but his self-command was always perfect."

One of the few men who dared to insult President Jackson to his face was James Buchanan. On the occasion of Buchanan's return to Washington in 1834, after serving as minister to Russia, he brought a young Englishwoman to the White House to meet the President. Buchanan raced up the stairs to Jackson's private rooms, barged in and found him "unshaved, unkempt in his dressing gown, with his slippered feet on the fender before a blazing wood fire, smoking a corncob pipe." When Buchanan brusquely asked Jackson to change his clothes before meeting his female friend, he later recalled that The Hero "rose, with his long pipe in his hand, deliberately knocking the ashes out of the bowl, and said, 'Buchanan (Buck-annan), I want to give you a little piece of advice, which I hope you will remember. I knew a man once who made his fortune by attending to his own business. . . . Tell the lady I will see her presently.'" A short time later he came downstairs smelling pleasantly and wearing his best suit.

When Congress was in session, Jackson tended to business in Washington. He found relaxation with his young guests and with horses. Once when he took two small boys riding, he said later, "They are the only friends I have who never pester me with their advice." For trips through town, he rode in a coach pulled by four swift dapple gray horses. But he had still other horses, racing steeds, that he kept in the White House stable. Negro jockeys were also kept at the White House and they rode the horses at local race tracks, where the racers were entered under the sponsorship of Jackson's nephew, Jack Donelson. Once when Jackson took a party out to the National Jockey Club to watch the White House horses, one of them ran wild. "Get behind me, Mr. Van Buren!" the crowd heard Jackson yell. "They will run over you, sir!" The political opposition later made use of this call.

For short vacations, Jackson's favorite haunt was Rip Raps, a breezy ocean island off Norfolk in Hampton Roads. The four-week hotel bill for the large Jackson entourage plus five of the eighteen White House servants came to less than one hundred dollars a week. Once when he traveled by boat down the Chesapeake to Rip Raps, a storm blew up. Small, stout George Washington Parke Custis, grandson of Martha Washington and father-in-law of Robert E. Lee, expressed his concern. "My good friend," Jackson said calmly, "you never traveled with me." Custis later told Blair about the remark and said that it reminded him of Julius Caesar's comment to a pilot who did not want to go out into a coming storm —"Why do you fear? You carry Caesar."

Jackson went home to the Hermitage at every opportunity,

though as the years lengthened he made these trips with foreboding. He found that Andy, Jr., was unfaithful to his wife, as well as being a liar and a poor manager. "My son," he wrote one time, "I regret to see that we are without seed wheat and that the negroes are without shoes in these heavy frosts." Andy ran up such debts that Jackson had to turn over much of his $25,000 Presidential salary to meet payments. At the same time, Jackson was a lavish spender on improving the Hermitage. He built an addition and when the house went up in flames on October 13, 1834, he spared no expense in rebuilding it. He was in later years saved from a pauper's grave only through the largess of Frank Blair.

As President, Jackson also took ceremonial trips. In the spring of 1833, for instance, he traveled to Fredericksburg, Virginia, to lay the cornerstone of a monument honoring Mary Ball Washington, mother of the first President. He was aboard ship at Alexandria, wedged in a chair between a table and a berth when a well-dressed young man approached him. Jackson assumed him to be a well-wisher and he held a hand out for the young man to press. Instead, the young man punched him in the face and pulled his nose. "What, sir! What, sir!" Jackson shouted while attempting to push the table out of the way. He felt a sharp chest pain. "I may have got a former broken rib injured against the table in a struggle to get to my feet," he told Van Buren afterward. Washington Irving, who was aboard, grappled with the assailant, who was found to be Robert B. Randolph, a cashiered Navy purser who had succeeded John Timberlake, Peggy Eaton's first husband, on the *Constitution*. Jackson had his hickory cane raised, but aides stopped him and Randolph managed to leap off the ship. Later when Randolph was brought to trial, Jackson wrote, requesting his release, "I have to this old age complied with my mother's advice to indict no man for assault or sue him for slander."

Later that summer he traveled to New England in a triumphant tour of the East Coast. He accepted the offer of the B. & O. line to ride the twelve-mile tracks into Baltimore and became the first President to travel by train. In Philadelphia, after his cheering reception, he let Dr. Philip Physick, the renowned physician, examine him. "I aim to do anything you think proper," he told the doctor, "except give up coffee and tobacco." Crowds everywhere were enormous. "I have bowed to upwards of two hundred thousand people today," he described his stop in New York. The bridge collapsed under the weight of the mob as he crossed to the Battery and two Cabinet members were among those flung into the water. In Boston Common, when Van Buren's horse would not respond to commands, Jackson jokingly told his hosts, "You've matched him with a horse even more non-committal than his rider." It was on this trip that Jackson was awarded a degree by Harvard. But not long afterward, when he reached New Hampshire, he suffered a physical collapse and was rushed back to Washington by steamboat, where doctors were so certain he would die that other Cabinet members showed increased interest in the friendship of Vice-President Van Buren. However, Jackson recovered in time to direct another major battle, the final assault on Biddle's Bank.

When he had first heard the news of his election victory, The Hero shook his hickory stick cane with the fervor of a political missionary who had received a mandate to attack the American "nobility system" and its staunchest defender, the Second Bank of the United States. Rather lugubriously, the initial reaction of both Clay and Biddle was that Jackson's triumph amounted to "something like popular ratification." But this soon gave way to determination to best him.

Even while the South Carolina "Nullies" were moving toward a showdown with him, Jackson was already setting the stage for the demise of the Bank. Biddle labored under the assumption that the Jackson veto of the Bank's recharter would somehow be overcome before the Bank was due to expire in 1836, and though his fight to make Clay President had failed, Congressional support for the Bank might still be raised to a point where another veto would be overridden. But Jackson was considering a new approach to throttle the Bank.

During the preceding Congress, he had asked for authority to remove government money from the Bank's vaults, money collected as taxes from citizens and used by the Bank without payment of interest to the Treasury. Congress had ignored him. But during the campaign, his determination spurted when he heard stories that Biddle was using Bank money for propaganda against Jackson and for bribing Congressmen to support the Bank.

He also had another reason. The Treasury had requested Biddle that year to advance $6,000,000 of government funds to retire 3 per cent government bonds. When Biddle asked for a postponement, Jackson became convinced that the Bank was in financial trouble. So in November 1832, he told his Cabinet of his plan to remove all government funds from Biddle's establishment. This precipitated a strong debate between Attorney General Taney and Treasury Secretary McLane, with the latter opposing the scheme. Jackson shut off McLane by closing the meeting, and almost immediately afterward, the South Carolina crisis bloomed. Until the Nullies were pacified, Jackson's sole Bank move during this period was to ask Congress in a Message to determine if the government's deposits in the Bank were safe.

The House responded early in March 1833, with a resolution affirming its belief in the Bank's sound financial health. However, the fact that a majority in the House would vote this way meant to a perennially suspicious Jackson that Biddle had succeeded in buying their souls. On March 19, he sent Cabinet members a memo with questions on the government's deposits and asked them to reply. Attorney General Taney, an early promoter of Jackson's removal proposal, provided no surprise in his reply: The Bank was not safe and its officers were secretive and dishonest because they were spending large sums to control the press and Congress. The slovenly Attorney General proposed that instead of forming another national bank to replace Biddle's Bank, government revenues should be distributed among "judiciously selected" state banks. Secretary of the Treasury McLane's ninety-one-page reply proposed a new national bank free of Mr. Biddle and the evils of the present charter. He opposed using state banks for revenue depositories because such banks were generally shaky propositions. McLane went on to point out that the 1816 charter provided that the President had no authority to remove government funds from the Bank. Only the Secretary of the Treasury was specifically permitted to do this, and when he did he was to report his reasons to Congress.

Months earlier, Jackson had decided to send Secretary of State Livingston to France as minister and to shift McLane into the State Department. McLane's reply on the Bank gave sudden impetus to this plan and on May 29, 1833, the changes were made. The new Treasury Secretary was William J. Duane, a Philadelphia lawyer and son of the editor of the fiery Jefferson era newspaper, the *Aurora*. Duane was outspoken in his anti-Bank views and Jackson believed he could continue his fight against Biddle with Duane's loyal support.

Ever-loyal Amos Kendall was sent on a mission to ask eastern bankers whether they would substitute for the Biddle Bank and take government deposits. Some expressed fear that Biddle would take punitive action against them, but most were eager to gain this lucrative business. Fortified with Kendall's report, Jackson presented it to his Cabinet on September 10, and announced that government funds were to be withdrawn from the Bank and deposited in selected state banks by October 1.

When Duane refused to comply, this came as no surprise to Jackson, for two days after Duane joined the Cabinet in June, he had boldly told Jackson that removal was neither wise nor legal. State banks were unsound, he argued, because they had printed paper silver certificates to an amount that was more than six times their silver reserve holdings. Given millions of Federal deposits, rampant inflation would result at best, he said, if they continued this reserve ratio; and at worst there would be catastrophe if all currency holders asked for redemption of their currency in silver. He could not, therefore, give Congress any valid reasons if he removed the funds from the Bank.

That Jackson did not strike him down with his cane or fire him on the spot was a mystery to those who knew his temper. This was hair-splitting to Jackson and some recalled how he had once bellowed at one man: "Hair-splitting is dangerous business!" But Jackson kept him on and attempted through letters and talks to change his mind. On his summertime triumphant tour of New England, he sent Duane a letter almost the size of a short volume and in it he deferentially sought to convince his Secretary. "In making to you, my dear Sir, this frank and explicit avowal of my opinions and feelings," he wrote, "it is not my intention to interfere with the independent exercise of the discretion committed to you by law over the subject."

But by September, Jackson was no longer willing to abide Duane's show of independence. "A secretary, sir, is merely an executive agent, a subordinate," he wrote Duane. The reply revealed no fear. "In this particular case, Congress confers a discretionary power, and requires reasons if I exercise it. Surely this contemplates responsibility on my part," Duane stated arrogantly. On the fourteenth of September, Jackson told Duane he should quit or carry out the removal order. Duane continued to refuse, to the delight of the opposition press, which had got wind of the controversy. Four days later Taney stayed up all night revising Jackson's "Paper" to his Cabinet, a restating of the principle first enunciated by Washington that Cabinet members served at the President's pleasure and under his direction. As Jackson now put it, the President had total responsibility for the Executive Branch and he controlled the activities of "his associates in the administration of the Government."

Not until the twenty-third did Jackson finally replace Duane with Taney, who was anxious to withdraw the funds from the Bank. As for Duane, said Jackson, writing to Vice-President Van Buren who first opposed, then tepidly supported withdrawal, "In his appointment, I surely caught a tartar in disguise, but I have got rid of him. . . . He is either the weakest mortal, or the most strange composition I have ever met with."

The battle was now joined. Taney started out by drawing money from the Bank to meet day-to-day government expenses. When new revenues became available, he put them on deposit in various state banks, or "pets," as the Biddleites called them. One of the pets was a bank in Baltimore in which Taney was a stockholder. Then as the new system grew less makeshift, he began the process of gradually withdrawing the remaining $10,000,000 in Federal deposits from the Bank.

Biddle was also busy, for he had no intention of losing by default. In a blaze of anger he labeled Jackson's removal order "a declaration of war," and told the President of his New York branch, "When we begin we shall crush the Kitchen Cabinet at once." To tighten his own vise on the economy in order to force Jackson to return the deposits, he began to present large quantities of state bank notes for redemption in specie. He also called in many loans in the South and West, producing hardship and a recession as he hoped he would, so that there would be a widespread outcry for public peace with the Bank. In addition, he spent the Bank's wealth recklessly to create a vocal army of businessmen who sent an endless number of petitions to Congress and visited the White House. St. Clair Clarke had written a favorable 830-page study of the Bank and Biddle bought several hundred copies for distribution at six dollars each, a dollar more than Congress paid for copies. For, as the author explained, "The Congress Committee jewed us down to five dollars, but it is really too little for the book."

One group called on Jackson and requested him to return Federal funds to the Bank to end the threatening contraction of capital. "Relief, sir!" Jackson shouted, in a voice he later called simulated rage. "Come not to me, sir! Go to the Monster. It is folly, sir, to talk to Andrew Jackson. The Government will not bow to the Monster.

Andrew Jackson yet lives to put his foot upon the head of the Monster and crush him to the dust."

When the Twenty-third Congress convened on December 2, 1833, the Legislative Branch also entered the removal fight. The Senate's Golden Age was on, with Webster, Calhoun and Clay in control of an Upper Chamber numbering twenty Democrats, twenty opponents of Jackson and eight in neither camp. It had been said that the men around Jackson gained his confidence because they hated the same people he did. This was also true of the Webster-Calhoun-Clay coalition, a tenuous bond focused on opposing Jackson. The House was only nominally in the hands of the Jackson Democrats, for it rejected Blair's *Globe* as its printer and named Calhoun's man and paper, Duff Green's *Telegraph*, instead. As for the Senate, its printers were Gale and Seaton, who edited Clay's paper, the *National Intelligencer*. Membership in that Congress included five future Presidents; Tyler and Buchanan in the Senate, and Polk, Fillmore and Pierce in the House.

Clay, the tall, sandy-haired man with gray merry eyes and overlarge mouth, with his snuffbox ever-present and an eager crowd about him to hear the latest political humor, was clearly the commanding figure just as he was as House Speaker in the War Hawk days of 1812. This session his thrashing arm emphasized the points his sonorous voice uttered in sixty speeches, in an effort to revive the Bank and rebuild his own chances for 1836.

He began his attack on Jackson with a resolution demanding that the President send the Senate the paper he had read to his Cabinet in September on the removal of government funds from the Bank. The Senate approved his resolution even though the newspapers had carried Jackson's Cabinet paper. However, Jackson had no intention of taking part in public humiliation. He denounced the request as an infringement of Presidential prerogatives. Next, Clay proposed two resolutions of censure. The first would condemn Jackson for firing Duane and appointing Taney merely to remove the deposits. The second would condemn him for his "unsatisfactory and insufficient" reasons for removing the money. Jackson understood censure to be as close to impeachment as the Senate could come, and his forces engaged in a three-month debate to throttle the Clay resolutions. But on March 28, 1834, Clay was victorious and Jackson was censured on the first resolution by a vote of 26 to 20 and on the second by 28 to 18. "False as hell!" Benton bellowed.

The Hero was so enraged that he dispatched a Special Message
to the Senate on April 17, protesting the censure and requesting
that his statement be inserted in the Senate Journal. It was the
Senate's turn to refuse. In his "Protest," Jackson offered the theory
that "the President is a direct representative of the American people." This was a long step beyond the Jefferson position that the
Presidency was one of three co-ordinate branches in the Federal
Government; and an opposite turn from the Jeffersonian belief that
the lower house of the Legislative Branch was most representative of the people.

Clay hoped to shame Jackson in the House as well as the
Senate. However, the House refused to concur in the censure. It
followed instead the resolutions offered by Ways and Means Committee Chairman James K. "Young Hickory" Polk. Polk's resolutions
proposed that the Bank not be rechartered, that deposits not be
returned but placed with state banks.

Clay was not yet finished, however. When Taney's name came
to the Senate for confirmation as Treasury Secretary in June 1834,
Clay accused him of "servile compliance" to Jackson and led the
fight that resulted in his rejection by a vote of 18 for and 28 opposed. Learning of Taney's defeat, Jackson cried, "The fate of
the Bank is sealed forever!" The rampaging Senator also took out
his venom on other Jackson nominees. These included House
Speaker Andrew Stevenson of Virginia who was rejected as minister to Great Britain, the nominee for governor of the Michigan
Territory, the Army paymaster and the collector of customs for
Mississippi. In 1835, when Jackson nominated Taney as associate
justice of the Supreme Court, the Senate held the nomination for
almost two months and then by a three-vote margin postponed the
nomination indefinitely. Jackson, who was in a Capitol room waiting for good news, called the Senate "damned scoundrels" when
a messenger brought him word of Taney's fate. Not until March
1836 did the Senate confirm Taney to a Federal post, this time approving him as successor to the late Chief Justice John Marshall, a
position Taney would hold for twenty-eight years.

The Bank fight was essentially over by mid-1834, with dire
effects to the nation and to Biddle but only glad political tidings
for Jackson. More than ever, the name of Jackson brought tears of
gratitude coursing down the cheeks of his growing army of admirers, for they saw him as their own valiant general against
monopoly and for widening opportunities, liberty and equality.

From the cold economic view, the consequences were unpleasant. Most of the "pet" banks immediately began a reckless expansion of loans with the deposit of Federal tax money in their vaults. Wildcat banks flourished, now that the Bank of the United States could no longer enforce paper money sanity. The result was an enormous speculation fever that overtook the nation and helped bring about the terrible depression of 1837. As for Biddle, he reorganized the Bank as the United States Bank of Pennsylvania in 1836, paying the state a bonus of $2,000,000. But he watched it dwindle in assets. In 1841 it went bankrupt. Biddle lost his own fortune, underwent arrest and trial for criminal conspiracy and was released on a technicality. He died a shell of a man at fifty-eight in 1844.

On June 30, 1834, when the dramatic first session of the Twenty-third Congress expired, Senator Benton kicked off that year's Congressional campaigns with an announcement that he would propose a resolution to expunge Jackson's censure from the Senate Journal. "The doughty knight of the stuffed cravat," as John Quincy Adams had characterized him, also announced he would renew this resolution at each succeeding session until this blotch on Jackson's reputation was removed. Senators who had engineered the vote of 27 to 16 not to receive the President's "Protest" against his censure were not easily frightened by the implied threat of retribution. However, they were well aware that although the censure and all the rest of the Bank squabble might be a dead issue in Congress, it could be the important issue of Jacksonians in that year's elections.

Clay's disastrous defeat in 1832 had induced the total collapse of the National Republican party. But a new party, the Whigs, arose from the floor when Clay, Webster and other National Republicans joined fortunes with the Anti-Masonic party of Thurlow Weed, William Seward and their Pennsylvania cohorts, across the New York border. Horace Greeley's *Whig Almanac* tied the coalition in with other forces in describing the Whig party. In addition to these two basic groups, he said, the Whigs contained the Nullifiers and those who opposed the Force Act against South Carolina; disgruntled Jacksonians who condemned the "immolation of Duane and the subserviency of Taney"; plus former apolitical citizens "now awakened from their apathy by the palpable usurpations of the Executive." When young Weed maneuvered himself into the boss seat of the Whigs, Clay was displeased because it had been Weed who had manipulated New York's electoral votes in 1824 and deprived him of being one of the three candidates considered for the Presidency by the House. As for Weed's use of the anti-Masonry issue, Clay said he was interested "in the pursuit of power without regard to the means of acquiring it."

Sheer statistics worked against the Whigs in 1834. For in the face of ever-lessening restrictions on suffrage, their appeal was only to the minority of citizens. The Whig army of eastern pro-Bank businessmen, western farmers and southern planters could not match in numbers the Jacksonian alliance of eastern anti-Bank businessmen, western and southern farmers plus a contradictory army of hard-money exponents in the East and paper-money exponents in the West, intellectuals in the East and anti-intellectuals in the West, and the foreign born in the East and anti-immigrants in the West. In addition, the Democrats had a left-wing element. These were the Locofocos, loudly anti-Bank, anti-protection, anti-monopoly and pro-hard money. This group was originally known as the Equal Rights party. Not until 1835 did they get their new name, as a result of a fight with Tammany conservative Democrats at a New York meeting. The newly invented friction matches were called "locofocos," and when the Tammany crowd tried to break up the meeting by turning off the gas jets, the Equal Righters struck locofocos to light candles and resume their meeting.

As usual, before breakfast each day, Frank Blair talked issues and propaganda with Jackson, and what the *Globe* printed served as a cue for all Jackson papers throughout the country. In the 1834 campaign, the Benton resolution and continuing attacks on the Bank received prominent attention in Blair's paper. Ridicule was also heaped on the Whigs, who were called opponents of "the people." Jackson was reported to have defined a Whig as a man who had no principle or trace of honesty and was entirely untrustworthy.

In spite of Blair's widely printed sulphurics and Jackson's great popularity, the Whigs did not suffer a disastrous defeat, though the Jacksonians gained comfortable margins in both houses. In the Twenty-fourth Congress, the Democrats held a 28 to 20 balance in the Senate and 145 to 98 in the House, a sufficient working majority. One consequence was that the Clay-Webster-Calhoun alliance in the Senate was blunted, if only temporarily. Another consequence of the 1834 election was that Jackson was able to install James Polk as Speaker of the House. In the preceding session of Congress, Jackson had tried to help "Young Hickory" become the successor to Speaker Stevenson, the rejected minister to Britain. But the House had slapped at Jackson by rejecting Polk and electing young John Bell, also of Tennessee, and a former Jacksonian. Many House members, though Democrats, did not consider Polk kindly. Sam Houston once described him as "a victim of the use of water as a beverage," an apt description that made him an oddity in a House filled with heavy drinkers and gun carriers. John Quincy Adams noted in his diary during this period that immorality was fairly commonplace. In 1834, for example, he wrote that Representative James Blair of South Carolina, an alcoholic, had killed himself after finding love letters from his wife to Governor Murphy of Alabama. He also said that Blair had shot at an actress while he was seated in a theater box. As for Polk, Adams said, he had "no wit, no literature, no elegance of language, no philosophy, no pathos, no felicitous impromptus, nothing that can constitute an orator but confidence, fluency and labor."

The Bank fight may have ended but other tumultuous matters arose during Jackson's last two years to keep the adrenaline of anti-Jacksonites pouring. In fact, Jackson admitted that rancorous Americans numbering more than five hundred wrote of their intention of murdering him. One actual attempt came on January 30, 1835, when he went to the Capitol for the funeral services of Representative Warren Davis of South Carolina. Afterward, Jackson was walking out the east end of the Capitol when a bearded stranger moved from behind one of the portico pillars and fired a pistol at him from a distance of six or eight feet. The gun missed fire and Jackson started for him with his hickory stick cane raised as a club. A shot from a second pistol also missed fire and Levi Woodbury, now Secretary of the Treasury, seized Jackson's arm before he could strike his would-be assassin. John Quincy Adams said the shots sounded "like a squib."

The gun-wielder turned out to be an insane house painter, Richard Lawrence, who was first tried and then sent to an asylum. Politics being so bitter a contest at the time, both the Whigs and Democrats tried to use the incident to promote party strength. Duff Green's *Telegraph* aided the Whigs by printing the charge that the assassination attempt had been a fraud designed to create sympathy for Jackson. A ballistics expert lent credence to this view when he reported that the odds against two successive misfires from Lawrence's gun were only 125,000 to one.

On the other hand, Frank Blair convinced The Hero that Lawrence was put up to the attempt by Whig Senator George Poindexter of Mississippi, a man who had made the motion in the Senate not to receive Jackson's "Protest" on his censure. Jackson bought Blair's charge because Poindexter frequently threatened his colleagues. In fact, Van Buren brought two guns to the Senate dais in case Poindexter attempted to kill him there. Affidavits were obtained from two men who swore they had seen Lawrence visit Poindexter's house shortly before the Capitol incident. These affidavits were printed in the *Globe*, and when Poindexter demanded an explanation from the President, Jackson ignored him. Poindexter then brought about a Senate investigation and after the affidavits were proved false, he was exonerated. However, Jackson still believed in his complicity, and by assiduous cultivation of the Mississippi legislature he was rewarded when the legislature did not return Poindexter to the Senate when his term expired on March 3, 1835. When Poindexter died, he suffered the embarrassment of being buried in the Jackson cemetery in Jackson, Mississippi.

During his Presidency, Jackson's sense of outrage and his firm hand revealed themselves in the conduct of foreign relations. His approach was set earlier in his effort to reopen the British West Indies to American trade. When the Prime Minister did not move swiftly enough to please him, he let word pass through Van Buren that he would ask Congress to establish reprisal action—non-intercourse with "Canaday." England complied not long afterward. Also King Bomba of Naples settled American claims in 1832 when five American frigates sailed into his bay with their cannons firing.

His approach to French problems was almost as extreme. For twenty years American Presidents had been unable to get France to pay for damages suffered by Americans during the Napoleonic Wars. Finally in 1832, France ratified a treaty, agreeing to pay 25,000,000 francs in six installments in exchange for the lowering of duties on French wines.

Jackson assumed that the issue was settled when Congress cut the tariff. However, the French Chamber of Deputies refused to make the required installment payments in 1833 and 1834. Jackson, who believed that a country's word should be its bond, grew incensed and ordered his new Secretary of State, John Forsyth, to threaten the French minister with war. Then in his Message of December 1834, he told Congress that the time had arrived to "take redress into our own hands . . . I recommend that a law be passed authorizing reprisals upon French property," if no action were taken by "the approaching session of the French Chambers."

Despite the fact that Congress would not authorize an increase in military strength, the French Government reacted to Jackson's threat by approving payment in April 1835. However, to save face, the French added the stipulation that payment depended on a satisfactory explanation of Jackson's language. But to this, Jackson angrily retorted that all foreign governments must understand "that we will not permit France or any, or all European governments to interfere with our domestic policy or dictate to the President what language he shall use in his Message to Congress."

As a result, both France and the United States recalled their ministers and relations between the two countries were suspended. However, they were again resumed after several months of mutual belligerence when Jackson told Congress in his Message of December 1835 that he had not intended in his previous Message "to menace or insult the Government of France." The French were willing to settle now, even though a following sentence of the Message read: "The honor of my country shall never be sustained by an apology from me for the statement of truth or the performance of duty."

Although Jackson never wavered in his belief in the rectitude of his fight with the Bank, certain results displeased him in 1835. Western speculators were on a rampage, using unbacked paper money from wildcat bank loans to buy extensive quantities of public land. In 1834, 4,500,000 acres of public land became private; in 1835, 12,000,000; and in 1836 some 20,000,000 acres would go. Jackson believed he had the answer in December 1835 when he asked Congress to prohibit the manufacture of all bank notes under twenty dollars. Since the average person traded below that figure, he believed, forcing such transactions to be conducted with gold and silver would "revive and perpetuate those habits of economy and simplicity."

However, even though he was stunned by the size of the bills presented him by contractors and suppliers rebuilding the burned Hermitage, it did not occur to him that the raging inflation had rapidly made twenty-dollar notes a commonplace currency. In fact, the continued sale of public land for bank notes helped make possible the extinction of the national debt in 1836. At the close of his first term, Congress had approved a Clay bill to distribute revenues collected from the sale of public land among the states. Even though Jackson opposed it on the ground that revenues should be used to retire the national debt, the House at the time had approved the bill by a vote of 96 to 40 and the Senate by 23 to 5. The bill went to the White House within ten days of the expiration of the Twenty-second Congress on March 2, 1833. Despite a Congressional support of more than two-thirds for the measure, Jackson ignored its existence. He had found that Article I, section 7, of the Constitution stated that any bill not signed and returned by him within ten days after he received it automatically became a law. But that same section also said that "unless the Congress by their Adjournment prevent its Return . . . it shall not be a Law." Jackson now ignored the land sales revenue distribution bill, and thus he effected the first instance of the "pocket veto."

In June 1836, when the national debt had finally disappeared, Jackson added to the inflationary fire by signing a bill providing for the distribution of the surplus revenue millions among the states. But only a few weeks later, on July 11, 1836, he took a deflationary step by issuing his Specie Circular. Henceforth, the government would accept only silver and gold as payment for public lands.

Speculators were quick to denounce the Specie Circular, as did the Whigs who were seeking campaign issues for that year's Presidential contest. Despite the Democratic majority, Clay pushed an annulment bill through Congress only to watch it die when Jackson used another pocket veto. The general could not be moved by statistics that a shortage of specie existed in the country. Nor could his obstinate mind be changed by the observation that the East was being drained of its specie by western speculators. Nor did the Administration show concern when people generally began demanding specie payment on non-public land matters, on the ground that if the Government insisted on specie for land payments there must be something wrong with paper money. Based to a large extent on wildcat paper circulation, the nation's economy grew steadily more shaky.

As the 1836 election approached, slavery also reared its head as an issue. The memory of the harsh Congressional debates involving slavery in the Missouri Compromise Act of 1820 had abated to the point where Virginia, Kentucky and North Carolina were considering gradual emancipation. However, this changed in August 1831 when Nat Turner, a slave in southeastern Virginia, led a rebellion that resulted in the death of fifty-seven white persons in the town of Jerusalem before it was crushed. Afterward, the southern tone hardened, while in the North the abolitionists led by William Lloyd Garrison and his newspaper, the *Liberator,* increased their attacks.

The spokesman for slavery, just as he had been for nullification, was John C. Calhoun. The astute Senator was aware that many Northerners did not take kindly to the efforts of the abolitionists, and a grand design now gained hold over him. He sincerely believed that he could win the Presidency in 1836 by combining his strong southern support with that of the white backlash in the North.

As Calhoun moved to strengthen his forces in Congress, so did the anti-slavers led by Representative John Quincy Adams. Calhoun was determined that Congress refrain entirely from legislating against slavery, and with a slave owner in the White House he did not expect a wrathful opposition from Jackson. He was right, for no Administration voice protested the establishment of a new House gag rule automatically laying all anti-slavery petitions on the table and thus removing them from consideration. However, he suspected the hand of Van Buren in the companion House rule that to interfere with slavery in the District of Columbia was inexpedient. Calhoun's fertile mind interpreted this to mean that inexpediency carried with it the connotation of "in the current period," and that the rule would permit the abolition of slavery in the capital at a future time.

Calhoun also set about to use the authority of the Federal Government to halt the increasing flood of abolitionist literature riding the mail routes into the South. This crisis reached fever pitch in 1835 in Calhoun's stronghold of South Carolina. When the mail steamer arrived in July at Charleston with a load of pamphlets from the American Anti-Slavery Society, local citizens forced open the post office, seized and publicly burned the propaganda. Postmaster Huger of Charleston wrote anxiously to Amos Kendall, the Kitchen Cabinet member now made Postmaster General, for advice whether such mail could be detained. Kendall, a fiery opponent of the Nullifiers, was also a slave owner, and he found himself torn between a defense of slavery and the Constitution's guarantee of freedom of the press.

"Upon a careful examination of the law," he wrote Huger, "I am satisfied that the postmaster general has no legal authority to exclude newspapers from the mail, nor prohibit their carriage or delivery on account of their character. . . . You inform me, that they are, in character, 'the most inflammatory and incendiary— and insurrectionary in the highest degree.'" Kendall then gave him a course to follow, one that counseled nullification of the Constitution. "We owe an obligation to the laws," he piously stated, "but a higher one to the communities in which we live." Later he clarified this further with the statement that the Federal Government had no right to deliver "incendiary" material through the Post Office Department if that material fomented slave insurrections.

Huger and other southern postmasters found authority in Kendall's words to tamper with the mail. Several states also passed laws banning the delivery of "incendiary" literature. But essentially the problem was national because the Post Office Department was a part of the Executive Branch, and the antagonists awaited Jackson's Message to Congress on the subject in December 1835.

The Hero would not condemn the land of his origin. He denounced the "unconstitutional and wicked attempts" of the antislavers to inflame the slaves and "produce all the horrors of a servile war." He also proposed a law "as will prohibit, under severe penalties, the circulation in the southern states, through the mail, of incendiary publications intended to instigate the slaves to insurrection."

In the Senate, Clay and Webster broke their alliance with Calhoun by castigating the proposal as a violation of the Constitution's First Amendment. Calhoun himself could not stomach the bill proposed by the Jackson forces, for it gave control over the delivery or exclusion of the mail to the Federal Government. His own bill contained a clause endorsing nullification and otherwise left censorship to the local postmaster, forbidding him to receive or deliver slavery literature in those states that prohibited it.

In the end, there was no legislation because the House and Senate could not agree. Calhoun failed to get his own bill through the Senate, but he nevertheless managed to arrange a serious problem for Vice-President Van Buren. He carefully organized his supporters so that a tie vote resulted on the Jackson proposal, considered by the abolitionists as bad as his own. And so the cautious Vice-President was smoked out. When he cast his ballot for the proposal, Van Buren lost for the near future what support he might have had from anti-slavers. By default and through Kendall's assertions, the southern states thus assumed the role of mail censors. They were to continue this activity until the Civil War.

The slavery issue also confronted Jackson in 1836 in the southwest area known as Texas. On March 2, 1836, Americans there had declared their independence from Mexico. A war with General Santa Anna followed, which included the wiping out of 187 Texans under Captain Travis at the Alamo by three thousand Mexicans; the slaughter of a Texas force at Goliad after the men surrendered; and the Battle of San Jacinto on April 21, 1836, where Sam Houston, Jackson's protégé, avenged the Alamo and Goliad by destroying the Mexican Army and capturing Santa Anna. When the Congress of the Lone Star Republic of Texas met in 1836, it petitioned the United States Congress for annexation of Texas into the Union.

In 1825, when Henry Clay was Secretary of State, he had instructed Joel Poinsett, American minister to Mexico, to buy Texas. However, the Mexican Government would not discuss this with him and shortly after Jackson became President, Poinsett was expelled for interfering in the internal affairs of Mexico. Jackson was as hungry for Texas as Clay had been, and to succeed Poinsett he named South Carolina-born Anthony Butler, a shady land speculator, giving him instructions to buy Texas and then California. To help Butler, Jackson with typical arrogance warned the Mexican Government that if it did not sell Texas, Americans there "will declare themselves independent of Mexico the moment they acquire sufficient numbers."

Butler personified the stereotype picture of a Texan of a century later with easy-found wealth, loud voice and bragging manner. Sam Houston was appalled at his selection, for he considered him a "swindler and gambler." One who made a study of Butler

called him "a national disgrace . . . personally a bully and a swash-
buckler, ignorant at first of the Spanish language and even the
forms of diplomacy, shamefully careless about legation affairs,
wholly unprincipled as to methods, and by the open testimony of
two American consuls openly scandalous in conduct."

When Butler, with red face and shouts, could not get the Mexican Government to part with Texas for $5,000,000, he wrote
Jackson that he could bring about the sale with several hundred
thousand dollars of bribes to the right Mexicans. Jackson's reaction was one of surprise—not because of the suggestion but because
Butler had not sent the letter in code. In his reply, he vaguely
authorized bribes but also warned Butler to give "these shrewd
fellows no ground to charge you with any tampering with officers
to obtain the cession through corruption." Butler failed to make
headway and as a last resort advised Jackson to seize Texas
outright. "What a scamp!" Jackson wrote on the back of the letter
Butler sent him. With that he recalled him and treated him to a
list of expletives of which "liar" was the mildest.

Sam Houston's victory at San Jacinto made a bribed purchase of Texas unnecessary in 1836. But this was a Presidential
election year, and with Webster and Adams in the lead northern
Congressmen were loudly denouncing a suspected southern plot
to spread slavery and increase the number of slave states. Mexico
had abolished slavery in 1829, they pointed out, and one result of
Houston's victory was to undo this act in Texas and reinstate the
institution. In fairness, the truth was that Mexico had exempted
the Texas province from manumission.

With Calhoun leading the southern contingency in demanding
not only recognition of the Republic of Texas but also annexation
and statehood, Jackson decided to forego his dream and play a
more cautious role. Any move favorable to Calhoun's exhortations
would serve only to diminish the chances of Van Buren for victory. So he remained a sphinx throughout the campaign and insured Van Buren of office.

But toward the end of his term, he could no longer remain inactive toward Texas, and made a backdoor move. Instead of a
straightforward recognition that might have brought on a fight,
he operated through the stealth of a rider to the Civil Appropriations Bill. The rider permitted the payment of a salary for an
American diplomatic representative to the Republic of Texas
whenever a President considered the time propitious to begin

diplomatic relations. Jackson took this step on March 2, 1837, a day before his Administration expired. But annexation and statehood would have to be the fight of another Administration.

In the fading period of Jackson's Administration there remained the unfinished business of expunging The Hero's censure from the Senate Journal. In January 1837, "Old Bullion" Benton made his supreme effort. One of the rooms off the Senate floor was known as "the hole in the wall" and Benton crammed it with liquor and choice foods in an attempt to befriend the opposition. Finally on January 16, after "the hole in the wall" had been restocked several times and after Daniel Webster had made a long plea to the Senate not to debase itself by removing the censure, the vote came. When the crowd in the galleries hissed Jackson's victory by a favorable 24 to 19 vote, Benton angrily demanded that the "Bank ruffians" be hauled down and punished. Ushers seized several spectators but Benton pointed only to one man and demanded that he be brought to the bar of the Senate. When the man entered dragged by the sergeant-at-arms, Benton moved for a vote that the culprit be discharged. This passed with only a single dissent, and the man walked up to the dais and called to Van Buren: "Mr. President, am I not to be permitted to speak in my own defense?" "Take him out!" the Chair ordered the sergeant-at-arms.

"The day is gone; night approaches, and night is suitable to the dark deed we meditate," Calhoun philosophized. In the shadowed Senate chamber, the clerk produced the Journal of March 28, 1834, containing the sharp rebuke of the President. Then the Chair ordered the clerk to draw a heavy black line around the original Resolution of Censure and write across its face—"Expunged by order of the Senate this sixteenth day of January in the Year of our Lord 1837." The learned Calhoun's comment on Benton's handiwork was: "Even a Roman Senator would not have done so until the time of Caligula and Nero." Later an unknown person stole the section of the Senate Journal containing the "expunged resolution" and it disappeared from history.

A tired and sick President attended Van Buren's inauguration on March 4. Yet he took great satisfaction in the enthusiasm of the crowd. "For once the rising was eclipsed by the setting sun," said Senator Benton, comparing the crowd's greater applause for

Jackson than for Van Buren. Afterward, Jackson used the hickory cane for support as he made his way to his coach and four dapple grays.

Henry Clay later commented that Jackson had "swept over the government, during the last eight years, like a tropical tornado."

☆ 8 ☆

MARTIN VAN BUREN

The Unfulfilled President

A rather eminent but sour observer once characterized dapper
and serene President Martin Van Buren as being "like Sosie of
Molière's *Amphitryon—l'ami de tout le monde.*" (The friend of all
the world.)

As a man who hoped for re-election even before his first inauguration, Van Buren would have desired nothing better than to
stroke the fluffy red sideburns that reached to his jaw and smile
benignly upon all voters as a friend . . . and have them smile
back.

Unfortunately, he could not. For he was the first President to
feel handcuffed by his predecessor's policies and activities. As the
hostage of the immediate past, he inherited the enemies of General Jackson, and men who had cowered before brazen Old Hickory straightened up for their delayed attack. As the chosen successor to Jackson, he also had the old man peering over his
shoulder to make certain he continued to follow his program. But
worst calamity of all, Jackson had busily prepared for him a
muddy, rock-strewn playing field on which to serve as President.
A Jackson-hastened economic depression came roaring onto the
scene simultaneously with the advent of Van Buren's Administration, and how to cope with it proved a painful four-year ordeal
for a friendly, laissez-faire Jeffersonian.

During his four years as President, Van Buren's name became
synonymous with the calamitous depression that saddened and
hungered a people normally given to exuberant optimism and
risk-taking adventurism. That he was not personally responsible
for the hard times made little difference to an opposition in search
of a scapegoat. Neither the remedies they proposed nor those he

advocated would have dented the severity of the economic distress or shortened its seven-year course. For neither he nor they considered that the powers of the President and the Federal Government might extend to the responsibility for attacking a nation-wide economic disaster at the individual level.

Most of all Van Buren wanted to be a friend of all voters because he yearned for an eight-year residence at the White House. It was his belief that if he followed the Presidential line of antagonizing no one, he would be rewarded with a second term. Only after two terms could he hope to make a gracious exit to Lindenwald, his post-operative estate at Kinderhook on the Hudson, where he wanted to play the role of the all-wise elder statesman, like Jefferson at Monticello, Madison at Montpelier and Jackson at the Hermitage.

This explains why he changed his political behavior of a lifetime when he became President. Throughout his long career he was a master at laying low any politician who stood in his path. Loyalty to a man or a party was not part of his code when weighed on a scale holding his ambitions. His career was based on dropping his political allegiance whenever his friends looked like losers, and then spreading himself over the winner like an octopus. Not for naught was he known as "the Little Magician," "the Red Fox" and "the American Talleyrand."

Yet, complained friends, when he became President he mistakenly cast aside the very political attributes that had brought him to the top. Senator Silas Wright of New York, his leader in the Upper Chamber, bewailed the fact that he did not consider the Presidency an extension of his own rough background in the Empire State's political jungle. At one time, as boss of the Albany Regency, a powerful New York coalition of upstate Republicans and Tammany Bucktails, Van Buren had held control over 6600 state jobs, 8000 military commissions and a glittering array of state contracts, each of which he doled out like a miser at usurious political interest rates. But as President, complained Wright, he proved totally inept when it came to using patronage to advance his small political program through Congress and manipulating the Federal spoils system in the states to enlarge his local following.

For two decades he had specialized in organizing large groups and controlling their most minute activities. As state senator, New York's attorney general, U. S. Senator, governor of New York, Jackson's Secretary of State, minister to England and Vice-President, he had mastered the details of his jobs and kept close watch over subordinates. But as Chief Executive, he refrained from even indirect leadership and control. When his Democratic party developed factions, he shut his eyes and did nothing to punish those responsible. When they joined with Whigs to make mincemeat of legislation, he would not read them out of the party. On his most important piece of legislation, to divorce the government from any connection with private banks, he did not lift a finger to help his Democratic leaders in Congress. Senator Wright said, "I was compelled to stand like a minuteman against the attacks, by way of amendment, of indiscreet friends and insidious enemies." Even his Cabinet Secretaries, a mediocre conglomerate inherited from Jackson (with the exception of Secretary of War Joel Poinsett), found themselves generally ignored and unsupervised. Although this system no doubt pleased some, others chafed under their lonely direction of "overwhelming" burdens. One Secretary invited a friend to visit him "if it be only to see a gentleman of leisure metamorphosed into a pack horse."

Van Buren especially wanted those eight years as President to culminate a lifetime of incessant effort to reach the top of the political heap. Always conscious of his humble beginning, inadequate education and the harsh political blackjacking he had to resort to in order to advance himself, he felt that two terms as President would fulfill his need to wipe out memories of the past and give him the status he believed he deserved.

Van Buren's quest for fulfillment had begun early. Born in 1782, he was the son of a poor tavernkeeper whose family came from Amsterdam to the Hudson in 1631 as indentured servants to the Van Rensselaer patroon. Along the way, the family gained its freedom and changed its original name of Van Buurmalsen to Van Buren because one member could not spell his name at a crucial legal time. Since New York taverns were used as polling places on election day, Van Buren could later claim he was born in a polling booth.

The poor lad's two best schoolhood friends were Billy Van Ness (Burr's second in his duel with Hamilton) and Hannah Hoes, his cousin, whom he married. Billy lived in the big house at Kinderhook where Washington Irving later wrote his Knickerbocker *History*. This was the house Van Buren triumphantly purchased a half century later as his statesman's manor. Their teacher in the village school was the source for the Washington Irving character Ichabod Crane.

To the great regret of his mother, Van Buren's schooling ended by his fourteenth year. Throughout his life, he spoke with a Dutch accent and a lisp and never learned the proper rules of written English or penmanship. John Randolph said he was always amused by the way Van Buren pronounced "conthiderable" for "considerable." DeWitt Clinton, while governor of New York, once commented that a letter written by State Senator Van Buren was not only impossible to read "but equally offensive to grammar and truth." When he was Secretary of State, Van Buren sent a memo on the Maysville Road Veto Message to President Jackson, who replied, "As far as I have been able to decipher it, I think it is one of the most lucid expositions of the Constitution . . . I have ever met with." One reason Van Buren had so little understanding with his Cabinet members when he was President was that they were unable to read the letters and memoranda he sent them.

Gnawing ambition and a disregard for the usual rules of politics moved the poorly educated boy ahead rapidly. At fourteen he was apprenticed to a local lawyer, at fifteen he spoke to his first jury, and before he was of age he served as a delegate to the state Republican convention and as campaign manager for Billy Van Ness's brother Johnny who was running for Congress. Johnny promised to support him for two years in New York City if he won, thus moving Martin from village to big-city politics. Unfortunately for Johnny, the House of Representatives expelled him for a conflict of interest because he was operating as a major in the local militia at the same time.

But in New York, Billy Van Ness employed Van Buren in his law firm and took him frequently to Richmond Hill, once the residence of George Washington and John Adams and now the home of Aaron Burr. It was a thrill to be welcomed by a man who had risen almost to the Presidency and was also the son of the second head of the College of New Jersey (later renamed Princeton). Burr was then Jefferson's Vice-President as well as "Our Chief" of Tammany, a vote-getting organization that met in the Long Room of Brom Martling's Tavern on Nassau Street. Van Buren won quick acceptance into the "Little Band," as the group of young men who surrounded Burr were called. Burr, who was kind to Van Buren, made him aware that the Little

Band and Tammany were devoted to the task of wresting political leadership in the state away from the coalition of the Livingston and Clinton families. These two families not only parceled out the top state jobs to themselves and relatives but controlled the rest of the state through their power over patronage and contracts. Burr was also important to the young Van Buren because he openly discussed political personalities and issues with him and the other young men. There were many humorous stories, such as the time Lady Washington told him she had named her tomcat Hamilton, after the New York Federalist leader. Hamilton, she said, had thirteen stripes on his tail—one for each colony. Burr also taught him that politics was synonymous with intrigue. A Van Buren critic in later years said that "if he could gain an objective as well by openness as intrigue, he would choose the latter."

It was in his association with Burr that Van Buren early established his basic political tenet that loyalty to others must be discarded when it conflicted with advancing one's career. He knew from Burr's successful career that loyalty was only for followers, not for leaders. Had not Burr frequently admitted that he was a Federalist supporter of Alexander Hamilton at one time and later a Republican supporter of George Clinton? In 1804, when Burr ran for governor of New York, he expected his young friend to work for him in the Kinderhook area. However, Van Buren, having determined that Morgan Lewis, the Livingston in-law, would defeat the Vice-President, came out for Lewis instead.

A short time later when Burr killed Hamilton in their duel and Governor George Clinton replaced Burr as Jefferson's second Vice-President, the Clintons and the Livingstons had a political falling out in New York. Lewis was counting on Van Buren's local help in 1808 in his re-election contest. But now the young Kinderhook operator switched his support to the Clinton candidate, Daniel D. Tompkins. "Happy Dan" Tompkins, as he was called, was probably the initiator of the politician's customs of remembering names, slapping backs and kissing babies. In gratitude for his victory, Tompkins did more than remember Van Buren's name and slap his back. He made him a surrogate judge in 1808 and gave him money to marry his cousin Hannah.

When Tompkins' chief sponsor, Vice-President George Clinton, died in 1812, family political control passed to nephew DeWitt Clinton, who was simultaneously mayor of New York and lieutenant governor as well as the "Peace party" Presidential candidate against President Madison that year. DeWitt Clinton was a person of substance, having been instrumental in establishing the state's public school system and having founded the Academy of Fine Arts, the New York Historical Association, the Literary and Philosophical Society and a hospital for the care of the insane. Later he would add to these by planning and developing the Erie Canal.

In 1812, Van Buren had won a seat in the state senate by fewer than two hundred votes over a Livingston in Columbia County. At that time, New York voters could not vote for President, and electors were chosen by the state legislature. For reasons never properly determined, DeWitt Clinton came to the conclusion that this legislative newcomer could advance his cause and he asked Van Buren to serve as his floor leader in the special session that would select Presidential electors. Van Buren agreed, even though he had campaigned as a war candidate and as a supporter of Madison. When New York's twenty-nine electoral votes went to Clinton, the Peace party and Federalist candidate, the young state senator's stock rose as "the Little Magician."

But shortly afterward when he determined that Clinton had no chance for 1816, he became a loud advocate of the war preparation measures advocated by Governor Tompkins, Clinton's protégé. Clinton was furious and broke with Van Buren, but Van Buren cared little because he was now known as a kingmaker. When he advocated the first conscription act in the country for amassing an army, the Madison Administration took notice of him and offered public praise for his patriotism. And when he told "Happy Dan" Tompkins he would support him for President in 1816, the governor became his enthusiastic admirer.

By now Van Buren had allied himself with Tammany Hall, whose members were known as "Bucktails" because they wore a buck's tail on their hats. In 1811, the Tammany tribes had abandoned the "Pig Pen," as Brom Martling's Tavern was called, for a new $11,000 wigwam, and the Bucktails made "Matty Van" the honorary Grand Sachem of the Eagle Tribe. Now when he told Tompkins he could count on Bucktail support for President, Happy Dan was willing to break with his sponsor Clinton and move into the Van Buren party. Tompkins went into the War of 1812 as a military commander to help his national reputation, and though he offered a commission to Van Buren, the senator remained a civilian. However, his friend Washington Irving accompanied the governor as his aide-de-camp. Ever whimsical, Irving wrote that Happy Dan's horse always threw him to the ground whenever a gun sounded, and his chief duty was to chase the steed and bring him back.

New York was an excellent proving ground for gutter politics by all parties. Elections were maneuvers in vote miscounting and stealing, demagogic appeals to the prejudices of voters, character assassinations and often physical violence. There was no way to remain in high office without such skulduggery. Tammany Hall was no worse or better than its competitors. Dedicated to the securing of graft through public contracts and jobs for its henchmen, Tammany operated under a state charter as a charitable body "for the purpose of affording relief to indigent and distressed widows and orphans."

By the time war ended in 1815, Van Buren had gained control not only of the legislative caucus but also of the state's patronage because of his power over the New York Council of Appointments. Men who clustered about him were now called "the Holy Alliance." Tompkins made him attorney general of New York that year and he retained his seat in the senate while he ran the state's legal arm. As he had promised, he saw to it that the New York legislative caucus nominated Happy Dan for President and Van Buren traveled to Washington to lobby in his behalf at the March 1816 Congressional nominating caucus. However, the best he could do for Tompkins was to engineer his selection as Monroe's running mate and Happy Dan served two terms as Monroe's Vice-President.

In 1815, Tompkins had shown his independence from Clinton by removing him from the office of mayor of New York City and appointing John Ferguson, the Grand Sachem of Tammany. But in 1817, Clinton was overwhelmingly elected governor to succeed Tompkins and in 1819 removed Van Buren from the post of attorney general. However, with the aid of the Bucktail wing of the Republicans, Van Buren still held control of the state legislature and the large patronage. Once when the Federalists had one more man in the Assembly than the Republicans, Van Buren had a Federalist ousted on the ground that many voters in his district had written "Hen" on their ballots instead of "Henry." When he learned that political enemies in opposition parties sought to make up and combine, he would go to each with false tales in order to keep their enmity alive. When he could not muster sufficient votes to kill a bill, he saw to it that it was re-written before passage into a jumble of nonsense.

Those who despised Van Buren made frantic efforts to prove that he was involved in political graft. It was known that he had amassed a fortune of $250,000 and controlled two newspapers, the Albany *Argus* and the New York *Advocate*. But no evidence of personal aggrandizement was ever uncovered, and Van Buren's claim that he made his money from a lucrative law practice went unchallenged. Nor could the Clinton Republicans make much gain from a charge of nepotism because of Clinton's own past record. As a result, with political impunity, Van Buren made his father-in-law, a hat-maker, the state treasurer; a brother-in-law, the state printer; a brother, a surrogate judge; another brother, clerk of the court; Ben Butler, his law partner, a district attorney; William Marcy, an editor on his New York paper, the adjutant general of New York.

On the national scene, Vice-President Tompkins felt so indebted to Van Buren that he feared offending him. Through pressure on the Monroe Administration, Van Buren obtained permission to use the Brooklyn Navy Band as the parade band for the Bucktails, had some New York postmasters fired and replaced with Bucktails, and by special prodding of Happy Dan won a Cabinet place for Smith Thompson, his lieutenant on the New York Supreme Court, as Monroe's Secretary of the Navy in 1818.

Tompkins' worst humiliation came in 1820 when Van Buren ordered him to return home and run for governor against DeWitt Clinton, even while serving as Vice-President. Tompkins did as he was told, though he lost when the Clintonians uncovered a shortage of $100,000 in his accounts during his previous terms as governor. However, Van Buren saved his hide with a two-day speech in the state senate and some swift alignments of his followers that resulted in an apology to Tompkins and an award of $12,000. But Happy Dan's spirit was broken by this experience and he crawled back to Washington for another four years as Vice-President—and a pathetic alcoholic ending.

When he became governor, Clinton hoped to extend his control over the New York delegation to Congress. However, he had to compete with Van Buren in this. In 1819, when a U. S. Senate seat became available, Clinton put up John C. Spencer as his candidate. But Van Buren humiliated him by pushing through the Republican legislature the re-election of Rufus King, a Federalist and the state's first Senator back in 1789. Then in 1821, when Clinton promoted the re-election of New York's other Senator, Nathan Sanford, who was one of his henchmen, Van Buren offered himself as a candidate and won the approval of the New York legislature.

He was two days short of his thirty-ninth birthday when he was sworn in as Senator on December 3, 1821. His Holy Alliance back at Albany ruled in his absence as the "Albany Regency" now, though it was known that he was still boss. Van Buren's wife Hannah had died in 1819 and he had parceled out their four sons to friends and relatives. As a young and carefree widower and a man of impeccable taste in clothes and manners, he was soon swept up by Washington's society leaders and matchmakers. But the only definite proposal of marriage he made came on a visit to Virginia in 1822 when he asked Ellen Randolph, granddaughter of Thomas Jefferson, to be his bride. According to Ellen's sister, she rejected the offer because she did not want to become a stepmother.

As a Senator, Van Buren gained a reputation for non-committalism. Rufus King said that when his colleague arrived at the Capitol, "he will not be there two weeks until he knows every man's opinion, but none will know his." Van Buren himself in his autobiography tells of the occasion when some Senators approached him and asked if he was of the opinion that the sun rose in the east. He replied: "As I never get up till after dawn I can't really say." A story became popular regarding a tariff speech he once made. A wool buyer in the audience remarked to his friend that it was "a very able speech." His friend agreed but added, "Mr. Knower! On what side of the tariff question was it?"

Yet despite this reputation, the pattern of his votes and speeches in the Senate revealed that he favored internal improvements, a high protective tariff, restrictions on slavery and a law against imprisonment for debt. His Senate desk was behind that of Senator Andrew Jackson, and one day when Van Buren stood up and reversed his vote on a measure, Jackson spun about and yelled, "You give way, sir!" In reply, Van Buren was off on a long and over-sincere explanation. "Before I had finished," he later recalled, "he stopped me and earnestly begged my pardon."

In 1824, he served as campaign manager for William Crawford

of Georgia in the Presidential contest against Jackson, Adams and Clay, and in payment the Georgia legislature nominated him for Vice-President. Afterward, he moved into the Jackson camp and became the Jackson party's Senate leader to hold President Adams up to ridicule and thwart his national program. As chairman of the Senate Judiciary Committee, he also went after John Marshall's Supreme Court. He attacked one proposal to relieve the justices of circuit court duty on the ground that in the secrecy of the Supreme Court rooms the incompetent judges were shielded by the abler judges. On circuit duty, he said, the judges would be exposed to public view and the people could see their poor quality.

DeWitt Clinton was also a strong Jackson supporter, and in fact had publicly acclaimed him in 1824 while Van Buren was busy with the Crawford campaign. This would have weakened Van Buren's authority within the Jackson party, but fortunately for him Clinton died in February 1828. That year Van Buren ran on the Bucktail ticket for governor against his old lieutenant, Smith Thompson, after whom he had named his youngest son (Smith Thompson Van Buren). Thompson was then an Associate Justice of the U. S. Supreme Court and the candidate of the Adams-Clay National Republicans. Van Buren won, but with only a plurality because the Anti-Masonic party had also entered a candidate. Thompson, who had wisely not resigned his Supreme Court seat to run for governor, returned to the Court and remained until his death in 1843.

Gossip had it that Van Buren had been offered the prime Cabinet post by Jackson even before he ran for governor. Denials were many on the part of Van Buren, who was sworn in as governor on January 1, 1829. He was soon involved in reorganizing the state's jobs to place his loyal followers into rewarding positions. When he named his lieutenant, Marcy, to the state Supreme Court, he wrote that the financially embarrassed Marcy "was so situated that I must make him a judge or ruin him."

He also attacked New York's banking problem and the many scandals then prevailing in the granting of charters to those who wanted to operate a bank. And to take the steam out of a rising political opponent named Thurlow Weed, who was using the agitation of Anti-Masonry to oppose Van Buren, he ordered the prosecution of the murderers of William Morgan, whose disappearance had given rise to the new political party. Then on March 12, 1829, after two months in office, he abruptly resigned to become Jackson's Secretary of State, to be followed as minister to Britain, Vice-President and political heir.

Friend and foe alike were agreed that Jackson had rigged the Presidential election for Van Buren. Matty Van had cultivated the old general with outlandish compliments, played on his prejudices and emotions and revealed excellent ability as loyal Secretary of State, party politician and spoilsman. His approach to Jackson was once described as "a perfect bedside manner." Along the way he demolished John C. Calhoun, The Hero's first-term Vice-President and enemy, and became his necessary replacement in the second term. It was, therefore, inevitable that he should be amply rewarded. Jackson had staged the Democratic national convention at Baltimore in May 1835, almost eighteen months before the election. The earlier he could settle the succession, he realized, the less possibility existed for a revolt. As it was, the legislatures of Alabama and Tennessee opposed Van Buren's nomination but Jackson forced him on the convention.

Nor was Jackson content merely to control the Presidential nomination. Colonel Richard Mentor Johnson, one of the young War Hawks of the Congress that had forced the War of 1812 on President Madison, had also to be installed at the Baltimore convention as Van Buren's running mate. It was Jackson's belief that the Whigs would put up a military candidate and Johnson would help offset that probability. The thick-set, handsome Kentuckian had fought at the Battle of the Thames, the river east of Detroit in Canada, and still bragged that he had killed Tecumseh, the brilliant Shawnee chief, who had fought on the side of the British. His Kentucky troops had returned from the war with razor strops they claimed had been cut from Tecumseh's carcass.

However, Jackson wanted "Tecumseh" Johnson on the ticket as Vice-President for a far more vital reason than his military background. Johnson, a colorful figure who sported a bright red waistcoat in public, posed a threat to Van Buren's nomination unless he were placated. Over the years since the war he had emerged as the darling of eastern radical and workingmen's groups because he had championed the downtrodden debtor class in his home state. He also laid claim to a reputation as the champion of religious liberty because as chairman of a U. S. Senate committee he had killed a proposal of religious extremists for legislation to bar the transportation of mail on Sundays.

But Johnson had a serious political drawback in the South that should have prompted Jackson and Van Buren to keep him off the ticket at all cost. While many southern planters were intimate with female slaves, they followed the planter's code and did so clandestinely. Johnson, however, openly flaunted his relationship with Negro girls. He made no secret of the fact that Julia Chinn, his mulatto housekeeper, was the mother of his two daughters. In fact, he not only gave them his name but he educated them well and found white husbands for them.

Upon Julia's death from cholera in 1835, he had selected a mulatto successor, and when she ran off with an Indian, he organized a hunt-down search. After catching her, he sold her as a slave and then brought her younger sister into his home as his "wife." A Kentuckian neighbor complained: "She is some eighteen or nineteen years of age and quite handsome, plays on the piano, calls him *my dear colonel* and is called *my dear* in return. How can he expect friends to sustain him when he shamelessly lives in adultery with a buxom young Negro wench?"

Despite Jackson's enormous prestige within the Democratic party, Southerners at the Baltimore convention did not take kindly to putting Johnson on the ticket with Van Buren. William Cabell Rives of Virginia, a U. S. Senator and formerly Jackson's minister to France, proved a persistent contender and when Johnson barely eked out the necessary two-thirds vote over him, hisses accompanied the announcement of his victory. The Virginia delegation, 108 strong, declared that the state would never accept the Kentuckian as a Democratic nominee.

Besides Virginia's opposition to Johnson as Vice-President, Van Buren soon found himself opposed by four Whigs. The Whig party, created in 1834 from a coalescence of the John Quincy Adams-Henry Clay National Republicans, the Thurlow Weed-Thaddeus Stevens Anti-Masonic party and the dissident anti-Jackson Democrats like John Bell of Tennessee and John Tyler of Virginia had condemned national conventions in 1836 as another form of the Congressional "King Caucus."

In its place, the Whigs had concocted a clever plan. State conventions in the four sections of the country were to nominate the strongest Whig available in their section. If each of these candidates could beat Van Buren in his area, this should force a play-off election in the House of Representatives, where the Whigs hoped to control the selection of the next President. In New England

the Whigs put up Senator Daniel Webster, "godlike" Dan the
Orator; the South nominated Senator Willie Mangum of North
Carolina to represent the Nullifiers and pro-slavery forces, even
though Mangum never tired of telling of his education at the
famous all-white Raleigh, North Carolina school run by John
Chavis, a freed Negro; western Whigs chose General William
Henry Harrison, the Whig military hero of 1812; and the Tennessee border nominated Senator Hugh White, Jackson's old In-
dian-fighting companion, who had broken with him over his hard-
money policy and who was now browbeaten into the Presidential
contest by his ambitious new wife, a former Washington boardinghouse keeper and divorcée.

It was a nasty campaign, the first in which candidates traveled
about to make speeches, distribute campaign biographies and praise
themselves. Colonel Johnson had not only a biography but also
a play to depict his bravery at the October 5, 1813, engagement
against the Indians and British at the Thames River. The cruelest
and most effective piece of literature was a biography of Van
Buren, written by a friend of Senator White and issued under Davy
Crockett's name. The so-called Crockett biography opened the
Jackson heir to sledgehammer ridicule and forevermore tarnished
Van Buren historically.

Said the ghostwritten biography about Vice-President Van Buren:
"When he enters the Senate chamber in the morning, he struts
and swaggers like a crow in the gutter. He is laced up in corsets,
such as women in a town wear and, if possible, tighter than the
best of them. It would be difficult to say from his personal appearance whether he was man or woman, but for his large red
and gray whiskers." He is "as opposite to General Jackson as dung
is to a diamond . . . secret, sly, selfish, cold, calculating, distrust-
ful, treacherous . . . It is said that at a year he could laugh on one
side of his face and cry on the other at one and the same time."

There were other charges against Van Buren that the Whigs
spread. They called him in the South the champion of free Negro
suffrage, and in areas where there was prejudice against immigrants they labeled him the friend of the Pope—"the fawning
sycophantic flatterer of a foreign tyrant." In areas where there
had been a great influx of European newcomers, the Whigs charged
Van Buren with being against immigrants, a charge he tried to
counteract with the distribution of his biography in German. This
book described him as having German (not Dutch) ancestors, a

German heart and a German mind. Thurlow Weed's Albany paper called Van Buren a "profligate, dangerous, demagogue, corrupt, pervert, prostitute and political huckster."

There were also whispering campaigns about Jackson's would-be successor. One widely spread story called him the illegitimate son of Aaron Burr. Old Kinderhook residents claimed to recall that Burr had frequented the Abraham Van Buren tavern on trips to and from Albany the year before Martin was born. John Quincy Adams believed this story and noted in his diary, "There is much resemblance in character, manner and even person, between the two." How else, asked some, could you explain the fact that when Burr returned penniless and in disgrace from Europe after his treason trial, Van Buren took him into his home and fed him? Other whisperers called Van Buren a midget. This reference to his size incensed Jackson, and even a half dozen years later he was writing: "Instead of a dwarf Dutchman, a little dandy who you might lift out of a bandbox, the people found him a man of middle size, plain and affable."

At last the national mudslinging ceased and the election results became known. In the popular vote, the multiple-candidate Whig plan almost succeeded, for Van Buren showed only a slim margin over his four regional opponents' total—762,678 to 735,250. But in the electoral total, where it counted, Van Buren had a clear majority with 170 of the 294 votes. Colonel Johnson was not so fortunate in his race for Vice-President. When Virginia refused to give her 23 electoral votes to him, his total was only 147, or one short of a majority. Jackson found the independent electors guilty of "depraved morals." This Virginia action pushed the contest into the Senate for settlement, as required by the Twelfth Amendment. And when Johnson defeated the rabid anti-Mason Whig, Francis Granger of New York, he became the only Vice-President in history to undergo this ordeal.

There was only a single triumphant moment for Van Buren during his entire four years as President. It came at his inauguration, a ceremony to which he rode with the ailing old Hero in an open four-wheel carriage made from boards off the body of the frigate *Constitution*. The fifty-five-year-old "Little Magician" gazed out upon the twenty thousand cheering Democrats crowded at the Capitol's East Portico and he found a mood of joy. Jackson, with whom the crowd was in complete emotional rapport, viewed the scene as a vindication of his own eight years in office. His watery

eyes studied Van Buren whom the Senate had rejected as his minister to Britain, and then they turned to Roger Taney, the unkempt Chief Justice of the Supreme Court, who had previously
been turned down by that same body as an Associate Justice.
Jackson later recalled proudly that here was Van Buren, "once
rejected by the Senate, sworn into office by Chief Justice Taney,
also being rejected by a factious Senate."

In his address, Van Buren called attention to his being the first
President born after the Revolutionary War. In his supreme
moment, he foresaw continuing prosperity everywhere in the land
and described his fellow Americans as "a great, happy and flour-
ishing people" with "an aggregate of human prosperity surely not
elsewhere to be found."

Little did he realize he was really astride a powder keg with
the angry fuse sputtering in his face. A month earlier, Senator
Tom Benton of Missouri had beckoned him into the privacy of the
Senate Finance Committee room to warn him about an approaching depression. "Your friends think you a little exalted in the head
on that subject," Van Buren scoffed at Old Bullion. This led the
hooknosed, pompous Benton to reply icily, "You will soon feel the
thunderbolt."

There was cause enough for the thunderbolt. By legislation and
edict, Jackson had been busily cutting the underpinnings from the
economy. Strangely, his actions in this area were immensely popular politically with the same people who would soon be ruined
financially by his folly. His successful fight against Nicholas Biddle's
Second Bank of the United States may have wrecked that mo-
nopolistic money structure. But it also destroyed the Bank's steady-
ing hand over the nation's credit and the value of paper money.

By vetoing the Bank's recharter and withdrawing government
funds from its branch vaults, Jackson flung wide open the door
to wildcat banks and round-the-clock printing of unbacked paper
money, to feed the national mania for speculation. The lines in
front of the land offices were so long that the expression "doing
a land-office business" developed. When loans fell due, banks obligingly extended additional credit to pay off the interest on the
first loan and provide paper funds to buy more land. In only
four years the sale of public land leaped 600 per cent in acreage
count, while the number of banks doubled to a total of 788 by
1837.

The Hero had also compounded the mess by his effort to com-

bat the wild inflation. The enormous paper profits reported induced even the poorest to take out loans and gamble on winning
a fortune in skyrocketing prices on public lands. Senator Benton
and Jackson agreed that something had to be done to correct this
situation. Said Benton: "I did not join in putting down the paper
currency of a national bank to put up a paper currency of a
thousand banks."

Jackson's response had been his Specie Circular of July 1836.
In an effort to halt land speculation and deal a blow at the
spread of unbacked paper money, he decreed that only gold or
silver would be acceptable payment for public land. This jarred
speculators, wildcat banks and even respectable banks. Eastern
conservative banks that promised to pay specie on demand for
their paper looked with horror at the flight of specie from the
East to the West with the promulgation of Jackson's Specie
Circular.

But Jackson also signed the Surplus Distribution Act, which
pulled on the economy from another direction. This act was a
promise by the government to distribute all Federal surplus revenue over $5,000,000 to the states, according to their representa-
tion in Congress. State and local governments assured of a windfall of $37,000,000 in four installments within the year immediately
went on a building binge of canals and roads with promises to pay
contractors from the Federal bounty when it arrived. Asked later
why he signed a bill that added inflationary fuel to overpapered
local economies, Jackson said he did so only because he believed
it was needed to help Van Buren win the 1836 election.

The depression swept in like a fury the same month Van Buren
was inaugurated and it lingered seven years after prostrating the
nation. Philip Hone, wealthy New York Whig, said that Americans
had come to believe they could run faster, jump higher and leap
further than any other people. But the depression sapped their optimism and extroverted nature, and left in its stead the first questioning of the economy's basic strength.

Within the week after Van Buren took office, the first financial
failures were reported. The cotton market had collapsed in England late in 1836. To raise cash, foreign investors had begun a
mad scramble for specie by unloading the American stocks they
held. This in turn drained whatever specie eastern banks had not
sent to the West to meet land purchase requirements. Then
frightened eastern depositors demanded that their accounts be

closed out by specie payment as promised. When the banks could not meet this, many were forced to close their doors.

During the first week in April, New York suffered more than one hundred commercial and bank failures. By the end of the month the number was too large to count. Producers, shopkeepers and consumers could not pay their bills. Factories shut down, throwing thousands out of work. The money plague fanned out to the West where speculators could not repay their loans and lost their property. Southern planters faced with a dead cotton market abroad and already heavily in debt to New Orleans and British merchants for next year's crop deserted their plantations by the hundreds. Many fled to Texas and it became common to refer to a missing planter as "G.T.T."—Gone to Texas. The American financial system had temporarily turned into a dead-end gully.

Unfortunately, the financial crash did not extend to prices, which continued high before receding slowly. A ton of coal cost $12, compared with less than half that price two years earlier. Flour had gone up almost threefold, from $5.62 a barrel to $18.25. As a result, unemployed people could not buy necessities and had to depend on private charity or starve. Suicide rates rose frighteningly; almshouses were soon overcrowded; prisons filled with the jobless who committed crimes so that they would be jailed and fed. In New York, five thousand persons attended a public protest meeting and a part of the crowd rioted afterward, smashing a flour warehouse and looting it. Riots by the poor and hungry also spread to Philadelphia, Baltimore and other cities. In Boston, businessmen met at Faneuil Hall where millionaire Abbott Lawrence condemned the Van Buren Administration and exhorted his audience with: "The time might come when the crew must seize the ship!"

Van Buren's reaction to the economic chaos was to ignore it. Congress was not to meet until December and in six months the trouble might disappear. But battle lines had formed immediately with the crisis: one side arguing for more inflation as a cure; the other, for even tighter money deflation. W. M. Gouge of the Treasury wrote Van Buren that the Specie Circular was "not powerful enough" rather than "too powerful . . . The disease under which the country is at this moment suffering is overtrading, produced by overbanking. The true remedy is to bank less and trade less." Jackson, fearing that his protégé would repudiate him, wrote him highly imaginative letters to keep him in line. "The people are everywhere becoming more aroused," he wrote from the isolation of the Hermitage, "and will sustain the Executive Government in any course that will coerce them to specie payments." The truth was that with paper money discredited and gold and silver vanished from commercial use, primitive bartering had returned as well as private printing of ticket money of exchange by businessmen in the cities. One card read: "This ticket will hold good for a sheep's tongue, two crackers and a glass of redeye."

The inflationists who opposed the Jacksonian financial policy were even more aggressive than Jackson in attempting to force their views upon Van Buren. On May 7, 1837, a fifty-man delegation representing New York merchants met with the President and bluntly insisted that he end the Specie Circular, "that unwise system which aimed at the substitution of a metallic for a paper currency." They also demanded that he recharter the Second Bank of the United States and continue payments to the states under the Surplus Distribution Act. Nicholas Biddle visited the White House to note the effect of the pressure put on the President and he reaffirmed the conclusion of the New Yorkers by calling Van Buren "profoundly silent upon the great and interesting topics of the day."

Van Buren still hoped for a quiet first term that would automatically pave the way to a second term and then to graceful retirement. But the continuation of the turmoil disturbed his equanimity, for the rich were threatening revolution unless he revived inflation and the poor were rioting for flour.

Not until two months after his inauguration when old, supposedly stable New York banks suspended specie payment on their notes did Van Buren publicly recognize the pervasive depression. The general banking collapse that followed on the heels of the May 10 action of the New York banks was threatening the stability of the Federal Government itself. For one existing law required that bank paper currency offered by individuals to pay taxes had to be backed by gold or silver. Another law required all "pet banks" that stored government revenues to pay hard money to the government upon demand.

With specie payments suspended, frantic government officials told Van Buren, the government would be unable to meet its bills and interest payments. Coupled with a reduction in expected revenues, the specie payment disavowal made the future look bleak indeed without Presidential action. It was at this juncture that Van Buren belatedly agreed that a general panic existed and took note of it by reluctantly calling a special session of Congress. However, he did not ask the legislators to come posthaste to Washington, but requested them instead to wait until September 4, more than three months away.

By September, the situation had worsened and the pressures on Van Buren to do something increased. Senator Rives, the disappointed candidate for the Democratic Vice-Presidential nomination, and Senator Nathaniel Tallmadge of New York arrived on the scene to lead the anti-Jacksonian Democrats. These two, who called their growing faction "Conservative Democrats," were actually leaders of the radicals, for what they advocated was an easy-money policy of unbacked paper money.

Months before—on March 15—Tallmadge had already revealed his hand to Van Buren. In a letter to the new President, he had brazenly warned him that the Whigs would win the 1838 Congressional elections unless he discarded Jackson's money policies, which he blamed for the depression. With Congress streaming into the Capitol, Tallmadge and Rives, without even a reprimand from the White House, immediately undertook to buttonhole Democratic Senator after Democratic Senator to vote alongside Whigs against continuing Jackson's Specie Circular. One Senator, Lewis Linn of Missouri, reported Tallmadge's great agitation as a lobbyist, and said he "trembled, walked the room, rubbed his hands together and recited." Tallmadge also invaded the lobbies of the House to ask Democratic members to oppose James K. Polk, the Van Buren choice to continue as Speaker, unless the President agreed to exclude Churchill C. Cambreleng from the House Ways and Means Committee and reform that committee "agreeable to the principle of the 'Credit System.'"

Tallmadge failed to defeat Polk. However, when his Conservative Democrats combined with the Whigs on economic matters, they could at will doom the Van Buren Democrats to a minority position. Tallmadge, who would later become a religious fanatic and devote his last years to writing religious tracts, possessed enormous powers to keep Congress in a state of agitation, even provoking duels between others. One duel involved young Jonathan Cilley of Maine, a Van Buren Democrat, who aroused the animosity of Henry A. Wise, a Virginia hothead Congressman who supported Rives and Tallmadge. William J. Graves of Kentucky, a friend of Wise, challenged Cilley to a duel for insulting Wise and killed him in February 1838.

By September 1837, the country was anxiously awaiting the President's Message to the Twenty-fifth Congress, for the summer had witnessed great suffering among the citizenry. What relief measures would he advocate? How did he propose to restore the economy? The answer came at last.

The domestic depression was really part of a worldwide financial crisis, Van Buren assessed, in an attempt to distribute some of the blame. Yet even so, he continued, the American economy would not have cracked up were it not for a wild overexpansion of business, excessive paper money, overextension of bank credit to poor risks, diversion of labor from farms, a drainage of gold from the United States to Europe and the foolish distribution of the Government's surplus revenues under the 1836 Surplus Distribution Act.

He refused to single out any chief culprit in the disaster but condemned the entire nation for greedily searching for unearned wealth. The "spirit of reckless speculation and the rapid growth among all classes of luxurious habits," he charged, were "founded too often upon merely fancied wealth." And now that the damage was done, what could the miscreants expect from him? "Those who look to the action of this government for specific aid to the citizen," he said bluntly, "lose sight of the ends for which it was created and the powers with which it is clothed . . . The less government interferes with private pursuits, the better for the general prosperity."

The shoe was on the other foot, he insisted. Rather than government helping citizens, it was the task of all to prevent the government from collapsing. No one should request the government's aid to help ease personal plight, but all had a duty to save the government. On this score, he had much to ask from Congress. He wanted bankruptcy action taken against the "pet banks" holding government revenues for suspending specie payment, approval to float a large Treasury note to meet current government expenses, the calling-off of the $9,000,000 fourth installment to the states due under the Surplus Distribution Act and the enactment of a Sub-Treasury or Independent Treasury measure to permit the government to store its funds in its own vaults.

"I feel as if I were on some other sphere," Daniel Webster complained after the Message, "as if this could not be America when I see schemes of public policy proposed, having for their object the convenience of government only, and leaving the people to shift for themselves." The President should use his authority to expand the economy, not induce further retrenchment, Webster argued. "Over-trading, over-buying, over-selling, over-speculation, over-production are terms I cannot well understand," he questioned the President's attack on the economic system. He would have Van Buren pay the last surplus installment due in October, return to depositing government funds in private state banks and establish a new paper currency instead of letting Senator Benton "embrace us in his gold and silver arms and hug us to his hard money chest."

Senator Henry Clay, gangling Kentuckian and the other Whig leader, followed a similar line of attack—"We are all—people, states, Union, banks—entitled to the protective care of a paternal government." In addition to defending paper money, he asked that the National Bank be re-established. In a mean fashion that was not his usual approach, Clay said that Van Buren had no more right to assume he had a mandate to oppose the Bank any more than he had to assume "that the people considered a little man of five feet with red face, sandy-colored whiskers, head inclined to baldness and downcast look, a model of human perfection."

Congress proceeded to pass the bulk of Van Buren's recommendations. However, it refused to approve the bill to declare bankrupt those specie-suspending banks holding government funds. "A war upon the whole banking system!" Tallmadge cried out effectively, while John Quincy Adams argued that the officers of those banks should be jailed as law violators. Van Buren considered his Sub-Treasury bill to divorce government from all private banking connections as his key piece of legislation, and suffered his worst defeat when this bill also failed. Primarily responsible for this were the lobbyists for the pet banks of special privilege. Although these pet banks incurred an expense in collecting government revenues and disbursing the receipts to pay government bills, they did not pay interest to the government for the millions stored in their vaults. These large sums they commonly lent to private parties at the going interest rates. So the permanent loss of this highly lucrative source of income was not a joyous prospect to the fifty-five banks involved. Tallmadge helped to kill the "Divorce Bill" by frightening other Congressmen with his scare call of "Locofoco, Fanny Wright and Tom Paine doctrines" in denouncing it. Fanny Wright was the era's zealous social reformer who openly advocated class warfare against "the booted and spurred riders."

In May 1837, when the banks suspended specie payment, the Treasury had begun to collect taxes directly and to store receipts in various government buildings. In a practical sense this made the Sub-Treasury Bill academic. However, Van Buren realized that without the divorce law, should the banks resume specie payment, the government would have to abandon its separate collection and storage if he wanted to avoid a continuous scrap with Congress.

Not until 1840 did the Sub-Treasury Bill pass Congress, and then only as a result of special events. In May 1838, Webster and Clay succeeded in pushing a bill through Congress repealing the Specie Circular. That same month when New York banks resumed specie payment with an assist from the Bank of England, which shipped a million pounds sterling to the United States, Van Buren seemed to be promoting a lost cause. However, a sharp economic tremor in 1839 in the midst of the depression forced the banks to suspend again. This lent credibility to the Democratic charge that state banks lacked stability.

Political infighting also aided its passage. When the Twenty-sixth Congress convened on December 2, 1839, the House membership stood at 120 Democrats and 118 Whigs, not counting the New Jersey delegation. Five New Jersey Whigs showed up bearing certification as Congressmen from the state's Whig governor, while five other New Jersey Democrats stepped forward at the same time to claim the identical seats. From the opening bell, the blasphemous, disordered debate that raged prevented the election of a Speaker and the organization of the House. Finally at the end of three days of anarchy, John Quincy Adams was chosen "Chairman" until a Speaker was elected. Two weeks of threats, fights and screaming followed before Whigs joined with southern Democrats to elect thirty-year-old Robert Hunter of Virginia, a Calhoun Democrat, as Speaker. Afterward, four months of the eight-month session evaporated in arguing the New Jersey dilemma before the five Democrats were seated. Sufficient votes then became available to pass the Sub-Treasury Bill.

When Van Buren finally signed it into law on July 4, 1840,

Frank Blair's *Globe* hailed it as "the Second Declaration of Independence." But the Act was repealed the following year by the next Administration, only to be reinstated in 1846. It then remained the law of the land until the Federal Reserve System produced a new solution in 1914.

The continuing depression plus a crop failure cast a dark shadow over Van Buren's Administration. But these were not the sole misfortunes to befall the ambitious President. His friends clamored for jobs but he could perform this service only by removing Jackson appointees. So he did little. Much more serious, the growing storm over slavery thrust him into a position where he could not avoid condemnation by both North and South. Dormant since the Missouri Compromise, the sectional argument had erupted again toward the close of the Jackson Administration and Van Buren inherited a pro-slavery program from his predecessor.

Jackson and Postmaster General Amos Kendall had brought about backstage rulings that effectively banned the delivery of "incendiary" (anti-slavery) literature through the mails in the South. In addition, the 1836 "gag rule" that had the blessing of The Hero automatically tabled anti-slavery petitions in the House. Not until December 3, 1844, through the continuous attacks of John Quincy Adams, was the House gag rule finally ended. Equally as emotion-laden was the question whether to annex Texas, the new slave pastureland recognized by Jackson.

Van Buren's quandary was enormous. He was essentially opposed to slavery, yet he was, as Senator John C. Calhoun put it, "a northern man relying on the South." It was better, he reasoned, to offer each section something tangible on slavery than to say nothing. That is why he became the first President to mention slavery in his inaugural address. In an attempt to balance off both sides, he had assured the North he would oppose the annexation of Texas; the South, that he would not end slavery in the District of Columbia nor "in the slightest interfere with it in the states where it exists." But he could not foresee that Calhoun would taunt the North ceaselessly, or that fanatic abolitionists would try to force Federal interference with the institution.

Van Buren and Calhoun had been sworn enemies since the days when Van Buren ruined the South Carolinian in the eyes of Jackson and succeeded him as The Hero's Vice-President and heir-apparent. As late as 1836, the dour Nullifier branded the

Jackson-Van Buren Democrats "a powerful faction held together by the hopes of public plunder." But only a year later when Van Buren proposed the Sub-Treasury Storage Bill, Calhoun walked into the White House to make amends. "Mr. President," he said in his tense manner, "you have removed the differences in our political relations. I have called to remove that of our personal differences." In Calhoun's imaginative philosophic view, Van Buren's proposal was a states' rights measure, while the Whig demand for a free paper inflationary currency was nationalism. Calhoun also considered the Sub-Treasury Bill as one that would sap northern capitalists, thereby increasing the economic strength of the South.

In the Senate, rigid, theoretical and humorless Calhoun hoped to trade on his reunion with Van Buren by getting the President to support his pro-slavery position. One Calhoun desire was to bring about a gag rule in the Senate similar to the one in the House. However, although Van Buren gave his tepid approval, Senate liberals under the leadership of Tom Benton successfully combatted Calhoun. "We gave notice, sir, that we were prepared to fight, yes, sir, to fight for freedom of debate," Benton jubilantly told Smith Thompson Van Buren, the President's youngest son. "We held out the prospect of the pistol, sir. Yes, sir, the pistol in one hand and the freedom of debate in the other, sir, and the other side shrank from the pistol, sir!"

Despite Calhoun's efforts to involve the Administration openly in a defense of slavery, Van Buren cautiously did little more than give him a warm smile. Calhoun had a complex plan to ensnare the President in a southern trap by forcing the Senate's views on him, and to this effect he introduced a group of Senate resolutions on December 27, 1837. These resolutions included one that asserted that the Union was a compact of the states and that the Federal Government had no authority to interfere in any manner with the exclusive power of the states over their domestic institutions. Another resolution placed slavery among the exclusive state powers, and still another declared that any refusal to annex a new territory or a state on the ground that slavery was a sin or immoral would, in effect, disenfranchise the slave states.

Van Buren found it wise to refrain from making comments on Calhoun's resolutions, and it was Henry Clay, leader of the Whigs, who finally stepped forward. An easy speaker, relaxed but colorful and dramatic, Clay pointed a long finger at the "cast-iron man" from South Carolina. Calhoun, he charged, had introduced "five or six as abstract resolutions, as a metaphysical mind can devise."

When Clay countered by offering his own mild resolutions, Calhoun descended to vile name-calling. He had trained himself to speak at the rate of 180 words a minute, and though his speaking voice was unmelodious his diction was such that his voice seemed to come from all parts of the Senate chamber at the same time. Clay possessed a defective mind, and was incapable of analyzing anything, said Calhoun to their colleagues. "He prefers the specious to the solid and the plausible to the true." Clay's robust reaction was as coarse as his adversary's tone. Calhoun was a man who led a clean personal life, he said, but his public life would result in his dying as a traitor or a madman. "His whole aim is to sow the seeds of dissension between the different parts of the Union, and thus prepare the way for its dissolution. His little clique, distinguished more by activity and paradoxes, rather than by numbers, is now busily endeavoring to propagate the notion that all the operations of the Federal Government, from the commencement, have been ruinous to the South, and aggrandizing the North. This, although forty years of the forty-eight, during which the Government has existed, have southern men directed the course of public affairs!"

Clay's milder resolutions passed, but the argument between the two did not subside. At the same time Clay came to the conclusion that he was not only doing Van Buren's work but he was also harming his own Presidential cause for 1840 in the South. So on February 4, 1839, he made a Senate speech in which he publicly espoused the position Van Buren had taken in his inaugural address. He said he opposed meddling with slavery in the capital and in the South. But he went even further and denounced the abolitionists for proposing immediate freedom for slaves. Abolition, he charged, would result in a violent war between whites and blacks "and beneath the ruins of the Union would be buried, sooner or later, the liberty of both races." He also insisted that the abolitionists had set back by a half century his work and that of others for gradual emancipation, and that their agitation had resulted in stimulating cruel and harsh treatment of Negroes throughout the South. No Senator was more pleased with his speech than Calhoun. Afterward, when Calhoun's cohort, Senator William Preston of South Carolina, told Clay that extremists on both sides were bound to condemn his speech, he said Clay's reply was: "I had rather be right than President."

In 1839, Van Buren entered the periphery of the argument when he sent a Message to Congress condemning the slave trade. Yet when an actual incident occurred he ended up opposing himself. This was the case of the Spanish slave ship, *L'Amistad,* carrying Negroes from Africa to Cuba. In June 1839, the slaves seized the vessel which was in turn taken by a U.S. ship off the coast of Connecticut. Fearing an emotional outpouring by northern agitators, Van Buren sent word to the U.S. district court considering the issues involved that if the court ruled for the Spanish slave importers, he would immediately thrust the Negroes aboard a frigate and deliver them to Cuba. This would preclude prolonged legal appeals and public clamor. However, despite his behind-the-scene activities, the case went to the Supreme Court where, with old John Quincy Adams defending the Africans, the Negroes were set free.

Even while Calhoun and Clay carried on over slavery and Americans were grimly trying to survive the worst of the depression, another Jackson albatross around Van Buren's neck came to life. During Jackson's Administration, Van Buren had opposed the appointment of Sam Swartwout as Collector of the Port of New York. But Swartwout, who had been an aide to Colonel Aaron Burr in his Southwest Conspiracy, was Jackson's personal friend and got the job. Suddenly in 1838 Swartwout stunned the nation by becoming the first government employee in history to abscond with more than a million dollars of public funds. Investigation revealed that General Swartwout's staff was no more honest than he, nor was the New York district attorney, William M. Price, who embezzled customhouse money and followed Swartwout safely to Europe.

The taint fell naturally on the incumbent President and he made a show of rectitude by naming his New York crony, Jesse Hoyt, as Swartwout's replacement to cleanse the New York customhouse from top to bottom. But Hoyt compounded the scandal by fleeing New York in 1841 with a $350,000 take. A subsequent Congressional investigation uncovered proof that he had stolen customs receipts for personal stock speculation and had corrupted the whole New York customhouse, defied the Secretary of the Treasury and entered into fraudulent relations with American importers. His five hundred patronage employees were found to be a wretched lot of grafters and bribe demanders.

During all this jarring hubbub another inherited Jackson program erupted to Van Buren's disadvantage. Jackson's ruthless policy of uprooting all Indian tribes east of the Mississippi and dragging them to reservations across the river was only in mid-passage when Van Buren entered office. In Florida, the Seminoles under a half-breed named Powell who called himself Osceola had proved especially warlike about accepting The Hero's displacement program. Jackson had sent General Winfield Scott to Florida to clean out the Everglades, but soon losing patience with him he hauled him out to appear before a court of inquiry on the charge of failing to prosecute the extirpation of the Seminoles with vigor. Scott rubbed many people the wrong way because of his outspoken nature. In 1809, General Wilkinson, Burr's traitorous partner, had court-martialed him for calling Wilkinson "as big a traitor as Burr." In 1817, after he called a Jackson order "mutinous," the two almost dueled. Then in 1828 when General Jacob Brown died, Scott was nasty to President Adams for passing him over and naming General Alexander Macomb as Brown's successor to command the 6000-man U. S. Army.

The Seminole chief Osceola was neither an angel nor a poor warrior. In one quick action, his Seminoles succeeded in killing the Federal agent in charge of their migration, the Army major detailed to move them and 107 of his 111 soldiers. When Van Buren became President, Osceola asked General Thomas S. Jesup, who had replaced Scott, for a flag of truce. But Jesup hoped for glory and treacherously seized him as a parole violator and shipped him to Fort Moultrie in Charleston Harbor, where he died in a prison cell in January 1838. National sympathy lay on the Seminole chieftain's side and the President found himself denounced as a tyrant.

In 1838, Van Buren sent Scott to convince 16,000 Cherokees in South Carolina and Tennessee that they should go West without a fight. The six and a half foot tall and 275-pound Scott learned the Cherokee language, lived with them and accompanied them part way to the Mississippi. But instead of winning praise for this peaceful move, Van Buren received only press brickbats. For in a period of general retrenchment, publication of figures showing government expenditures of $14,000,000 for the Cherokee move and the continuing war with the Seminoles brought condemnation on Van Buren for being a wastrel.

On the northern border, the Canadian line erupted into two worrisome situations that might have led to another war with England. In both instances, Van Buren maintained an unswerving neutral policy which hotheads described as cowardice.

Discontent had arisen in Canada with the lack of adequate local political liberties and authority. Late in 1837, William L. Mackenzie led a rebellion in Upper Canada and Louis J. Papineau led another in Lower Canada. Upper Canada, which centered about Toronto, did not sweep Mackenzie into power, nor did Lower Canada, centering about Quebec, put Papineau in charge. Both men had to flee into the United States to avoid capture, and Mackenzie continued the rebellion from Buffalo where he recruited American volunteers for his army.

International violence came in December 1837, when at the instigation of Mackenzie his American "Patriots" seized Navy Island, a Canadian possession just above Niagara Falls. Mackenzie established a provisional government on the island, produced a flag and great seal and issued paper money. Within a month, several hundred Patriots were on Navy Island under arms and ready for war. To get supplies they chartered the steamer *Caroline*. Canadian Loyalists, learning this, crossed over to Schlosser, on the U.S. shore one night, killed an American guarding the ship, and towed the *Caroline* to the middle of the river where they set fire to her and sent her to drift over the Falls.

An immediate outcry was heard throughout the United States over this violation of American territory, though nothing was said of the capture of Navy Island. Henry Clay called the seizure of the *Caroline* "a most unparalleled outrage," and forgetting the trouble he had caused in 1812 as leader of the War Hawks, he said that "if it should be war with Great Britain . . . it would be a just war."

However, the sobering status as President put Van Buren above reckless words and deeds. Almost all of the small American Army was engaged in Indian affairs in the South and could not be shifted to the Canadian border. In addition, he knew that he was without power to call out state militias to prevent forays into Canada. Nevertheless, on January 5, 1838, he issued a proclamation declaring that all violators of American neutrality would be punished. Then he quickly asked Congress for a neutrality act giving him authority to call out state militias to guard against attacks on friendly nations by American citizens. Congress complied and gave him this additional Presidential power in March.

At the same time that he issued his January proclamation, Van Buren sent General Scott by himself to the border to bring about a settlement. Scott, whose size alone commanded respect, succeeded on January 13 in getting the American Patriots on Navy Island to abandon the island and return to the United States. This single act broke the back of the hopeful plan of border states to wrest Canada from Britain, though sporadic and serious fighting continued a few years. Many British ships on the St. Lawrence were fired upon and some were destroyed. In May 1838, Patriots attacked and ruined the British steamer *Sir Robert Peel* at Oswego on Lake Erie and in November they mounted a large attack on the town of Prescott across the St. Lawrence from Ogdensburg, New York. In total, Canadian authorities arrested 900 Americans and executed several. At one time Van Buren planned to send his son John and Senator Wright to Canada to seek the release of Americans captured at Prescott, but he abandoned the idea because it would give the impression he did not believe in his own policy of neutrality. Mackenzie, who continued his recruiting efforts at Buffalo and elsewhere, was arrested, indicted, tried and convicted in 1839. When Van Buren refused to pardon him until he served two-thirds of his sentence, border state papers denounced him as "a British tool." Presidential neutrality was so unpopular that large-scale defections in Democratic ranks took place from New York to Michigan. In Van Buren's own bailiwick of New York, for example, "Little Billy" Seward, the Whig candidate, trounced the President's lieutenant and incumbent governor, "Big Bill" Marcy in the 1838 election.

By 1840 the *Caroline* affair was beginning to fade as an emotional issue when in November a Canadian named Alexander McLeod bragged in an American tavern that he had killed an American aboard the ship. He was thrown into jail and despite British diplomatic demands that he be released, Van Buren refused, declaring that the national government lacked jurisdiction over New York courts. McLeod was later discovered to be a liar.

Canadian rebellion was not the sole cause of friction along the northern border, for the "Aroostook War" of 1838 also required much Presidential attention. The 1783 Treaty of Paris establishing peace between the United States and Britain had placed the northeastern boundary between Maine and Canada "along the Highlands which divide those rivers that empty themselves into the

River St. Lawrence from those that fall into the Atlantic Ocean."
The treaty map delineating the exact line was unfortunately mis-
placed.

However, the definition seemed clear until the wealth of the
area between the St. Lawrence and the Atlantic Ocean was ex-
plored. Rich timberlands existed south of the St. John River and
Maine citizens claimed the area through the river zone to the
north. Canada, however, argued that the St. John emptied into
the Bay of Fundy, north of the waters where the Bay became
technically the Atlantic Ocean. To this, the State Department
countered that the Bay was actually a part of the Atlantic, even
though that span of water had a different name. Therefore, said
the U. S. Government, the St. John River emptied into the Atlantic Ocean.

The St. John dispute had erupted earlier during the John
Quincy Adams Administration in 1826. Both countries had then
agreed to the King of Holland as arbiter, and the King cautiously
ruled that the 1783 Treaty was "inexplicable." His final decision
was a compromise, awarding two-thirds of the area in question
to Canada. To this the British Government assented, but the state
of Maine refused.

In 1838, when Americans and Canadians took to shooting at
each other in the disputed territory, Britain called off the Dutch
settlement. After this, Canadian timber cutters rushed into the
Aroostook River Valley to cut the trees. Maine responded by calling out the Maine militia and voting almost a million dollars to
fight the "Aroostook War." In short order most of the territory fell
into the hands of Maine militiamen who were soon busily engaged building impregnable fortresses.

While Van Buren told Maine's leaders that he was proposing
arbitration to Britain and that they should not kill Canadians,
Henry Clay again spoke in favor of a "just war." And despite the
shaky condition of the government, Congress authorized Van
Buren to call out 50,000 volunteers and gave him $10,000,000 to
carry out needed activities.

Although reports came that New Brunswick and Nova Scotia
were preparing for war with the United States, Van Buren made no
effort to build up a combative military force. Instead, he again
called on General Scott to go to the troubled area for a last effort
to settle the dispute. Scott traveled north, made friends with members of the Maine legislature and held long conversations with
Lieutenant Governor Harvey of New Brunswick. Afterward, Van

Buren's personal friend, Governor John Fairfield of Maine, agreed
to withdraw his militia from the Aroostook Valley, while Harvey
gave assurances that Canadian troops would also stay out pending
an arbitration settlement. But instead of local pleasure at the announcement, the reaction in Maine was one of angry contempt
for the President and an immediate swelling of Whig ranks.

On another border, Van Buren's policy won him many friends.
This was in the West where distrust of an Easterner had cost him
the sixty electoral votes of Kentucky, Tennessee, Indiana and Ohio
in 1836. The West loomed large in his hopes for 1840, and whether
from a late-developed conviction or from design, he espoused the
frontier land program of Senator Benton. With the Clay Whigs
hammering away against low selling prices for public lands, Benton had been promoting the opposite policy. Chief among his
planks were Pre-emption and Graduation. Pre-emption would
grant squatters the right to buy their land for $1.25 an acre, no
matter how much others were willing to bid for it. Graduation
would periodically lower the price of land the longer it remained
unsold.

A Graduation bill could not get through the House, but temporary Pre-emption became law in 1838. However, Van Buren was to
find that while his stand gained him western support it cost him
eastern backing.

As the time for the 1840 campaign approached, Whig leaders
determined to avoid issues and concentrate on ridiculing Van
Buren. A depression-weary and border-wary people found him an
easy target for such criticism. Gross smears spread of the way he
lived as President. Whigs accused him of limitless spending sprees
of public money on himself while enforcing retrenchment on the
rest of the population.

As a Whig pointed out: "The cry of aristocracy takes with certain folks." The pendulum had swung from a point where the
people wanted a White House occupant to be wealthy, cultured
and snobbish to the other extreme where a man who did not
campaign in old clothes was considered with suspicion. Here was
Van Buren, unfortunately described as "rather an exquisite in appearance. His complexion was a bright blend and he dressed
accordingly." On one occasion he was pictured as wearing "an
elegant snuff-colored broadcloth suit with a velvet collar, his cravat
was orange with modest lace tips; his vest was of a pearl hue;

his trousers white duck; his shoes were morocco; his neat-fitting gloves were of yellow kid; his long-furred beaver hat with broad brim was of a Quaker hue." Attacks on Van Buren's colorful clothing led to a funereal restyling of men's attire that lasted until the mid-twentieth century.

When he became President, he found the White House shabby and spent $27,000 patching it here and there. This was a third of the sum Jackson had spent on the Executive Mansion, yet the Van Buren expenditure was made to appear as a tremendous waste of public money. He saved half his annual $25,000 salary, but imaginative Whigs pictured him as living like royalty. At the same time, Whigs made much sport of Vice-President Johnson, spreading stories of his mulatto concubine and his unusual between-Congressional-sessions activities. There was no need to embellish the stories about Johnson because they were true. When Congress adjourned he rushed back to Kentucky where he ran an inn with his young consort and sold watermelons to travelers. He was growing stout and gray and his speeches were becoming unbearably long and incoherent. Anyone could make him remove his shirt by asking to see the wounds he suffered at the Battle of the Thames.

A speech on the House floor by Representative Charles Ogle of Pennsylvania severely damaged Van Buren's dwindling reputation. Ogle described Van Buren's White House as "a palace as splendid as that of the Caesars, and as richly adorned as the proudest Asiatic mansion." Representative Levi Lincoln, who almost choked with choleric rage defending the shabbiness of the White House, replied that "in many of the rooms the gentleman would not lodge his Negro, if he kept one." He said the anteroom had "no mirror, no table except an old pine one in the corner and an old worn-out sofa worth five dollars."

Representative Ogle was further describing the "palace pile" as "170 feet front and 86 feet deep" and standing on twenty acres "surrounded by firmly built stone walls and lanceolated iron railings, with imposing portal abutments and well-barred iron gates." He said that the interior of the palace was crowded "with the costly fripperies of Europe." Then in words that would be read from border to border in a bestseller giveaway pamphlet, he added, "How delightful it must be to a genuine Locofoco to eat his pâté de foie gras, dinde désossée and salade à la volaille from a silver plate with a golden knife and fork. And how exquisite to sip with a golden spoon his soup à la reine from a silver tureen." Silver plates and gold knives and forks: these words were so repetitiously spouted that their mere mention immediately conjured up Van Buren's name.

There was just the slightest element of truth in the Whig stories about the so-called aristocrat in the White House, for the part of the Presidency that Van Buren enjoyed most was serving as the nation's Number One host. No one was a more affable host than he, even to those who were publicly denouncing him. And no one enjoyed the music more than he when the Marine Band struck up "Hail to the Chief," "Who'll Be King but Charlie" and a host of other sprightly airs in major keys.

While Whigs attacked him as an aristocrat, they were immensely pleased when he invited them to Presidential dinners and parties. John Quincy Adams, whose own Administration had been ruined by the vicious, disrupting attacks of the then Senator Van Buren, was a frequent guest at the White House. After one occasion, Adams wrote in his diary that the President "was, as usual, courteous to all, and particularly to me." Henry Clay left his name-calling behind on the Senate floor to come to the White House for a pleasant evening with the man he had just slandered. He said of Van Buren: "An acquaintance with him of more than twenty years' duration has inspired me with a respect for the man, although . . . I detect the magistrate." Van Buren was too shrewd to mistake the eagerness of politicians to attend his parties for friendship. Once during a levee, Clay sauntered up to him and remarked, "It must be pleasant to be surrounded by so many friends." Van Buren gave him a broad smile and replied, "Well, the weather is very fine." Many believed that with a man so friendly and relaxed, it would be simple to get him to divulge his thoughts on various matters. The bearded Whig poet, Henry Wadsworth Longfellow, had this notion, but afterward wrote to his father: "We talked about the weather, the comparative expense of wood and coal as fuel, and the probability that as the season advanced it would grow milder!"

One sign of a more high-toned atmosphere than that of his predecessor was his effort to restrict his guest list at levees. Captain Frederick Marryat described the change since Van Buren moved into the White House: "The police are now stationed at the door to prevent the intrusion of any improper person. A few years ago, a fellow would drive his cart, or hackney coach, up

to the door, walk into the saloon in all his dirt, and force his
way to the President, that he might shake him by one hand,
whilst he flourished his whip with the other. The revolting scenes
which took place when refreshments were handed round, the injury done to the furniture and the disgust of the ladies, may well
be imagined."

The widower President had no White House hostess until 1838,
when his eldest son Abraham married. Abraham was his private
secretary and his bride was lovely Angelica Singleton, niece of
Andrew Stevenson, the minister to Britain. She was also a close
relation of Dolley Madison and Senator William Preston, the
South Carolina Nullifier. Angelica introduced the hoop skirt, which
became the fashion rage. But she was otherwise the object of
much mouth-covered criticism by Washington society matrons because she wore three large ostrich plumes in her hair and received
White House guests while seated in a chair set on a raised platform.

Another Van Buren son, twenty-seven-year-old John, was to be
feared by the Whigs for more than a decade as a possible Presidential candidate. John was tall, handsome, charming and a gifted
speaker. A Whig press campaign tried to cut him down to size
by labeling him "Prince John." Prince John acquired this nickname originally because of a trip he made to Europe where he
was the dancing companion of the small, dumpy Princess Victoria
of Great Britain.

At the same time that the Whigs attacked Van Buren as an
aristocrat, they were also blistering him as a dangerous radical.
Workers were then slaving on farms from sunup to sundown and
in factories from six to six. Early in 1840 when Van Buren decreed a ten-hour day for laborers and mechanics on public works
projects, he was roundly condemned by business leaders for being
in league with left-wing Locofoco elements.

When Van Buren ran for re-election in 1840, he did not have
a chance against "Old Tippecanoe" Harrison. Nevertheless, when
he lost by a four to one electoral margin, he sincerely believed
his defeat was occasioned by Whig vote frauds. Still discounting
the severity of the depression, which was his chief legacy from
Jackson, he told the nation in his farewell address that he was
pleased that the country was in a state of "health, plenty and
peace."

He was certain as he set out for his acquired Van Ness estate in Kinderhook that he would be back because "the sober, second thought of the people is never wrong, and always efficient." But he was destined, after only a single term, to three unsuccessful efforts to recapture the Presidency and to the worst fate of all for a would-be elder statesman—being ignored and forgotten.

☆ 9 ☆

WILLIAM HENRY HARRISON

Old Whitey, Clodhopper President

Before the 1836 election, William Henry Harrison wrote from Ohio to his old friend, Stephen Van Rensselaer, the postmaster at Albany, New York: "I am the clerk of the Court of Common Pleas of Hamilton County at your service. But I have news still more strange to tell you, if you have not already heard. Some folks are silly enough as to have formed a plan to make a President of the United States out of this Clerk and Clodhopper."

The wonder is great that a man could have made the tremendous leap from this lowly position to the rank of his country's first citizen. But a greater wonder is why, outside of ego satisfaction, he should have desired the job. For his view of the Presidency was that the Chief Executive Tree should be topped, trimmed and sapped and a figurehead carved from the remains. "It is preposterous to suppose," he told the nation at his inauguration, "that the President . . . could better understand the wants and wishes of the people than their own immediate representatives." He would limit the President to a single term and make him inferior in power to Congress. The President must not promote a program through Congress, he insisted, vowing to prevent the formation of an Executive party within Congress to do his bidding. It was also his belief that the Founding Fathers committed a serious blunder when they did not make the Secretary of the Treasury "entirely independent of the Executive." On questions relating to the public revenue, he declared, "the further moved it may be from the control of the Executive, the more wholesome the arrangement."

Being on the public payroll was an obsession with General Harrison. From the Battle of the Thames, which he commanded on October 5, 1813, until his letter to Van Rensselaer, he had already run for ten offices. In seven of these contests, he suffered defeat, though his victories made him a member of the U. S. House of Representatives, the Ohio Senate and the U. S. Senate. His percentage was higher on landing appointive posts, with five successes out of twelve tries: secretary of the Northwest Territory, territorial governor of Indiana, major general in the U. S. Army, Indian commissioner, and minister to Colombia. President John Quincy Adams, badgered by Harrison for appointments, noted in his diary: "This person's thirst for lucrative office is positively rabid." He called him a man with an "active but shallow mind, a political adventurer not without talents but self-sufficient, vain and indiscreet. He has withal a faculty of making friends and is incessantly using them for their influence in his favor."

Harrison's maxim was *Nil Desperandum*. Born into an elite Virginia tidewater family and cousin of John Randolph, he did not appear to be a potential candidate for the desperation that frequently jarred his existence. Stout and gouty Benjamin Harrison, signer of the Declaration of Independence and a governor of Virginia, doted on William, his seventh and youngest child. After a classical education in Virginia, William went to Philadelphia to study medicine under Dr. Benjamin Rush, also a signer of the Declaration and the most renowned physician of his time. Rush's medical course consisted of two series of lectures each running sixteen weeks, after which students returned to their communities to commence operating on the local sick. William took only half the course lectures, enough to enable him to be his own doctor and minister to the numerous ailments that afflicted him throughout his life.

Soldiering interested him more than slaughter on the operating table and in 1791, he induced President Washington, his father's longtime companion, to commission him as an Indian fighter. When the Sixth Congress assembled in Philadelphia in 1799, he was there as a delegate from the Northwest Territory. Here he played a key role in winning approval for a split of the territory into Ohio and Indiana. Once this was done, he induced President John Adams to appoint him governor of the Indiana Territory in 1800 and he resigned as delegate at twenty-seven. It was during his dozen-year reign as absolute dictator over Indiana that he defeated The Prophet, brother of Tecumseh at Tippecanoe, Indiana, on November 7, 1811. This Wabash engagement won him romantic fame for a defensive action that he had provoked.

With the coming of the War of 1812, Harrison saw an opportunity for further glory. He began what turned out to be almost two decades of requests for appointment help from Henry Clay. Speaker Clay, then leader of the War Hawks, acted on one request and asked President Madison to name Harrison head of the American Army in the West. This did not come about and Harrison entered the fighting as a major general in the Kentucky militia, Clay's home state.

Having got into the fighting, Harrison revealed an astounding unsureness as a soldier in his letters to Clay during the summer of 1812. General Hull had surrendered Detroit without firing a shot and the British seemed on the verge of taking over the entire West. On August 29, Harrison wrote that his army was "in spirit equal to any that Greece or Rome ever boasted of, but destitute of artillery, of many necessary equipments, and absolutely ignorant of any military evolution." The following day he sent Clay a frenzied letter, beseeching him to leave his legislative work and come West to advise him how to operate his forces. "Your advice and assistance in determining the course of operations for the Army . . . will be highly useful." He complained bitterly that Clay was indeed responsible for getting him and the country into the war fiasco and therefore Clay should save both. "For God's sake, then," his pen cried, "come on to Piqua as quickly as possible."

But he settled down after that, though he underwent criticism because he let subordinates have full play and he would not enforce harsh discipline. When deserters were hauled back to camp, he refused to shoot them, sending them instead to guardhouse stays of two or three weeks. He was more or less surrounded by the three Johnson brothers—John, James and Richard Mentor—Kentucky admirers of Henry Clay. John was his aide, and James and Richard were field colonels. The latter two diluted Harrison's chief claim to wartime fame as the victor at the Battle of the Thames by loudly asserting they had done all the work.

A disagreement with Secretary of War John Armstrong led to Harrison's resignation from the Army in 1814. But he was once more back in public service when he won a House seat from Ohio in 1816. Before he left the House in 1819, he incurred the undying hatred of Andrew Jackson by voting to censure him for his brutality against the British and Spaniards in Spanish Florida during the Seminole fighting of 1818. Home again, Harrison found a place in the Ohio Senate, and after losing a race for the U. S. House of Representatives, he won the approval of the Ohio legislature in 1825 to take a seat as U. S. Senator.

In 1828, when President John Quincy Adams found it difficult to convince other National Republicans that it was their patriotic duty to be his running mate in that year's campaign against Jackson and Calhoun, Harrison fought strenuously for the Vice-Presidential berth. His unrelenting effort made Clay for the first time regard his entreaties with both suspicion and disgust.

When Richard Rush, the Treasury Secretary and son of Harrison's old medical school teacher, reluctantly agreed to run with Adams, Harrison turned his attention to other possibilities. Head of the Army Major General Jacob Brown died in 1828, and Congress was on the verge of abolishing the post of commanding general when Senator Harrison successfully opposed such action. He then pressured the Administration to appoint him as Brown's successor, but the President and the Cabinet had already narrowed down the choice to either Brigadier General Alexander Macomb or Winfield Scott. Four of the six Cabinet members favored Scott, but Adams named Macomb because Scott had once challenged General Edmund Gaines to a duel. After Macomb was named, Secretary of State Clay felt remorseful, and as conciliation he sent Harrison to Bogotá, Colombia, as minister to Simón Bolívar. This was a lucrative post, paying $18,000.

It did not take Harrison long to discover that the fiery liberator of South America was running a tight dictatorship. He reported a street sight of "long strings of manacled wretches goaded on by the bayonet." Hardly a discreet type, he wrote Bolívar on September 27, 1829, that he was praying against Bolívar's continuation of "monarchial advisers and for the return of republicanism." His life was in immediate danger, and he was accused by Bolívar of plotting his assassination. President Jackson had recalled Harrison that summer, but he let him face threats and outrages by deliberately withholding a pickup boat from going after Harrison until early the next year.

Despite his high rate of pay, Harrison returned to his large, well-furnished house at North Bend, Ohio, in serious financial trouble. One of his six sons, William, Jr., had become an alcoholic and was heavily in debt. Harrison shouldered his bills, but a short time later when his own iron foundry failed, he had additional debts of $20,000. There was common talk that he had turned to moonshining to pick up cash. In 1830, he ran desperately for governor, U. S. Senator and Representative, dismally losing all three contests. Nicholas Biddle's Bank saved him from catastrophe with a timely loan of $19,000, even though it was apparent he would never be able to repay it. It was in the midst of all his anguish in 1833 that the wife of his third son, John Scott Harrison, gave birth in the North Bend house to a son, Benjamin, who would one day become the twenty-third President. Then in 1834, kind friends arranged a minor sinecure for the sixty-one-year-old Harrison as clerk of the county court of common pleas so he could vegetate in genteel want during his few remaining years.

When the 1836 election approached, Mr. Whig himself, Senator Henry Clay, took himself out of contention. Having lost two Presidential elections already—in 1824 and 1832—Clay wanted to bide his time and run again when the Jackson image over the Democratic party had faded. In addition, the recent death of his daughter Anne, the last of his six girls, had temporarily removed his appetite for another political contest.

It was then that the Whig leaders conceived the unusual scheme of running four candidates against Martin Van Buren, each to be nominated by a state convention and to run primarily in his section of the country. Harrison was suddenly astounded to find himself pulled out of limbo, dusted off and thrust into the public limelight as the Whig candidate in the West. "How little we can judge our future destinies," he wrote to Clay in a happy daze.

Nicholas Biddle, not yet ruined by Jackson's war on his Bank of the United States, took charge of the Harrison campaign. His utter contempt for the county clerk, who clung to his job, was revealed in a letter of instructions he sent to Harrison's local manager. It read: "Let him say not a single word about his principles, or his creed—let him say nothing—promise nothing. Let no Committee, no convention—no town meeting ever extract from him a single word about what he thinks now, or what he will do hereafter. Let the use of pen and ink be wholly forbidden as if he were a mad poet in Bedlam."

Despite Biddle's orders, Harrison would not abide being treated like an idiot. The Democrats were proclaiming him an "imbecile and dotard" and red-vested Colonel Richard Johnson, Van Buren's running mate, was telling crowds that he and not Harrison was the hero of the Battle of the Thames. Harrison permitted ghost-writers to answer five political questions put to him by Whig House member Sherrod Williams of Kentucky. Among the double-talk replies were his opposition to Federally-financed internal im-provements—except those of national importance—and his opposi-tion to a new Bank of the United States—unless it were needed. But Harrison's ego was too large to permit him to sit out the biggest event of his life while supposedly astute politicians made up and answered questions in his behalf.

A three-month tour followed into New York, Pennsylvania, New Jersey, Maryland and Virginia, with fifty receptions, banquets and speeches. Whigs in Ohio had given him a nickname, "Old Buck-eye," in an effort to help voters identify him. But "Old Buckeye" didn't catch on with the crowds and it was replaced by the spontaneous development of "Old Tippecanoe" and "Old Tip." Every Whig community wanted to give him a testimonial dinner or stage a public celebration of the 1811 Battle of Tippecanoe, and he joined in enthusiastically, though a Whig paper reported that "he does not look in very firm health." One description of him found him "a small and rather sallow-looking man, who does not exactly meet the associations that connect themselves with the name general." But his personality was praised, especially the "simplicity of his manners . . . utter want of any show . . . copious fund of eloquence." He needed the last to help explain away his support of a bill in the Ohio Senate that said criminal offenders should not be whipped but should be "sold to any person who would pay their fine and costs."

The Whig multiple candidates plan failed to throw the 1836 election into the House. But one factor stood out. Harrison amassed twenty-two more electoral votes than his three fellow Whig candi-dates combined. A few thousand more votes and he would have captured Pennsylvania and New York from Van Buren, and with only 128 more votes in Rhode Island, he would have become President in 1836. If his health held out, he was a man to watch in 1840.

While Harrison returned to his clerk's job with an elevated salary of $6000 a year, and to dreams of 1840, the Great De-pression of '37 came crashing onto the scene. The continuing hard times raised Whig hopes for victory in the forthcoming Presi-dential contest, and Henry Clay decided that the time was ap-proaching to cap his illustrious career with the Presidency. "Harry of the West," "Prince Hal," "The Millboy of the Slashes" and the "Kentucky Hotspur," as friend and foe called him, took on a triumphant air. One evening in 1838 he strolled up to Van Buren in the White House and jovially remarked that he wanted to make certain the Executive Mansion "would be likely to be in a tenantable condition about three years hence." With false political modesty, he told a reporter: "I shall again be *forced* into the Presidential arena." And to his son, Henry Clay, Jr., he wrote, "There is everywhere an irresistible current setting in towards me."

No doubt Washington politicians would have agreed that if tall, spare Clay with the mouth that extended almost from ear to ear and little, round Van Buren were the 1840 candidates, it would be a campaign between two clever wits. Still anecdoted was the 1834 episode between the two in the U. S. Senate when Clay made a speech against President Jackson's removal of government deposits from Nick Biddle's Bank. To a packed gallery, Clay's sonorous voice and dramatic manner were in full display as he accused Jackson of having defrauded the nation. As he spoke, he left his place and walked up the aisle until he faced Vice-President Van Buren on the dais. In a cracking emotional tone, he pleaded with him to go to his friend in the White House and beg Jackson to return the funds to the Bank. All the while, Van Buren sat in silence, his eyes glued on Clay's face and his head nodding. Afterward, Clay returned to his seat and fell into it, exhausted. A moment later the Vice-President put down his gavel and rose from his place on the dais. Purposefully, he strode toward Clay and spectators gasped as the climax neared. Finally he reached Clay's side. "Mr. Clay," he lisped in his Dutch accent. Clay leaned forward expectantly. "Mr. Clay, may I borrow a pinch of your excellent snuff?" Clay held out his box of fine old Maccoboy and Van Buren put a pinch to his nostrils with a snappy twirl of his fingers while Clay sat poised. But now Van Buren merely bowed and sauntered casually from the chamber to the accompaniment of a wave of laughter that brought a crimson blush to Clay's face.

Eighteen-forty was also on the mind of Thurlow Weed, the tall, dark New Yorker, the boss of the Whig party who combined political victories with lucrative government contracts. Weed, who passed out eighty thousand cigars to win friends, had come to the conclusion that even a million cigars would not help install Clay as President. There was only one word to describe Clay. He was "unavailable." His two previous defeats gave his name a losing sound; his tariff compromise of 1833 had alienated New England Whigs; his nationalism, southern Whigs; his hassles with Calhoun over slavery, every slaveholder in the country; his proposal to sell public land at highest auction prices had antagonized the West.

Weed also found "Black Dan," "Godlike Dan" Webster too closely associated with New England to be a national candidate. Who remained as candidates? There were only two—aging Harrison and mountainous General Winfield Scott, who was making a name for himself settling troubles with the Southern Indians and Canadian border hotheads. Which of the two Weed really favored became apparent when he conversed with Webster and offered him the Vice-Presidential berth under Harrison. Webster grew choleric at the suggestion that he place himself second to a man far inferior to him in ability and experience, and when he refused he realized he had no chance to fight Weed's decision further.

By 1839, Harrison knew he was among the top runners and he feigned embarrassment in writing to Clay about the situation. "A few years ago," he said, "I could not have believed in the possibility of apparent rivalry to you. I confess that I did covet the second [the Vice-Presidential nomination in 1828] but never the first office in the gift of my fellow citizens." He wrote again, expressing relief that Clay bore him no animosity and he asked for advice on what to do for a Spanish jackass that had become impotent. Clay was renowned throughout the stock-breeding world for his blooded donkeys and bulls.

In the fall of 1839, Clay visited New York to tie up convention support for himself. Anti-Masonic Representative Millard Fillmore of Buffalo, a henchman of Thurlow Weed, wrote to the boss from Washington of the potential danger of Clay unless his candidacy were smashed. Weed passed out stern warnings to his boys to ignore Clay when he reached New York and give him no receptions or publicity. But Van Buren, who was at Saratoga Springs at the time, arranged with the Tammany crowd to give Clay a tremendous welcome. In President Van Buren's view, Clay would be easy to beat in 1840 and anything to promote Clay's candidacy would pay dividends to the Democrats in the final showdown. With the Tammany greeting disguised so that the Whig Clay could not tell that Democrats were cheering him, Clay believed he was enormously popular in New York. This upset Weed who had hoped that a chilly reception would have convinced Clay that he had no chance. Weed therefore decided to confront Clay personally.

There was much the former farmhand, roustabout, tavern pot-boy and reporter could complain of to "Mr. Whig." Clay's image was bad, primarily because he had taken a definite stand on so many important issues where there were deep sectional differences. Besides, he was a Mason. He was also known as a man who swore, drank, and gambled—and he talked too much and dashed off too many letters. When he finished his recounting of Clay's weaknesses, Weed bluntly demanded that he remove himself as a Presidential candidate.

Clay's refusal led Weed to take public action in New York to destroy him there. The Weed technique became known as the "Triangular Correspondence." He had men in three different cities exchange letters, each saying for publication: "Do all you can for Mr. Clay in your district, for I am sorry to say he has no strength in this."

The climax of the Harrison-Clay drama came at the beginning of December, when Whigs poured into Harrisburg, Pennsylvania, for the first national Whig convention in history. Four years earlier the Whig boss's opinion that a national convention was a form of "King Caucus" had been a convenience to have state legislatures nominate four Whig candidates for President. Such a convention was now a necessity because the selection of a single nominee would forestall Clay's nomination by state legislatures.

By December 4 when the 254 delegates from twenty-two states crowded into the Harrisburg Lutheran Church, Weed was worried because Clay had a strong plurality of delegates. To the various delegations, he and his top lieutenant, New York's governor, "Little Billy" Seward, pointed out that much of Clay's strength lay in delegations from states that would support Van Buren. Seward, an excellent speaker and an odd-looking man with his huge, beaked nose, tried to sound convincing when he said that the New York delegation was supporting General Winfield Scott for the nomination. But there was little question where the true sentiments of the New Yorkers lay.

Because of the personal sentimental attachment of delegates to Clay, Weed proceeded with a clever plan to handle the nomination behind the scenes. What he proposed was that each state delegation appoint a three-man committee to meet with similar committees from other delegations to exchange views on candidates. Then each committee would report back to its delegation and a vote would be taken there on candidates. A "unit rule" would be enforced, with the majority vote of a delegation representing the state. The process would then be repeated until one candidate gained a majority, at which point the committees would report to the convention that they had agreed on a candidate.

A long floor debate developed over the Weed proposal, but it was finally railroaded through over the hoarse opposition of Clay's cousin, Cassius M. Clay, the noted anti-slavery Southerner. Weed's stratagem revealed its value shortly afterward when the first private ballot under the unit rule took place. The informal count without the rule would have given Clay more than the needed majority. But the unit rule compressed his strength to a vote of 103, while Harrison had 94 and General Winfield Scott 57.

Weed had now bought time to increase the Harrison vote at the expense of the Clay total. But a strange thing happened. Several ballots later only Connecticut and Michigan had decided to drop Clay. However, they switched to Scott instead of to Harrison! The job now became one of lowering the boom on Scott as well as on Clay, and Thaddeus Stevens, Weed's Pennsylvania cohort, was given the assignment. By careful accident, Stevens managed to drop a letter from Scott in the area of the Virginia delegation. The letter stated that Scott hoped to conciliate New York abolitionists.

The hoped-for results developed. Scott votes poured into the Harrison camp. On Friday, December 6, the committees were able to report to the convention that they had agreed upon a candidate: Harrison had 148, Clay 90 and Scott 16.

The losing candidates took the decision with ill grace. General Scott later growled: "I could have been elected as easily as I could walk down these stairs." Clay, with a premonition of bad news, was in his cups at Brown's Indian Queen Hotel in Washington when a messenger brought word of Harrison's nomination. His homely long face did not reveal its usual ear-to-ear jovial smile. Nor did the loose-jointed Senator stride out with his swinging gait; he lifted his legs by spasmodic jerks and cried out: "My friends are not worth the powder and shot it would take to kill them! . . . I am the most unfortunate man in the history of parties; always run by my friends when sure to be defeated, and now betrayed for a nomination when I, or anyone, would be sure of an election."

Once the Whig Presidential nomination was settled, Weed turned to the task of selecting a Vice-Presidential nominee. As the major part of the ticket, Harrison could be promoted to represent the West, the anti-Masons and abolitionists. He could also represent the war hero department. What was needed now to round out the ticket was a pro-slavery southern states'-righter. Southern states had been apathetic toward the Whigs, he noted. Four states had sent no delegates to the convention while only one of Louisiana's eleven had come to Harrisburg. With a Southerner on the ticket, the Calhoun country might find the Whigs more alluring.

Weed was also confronted by a need to create unity in the party. When Harrison won, the Clay delegates had shown clearly their anger and grief. One expressed the view of the lot when he remarked: "Just think of a man such as Mr. Clay after thirty years of such service as no man has rendered to the Republic except Washington . . . cast aside."

Weed began by offering the Vice-Presidential nomination to active Clay backers. Former Senator John M. Clayton of Delaware scowlingly turned him down, as did former Senator B. Watkins Leigh of Virginia. Weed also tried to hand it to Clay's friend and fellow Senator from Kentucky, John Crittenden, only to meet with a similar show of disdain. Senator Willie Mangum of North Carolina was another who would not accept the Vice-Presidential nomination. Nor would Senator Nathaniel Tallmadge of New York, the leader of the conservative Democrats, who had worked closely with Clay to thwart the Van Buren measures in the Senate.

Now in a quandary, Weed fortunately found a nominee. His man was former Senator John Tyler of Virginia, a suspected Democrat even though he called himself a Whig because he opposed every feature of Clay's American System. As an extreme states'-righter, Tyler was against a national bank, a protective tariff and Federally-financed internal improvements. A courageous man, he was the only Senator to have dared to vote against the Jackson Force Bill to invade South Carolina, if necessary, to end defiance of the tariff law. Someone once pointed out that his "fetish was consistency." So severe a doctrinaire was he that no matter how much circumstances might have changed, he would not amend or compromise his hardened views.

Weed could almost hear Tyler panting after the Vice-Presidency. In 1836, he had run for Vice-President under the Senator Hugh White part of the four Whig candidates scheme. In fact, Tyler may have professed a fondness for Clay, but in reality those who knew him well declared he had only animosity toward "Harry of the West." For Tyler believed that if Clay had not supported the other Whig Vice-Presidential nominee, Francis Granger of New York, Tyler would have defeated Richard Mentor Johnson, the Democratic nominee.

A generation earlier, Benjamin Harrison and John Tyler, Sr., had been bitter political enemies in Virginia. Now their sons were running on the same political ticket. Why Tyler? Weed bluntly gave his answer: "We could get no one else to accept." So it was "Tippecanoe and Tyler, too."

The Democrats did not meet for their Baltimore national convention until May 5, five months later. For the first time the party officially called itself the Democratic party, dropping the Democratic-Republican title that had come down since the days of Jefferson. This was not a peaceful convention because Weed would not permit the Democrats to operate without his interference. He arranged for thirty thousand Whigs to descend on Baltimore at the same time that the Democrats were meeting and to frighten them out of town, if possible. The Whig bands, the noise, parades, speeches drowned out the Democratic show, and when some Democrats protested, muscular Whig bullies stepped forward. Luckily, the many brawls resulted in only a single killing.

Meanwhile, the Democratic convention was holding its sessions and nominated President Van Buren unanimously for a second term. Because of the seething resentment of Southerners against Vice-President Johnson, the convention nominated no second man, but left the second place open for state legislatures to fill. Jackson had been promoting James K. "Young Hickory" Polk as Van Buren's running mate, but Polk preferred a future time when there was more likelihood of success.

Unlike the Whigs, the Democrats offered a platform of principles, calling for a national government limited in power, no special protective tariffs for manufacturers and no Federally-financed internal improvements. Many Whig Congressmen had promoted legislation to have the Federal Government assume the debts of the states. The Democratic platform opposed this. To win southern support, the Democrats offered a plank vowing that Congress should not interfere with slavery; to win support of immigrant groups, a plank declared opposition to all restrictions on naturalization.

There is little argument that the 1840 campaign was the strang-
est one in American history. Harrison was elated when messengers
came the sixteen miles west of Cincinnati to North Bend with word
of his nomination. But he soon felt he was in a trap of sorts when
a three-man committee made an appearance with the expressed
purpose of handling all questions pertaining to his views and con-
serving his health. When the Democrats heard about the proposed
campaign blackout for the Whig candidate, they scoffed at him as
"General Mum" and at his trio as "Harrison's Conscience-Keeping
Committee." Other names followed. He was "Granny," "the old
lady" and "the superannuated and pitiable dotard" to the Democratic press. Jackson labeled him "the Mock Hero." Van Buren wasn't
immune to names; the Whig press, including Weed's own editor,
twenty-eight-year-old Horace Greeley, and the editor of the New
York scandal sheet, the *Herald,* who was a young man named
James Gordon Bennett, derisively called the President "Martin Van
Ruin," "Matty" and "Sweet Sandy Whiskers."

Besides name-calling, the campaign was fought at other levels.
On a minor level, were the issues. Van Buren's chief campaign
aides—Amos Kendall, who had resigned as Postmaster General to
be his campaign manager; Senator John C. Calhoun; Hannibal
Hamlin, the Maine anti-slaver; John A. Dix, a member of Van
Buren's Albany Regency in New York; and his Senate leader, Silas
Wright—had hoped that the issues would form the main area of
campaign contention with Harrison and his three-man committee.
From the start, Democrats spoke frequently about the blessings
of the Sub-Treasury Act and the important step forward for workingmen when Van Buren decreed the ten-hour day for Federal
employees on construction work.

But Weed considered specific issues a dangerous manner of campaigning, and he would have none of it. If the Democrats wanted
to talk about specific legislation that was their business. The Whig
answer to this would be to attack the Democrats and not their
position. In this way, votes would not be lost. How effective this
technique was came clear from comments of voters. One commented: "As to what the Sub-Treasury really was, I had not the
remotest idea; but I knew this—that it was the most wicked outrage ever committed by a remorseless tyrant upon a long-suffering
people."

Years before, Weed had reached the conclusion that his own

reactionary beliefs were too narrow a framework on which to create a successful national political party. For example, he opposed universal white manhood suffrage, a position that would hardly have won wide support. It was as long ago as 1834 that he saw the folly of bossing a party that did not contain every shade of political view. "The longer we fight Jacksonianism with our present weapons, the more it won't die," he wrote. Jackson had the base Weed wanted.

Governor Seward, the small, sloppy man with stiff red hair and the eagle-beak nose, who said of Weed, "I never knew that dictators could be such amiable people," gave the boss the new line. The Whigs would simply have to profess to be more democratic than the Democrats if they were to win a national election. "We should assail aristocracy, remove the barriers between the rich and the poor, break the control of the few over the many, extend the largest liberty to the greatest number," said Seward. Weed agreed, though unlike Seward he was personally opposed to using this approach beyond the campaign promises period.

The entire Whig campaign took on the Seward approach. Yet it came about by accident. One disgruntled Clay supporter at Harrisburg had jeered at Harrison's qualifications in an interview with a Baltimore newsman. In turn, the reporter offered his formula how to get Harrison to relinquish the nomination. When his suggestion was printed in the Baltimore *Republican* on March 23, 1840, a fever overtook the nation. "Upon condition of his receiving a pension of two thousand dollars, a barrel of cider, General Harrison would no doubt consent to withdraw his pretensions and spend his days in a log cabin on the banks of the Ohio," was the advice.

Instead of taking umbrage at this remark, a Harrison Whig reporter, Richard E. Parker of Harrisburg, was immediately struck with the idea that this could result in political gold. Whig leaders quickly agreed and the campaign die was cast. Harrison was pictured as a simple person living in a log cabin where the latch string was always out and where Harrison and his friends drank hard cider, the poor man's drink. That Harrison was actually a Virginia aristocrat who lived in a sixteen-room house on a 3000-acre estate and would not drink hard cider was carefully ignored by the Whigs in creating a new image for the "Farmer from North Bend."

In contrast, Representative Ogle's harangue on Van Buren in the

House was reprinted with the title "The Royal Splendor of the President's Palace," and then widely distributed. "In his dining room do we find hog and hominy, or schnitz, knep and sourcrout? No, sir, no. All these substantial preparations are looked upon by gourmands, French cooks and locofoco Presidents as exceedingly vulgar, and fit only to be set before 'Bank Whigs.'" On the other hand, Ogle pictured Harrison as the epitome of the simple farmer, totally unlike the "lily-fingered aristocrat" who used perfume on his fingers, flirted with the Duchess of Westmorland, ate from silver plates with gold spoons and was a slacker in 1812 . . . "I wonder where he fought his battles?" Ogle sneered.

But the Whigs did more than conduct their campaign of simplicity in the press. From one end of the country to the other, they created a passion play in which they were their own actors, with the cider barrel and the log cabin as their chief props.

The idea was first tested at New York rallies where a large log cabin served as reception hall for guests who came dressed in homespun and guzzled hard cider. Governor Seward traveled in an old green wagon and Joseph Hoxie, a quiet and sedate merchant of wealth, came forward as leader of the songfest. Hoxie proved a sensation, especially with one song bellowed to the tune of "The Little Pig's Tail." The crowds demanded endless choruses of—

> For Tippecanoe and Tyler, too—Tippecanoe and Tyler, too;
>   And with them we'll beat little Van, Van,
>   Van is a used-up man;
>   And with them we'll beat little Van.

So successful were the New York rallies that they were staged in hundreds of cities, towns and villages East and West. Whigs took to wearing coonskin caps, old clothes and carrying a canteen of cider hanging from their necks. Before this year, women never attended political rallies. Now Whig leaders pleaded with them to come. In a typical rally, log cabins of various sizes were put on display. Barrels of cider were rolled out and everyone was gay. Afterward, there were a few short, general speeches about the old general at his log cabin where "the latch-string is never in and where everyone is invited." Then came the songfest lasting hours. It was like a revival meeting in the setting of a barbecue, or an excursion. The more ungrammatical the speakers the louder was the applause. Local vernacular was also a boon to speakers and three favorite speakers to Whig audiences were "Honest Abe Lincoln, the Log Splitter," "Henry Wilson, the Natick Cobbler" and "Tom Corwin, the Wagon Boy." Sometimes there were big paper or tin balls, six to fifteen feet high, with Whig sayings plastered on them. Whigs rolled the balls from town to town, and some went hundreds of miles. The idea for the balls originated as an effort to ridicule Senator Thomas Hart Benton, who had bragged when the Senate finally expunged the Jackson censure from its Journal, "Solitary and alone, I set this ball in motion."

One ball song went:

> What has caused the great commotion, motion, motion,
> Our country through?
> It is the ball a-rolling on
> For Tippecanoe and Tyler, too,
> Tippecanoe and Tyler, too.
> And with 'em we'll beat Little Van, Van, Van.
> Van is a used-up man,
> And with 'em we'll beat Little Van.

It was impossible to lose sight of the log cabin motif. Towns erected large models, businessmen put small models in their shop windows, men wore them on watch chains, women on earrings. Even the Whig paper edited by Horace Greeley was called *The Log Cabin*. The E. C. Booz Company of Philadelphia bottled Old Cabin Whisky in glass log cabins and people began calling whisky "booze." Woodcarvers did a brisk business selling likenesses of Old Tip on a horse or at the door of his log cabin.

But it was the incessant songfests that infuriated the Democrats most. A Democratic editor wailed: "Some of the songs I shall never forget. They rang in my ears wherever I went, morning, noon and night. Men, women and children did nothing but sing. It worried, annoyed, dumbfounded, crushed the Democrats. It was a ceaseless torrent of music, still beginning, never ending. If a Democrat tried to speak, argue or answer anything that was said or done, he was only saluted with a fresh deluge of music." From the Hermitage, General Jackson let out a roar, calling the Whig campaign equal to a claim that American voters "are unfit for self-government and can only be led by hard cider, coons, log cabins and big balls by the demagogues, as can the lowing herd be by his keeper and a baskett [sic] of salt." But the Whigs went on singing:

> From the White House, now Matty,
> Turn out, turn out,
> From the White House, now Matty,
> Turn out.

The Whig watchers were carefully guarding "the honest old farmer of Ohio" but he was beginning to squirm under their guardianship as the warm summer of 1840 appeared. He wrote a letter with his views on issues to Gulian C. Verplanck of New York, who had left the Democrats when Jackson removed the government deposits from the national bank. However, Verplanck found the letter enclosed in another by Edward Curtis, a New York lieutenant of Daniel Webster's. Curtis warned Verplanck not to publish Harrison's letter because it would "accomplish far more harm than good."

There seemed little point in turning Harrison loose so long as the *Democratic Review* was whining as it did in its June 1840 issue, "We have taught them how to conquer us!" It was a case of "out-Heroding of Herod," said the *Review*. Nor was there reason for Harrison to participate directly when local Whigs were making such exacting plans to get out the vote. Honest Abe Lincoln, the Log Splitter, and a Whig county chairman, prepared the following guide: "Divide county into small districts, and . . . appoint in each a subcommittee, whose duty it shall be to make a perfect list of all the voters in their respective districts, and to ascertain with certainty for whom they will vote . . . keep a constant watch on the doubtful voters, and from time to time have them talked to by those in whom they shall have the most confidence. . . . On election days see that every Whig is brought to the polls."

Like a giant chorus, the tide of an expected victory brought closed ranks to the Whigs. Webster at first considered the campaign with contempt, but fell in line to the point where he made several speeches with the log-cabin focus. He pointed out that his sisters and brothers had been born in a log cabin and expressed regret that he had not. "The man who calls me an aristocrat—*is a liar!*" the master of the spacious and formal estate of Marshfield warned crowds. Astute Whigs believed that Webster was campaigning for Harrison not from conviction but from a desire to control him afterward. This reason was also advanced for the late but strong effort by Clay in Harrison's behalf. Clay had earlier expressed anger at the demagogic approach and said he opposed "appealing to the feelings and passions of our countrymen, rather than to their reasons and judgments." The truth was that neither Clay nor Webster could allow the other to move ahead.

The Democrats at last found an issue that worried the Whigs. Earlier thrusts by the Democrats had been the old charge that Harrison had favored selling criminals in Ohio into slavery, continuing attacks on his mental abilities, plus the dredging up of a Winnebago squaw who said Old Tip was the father of her three half-breed sons. These charges did not disturb the Whigs, but one questioning his health did. Dr. Daniel Drake, a Whig physician in Cincinnati, let out a nation-wide broadside at the Democratic whispering campaign that Harrison was dying. Dr. Drake declared him filled with "vivacity and almost youthfulness of feelings." He is "subject to no diseases but periodic headache." But when this statement did not end the whispers, the Whigs decided that their man must leave his log cabin and show himself in public.

Harrison first went to Fort Meigs where the Whigs hoped his appearance would still the rumors. For this occasion on June 11, he "changed his tall silk hat for a broad-brimmed one, the rest of his garb a plain frock coat, bombazine stock, black silk vest and blue pantaloons." He was the old, kindly farmer to the enthusiastic crowd that watched the short, wan-faced nominee as he stood under a broiling sun for an hour and orated generalities in "trumpet-like tones." He enjoyed himself so much that he also spoke at Cleveland and Columbus and would have gone on to Springfield, Ohio, if word had not reached him of the death of his thirty-four-year-old son Benjamin on June 9.

Again in July he made another campaign swing, and he was greeted everywhere with log cabins, cider and songs. Speakers extolled his Tippecanoe and Thames battles as more decisive than Jackson's Battle of New Orleans. By now his writing crew had prepared a seven-point statement on Harrison's ideas on the Presidency, and this was given press coverage. His statement contained a promise to serve only one term, give up any authority to control the national treasury, avoid using his office to influence elections, limit the use of the veto power, "never suffer the influence of his office to be used for partisan purposes," tell the Senate when asked his reasons for removing officials and never permit the President "to become a source of legislation."

The man who wanted to be a figurehead President visited two dozen places that fall. It wasn't necessary for him to talk much because the songfests, cider-drinking, ball-rolling and log-cabin inspecting occupied most of the time. His chief function was to stand erect and move briskly about to show good health. The crowds were tremendous at every stop. Whig papers began to measure the mobs in acres. Ten acres of people greeted him at one meeting. At Erie, when asked the length of the procession, the marshal replied: "The other end is forming somewhere in the state of New York." At Dayton, more than 100,000 persons were present. The occasion was also a celebration of the September 10, 1813, anniversary of Oliver Hazard Perry's Lake Erie victory, and, of course, it could truthfully be said that it was to Harrison that Perry had sent his message: "We have met the enemy and they are ours." It was at Dayton also that he explained his stand on national finance. "Methinks I hear a soft voice asking, 'Are you in favor of paper money?' . . . I am." Earsplitting roars went up. At some stops he attacked the Democrats as aristocrats: "I believe and I say it in truly democratic feeling that all the measures of the government are directed to the purpose of making the rich richer and the poor poorer." Besides this attempt at class warfare, which pleased Whig leaders, he sometimes said things that horrified them. At Carthage, Ohio, he told the immense gathering that the people could petition Congress to redress any grievance—even slavery. Many southern Whigs immediately denounced him as an abolitionist.

A new word, "O.K.," entered the language during the campaign. Both sides claimed its origin. One story was that a non-speller of Whig sentiment, in reporting a local election where the Whigs won, said the verified returns were "Oll Korrect." Whig editors picked up the initials and first used them as a victory sign. The version of the Democrats was that the *New Era* party publication in New York had shortened "Old Kinderhook" for Van Buren to O.K. "We will say to you, Martin Van Buren, O.K., you can remain in the White House for another four years."

As the campaign neared its climax, the Democrats kept saying that "the bubble would burst." But some, like Jackson, believed that only a miracle could save the Democrats. He was furious when John Eaton, Peggy's husband, came out for Harrison. Taking along

an extra supply of "Matchless Sanative," the patent cough medicine he used to doctor his advanced case of tuberculosis, Jackson
took to the Tennessee hustings for Van Buren. In a frenzied bit of
stumping, he transmitted germs by kissing babies, shaking hands
with Jackson worshippers, autographing papers and haranguing
crowds at mammoth barbecues.

But it was no use, for the election results gave Harrison 1,275,016
votes to Van Buren's 1,129,102. The electoral vote was far more
one-sided with 234 going to Harrison and only 60 for the defeated
President. A western Democratic editor moaned: "Sung down, lied
down, drank down." When it was over, an observer noted: "If one
could imagine a whole nation declaring a holiday or season of rollicking for a period of six or eight months, and giving themselves
up during the whole time to the wildest freaks of fun and frolic,
caring nothing for business; singing, dancing and carousing night
and day, he might have some faint notion of the extraordinary
scenes of 1840."

Jackson felt crushed and was barely able to say, "I do not yet
despair of the Republic. Rally round Mr. Van Buren and elect him
by a triumphant majority should he live to November 1844." As
for Van Buren, he believed he had been swindled out of victory
by voting frauds. This was true in New York where Weed's
crooked poll workers combined with an invasion of voting ringers
from Pennsylvania. The accusing Democratic finger pointed first
to Weed and then to Thaddeus Stevens, known to Democrats as
"a notorious Whig Election 'Specialist'" and "the Pennsylvania
Devil for Cheating." Said Van Buren: "All that was needed to
make a system used with success in a ward or a city applicable
to the Union was money, men and time." As an afterthought, Jackson declared that the Whigs had also won because of corruption,
plus British interference in order to get a President to "unite with
her in her corrupt views, put down our republican system and
build upon its ruins a great consolidated government to be ruled
by the corrupt money power of England and America."

Harrison's victory signaled the striking of the war gong between
Clay and Webster. Each looked forward to controlling him and his
Administration, determining policy, placing lieutenants in key posts
and managing the operations of the Executive Branch.

No doubt Webster gulped shortly after the election when he
learned that Harrison planned to go down to the Blue Grass country

south of Cincinnati for a visit. For this was Clay country and it portended favoritism on Harrison's part toward his rival. However, Harrison was going to Kentucky to talk to "the Old Duke," Charles Wickliffe, purportedly about a land company. He wrote Clay, "I shall set out for Louisville in the mail boat tomorrow" (November 16, 1840). He said that on his brother's land claim, bought for $5000, "W. [Wickliffe] now offers $11,000 for it." He had no intention of meeting with Clay because he had heard reports that many Whigs considered him to be Clay's lackey, and he suggested that Clay send a friend to ask questions for him in a Frankfort meeting. As for Clay, he saw the visit as fraught with danger for him because Wickliffe, an officer in the War of 1812, a former Congressman and governor of Kentucky, was his chief political enemy at home. Reasoning that the old man was probably agreeing to turn over frontier patronage to Wickliffe, he rushed to Frankfort where he met Harrison and took him home with him the forty miles to Ashland, near Lexington.

Clay was a gracious host, and Harrison was unable to muster courage to leave him. For almost a week Clay held long talks with him. Harrison tried to pay him off quickly by offering to make him Secretary of State, but Clay brushed this aside. He would be satisfied to be the boss of Congress and to have some of his friends become part of Harrison's official family. Harrison agreed to appoint Senator John J. Crittenden of Kentucky as his Attorney General and John Bell of Tennessee as Secretary of War. Clay was most persistent about having former Senator John M. Clayton named Treasury Secretary, for Clayton was a strong Bank man. Harrison deferred action, for he had almost reached Webster's conclusion that the rechartering of the national bank was a dead issue and shouldn't be revived. During the week, Harrison attended a rally at Versailles, a short distance west of Lexington, and after long praise of his host he said that if the Constitution would permit it, he would make Clay President and retire to his farm. He also emphasized to Clay in private that the two were in perfect agreement on all public issues. This so pleased Prince Hal that he departed for Washington at the beginning of December, 1840, to attend the last session of the Twenty-sixth Congress, and left Harrison still in Lexington.

Clay could never handle success. In Washington, even his fellow Whigs were embarrassed by the rough way he handled Van Buren in the lame duck session. "Clay crows too much over a fallen foe,"

John Quincy Adams commented. He succeeded in ousting the Democratic Blair and Rives team as the Senate's printer and bellowed that Blair had libeled him for ten years. Senator William King of Alabama jumped up to defend Blair and a duel between him and Clay was barely averted. As for Van Buren and his Sub-Treasury Act, Clay rubbed his palms together and said that the defeated President was like "a convicted criminal with a rope around his neck." Senator Wright demanded to know why Clay didn't propose to tear down the White House and erect a log cabin for the man who had qualified himself for the Presidency by drinking hard cider.

Late in January 1841, Harrison collected a few of his possessions for the journey to Washington. His wife Anna showed little enthusiasm. In fact, her comment on first hearing of his victory had been: "I wish that my husband's friends had left him where he is, happy and contented in retirement." She now claimed ill health and said she would not go to Washington until May.

On January 26, Harrison made a prophetic farewell speech at Cincinnati before embarking on the steamboat *Ben Franklin* for Pittsburgh. In his party were his daughter-in-law, Jane Findlay Harrison, widow of his son, William, Jr., who would serve as his White House hostess, three young grandsons and Charles S. Todd, editor of Harrison's campaign paper, the Cincinnati *Republican*. To the large gathering, he said in closing: "Gentlemen and fellow citizens, perhaps this may be the last time I may have the pleasure of speaking to you on earth or seeing you. I will bid you farewell, if forever, fare thee well."

All the way to Pittsburgh bonfires lighted the shoreline. His grandsons were lost for a time in Pittsburgh, and later admitted they had gone to three church services so they could stare at the girls. The party then went by coach to Maryland, stopping for ceremonies at Hagerstown and Frederick. At the latter place, Harrison climbed onto a train for a ride to Baltimore. Here so many thousands shook his hand that it swelled and he affirmed a rule not to shake hands when he reached Washington.

The B. & O. carried him to Washington on February 9, the day of his sixty-eighth birthday. The Democrats said that he brought the heavy snowstorm that hit the capital that day and pointed to the bad omen of the Senate scroll with "E Pluribus Unum" on it that had fallen at the time of his arrival. Another bad omen they claimed, was a rope made of the flags of all the states and strung across Pennsylvania Avenue that had broken. Blair's *Globe* reported that when he reached Pennsylvania Avenue he was greeted by an immense crowd and "a multitude had their pockets picked in the course of five minutes."

Harrison's arrival heralded the beginning of the symphony of the office seekers and the climactic struggle between Clay and Webster to pin his hide on their wall. John Quincy Adams said of the bulging crowd in Washington that it consisted chiefly of the "wolves of the antechamber, pushing for office." These hungry Whigs numbered in the thousands, and from all hamlets and towns in the country they had "rushed pell-mell to Washington, every man with a raccoon's tail on his hat." Gadsby's Tavern, where Harrison registered, was so bursting with them that the dining room was converted into a dormitory and a crude shed was built in the courtyard as an eating hall. Senator Silas Wright described Gadsby's of that period as the place "where loafers assemble from all parts of the Union, where all the meats taste alike and the bells ring from morning to night."

Harrison was no sooner inside the door when Senators surrounded him to clamor for Cabinet posts. Weed had to be paid off promptly and Harrison made the significant gesture of naming the boss's man, Francis Granger, as Postmaster General in charge of the bulk of available patronage. To Clay, who continued to urge him to name Clayton as Treasury Secretary, Harrison listened politely, then showed a temper for the first time when he suddenly snapped: "Mr. Clay, you forget that I am President!" Harrison finally gave the Treasury job to former Senator Thomas Ewing of Ohio who had defeated him in 1830 for the Senate seat. Ewing, who was soon to be called "the butcher," because of the way he chopped Democrats off the public payroll, had fought at the Battle of the Thames under Harrison. History would also know him as the man who adopted young William Tecumseh Sherman, the son of his late best friend.

Ewing's appointment was regarded by Whigs as a victory for Webster. Then Harrison compounded matters by appointing Webster as Secretary of State, the post rejected by Clay. That he had named Webster solely to gain a respite from his many demands soon became apparent. Senator William C. Rives, a leader of the conservative Democrats who had joined the Whigs, came to talk patronage for his group, and to Rives Harrison confided that he really preferred him to Webster as Secretary of State.

Although he was personally disheartened by the results of the election, Van Buren was anxious to bring about a smooth transition from his Administration to the next. He broke tradition by taking his entire Cabinet to Gadsby's Tavern to visit Harrison and he also invited the President-elect to one of his exclusive Saturday night dinners. It was here that Harrison showed his vexation with the pulling and hauling to which Clay and Webster were subjecting him. There were only a few Whigs present and directly across the table from Harrison sat Senator Thomas Hart Benton, the extreme Democratic partisan. "Benton," Harrison called across to him, "I beg you not to be harpooning me in the Senate. If you dislike anything in my Administration, put it into Clay or Webster. But don't harpoon me." Benton said he would do what Harrison desired.

By mid-February when he had completed his Cabinet by naming George Badger as Navy Secretary, Harrison announced a rule— No quarrels or arguments before March 4, only fun. Van Buren noticed his unusual lack of seriousness. "The President is the most extraordinary man I ever saw," Van Buren remarked. "He does not seem to realize the vast importance of his elevation. He talks and thinks with such ease and vivacity. He is as tickled with the Presidency as is a young woman with a new bonnet." On a visit to the Capitol, he stood about joking with both Democrats and Whigs. One Congressman introduced him to Representative Lewis Williams of North Carolina with the remark that "Mr. Williams is the oldest member and is called 'the Father of the House.'" Harrison replied, "Mr. Williams, I am glad to see the Father of the House and the more so because you have a very unruly set of boys to deal with, I know." When Harrison was introduced to the editor of the *Madisonian*, the conservative Democratic newspaper in Washington, he said, "Happy to see you, Mr. Allen. You are a good-looking chap for these parts, but there's hardly enough raw material in you for the girls beyond the Alleghenies!"

With the completion of his Cabinet, the pressure for jobs temporarily shifted to Harrison's Secretaries. "I could not be more hunted after and hunted down than I am," Attorney General Crittenden complained. Other Secretaries also admitted to the same torture. The temporary shunting of job seekers to the Cabinet should have given Harrison a needed rest. But he was on the banquet go all the time. There was one on February 15 with old military buddies. At another one, his rule prescribing fun was jolted when one man extolled himself and his claims for a top job and finally asked the weary Harrison for his comments. "The ham is excellent," Harrison drily replied.

By now Harrison realized he had come too early to Washington, and the prospect of another two weeks in the Whig victory atmosphere seemed unbearable. So he fled the political scene for Richmond, Virginia. But an endless line came through the Powhatan House to exchange greetings with him, and on February 20 he attended an immense party in his honor at the large log cabin erected by the Richmond Tippecanoe Club in the public square. In company with John Tyler, his Vice-President, who now came forward to greet him, he attended a military parade and after eating at Military Hall, he replied to a toast by giving his view of slavery. He stoutly insisted he had never been an abolitionist, as some were claiming. His memory was poor, for in 1790 he had been an active member of the Methodist-Quaker Humane Society of Richmond, which had been an abolitionist society.

Again, the noise and the crowds were tiring and he went to his ancestral home at Berkeley on the James River. In the quiet of his mother's room in the hundred-year-old brick mansion, he scribbled page after page of what would be his inaugural address. Then traveling with Tyler, Secretary of the Navy Badger, his grandnephew, Henry Harrison of Berkeley, who was to serve as his secretary, and with daughter Anna Tuthill Taylor, the ninth of his ten children, whose husband had been his substitute court clerk, he returned to Washington.

Philip Hone, the observant Whig merchant from New York, saw Harrison on the street and wrote, "Passing through the crowd on Pennsylvania Avenue was an elderly gentleman dressed in black and not remarkably well dressed, with a mild benign countenance, a military air, but stooping a little, bowing to one, shaking hands with another and cracking a joke with the third . . . the man among men, the sun of the political firmament."

This time Harrison could not stomach the thought of moving back to Gadsby's Tavern. Aware of the pounding he would get from job hunters, President Van Buren had sent him a remarkable offer that he could not accept. Van Buren told him he would vacate the White House early and let Harrison move in before his inauguration. Instead of this, Harrison moved into the home of William W. Seaton, the mayor of Washington. What must have made Clay worry about Harrison's new residence was the fact that Daniel Webster also lived with the Seatons.

It wasn't long before Webster had Harrison's inauguration speech and took on the task of editing it. The pretentious writing and the hodgepodge of ideas was a nightmare. Mrs. Seaton came upon Webster sprawled in a chair and asked why he looked so weary. "Madam," he told her, "within twelve hours I have killed seventeen Roman proconsuls as dead as smelts, every one of them!"

Because it became known that Webster was editing his speech, Harrison thought it prudent to pass it to Clay for further pruning afterward. However, Clay made only a few changes because Harrison's friends had warned him that the elimination of any more classical allusions would hurt Old Tip's feelings.

The great day finally arrived, a bitterly cold morning with a whistling northwest wind. The Whigs had decided that despite the friendliness between Van Buren and Harrison, politics dictated that Little Van not be invited to the inauguration. On March 4, Van Buren was observed "walking placidly down the Avenue as unconcerned as any private citizen in the crowd."

Harrison climbed onto Old Whitey, his large white horse, that morning after rejecting suggestions that he wear a coat and hat. Personal friends on either side of his white charger escorted him to the Capitol, where he appeared at the Senate chamber and shook hands with Tyler who had just been sworn in. After Tyler's short address, they marched to the eastern portico to face the cheering throng of fifty thousand persons, almost all of whom were wrapped in fur coats and heavy shawls. Harrison again refused to don a coat, and he began the 8500-word inaugural address, the longest in history. In one hour and forty minutes, he told the crowd of his intention to be a figurehead President and he defined what that would be. Among the classical allusions that had escaped Webster's inkpot was his citation of a Roman proconsul who noted the difference between the behavior of politicians before and after they assumed public office. No one need fear this from him, he said, for he would serve only one term, severely limit Presidential powers, avoid encroaching on the Legislative Branch, give Congress control over currency and refrain from employing an "Executive party" in the Capitol. One paragraph from the close of his address be stopped to take the oath of office administered by Chief Justice Roger Taney. Then he completed the last sentences,

finishing to a burst of cheers. The cheers were for him and not
for what he said, for newsmen reported that the crowd had not
paid attention to his address. Instead, the onlookers rudely talked
aloud about patronage and legislation.

By the time he finished, Harrison was thoroughly chilled and his
thin lips were blue. Yet again he refused a wraparound and insisted on riding Old Whitey to the Executive Mansion at the head
of the two-mile long gathering of floats and marchers in the inaugural parade. Fellow Whigs marveled at his stamina when he
spent the afternoon, following the parade, as host at the White
House reception and then attended two parties that evening plus
his ten-thirty P.M. appearance at the inaugural ball, where he
greeted Webster and Clay at the punch bowl and saluted General
Scott in his full dress uniform "with heavy epaulettes and yellow
plumes."

Harrison began his term with a heavy chest cold, but this did
not deter Clay and Webster from pressuring him to gain control
over his Administration. Nor did it bring any display of decency
among the clamoring office seekers who now crowded the White
House and waved letters of recommendation in the old man's
face. Duff Green, editor for Calhoun, pestered Harrison relentlessly for the post of minister to the Republic of Texas. Finally,
to get rid of him, Harrison named him governor of Florida. But
Green was back the next day importuning the President for an
appointment for his son. Webster was in the best position to promote friends for the diplomatic service. No matter who else he
might have desired to put into the key diplomatic post as minister
to Great Britain, Harrison frankly pacified Webster by naming
Edward Everett of Massachusetts. At one gathering, Harrison emo-
tionally told an old friend from Cincinnati, "I am glad with all
my heart to see you, for I know that you do not want an office."

The patronage fight even invaded the Cabinet room. Webster
refused to drop his demand that his friend James Wilson of New
Hampshire be appointed governor of the Iowa Territory, even
though Harrison hinted that his own friend, John Chambers, who
had been his aide-de-camp in the War of 1812, was in line for it.
At one Cabinet meeting, Webster informed Harrison that the Secretaries had taken a vote and decided that Wilson should have
Iowa. Harrison scribbled something on a piece of paper, then
handed the sheet to Webster with the request that he read it

aloud. Webster read: "William Henry Harrison, President of the United States."

Harrison then rose and announced fiercely, "And 'President of the United States' tells you, gentlemen, that by God, John Chambers will be governor of Iowa!" Chambers won the nomination and Wilson had to be satisfied with the job of surveyor general of the Territory.

Francis Blair, writing to Jackson on April 4, 1841, described a White House scene witnessed by General Alexander Hunter, marshal of Washington. "The President wanted to have a meeting of his Cabinet but could not go into a room where he was not pressed by the crowd. Hunter expostulated but in vain. He prepared to rally a force to drive out the intruders, but suggested to the President first to make a speech to them, stating his conditions. This he did, told them it was impossible to attend to their claims upon him as public business imperiously required his time. The Spoils men, however, refused to quit unless he would then receive their papers and pledge himself to attend to them. He capitulated, and first all his pockets were filled with papers, then his hat, then his arms, and finally Hunter was loaded; and both marched up stairs with as much as they could carry. It was with difficulty then that the House was cleared."

But the White House could not be cleared of the incessant struggle between Webster and Clay. The short "confirmation" session of the Senate was to expire on March 15, and Clay clamored for Harrison to call the Twenty-seventh Congress into immediate special session instead of waiting until December. Webster quickly voiced strong objection, for he understood Clay's reason. So long as Congress was not in session, Webster would be able to exert unopposed influence over the President. With Congress in Washington, Clay would gain the whiphand.

As for Harrison, he was not anxious to have Congress in town, even though Clay's argument for a swift Whig attack on the financial problems of the continuing depression seemed plausible. Nor were the Senate Whigs enthusiastic about spending the spring and summer in the capital. A caucus poll showed that only two members were behind Clay. But he came with his loose-jointed stroll into the caucus room at one meeting, "speaking as he went, in triumphant manner," and when the final vote was taken only two members opposed the calling of a special session.

While this argument was proceeding, Webster and Clay were

also fighting to install their own henchmen in the lucrative post of Collector of the Port of New York. Clay's man was a Whig hack named Robert C. Wetmore, while Webster's choice was Edward Curtis, formerly a Democrat but more recently a Weed man at the Harrisburg convention. Curtis, who managed to be both a Webster and a Thurlow Weed lieutenant, had played a conspicuous role at the convention in keeping Clay from winning the nomination.

When the Webster pressure failed to win an early nod from the President, Weed wrote privately to Clay to gain his support. Don't oppose Ed Curtis and be assured that Curtis' services will be available for you in 1844, Weed wrote. This letter so infuriated Clay that he almost blew the Whigs apart with his threat to show the letter to Webster, who was also making plans for 1844. However, calming down, he played the game with his usual directness and spoke to Harrison about dropping Curtis as a possible appointee. Curtis, who was aware of what was going on regarding his and other appointments, reported from Washington that "Gen[1]. Harrison gives signs of a disposition to have some voice in the matter. . . . However arrogant this . . . and however foolish not to leave it to the editors and office seekers, it is well ascertained that the old man, thro. the weakness incedent [sic] of waning life, is immovable upon this point."

The Senate quit on Monday, March 15, before Harrison had made any decision about the call for a special session or about the Curtis appointment. A few days later Curtis wrote Weed about Clay: "He visited our dinner table on Tuesday, drank, laughed, joked and was happy for hours, & at night bid me goodbye with a hearty shake of the hand & God bless you, Curtis—God bless you, and the next morning went to General Harrison to make his final protest in the most decisive terms against me—left town that day, & from Baltimore wrote to Gen. H. not to appoint that d—d fellow Curtis."

A playback of actual events shows that Clay went to see Harrison for a final showdown on Curtis. But when this proved inconclusive, he sent Harrison a letter on March 13, concentrating this time on his other demand, that the President call an "Extra Session." He went so far as to enclose a proclamation that Harrison could use to recall Congress. That day Harrison reached the decision that Clay had gone too far and he wrote an angry reply. Clay lacked generosity, he complained, and failed to realize that the President had to consult others besides the Kentucky Senator. "You use the privilege of a friend to lecture me . . . . You are too impetuous." He could not call a special session, Harrison went on, because the Tennessee delegation was incomplete and uninstructed. He also told Clay he preferred letters from him "to a conversation in the presence of others." Clay sent his reply to Harrison. It was one for the historic record with Clay strangely insisting that he had never dictated about patronage, never demanded that Harrison appoint any of his friends to any offices and never said that Curtis should not be given an appointment.

Two days later a friend found Clay pacing his room "in great perturbation," with Harrison's crumpled letter in his hand. "And it has come to this!" Clay roared. "I am civilly but virtually requested not to visit the White House, not to see the President personally but hereafter only communicate with him in writing. . . . Here is my table loaded with letters from my friends in every part of the Union applying to me to obtain offices for them, when I have not one to give, nor influence enough to procure the appointment of a friend to the most humble position." He left town shortly afterward, and never saw Harrison again.

With Clay gone, Harrison now made decisions on the two troubles between him and the Senator. First he made a show of asking for the Cabinet's advice on the port collector's post. A four-man committee (Ewing, Badger, Bell and Granger) reported in favor of Curtis. This served to make a decision simple and he bowed in favor of the Webster-Weed man. The Curtis appointment also pleased Abbott Lawrence, the New England cotton mill magnate, who had given Harrison a $5000 loan at the beginning of his Presidency. In addition, Harrison issued a call for a special session of Congress, but he tempered his pro-Clay decision by delaying the commencement date until May 31.

Despite the continuation of his chest cold, the Webster-Clay squabble and the mob milling about in the White House, Harrison attempted to do some work. British papers had been demanding war if the United States did not release Alexander McLeod, the self-incriminating Canadian who claimed he killed an American crew member of the *Caroline* during the Canadian Rebellion. Harrison dispatched Attorney General Crittenden to New York to get the New York court indictment quashed. This infuriated Governor Seward who insisted that the McLeod affair was a local court matter and no business of the Federal Government. However, Seward promised Crittenden he would pardon McLeod.

By the time he had been in office only two weeks, Harrison was already growing apprehensive about the Whig spoils system. His Cabinet had decided to remove every Democrat and with Ewing and Granger in the lead, Whigs were inserted into small and large jobs throughout the Federal service. In six months, Granger would be boasting that he removed 39 of the 133 Presidential postmasters and 2500 lesser postmasters, while Ewing would be justifying his wholesale firing of Democrats on the ground that "the offices had become for the most part filled with brawling offensive political partisans of a very low moral standard."

Harrison first involved himself in the spoils system when he sent a strong memo on Presidential policy to department heads. He ordered an end to the practice of forcing government employees to make political payments to party "tax" collectors. Any payment would result in dismissal, he said. Another order forbade civil servants from "partisan participation in popular elections" or from receiving pay for party duties.

These orders did not meet with the approval of his Cabinet, and when his Secretaries told him on March 22 of the party decision to fire all Democrats, his reaction startled them. They stared as he leaped to his feet, thrust out a fist and shouted, "So help me, God, I will resign my office before I can be guilty of such iniquity!" Later he told an Indiana Congressman, "They are urging the most unmerciful proscription, and if they continue to do so much longer, they will drive me mad!"

To counteract the trend, he went to the offices of his Secretaries and examined personnel matters on the spot. No one was to be fired without cause, he warned them. He also requested former Cabinet members to submit an analysis of the individual employees they had known. To guard against stealing, the common charge at the time against public employees, he ordered collecting and disbursing officers to maintain up-to-the-minute open records and to supply him with detailed statements on spending for public works then under way.

Harrison's troublesome cough subsided somewhat a week after his inauguration. However, he did not feel well because his carefully maintained health program had been badly upset by the change in routine. Never robust physically, he had previously managed a normal existence by exercising regularly, keeping decent hours, eating simply and enforcing a regimen free of mental worries. Since coming to Washington, he had not been able to follow these rules.

To get some exercise, he rose early each day and walked to the market to buy meat and fish. One morning he visited Washington's only bookshop and complained loudly to the proprietor that he had not been able to find a Bible in the White House. "The Bible ought to be part of the furniture of the house," he insisted. This interest in religion was manifested by his Sunday routine of attending Episcopal services in the morning and Presbyterian services in the evening.

On one occasion while out for a walk, he was caught in a cloudburst and returned soaking wet to the White House. Then instead of spending the rest of the day indoors, he walked through the slush to nearby Octagon House to offer Colonel John Tayloe a diplomatic post. Tayloe's son had been Harrison's secretary when he was minister to Colombia.

At five P.M. on March 26, Dr. Thomas Miller walked up the White House stairs to the second floor to examine an ailing President. He found Harrison out of bed and complaining of fatigue and mental anxiety. Harrison said his coughing and sniffing had been with him since the inauguration. He told Miller about his own medical background and said he usually was his own doctor. He listed his longtime ailments as neuralgia, which bothered his stomach, heart and extremities; dyspepsia, which he tried to control by keeping to a meat diet; and chronic constipation. He added that dyspepsia had been severe since he moved into the White House, but he was attempting to control it by resorting to an almost starvation diet.

Miller decided not to give him any medicine. Harrison was to stay in bed until he was recovered, do no work and avoid excitement. Miller said he would return that evening for another look, but when he came back, Harrison was in the parlor having a loud happy time with old wartime buddies. The President assured Dr. Miller he was almost completely recovered and would be in fine shape by morning. The doctor still thought that Harrison should follow his advice, but it was impossible to force his view on the President of the United States.

Harrison wrote that night to his son, John Scott Harrison, asking him to "send on Bacon, Beef, etc., etc., (Lard)." He made no mention of illness, but called attention to his duties and said he met with his Cabinet every morning at eleven-thirty A.M. The next day Harrison's troubles were far more serious. That Saturday morning he took a stroll about the White House grounds, went to market, saw a visitor in his office and escorted him to the Avenue. He was sitting in a Cabinet meeting at one P.M. when he was suddenly stricken with a shaking chill that lasted fifteen minutes. This time he was carried to bed and a nurse named Fanny was placed in charge.

That evening the doctor decided he was too old to bleed, but something was required to take care of what the doctor called "bilious pleurisy." The substitute technique was to "cup" him. The cupping process involved turning a cup over a lighted candle, then setting the hot cup over the skin. As the cup cooled, the skin beneath was "drawn in a lump into the cup." The following day he ran a high fever and he was so parched that he drank water almost compulsively.

A few days later he appeared to be gaining strength. He wrote a letter on patronage to Ed Curtis—his last letter—and ordered Curtis to employ a seaman who had served aboard the *Montilla,* the ship that had carried him home from Colombia in 1830. Then he called for the new Bible he had purchased after announcing he would become a communicant at St. Johns Episcopal Church across Lafayette Park from the White House grounds. When the Bible was brought to him, he asked that the 103rd Psalm be read and he thanked the Lord for His mercy. He seemed "overpowered with emotion."

After that his condition steadily worsened. "Ah, Fanny," he told his nurse, "I am ill, very ill, much worse so than they think me."

Four doctors now came to see what they could do for him. What they did in the name of medical care was criminal. They drew a great deal of blood from him with their suction cups. Then they blistered his skin with stinging ointments. Down his throat went harsh purgatives—rhubarb, castor oil and calomel. In addition, he was administered opium, brandy and camphor, and when his skin turned jaundiced, crude petroleum and Virginia snakeweed were added to the tortures. At one point in his delirium, Harrison cried out, "It is wrong. I won't consent—it is unjust. These applications, will they never cease?" He asked that Colonel George Croghan, who had commanded Fort Stephenson and Detroit in the War of 1812, be brought to him and when Croghan appeared, Harrison pleaded, "I can't stand it. . . . I can't bear this. . . . Don't trouble me."

The always efficient Colonel Todd of the Cincinnati *Republican* and recently appointed minister to Russia employed himself writing out frequent sickroom bulletins for the *National Intelligencer.* All day Saturday, April 3, the reports were pessimistic. By six P.M., the four doctors agreed he would not live. Shortly after midnight, he groaned and Dr. N. W. Worthington listened to his final words—"Sir," Harrison cried out, "I wish you to understand the true principles of the government! I wish them carried out. I ask nothing more."

Colonel Todd's report of his death at twelve-thirty A.M. on April 4, exactly a month after his inauguration, noted: "Topical depletion, blistering and appropriate internal remedies subdued in a great measure the diseases of the lungs and liver, but the stomach and intestines did not regain a healthy condition."

Every doorknocker in Washington was covered with black crepe after the news spread. Harrison's remains were taken to the East Room where twenty-four clergymen and twenty-four pallbearers surrounded his coffin. Then his body was taken to the Capitol to rest in state. Newspapers noted the irony that his funeral was far better organized than his inauguration. It also "occasioned even a greater concourse than the inauguration," said one report. "Every steamboat, train, coach and carriage poured crowds into the city where bells were constantly tolled and minute guns fired." The crowds cried in sympathy for his charger, Old Whitey, a forlorn appearing beast who walked riderless in the procession with boots set backward in the stirrups.

Asked to comment on the first Presidential death in office, General Jackson at the Hermitage blasphemed: "A kind and overruling Providence has interfered to prolong our glorious Union. For surely Tyler will stay the corruption of this clique who has got into power by deluding the people by the grossest of slanders . . . and hard cider."

☆ 10 ☆

JOHN TYLER

The Challenged Heir

At dawn on April 5, 1841, a persistent rapping at his Williamsburg, Virginia, door brought a sleepy man in nightgown and cap down the stairs to investigate. He was a long, thin man with a long, thin face, a long, thin nose and bright eyes like an eagle. He took a long, thin look at the two early callers until he learned their mission. One was Fletcher Webster, the young son of Secretary of State Daniel Webster and the department's chief clerk, while the other was a Mr. Beall, an employee of the U. S. Senate. The Vice-President must come to Washington without delay, Webster relayed the Cabinet's request. President Harrison had expired at twelve-thirty the day before.

Thus began John Tyler's tempestuous ascension to First Citizen of the Land and four years of cannonading warfare between him and Senator Henry Clay to determine who would direct the Federal Government. In the course of Tyler's chaotic term, he was thrown out of the Whig party that had made him Harrison's running mate, mobs invaded the White House grounds with guns and bugles, "indignation meetings were everywhere held," and "the fires of a thousand effigies lighted the streets of the various cities." As Clay's newspaper organ, the Lexington *Intelligencer,* put it: "If a God-directed thunderbolt were to strike and annihilate the traitor, all would say that 'Heaven is just.'" Representative Millard Fillmore, the overweight but handsome Whig boss of Buffalo, jeeringly appraised the fight between the two men in this fashion: "I have heard of but two Tyler men in this city [Buffalo, New York], and I need not add that both are applicants for office."

Nevertheless, the blunt truth was that when the smoke of the battle eventually faded, Tyler was not on his back with the foot of the victorious Clay on his chest. At a price of frequent attacks of indigestion and diarrhea, he won the right for all Vice-Presidents to be called and empowered as "President" and not as "Acting President" when the elected Chief Executive died in office.

In addition, by his bold use of the President's veto power, he offset the great legislative strength massed against him by Clay. As the Richmond *Whig* assessed on one occasion the ease with which he was able to nullify the positive action of the House and Senate: "Again has the imbecile, into whose hands accident has placed the power, vetoed a bill passed by a majority of those legally authorized to pass it." Ten times did he veto bills, tearing the heart out of the Whig legislative program; and unable to muster the necessary two-thirds of each house to override his vetoes, the Whigs were reduced to screaming in futile fury, instituting idiotic impeachment proceedings and gaining a modicum of revenge by rejecting more than a hundred of his nominations submitted to the Senate for confirmation.

Henry Clay was in Kentucky when Harrison died. In a letter he wrote afterward to one of Tyler's close friends, he referred to the Virginian as the "Vice-President" and said that he would be administering a "regency" until the next election. Tyler was simply an accident and a "flash in the pan" who would be without real power or influence.

Then there was John Quincy Adams, "Old Man Eloquent," who wrote in his diary on April 4, 1841: "This day is in every sense gloomy." Word had reached him of Harrison's passing and the thought that Tyler would now become "Acting President of the Union," as he put it, galled him. In his corrosive style, he wrote: "Tyler is a political sectarian of the slave-driving, Virginian, Jeffersonian school, principled against all improvements, with all the interests and passions and vices of slavery rooted in his moral and political constitution—with talents not above mediocrity, and a spirit incapable of expansion to the dimensions of the station upon which he has been cast by the hand of Providence."

When he heard the news of Harrison's death, Tyler reacted with a calmness and swiftness that betokened a man who had prepared himself beforehand for just this eventuality. Shortly after Fletcher Webster roused him, he sped on horseback to Richmond where he boarded the train and arrived in Washington at five A.M., Tuesday, April 6, only fifty-three hours after Harrison had expired.

This breakneck speed had purpose behind it. Obviously, Tyler realized that if he did not create a new status for himself posthaste, other political leaders would designate a smaller role for him, from which he would later be unable to extricate himself.

By mid-morning, he had established himself at Brown's Indian Queen Hotel, where the rate was $1.50 a day with brandy and whisky free. Once he checked in, he sent word to all Cabinet members to come immediately. All were in town except Secretary of the Navy George Badger and they said they would come. Tyler gave no thought to their friendship for him. He knew they had been forced on Harrison by Clay, Webster and Thurlow Weed, and he was well aware that from Secretary of State Webster down, the six Secretaries considered him with contempt, as a pigmy on the king's throne. They were a representative sample of the entire Whig party leadership, a broad conglomeration that had always oppressed Tyler whenever he found himself in their company. At such times, he said, he felt choked "surrounded by Claymen, Webster-men, anti-Masons, original Harrisonians, old Whigs and new Whigs—each jealous of the others."

The Cabinet was the first group he had to bring into line to avoid a revolution against his plans. The Secretaries had met after Harrison's death and it was common knowledge they had concluded that "Mr. Tyler, while performing the function of President bear the title of 'Vice-President Acting President.'" According to John Tyler, Jr., who had accompanied his father to Washington to serve as his private secretary, Tyler's first meeting with the Cabinet bore out the intended arrogance toward him. Webster lost little time telling Tyler that the late President Harrison had always relied on the majority vote of the Secretaries on all matters relating to the Administration.

Tyler's response to what he called "this exhibition of adamantine cheek" was savage. "I can never consent to being dictated to," he turned on Webster. "I, as President, shall be responsible for *my* Administration. I hope to have your hearty co-operation in carrying out its measures. So long as you see fit to do this, I shall be glad to have you with me. When you think otherwise, your resignation will be accepted." No recorded protest developed.

Long before, Tyler had developed a dislike for Webster that was based on the entirely incorrect premises that Webster had been a member of the 1814 Hartford Convention of New England disunionists and was later the Congressional hatchetman of President John Quincy Adams, "The mere fact that Daniel Webster, a Hartford Conventionist, has been his [Adams'] mouthpiece," Tyler once cursed Webster, "has always been with me enough to damn him."

Despite his detestation for the Harrison Cabinet, Tyler realized the need for government continuity. At his leisure he would find loyal replacements and in the meantime he would operate chiefly through his own backstairs "Kitchen Cabinet" of old Virginia friends such as wrinkled thirty-four-year-old Representative Henry A. Wise, Tom Dew, head of William and Mary, and Nathaniel Tucker, novelist-lawyer and half-brother of John Randolph. When the Cabinet agreed to stay, and under his own terms of subservience, he knew that he had successfully walked across the first burning coal bed.

Beyond the Cabinet lay the public and the politicians, and Tyler acted with assurance to win their acceptance of him as a full President, with all the prerogatives as well as the title of Chief Executive. Newspapers and influential politicians were already referring to him as an Acting President, but this view had not spread because the news of Harrison's death still stunned and numbed the nation.

A reading of Article II, section 1, of the Constitution convinced some constitutional lawyers that the unique situation in which Tyler found himself did not permit him the legality of being more than an Acting President. Pertinent paragraph 5, as vague as other parts of the Constitution when a crisis arose, read: "In Case of the Removal of the President from Office, or of his Death, Resignation, or Inability to discharge the Powers and Duties of the said Office, the same shall devolve on the Vice-President." Their argument was that the word "same" referred to the "Duties of the said Office," not to the Office itself.

As a strict constructionist, had Tyler not been personally involved he would undoubtedly have joined in this opinion. However, his strong ego, vanity and the enormous opportunity of fulfilling his wildest dream made him take the opposite course. "Same" did not refer to the "Duties of the said Office," he said bluntly. "Same" referred to "Office"; and a proper reading of the paragraph was: "In Case of the Removal of the President from Office . . . the same shall devolve on the Vice-President."

Tyler believed that the oath he had taken for Vice-President a month earlier covered his elevation to the Office of President. But he realized that a new oath ceremony would solidify his own view that he was a full President as well as dramatize this situation to the nation. Besides, it would go far to stifle the legal loophole seekers.

Chief Justice Roger Taney, in Baltimore at the time, refused to administer the oath of office to him. But Chief Judge William Cranch of the Circuit Court of Appeals for the District of Columbia, nephew of John Adams and one of his "midnight" nominations, was amenable and the ceremony took place at noon at Brown's Indian Queen Hotel before his Cabinet on the day of his arrival in town. Cranch later said Tyler told him he wanted the ceremony because "doubts may arise and for greater caution."

Even Harrison's funeral served his cause. Despite his low opinion of Harrison, Tyler managed a sad face at the funeral rites on April 7. Newspaper reports described him as "visibly affected" as he walked in slow cadence down the Avenue behind Old Whitey, the general's horse, the casket and Harrison's relatives who were to take the body back to Harrison's wife at North Bend, Ohio, for burial. Then to symbolize that the old had given way to the new, Tyler issued a Presidential proclamation afterward, ordering Friday, May 14, set aside as a national day of praying and fasting.

Tyler's next move to consolidate his position was to issue an inaugural address to the nation on April 9. This was a poorly worded address, obviously written hurriedly. Yet it served his purpose, for in it he boldly referred to "my Administration." Other than this, the chief point of his inaugural address was an ominous statement to Whig leaders that he would focus his Presidential efforts on strengthening states' rights and preventing the extension of Federal authority.

Five days later, Tyler took his most symbolic step when he moved out of the Indian Queen and into the White House. Since the Executive Mansion was the residence of Presidents and not of a Vice-President Acting President, Tyler intended that this move would go far to win him acceptance as President.

The most crucial test was yet to come. This would take place at the end of May when the special session of the Twenty-seventh Congress would convene. Tyler knew that instead of permitting the regular session to come in December 1841, Clay had badgered Harrison into calling the special session for May 31. Tyler also knew the reason—that with Congress away all spring, summer and fall, Clay had been concerned that Secretary of State Webster would have been able to make himself supreme over the government.

Because the special session would soon pour legislators into Washington, Tyler found it advisable to give the impression he esteemed Clay as an eminent statesman. He now went out of his way to praise Clay to men who might be in touch with him. For instance, on May 8, 1841, Treasury Secretary Thomas Ewing wrote to Clay: "No man can be better disposed [toward you] than the President. . . . He speaks of you with the utmost kindness and you may rely upon it his friendship is strong and unabated."

Part of the final and most crucial test came in the House on May 31, the day of assembly, when Representative John McKeon of New York questioned the legality of designating him as President Tyler. But Tyler's commander in the House, Representative Henry Wise, the most important member of his "Kitchen Cabinet," was on his feet long ready for McKeon's move. Wise, the hot-headed, argumentative, duel-threatening Virginian, quickly offered a countering resolution asserting that Tyler was President "by the Constitution, by election and by the Act of God." No one wanted to tangle with the tall, lean man with piercing eyes who once publicly poked a finger in the eye of former Speaker James K. Polk and called him foul names. Moreover, it was the first day of the session and no one proposed to mar the day. So expected opposition to Tyler did not come forward and Wise's resolution passed handily.

In the Senate, the decision rested on the whim of Henry Clay. How well Tyler's campaign of friendship had succeeded with Clay became evident on June 1, when the Senate took up the question of Tyler's status. Senator William Allen of Ohio proposed that the Senate communicate with Tyler as "the Vice-President, on whom, by the death of the late President, the powers and duties of the Office of President have devolved." However, when Clay offered no encouragement to the Allen Resolution, it was defeated by a vote of 38 to 8.

Almost two months earlier, Tyler had written: "I am under Providence made the instrument of a new test which is for the first time to be applied to our institutions." Now he could say without contradiction: "I am the President of the United States."

Having accomplished his first objective, Tyler was already thinking of a second—to make an outstanding record as President. Unfortunately, this was of a different order from his struggle to establish himself as President. First of all, he had no control over his political party, a matter that had ballooned to prime importance for a President with the advent of Jackson's regime. Second, he had no control over Congress or its key committees. And third, he could not bring himself to proceed beyond the Jeffersonian political bible, which classified as original sin any attempt by a President to provide Congress with finished legislation to consider instead of general, gentle suggestions.

If Tyler lacked these vital powers, there was one man who held them and planned to use them. Shortly after Harrison's election, Whig leaders and Harrison had firmly agreed that "Prince Hal" of Kentucky would succeed the old general after a single term. This had immediately re-established Clay as Mr. Whig himself and his authority extended throughout the party and the Congress. Moreover, Clay had a well-detailed program, his so-called American System, ready to promote at the first opportunity, and the high regard of the American people that made him the most popular American of his era. Had Harrison, the Old Farmer of North Bend, lived, he would have offered no obstacles to the enactment of Clay's American System because he believed in it.

But now that Harrison was dead and humorless Tyler was trying to assert himself, Clay was well aware that his claim check for 1844 might be torn up unless he destroyed Tyler. Clay knew that Tyler, once tasting the power and glamour of the Presidency, would want another four-year drink. In addition, by using the appealing setting of the White House, Tyler already possessed a powerful lever for competing with Clay for the Whig nomination in 1844. Then again, any positive reputation Tyler should gain during the next four years could come only at Clay's expense.

So while Tyler might be called "Mr. President," he must be limited to the role of a figurehead President. The Virginia states'-rights extremist must be taught to regard Clay as the master of his Administration and to give more than mere lip service to the twelve-year-long Whig battle cry of "Executive Usurpation" that had welded the party together against Jackson and Van Buren.

The struggle that now unfolded between Clay and Tyler was not one between old friends in sudden competition. For years, they had been on a collision course and both recognized that they stood poles apart in their philosophy of government and their interpretation of the Constitution. Tyler had no business calling himself a Whig, for by 1840 it was abundantly clear that the main-line Whigs were nationalists who supported Clay's American System calling for another Biddle-type Bank, protective tariffs for American industry, Federal internal improvements, plus the development of towns and cities and the weakening of the institution of slavery.

Most of Tyler's friends in the South, who had become Whigs because of Jackson's policies on banking and currency and the right of nullification, had by now returned to the Democratic fold, following the lead of John C. Calhoun. The Whigs had never felt comfortable with these Democratic turncoats and had referred to them as the "Awkward Squadron."

Only inertia had kept Tyler from making the switch back to the Democrats with his friends, for on no point did he agree with the Whig mainstream. The nationalism that Clay and John Quincy Adams preached was the devil himself to Tyler. "The Government was created by the states," he once explained his extreme stand. "It is amenable to the states, is preserved by the states and may be destroyed by the states." Any time the states desired, he said, they "may strike you [the Federal Government] out of existence by a word; demolish the Constitution and scatter its fragments to the wind."

It was the luck of his inertia that made him Vice-President and then President. When the Whigs later came to question how they could have put a man like Tyler on the 1840 ticket with Old Tippecanoe Harrison, one answer was that there had been a mistaken notion that he was an ally of Clay. Tyler had attended the Whig convention, which had cruelly euchred Clay from winning the Presidential nomination. Recalled Horace Greeley, the New York *Tribune*'s editor, "When it was announced that Mr. Clay was defeated, he (Tyler) cried (so it was reported); and that report (I think) gave him the nomination for Vice-President as a sop to Clay."

Tyler later denied he had ever shed a tear over Clay. He labeled the story of the inane reason for giving a man a top nomination as "the greatest of the falsehoods propagated" against himself. Yet there is ample evidence that his supposed shedding of tears over Clay made his selection a simple matter by a guilt-ridden convention.

Despite the conclusion of the 1840 Whig convention that Tyler and Clay were soulmates, their differences extended far beyond their political philosophies. In a broad sense, Tyler was a member of the slow-moving, genteel "minuet" political school that had existed before Jackson so ruthlessly modernized politics. The minueters claimed they had entered politics solely as a public duty and were forever complaining of the agonies and expenses they suffered to fulfill their duty. On the other hand, Clay found politics the most exciting part of his life, the place where personal ambitions might achieve the highest honor the nation could bestow. Power was to him as important as breathing. Most Americans found the Kentuckian an exciting figure. Abraham Lincoln once called Clay, "My beau ideal of a statesman, the man for whom I fought all my humble life."

Clay was the Great Pacificator, the Great Compromiser, the man who found the common ground on which opposing forces could jointly stand. Tyler had rigid rules of thought and conduct, and deviation from them was unthinkable. Tyler had a courtly veneer, bowing and smiling, pretending not to hear offensive remarks. He was quiet and a prude who found the waltz outrageously intimate, while Clay was loud and friendly, gambled heavily, drank too much on occasion and was too attentive to young women. Yet surprisingly, Tyler put little stock in formal religion, while Clay never went to bed without first dropping to his knees, touching his fingertips and reciting, "Now I lay me down to sleep . . ."

Tyler's rules of thought and conduct came secondhand from others, hence the rigidity with which he practiced them. He derived his standard of polite conduct from Lord Chesterfield's letters to his son. "Half the success in life depends on manners," Tyler once wrote his own son Robert. His laissez-faire economic views were memorized gobs of Adam Smith's *Wealth of Nations* and his political views were those of his idol, Thomas Jefferson, who demanded in his written words the strictest construction of the Constitution, states' rights and legislative supremacy. Unfortunately, Tyler in action was more Jeffersonian than Jefferson, for the father of the Republican party had been sufficiently practical and flexible to cast aside his own philosophy when logic demanded.

Tyler was born in Charles City County in the snob set James River Tidewater in 1790, while Henry Clay had started life thirteen years earlier in nearby Hanover County, the son of a Baptist preacher in the poor neighborhood known as "The Slashes." Tyler's father had been a college roommate of Jefferson, and later became a state judge, governor and Federal judge.

Tyler went to fashionable William and Mary College, graduating at seventeen, while Clay confessed to only three years of schooling and these from a drunken Englishman who had been his teacher. Throughout his life, Clay regretted not having learned Greek and Latin, which politicians of his era used so effectively in Congressional debate to give off the aura of culture. Nevertheless, Clay managed to gain a unique education by serving as the fifteen-year-old secretary to George Wythe, the Chancellor of Virginia, outstanding national lawyer, signer of the Declaration of Independence and member of the Constitutional Convention of 1787. Wythe directed Clay's readings in the law and classics, filled him with ambition and showed him how to brazen through local mores when Wythe, a bachelor, freely admitted to anyone that the young mulatto he was raising in his home was his own son. Five years later, after passing the bar, Clay moved to Lexington, Kentucky, "the land of lawsuits and horses," and the "Athens of the West," to rush into his half century of law, stock breeding and politics.

Tyler was also a young man in a hurry. At twenty-one, he was already in the Virginia House of Delegates, and at twenty-six he went to Congress. It was 1816 and he gazed with awe upon Speaker Henry Clay, twice already a member of the Senate, the engineer of what was called "Mr. Clay's War of 1812" and a member of the American diplomatic brigade for peace at Ghent in 1814.

Tyler's unbending principles and independence of party labels were apparent while he served in the House. They were also apparent when he became Virginia's governor in 1825 and when he entered the Senate in 1827 replacing bitter-tongued John Randolph. He voted to censure General Jackson in 1819 for his role in the Seminole fighting, supported him for President in 1828 and 1832, approved of his veto of the Second Bank's recharter, then condemned him for withdrawing government funds from the Bank before its charter expired in 1836. He was the only Senator who dared vote against Jackson's Force Bill, the proposal to use military force to bring tariff law compliance from the South Carolina Nullifiers.

As for his political relations with Clay, he opposed the Clay-promoted Missouri Compromise, his candidacy for President in 1824 and 1832, but considered him a hero in 1833 for his tariff-lowering measure known as the Clay Compromise Tariff Act of 1833. In turn, Clay saw to it that Tyler got only meager support when he ran for Vice-President in 1836 on the Whig ticket. Then in 1839, when Tyler ran again for the Senate, Clay threw his support to William C. Rives, a conservative Democrat. When neither Tyler nor Rives gained a majority after twenty-eight ballots, Virginia's Assembly gave up and the state was without its second Senator until 1841.

It was not that Tyler had deceived the Whigs in 1840 about his regard for Clay and his principles. "I was perfectly and entirely silent in that convention," he said. "I was wholly unquestioned about my opinions." No one cared what he thought because Whig strategists planned a campaign to fool the voters and avoid issues, relying on the nonsense approach of log cabins, hard cider and songfests to defeat Van Buren. All that mattered was that Tyler was from the South and Virginia had twenty-three electoral votes. "And we'll vote for Tyler, therefore, Without a why or wherefore," went the unconcerned refrain from a popular Whig campaign song.

Tyler had planned to sit out the campaign at home with his wife Letitia, who had suffered a paralytic stroke the previous year. But when he heard that the Democratic Vice-President "Tecumseh" Johnson, who was running again, was drawing crowds, he made his own independent swing to Ohio in September. Hecklers in audiences pestered him about his views, and it cost him dearly to mutter his standard reply: "I am in favor of what General Harrison and Mr. Clay are in favor of." Once when Tyler wrote a reply to Pennsylvania Democrats who wanted to learn his view of a Third Bank of the United States, Washington Whigs would not release his reply on the ground that "Mr. Tyler's opinions were already too well known to need a response." In the words of one Virginian, a declaration of truth by the Whig ticket would have shown that "Tip was Bank, Ty was anti-Bank; Tip was tariff, Ty was anti-tariff . . . In fact, fellow citizens, Tip is Whig, Ty is Democratic."

After the election of Harrison, Whig leaders were sorry for the first time that they had put Tyler on the ticket. For Tyler had played a cipher role, with his own state voting for Van Buren instead of the Whig ticket. There was also momentary after-doubt about the wisdom of taking Tyler when the leadership took a close look at Harrison's state of health. The patronage pushing and shoving the old general went through led one Whig to conjecture that he would be "devoured by the divided pack of his own dogs." Henry Clay, who had fought with him over Cabinet appointments and the need for a special session of Congress, said he looked "somewhat shattered" in appearance after the election. Following Harrison's visit to Lexington, Clay wrote on December 8, 1840: "He is much broken, but his mind retains all its strength and vigor." Webster later said he had concluded from a similar study that Harrison was in poor physical condition. Nevertheless, they and other ranking Whigs could not believe that anything fatal would occur, and so they gave no further thought to Tyler. However, there was one man who did and he wrote to Tyler with predictions about the future. The man was Littleton Tazewell, Tyler's personal friend, former Senator and Virginia governor and a Jacksonian who had joined the Whigs and then returned to the Democrats.

Tazewell wrote to Tyler his belief that Harrison would soon die and he forecasted immense troubles for Tyler. The Vice-President-elect recollected Tazewell's comments afterward and said, "He spoke of violent assaults to be made upon me unless I yielded my conscience, judgment—everything, into the hands of the political managers . . . and even anticipated my resignation as a measure to be forced upon me." Because Tyler was a methodical man, there is good reason to believe that Tazewell's prophecy precipitated some thought about his future course of action should Harrison die.

Harrison came to Virginia in February 1841 to escape the spoilsmen of Washington and Tyler accompanied him back to the capital as an insignificant part of his entourage. While the crowds roared and followed Harrison to his pre-inaugural stay with Mayor Seaton, Tyler went quietly to Brown's Indian Queen Hotel. Harrison had discussed nothing with him and made no plans to hold a meeting with him in the future. The truth was that they had little in common.

On Inauguration Day, Tyler took his oath of office in the Senate chamber before members of both houses, the Supreme Court, the diplomatic corps and crowded galleries. Then he delivered a five-minute address that Senator Benton characterized as "appropriately brief." It was just as well that Harrison was conversing in a loud voice in the anteroom and then in the Senate chamber with enthusiastic well-wishers during Tyler's speech. For Tyler's words were a glorification of states' rights. Afterward when the procession was arranged, Tyler joined the others for the walk to the east portico of the Capitol where Harrison's time of glory took

place. Then upon the completion of Harrison's wretched and over-
long address in the bitter cold, Tyler returned to the Senate chamber to preside over the confirmation of the new President's Cabinet
choices.

Once this chore was done, he ignored the gala inauguration
balls to return to Williamsburg. No one noticed that evening that
the Vice-President was not in Washington.

When the Twenty-seventh Congress met in special session eight
weeks after Tyler took the oath as President, Clay's control
over the Legislative Branch was impressive. The Whig majority
stood at forty-nine in the House and seven in the Senate, and with
few exceptions the legislative Whigs considered Clay to be their
Grand Sachem, even though they helped in rejecting him as the
party's Presidential candidate in 1840. From Speaker John White
of Kentucky, Clay's henchman, down through the backbench
Whigs, the House looked to Clay for guidance as much as the
Upper Chamber did. As the Washington correspondent of the
New York *Herald* noted, "He predominated over the Whig party
with despotic sway. Old Hickory himself never lorded it over his
followers with authority more undisputed, or more supreme. Mr.
Clay's wish is a paramount law to the whole party."

Tyler blundered at the outset in dealing with Clay. In a letter of
April 30, 1841, at a time when he believed he needed Clay's support to be recognized as a full President, he had mentioned the
Bank issue. But instead of bluntly reasserting his view that another
national bank in the image of the Biddle structure was unconstitutional, he weakly pleaded with Clay: "As to a Bank—I would not
have it urged prematurely." However, should Clay insist upon
one, Tyler continued, he hoped that the Kentucky Senator would
"consider whether you cannot so frame a Bank as to avoid all
constitutional objections." He also promised his entire lack of "intention to submit anything to Congress on this subject." The net
impression of his letter was that he would be a pushover for whatever Clay wanted to do.

Tyler's second blunder was his Message to Congress on June 1.
Mentally, he had not yet made the transition from the Capitol to
the White House. This would come as soon as his ego understood
the latent powers of his new office. So with the Presidency still a
vague enemy to his mind, he assured Congress that he considered
it the more "immediate representatives of the states and the peo-

ple." Certainly the results of the last election showed that former President Van Buren's Sub-Treasury plan had been "plainly condemned by the voice of the people." But instead of presenting Congress with his own specific plan to replace the Sub-Treasury government vault system with another for the collection and disbursement of public funds, he begged Congress for ideas. "It is incumbent upon Congress to devise a plan," he said, adding that his only role would be "the ultimate power of rejecting any measure which may in my view of it conflict with the Constitution." Yet even this threat of a possible veto he softened by saying that it was "a power . . . which I will not believe any act of yours will call into requisition."

Within the week, Clay took up the leadership void. First, he put his key helpers on important committees and awarded himself the chairmanship of the Senate Finance Committee where all banking and tariff legislation would go. Then, on June 7, he presented a resolution for a legislative agenda of six proposed measures, which he said would be the labor of that session. Among his proposals were the repeal of the Sub-Treasury Act, the incorporation of a Third Bank of the United States, a step-up in tariff rates, the authorization of a Treasury loan because government revenues during the continuing depression were inadequate, and the distribution to the states of the money taken in from the sale of public land. To show his mastery, Clay had inserted in the resolution Congress approved the statement that any postponement of his bills would "be materially detrimental to the public interest." Senator Silas Wright of New York, leader of the Democrats, wrote to Van Buren that Clay "is much more imperious and arrogant with his friends than I have ever known him, and that, you know, is saying a great deal."

There was agreement between Tyler and Clay on only the first subject on the Clay agenda before the savage battle erupted. This was the repeal of the Sub-Treasury Act, which the Whigs hailed with a boisterous parade up and down Pennsylvania Avenue that highlighted a coffin labeled "Sub-Treasury Plan." But the question was now: Who would collect and disburse Government revenues if the Government were barred from this function?

On June 3, when Treasury Secretary Thomas Ewing sent his report to Congress recommending the repeal of the Sub-Treasury Act, he also recommended the creation of a "fiscal agent of the United States." This prompted Clay to push a resolution through the Senate ordering Ewing to supply a plan for a fiscal agent, or a privately operated, publicly involved new bank. This in turn led Ewing to approach Tyler for instructions on what to do to satisfy Clay.

Tyler now found himself in an uncomfortable position because his personal principles, his growing ego and his desire to maintain friendly relations with the Whig leadership were suddenly in conflict with each other. But his agility and concern soon revealed a path out of his troubles. For the moment, at least he appeared to have lighted upon an adequate solution when he blew the dust off a states'-rights bank plan once offered by Senator Hugh White of Tennessee. The White Plan agreed with Tyler's view that Congress lacked authority to establish a national bank to operate throughout the country and locate branches where it desired. However, said the hair-splitting White, Congress did have authority to legislate for the District of Columbia if it desired. Therefore, it would be constitutional for Congress to charter a bank to be incorporated in the capital. This bank could then establish branches throughout the country with the consent of the states involved.

Led by Webster, the Cabinet heartily endorsed the White-Tyler plan, for it not only met Tyler's states'-rights strictures but it also made possible a bank that could operate nationally. Tyler's sole objection was that the District Bank Plan, as it was called, permitted the bank to discount local promissory notes. Tyler said he had no objection to the Bank's dealing in bills of exchange, but dealing in discounting of notes was another matter even though the general effect of both was identical. However, he did not insist that Ewing remove the discounting provision from the bill.

On June 12, Ewing submitted the District Bank Bill to Congress with every hope that a Third Bank would soon become law. But trouble came almost immediately. Senator Silas Wright made an astute observation on a possible cause of the earthquake. Clay was "made for a minority, not a majority," and his basic role in politics, said Wright, was to act as "chief fault-finder and tearer downer of other people's measures."

Clay could not tolerate any demand that came from an inferior, especially one who intended to be his rival for 1844. Nor could he swallow any outside proposal for a bank, a subject that had belonged to Clay since 1816. Moreover, to thread a philosophic needle and stitch a clumsy patch on velvet, as Tyler was proposing through Ewing, was intolerable to Clay. The bank must be national and supreme over other banks, just as Hamilton's Bank of 1791 and the Second Bank of 1816 were. Hiding behind the sham of making it appear to be a local institution of Washington, D.C., was outrageous, even though it would be as effective a proposal.

Tyler soon learned of Clay's views when he invited him to the White House. "What a bank would be that!" Clay exploded, bluntly exclaiming that he would not promote the plan. According to one of Tyler's sons, his father reacted with equal anger. Unfortunately, the son's memory of Tyler's reply was the following stilted hodgepodge: "Then, sir, I wish you to understand this—that you and I were born in the same district; that we have fed upon the same food and breathed the same natal air. Go you now then, Mr. Clay, to your end of the avenue, where stands the Capitol, and there perform your duty to the country as you shall think proper. So help me God! I shall do mine at this end of it as I think proper."

When the Ewing Bill reached Clay's committee, he tossed it aside and substituted his own bill. In his committee report of June 21, Clay's proposed bank was based on his belief that Congress as the legislature for the entire nation possessed authority to charter a bank that could establish branches wherever it wished. It need not first acquire the consent of a state to operate a branch there, as the Ewing Bill required. Nor would it have to go through the fiction of incorporating itself as a local District of Columbia bank before spreading its wings over other areas of the country.

Tyler's reaction was a martyr's cry. "I am placed upon trial," he said. "Those who have all along opposed me will . . . leave me impotent and powerless. Remember always that that power claimed by Mr. Clay and others is a power to create a corporation to operate *per se* over the Union. This from the first has been the contest."

An outsider reading both bills would have been shocked by the enmity engendered. For the ends were similar, considering that Clay's bill would establish the central bank in the District of Columbia. And the differences narrowed further when Clay made a count and saw that he lacked sufficient votes to plunge his bill through Congress. Senator Wright observed that Tyler in desperation was making offers of patronage to various Whigs, and "the power of Executive influence has never been so susceptible in our body since I have been in it, as it is now," he exaggerated.

Representative John M. Botts of Virginia, powerful in build, speech and aggressive manners, played the role of peacemaker. A trusted friend of Tyler, he had fought alongside him to have him returned to the Senate in 1839 when Clay supported the candidacy of William C. Rives, the conservative Democrat. Botts had also been Tyler's roommate at Brown's Indian Queen Hotel. Botts now came to the White House to talk to Tyler about his proposed compromise amendment, and he returned to the Capitol to tell Clay that Tyler had given his consent.

Under the Botts Amendment, the bank would not be permitted to establish branches without the assent of the states, just as Tyler had proposed. However, there was a big difference. The Botts Amendment stated that if a state legislature did not object to the establishment of a bank branch in its first session after the passage of the Bank Bill, then it would be assumed that the state had consented.

Clay saw little weakening of his own position by this amendment, and after the Whig caucus consented, the Senate passed the Clay bill with the Botts Amendment by a vote of 26 to 23. Then on August 6, after the House Whigs stifled debate and pushed the bill through in only four days, by a vote of 131 to 100, it traveled to the White House. "We all earnestly recommended the President to sign the Bill," Webster wrote after a Cabinet meeting.

When Tyler did not take immediate action, the New York *Herald* reported: "Nothing is thought of, dreamed upon, or sworn about now but the fate of the Bank Bill. Politicians discuss it morning, noon and night—in the avenue, in the House, over their lunch at the refectory, in the Capitol, over their coffee, their wine. The ladies talk of it on all occasions among themselves and to the gentlemen. It is a favorite topic with the hackney coachman." Botts said the President would sign the bill, though his growing doubts were revealed by the exhortation he sent Tyler—"If you can reconcile this bill to yourself, all is sunshine and calm; your Administration will be met with the warm, hearty, zealous support of the whole Whig party." Then there was the quoted comment of Robert Tyler, the President's twenty-four-year-old son, thrilled by the limelight and the attention old politicians paid to his words. In the House lobby, he loudly told a New York Congressman, "To

suppose that my father could be gulled by such a humbug compromise as the bill contains is to suppose that he is an ass."

On August 15, the ninth of his ten-day leeway on legislation,
Tyler went to church to "pray earnestly and devoutly to be en-
lightened as to my duty." But his close friends already knew his
course. Their smug assurance that he would veto the bill had led
Clay to a flash of fury at a dinner and the promise that if he did,
"I will live to be a hundred years and devote them all to the
extermination of Tyler and his friends!"

On the last day of grace, John Tyler, Jr., twenty-one years old
and his father's secretary, traveled up Capitol Hill with a Message
from the President. Young Junior, fast becoming an alcoholic and
in his father's words, "part a madman," left the Message at the
Senate door. Shortly afterward, when it was read aloud, it was
found to be a veto of the Bank Bill. Gallery spectators hooted and
booed, and hooknosed Democratic Senator Benton, pleased with
the veto, screamed out a demand that the sergeant-at-arms "arrest the bank ruffians for insulting the President." As a group,
the Democrats had gone along with Clay's bill, said young Sam
Tilden of New York, solely for the purpose of causing mischief.
Only the Calhoun Democrats had not joined in, for as Calhoun
put it, "As far as we are concerned they are all Whigs alike,
whether Tyler Whigs or Clay Whigs."

The reading of the Veto Message revealed Tyler's stated objections, but it failed to disclose his real objection. He said that
Congress had no power to give the bank the right to discount local
promissory notes, that this power was not necessary to collect,
keep and disburse government revenues. Far more important, he
said, Congress lacked power "to create a national bank to operate
per se over the Union." In addition, he objected to the Botts
Amendment because of its negative approach to the establishment
of branches. States should have the right to declare in a positive
manner whether they wanted a bank branch, and the issue should
not be decided on the basis of a state's failure to legislate the
branch's exclusion.

Tyler's real objection was more complex. The Presidential fever
was in him and he hoped for an elected term when his present
term expired. Had he signed the bill, this action would have been
widely interpreted to mean that he was a Clay rubber stamp. The
veto was a mark of independence.

The Democrats were wild with joy at the veto. That night a

Democratic contingent led by Senators Buchanan, Benton and Calhoun called on Tyler to congratulate him on his "patriotic and courageous" action. Tyler, in the flush of popularity, even though it came dubiously from the political opposition, had servants and slaves bring out the best of his ample liquor stock. But as the hours passed on, he watched the false "congratulations gradually descend into convivial hilarity." Later that night a different group came. A drunken Whig mob stumbled down the Avenue after midnight, approached the Executive Mansion with blunderbusses, drums and trumpets and shouted, "Down with the veto!" Crippled Mrs. Tyler, indoors on the second floor, feared for her life as did the other ladies of the household. Then, on the street, Tyler was treated to being burned in effigy.

The Whig leaders were not speechless for long following the veto of the Bank Bill. "Poor Tippecanoe!" cried Philip Hone, New York Whig businessman. "It was an evil hour that 'Tyler too' was added to make out the line. There was rhyme, but no reason to it." Clay party attacks grew so vehement that the Washington *Madisonian*, the conservative Democratic paper that had become Tyler's organ, reported: "The vocabulary of the language seems to have been ransacked for words to express their angry denunciation."

All eyes were on Clay after the veto. He would know how to demolish the upstart, said his friends, as he set the Congressional machinery in motion to override Tyler's astounding veto. But though Clay owned a majority of members, this was not enough and he failed by seven votes to get the necessary two-thirds needed to override the veto in the Senate. His chagrin was immense and his anger electric, once his loss to Tyler was apparent. If the Whig convention had known that Harrison would die, he told his colleagues and the world, not a single delegate would have voted for Tyler. As for Tyler's newly found friends among the Democrats who had serenaded him upon his veto, Clay scoffed that they would ever prove to be the true-blue variety. As one observer noted Clay's amazing gift of mimicry on this occasion: "He recited the speeches he supposed were delivered on that occasion by Democratic Senators to the Whig President, imitating the style of the different orators, especially Calhoun, Benton and Buchanan, in so striking and artistic a way as to win the involuntary applause even of some of the victims." All he had achieved by his veto, Clay jeered, was the fashioning of a tiny clique who were "beating up for recruits and endeavoring to form a third party, with materials so scanty as to be wholly insufficient to compose a decent corporal's guard." This last expression immediately caught fire with Tyler's friends, who henceforth referred to themselves as the "Corporal's Guard."

Clay had other thoughts on the veto. Only five years earlier, he pointed out, Tyler had resigned his Senate seat rather than obey the instructions of the Virginia legislature to vote to expunge the Jackson censure from the Senate Journal. Since Tyler had said in his first Message to Congress that its members were the more "immediate representatives of the states and the people," and since Congress had passed the Bank Bill, by the same logic Tyler should have resigned the Presidency if he could not sign the bill. Clay also said that in Tyler's inaugural address, he had agreed to a bank and had promised to "resort to the fathers of the great Republican school for advice and instruction." On this basic, Clay said, Tyler should have paid attention to Madison, the leading "father," who in 1816 had regarded "the question of the power to establish a national bank was invariably settled." Unfortunately for Clay's thesis, Madison had also led the fight against the First Bank back in 1791. However, Clay might have strengthened his argument by quoting Madison during the Constitutional Convention of 1787 when he said, "No man would be so daring as to place a veto on a law that had passed with the assent of the legislature."

Afterward, Clay proposed an amendment to the Constitution so that a simple majority vote would override a veto. He pointed out that Tyler's veto was equal in strength to the vote of nine Senators and forty Representatives, and that historic precedent revealed that the mere threat of a veto controlled Congress, for no veto had been overridden. In a scoffing reply, Senator James Buchanan said that Clay's fallacy "from beginning to end, consists in the assumption that Congress in every situation and under every circumstance, truly represents the deliberate will of the people." It was the President instead who did, said the man who would one day forget his own words. And what was this terrible veto power that Clay feared? he asked. It created nothing new, altered no law and ended no existing institution.

The Whigs were by now concerned about the development of a permanent breach and a new effort was undertaken by friends of Tyler and Clay to restore a semblance of party unity. Senator

Rives, Tyler's rival for the Senate in 1839, was now a Whig and
the only Senator a member of the Corporal's Guard. To Rives,
Tyler gave his renewed specifications for an acceptable bank.
Again he insisted that it be incorporated in the capital where
Congress had unquestionable power to legislate local matters, that
it be denied discounting authority and be permitted to establish
branches after the specific approval of the states.

On August 18, he met with Senator John Berrien of Georgia
and Representative John Sergeant of Pennsylvania after telling
both men he doubted the propriety of a conference between the
Chief Executive and members of Congress. Berrien had been a
Jackson Attorney General before turning Whig, and Sergeant had
been Clay's running mate in 1832. Sergeant was one of the commissioners named to the ill-fated Panama Congress in 1826 and
was also a leading authority on banking, the chief adviser and a
director of Biddle's Second Bank of the United States, an excellent
Supreme Court lawyer who had once rejected a proffered seat on
the Court as well as an invitation from Harrison to join his
Cabinet.

Tyler repeated to both men what he had told Rives, but he
refused to become more specific. Afterward, he told Webster and
Ewing to meet with them and spell out the details of what he
would accept. Webster's memorandum of this meeting with Tyler
read that the approved framework for a new legislative measure
was "to make a bank of issue, deposit and exchanges, without
power of discounting promissory notes. And for such a bank he did
not intimate that he requested the assent of the states. I took a
carriage and came immediately to the Capitol and saw Messrs
B and S; suggested to them the provisions and modifications which
I supposed would ensure the President's signature."

Ewing's diary confirmed Webster's memo, and on this basis Sergeant wrote a new bank bill, called the Fiscal Corporation Bill.
Sergeant then proceeded to ram the bill through the House in three
days with sharp opposition coming only from two members of
Tyler's Corporal's Guard, Henry Wise of Virginia and James Roosevelt of New York. When the bill came to the Senate, Clay found it
objectionable because it lacked a strong national character, but he
finally agreed to support it for the sake of having a bank. "Tyler
dares not resist," he told James Lyon of Richmond, brother-in-law
of Wise, who was the chief member of the Corporal's Guard. Certainly with Webster and Ewing saying publicly that Tyler ap-

proved the bill there would be no trouble this time. But Lyon
stunned him by replying that Tyler considered the bill unconstitutional, "and I will tell you that when he thinks he is right, he is
as obstinate as a bull."

While the bill was before the Senate, Attorney General Crittenden held a supper party for Whigs. Late that night a drunken
delegation was deputized to go to the White House and ask Tyler
to join the fun. Clay stood at the door when Tyler entered. "Well,
Mr. President," he asked, "what are you for, Kentucky whisky or
champagne?" Others present sensed that Clay had asked whether
Tyler was for a Clay bank or a localized Tyler bank of this second
go-around. "Champagne," Tyler replied. Clay then treated him to a
recital from Shakespeare's Richard III, emphasizing the lines:

> Conscience is but a word that cowards use,
> Devis'd at first, to keep the strong in awe.

In the Senate, Benton called the bill the "Corposity" and Buchanan called it the "Kiteflying Fiscality." But the Whigs were
united and on September 2 the Senate voted its approval, 27 to
22.

The capital was again the scene of suspense when the bill
traveled to the White House for Tyler's decision. But to those on
the inside there was little need to guess what Tyler would do, even
though Webster and Ewing were referring to the bill as the President's measure. One indication of Tyler's intent was his effort to
have consideration of the bill postponed while it was moving
through Congress. Another was the vehemence with which members of the Corporal's Guard attacked the legislation. Still another
indication was the rage he revealed when he learned that his
friend Botts had turned on him. On the day that Tyler vetoed
the first Bank Bill, Botts had prophesied that he would in order
to win acceptance by the Democrats. In Botts' letter, which was
published, Tyler read that Botts predicted he would become "an
object of execration with both parties." There was also a deprecating reference to him as "Captain Tyler." It was known that Tyler
had served only a few months during the War of 1812, and despite
his lack of action he had taken his veteran's bonus of 160 acres of
land in Iowa and made himself eligible for a monthly pension.
What made the "Captain Tyler" especially galling to the President
was the story of his company's reaction to the false report that

British soldiers were approaching. The men were stationed at William and Mary College and when the rumor came they fled, falling down a flight of stairs into such a tangled heap at the bottom that it took a long while to separate them. Said Webster of the Botts letter, Tyler came to the State Department and "sat an hour, and complained very much of the ill treatment which he received from Mr. Botts and other Whigs. He appeared full of suspicion and resentment. I began to fear another veto."

Tyler's Veto Message came to Congress on September 9. As ghostwritten by Representative Wise, he confessed to a soul-searching that had compelled him "to differ from Congress a second time in the same session." Again he entered his chief objection to permitting the bank to operate *per se* over the Union by virtue of the unaided and assumed authority of Congress as a national legislature, as distinguishable from a bank created by Congress for the District of Columbia as the local legislature of the District." He also objected to the provision permitting the bank to deal in bills of exchange on the ground that the bank would "indulge in mere local discounts under the name of bills of exchange."

Charges and countercharges flew whether Tyler had foully deceived the Whigs; whether he had told Sergeant, Berrien, Webster and Ewing what would be an acceptable bill and then doublecrossed them. There is little question that Tyler changed his mind along the way partly because of wounded pride at his treatment by Botts and Clay, partly because of his desire to pick up Democratic support for his re-election but chiefly because any national bank dealing in Government revenues went against his philosophic grain. However, in defending his action, Tyler was not above twisting the truth. For instance, he insisted later that he knew dirty work was afoot when Webster and Ewing failed to show him the bill before it was considered by the House. But a Webster memorandum said: "The President wished me to get him a copy of the bill before it was introduced, I did so, went with it to him, and read it over with him. . . . He said he did not wish it to be called a bank. I sat down at his table, struck out bank and wrote the title as it finally passed. He wished a reduction of capital from 30 millions to 20, or 15—pressing the latter—and he wished the corporation to be restrained from selling the U.S. stocks except by authority of Congress. And he suggested no other alterations whatever. I went immediately to my lodgings on Capitol Hill, sent for

Mr. S[ergeant] and . . . showed him the prepared alterations. He copied the title in his own handwriting, and afterwards told me that he reduced the capital to 21 millions."

The second veto ruptured all relations between Tyler and the Whigs. From every part of the nation came letters to the White House threatening Tyler with assassination; Whig papers denounced him in rough terms; and Whig rallies by the dozens burned "Cap'n Tyler" in effigy. Botts added ammunition by a wild speech to the House on September 10, charging that Tyler had offered him a bribe in exchange for his aid in helping Tyler win two terms on his own after his inherited term expired.

Henry Clay's conclusion was that the Administration must be wrecked and Tyler driven from office. His keen memory brought back the scene of an extremely bitter and self-righteous Senator Tyler opposing Jackson's recess appointments to the Turkish mission. Certainly any man who was so outraged because a President appointed aides while Congress was not in session and thus unable to confirm or reject them would remain true to his principles. Surely he would make no recess appointments now that he was President.

Clay laid his plan accordingly. The special session would adjourn on September 13, only a few days away. What if the Cabinet resigned suddenly? Tyler would be unable to form a new Cabinet before Congress went home. Then his unwillingness to make recess appointments would make the government inoperative and he would resign. In this instance, the line of succession would pass to Clay's supporter, Samuel L. Southard, the Senate's Pro Tem. Southard, a tactless, high-pitched-voiced New Jerseyite, had already been a member of the Monroe and Adams cabinets and held the unique distinction of serving with his father, Henry Southard, in the same Congress.

On Thursday, September 9, Secretary of the Navy Badger had the rest of the Cabinet come to his house for a supper strategy meeting. When Webster found Clay present, he left. The decision was made that night and on September 11, all members of the Cabinet except Webster resigned. Webster had met with the Massachusetts Congressional contingent, and, said "Old Ebony," as John Quincy Adams was now called, "We all agreed that Mr. Webster would not be justified in resigning at this time; but we all

felt that the hour for the requiem of the Whig party was at hand."
As a Whig leader in his own right, Webster could not resign without making it appear that he was subservient to Clay. Furthermore,
he was hoping to write a treaty with Britain concerning the Maine
border, the boundary west of Lake Superior and the African slave
trade abolition.

When the letters of resignation came to Tyler that Saturday
afternoon, he showed no surprise, for members of the Corporal's
Guard had been made privy to Clay's scheme and reported it to the
White House. "We are on the eve of a Cabinet rupture," wrote
Wise, who detested Webster and was sorry he had not resigned
with the others. "We can part friendly with Webster by sending
him to England [as minister]. Let us, for God's sake, get rid of
him on the best terms we can," he urged.

After the others had resigned, Webster, who knew the dislike
the pro-slavery, states'-rights clique had for him, asked Tyler,
"Where am I to go, Mr. President?"

"You must decide that for yourself, Mr. Webster," Tyler replied.

Webster then said, "If you leave it to me, Mr. President, I will
stay where I am."

Tyler leaped up and held out his hand. "Give me your hand on
that, and now I will say to you that Henry Clay is a doomed man."

As Tyler summarized the situation, "It was declared to him
[Webster] that if he would resign, I would necessarily have to
vacate the Government by Saturday night, and thus Whig rule be
thoroughly re-established." But Tyler had long prepared to drop
his Cabinet and had given thought to replacements for his inherited
Secretaries. With speed that must have made Clay gulp, he dispatched a new Cabinet slate to the Senate, and with that body
still in session the Senate felt itself obliged to confirm the new
members. Clay's shallow scheme had failed.

It was Clay's move now. On September 13, the day for adjournment, the Whigs met in caucus and approved a paper written by
Representative John P. Kennedy of Maryland, the well-known novelist, for the expulsion of Tyler from the party. Tyler was now a
man without a party, for the Democrats would not accept him
even though they enjoyed his vetoes. As one writer noted, the
Democrats "loved the sin, but not the sinner."

The action of the caucus also became the signal for Whig newspapers to institute a campaign of vilification as rough as any Presi-

dent faced. Henceforth to the Whig press, Tyler was "the Executive Ass," "the Accident of an Accident," "the Second Benedict Arnold," "ingrate," and "reptile-like."

Long afterward, that special session of the summer of 1841 was known as the "Dog Days Session" because of the abominable summer heat and humidity that provided a hell-hole setting for the thunderous tumult and flying mud occasioned by the bank vetoes and Cabinet resignations. Some months later when Charles Dickens paid a call on Tyler at the White House, he said of the President: "He looked somewhat worn and anxious, and well he might be, being at war with everybody."

Yet that Dog Days Session entailed more than a war between the Executive and Legislative branches. Clay may have lost the battle of the bank, but he still hoped to win other items on his legislative agenda. Chief among these items were the raising of import duties to a respectable level of protection and the establishment of his distribution scheme, which would distribute public land sales revenues among the states. But again Tyler loomed as a mammoth stumbling block, publicly declaring Clay's own Compromise Tariff Act of 1833 as Holy Writ and beyond alteration. As for Distribution, while Tyler said it would be one solution to keep the debt-ridden states from collapsing, he opposed letting these revenues go to the states if it meant raising tariff duties to make up for this generosity in order to keep the Federal Government afloat.

Since there was a greater chance of winning Distribution, Clay pushed this rather than a new protective tariff measure. But even to get this through Congress required the full use of all the legislative skills he had amassed during his decades in Washington. Perhaps the smoothest display in American history of the art of logrolling was evidenced at this time.

At the outset, impresario Clay's count of noses revealed that Distribution was doomed to failure, if put to an immediate vote. Western opposition was strong because Clay had been talking for years about selling public land at the highest prices bidders would pay. What western Congressmen wanted was Pre-emption, or a law giving settlers the right to buy their land at a minimum price. On the other hand, eastern members were little interested in Distribution without top selling prices for public land, in order that their states' share of the proceeds would be high. Actually, what had top legislative priority for eastern Congressmen was a new bankruptcy law. An earlier national bankruptcy act had been passed in 1800 because of the disgraceful debtors' prison situation. But when times were prosperous in 1803, that act had been repealed. Now in 1841, with a total population of only 16,500,000 persons, more than 400,000 bankruptcies had resulted from the "Van Buren" Depression of 1837, and the clamor was loud for Federal relief for debtors.

Clay recognized the work that was cut out for him if he were to win a Distribution bill. He would have to promote three separate and unrelated bills. To gain western support, he told frontier legislators that if they voted for a new national bankruptcy bill and for a Distribution bill, they could have their Pre-emption bill. What he proposed giving them was the long-floundering Benton "Log Cabin" plan, permitting squatter-settlers to buy 160 acres of the land they were on at $1.25 an acre. Then to roll the legislative log in the other direction, he told eastern members they could have their bankruptcy bill if they supported the West's demand for cheap land and the Distribution bill.

New York Whig boss, Thurlow Weed, who had kept Clay from the Presidency in 1840, came down from his headquarters to help the Kentuckian at logrolling. The large, stoop-shouldered boss was seen in both the House and Senate chambers spreading the Clay gospel to members, "his long arms draped around their shoulders." And in the end, the pieces fell into place.

The Log Cabin Pre-emption Bill passed with eastern support and became the landmark law in the settlement of the West. Yet Clay, who made this heroically democratic measure possible, never received due credit for it because he had merely made it the carrot enticement to gain support for his Distribution bill.

When the bankruptcy bill then passed with western support in exchange for Pre-emption, Clay believed he had fulfilled his obligations to sectional interests. But now his enemy in the White House insisted on being heard. Tyler's intermediaries delivered the ominous news that he had raised the price Clay would have to pay if he hoped to avoid a veto of his Distribution bill. "The Great Pacificator," as Tyler and others had nicknamed Clay for his Compromise Tariff Act of 1833, must tie Distribution to that tariff law.

Clay's 1833 Tariff Act, with its gradually reduced duty rates, was to drop to the maximum 20 per cent import tax on value on July 1,

1842. It was Clay's determination to write a new tariff bill before that date, raising the ad valorem rates to a high protective level. But now Tyler was proposing to out-logroll him. For what Tyler demanded was that Clay write into his Distribution bill a provision suspending Distribution if the duty rates ever exceeded the 20 per cent maximum of the 1833 Tariff Act. In other words, he would not permit Clay to use Distribution to force him to accept a protective tariff rate.

Clay fumed and roared at being out-tricked by "His Accidency, Cap'n Tyler." But realizing he had no alternative, he agreed to cripple his Distribution bill with the hateful amendment on the tariff. And on this basis, Tyler signed the bill.

When the first regular session of the Twenty-seventh Congress convened early in December 1841, Tyler made a belated attempt to appease Clay by proposing the abdication of Presidential authority over public funds. Throughout the Jackson assault on the Second Bank and afterward, the Whigs had mouthed to triteness the shrill war cry of "Separate the Purse from the Sword." Tyler had paid lip service to this catchphrase in his inaugural address with his comment that so long as "the President can exert the power of appointing and removing at his pleasure the agents selected" for the custody of public revenues, "the Commander-in-Chief of the Army and Navy is in fact the treasurer."

What Tyler now proposed to Congress in his Message of December 7, 1841, was a "Board of Exchequer" to receive, hold and disburse public revenues "safe from Executive control." The Board members would be appointed by the President with the consent of the Senate, but they would be removable solely for disability, incompetence or neglect of duty. To protect against patronage removals, the President would have to submit reasons to the Senate on any removal. As for the Exchequer Board's scope and methods, it would have power to establish agencies throughout the states to buy and sell bills of exchange, accept public deposits of specie up to $15,000,000 and issue its own specie-backed paper money to this limit.

Here was an opportunity for the Congressional Whigs to take Tyler at his word and let him abdicate his authority over finance. But Clay would not approve anything that Tyler proposed and saw to it that the bill was first tabled then roundly defeated.

Another clash was soon in the making because the Whigs were

determined to have both Distribution and a protective tariff, even though Clay's Distribution Act barred the latter. Opportunity arose when Tyler sent Congress a Special Message on March 8, 1842, expressing his alarm at the government's deteriorating financial position. The national debt had already reached $13,500,000 at the beginning of the year and an additional deficit of $3,000,000 more was forecast for 1842. Congress had approved a $12,000,000 Treasury loan during the special session, but the public and the banks had subscribed to less than half the Treasury bonds.

When Congress blithely ignored Tyler's demand that it take immediate steps to correct this situation, he sent a second Special Message on March 23. This time he specifically requested that in view of the emergency the rates on some products be raised above the 20 per cent duty in the beloved Clay Compromise Tariff Act of 1833. He also pointed out that this would automatically halt the distribution of public land sales revenues, as was required by the Clay Distribution Act of September 1841.

The Congressional Whigs now attempted to legislate higher tariff rates while continuing Distribution. Representative Millard Fillmore, chairman of the House Ways and Means Committee, first prepared a bill that froze existing rates until August. (The lower 20 per cent maximum would not become effective until July 1.) Fillmore's bill also contained a provision to the effect that his measure did not suspend Distribution.

When this bill reached Tyler's office on the second floor of the White House, he promptly vetoed it as unsound legislation. His Veto Message that made Whigs gag spoke of his "embarrassments" in taking his action, in view of "the superior wisdom of the legislature."

The furious Whigs now rushed through a new tariff bill to replace the 1833 Act. Tariff rates were raised to the level of the "Black" 1832 Tariff Act, which had prompted South Carolina's nullification action that year. In addition, the new tariff bill again ordered the retention of Distribution. This time when the bill reached the White House, Tyler applied his fourth veto despite the plea of Webster that the "awful" state of the economy justified its approval.

When his Veto Message reached Capitol Hill, the angry Whigs did not glumly accept the verdict, even though they lacked the votes to override his veto. The House referred the Message to a special committee under the chairmanship of John Quincy Adams, and on August 16, the committee report censured Tyler for Executive dictatorship.

After recommending that the Constitution be amended to permit a simple Congressional majority in each house to override a veto, the committee declared that Tyler actually deserved to be impeached but that such action would "prove abortive." Among the specific high crimes charged to Tyler were: (1), that he had agreed to the two bank bills and then vetoed both; and (2), that he was using the veto power in a deliberate effort to ruin the Whig party.

When the House approved the Adams Committee report, Tyler sent a sharp protest the following day, demanding that his statement be placed in the House Journal. "I have been accused without evidence and condemned without a hearing," he said. "I am charged with violating pledges . . . with usurping powers not conferred by law, and, above all, with using the powers conferred upon the President by the Constitution from corrupt motives and unwarranted ends."

Tyler's demand that his protest be inserted in the House Journal brought joy to his former friend Botts. The Virginian recalled that Tyler had voted for the Senate resolution to bar from the Senate Journal Jackson's protest of 1834 against Senate censure. Botts now used the identical Senate resolution to keep Tyler's protest out of the House Journal.

Botts also went further. By resolution, he moved to impeach Tyler, the first such action brought against a President. However, most of his Whig colleagues considered this unwise because "it might invest nothingness with consequence" and swing public opinion behind Tyler. So the vote on Botts' resolution found only 83 in favor and 127 opposed. Over in the Senate, Whigs considered passing a vote of "no confidence" in Tyler. But this was abandoned when Clay pointed out that if this "English usage" were approved, it would only serve to make Tyler "laugh in your face."

In the end, it was the Congressional Whigs who won the fight of 1842 for the protective tariff but only because they gave in to Tyler on Distribution. The government required revenue to stay afloat and the Whigs could not bring themselves to total irresponsibility, no matter how strong their hatred of Tyler. So by a small margin in both houses, they now won approval for a protective tariff bill that did not contain a provision ordering the continuation of Distribution. Then to save face, they passed a separate Distribution bill that made no mention of any suspension of payments to states when tariff rates rose. "Judas Iscariot," as Greeley's New York *Tribune* called Tyler, signed the new tariff bill on August 30, 1842, even though it ended the low duty rate of the 1833 Act. At the same time he pocket-vetoed the Distribution bill. So the result was that the country was once more operating under a protective tariff while Distribution was as dead as the bank issue.

Condemned by the Whigs as an "imbecile" for ending Distribution, Tyler also found himself berated by southern free-trade Democrats for approving the 1842 Tariff Act. In the words of Calhoun's *Columbian South Carolinian* paper, the President had signed "the most flagrantly protective, fraudulent and unconstitutional tariff bill that has ever passed."

If Tyler found himself tied, flogged and dragged through the cinder bed in his relations with Congress on legislation, in other Presidential duties he enjoyed a more comfortable existence as well as success. The long fight to subdue the Florida Seminoles finally ended in 1842. In December of that year, he moved also with sureness in foreign affairs when Prince Haolilio of the Sandwich Islands (later known as Hawaii) came to Washington. Tyler, who like other Washingtonians called the Prince "Hallelujah," made a preliminary gesture through conversation to annex the group of volcanic and coral Pacific islands. Hallelujah had no objection to this but was more concerned at the moment with French designs on his islands. Tyler took action on this issue on December 20 by sending a Webster-written warning to European powers to keep hands off the islands. In this extension of the Monroe Doctrine, which Tyler's friends proudly called the Tyler Doctrine, Tyler notified the powers that if they tried "to take possession of the islands, colonize them and subvert the native government," they would "create dissatisfaction on the part of the United States." Success was capped by France's abstinence from seizing Hawaii.

Inexplicably, Tyler had remarkable success with treaties. Of the fifteen he submitted to the Senate, only two were rejected. Those rejected were a treaty to annex Texas and another to regulate commercial relations with the German Customs Union (Zollverein). Tyler was to win Texas annexation later by another route, but the German Customs Union treaty could not be revived so long as it set tariff rates not previously authorized by Congress. Two other treaties were so amended that the countries involved would not agree to the changes, while a fifth treaty was sent to the Senate Foreign Relations Committee and pigeonholed.

One major diplomatic success was the Cushing Treaty of Wanghia negotiated with China in 1844. Representative Caleb Cushing of Massachusetts, a tall, awkward man whom the Washington ladies considered a "tongue-tied bore," had been a member of Tyler's Corporal's Guard. When he retired from Congress after the 1842 session because he knew he could not win another term, Tyler attempted without success to bring him into his Cabinet. The record shows that at one-thirty A.M. on March 4, 1843, Tyler sent Cushing's nomination as Secretary of the Treasury into the Senate chamber. A Presidential custom was to come in person to the Capitol as a session neared its end and sign or veto bills before adjournment. Tyler was in the Vice-President's Capitol chamber off the Senate floor at the time and a short while later he was notified that the Senate had rejected his nominee by a vote of 27 to 19. In a poorly controlled rage, he resubmitted the Cushing nomination, which the Senate promptly rejected 27 to 10. Stubbornly, Tyler scribbled on a scrap of paper, "I nominate Cushing as Secretary of the Treasury," and sent it inside the chamber. This third attempt convinced him that he should quit, for the vote was 29 to 2.

During that same night, Congress, at the request of Daniel Webster who had many friends in the China trade, approved a bill providing $40,000 to send an agent to negotiate commercial relations with the Chinese Empire. Tyler immediately nominated as agent Edward Everett, then minister to Britain, and Everett won confirmation. However, when Everett refused to leave his post so that Webster might succeed him, Tyler gave Cushing a recess appointment as agent on the China mission. Senator Benton in a rage pointed out that Tyler had called recess appointments unconstitutional, and furthermore, Cushing would never win confirmation if the Senate were in session. However, Tyler found a split-hair precedent set by George Washington, who had ruled that when a senatorially-confirmed appointee declines his position after the Senate has adjourned, this created a valid authority for making a recess appointment to the office.

At any event, Tyler dispatched Cushing to the Orient and the resulting Cushing Treaty of July 3, 1844, opened American relations with China. Cushing did not find his task too difficult because China had recently undergone a three-year Opium War

with Britain (1839–1842) triggered by the British refusal to abide
by the decision of the Chinese Government to prohibit the opium
trade. Afterward, the 1842 Sino-British treaty had opened five ports
to British trade and residence, ceded Hong Kong to the British
Empire and permitted the "foreign devils" to sell opium to Chinese
citizens. Under the theory that if other foreign devils were given
the same privileges they would fight among themselves, China
then agreed by treaty to grant the United States the "most favored
nation" clause, which guaranteed equal commerical rights with the
British on foreign trade. In addition to opening the five ports to
American residence, China granted the United States the right of
extraterritoriality, or the right of Americans accused of crime in
China to be tried under American law by Americans.

Certainly the major diplomatic effort of the Tyler Administration
involved Great Britain, with whom relations had grown unpleasant
under preceding administrations. The *Caroline* incident and the
McLeod case were still not settled; American sympathizers through
the guise of organizations called "Patriotic Societies" and "Hunters
Lodges" were continuing to invade Canada and assist anti-govern-
ment rebels; and the border between Maine and New Brunswick
remained a zone of contention.

Fortunately, Tyler had an excellent Secretary of State in Daniel
Webster who was dedicated to effecting good relations with the
British. On the other side of the Atlantic good fortune also appeared in 1841 with the fall of the Ministry of Viscount Melbourne,
for this removed Melbourne's obstreperous Foreign Minister, Lord
Palmerston. Incoming Prime Minister Sir Robert Peel installed
friendly Lord Aberdeen as Foreign Minister, and Lord Aberdeen
chose Lord Ashburton as the British plenipotentiary to the United
States to settle outstanding differences between both nations. Lord
Ashburton was the former Alexander Baring, partner in the banking firm of Baring Brothers and an agent on many occasions in
Europe for the Second Bank of the United States and the
American Treasury Department. Ashburton also had other advantages to bring to his assignment. He was a personal friend of
Secretary Webster and his wife was an American, the daughter of
former Senator William Bingham of Pennsylvania who was the
richest American of his day.

Ashburton arrived in Washington in the spring of 1842 and he
and Webster were soon busily negotiating. First to be settled were

the *Caroline* sinking and the McLeod case. Alexander McLeod, the Canadian arrested in November 1840 because he said he had killed an American when the *Caroline* was towed from the American shore by Canadians, burned and sent over Niagara Falls, was to be tried in a New York State court. Previously, the British had sent several stiff protests to Washington and Webster had attempted to get him released or remanded to a Federal court. Tyler had sent harsh letters written by Webster for his signature to Governor Seward and in turn received angry replies from the governor. Finally when the case came to court, McLeod had a provable alibi that he was far from the scene and in addition was a congenital liar.

With McLeod's quick acquittal, Ashburton agreed to Webster's request that he express his deep regret publicly because his government had not previously offered "some explanation and apology" for the *Caroline* sinking. In return, Webster went to Capitol Hill where his lobbying effort was rewarded by a bill passed in August 1842 to give Federal courts jurisdiction in cases where aliens committed crimes under the authority of a foreign government.

For the most part, Webster and Ashburton negotiated informally, ignoring protocol and the usual "unnecessary mystery and mummeries of negotiations." Over the dining and conference tables, they discussed the Oregon boundary problem, though they failed to reach any agreement. However, they were able to reach a compromise on the boundary line between Minnesota and Canada running from Lake Superior westward to the Lake of the Woods. The original British claim included Duluth, while Webster countered with a claim reaching halfway around the north of Lake Superior. In the give and take, Webster would not budge further south than the line going west from the point where Pigeon River entered Lake Superior and proceeding through Rainy Lake to the Lake of the Woods. Webster's obstinacy was based on the fact that he and Tyler had heard that the world's richest iron ore deposits—in the Mesabi Range—lay below this line. Ashburton, who was not aware of this mineral wealth, did not put up a strong argument.

The two negotiators also made some changes in the New York and Vermont boundaries with Canada. At the behest of the military, Webster saw to it that strategic Rouse's Point, on Lake Champlain below Montreal on the St. Lawrence, was made part of New York. The question of suppressing the African slave trade also came under discussion. Slave ships were illegally flying the

American flag and using American papers, and Ashburton requested the right of visit and search of American vessels where
the slave trade was suspected. To Tyler, this smacked of a limitation on freedom of the seas and conjured up memories of British
boarding parties earlier in the century on the hunt for sailors to
impress into the British Navy. The final agreement written into
the treaty provided that each nation would station a naval fleet
in African waters "for the suppression of the slave trade."

On another slavery issue, the two could reach no unified position. This involved the *Creole,* an American vessel carrying slaves
from Virginia to New Orleans. In October 1841, the slaves aboard
her had mutinied and forced the crew to take them to Nassau in
the British Bahamas, where most were given their freedom. Tyler
entered a strong protest at British unwillingness to return the
slaves, but Ashburton said he lacked instructions from London to
negotiate this matter.

The major effort between Webster and Ashburton related to the
Maine-New Brunswick boundary, under bitter controversy since
the outbreak of the "Aroostook Valley War" in 1838. Ashburton had
been instructed to settle for no less than a territorial division that
would provide the British with a good all-weather road to run
military supplies from Halifax to Quebec, and he came well-
heeled with funds to spread among Americans who could help
his cause. At the same time, the state of Maine demanded all
12,000 square miles of the land in dispute, with her commissioners
loud and stubborn in their refusal to yield an inch. In fact, their
opposition to any compromise was so flinty that Ashburton became
sufficiently discouraged as to believe his only course was to dis-
continue negotiations. "I contrive to crawl about in these heats
by day and pass my nights in sleepless fever," he wrote Webster
on July 1. "In short I shall positively not outlive this affair, if it
is to be much prolonged."

At this point, Tyler entered the scene by asking Ashburton to
come to the White House for a pep talk. Webster noted this interview with the summary that "the President has pressed upon
him in the strongest manner the necessity of staying till every
effort to effect the great object of his mission shall have been
exhausted. The President feels that if the mission should return,
rebus infectis, the relations of the two countries will be more than
ever embarrassed."

The answer where to set the northeastern border depended on

the lines drawn on the maps used by the original negotiators in 1782–1783. Unfortunately for the Maine claimants, the handiwork of Benjamin Franklin, John Jay and John Adams in negotiation with Richard Oswald, the British representative, was not to be found in the American archives. Webster, realizing he needed a map to buttress the American case, asked his friend Jared Sparks, professor at Harvard and a biographer of George Washington, to help him. Sparks reported, while the Ashburton negotiations were beginning, that he had once seen a map in the French archives that showed Franklin's "strong red line" on a 1783 Mitchell's Map of North America. The strong red line, said Sparks, drawing one from memory on a clean map for Webster, supported the British claim to the Aroostook Valley and other areas claimed by Maine. Webster also did some independent hunting and he bought an old map from a secondhand dealer that had a red line drawn on it that rather coincided with the free-hand red line drawn by helpful Sparks. To Webster, who later asserted he was unaware that both red-line maps had nothing to do with the 1783 Peace Treaty, the Maine claim was suddenly poor and anything he negotiated above the so-called Franklin red line would be a gift on the part of the British.

On the other hand, the British archives contained a true boundary map made by Richard Oswald for George III. Had Webster or any other American bothered to read the course of debates in Parliament in 1839, he would have found this map mentioned. At the time, Lord Palmerston took a look at the map and gulped, for the Oswald map gave the entire disputed territory to the United States. Palmerston, ever protective of his country's empire, had hastily ordered the map made unavailable and gave it a seques-tered classification. So while Webster claimed he was concerned that Ashburton would learn about his red-line maps, Ashburton was worried to distraction that Webster would demand to see the Oswald map.

Once Ashburton left Tyler's office with the President's request that he continue negotiations, Webster went to work to end the lobbying by the Northeasterners. First, he sent Sparks to Augusta, Maine, to reveal his hand-drawn red-line map to the Maine and Massachusetts commissioners, in order to frighten them. Massa-chusetts' interest in the boundary stemmed from the fact that when Maine separated herself from Massachusetts and became a state in 1820, Massachusetts retained half-interest in her public

lands. Then he armed F. O. J. "Fog" Smith, an unprincipled sol-
dier-of-fortune, with $17,000 and sent him to Maine to bribe editors
to drop their opposition to a compromise settlement. The money
came from the Secret Service Fund, special money appropriated
to the President for use at his discretion on secret projects. The
large circulation *Eastern Argus* of Portland had opposed giving
up an inch of territory. But after a visit from Fog Smith, the
editor came out for "an honorable settlement."

As a result of the free flow of money and the disclosure of
the red-line maps, the Maine and Massachusetts commissioners
agreed to a compromise that gave Canada 5000 of the disputed
12,000 square miles; land that properly belonged to Maine. In addition, the two states agreed to an indemnity of $125,000 each for
the loss of the land they had claimed.

With the commissioners and newspapers willing now to surrender
United States territory, Webster and Ashburton signed the treaty
on August 9, 1842. Then on August 20, when the Senate gave
its consent by a vote of 39 to 9, the Webster-Ashburton Treaty
once more put the United States and England on temporary good
terms. Angriest about the treaty was Senator Benton who charged
Webster with having brought many Senators into the negotiations
directly and wined and dined them in order to control their later
vote. "I have reasons to think that this treaty has been ratified
out of doors!" he complained. "A solemn bamboozlement . . . a
shame and an injury," he described the treaty.

In 1846, when the Secret Service Fund became the subject of
a House investigation, Tyler and Webster were called as witnesses and denied such payment. In a masterful display of thunderous anger, Webster "grit his teeth, scowled, stamped and roared
forth" against Representative Charles J. Ingersoll, a Pennsylvania
Democrat who wanted him impeached retroactively. He called
Ingersoll "a man or thing" and told him, "I now leave the gentleman with the worst company I know on the face of the earth—I
leave him with himself!"

Tyler's successes in diplomacy came in the midst of the fratricidal
warfare between himself and his former Whig brothers, a war
that did nothing to advance the reputation of either side. So unpopular was the thin Virginian that when a flu epidemic struck
the nation, it was commonly called the "Tyler Grippe." Tyler re-

plied to such attacks by denouncing them as "the abuse of the malignants . . . I only hear them to despise them." As for the Whigs, the country was so sick of the party's skirmishes and battles with the President that the 1842 Congressional elections altered the previous Whig majority of sixty in the House to a Democratic majority of eighty in the Twenty-eighth Congress. Tyler's Corporal's Guard was almost entirely turned out, too, yet he hailed the Democratic landslide as "the greatest political victory ever won within my recollection . . . achieved entirely upon the vetoes of the bank bills."

Clay, the leader of the Whig army against Tyler, was also gone from Washington, having retired on March 31, 1842, to straighten out vexing financial problems and prepare his candidacy for the 1844 Presidential contest. His wife Lucretia required personal attention because their oldest son, Theodore, was definitely insane, the result, Clay said, of a carriage mishap. Their second son, Thomas, who had languished in a Philadelphia jail at the time Clay was serving as Secretary of State to President John Quincy Adams, had now ruined the family hemp business and $20,000 in unpaid bills needed Clay's immediate attention; and above all their troubles Lucretia felt an undiminishing sadness caused by the death of their six daughters.

In his farewell address to the Senate, Clay wrung the hearts of his listeners on the floor and in the packed galleries. Said the Sage of Ashland in reviewing his long career to his openly weeping audience: "I migrated to the state of Kentucky nearly forty-five years ago. I went there as an orphan who had never recognized a father's smile." He asked forgiveness for his arrogance and said he had always tried to act in the nation's best interest. When he finished a vast silence descended and the Senate adjourned for the day in his honor.

Perhaps it was the Tyler imbroglio with the Whigs; perhaps it was merely the times, when the great broadening of the electorate brought a more common type of politician to Washington; but in the Twenty-eighth and succeeding Congresses a noticeable drop in manners and ethics characterized the membership. The Senate made liquor available to its associates and Senate Pro Tem Willie Mangum appropriately charged it to the Senate's fuel account. Visitors flocked to the House to watch Representative William "Sausage" Sawyer of Ohio climb the Speaker's rostrum to stuff himself with his daily diet of sausages. Fights were common on the

House floor and on one occasion a bullet from a fired pistol broke one man's leg. Good times had begun to reappear and the special interests sent armies of lobbyists to roam Capitol halls to "buy" Congressmen who would aid them in getting contracts, grants and private bills. Thurlow Weed was commonly referred to as "the Lucifer of the lobbyists." Double standards invaded the ranks of the idealists, witness the false claims for mileage by men such as Senator Benton. Actually the precedent had been set in the First Senate in 1789 by Senator William Johnson who lived in New York, the capital, as the first head of Columbia College and represented Connecticut. Johnson had augmented his $6.00 a day Congressional salary with mileage claims for faked trips to Connecticut.

This lack of morals also extended to the Executive Branch, where patronage appointees since Jackson's time had shown less regard for their duties than for their pocketbooks. This was especially the case in the customhouses and the land office where sordid collusion with private interests was commonplace.

The spoils hunters who had crowded into the White House and hurried Harrison into his grave were still in evidence when Tyler became President. Tyler attempted to drive them away by issuing a statement that he would "remove no incumbent from office . . . except where such officer has been guilty of an active partisanship or by secret means has given his official influence to the purposes of party." Later he added to this rule with another requiring job seekers to apply to department heads and not to him.

But Tyler's initial ideals for government service were short-lived; first, because he found himself surrounded by a civil service of enemies; and second, because he wanted another term as President and this required wholesale patronage appointments.

By 1842, he had begun to play a double game. On the one hand, he hoped to capture the Democratic Presidential nomination in 1844. And on the other, he made initial moves to form a third party consisting of states'-right Whigs, pro-slavery southern Democrats and conservative northern Democrats. This led him to make unusual offers to key Democrats with a view to winning their support or removing them from competition.

When Supreme Court Justice Smith Thompson died in 1843, Tyler made the astonishing offer of the vacant seat to ex-President Van Buren. Senator Silas Wright, Democratic leader in the Upper

Chamber, to whom this offer to Van Buren was broached, replied, "Tell Mr. Tyler for me that if he desires to give this whole country a broader, deeper, heartier laugh than it has ever had and at his own expense, he can effect it by making that nomination."

Tyler later offered this same seat to Wright and the post of Navy Secretary to former Speaker James K. Polk. Both rejected the offers, for they understood Tyler's purpose to get them out of his political path. Tyler also made overtures to appease wordy Senator Benton by appointing his son-in-law, Lieutenant John C. Frémont, commander of the Oregon exploring expedition. He also gave Amos Kendall, Jackson's Kitchen Cabineteer, a government printing contract and named the old general's nephew, Andrew Jackson Donelson, United States minister to Texas.

As time went on, Tyler went to great lengths to build a loyal force in the government service. Edward Curtis, the Webster crony appointed by Harrison as Collector of the Port of New York, was fired and wholesale changes were made in that 500-job office. Jonathan Roberts, Collector of the Port of Philadelphia, was also expelled along with thirty-one employees whom Tyler's son called "the very scum of Philadelphia." This same fate befell Robert C. Wetmore, whom Clay had promoted for the post Curtis got. Wetmore was removed as Navy agent in Brooklyn and stigmatized as "incompetent."

By the spring of 1843, Tyler decreed an official axing of government employees who did not show enthusiasm for him and his policies. In a letter to Treasury Secretary John C. Spencer, an avid job seeker himself, Tyler wrote: "We have numberless enemies in office and they should forthwith be made to quit. The changes ought to be rapid and extensive and numerous—but we should have some assurances of support by the appointees. Glance occasionally at the Marshals and D. Attorneys and let me hear from you."

Besides patronage appointments, Tyler attempted to develop local Tyler organizations in New York City, Philadelphia and elsewhere. In New Orleans, for instance, four hundred joined the Tyler Club but it soon became apparent that they expected government jobs as a *quid pro quo*. In New York, Tyler infiltrated the Tammany organization, which was always amenable to dollar loyalty to any rich provider. He also let it be known that he favored the Democratic candidate for mayor and then played a third role by inducing friends to establish themselves as an independent Tyler force in state politics. After failing to buy control of James Gordon Bennett's New York *Herald,* Tyler acquired his own newspaper, the New York *Union,* under the editorship of Mordecai Noah, outstanding Tammany editor who also directed the Tyler Committee. However, a fight developed among the New York Tyler supporters over Noah, primarily because he was Jewish. Finally, Noah agreed to leave his posts when word reached him that Tyler would appoint him consul general at Constantinople. But Tyler made no such appointment because he would not compromise his own dictum against giving government jobs to editors. After Noah's departure, the *Union* was combined with the *Aurora,* a libelous sheet that had run a story claiming that Webster had raped a girl who had wandered into the State Department. Tyler also depended on the good will of Bennett's paper in New York and was the source for many of the scoops that appeared in the *Herald.* However, in time Bennett turned on Tyler just as he turned on Thurlow Weed, whom he had once supported. After Weed had retracted a story in his own Albany paper because of a libel suit, Bennett captioned the story of Weed's trip abroad with —"A Common Liar Goes to England."

Tyler realized the importance of rallies to whip up support for himself and made such suggestions to out-of-town supporters. To cloak himself with the common touch, he asked that he be referred to as "Honest John." However, rally posters labeled him "Old Veto." The biggest rally planned for him was held at the Broadway Tabernacle in the winter of 1843 and resulted in the fiasco of indiscriminate cheering for him, Van Buren, Clay and "a celebrated lady who conducted a harem in one of the streets which radiate from Broadway."

The Democrats and Whigs had no intention of sitting still while Tyler turned the government upside down. More than a hundred of his nominees failed to win Senate confirmation, an all-time record among Presidents. Among these were five nominations to the Supreme Court and four to his Cabinet. Diplomatic rejections were even more numerous, with Henry Wise the outstanding rejection, failing to be confirmed as minister to France. At the lower levels, of course, the opposition could not combat the firings and hirings where Senate confirmation was not needed. Among other things, this safety permitted Tyler to put a large number of his relatives on the payroll. It was remarkable that as many nominees won Senate approval as did, for as Calhoun noted, Tyler lacked even "one open advocate in the Senate; and not more than four or five in the House." The Administration, said Calhoun, was "unsteady, without fixed purpose of any kind, except to create a third party."

But Tyler did acquire a policy purpose as his term lengthened, and this was to annex California and Texas. Webster saw California as a way station for China traders and whalers, and although he showered Mexico with threats, demands and purchase offers, the Mexican Government would not part with California.

After Webster completed his treaty work with Lord Ashburton in 1842, it was apparent to him that Tyler already was making plans to bring the Republic of Texas into the Union. Texas, gaining her independence from Mexico at the Battle of San Jacinto on April 21, 1836, and winning recognition from "Old Hickory" Jackson in March 1837, had been kept at arm's length by Van Buren, who did not relish the idea of adding another slave state or going to war with Mexico in her behalf. To Webster, as to most northern Whigs, Democratic Van Buren was a man to be detested but his Texas policy was satisfactory.

Now he saw that policy about to be overturned by Tyler and he could not bring himself to participate in spreading slavery. Moreover, as a solid Whig, Webster realized that Tyler had reverted to the southern states'-rights Democrats in his views, and because of his Presidential ambitions for 1844 was "quite disposed to throw himself into the arms of the Locofoco [left-wing New York Democratic] party."

When Webster resigned on May 8, 1843, Tyler's pleasure and relief were obvious to those about him. Quickly, he shifted Secretary of the Navy Abel P. Upshur, his old Virginia friend and slavery defender, to the State Department and the two began a collaboration to annex Texas.

Upshur believed there was no time to waste, for reports showed that Britain was attempting to establish a close relationship with Texas. And in return, Texas appeared to be moving into the British orbit. Texas President Sam Houston later said he had "coquetted a little with Great Britain" in order to make the U. S. Senate jealous and more pliable to a treaty of annexation. Uncertain as to the seriousness of the British-Texas association and the price England planned to exact from Houston, Tyler sent Duff Green, Calhoun's public relations man and editor, to London as roving envoy to find out. Green sent back a report that the association was serious and that England had agreed to forget about interest payments on her loan to Texas if the Republic would abolish slavery.

Tyler and Upshur now made several moves. Upshur assessed the attitude of the Senate and concluded that annexation of Texas would win the support of at least the necessary two-thirds. England was sent a warning that if American slaves ran away to Texas, the United States intended to employ "hot pursuit" to return them to their masters and would brook no outside interference. Mexico was told that because she had made no attempt to force Texas to return to her control, she must now recognize the Republic above the Rio Grande and had no legal protest if the United States associated with Texas. The Administration also informed Sam Houston that it would negotiate a treaty of annexation without delay.

At first, Houston played coy and rejected the overture. Then when he thought Tyler and Upshur had gasped enough with anxiety, he ordered Isaac Van Zandt, the Texas agent in Washington, to collaborate in negotiating the treaty.

By February 1844, Upshur and Van Zandt were at the point of settling the last minor details, while Tyler had taken on the propaganda role to pave the way for the acceptance of annexation by the Senate and the people. To the question whether annexation was predicated on spreading slavery, Tyler's reply was that the addition of Texas was in the interest of the entire nation. From the strategic value alone, he argued, the United States would have enemies both to the north and south if trouble arose with Britain and Texas were allied to the English. He also used the scare technique in his December 1843 Message to Congress, saying that Mexico had threatened war if annexation negotiations were made. Surely, he added, "the representatives of a brave and patriotic people" would not cringe before weak Mexico.

On February 28, Tyler and a prominent array of Washingtonians were invited by Captain Robert Stockton to be his guests on a Potomac excursion aboard the new steam frigate *Princeton*, invented by John Ericsson, who later produced the Civil War ironclad, the *Monitor*. There were about 350 aboard the vessel as she pulled away from the dock, including Dolley Madison, that heavily rouged and snuff-pinching relic of a bygone era, Tyler, his Cabinet, members of Congress, military officers, diplomats and others. In mid-afternoon, as the *Princeton* neared Mount Vernon, dinner was served in the salon and champagne toasts abounded.

Afterward, the captain agreed to fire his large gun in esteem for the first President and many followed him up to the main deck to witness the firing. Tyler started to join the throng, but he paused at the foot of the ladder to listen while his son-in-law, William Waller, finished singing a song. He heard the gun go off and a moment later a hysterical officer, his face "blackened with powder," came down the ladder and screamed for a doctor. When Tyler investigated, he found that the gun had exploded, killing Upshur, Secretary of the Navy Thomas Gilmer, a commodore, Tyler's personal valet-slave, two seamen, a former American diplomat and a prominent New York socialite named David Gardiner. He also discovered Senator Benton wandering about in a daze, his hearing permanently lost in one ear. Tyler might have suffered the fate of Upshur and the other dead had he not stayed behind to listen to a song.

While Tyler was still shocked by the *Princeton* disaster, his erratic and bragging chief adviser, Henry Wise, saw Senator George McDuffie of South Carolina and remarked that Calhoun would make an excellent successor to Upshur. Wise gave the impression that Tyler had decided to make the offer and when he left, McDuffie sent Calhoun a letter with this conclusion.

Afterward, Wise stopped in the White House and by a strange coincidence Tyler told him that one of the last men he would appoint to the State Department was Calhoun. Wise panicked, confessed his conversation with McDuffie and threw himself on Tyler's mercy. Tyler reacted with anger and a flow of uncomplimentary words. But finally he agreed to appoint Calhoun because to do the opposite would antagonize McDuffie and Calhoun's friends and endanger the Texas treaty.

Calhoun had a microscopic regard for Tyler and under different circumstances he would not have associated with Tyler any more than Tyler would have with him. But Calhoun was a beaten man at the time the President's letter of notification reached him and he accepted the State Department with alacrity. When the Tyler-Clay clash had come in 1841, Calhoun sensed that the outcome would strangle both politically. As a result, Calhoun's hopes rose and he was determined to become the Democratic Presidential nominee in 1844. His supporters built organizations in several cities

and flooded Virginia and other states with a biography of Calhoun written anonymously by the subject! However, after defeats
to his candidacy in New York and Massachusetts and after watching his henchmen fail in their attempt to organize the House of
Representatives in the Twenty-eighth Congress, he withdrew from
the race in December 1843. Calhoun's hope now was to make a
record as Secretary of State that would make him a front-runner
for 1848.

The Upshur-Van Zandt annexation treaty required a few last-
minute changes before Calhoun rushed it to the Senate on April 22,
1844. Houston had refused to accept it until Tyler agreed to station a naval force in the Gulf of Mexico and a large army on the
southwestern frontier to ward off any Mexican attacks. Now that
this had secretly been accomplished, Houston found no objections
to the treaty terms, which stated that Texas must first enter the
Union as a territory, and cede its public lands to the United States
in return for the Federal assumption of the Texas Republic's
national debt of $10,000,000. No mention was made of boundaries.

Disaster came within the week. Both Clay and Van Buren,
leaders of the Whigs and Democrats, opposed annexation in letters
made public on April 27. "Annexation and war with Mexico are
identical," Clay charged and Van Buren agreed. Then a Calhoun
blunder reached public attention. Sir Richard Pakenham, British
minister to Washington, had passed along his government's expressed interest in abolishing slavery everywhere. On April 18,
Calhoun sent him a reply, calling slavery a blessing both to the
slaves and "to the peace, safety and prosperity of those states of
the Union in which it exists." Calhoun went on to assess the annexation of Texas as vital to American peace, because abolition
would endanger the South's security as well as that of the rest
of the nation.

The stupidity of the Calhoun reply to Pakenham was readily
evident to Tyler, but he could not suppress it for Calhoun had sent
a copy of the letter to Congress and Senator Benjamin Tappan
of Ohio had leaked it to the press. Thus all of Tyler's efforts to
establish the national character of the annexation went down the
drain through Calhoun's emphasis on slavery. Northern and western Senators could not be expected to support the treaty at this
time if its true results were to extend slavery and chance a war
with Mexico on that account. Senator Benton crowned his long
speech against annexation with a picture of the war aspect in-

volved in the treaty and he charged that the treaty-making power did not extend to granting authority to make war. An angered Tyler later described him as "the most raving political maniac I ever knew."

In an attempt to undo some of the damage, Tyler sent the Senate a Message, calling for annexation "in the interest of every portion of the country." Then a short time later he sent a second Message, on May 16, in which he warned that if the Senate did not approve the treaty the opportunity for annexation would be gone forever. But his explanations and threats proved ineffective, for on June 8, 1844, the Senate rejected the treaty by a vote of 16 in favor and 35 opposed.

Even this verdict did not deter Tyler from continuing the fight. In fact, he now dropped his rigid principles in order to achieve his goal. He had to have annexation both for the historic reputation he believed would be his and for the great rise in international status he thought would accrue to the United States. This status, he explained, would result directly from "the monopoly of the cotton plant" that Texas would help the nation achieve. "That monopoly, now secured," he wildly conjectured, "places all other nations at our feet. An embargo of a single year would produce in Europe a greater amount of suffering than a fifty years' war. I doubt whether Great Britain could avoid convulsions."

If Tyler could not obtain annexation through the treaty-making process, he would still get it, even if he had to take unprecedented action. He would try to get it through the ruse of a joint resolution by Congress. This he attempted on June 10, only two days after the Senate rejected the treaty, when he sent the House all the papers he had submitted to the Senate for its closed executive sessions on the treaty plus others in his possession. His request to the House now was that it play a role in foreign relations determination for the first time and pass a resolution favoring annexation. When Senator Benton heard of this, he treated Tyler to a scathing attack in a Senate speech, condemning the President for attempting to circumvent the Senate's constitutional rights over treaties by bringing the House into their consideration.

There wasn't time for the House to act before adjournment. Yet the release to the House and the public of the contents of the Presidential papers kept annexation alive in the press during that summer and fall. More than that, Tyler's relentless efforts made annexation of Texas the key issue of the Presidential campaign.

And his revenge on Clay was complete when the softening of Clay's original stand against annexation cost him northern votes, dooming Clay's Presidential campaign against the 1844 Democratic nominee, James K. Polk.

After his own withdrawal from the Presidential race and after Polk's victory over Clay that November, Tyler sent a Message to the lame-duck Congressional session in December 1844, hailing Polk's victory as a mandate for the admission of Texas.

The House now acted upon Tyler's request of the previous summer and passed a joint resolution authorizing the President to invite the Republic in the Southwest to join the Union. Under the terms of this resolution, Texas would come in as a state and not a territory; a total of four new states could be created from Texas with her consent; all of these new states north of 36°30′ were to bar slavery; Texas would not have to turn over her public lands to the Federal Government but she would have to pay her own debts.

Trouble arose when the joint resolution reached the Senate. Affronted by this invasion of the Senate's exclusive treaty power, the Senate Foreign Relations Committee returned an adverse report to the floor. Then truculent Benton called for a return to the established method with his resolution authorizing the President to negotiate a treaty with Texas.

At this point tiny Senator Robert J. Walker of Mississippi, an ardent supporter of Texas statehood, offered a compromise plan. Why not combine Benton's resolution and the resolution passed by the House into a single bill? By this scheme, when Polk was inaugurated he could decide whether to use the House resolution and invite Texas into the Union directly or negotiate a new treaty and then submit it to the Senate. Benton agreed when Walker assured him that Polk would negotiate a treaty. On this basis, the Walker Resolution squeaked by the Senate 27 to 25 and won quick House approval.

When Tyler signed the new joint resolution on March 1, 1845, he sent Calhoun to ask Polk which method he preferred—direct and simple admittance or the drafting of a new treaty. When Calhoun reported back that "Mr. Polk declined to express any opinion," Tyler breathed a sigh of relief. The bill he had signed said that *the President* should decide which method to use and he would still be President for a few days. So on March 3, the day before

Polk's inauguration, Tyler engaged in duplicity by acting on the House proposal alternative. He forwarded an invitation to Texas that day to become a state. Tyler's long struggle had ended in success.

The explosion aboard the *Princeton* did more than kill several persons and bring Calhoun ("the great 'I Am,'" as Tyler called him) into the Cabinet. It also brought him his second wife, Julia Gardiner of Long Island.

Letitia Tyler, paralyzed by a stroke, had come downstairs in the White House on only one occasion, and that was when one of her daughters married. The task of serving as Presidential hostess had been delegated to twenty-five-year-old Priscilla Cooper Tyler, wife of the President's son Robert. Priscilla had been on the stage with her father, Thomas Cooper, the well-known star, who was the adopted son of the British philosopher William Godwin, father of Mary Shelley. Cooper and Priscilla had been reduced to bleak poverty by the depression of 1837 and the competition of the likes of Tyrone Power and the Kembles. But fortunately, Robert Tyler saw Priscilla play Desdemona in Shakespeare's *Othello* in Richmond, went backstage to meet her, courted her and made her his bride.

When Tyler became President, old Tom Cooper, a vociferous rooter for Van Buren, was given a sinecure as military storekeeper at an arsenal, while Priscilla presided at social affairs. Dolley Madison, who lived only on the other side of Lafayette Park, tutored her in protocol and the young hostess suffered only a single embarrassing evening. This was in May 1841, when she fainted at the table. Daniel Webster, seated next to her and looking like his usual "cathedral in britches," lifted her in his arms and began to carry her from the room. Her concerned husband dashed after them with a pitcher of ice water and in his excitement threw the water in Webster's face while trying to revive her. "Poor Mr. Webster had to be shaken off, dried and brushed before he could resume his place," she said later.

Despite the regular political knocks he took, Tyler let nothing interfere with his social existence. There were two receptions a week, two formal dinners a week with twenty guests at the first and forty at the second, a monthly public levee when Congress was in session, special receptions in the oval Blue Room on Inde-

pendence Day and New Year's Day, an every evening informal reception until ten P.M. in the Green Room for friends, occasional
balls and bi-weekly summertime garden concerts by the Marine
Band to which the public was invited. Tyler, who enjoyed writing
sonnets and fiddling, liked to invite literary personalities to the
White House and sometimes rewarded them with jobs. Washington Irving became his minister to Spain and John Howard Payne,
author of "Home Sweet Home," consul to Tunis. Edgar Allan Poe,
then in his Philadelphia period, came one night to the White House
with hopes of landing a job in the Philadelphia customhouse. But
his opportunity vanished when he became drunk while with Tyler.

There was no secret that Mrs. Tyler was gradually fading, and
when she died on September 10, 1842, Tyler concentrated on his
work to spare himself from some of the gloom. He rose at five A.M.
and worked until past three P.M. at his second-floor desk without
pause. Then after four P.M. dinner, he sat at his desk until dusk
when he saw politicians on business. Bedtime came at ten o'clock.

One of the victims of the *Princeton* disaster of February 1844
was David Gardiner, wealthy New Yorker, whose daughter, Julia,
had been aboard the vessel at the time. Tyler had first met her
at a White House reception in January 1842 and those close by
said he paid her "a thousand compliments" even though his wife
was still alive. Julia was the belle of the ball in Washington and
the recipient of numerous proposals from politicians, judges and
military officers. Even John Tyler, Jr., pursued her, carefully re-
fraining from telling her he was married. Representative Francis
Pickens of South Carolina, later as Civil War Governor to test wills
with Lincoln over Fort Sumter, wrote Julia that if she married
him she would be attended by "ever so many niggers."

Just a few months after Mrs. Tyler's death, Julia came to the
New Year's Day, 1843, White House levee. Tyler remembered her
and found her fascinating. Several times during the following few
weeks he invited her family as his guests. One night, to the embarrassment of Tom Cooper, he flirted with her over cards in
the Red Room and chased her down the stairs to claim a kiss. He
proposed at the White House Washington Birthday Ball in February 1843, but she did not accept for he was fifty-three and she
twenty-three.

However, he refused to accept her verdict and sent her love
letters and sonnets. Gossip spread about them, but so much had
already been said about him that he did not care. A Congressman

reported that the Lower Chamber had been "in an uproar all day" discussing the romance.

So matters continued until her father was killed on the *Princeton*. Several weeks later she accepted Tyler, who had become her father-substitute, and the marriage took place in New York in June 1844.

During the remaining eight months of Tyler's term, the social season was almost royal, though much work had to be done to make the White House presentable. Congress, at odds with Tyler, had consistently failed to provide maintenance or improvements funds. Tyler was forced to pay for light and fuel and the Executive Mansion grew steadily seedier. Nor was he pleased by the gouging he suffered from local merchants. "I am heartily tired of the grocers here who exact high prices for everything," he complained of his special lot in Washington. An observer who studied the condition of the White House reported it to be "a contemptible disgrace to the nation." The White House pillars were "besplattered with saliva of tobacco," the floors covered with "patched carpets," "three-inch stumps of wax lights in the sockets of magnificent chandeliers, the splendid drapery falling in tatters" and the East Room chairs so rotten that they "would be kicked out of a brothel."

When Congress rejected a request to provide a $20,000 appropriation in 1844 to fix up the President's residence, Tyler and Gardiner money was used, in order that the second Mrs. Tyler reign with dignity. And a reign it was, with a court of "ladies in waiting" copied from what she had seen at the French court of Louis Philippe, then ruling France. She wore a diamond star on her forehead, though while mourning for her father she changed this to a black onyx. She acquired a greyhound, dressed her coachmen in expensive black suits with velvet bands, held gay parties at which she introduced the polka to Washington and found an obliging public relations man to get her widespread newspaper coverage of her ship christenings, exclusive dinner parties and daily doings. In addition, her public relations man, F. W. Thomas of the New York *Herald*, always described her as "beautiful . . . rosy as a summer morning . . . a spirit of youth and poetry, and love and tenderness." In queenly fashion, she accepted expensive gifts from admirers and extended the White House franking privilege to all her relatives. John Quincy Adams, who attended some Executive Mansion affairs, was appalled by the December-May match of the Executive lovebirds, and although he found no fault with their hospitality, he said that Tyler's "dull remarks were quoted for wit and his grave inanities passed off for wisdom."

Tyler's courtship of Julia had continued apace with his plans to launch a third party. In an effort to create public sympathy for himself, he denounced the Twenty-seventh Congress at every opportunity as a "Do-Nothing Congress." In June 1843, he left Washington for what he hoped would be a swing throughout the North to test public reaction to him. The stated reason for the trip was to attend the commemoration of the completion of the Bunker Hill Monument on June 17.

Along the way he made frequent stops and was heartened by the large turnouts that, to him, belied the pommeling he was getting from Congress. At Baltimore, Wilmington and Philadelphia, the size of the crowds displeased Whig papers, and their general excuse was to write off the warm receptions as "curiosity to see a Chief Magistrate of the Union." More than sixty thousand turned out to welcome him to New York and the parade in his honor took an hour and a half to pass. A Whig paper coldly assessed what in its estimation had occurred by this description: "The President was drawn in a barouche uncovered through the streets, and from 4 o'clock P.M. to 8½ P.M. he was exhibited to the public gaze." At Stonington, Connecticut, five hundred girls met him with bouquets, and after calling them "the sweetest flowers that Connecticut can possibly produce," he kissed each in turn.

Tyler did not know what to expect in Rhode Island because of his role in Dorr's Rebellion. About the time he became President, a great restlessness had spread over the little state because Rhode Island's constitution, which was actually the charter grant by Charles II in 1663, prevented most citizens from meeting voting qualifications. Finally in 1841, a mass meeting led by Thomas Dorr drew up its own constitution, which contained a provision establishing universal white manhood suffrage. Then the dissidents established a state government with Dorr as governor.

Sam King, the legal governor under the charter, reacted by calling on the state militia to support him. Since Dorr also had troops, a civil strife seemed imminent. But both sides delayed by calling on President Tyler for help.

When the requests had come to the White House, Tyler realized that if he backed King it would appear as though he opposed extending the suffrage. Then again, if he backed Dorr, he would be opposing the legal government. His communicated decision was that if civil war erupted he would have to send Federal troops to aid the charter government. At the same time, he told Governor King to call a convention and broaden voter ranks.

Tyler dispatched the Secretary of War to the scene under orders to use his troops if a rebellion broke out. The period of jitters had descended when Dorr established the various government agencies of his government in Providence in May 1842. King proclaimed martial law and again requested Tyler to provide armed intervention. But Tyler would not. Finally that summer, the state militia attacked Dorr's army and the rebel army fled in panic. Afterward, the charter government called a convention to make a new constitution and modernize the undemocratic relic of the seventeenth century. Nevertheless, the Dorrites denounced Tyler for using the authority of the Federal Government in behalf of the archaic state government.

Tyler was now pleasantly surprised on his trip north to find his reception in Providence "enthusiastic in the extreme." Then he finally arrived in Boston by train and on June 17 he was feted with another immense parade, a banquet and Daniel Webster's superb oration on Bunker Hill. Tyler intended to return to Washington via Springfield, Albany, Buffalo, Cleveland and Cincinnati. But his Attorney General, Hugh S. Legaré, a southern legal giant, died in Boston and Tyler canceled his western political swing to return to Washington.

By 1844, Tyler estimated that if he started a third party he would begin with a following of about 150,000 persons. In several cities and states, his Tyler Clubs won publicity by endorsing him for President, and the small Tyler press attempted to whip up popular enthusiasm for their man. In the spring, he decided to stage his own national convention. Under his direction, a large group of Tylerites met in Washington in April, "spontaneously assembled," said the Tyler press, and a call went out to "Democratic-Republicans" in all states to attend a national convention for their man in Baltimore on May 27, the same day the Democratic convention was to meet.

It was a strange gathering that met at Calvert Hall in Baltimore. Leaders had come through Washington en route, stopping at the White House for instructions. The trimmings were in evidence in the hall—the bunting, flags, restless delegates a thousand strong and overhead the campaign slogans: TYLER AND TEXAS and RE-ANNEXATION OF TEXAS—POSTPONEMENT IS REJECTION. But Judge White of Connecticut, the convention's chairman, failed to stress the third-party aspect of the meeting in his address. Instead, he praised Tyler for rescuing the Democratic party "from the prostrate condition in which it was left in 1840."

Only an hour was required to nominate Tyler unanimously, and on May 30 when he accepted the nomination, he spoke oddly of the gathering as a "Democratic convention." He also displayed a bit of self-pity in speaking of his trials in office—"Every harsh appellation was employed in connection with my name—mobs assembled at midnight at the door of the Presidential Mansion, and the light of burning effigies threw its glare along the streets of some of our cities." His chief reason for running now, he said, was to bring Texas into the Union.

As the campaign began, it was obvious to all that he did not have a chance. Yet his continuation as a candidate was bound to cost James K. Polk, the Democratic candidate, some votes in his contest with Henry Clay. Senator Robert J. Walker of Mississippi, chairman of the Democratic party's Executive Committee, was sent as an emissary by the Jackson-Polk camp to learn Tyler's price for withdrawing from the race.

He talked with Tyler for hours and later wrote Polk that he considered it "a most disagreeable duty." Tyler spoke of Jackson "in terms of deep affection," wrote Walker, and his only concern about withdrawing was the fate of his friends and supporters. Since Polk was also for annexation of Texas, he had no political animosity toward him. All he wanted, Tyler told Walker, were assurances from Polk that he would accept the Tylerites back into the Democratic party "as brethren and equals."

Polk considered sending Tyler a letter on this score until Jackson warned him that such a letter from Polk or Jackson would gain them notoriety "just as Adams and Clay's bargain" of 1824. Instead, said Jackson, he would write a letter to his old White House aide, Major William B. Lewis, and Lewis would show it to Tyler.

All this was accomplished. Tyler read that his withdrawal was "the certain means of electing Mr. Polk and ensuring a consummation of all the leading measures" Tyler favored. For this, said Jackson, Tyler and his friends, "true friends of the country," would be welcomed with open arms back into the Democratic fold and "all former differences forgotten." So on August 20, 1844, Tyler formally withdrew from the Presidential race, once more becoming a Democrat.

After this, his chief interests centered on annexing Texas and in providing his young wife with a gala social season. Finally on March 3, 1845, these two goals achieved, Old Veto moved from the White House. That day Congress accomplished what it had failed to do in his four years in office. He had vetoed a bill to construct some revenue cutters and Congress passed the bill over his veto.

In his last talk, Tyler told well-wishers who had come to say farewell: "In 1840 I was called from my farm to undertake the administration of public affairs, and I foresaw that I was called to a bed of thorns. I now leave that bed, which has afforded me little rest, and eagerly seek repose in the quiet enjoyments of rural life. I rely on future history to award me the meed due to honest and conscientious purposes to serve my country."

With the departure of John Tyler from the White House, the epoch of the Founding Presidents ended. The last major area of dispute surrounding the awesome Office was settled; the institution, firmly established; and the focal point for guiding the nation through its turbulent future remained as the legacy of the ten men who first occupied the Presidency.

SELECTED BIBLIOGRAPHY

GEORGE WASHINGTON

AMES, SETH, ed., *Works of Fisher Ames*, 2 v., Boston, 1854

BACHE, BENJAMIN F., *Remarks Occasioned by the Late Conduct of Mr. Washington*, Philadelphia, 1798

BAKER, WILLIAM S., *Washington After the Revolution, 1784–1799*, Philadelphia, 1898

BALLAGH, JAMES C., ed., *The Letters of Richard Henry Lee*, 2 v., New York, 1911–1914

BANCROFT, GEORGE, *The History of the Formation of the Constitution of the United States*, New York, 1903

BASSETT, JOHN S., *The Federalist System, 1789–1801*, New York, 1906

BEARD, CHARLES A., *An Economic Interpretation of the Constitution*, New York, 1913

————, *The American Political Battle*, New York, 1928

BELOFF, MAX, *The Federalist*, New York, 1948

BEMIS, SAMUEL F., *Jay's Treaty*, New York, 1923

————, *The Pinckney Treaty*, Baltimore, 1926

BOWERS, CLAUDE G., *Jefferson and Hamilton; the Struggle for Democracy in America*, Boston, 1925

BRACKENRIDGE, H. M., *Incidents of the Insurrection in the Western Parts of Pennsylvania in the Year 1794*, Philadelphia, 1795

BURNETT, E. C., *Letters of Members of the Continental Congress, 1774–1789*, 8 v., Washington, 1921–1936

BURT, ALFRED L., *The United States, Great Britain and British North America, 1783–1812*, New Haven, 1940

CALLENDER, JAMES T., *The History of the United States for 1796*, Philadelphia, 1800

CAREY, MATHEW, *A Short Account of the Malignant Fever Lately Prevalent in Philadelphia*, Philadelphia, 1793

CARROLL, J. A. and ASHWORTH, M. W., *George Washington*, v. 7, New York, 1957

CHANNING, EDWARD, "Washington and Parties, 1789–1797," *Proceedings of the Massachusetts Historical Society*, v. 47, Boston, 1914

COBBETT, WILLIAM, *Porcupine's Works*, 12 v., London, 1801

CONWAY, MONCURE D., *Omitted Chapters of History in the Life of Edmund Randolph*, New York, 1888

CORWIN, EDWARD S., *French Diplomacy and the Alliance of 1778*, Princeton, 1916

Coxe, Tench, A View of the United States of America, Philadelphia, 1794

Cunliffe, Marcus, George Washington: Man and Monument, Boston, 1958

Curtis, George Tichnor, History of the Origin, Formation and Adoption of the Constitution of the United States, 2 v., New York, 1889–1896

Custis, G. W. P., Recollections and Private Memoirs of Washington, Philadelphia, 1860

Daniel, Peter V., ed., A Vindication of Edmund Randolph, Written by Himself and Published in 1795, Richmond, 1855

Decatur, Stephen, Jr., Private Affairs of George Washington from the Records and Accounts of Tobias Lear, Esq., his Secretary, Boston, 1933

DeConde, A., Entangling Alliance; Politics and Diplomacy under George Washington, Durham, North Carolina, 1958

Drake, Francis S., Life and Correspondence of Henry Knox, Boston, 1873

Elliot, Jonathan, Debates in the Several State Conventions in the Adoption of the Federal Constitution, 5 v., Philadelphia, 1906

Farrand, Max, ed., The Records of the Federal Convention of 1787, 4 v., New Haven, 1937

Fauchet, Joseph, A Sketch of the Present State of Our Political Relations with the United States of America, Philadelphia, 1797

Fiske, John, The Critical Period of American History, 1783–1789, Boston, 1888

Fitzpatrick, John C., ed., The Diaries of George Washington, 4 v., Boston, 1925

————, The Writings of George Washington, 39 v., Washington, 1931–1934

————, George Washington Himself, Indianapolis, 1933

Ford, Paul L., The True George Washington, Philadelphia, 1896

Freeman, Douglas S., George Washington, 6 v., New York, 1948–1954

Freneau, Philip, Letters on Various Interesting and Important Subjects, Philadelphia, 1799

Gibbs, George, Memoirs of the Administrations of Washington and John Adams, Edited from the Papers of Oliver Wolcott, 2 v., New York, 1846

Griswold, Rufus W., The Republican Court, or American Society in the Days of Washington, New York, 1854

Hamilton, John C., ed., The Works of Alexander Hamilton, 7 v., New York, 1850–1851

Hamilton, S. M., ed., Letters to Washington and Accompanying Papers, 5 v., Boston, 1902

Hazen, C. D., Contemporary American Opinion of the French Revolution, Baltimore, 1897

Henry, William Wirt, Patrick Henry; Life Correspondence and Speeches, 3 v., New York, 1891

Holdsworth, John T., The First Bank of the United States, Philadelphia, 1911

Hughes, Rupert, George Washington, 3 v., New York, 1926–1930

Hunt, Gaillard, ed., Debates of the Federal Convention of 1787, Reported by James Madison, New York, 1908

Irving, Washington, Life of George Washington, 5 v., New York, 1855–1859

Jay, William, Life of John Jay, 2 v., New York, 1833

Jensen, Merrill, The New Nation, A History of the United States During the Confederation, 1781–1789, New York, 1950

JOHNSON, HENRY P., ed., *Correspondence and Public Papers of John Jay,* 4 v.,
     New York, 1890–1893
KING, CHARLES R., ed., *The Life and Correspondence of Rufus King,* New
     York, 1894–1900
LINCOLN, BENJAMIN, "Journal of Benjamin Lincoln," *Massachusetts Historical
     Society Collections Third Series,* v. 5, 1836
LODGE, HENRY CABOT, *Life and Letters of George Cabot,* Boston, 1877
————, *Alexander Hamilton,* Boston, 1882
————, ed., *The Federalist,* New York, 1886
————, *George Washington,* 2 v., Boston, 1889
————, ed., *Works of Alexander Hamilton,* 12 v., New York, 1904
MACLAY, EDGAR S., ed., *The Journal of William Maclay,* New York, 1890
MARSHALL, JOHN, *George Washington,* 5 v., Philadelphia, 1804–1807
MITCHELL, BROADUS, *Alexander Hamilton,* 2 v., New York, 1957–1962
MONROE, JAMES, *A View of the Conduct of the Executive of the United States,*
     Philadelphia, 1797
MORRIS, ANNE C., ed., *The Diary and Letters of Gouverneur Morris,* 2 v., New
     York, 1888
PICKERING, OCTAVIUS and UPHAM, C. W., *Life of Timothy Pickering,* 4 v.,
     Boston, 1867–1873
SCHACHNER, NATHAN, *Alexander Hamilton,* New York, 1946
SPARKS, JARED, *Life of Gouverneur Morris,* 3 v., Boston, 1832
————, ed., *Writings of George Washington,* 12 v., Boston, 1834–1837
STEPHENSON, N. W. and DUNN, W. H., *George Washington,* 2 v., New York,
     1940
THACH, C. C., *Creation of the Presidency,* Baltimore, 1922
TWINING, THOMAS, *Travels in America One Hundred Years Ago,* New York,
     1894
WARREN, CHARLES, *The Making of the Constitution,* Boston, 1928
WHITE, LEONARD, *The Federalists; A Study in Administrative History,* New
     York, 1948
WINGATE, CHARLES, *Life and Letters of Paine Wingate,* 2 v., Medford, Massa-
     chusetts, 1930
WOODWARD, W. E., *George Washington: The Image and the Man,* New York,
     1946

JOHN ADAMS

ADAMS, BROOKS, "The Convention of 1800 with France," *Proceedings of the
     Massachusetts Historical Society,* v. 44, 1911
ADAMS, CHARLES FRANCIS, *Letters of John Adams Addressed to His Wife,* 2 v.,
     Boston, 1841
————, *Letters of Mrs. Adams, Wife of John Adams,* Boston, 1848
————, *Works of John Adams,* 10 v., Boston, 1850–1856
————, *Life of John Adams,* 2 v., Boston, 1874
ADAMS, JAMES TRUSLOW, *The Adams Family,* Boston, 1930
ALLEN, GARDNER, *Our Naval War with France,* Boston, 1909

ANDERSON, FRANK M., "Contemporary Opinion of the Virginia and Kentucky Resolutions," *American Historical Review*, v. 5, October 1899, January 1900

AUSTIN, JAMES, *The Life of Elbridge Gerry*, 2 v., Boston, 1827–1829

BEVERIDGE, ALBERT J., *Life of John Marshall*, 4 v., Boston, 1916–1919

BROWN, WILLIAM G., *The Life of Oliver Ellsworth*, New York, 1905

BUTTERFIELD, LYMAN, ed., *The Diary and Autobiography of John Adams*, 4 v., Cambridge, 1961

CALLENDER, JAMES T., *The Prospect Before Us*, Philadelphia, 1800

CAPPON, LESTER J., ed., *Adams-Jefferson Letters*, 2 v., Chapel Hill, 1959

CHEETHAM, JAMES, *An Answer to Alexander Hamilton's Letter Concerning the Public Conduct and Character of John Adams*, New York, 1800

CHINARD, GILBERT, *Honest John Adams*, Boston, 1933

CLARK, MARY E., *Peter Porcupine in America*, Philadelphia, 1939

CUSHING, HENRY A., ed., *The Writings of Samuel Adams*, 4 v., New York, 1904–1908

DAUER, MANNING J., *The Adams Federalists*, Baltimore, 1953

DONNAN, ELIZABETH, ed., *Papers of James A. Bayard, 1796–1815*, Washington, 1915

FORD, W. C., "Letters of William Vans Murray to John Quincy Adams," *American Historical Association Annual Report for 1912*, Washington, 1913

GIBBS, GEORGE, *Memoirs of the Administrations of Washington and John Adams, Edited from the Papers of Oliver Wolcott*, 2 v., New York, 1846

HARASZTI, ZOLTÁN, *John Adams and the Prophets of Progress*, Cambridge, Massachusetts, 1952

HARLOW, R. V., *History of Legislative Methods in the Period Before 1825*, New Haven, 1917

HUNT, GAILLARD, ed., *The First Forty Years of American Society, Portrayed in the Family Letters of Mrs. Margaret Bayard Smith*, New York, 1906

KURTZ, STEPHEN, *The Presidency of John Adams*, Philadelphia, 1957

LANGDON, JOHN, *Letters of Washington, Adams, Jefferson and Others Written to John Langdon*, Philadelphia, 1880

LOGAN, DEBORAH N., *Memoirs of Dr. George Logan of Stenton*, Philadelphia, 1899

MAYO, LAWRENCE S., *John Langdon of New Hampshire*, Concord, New Hampshire, 1937

MILLER, JOHN C., *Crisis in Freedom, The Alien and Sedition Acts*, Boston, 1951

———, *Alexander Hamilton, Portrait in Paradox*, New York, 1959

MITCHELL, STEWART, ed., *New Letters of Abigail Adams, 1789–1801*, Boston, 1947

MORSE, JOHN T., *John Adams*, Boston, 1899

PICKERING, OCTAVIUS and UPHAM, C. W., *Life of Timothy Pickering*, 4 v., Boston, 1867–1873

SMITH, JAMES M., *Freedom's Fetters: The Alien and Sedition Laws and American Civil Liberties*, Ithaca, 1956

SMITH, PAGE, *John Adams*, 2 v., New York, 1962

STEINER, BERNARD C., *Life and Correspondence of James McHenry*, Cleveland, 1907

WALSH, CORREA, *The Political Science of John Adams,* New York, 1915

WARFIELD, E. D., *The Kentucky Resolutions of 1798,* New York, 1887

WHARTON, ANNE H., *Social Life in the Early Republic,* Philadelphia, 1902

WHITE, LEONARD, *The Federalists; A Study in Administrative History,* New York, 1948

WORTMAN, TUNIS, *A Solemn Address to Christians and Patriots, Upon the Approaching Election,* New York, 1800

THOMAS JEFFERSON

ADAMS, HENRY, *Documents Relating to New England Federalists, 1800–1815,* Boston, 1877

————, *Life of Albert Gallatin,* Philadelphia, 1879

————, ed., *Writings of Albert Gallatin,* 3 v., Philadelphia, 1879

————, *John Randolph of Roanoke,* Philadelphia, 1882

————, *History of the United States During the Administrations of Jefferson and Madison,* 9 v., Boston, 1889–1891

BECKLEY, JOHN, *Address to the People of the United States; With an Epitome and Vindication of the Public Life and Character of Thomas Jefferson,* Philadelphia, 1800

BEVERIDGE, ALBERT J., *Life of John Marshall,* 4 v., Boston, 1916–1919

BOWERS, CLAUDE G., *Jefferson in Power,* Boston, 1936

BOYD, JULIAN P., ed., *Papers of Thomas Jefferson,* 17 v., Princeton, 1950–1965

BRADY, J. P., *Trial of Aaron Burr,* New York, 1913

BROWN, EVERETT S., *The Constitutional History of the Louisiana Purchase,* Berkeley, 1920

BRUCE, WILLIAM C., *John Randolph of Roanoke,* 2 v., New York, 1922

BURR, AARON, *Private Journal,* 2 v., Rochester, 1903

CHANNING, EDWARD, *The Jeffersonian System, 1801–1811,* New York, 1906

CHINARD, GILBERT, *Thomas Jefferson, The Apostle of Americanism,* Boston, 1929

CORWIN, EDWARD S., *The Doctrine of Judicial Review,* Princeton, 1914

COTTON, J. P., ed., *Constitutional Decisions of John Marshall,* 2 v., New York, 1905

CRANCH, WILLIAM, *Reports of Cases Argued and Adjudged in the Supreme Court of the United States, 1801–1808,* 6 v., New York, 1812

DAVIESS, JOSEPH H., *A View of the President's Conduct Concerning the Conspiracy of 1806,* Frankfort, 1807

DAVIS, MATTHEW L., ed., *Memoirs of Aaron Burr,* 2 v., New York, 1836

DODD, WILLIAM, *Life of Nathaniel Macon,* Raleigh, 1903

DONNAN, ELIZABETH, ed., *Papers of James A. Bayard, 1796–1815,* Washington, 1915

FORD, P. L., ed., *The Writings of Thomas Jefferson,* 12 v., New York, 1892–1899

GARLAND, HUGH, *Life of John Randolph of Roanoke,* 2 v., New York, 1851

HARLOW, R. V., *History of Legislative Methods in the Period Before 1825,* New Haven, 1917

HASKINS, CHARLES, *Yazoo Land Companies*, New York, 1891

HASTINGS, HUGH, ed., *Public Papers of George Clinton*, 10 v., New York, 1899–1914

HAY, THOMAS R. and WERNER, M. R., *The Admirable Trumpeter; A Biography of General James Wilkinson*, New York, 1941

HIRST, FRANCIS W., *Life and Letters of Thomas Jefferson*, New York, 1926

JACOBS, JAMES R., *Tarnished Warrior; Major-General James Wilkinson*, New York, 1938

JENNINGS, WALTER W., *The Arms Embargo, 1807–1809*, Iowa City, 1921

KENNEDY, JOHN P., ed., *Memoirs of the Life of William Wirt*, 2 v., Philadelphia, 1849

LIPSCOMB, ANDREW A., ed., *The Writings of Thomas Jefferson*, 20 v., Washington, 1904–1905

MALONE, DUMAS, *Thomas Jefferson*, 2 v., Boston, 1948

MAYO, BERNARD, *Jefferson Himself*, Boston, 1942

MORSE, JOHN T., *Thomas Jefferson*, Boston, 1899

MOTT, FRANK L., *Jefferson and the Press*, Baton Rouge, 1943

MUZZEY, DAVID, *Thomas Jefferson*, New York, 1919

NOCK, ALBERT JAY, *Jefferson*, New York, 1926

PARTON, JAMES, *Life and Times of Aaron Burr*, New York, 1858

————, *Life of Thomas Jefferson*, 2 v., Boston, 1874

PLUMER, WILLIAM, *Memorandum of Proceedings in the United States Senate, 1803–1807*, Ann Arbor, 1923

POORE, BENJAMIN PERLEY, *Perley's Reminiscences of Sixty Years in the National Metropolis*, Philadelphia, 1886

PRENTISS, H. P., *Timothy Pickering as the Leader of New England Federalism, 1800–1815*, Salem, 1934

RANDALL, HENRY S., *The Life of Thomas Jefferson*, 3 v., New York, 1858

RANDOLPH, SARAH, *The Domestic Life of Thomas Jefferson*, New York, 1871

ROBERTSON, DAVID, Stenographer, *Trials of Aaron Burr for Treason and for a Misdemeanor*, 2 v., Philadelphia, 1808

SCHACHNER, NATHAN, *Aaron Burr*, New York, 1937

————, *Thomas Jefferson*, 2 v., New York, 1951

SEARS, L. M., *Jefferson and the Embargo*, Durham, 1927

STEVENS, JOHN A., *Albert Gallatin*, Boston, 1899

TAYLOR, JOHN, *A Definition of Parties*, Philadelphia, 1794

WATSON, THOMAS E., *Life and Times of Thomas Jefferson*, New York, 1903

WHARTON, ANNE H., *Social Life in the Early Republic*, Philadelphia, 1902

WHITE, LEONARD, *The Jeffersonians*, New York, 1951

WILKINSON, JAMES, *Memoirs of My Own Times*, 3 v., Philadelphia, 1816

JAMES MADISON

ADAMS, HENRY, ed., *Writings of Albert Gallatin*, 3 v., Philadelphia, 1879

————, *History of the United States During the Administrations of Jefferson and Madison*, 9 v., New York, 1889–1891

ADAMS, JOHN QUINCY, *The Life and Character of James Madison* (Pamphlet), Boston, 1816

————, *The Lives of James Madison and James Monroe*, Boston, 1850

ANDERSON, DICE R., *Insurgents of 1811*, 2 v., Washington, 1911

————, *William Branch Giles*, Menasha, Wisconsin, 1914

ARMSTRONG, JOHN, *Notices of the War of 1812*, 2 v., New York, 1836

AUSTIN, JAMES, *The Life of Elbridge Gerry*, 2 v., Boston, 1828–1829

BALINSKY, ALEXANDER, *Albert Gallatin: Fiscal Theories and Practices*, New Brunswick, 1958

BOBBÉ, DOROTHIE, *DeWitt Clinton*, New York, 1933

BRANT, IRVING, *James Madison*, 6 v., Indianapolis, 1941–1961

BURNS, EDWARD M., *James Madison, Philosopher of the Constitution*, New Brunswick, 1938

BUTLER, N. M., *Influences of the War of 1812*, Baltimore, 1888

CLARK, ALLEN C., *Life and Letters of Dolly Madison*, New York, 1914

COLES, HARRY L., *The War of 1812*, Chicago, 1965

COLTON, CALVIN, ed., *The Works of Henry Clay*, 6 v., New York, 1857

CUTTS, JAMES MADISON, "Dolly Madison," *Records of the Columbia Historical Society*, v. 3, 1898

CUTTS, LUCIA B., ed., *Memoirs and Letters of Dolly Madison*, New York, 1888

DALLAS, A. J., *An Exposition of the Causes and Character of the Late War*, Washington, 1815

DALLAS, GEORGE M., ed., *Life and Writings of A. J. Dallas*, Philadelphia, 1871

DWIGHT, THEODORE, *History of the Hartford Convention*, New York, 1833

GALES, JOSEPH, *Recollections of the Civil History of the War of 1812, By a Contemporary*, Washington, 1857

GALLATIN, ALBERT, *Considerations on the Currency and Banking System of the United States*, Philadelphia, 1831

GAY, SIDNEY, *James Madison*, Boston, 1884

HANSON, ALEXANDER, *Reflections Upon the Late Correspondence between Mr. Secretary Smith and Francis James Jackson*, Baltimore, 1810

HUNT, GAILLARD, ed., *Writings of James Madison*, 9 v., New York, 1900–1910

————, ed., *The First Forty Years of American Society, Portrayed in the Family Letters of Mrs. Margaret Bayard Smith*, New York, 1906

HUTCHINSON, W. T. and RACHAL, W. R., eds., *The Papers of James Madison*, 4 v., Chicago, 1962–1965

JENNINGS, PAUL, *A Colored Man's Reminiscences of James Madison*, Brooklyn, 1865

KOCH, ADRIENNE, *Jefferson and Madison*, New York, 1950

LOSSING, BENSON, *Pictorial Field Book of the War of 1812*, New York, 1868

MADISON, JAMES, *Letters of Helvedius*, Philadelphia, 1796

————, *Letters and Other Writings* (Congress Edition), 4 v., Philadelphia, 1865

MORISON, SAMUEL E., "The Henry-Crillon Affair of 1812," *Massachusetts Historical Society Proceedings*, v. 69, 1950

PERKINS, BRADFORD, *Prologue to War, 1805–1812*, Berkeley, 1861

RIVES, WILLIAM C., *History and Times of James Madison*, 3 v., Boston, 1859–1868

ROOSEVELT, THEODORE, *Naval War of 1812*, New York, 1903

STEVENS, JOHN A., *Albert Gallatin*, Boston, 1899

SWAIN, JAMES B., ed., *Life and Speeches of Henry Clay*, New York, 1843

UPDYKE, FRANK, *The Diplomacy of the War of 1812*, Baltimore, 1915

WHITE, LEONARD, *The Jeffersonians*, New York, 1951

JAMES MONROE

ADAMS, CHARLES FRANCIS, ed., *Memoirs of John Quincy Adams*, 12 v., Philadelphia, 1874–1877

ADAMS, JOHN QUINCY, *The Duplicate Letters, the Fisheries and the Mississippi*, Washington, 1822

————, *Lives of James Madison and James Monroe*, Boston, 1850

APTHEKER, HERBERT, *American Negro Slave Revolts*, California U. Studies in History, Economics and Public Law, #501, 1943

BALDWIN, JOSEPH G., *Party Leaders*, New York, 1855

BASSETT, JOHN SPENCER, *Life of Andrew Jackson*, 2 v., New York, 1911

————, ed., *Correspondence of Andrew Jackson*, 6 v., Washington, 1926–1935

BEMIS, SAMUEL F., *Latin American Policy of the United States*, New York, 1943

————, *John Quincy Adams and the Foundations of American Foreign Policy*, New York, 1949

BROWN, EVERETT S., ed., *The Missouri Compromises and Presidential Politics, 1820–1825*, St. Louis, 1926

BRUCE, WILLIAM C., *John Randolph of Roanoke*, 2 v., New York, 1922

BUTLER, BENJAMIN F., *Sketches in the Life and Character of William H. Crawford*, Albany, 1824

CARROLL, JOSEPH C., *Slave Insurrections in the United States, 1800–1865*, Boston, 1938

COLTON, CALVIN, ed., *The Works of Henry Clay*, 6 v., New York, 1857

COOPER, THOMAS, *Life and Character of William H. Crawford*, Albany, 1824

CORWIN, EDWARD S., *John Marshall and the Constitution*, New York, 1919

CRALLÉ, RICHARD K., ed., *The Works of John C. Calhoun*, 6 v., Charleston, 1851–1856

CRESSON, WILLIAM PENN, *James Monroe*, Chapel Hill, 1946

DANGERFIELD, GEORGE, *The Era of Good Feelings*, New York, 1952

————, *The Awakening of American Nationalism, 1815–1828*, New York, 1965

ELLET, ELIZABETH F., *Court Circles of the Republic from Washington to Grant*, Hartford, 1869

FORD, W. C., "John Quincy Adams and The Monroe Doctrine," *American Historical Review*, v. 7, July 1902, and v. 8, October 1902

————, "Letters of Monroe," *Proceedings of the Massachusetts Historical Society*, v. 42, 1909

————, ed., *The Writings of John Quincy Adams*, 7 v., New York, 1913–1917

FORNEY, JOHN W., *Anecdotes of Public Men*, New York, 1873

GILMAN, DANIEL C., *James Monroe*, Boston, 1885

GOODRICH, SAMUEL G., *Recollections of a Lifetime*, 2 v., New York, 1857

HAMILTON, S. M., ed., *Writings of James Monroe*, 8 v., New York, 1898–1903

JAMES, MARQUIS, *The Life of Andrew Jackson*, 2 v., Indianapolis, 1938

JAMESON, J. F., ed., "Correspondence of John C. Calhoun," *Annual Report, American Historical Association*, v. 2, 1899

MOORE, GLOVER, *The Missouri Controversy, 1819–1821*, Lexington, 1953

MORGAN, GEORGE, *The Life of James Monroe*, Boston, 1921

PERKINS, DEXTER, *The Monroe Doctrine: 1823–1826*, Baltimore, 1933

REZNECK, SAMUEL, "The Depression of 1819–22, A Social History," *American Historical Review*, v. 39, October 1933

ROTHBARD, MURRAY N., *The Panic of 1819*, New York, 1962

SHIPP, JOHN E. D., *Giant Days, or the Life and Times of William H. Crawford*, Americus, Georgia, 1909

SPARKS, W. H., *Memories of Fifty Years*, Philadelphia, 1870

TATUM, EDWARD L., *The United States and Europe, 1815–1823*, Baltimore, 1936

TURNER, FREDERICK J., *Rise of the New West, 1819–1829*, New York, 1906

VAN DEUSEN, GLYNDON G., *The Life of Henry Clay*, Boston, 1937

WHITAKER, ARTHUR P., *The United States and the Independence of Latin America, 1800–1830*, Baltimore, 1941

WHITE, LEONARD, *The Jeffersonians*, New York, 1951

WILMERDING, LUCIUS, *James Monroe, Public Claimant*, New Brunswick, 1960

WILTSE, CHARLES, *John C. Calhoun, Nationalist*, 3 v., Indianapolis, 1944–1951

JOHN QUINCY ADAMS

ADAMS, CHARLES FRANCIS, ed., *Memoirs of John Quincy Adams*, 12 v., Philadelphia, 1874–1877

BASSETT, JOHN S., *Life of Andrew Jackson*, 2 v., New York, 1911

————, ed., *Correspondence of Andrew Jackson*, 6 v., Washington, 1926–1935

BEMIS, SAMUEL F., *John Quincy Adams and the Foundations of American Foreign Policy*, New York, 1949

————, *John Quincy Adams and the Union*, New York, 1956

BROWN, EVERETT S., "The Presidential Election of 1824–25," *Political Science Quarterly*, v. 4, 1925

CARROLL, EBER M., "Politics During the Administration of John Quincy Adams," *South Atlantic Quarterly*, v. 23, 1924

————, *Origins of the Whig Party*, Durham, North Carolina, 1925

CLARK, BENNETT CHAMP, *John Quincy Adams: Old Man Eloquent*, Boston, 1932

COIT, MARGARET, *John C. Calhoun*, Boston, 1950

COLTON, CALVIN, ed., *The Works of Henry Clay*, 6 v., New York, 1857

CRALLÉ, RICHARD K., ed., *The Works of John C. Calhoun*, 6 v., Charleston, 1851–1856

CRESSON, WILLIAM PENN, *James Monroe*, Chapel Hill, 1946

DANGERFIELD, GEORGE, *The Era of Good Feelings*, New York, 1952
————, *The Awakening of American Nationalism, 1815–1828*, New York, 1965
FORD, W. C., "John Quincy Adams and The Monroe Doctrine," *American Historical Review*, v. 7, July 1902, and v. 8, October 1902
————, ed., *The Writings of John Quincy Adams*, 7 v., New York, 1913–1917
JAMES, MARQUIS, *The Life of Andrew Jackson*, 2 v., Indianapolis, 1938
JAMESON, J. F., ed., "Correspondence of John C. Calhoun," *Annual Report, American Historical Association*, v. 2, 1899
MONROE, JAMES, "Monroe on the Adams-Clay 'Bargain,'" *American Historical Review*, v. 42, January 1937
NEVINS, ALLAN, ed., *The Diary of John Quincy Adams, 1794–1845*, New York, 1928
POWELL, J. H., *Richard Rush, Republican Diplomat*, Philadelphia, 1942
REMINI, ROBERT V., "Martin Van Buren and the Tariff of Abominations," *American Historical Review*, v. 63, 1958
SHIPP, JOHN E. D., *Giant Days, or the Life and Times of William H. Crawford*, Americus, Georgia, 1909
STYRON, ARTHUR, *The Cast-Iron Man, John C. Calhoun and American Democracy*, New York, 1935
THOMPSON, C. S., *The Rise and Fall of the Congressional Caucus*, New Haven, 1902
VAN DEUSEN, GLYNDON G., *The Life of Henry Clay*, Boston, 1937
WEBSTER, DANIEL, *Writings and Speeches of Daniel Webster*, 18 v., Boston, 1903
WEED, HARRIET A., ed., *Autobiography of Thurlow Weed*, Boston, 1883
WILTSE, CHARLES, *John C. Calhoun, Nationalist*, 3 v., Indianapolis, 1944–1951

ANDREW JACKSON

ADAMS, CHARLES FRANCIS, ed., *Memoirs of John Quincy Adams*, 12 v., Philadelphia, 1874–1877
BANCROFT, GEORGE, "The Bank of the United States," *North American Review*, v. 33, January 1831
————, *Martin Van Buren*, New York, 1889
BASSETT, J. S., *Life of Andrew Jackson*, 2 v., New York, 1911
————, ed., *Correspondence of Andrew Jackson*, 6 v., Washington, 1926–1935
BEMIS, SAMUEL F., *John Quincy Adams and the Union*, New York, 1956
BENTON, THOMAS HART, *Thirty Years' View*, 2 v., New York, 1858
BLAIR, FRANCIS P., *General Jackson and James Buchanan*, n.p., 1856
BOUCHER, C. S., *The Nullification Controversy in South Carolina*, Chicago, 1916
BRADLEY, CYRUS P., *Biography of Isaac Hill*, Concord, New Hampshire, 1835
BUTLER, W. A., *Martin Van Buren, Statesman and Man*, New York, 1862
CARROLL, EBER M., *Origins of the Whig Party*, Durham, North Carolina, 1925
CATTERALL, R. C. H., *Second Bank of the United States*, Chicago, 1903
CHAMBERS, W. N., *Old Bullion Benton*, Boston, 1956

COBBETT, WILLIAM, *Life of Andrew Jackson*, London, 1834

COIT, MARGARET, *John C. Calhoun*, Boston, 1950

COLTON, CALVIN, ed., *Private Correspondence of Henry Clay*, New York, 1855

CRALLÉ, RICHARD K., ed., *The Works of John C. Calhoun*, 6 v., New York, 1854–1857

CROCKETT, DAVID, *The Life of Martin Van Buren*, Philadelphia, 1835

————, *Life of Colonel David Crockett, Written by Himself*, Philadelphia, 1859

CURRENT, RICHARD N., "John C. Calhoun, Philosopher of Reaction," *Antioch Review*, Summer, 1943

CURTIS, GEORGE T., *Life of Daniel Webster*, 2 v., New York, 1870

DAVIS, C. A., *Letters of J. Downing, Major*, New York, 1834

DEEMS, C. F., ed., *Autobiography of Peggy Eaton*, New York, 1932

DEWEY, D. R., *The Financial History of the United States*, Washington, 1909

EATON, CLEMENT, *Henry Clay and the Art of American Politics*, Boston, 1957

EATON, JOHN H., *Life of Andrew Jackson*, Philadelphia, 1828

EMMONS, WILLIAM, *Authentic Biography of Col. Richard M. Johnson of Kentucky*, Boston, 1833

EVERETT, A. H., *The Conduct of the Administration*, Boston, 1831

FOREMAN, GRANT, *Indian Removal*, Norman, Oklahoma, 1953

FORNEY, J. W., *Anecdotes of Public Men*, 2 v., New York, 1873

FUESS, C. M., *Daniel Webster*, 2 v., Boston, 1930

GAMMON, S. R., *The Presidential Campaign of 1832*, Baltimore, 1922

GARLAND, HUGH A., *Life of John Randolph of Roanoke*, New York, 1851

GORDON, T. F., *The War on the Bank of the United States*, Philadelphia, 1834

GOUGE, W. M., *A Short History of Paper Money in the United States*, Philadelphia, 1833

GOVAN, T. P., *Nicholas Biddle*, Chicago, 1959

GREEN, DUFF, *Facts and Suggestions, Biographical, Financial and Political*, New York, 1866

HAMILTON, JAMES A., *Reminiscences*, New York, 1869

HEALEY, G. P. A., *Reminiscences of a Portrait Painter*, Chicago, 1894

HILL, ISAAC, *Brief Sketch of the Life, Character and Services of Major-General Andrew Jackson*, Concord, New Hampshire, 1828

HOLDSWORTH, J. T. AND DEWEY, D. R., *The First and Second Banks of the United States*, Washington, 1910

HOUSTON, DAVID F., *A Critical Study of Nullification in South Carolina*, Cambridge, 1896

HUNT, GAILLARD, ed., *The First Forty Years of American Society, Portrayed in the Family Letters of Mrs. Margaret Bayard Smith*, New York, 1906

JAMES, MARQUIS, *The Life of Andrew Jackson*, 2 v., Indianapolis, 1938

JAMESON, J. F., ed., "Correspondence of John C. Calhoun," *Annual Report, American Historical Review*, v. 2, 1899

JENKINS, J. S., *History of Political Parties in the State of New York*, Auburn, New York, 1849

————, *Life of John Caldwell Calhoun*, Auburn, New York, 1850

KENDALL, AMOS, "Anecdotes of General Jackson," *Democratic Review*, v. 11, September 1842

————, *Life of Andrew Jackson*, New York, 1843–1844

LAWRENCE, RACHEL JACKSON, "Andrew Jackson at Home," *McClure's Magazine*, v. 9, July 1898

LUMPKIN, WILSON, *The Removal of the Cherokee Indians from Georgia*, 2 v., New York, 1907

MARTINEAU, HARRIET, *Retrospect of Western Travel*, 2 v., London, 1838

McCARTHY, CHARLES, "The Antimasonic Party," *American Historical Association Reports*, v. 1, 1902

McCORMAC, E. I., *James K. Polk*, Berkeley, 1922

McGRANE, R. C., ed., *Correspondence of Nicholas Biddle*, Boston, 1919

PARTON, JAMES, *Life of Andrew Jackson*, 3 v., New York, 1859–1860

POAGE, G. R., *Henry Clay and the Whig Party*, Chapel Hill, 1936

POLLACK, QUEENA, *Peggy Eaton: Democracy's Mistress*, New York, 1931

POORE, BEN, *Perley, Perley's Reminiscences*, 2 v., Philadelphia, 1886

REMINI, ROBERT V., *The Election of Andrew Jackson*, New York, 1964

SARGENT, NATHAN, *Public Men and Events*, 2 v., Philadelphia, 1875

SCHLESINGER, ARTHUR M., JR., *Age of Jackson*, Boston, 1945

SCOTT, M. M., *Memoir of Hugh Lawson White*, Philadelphia, 1856

SELLERS, C. G., *James K. Polk, Jacksonian, 1795–1843*, New York, 1957

SMITH, W. B., *Economic Aspects of the Second Bank of the United States*, Cambridge, 1953

SMITH, W. E., *The Francis Preston Blair Family in Politics*, 2 v., New York, 1933

STEINER, B. C., *Life of Roger Brooke Taney*, Baltimore, 1922

STICKNEY, WILLIAM, ed., *Autobiography of Amos Kendall*, Boston, 1872

STORY, W. W., ed., *Life and Letters of Joseph Story*, Boston, 1851

STYRON, ARTHUR, *The Cast-Iron Man, John C. Calhoun and American Democracy*, New York, 1935

SUMNER, W. G., *Andrew Jackson, Symbol of an Age*, Boston, 1882

SWIFT, LINDSAY, *The Great Debate Between Hayne and Webster*, Boston, 1898

TURNER, FREDERICK J., *The Frontier in American History*, New York, 1921

————, *The United States, 1830–1850*, New York, 1935

VAN DEUSEN, GLYNDON G., *The Life of Henry Clay*, Boston, 1937

————, *The Jacksonian Era, 1828–1850*, New York, 1959

VAN DEUSEN, JOHN G., *The Economic Bases of Disunion in South Carolina*, New York, 1928

VAN TYNE, C. H., ed., *Letters of Daniel Webster*, New York, 1902

WESTON, FLORENCE, *The Presidential Election of 1828*, Washington, 1938

WHITE, LEONARD, *The Jacksonians*, New York, 1951

WILTSE, CHARLES M., *John C. Calhoun, Nationalist*, 3 v., Indianapolis, 1944–1951

MARTIN VAN BUREN

ALEXANDER, HOLMES, *The American Talleyrand*, New York, 1935

BANCROFT, GEORGE, *Martin Van Buren to the End of His Public Career*, New York, 1889

BARNES, T. W., *Memoir of Thurlow Weed*, Boston, 1884

BENTON, THOMAS HART, *Thirty Years' View*, 2 v., New York, 1854

BLAKE, H. V., *History of the Tammany Society or Columbia Order*, New York, 1901

BOWERS, CLAUDE G., *Party Battles of the Jackson Period*, Boston, 1922

BUTLER, HARRIETT A., ed., *A Retrospect of Forty Years of William Allen Butler*, New York, 1911

BUTLER, WILLIAM A., *Martin Van Buren*, New York, 1862

COLTON, CALVIN, ed., *The Works of Henry Clay*, 6 v., New York, 1857

COREY, ALBERT B., *The Crisis of 1830–1842 in Canadian-American Relations*, New Haven, 1941

CROCKETT, DAVID, *The Life of Martin Van Buren*, Philadelphia, 1835

DAVIS, MATTHEW L., ed., *Memoirs of Aaron Burr*, 2 v., New York, 1855

DAWSON, MOSES, *Sketches in the Life of Martin Van Buren*, Cincinnati, 1840

ELLIOTT, C. W., *Winfield Scott: The Soldier and the Man*, New York, 1937

EMMONS, WILLIAM, *The Biography of Martin Van Buren, Vice-President of the United States*, Washington, 1835

FITZPATRICK, JOHN C., ed., "Autobiography of Martin Van Buren," *Annual Report, American Historical Association for 1918*, Washington, 1920

FOOTE, HENRY S., *Casket of Reminiscences*, Washington, 1874

GARRATY, J. A., *Silas Wright*, New York, 1949

GILLET, R. H., *Life and Times of Silas Wright*, Albany, 1874

HILDRETH, RICHARD, *The Contrast: or, William Henry Harrison versus Martin Van Buren*, Boston, 1840

HOLLAND, WILLIAM M., *The Life and Political Opinions of Martin Van Buren*, Hartford, 1836

HOYT, EDWIN P., *Martin Van Buren*, Chicago, 1964

IRELAND, JOHN R., *History of the Life and Times of Martin Van Buren*, Chicago, 1887

IRVING, P. M., ed., *Life and Letters of Washington Irving*, 4 v., New York, 1862–1863

JAMES, MARQUIS, *The Life of Andrew Jackson*, 2 v., Indianapolis, 1938

JENKINS, J. S., *Life of Silas Wright*, Auburn, New York, 1847

————, *History of Political Parties in the State of New York*, Auburn, New York, 1849

————, *Lives of the Governors of the State of New York*, Auburn, New York, 1851

KASS, ALVIN, *Politics in New York State, 1800–1830*, Syracuse, 1965

KINLEY, DAVID, *The Independent Treasury of the United States and Its Relations to the Banks of the United States*, Washington, 1910

LYNCH, DENIS T., *An Epoch and a Man: Martin Van Buren and His Times*, New York, 1929

MACKENZIE, WILLIAM LYON, *The Life and Times of Martin Van Buren*, Boston, 1846

MANN, J. B., *An Appeal to the Locofocos*, Boston, 1840

MARTINEAU, HARRIET, *Society in America*, London, 1837

MAYO, ROBERT, *A Word in Season: or, A Review of the Political Life and Opinions of Martin Van Buren*, Washington, 1840

McGRANE, R. C., *The Panic of 1837*, Chicago, 1924

M'ELKINEY, THOMAS, *Life of Martin Van Buren*, Pittsburgh, 1853

MEYER, LELAND W., *The Life and Times of Col. Richard M. Johnson of Kentucky*, New York, 1932

NEVINS, ALLAN, ed., *Diary of James K. Polk*, New York, 1929

OGLE, CHARLES, *The Pretended Democracy of Martin Van Buren*, Boston, 1840

REMINI, ROBERT V., *Martin Van Buren and the Making of the Democratic Party*, New York, 1959

REZNECK, SAMUEL, "The Social History of an American Depression, 1837–1843," *American Historical Review*, v. 40, October 1934

SCOTT, WINFIELD, *Memoirs of Lt.-Gen. Scott, LL.D.*, 2 v., New York, 1864

SHEPARD, EDWARD M., *Martin Van Buren*, New York, 1899

STAPLES, ARTHUR, ed., *The Letters of John Fairfield*, Lewiston, Maine, 1922

STICKNEY, WILLIAM, ed., *Autobiography of Amos Kendall*, Boston, 1872

STODDARD, WILLIAM O., *Andrew Jackson and Martin Van Buren*, New York, 1887

TIFFANY, ORRIN E., "Relations of the United States to the Canadian Rebellion of 1837–1838," *Buffalo Historical Society Publications*, v. 8, Buffalo, 1905

VAN BUREN, MARTIN, edited by his sons, *Inquiry into the Origin and Course of Political Parties in the United States*, New York, 1867

VAN DEUSEN, GLYNDON G., *The Life of Henry Clay*, Boston, 1937

————, *Thurlow Weed, Wizard of the Lobby*, Boston, 1947

————, *The Jacksonian Era, 1828–1848*, New York, 1959

WHITE, LEONARD, *The Jacksonians*, New York, 1963

WILLIAM HENRY HARRISON

BAKER, G. H., ed., *The Works of William H. Seward*, 5 v., New York, 1853–1854

BARNES, T. W., *Memoir of Thurlow Weed*, Boston, 1884

BAYARD, SAMUEL J., *A Short History of the Life and Services of General William Henry Harrison*, Seneca Falls, New York, 1840

BURR, S., *Life and Times of William Henry Harrison*, Philadelphia, 1840

CLEAVES, FREEMAN, *Old Tippecanoe*, New York, 1939

COLTON, CALVIN, ed., *Private Correspondence of Henry Clay*, New York, 1857

————, ed., *Works of Henry Clay*, 6 v., New York, 1857

EATON, CLEMENT, *Henry Clay and the Art of American Politics*, Boston, 1957

GOEBEL, DOROTHY, *William Henry Harrison: A Political Biography*, Indianapolis, 1926

GREEN, JAMES A., *William Henry Harrison*, Richmond, 1941

GUNDERSON, ROBERT G., *The Log-Cabin Campaign*, Lexington, 1957

HARRISON, WILLIAM HENRY, "General Harrison's Speech at the Dayton Convention," September 10, 1840, Boston, 1840

————, "Remarks of General Harrison, Late Envoy Extraordinary and Minister Plenipotentiary of the United States to the Republic of Colombia, On Certain Charges Made Against Him by That Government," n.p., n.d.

————, "Harrison's Great Speech at the Wonderful 'Log Cabin' Campaign Meeting at Fort Meigs in 1840," *Ohio Archeological and Historical Quarterly*, v. 17, Columbus, 1908

HILDRETH, RICHARD, *The Contrast: or, William Henry Harrison versus Martin Van Buren*, Boston, 1840

JACKSON, ISAAC R., *The Life of William Henry Harrison*, Philadelphia, 1840

KNIGHT, T. A., *Tippecanoe*, Cleveland, 1940

MAYO, BERNARD, *Henry Clay*, Boston, 1937

NORTON, ANTHONY B., *The Great Revolution of 1840. The Log Cabin and Hard Cider Campaign*, Mount Vernon, Ohio, 1888

POAGE, G. R., *Henry Clay and the Whig Party*, Chapel Hill, 1936

SEWARD, FREDERICK W., ed., *An Autobiography of William H. Seward*, 3 v., New York, 1891

TODD, CHARLES S., *Sketches of the Civil and Military Services of William Henry Harrison*, Cincinnati, 1847

VAN TYNE, C. H., ed., *Letters of Daniel Webster*, New York, 1902

WEBSTER, DANIEL, *Works of Daniel Webster*, 6 v., Boston, 1853

WEBSTER, HOMER J., *William Henry Harrison, Administrator of the Indiana Territory*, Indianapolis, 1907

JOHN TYLER

ABELL, A. G., *Life of John Tyler*, New York, 1844

AMBLER, C. H., ed., *Diary of John Floyd*, Richmond, 1918

BURRAGE, HENRY S., *Maine and the Northeast Boundary Controversy*, Portland, 1919

CHITWOOD, O. P., *John Tyler: Champion of the Old South*, New York, 1939

COLE, A. C., *The Whig Party in the South*, Washington, 1913

COLTON, CALVIN, ed., *The Works of Henry Clay*, 6 v., New York, 1857

COREY, ALBERT B., *The Crisis of 1830–1842 in Canadian-American Relations*, New Haven, 1941

CUMMING, HIRAM, *The Secret History of the Perfidies, Intrigues and Corruption of the Tyler Dynasty*, New York, 1845

CURRENT, RICHARD N., "Webster's Propaganda and the Ashburton Treaty," *Mississippi Valley Historical Review*, v. 34, October 1957

DICKENS, CHARLES, *American Notes*, Boston, 1871

EATON, CLEMENT, *Henry Clay and the Art of American Politics*, Boston, 1957

FUESS, C. M., *Daniel Webster*, 2 v., Boston, 1930

GOEBEL, DOROTHY, *William Henry Harrison: A Political Biography*, Indianapolis, 1926

HARRISON, GEORGE P., *Westward Expansion, 1841–1950*, New York, 1906

LAMBERT, O. D., *Presidential Politics in the United States, 1841–1844*, Durham, 1936

LANMAN, CHARLES, *Private Life of Daniel Webster*, New York, 1852

MORGAN, ROBERT J., *A Whig Embattled: The Presidency under John Tyler*, Lincoln, Nebraska, 1954

MOWRY, ARTHUR M., *The Dorr War*, Providence, 1901

OGG, F. A., *The Reign of Andrew Jackson*, New Haven, 1919

PHILLIPS, U. B., *The Southern Whigs, 1834–1854*, New York, 1910

REEVES, JESSE S., *American Diplomacy under Tyler and Polk*, Baltimore, 1907

SCHURZ, CARL, *Life of Henry Clay*, 2 v., Boston, 1892

SEAGER, ROBERT, *And Tyler Too*, New York, 1963

SIMMS, H., *Rise of the Whigs in Virginia, 1824–1840*, Richmond, 1929

SMITH, JUSTIN H., *The Annexation of Texas*, New York, 1941

STENBERG, R., "Intrigue for Annexation," *Southwest Review*, v. 25, October 1939

TURNER, FREDERICK J., *The United States, 1830–1850*, New York, 1935

TYLER, LYON G., ed., *Letters and Times of the Tylers*, 3 v., Richmond, 1884–1896

———, *Parties and Patronage in the United States*, New York, 1891

———, ed., "Some Letters of Tyler, Calhoun, Polk, Murphy, Houston and Donelson," *Tyler's Quarterly Historical and Genealogical Magazine*, v. 9, 1927

TYLER, ROBERT, *A Reply to the Democratic Review*, New York, 1845

WEBSTER, DANIEL, *Works of Daniel Webster*, 6 v., Boston, 1853

WISE, BARTON, *Life of Henry A. Wise of Virginia*, New York, 1899

WISE, HENRY A., *Seven Decades of the Union*, Philadelphia, 1881

GENERAL

AMES, HERMAN, *State Documents on Federal Relations, 1789–1861*, New York, 1907

BATES, ERNEST S., *The Story of Congress*, New York, 1936

BEMIS, SAMUEL F., *American Secretaries of State and Their Diplomacy*, 10 v., New York, 1923

———, *A Diplomatic History of the United States*, New York, 1942

BINKLEY, WILFRED E., *Powers of the President*, New York, 1937

———, *American Political Parties*, New York, 1943

BOLTON, SARAH, *Famous American Statesmen*, New York, 1888

BOUDIN, LOUIS, *Government by Judiciary*, 2 v., New York, 1932

BURDETTE, FRANKLIN L., *Filibustering in the Senate*, Princeton, 1940

BUTLER, CHARLES, *The Treaty-Making Power of the United States*, 2 v., New York, 1902

CARTER, CLARENCE E., ed., *The Territorial Papers of the United States*, 20 v., Washington, 1934

CHANNING, EDWARD, *A History of the United States*, 6 v., New York, 1905–1925

CORWIN, EDWARD, *The President's Control of Foreign Relations*, Princeton, 1917

——— and KOENIG, C. W., *The Presidency Today*, New York, 1956

CRANDALL, SAMUEL B., *Treaties, Their Making and Enforcement*, Washington, 1917

DAVIS, JOSEPH E., *Essays in the Early History of American Corporations*, 2 v., Cambridge, 1917

DENNISON, ELEANOR E., *The Senate Foreign Relations Committee*, London, 1942

DEWEY, D. R., *Financial History of the United States*, New York, 1936

DIMOCK, MARSHALL E., *Congressional Investigating Committees*, Baltimore, 1929

DORFMAN, JOSEPH, *The Economic Mind in American Civilization*, New York, 1959

FINER, HERMAN, *The Presidency*, Chicago, 1960

FOLLET, M. P., *The Speaker of the House of Representatives*, New York, 1896

American State Papers, Documents: Foreign Relations, Finance, Indian Affairs, etc., 38 v., Washington, 1832–1861

HART, ALBERT BUSHNELL, ed., *American History Told by Contemporaries*, 5 v., New York, 1897–1929

————, *The American Nation: A History from Original Sources*, 28 v., New York, 1904–1918

HATCH, LOUIS C. and EARLE L. SHOUP, ed., *History of the Vice-President of the United States*, New York, 1934

HAYNES, GEORGE, *The Senate of the United States*, 2 v., Boston, 1938

HERRING, E. P., *Presidential Leadership*, New York, 1940

HINSDALE, MARY L., *A History of the President's Cabinet*, Ann Arbor, 1911

HOFSTADTER, RICHARD, *The American Political Tradition*, New York, 1948

HYMAN, SIDNEY, *The American President*, New York, 1954

KERR, CLARA, *Origin and Development of the United States Senate*, Ithaca, 1895

KROUT, JOHN A. and FOX, DIXON R., *The Completion of Independence, 1790–1830*, New York, 1944

LEARNED, H. B., *The President's Cabinet*, New Haven, 1912

MALLOY, WILLIAM M., compiler, *Treaties, Conventions, International Acts, Protocols and Agreements Between the United States and Other Powers, 1776–1923*, 3 v., Washington, D.C., 1904

MARX, RUDOLPH, *The Health of the Presidents*, New York, 1961

McCONACHIE, LAUROS G., *Congressional Committees*, New York, 1898

McLAUGHLIN, ANDREW C., *A Constitutional History of the United States*, New York, 1935

McNEIL, NEIL, *Forge of Democracy, the House of Representatives*, New York, 1963

MILLER, DAVID H., ed., *Treaties and Other International Acts of the United States*, v. 1–4, Washington, 1931

PARRINGTON, VERNON L., *Main Currents in American Thought*, 3 v., New York, 1927–1930

POLLARD, JAMES E., *Presidents and the Press*, New York, 1947

RICHARDSON, JAMES D., ed., *A Compilation of the Messages and Papers of the Presidents*, 10 v., Washington, 1897–1898

ROGERS, LINDSAY, *The American Senate*, New York, 1926

ROSSITER, CLINTON, *The American Presidency*, New York, 1960

SINGLETON, ESTHER, *Story of the White House*, 2 v., New York, 1907

STANWOOD, EDWARD, *History of Presidential Elections*, Boston, 1884

————, *History of the Presidency*, Boston, 1898

TAUSSIG, F. W., *The Tariff History of the United States*, New York, 1931

TURNER, FREDERICK J., *The Significance of Sections in American History*, New York, 1932

An impressive number and variety of American newspapers ranged through the period of the Founding Presidents. Among those read for the flavor of the times and for their partisan observations were: The Albany *Argus*, Albany *Evening Journal*, Baltimore *American*, Baltimore *Republican*, Boston *Advertiser*, Boston *Gazette*, Frankfort *Argus*, Hartford *Courant*, New Hampshire *Gazette*, New York *American*, New York *Herald*, New York *Post*, New York *Tribune*, Philadelphia *Aurora*, Philadelphia *Gazette of the United States*, Philadelphia *General Advertiser*, Philadelphia *National Gazette*, Richmond *Enquirer*, Washington *Gazette*, Washington *Globe*, Washington *Madisonian*, Washington *National Intelligencer* and the Washington *National Journal*.

Among the magazines of particular interest to students of this period: *American Antiquarian Society Proceedings*, *American Historical Review*, *Century Magazine*, *DeBow's Review*, *Democratic Review*, *Magazine of American History*, *Maryland Historical Magazine*, *Massachusetts Historical Society Proceedings*, *Mississippi Valley Historical Review*, *Niles' Register*, *North American Review*, *Pennsylvania Magazine of History and Biography*, *Southern Literary Messenger* and the *William and Mary College Quarterly Historical Magazine*. In addition, of enormous value were the proceedings of Congress as accounted in the Annals of Congress (1789–1824), Register of Debates (1824–1837) and the Congressional Globe (1833–1873).

For first-hand portrayals, the letters, diaries and documents of the following found in the Manuscripts Division of the Library of Congress were consulted.

The Papers of:
    Nicholas Biddle
    Blair Family
    Breckinridge Family
    Henry Clay
    Elbridge Gerry
    Duff Green
    Alexander Hamilton
    Andrew Jackson
    Thomas Jefferson
    Richard Mentor Johnson
    James McHenry
    James McLean
    James Madison
    James Monroe
    James Polk
    John Randolph
    William C. Rives
    Samuel Smith
    Roger B. Taney
    Martin Van Buren
    George Washington
    Daniel Webster
    Gideon Welles
    Oliver Wolcott

INDEX